# INTRODUCTION TO DATA MINING and ANALYTICS

## WITH MACHINE LEARNING IN R AND PYTHON

**KRIS JAMSA, MBA, PhD**

JONES & BARTLETT LEARNING

*World Headquarters*
Jones & Bartlett Learning
5 Wall Street
Burlington, MA 01803
978-443-5000
info@jblearning.com
www.jblearning.com

Jones & Bartlett Learning books and products are available through most bookstores and online booksellers. To contact Jones & Bartlett Learning directly, call 800-832-0034, fax 978-443-8000, or visit our website, www.jblearning.com.

Substantial discounts on bulk quantities of Jones & Bartlett Learning publications are available to corporations, professional associations, and other qualified organizations. For details and specific discount information, contact the special sales department at Jones & Bartlett Learning via the above contact information or send an email to specialsales@jblearning.com.

Copyright © 2021 by Jones & Bartlett Learning, LLC, an Ascend Learning Company

All rights reserved. No part of the material protected by this copyright may be reproduced or utilized in any form, electronic or mechanical, including photocopying, recording, or by any information storage and retrieval system, without written permission from the copyright owner.

The content, statements, views, and opinions herein are the sole expression of the respective authors and not that of Jones & Bartlett Learning, LLC. Reference herein to any specific commercial product, process, or service by trade name, trademark, manufacturer, or otherwise does not constitute or imply its endorsement or recommendation by Jones & Bartlett Learning, LLC and such reference shall not be used for advertising or product endorsement purposes. All trademarks displayed are the trademarks of the parties noted herein. *Introduction to Data Mining and Analytics* is an independent publication and has not been authorized, sponsored, or otherwise approved by the owners of the trademarks or service marks referenced in this product.

There may be images in this book that feature models; these models do not necessarily endorse, represent, or participate in the activities represented in the images. Any screenshots in this product are for educational and instructive purposes only. Any individuals and scenarios featured in the case studies throughout this product may be real or fictitious, but are used for instructional purposes only.

17830-2

**Production Credits**
Director of Product Management: Laura Pagluica
Product Manager: Edward Hinman
Product Assistant: Melissa Duffy
Product Coordinator: Paula Yuan-Gregory
Tech Editor: Robert Shimonski
Senior Project Specialist: Dan Stone
Digital Project Specialist: Angela Dooley
Marketing Manager: Michael Sullivan
Product Fulfillment Manager: Wendy Kilborn
Project Management: codeMantra U.S., LLC
Cover Design: Scott Moden
Text Design: Scott Moden
Senior Media Development Editor: Troy Liston
Rights Specialist: Rebecca Damon
Cover Image (Title Page, Part Opener, Chapter Opener):
 © Patra Kongsirimongkolchai/EyeEm/Getty Images
Printing and Binding: LSC Communications

**Library of Congress Cataloging-in-Publication Data**
Library of Congress Cataloging-in-Publication Data unavailable at time of printing.

LCCN: 2019955670

6048

Printed in the United States of America
24 23 22 21 20   10 9 8 7 6 5 4 3 2 1

# DEDICATION

Debbie,
    You are the love of my life…

# BRIEF CONTENTS

Preface .................................................................. xiii
About the Author ......................................................... xviii
Contributors ............................................................. xviii

| | | |
|---|---|---|
| 1 | Data Mining and Analytics | 1 |
| 2 | Machine Learning | 44 |
| 3 | Databases and Data Warehouses | 75 |
| 4 | Data Visualization | 102 |
| 5 | Keep Excel in Your Toolset | 159 |
| 6 | Keep SQL in Your Toolset | 211 |
| 7 | NoSQL Data Analytics | 291 |
| 8 | Programming Data Mining and Analytic Solutions | 344 |
| 9 | Data Preprocessing and Cleansing | 411 |
| 10 | Data Clustering | 446 |
| 11 | Classification | 485 |
| 12 | Predictive Analytics | 530 |
| 13 | Data Association | 563 |
| 14 | Mining Text and Images | 591 |
| 15 | Big Data Mining | 609 |
| 16 | Planning and Launching a Data-Mining and Data-Analytics Project | 628 |

GLOSSARY ................................................................. 645
INDEX .................................................................... 657

# TABLE OF CONTENTS

Preface . . . . . . . . . . . . . . . . . . . . . . . . . . . . . . . . . . . . . . . . . . . . . . . . . . . . . . . . . . xiii
About the Author . . . . . . . . . . . . . . . . . . . . . . . . . . . . . . . . . . . . . . . . . . . . . . . xviii
Contributors . . . . . . . . . . . . . . . . . . . . . . . . . . . . . . . . . . . . . . . . . . . . . . . . . . xviii

## 1  Data Mining and Analytics — 1

Data Mining Versus Machine Learning . . . . . . . . . . . . . . . . . . . . . . . . . . . . . . . 3
Data Mining Versus Data Science . . . . . . . . . . . . . . . . . . . . . . . . . . . . . . . . . . 4
Data Mining Versus Statistics . . . . . . . . . . . . . . . . . . . . . . . . . . . . . . . . . . . . . 4
Data Visualization . . . . . . . . . . . . . . . . . . . . . . . . . . . . . . . . . . . . . . . . . . . . . 4
Visual Programming . . . . . . . . . . . . . . . . . . . . . . . . . . . . . . . . . . . . . . . . . . . 11
Business Intelligence . . . . . . . . . . . . . . . . . . . . . . . . . . . . . . . . . . . . . . . . . . 15
Programming Data Mining and Machine Learning . . . . . . . . . . . . . . . . . . . . . 17
Understanding the Role of Databases . . . . . . . . . . . . . . . . . . . . . . . . . . . . . . 17
A Word on Data Sets . . . . . . . . . . . . . . . . . . . . . . . . . . . . . . . . . . . . . . . . . . 18
Data Cleansing and Wrangling . . . . . . . . . . . . . . . . . . . . . . . . . . . . . . . . . . . 19
Text and Photo Data Mining . . . . . . . . . . . . . . . . . . . . . . . . . . . . . . . . . . . . . 19
Data Clustering . . . . . . . . . . . . . . . . . . . . . . . . . . . . . . . . . . . . . . . . . . . . . . 20
Data Classification . . . . . . . . . . . . . . . . . . . . . . . . . . . . . . . . . . . . . . . . . . . . 23
Predictive Analytics . . . . . . . . . . . . . . . . . . . . . . . . . . . . . . . . . . . . . . . . . . . 25
Data Association . . . . . . . . . . . . . . . . . . . . . . . . . . . . . . . . . . . . . . . . . . . . . 27
Big Data Mining and Analytics . . . . . . . . . . . . . . . . . . . . . . . . . . . . . . . . . . . 29
Excel Still Matters . . . . . . . . . . . . . . . . . . . . . . . . . . . . . . . . . . . . . . . . . . . . . 30
Future of Data Mining and Analytics . . . . . . . . . . . . . . . . . . . . . . . . . . . . . . . 31
Hands-on Data Mining and Analytics with Weka . . . . . . . . . . . . . . . . . . . . . . 31
    Cleansing Data with Weka . . . . . . . . . . . . . . . . . . . . . . . . . . . . . . . . . . . . 31
    Visualizing Data within Weka . . . . . . . . . . . . . . . . . . . . . . . . . . . . . . . . . . 33
    Identifying Prediction Variables with Weka . . . . . . . . . . . . . . . . . . . . . . . . 33
    Clustering Data with Weka . . . . . . . . . . . . . . . . . . . . . . . . . . . . . . . . . . . 35
    Classifying Data with Weka . . . . . . . . . . . . . . . . . . . . . . . . . . . . . . . . . . . 36
Performing Data Association within Weka . . . . . . . . . . . . . . . . . . . . . . . . . . . 40

## 2  Machine Learning — 44

Machine Learning Versus Artificial Intelligence . . . . . . . . . . . . . . . . . . . . . . . 46
Types of Machine Learning . . . . . . . . . . . . . . . . . . . . . . . . . . . . . . . . . . . . . 46
Underlying Machine-Learning Algorithms . . . . . . . . . . . . . . . . . . . . . . . . . . 47
Understanding the Supervised Learning Process . . . . . . . . . . . . . . . . . . . . . 48
    Specifying Training and Testing Data Sets . . . . . . . . . . . . . . . . . . . . . . . . 49
    Testing Your Machine-Learning Model . . . . . . . . . . . . . . . . . . . . . . . . . . . 52
Classifying Email as Valid or Spam . . . . . . . . . . . . . . . . . . . . . . . . . . . . . . . . 53
Clustering Stock Data . . . . . . . . . . . . . . . . . . . . . . . . . . . . . . . . . . . . . . . . . 56

## TABLE OF CONTENTS

Scaling Data-Set Values.................................................................... 57
Understanding Dimensionality Reduction............................................ 59
    Primary Component Analysis......................................................... 60
    Linear Discriminant Analysis.......................................................... 63
Mapping Categorical Variables........................................................... 64
Hands-on Google TensorFlow Programming Library............................ 69

### 3 Databases and Data Warehouses — 75

Databases Store Things (aka Entities).................................................. 78
    Entity Relationship Diagrams......................................................... 79
    Entities Have Attributes................................................................ 79
Database Models................................................................................ 79
    Conceptual Database Model........................................................ 80
    Logical Database Model............................................................... 81
    Physical Database Model.............................................................. 82
Database Schemas............................................................................. 85
A Word on Normalization................................................................... 85
Common Database Types................................................................... 87
    Relational Database Management Systems.................................. 87
    NoSQL Database Management Systems...................................... 88
    Object-Oriented Database Management Systems........................ 88
    Graph Database Management Systems....................................... 89
Data Warehouses............................................................................... 91
Data Marts.......................................................................................... 93
Revisiting Schemas............................................................................. 93
Data Lakes.......................................................................................... 95
Hands On—Creating Entity Relationship Diagrams Using Lucidchart.... 96

### 4 Data Visualization — 102

Visualization Best Practices................................................................ 104
Selecting the Correct Chart for the Right Purpose............................. 105
Integrating Data Visualizations into Web Solutions............................ 106
    Creating a Simple Static Chart..................................................... 107
    Creating a Real-Time Dynamic Chart........................................... 111
Time-Based Comparison Charts........................................................ 111
    Line Chart.................................................................................... 111
    Multiline Charts........................................................................... 113
    Top $x$-Axis Line Chart................................................................ 113
    Dual $y$-Axis Chart..................................................................... 116
    Area Chart................................................................................... 118
Category-Based Comparison Charts.................................................. 119
    Bar and Column Charts............................................................... 120
    Clustered Bar and Column Charts............................................... 121
    Radar Chart................................................................................. 122
    Combo Chart............................................................................... 122
    Diff Chart..................................................................................... 122
    Waterfall Chart............................................................................ 125
Composition Charts........................................................................... 125
    Pie Chart..................................................................................... 126
    Donut Chart................................................................................ 129
    Sunburst Chart............................................................................ 130
    Stacked Bar and Column Charts................................................. 130

| | |
|---|---|
| Stacked Area Chart | 132 |
| Treemap Chart | 134 |
| Funnel Chart | 135 |
| Pyramid Chart | 136 |
| Correlation Charts | 136 |
| Scatter Chart | 136 |
| Bubble Chart | 137 |
| Dashboard Charts | 138 |
| Gauge Chart | 138 |
| Calendar Chart | 139 |
| Candlestick Chart | 141 |
| Distribution Charts | 142 |
| Histogram Chart | 142 |
| Box and Whisker Charts | 145 |
| Geocharts | 146 |
| Big Number | 149 |
| Plotting Data Using the Python and R Programming Languages | 149 |
| Tables Still Communicate Effectively | 150 |
| Hands-on Data Visualization Using Tableau | 150 |
| Getting Started with Tableau | 150 |
| Creating a Sales Dashboard | 152 |

## 5 Keep Excel in Your Toolset — 159

| | |
|---|---|
| Sorting Data Values | 160 |
| Filtering Data | 161 |
| Charting Data with Excel | 164 |
| Conditional Formatting | 167 |
| Understanding File Formats | 170 |
| Comma-Separated Value Files | 170 |
| Open Document Specification Files | 170 |
| Portable Document Format Files | 171 |
| Extensible Markup Language Files | 172 |
| JavaScript Object Notation Files | 172 |
| Excel Files | 174 |
| Leveraging Excel Statistical Functions | 174 |
| Determining the Arithmetic Mean with AVERAGE | 175 |
| Determining the Arithmetic Mean for Mixed Data Using AVERAGEA | 175 |
| Determining the Arithmetic Mean for Values Meeting a Specific Condition Using AVERAGEIF and AVERAGEIFS | 177 |
| Eliminating the Impact of Outliers on the Mean Using TRIMMEAN | 178 |
| Calculating the Geometric Mean with GEOMEAN and the Harmonic Mean with HARMEAN | 179 |
| Determining the Median Value Using MEDIAN | 180 |
| Determining the Maximum and Minimum Values Using MAX and MIN | 181 |
| Determining the Quartile Values Using QUARTILE | 183 |
| Determining the $n$th Largest and Smallest Value in a Data Set Using LARGE and SMALL | 184 |
| Counting the Number of Cells Using COUNT | 184 |
| Calculating by How Much Data-Set Values Differ from Their Mean Using VAR and STDEV | 185 |
| Determining the Sum of Squared Deviations Using DEVSQ | 188 |
| Determining Variability Using AVEDEV | 188 |
| Determining the Correlation Coefficient Using CORREL | 188 |
| Determining the Covariance Using COVARIANCE.S and COVARIANCE.P | 190 |
| Determining the Slope and Intercept of a Line That Represents a Data Set Using SLOPE and INTERCEPT | 191 |

Determining an Equation for a Line Using LINEST ............................................. 193
Determining the Equation for a Curve Using LOGEST ........................................ 193
Determining Frequency Counts for Data-Set Values Using FREQUENCY ......................... 194
Hands-on: Data Analysis Using Excel........................................................ 196
Performing What-If Processing Using Excel Goal Seek ..................................... 196
Forecasting Future Results with a Forecast Sheet........................................ 198
Excel Pivot Tables .................................................................... 200

## 6  Keep SQL in Your Toolset                                                         211

Understanding SQL Query Types: DDL, DCL, and DML ........................................... 213
SQL Database Vendors ..................................................................... 222
Using SELECT to Retrieve Rows (Records) from a Table..................................... 225
Limiting the Number of Rows SELECT Returns.............................................. 229
Sorting Your Query Results ............................................................... 229
Selecting Only Records that Meet a Condition............................................. 231
Using the SQL Relational Operators.................................................... 232
Using Logical Operators for Complex Conditions....................................... 237
Specifying Different Field Names with Query Results Using AS ......................... 241
Using the SQL Built-in Aggregate Functions .............................................. 243
Performing Arithmetic Operations......................................................... 245
SQL Arithmetic Functions ................................................................ 247
Grouping Query Results Using GROUP BY ................................................... 250
Using HAVING to Specify a Condition with GROUP BY .................................... 251
Using GROUP BY ROLLUPs and Cubes..................................................... 252
Joining One Table to Another ............................................................. 255
Using Table Alias Names .............................................................. 257
Understanding JOIN Types............................................................. 257
Understanding SQL Query UNION and INTERSECT Operations .................................. 262
Importing and Exporting Database Data.................................................... 263
Importing Data from a File ........................................................... 263
Importing Data from a Spreadsheet..................................................... 264
Importing Data from Another Database Table ........................................... 264
Exporting Data to a File ................................................................. 265
Exporting Data to a Spreadsheet....................................................... 266
Performing Extract, Transform, and Load Operations ...................................... 266
Using a Cloud-Based Database ............................................................ 267
Using the phpMyAdmin Utility ............................................................ 267
Using a Cloud-Based Managed Database Service ............................................ 268
Creating Database Tables................................................................. 268
Inserting Data into a Database Table..................................................... 271
Updating Data Within a Database Table ................................................... 272
Deleting Records from a Database Table .................................................. 274
Dropping (Deleting) a Table or Database ................................................. 275
Nesting a SELECT Query .................................................................. 276
Using an Index to Improve Query Performance ............................................. 277

## 7  NoSQL Data Analytics                                                             291

Understanding JSON ...................................................................... 292
JSON Field Data Types................................................................. 293
JSON Is Self-Describing, Human Readable, Language Independent, and Lightweight ....... 294
Storing Multiple Values Using a JSON Array ........................................... 295

Nesting JSON Objects . . . . . . . . . . . . . . . . . . . . . . . . . . . . . . . . . . . . . . . . . . . . . . . . . . . . 295
JSON Is Self-Describing . . . . . . . . . . . . . . . . . . . . . . . . . . . . . . . . . . . . . . . . . . . . . . . . . 295
Storing JSON Objects . . . . . . . . . . . . . . . . . . . . . . . . . . . . . . . . . . . . . . . . . . . . . . . . . . 296
Validating JSON Content . . . . . . . . . . . . . . . . . . . . . . . . . . . . . . . . . . . . . . . . . . . . . . . 296
Getting Started with MongoDB . . . . . . . . . . . . . . . . . . . . . . . . . . . . . . . . . . . . . . . . . . . . . . . 298
Using the MongoDB Graphical User Interface . . . . . . . . . . . . . . . . . . . . . . . . . . . . . . . . . . . 301
Using Third-Party MongoDB GUIs . . . . . . . . . . . . . . . . . . . . . . . . . . . . . . . . . . . . . . . 302
Querying a MongoDB Collection . . . . . . . . . . . . . . . . . . . . . . . . . . . . . . . . . . . . . . . . . 302
Using Relational Operators Within a Query . . . . . . . . . . . . . . . . . . . . . . . . . . . . . . . . . 304
Using MongoDB Logical Operators . . . . . . . . . . . . . . . . . . . . . . . . . . . . . . . . . . . . . . . 306
Sorting Your Query Results . . . . . . . . . . . . . . . . . . . . . . . . . . . . . . . . . . . . . . . . . . . . . 308
Using MongoDB Arithmetic Operators . . . . . . . . . . . . . . . . . . . . . . . . . . . . . . . . . . . . 309
Using MongoDB Arithmetic Functions . . . . . . . . . . . . . . . . . . . . . . . . . . . . . . . . . . . . 309
Limiting the Number of Documents a Query Returns . . . . . . . . . . . . . . . . . . . . . . . . 309
Grouping MongoDB Query Results . . . . . . . . . . . . . . . . . . . . . . . . . . . . . . . . . . . . . . . 311
Inserting Data into a MongoDB Collection . . . . . . . . . . . . . . . . . . . . . . . . . . . . . . . . . 314
Updating a MongoDB Document . . . . . . . . . . . . . . . . . . . . . . . . . . . . . . . . . . . . . . . . . . . . 316
Deleting MongoDB Documents . . . . . . . . . . . . . . . . . . . . . . . . . . . . . . . . . . . . . . . . . 316
Creating and Dropping MongoDB Collections and Databases . . . . . . . . . . . . . . . . . . 317
Revisiting MySQL and JSON . . . . . . . . . . . . . . . . . . . . . . . . . . . . . . . . . . . . . . . . . . . . . . . 319
Using an Index to Improve MongoDB Query Performance . . . . . . . . . . . . . . . . . . . . . . . . 319
Importing and Exporting Data to and from a MongoDB Database . . . . . . . . . . . . . . 321
Performing SQL Queries on a MongoDB Database . . . . . . . . . . . . . . . . . . . . . . . . . . 322
Distributing a MongoDB Database Using Shards . . . . . . . . . . . . . . . . . . . . . . . . . . . . 323
Replicating a MongoDB Database Using Replica Sets . . . . . . . . . . . . . . . . . . . . . . . . 325
Using the MongoDB Connector for Business Intelligence . . . . . . . . . . . . . . . . . . . . . 326
Other Popular NoSQL Databases . . . . . . . . . . . . . . . . . . . . . . . . . . . . . . . . . . . . . . . . . . . . 327
CouchDB . . . . . . . . . . . . . . . . . . . . . . . . . . . . . . . . . . . . . . . . . . . . . . . . . . . . . . . . . . . . 327
Redis . . . . . . . . . . . . . . . . . . . . . . . . . . . . . . . . . . . . . . . . . . . . . . . . . . . . . . . . . . . . . . . 330
Amazon DynamoDB . . . . . . . . . . . . . . . . . . . . . . . . . . . . . . . . . . . . . . . . . . . . . . . . . . 332
Cassandra . . . . . . . . . . . . . . . . . . . . . . . . . . . . . . . . . . . . . . . . . . . . . . . . . . . . . . . . . . . 333
HBase . . . . . . . . . . . . . . . . . . . . . . . . . . . . . . . . . . . . . . . . . . . . . . . . . . . . . . . . . . . . . . 333
RocksDB . . . . . . . . . . . . . . . . . . . . . . . . . . . . . . . . . . . . . . . . . . . . . . . . . . . . . . . . . . . . 335
Hands-on: MongoDB Managed Service and MongoDB Charts . . . . . . . . . . . . . . . . . . . . . 335
Using Charts Within Atlas . . . . . . . . . . . . . . . . . . . . . . . . . . . . . . . . . . . . . . . . . . . . . . 338

# 8  Programming Data Mining and Analytic Solutions     344

Getting Started with Python . . . . . . . . . . . . . . . . . . . . . . . . . . . . . . . . . . . . . . . . . . . . . . . . 347
Leverage the Many Python Tutorials . . . . . . . . . . . . . . . . . . . . . . . . . . . . . . . . . . . . . 350
Python Assignment Operator . . . . . . . . . . . . . . . . . . . . . . . . . . . . . . . . . . . . . . . . . . . 350
Python Variable Names . . . . . . . . . . . . . . . . . . . . . . . . . . . . . . . . . . . . . . . . . . . . . . . . 350
Creating and Executing Python Scripts . . . . . . . . . . . . . . . . . . . . . . . . . . . . . . . . . . . 351
Commenting a Python Script . . . . . . . . . . . . . . . . . . . . . . . . . . . . . . . . . . . . . . . . . . . 352
Python Variables Are Dynamic . . . . . . . . . . . . . . . . . . . . . . . . . . . . . . . . . . . . . . . . . . 352
Python Operators . . . . . . . . . . . . . . . . . . . . . . . . . . . . . . . . . . . . . . . . . . . . . . . . . . . . . 353
Relational Operators . . . . . . . . . . . . . . . . . . . . . . . . . . . . . . . . . . . . . . . . . . . . . . . . . . 353
Python Lists . . . . . . . . . . . . . . . . . . . . . . . . . . . . . . . . . . . . . . . . . . . . . . . . . . . . . . . . . 354
Python Groups Statements Based upon Statement Indentation . . . . . . . . . . . . . . . . 356
Conditional Processing within Python . . . . . . . . . . . . . . . . . . . . . . . . . . . . . . . . . . . . 357
Logical Operators . . . . . . . . . . . . . . . . . . . . . . . . . . . . . . . . . . . . . . . . . . . . . . . . . . . . . 358
Iterative Processing . . . . . . . . . . . . . . . . . . . . . . . . . . . . . . . . . . . . . . . . . . . . . . . . . . . 358
Python Supports Functions . . . . . . . . . . . . . . . . . . . . . . . . . . . . . . . . . . . . . . . . . . . . . 360
Leveraging Python's Built-In Functions . . . . . . . . . . . . . . . . . . . . . . . . . . . . . . . . . . . 363
Python Is Object Oriented . . . . . . . . . . . . . . . . . . . . . . . . . . . . . . . . . . . . . . . . . . . . . . 364

## TABLE OF CONTENTS

    Understanding Python Modules. . . . . . . . . . . . . . . . . . . . . . . . . . . . . . . . . . . . . . . . . . . . . . . . . . . . . 365
    Understanding and Importing Packages . . . . . . . . . . . . . . . . . . . . . . . . . . . . . . . . . . . . . . . . . . . . . 366
    Understanding Python Dataframe Objects. . . . . . . . . . . . . . . . . . . . . . . . . . . . . . . . . . . . . . . . . . . 369
    Using the pandas Package for Numerical Data Structures . . . . . . . . . . . . . . . . . . . . . . . . . . . . . 370
    Using the plot.ly Package to Create Visualizations. . . . . . . . . . . . . . . . . . . . . . . . . . . . . . . . . . . . 372
    Using the matplotlib Package to Create Visualization . . . . . . . . . . . . . . . . . . . . . . . . . . . . . . . . . 372
    Using the numpy Package for Numerical Calculations . . . . . . . . . . . . . . . . . . . . . . . . . . . . . . . . 374
    Using the sklearn Package for Machine Learning and Data Mining . . . . . . . . . . . . . . . . . . . . . 375
Getting Started with R. . . . . . . . . . . . . . . . . . . . . . . . . . . . . . . . . . . . . . . . . . . . . . . . . . . . . . . . . . . . . . . . 376
    Creating Variables in R. . . . . . . . . . . . . . . . . . . . . . . . . . . . . . . . . . . . . . . . . . . . . . . . . . . . . . . . . . . 380
    Comments in R . . . . . . . . . . . . . . . . . . . . . . . . . . . . . . . . . . . . . . . . . . . . . . . . . . . . . . . . . . . . . . . . . 381
    Using R's Built-in Functions . . . . . . . . . . . . . . . . . . . . . . . . . . . . . . . . . . . . . . . . . . . . . . . . . . . . . . 381
    Getting Additional Help in R. . . . . . . . . . . . . . . . . . . . . . . . . . . . . . . . . . . . . . . . . . . . . . . . . . . . . . 382
    Operators within R . . . . . . . . . . . . . . . . . . . . . . . . . . . . . . . . . . . . . . . . . . . . . . . . . . . . . . . . . . . . . . 382
    Logical Operators . . . . . . . . . . . . . . . . . . . . . . . . . . . . . . . . . . . . . . . . . . . . . . . . . . . . . . . . . . . . . . . 384
    Conditional Operators in R. . . . . . . . . . . . . . . . . . . . . . . . . . . . . . . . . . . . . . . . . . . . . . . . . . . . . . . 385
    Repeating Statements with for, while, and repeat. . . . . . . . . . . . . . . . . . . . . . . . . . . . . . . . . . . . 386
    Storing a List of Values as a One-Dimensional Vector. . . . . . . . . . . . . . . . . . . . . . . . . . . . . . . . . 389
    Storing Multidimensional Values in an Array. . . . . . . . . . . . . . . . . . . . . . . . . . . . . . . . . . . . . . . . 391
    Using a Dataframe to Store a Data Set . . . . . . . . . . . . . . . . . . . . . . . . . . . . . . . . . . . . . . . . . . . . . 393
    Defining Your Own Functions . . . . . . . . . . . . . . . . . . . . . . . . . . . . . . . . . . . . . . . . . . . . . . . . . . . . 395
    Using R Packages. . . . . . . . . . . . . . . . . . . . . . . . . . . . . . . . . . . . . . . . . . . . . . . . . . . . . . . . . . . . . . . 397
    Object-Oriented Programming with R . . . . . . . . . . . . . . . . . . . . . . . . . . . . . . . . . . . . . . . . . . . . . 398
Hands-On Visual Studio . . . . . . . . . . . . . . . . . . . . . . . . . . . . . . . . . . . . . . . . . . . . . . . . . . . . . . . . . . . . . . 399
    Using Visual Studio to Create a Regression Program . . . . . . . . . . . . . . . . . . . . . . . . . . . . . . . . 405

## 9   Data Preprocessing and Cleansing     411

Understanding and Measuring Data Quality. . . . . . . . . . . . . . . . . . . . . . . . . . . . . . . . . . . . . . . . . . . . . 412
    Common Data Validation Techniques. . . . . . . . . . . . . . . . . . . . . . . . . . . . . . . . . . . . . . . . . . . . . . 414
    Determining Whether to Correct or Delete Records. . . . . . . . . . . . . . . . . . . . . . . . . . . . . . . . . . 426
Understanding the Role of Data Governance . . . . . . . . . . . . . . . . . . . . . . . . . . . . . . . . . . . . . . . . . . . 427
    Using a Data-Governance Framework. . . . . . . . . . . . . . . . . . . . . . . . . . . . . . . . . . . . . . . . . . . . . 427
    Understanding Data Stakeholders, Owners, Stewards, and Custodians . . . . . . . . . . . . . . . . 429
    Understanding the Data Lifecycle. . . . . . . . . . . . . . . . . . . . . . . . . . . . . . . . . . . . . . . . . . . . . . . . . 429
Revisiting Extract, Transform, and Load Operations. . . . . . . . . . . . . . . . . . . . . . . . . . . . . . . . . . . . . . 430
Data Wrangling Defined . . . . . . . . . . . . . . . . . . . . . . . . . . . . . . . . . . . . . . . . . . . . . . . . . . . . . . . . . . . . . 430
    Leveraging a Data-Wrangling Tool. . . . . . . . . . . . . . . . . . . . . . . . . . . . . . . . . . . . . . . . . . . . . . . . . 430
    Creating Your Own Custom Data Wrangler in Python. . . . . . . . . . . . . . . . . . . . . . . . . . . . . . . . 431
Leveraging the Data Quality Assessment Framework . . . . . . . . . . . . . . . . . . . . . . . . . . . . . . . . . . . . 436

## 10   Data Clustering     446

Common Clustering Approaches. . . . . . . . . . . . . . . . . . . . . . . . . . . . . . . . . . . . . . . . . . . . . . . . . . . . . . 447
Understanding K-Means Clustering. . . . . . . . . . . . . . . . . . . . . . . . . . . . . . . . . . . . . . . . . . . . . . . . . . . 448
    Using K-Means++. . . . . . . . . . . . . . . . . . . . . . . . . . . . . . . . . . . . . . . . . . . . . . . . . . . . . . . . . . . . . . . 453
    Hierarchical Cluster . . . . . . . . . . . . . . . . . . . . . . . . . . . . . . . . . . . . . . . . . . . . . . . . . . . . . . . . . . . . . 456
    Understanding DBSCAN Clustering . . . . . . . . . . . . . . . . . . . . . . . . . . . . . . . . . . . . . . . . . . . . . . . 462
Set Aside Cluster-Shape Biases . . . . . . . . . . . . . . . . . . . . . . . . . . . . . . . . . . . . . . . . . . . . . . . . . . . . . . . 465
    Viewing the Cluster Assignments. . . . . . . . . . . . . . . . . . . . . . . . . . . . . . . . . . . . . . . . . . . . . . . . . 468
Identifying Data Outliers . . . . . . . . . . . . . . . . . . . . . . . . . . . . . . . . . . . . . . . . . . . . . . . . . . . . . . . . . . . . . 471
Hands-On: K-Means and Hierarchical Clustering in Excel Using Solver. . . . . . . . . . . . . . . . . . . . . 473
    K-Means Clustering Using Solver. . . . . . . . . . . . . . . . . . . . . . . . . . . . . . . . . . . . . . . . . . . . . . . . . 474
    Hierarchical Clustering Using Solver. . . . . . . . . . . . . . . . . . . . . . . . . . . . . . . . . . . . . . . . . . . . . . . 479

# TABLE OF CONTENTS

## 11  Classification — 485
Applying the K-Nearest Neighbors (KNN) Classification Algorithm — 488
    Understanding the Confusion Matrix — 494
    Predicting Wine Types Using KNN — 497
Predicting Breast Cancer Malignancy Using KNN — 500
Classification Using Naïve Bayes — 502
Classification Using Logistic Regression — 506
Classification Using a Neural Network — 509
Classification Using Decision Trees — 511
    Viewing the Decision Tree — 513
Classifying Data Using Random Forests — 514
    Classifying Data Using a Support Vector Machine — 517
Hands-on: Real-World Data Sets — 521
    Data Sets from Kaggle — 523
    Filtering Non-Numeric Data — 525

## 12  Predictive Analytics — 530
Understanding Linear Regression — 532
    Looking at a Simple Example — 533
    Looking at a Real-World Example of Simple Linear Regression — 537
    Multiple Linear Regression — 539
    Looking at a Real-World Multiple Linear Regression — 540
Decision Tree Regression — 543
Random Forest Regression — 546
K-Nearest-Neighbors Regression — 548
Polynomial Regression — 550
Hands-on: RapidMiner — 553

## 13  Data Association — 563
Understanding Support, Confidence, and Lift — 564
    Calculating the Association Measures — 566
Associating Real-World Data — 568
FP-Growth Association Using RapidMiner — 571
Data-Set Summaries and Correlation — 574
Hands-on: Data Mining with Orange — 579
    Performing Predictive Analysis within Orange — 586

## 14  Mining Text and Images — 591
Getting Started with Text Mining — 592
    Performing Sentiment Analysis — 592
    Text Processing in Python — 594
    Using the Natural Language Toolkit — 597
    Clustering Related Text — 598
Getting Started with Image Mining — 601
    Creating a Simple Facial Recognition Application — 601
    Handwriting Classification — 604
Hands-on: Facial Recognition Using OpenCV — 606

## 15 Big Data Mining — 609

The V's of Big Data.................................................................. 613
Big Data Requires a Big Number of Servers ................................................. 613
Understanding the Role of File Systems ................................................. 614
Bring the Process to the Data.................................................... 614
Enter MapReduce .................................................................. 617
    Looking at a Simple MapReduce Example ..................................... 617
Hands-On: Performing MapReduce Options Using MongoDB............................ 621

## 16 Planning and Launching a Data-Mining and Data-Analytics Project — 628

Creating an Enterprise Data Ecosystem ................................................. 629
Defining Your Data Goal.............................................................. 629
    Establishing a Data Governance Board ........................................ 630
Identifying and Accessing Key Data Sources ................................................. 631
Establishing Data Quality Expectations................................................. 632
Identifying Your Data Toolsets ................................................. 633
    On-Premise, Cloud, or Managed Services............................................ 633
Identifying Security Considerations ................................................. 633
    Identifying Data Controls and Logging ........................................ 633
Creating a "SMART" Approach ................................................. 634
Making Your Business Case........................................................ 634
Applying Plan, Do, Check, and Act ................................................. 637
Leveraging SWOT Analysis................................................. 637
Strive to Deliver Self-Service Solutions That Empower Others ............................. 637
Hands-On: Documenting Projects Using Jupyter Notebook............................ 638

**GLOSSARY** ........................................................ 645
**INDEX** ........................................................ 657

# ADDITIONAL RESOURCES

## Cloud Desktop

This textbook is accompanied by a Navigate 2 Premier Course that includes access to a Cloud Desktop with lab exercises. Cloud Desktops are browser-based lab environments where students have a chance to extend their learning beyond the textbook with real software on live virtual machines. Visit go.jblearning.com/JamsaData to learn more.

# PREFACE

Data analysts are dealing with more data today than ever before, and conservatively, that amount of data will continue to double every two years for many years to come. With ever-growing amounts of data come many opportunities for discovery. However, as the volume of data increases, so too do the challenges of discovering trends and patterns, as well as expressing such findings in a meaningful way to others. To store, analyze, and visualize data, analysts use SQL, NoSQL, and graph databases; Excel; data-mining tools; and machine-learning as well as big-data tools. This book examines these concepts and tools, introducing each and then using hands-on instruction to develop the skills you will need to perform real-world data-mining and analytic operations. Machine-learning and data-mining operations normally make extensive use of Python and R programming. As such, this book uses each. If you have not programmed before, relax – this book presents the programming skills you will need and introduces Visual Programming environments, such as Weka, Orange, and RapidMiner, which let you perform data mining and machine learning without having to write code!

Chapter 1 examines data mining, the process of identifying patterns that exist within data, and machine learning, the use of data pattern recognition algorithms, which allow a program to solve problems. With the data-mining patterns in hand, data analysts can apply them to other data sets. Think of the actual "mining" as the search for the data patterns, as opposed to the subsequent use of the patterns. The data-mining process may involve the use of statistics, database queries, visualization tools, traditional programming, and machine learning. Machine learning is the use of a programming language to solve problems, such as clustering, categorization, predictive analysis, and data association. As you will learn in Chapter 1, machine-learning solutions solve complex problems by using data to drive discovery, using only a few lines of code.

Chapter 2 drills deeper into machine learning, the use of data pattern recognition algorithms to solve problems. Developers classify machine-learning algorithms as supervised, unsupervised, reinforced, and deep learning. Supervised learning is the use of an algorithm that uses labeled data to produce a training data set an algorithm can use to learn how to identify patterns. Common solutions that use supervised learning include data classification. Unsupervised learning is the use of an algorithm to identify patterns within data that do not have labeled elements that can be used to create a training data set. Common solutions that use unsupervised learning include data clustering and data association. Reinforced learning is the use of feedback loops to reward correct predictions and to punish mistakes. Finally, deep learning is a hierarchically structured process that leverages layers of machine learning, for which the output of one layer becomes the input to the next in order to drill down into a lower-level result.

Chapter 3 examines databases, data warehouses, and data lakes. At the heart of most data applications are databases. Whether an application analyzes big data, mines data using machine learning, or drives real-time dashboards, data are at the center of the processing performed. For the past 50 years, relational (table-based) databases have been the mainstay of data operations. Because developers normally use Structured Query Language (SQL) to interact with relational databases, developers generally refer to relational databases as SQL databases. With the advent of mobile and web applications that frequently deal with documents, videos, audios, and other unstructured data, developers today often turn to NoSQL databases, such as MongoDB—so named because it can handle humungous amounts of data. To align database operations with object-oriented programming practices, database developers have implemented object-oriented database management systems. Although such databases have not yet achieved tremendous market adoption, key database solutions, such as Oracle, now integrate object-oriented concepts into their query language. Finally, real-world objects have a wide range of relationships, which traditional databases cannot readily represent. As such, developers are starting to migrate to graph databases, which are designed to handle such numerous relationships. The chapter introduces object-oriented and graph databases. Databases are normally ideal for transactional operations, such as storing e-commerce sales, inventory levels, employee timecard processing or payroll operations, and other read and write operations. Business dashboards and decision support tools, in contrast, typically require only a subset of a company's data, normally perform read-only operations, and must provide fast answers to analytic queries. To drive such operations, developers normally use a data warehouse. Depending on the business requirements and the data warehouse size and complexity, developers often decompose the data warehouse into smaller, specialized data marts. Recently, big data applications bypass databases and instead connect to data files directly, a process for which developers refer to the file as a data lake. Such processing is well suited for interacting with large binary objects (which developers call blobs), as well as audio and video data.

Chapter 4 examines data visualization, the visual representation of data with the goal of improving communication. Data analysts have a wide range of communication tools available to represent data, from tables, to charts and graphs, to the display of a big number. Throughout Chapter 4, you will examine many of these tools in detail and learn when the use of each is appropriate. You will examine many different visualization tools, which include Excel, Tableau, and Google Charts. Creating quality visualizations is both an art and a science. This means a quality chart uses color effectively, integrates complementary fonts, and highlights points of interest to communicate a message—the art of visualization. Likewise, quality visualizations use the correct chart for the right purpose—the science of visualization. Creating quality charts takes time and effort. As you will learn in Chapter 4, you should be prepared to revise your charts based on feedback you receive from others. Over time, you will learn your audience's preferences.

Chapter 5 examines data mining and analysis using Excel. Despite the recent explosive growth of machine-learning and data-mining tools and solutions, Excel remains the most widely used data-analysis program. Using Excel, data analysts model complex data, create visualizations, cleanse data, and more. Often, one of the first steps a data analyst performs when he or she receives a new data set is to open and examine it within Excel. Chapter 5 examines common data operations using Excel, as well as key built-in Excel functions.

Chapter 6 examines SQL. For over 50 years, SQL has been the primary way database developers create and manipulate table-based relational databases. In fact, developers often refer to relational databases as SQL databases. Chapter 6 examines SQL operations in detail. As you will learn, SQL is the language you will use to speak (interact) with a database and the tables it contains. SQL provides queries that let you create databases, then create tables within the database, and then to insert, update, and delete data records within those tables. Many software companies, such as Oracle, Microsoft, and even Amazon, provide implementations of SQL database systems. Each of these systems provides different capabilities. At their core, you will find that all such systems support the base set of SQL queries. To perform data mining and analytics, it is important that you understand SQL. As you will learn, an SQL database (or data warehouse within a database) is often the source of the data that data-mining and data analytic tools access. Having the ability to query and manipulate underlying data will increase your ability to independently complete your data-mining and data analytic work. Further, as you will learn, using SQL operations, such as JOINs, GROUP BY with rollups, and nested SELECTs, you can create query results well suited for immediate analysis. Chapter 6 will provide you with the foundational SQL knowledge you need.

Chapter 7 examines NoSQL databases. For the first 50+ years of computing, database developers made extensive use of SQL relational (table-based) databases. The explosive growth of web- and mobile-based applications, however, has introduced challenges to traditional databases, such as the need to store audio, video, or other unstructured data. In response to these demands, NoSQL databases have emerged, so named because they do not use SQL. Instead, NoSQL databases use query mechanisms that are not SQL. Further, unlike relational databases that store data with tables, NoSQL databases store data in a less structured way, often using JavaScript Object Notation (JSON) to store objects. This chapter examines NoSQL database processing through the popular MongoDB database and briefly introduces additional NoSQL databases, which include Redis, CouchDB, Casandra, and others. As you will learn, the cloud makes it very easy for you to set up and run these databases.

Chapter 8 examines Python and R programming in detail. Throughout this text, you will make extensive use of the Python and R programming languages to perform data-mining and machine-learning operations. Both Python and R are very powerful programming languages with a wide range of capabilities and features. Chapter 8 introduces the fundamental concepts you need to know in order to understand the programs this text presents. The chapter's goal is to get you up and running with each quickly.

Chapter 9 examines data cleansing, the process of detecting, correcting, and removing errors and inconsistences from data. Database developers today face greater amounts of data from more sources than ever before. Unfortunately, the many sources of data bring with them a greater chance of bad data. The decades-old adage of "garbage in, garbage out" remains an ever-present data threat. Data analysts and database developers must be constantly aware of bad data risks and must work to put in place safeguards against factors that reduce the quality of data and, ultimately, reduce the quality of the decisions made that are based upon such data. Errors within data may be the result of bad user input, which may include incorrect spelling, numeric entry errors, inconsistent abbreviation of names and addresses, and so on. Likewise, some errors may occur due to a faulty sensor on an Internet of Things (IoT) device or a noisy data transmission line. Regardless of the cause of the error, the goal of data cleansing is higher quality data. Data cleansing is normally not a one-time event. Database developers and data analysts must constantly monitor and assess the quality of incoming data. The database developers may create and execute queries to clean up the data, which they then integrate into one or more data-cleansing scripts, which can run automatically in the future. Chapter 9 examines data cleansing in detail.

Chapter 10 examines data clustering, the process of grouping related data. Often, one of the first steps a data analyst will perform when analyzing new data is to decompose a large data set into smaller groups of related data elements called clusters. The concept of clustering is that an item in one cluster more closely resembles other items in that cluster than it does items in another cluster. Clustering uses unsupervised learning, in that it works with unlabeled data that have not been assigned to a category or group—the clustering process will form such groups. There are two main types of clustering solutions. Hard clustering restricts each point to residing in only one cluster. Soft clustering algorithms, in contrast, allow points to reside in multiple clusters. As you perform cluster analysis, you will find that some values fall outside of all clusters—making the points outliers. Chapter 10 discusses ways to best deal with such values.

Chapter 11 examines data classification, the process of assigning data to a specific group. When data analysts mine data, they must often put data into specific groups (such as a pet is a dog, cat, or horse) or determine if an object is or is not something (such as a loan being approved or disapproved). With respect to data mining, classification is the use of a supervised machine-learning algorithm to assign an observation into a specific category. Classification algorithms work by examining an input "training set" of data to learn how the data values combine to create a result. Such a training set, for example, might contain heights, weights, colors, and temperaments of different dogs and the resulting breeds, or it might contain the sizes, shapes, dimensions, and locations of tumors that are malignant, as well as similar data for tumors that are benign. In other words, the training data contain predictive values and the correct classification results. After the algorithm learns from and models the test data, a "test" data set (for which the correct results are known) is tested against the model to determine its accuracy, such as 97%. With knowledge of the accuracy in hand, the data analyst can then use the model to classify other data values. Normally, the training set and testing set come from the same data set of values that are known to be correct or observed. The data analyst will specify, for example, that 70% of the data will be training data and 30% will be used for testing. Across the web, you can find many different data sets of known or observed data that you can use to try different classification algorithms. Chapter 11 uses several commonly used classification algorithms.

Chapter 12 examines predictive analytics—the use of data to predict a future result. As you might imagine, being able to analyze data to determine such historical facts is very important and very valuable to businesses. To perform descriptive analytics, you can use statistical tools to generate metrics, you can use visualization tools to chart data, you can use clustering to group data, and more. Chapter 12, however, is about using data to predict future events—predictive analytics. In Chapter 11, you will examine one form of predictive analytics: classification. Using supervised learning, you can predict in which class (category) an object should reside, given predictor variables. Classification works with discrete categories, meaning data that have finite values, such as the type of car, breed of dog, color of hair, number of students (you cannot have a fractional student), and so on. In contrast, continuous values have an infinite set of values, such as a company's projected revenue, the average basketball player's height, and the range of temperatures in Phoenix. Chapter 12 focuses on predicting continuous values using a technique called regression, the goal of which is to produce an equation that you can then use to predict results.

Chapter 13 examines how to use association to identify patterns within data sets, such as the items a customer often purchases together at a grocery store, the links on a website upon which a customer clicks before making a purchase, and the snacks a fan purchases together at a ballgame. As you will learn, one of the most well-known association applications is the shopping cart problem, which identifies the association between buying diapers and beer. You can think of this association process as looking in each shopping cart as customers leave the market and taking note of the items they bought. By noting that many of the carts that contained diapers also contained beer, you form an association. Data analysts often refer to this process as market basket analysis. In Chapter 13, you will perform association operations.

Chapter 14 examines text and image data mining. Such text and image data are ripe for data mining. Companies, for example, collect and mine Twitter posts, email messages, and other forms of customer feedback. Further, government organizations make extensive use of image and facial recognition. In general, text and image mining include many of the data-mining operations you have performed throughout this text: clustering, classification, and prediction. Chapter 14 examines text and image processing in detail.

Chapter 15 examines big data mining and analytics. The term "big data" applies to data sets that exceed the size our data programs can hold. For Excel, that might be a data set that is larger than the available memory, and for MySQL, that might be the size of the largest file supported by the underlying operating system. The point is, most software applications have size limits, which the size of big data solutions exceed. As you will learn, to store big data, developers often use distributed file systems and distributed databases. To perform processing on such distributed data, Chapter 15 examines the MapReduce process, a programming technique that brings the processing to be performed to the remote servers. Using MapReduce operations, you can quickly perform queries on distributed data. In the future, the greatest source of data will be devices on the IoT. Looking forward, big data is only going to become bigger and the demand for big data solutions that Chapter 15 presents greater.

Chapter 16 examines the steps an analyst should perform to plan and launch a data-mining and data-analytic process. Throughout this text, you will examine many data-mining and data-analytics operations. If someone asks you to cleanse data, create a predictive model, or cluster related data, you will know how to technically achieve it. That said, many organizations are new to data mining and data analytics, and beyond their initial efforts, most organizations are, at best, still performing such operations on a one-off or ad hoc process. Companies that become successful with data analytics will put together and deploy a formal data plan. Chapter 16 presumes that because you may now have the most data-analytic and data-mining knowledge and skills in your company, you will be asked to lead the company's data projects. To help you get started, this chapter addresses key issues you should consider and recommends practices you should implement.

# ABOUT THE AUTHOR

**Dr. Kris Jamsa** wrote his first computer program in Algol, using punched cards, while attending the U.S. Air Force Academy. Since then, he has spent his career wrangling data and programs that use it. Jamsa has a PhD in computer science, a second PhD in education, and master's degrees in computer science, information security, project management, education, and business. He is the author of 115 books on all aspects of programming and computing.

Kris lives with his wife, Debbie, on their ranch in Prescott, Arizona. When he is not in front of a computer screen, you can find him spending time with their horses, dogs, and grandkids.

# CONTRIBUTORS

Many people have contributed valuable assistance in the development of this book. The author and publisher would like to thank the reviewers whose feedback helped shaped the text in many ways:

Ramachandra B. Abhyankar, PhD, Indiana State University

David C. Anastasiu, PhD, San Jose State University

Darius M. Dziuda, PhD, Central Connecticut State University

Peter V. Henstock, PhD, Harvard University

Ching-Yu Huang, PhD, Kean University

Adam Lee, PhD, University of Maryland

Smiljana Petrovic, PhD, Iona College

Ron Price, MBA, Spokane Falls Community College

Anthony Scime, DA, State University of New York

Junping Sun, PhD, Nova Southeastern University

B.S. Vijayaraman, PhD, The University of Akron

Haibo Wang, PhD, Texas A&M International University

Youlong Zhuang, PhD, Columbia College of Missouri

We would also like to express our gratitude to the technical editor, Robert Shimonski, of Northwell Health, for his guidance and expertise.

# CHAPTER 1

# Data Mining and Analytics

## Chapter Goals and Objectives

- Define and describe data mining.
- Define and describe machine learning.
- Define and describe data visualization.
- Locate, search, and use common data-set repositories.
- Define and describe data quality.
- Define and describe the common data-mining and machine-learning applications: clustering, classification, predictive analytics, and association.

Since the Census Bureau first began to collect data about households in the 1890s, the operations performed on data to extract information and knowledge have been known as data processing. For decades, programmers were called data programmers and the individuals who loaded tapes in the data center, data operators. Over the years, the focus on data somewhat went away—programmers (not "data programmers") wrote programs that performed specific processing (as opposed to "data processing").

As the use of big data, data mining, and machine learning began to explode, the word data quickly came back in vogue. There are now data analysts, data programmers, data wranglers, data engineers, data miners, data statisticians, and data scientists. The point is, data analytics is here to stay.

This chapter introduces data mining, the process of identifying patterns that exist within data. By the time you finish this chapter, you will understand the following key concepts:

- Data mining is the process of identifying patterns within data.
- Data mining may involve the use of statistics, database queries, visualization tools, traditional programming, and machine learning.

- **Machine learning** is the use of data pattern-recognition algorithms to solve problems. There are two primary forms of machine learning: supervised and unsupervised. In supervised machine learning, the algorithm examines a **training data set** to learn how to identify patterns. **Unsupervised learning**, in contrast, does not use a training data set.
- **Data visualization** is the use of charts and graphs to represent data. Analysts use many different charts to represent data. The key is knowing which chart to use when.
- To provide sample data sets you can use with data-mining and machine-learning algorithms, many sites on the web provide downloadable files. Two of the most commonly used data-set repositories are the University of California Irvine (UCI) data-set repository and the Kaggle website.
- **Visual programming** is the process of specifying processing by dragging and dropping different objects on to a workspace, as opposed to using programming-language statements. This text presents the RapidMiner and Orange visual-programming environments.
- **Business intelligence** is the use of tools (data mining, machine learning, and visualization) to convert data into actionable insights and recommendations.
- Most modern programming languages provide software libraries programmers can use to create data-mining and machine-learning solutions. Due to their popularity and common use, this text makes extensive use of Python and R.
- The vast volume of data is not only leading database developers to NoSQL databases, it also has them thinking about who should administer databases. One of the cloud's new key capabilities is database as a service (DBaaS) for which a managed-service provider spins up and administers the database so that the customer need only worry about their applications and not the management of the underlying infrastructure.
- The first step that data analysts perform with new data is to cleanse the data to eliminate duplicate records, resolve null or not-a-number (NaN) values, identify outliers, and more. There are many ways an analyst can clean data, which may include the use of Excel, a programming language, or even a third-party tool.
- **Data quality** is a measure of the data's suitability for use. Data analysts calculate quality by considering factors such as:
  - Accuracy: the degree to which the data correctly represent the underlying real-world values, such as all temperatures from a sensor being in the correct range.
  - Completeness: the degree to which the data represent all required values, such as a data set that should contain an hour of data, for a sensor that reports every second, having 100% of the data values.
  - Consistency: the degree to which similar or related data values align throughout the data set, such as each occurrence of an address having the same ZIP code.
  - Conformity: the degree to which the data values align with the company's business rules, such as the company will measure and store sensor values in 1-second intervals.
- Data clustering is the process of grouping related data-set items into one or more clusters. **Clustering** uses unsupervised machine learning for which the underlying algorithm does not use a training data set.

- Data classification is the process of assigning data to matching groups (categories), such as a tumor being benign or malignant, email being valid or spam, or a transaction being legitimate or fraudulent.
- **Predictive analytics** is the use of data to predict what will happen in the future.
- **Data association** is the process of identifying key relationships between variables. One of the best-known data-association problems is market-basket analysis, which examines items in a customer's shopping cart to determine if the presence of one item in the cart (called the antecedent) influences the addition of a second item (called the consequent).
- Data analysts still make extensive use of Excel. By installing add-ins, such as Solver, analysts can perform many data-mining operations from within Excel.
- Weka (Waikato Environment for Knowledge Analysis) is a data-mining tool created at the University of Waikato in New Zealand. Using Weka, you can perform **data cleansing**, clustering, classification, prediction, and visualization.

# Data Mining Versus Machine Learning

Data mining is the process of identifying patterns that exist within data. With the patterns in hand, data analysts can apply them to other data sets. Think of the actual "mining" as the search for the data patterns, as opposed to the subsequent use of the patterns. The data-mining process may involve the use of statistics, database queries, visualization tools, traditional programming, and machine learning.

Machine learning is defined as the use of data pattern-recognition algorithms that allow a program to solve problems, such as clustering, categorization, predictive analysis, and data association, without the need for explicit step-by-step programming instructions to tell the algorithm how to perform tasks. In this way, machine-learning solutions can solve complex problems by using data to drive discovery, by using only a few lines of code.

Because data mining often (but not always) makes extensive use of machine learning, the two terms often appear together. Common tools you will use for data mining include:

- Databases such as MySQL or MongoDB
- Excel
- Visualization tools such as Tableau
- Business intelligence tools such as Microsoft Power BI
- Programming-language solutions
- Data-mining tools such as RapidMiner, Orange, and Weka

In contrast, to perform machine-learning operations, you will use tools that include:

- Python and R programming solutions
- Visual-programming tools, such as RapidMiner and Orange
- Excel third-party add-ins, such as Solver

## Data Mining Versus Data Science

Data mining is the process of identifying patterns that exist within data. Data science is the use of statistics, programming, scientific methods, and machine learning to extract knowledge from a data set. As you can see, the definitions of data mining and data science are very similar. In fact, the two terms are often used interchangeably.

A data scientist, therefore, is an individual who analyzes and interprets data. Again, you will find the terms data scientist and data analyst quite similar. Both will use data-mining tools to gain insights into one or more data sets.

## Data Mining Versus Statistics

Data mining is the process of identifying patterns that exist within data. Statistics is the collection, analysis, modeling, and presentation of data. Statistics is one component of data mining, meaning it is one tool in the data analyst's tool kit. Having knowledge and understanding of statistics will help a data analyst better understand the behind-the-scenes processing of many of the data-mining and machine-learning algorithms that this text presents. That said, the good news is that you don't have to be a statistician to use the tools.

As discussed, Excel remains one of the most widely used data-analytics tools. Admittedly, having statistical skills can only benefit you as you use data-mining tools. That said, many data analysts find success with only a basic understanding of statistical processes. Chapter 5, "Keep Excel in Your Toolset," examines many of the statistical functions built into Excel.

## Data Visualization

A few years ago, big data was the exception—now it is the norm. One of the first steps data analysts perform to identify patterns within data is to represent the data visually, using charts and graphs. Likewise, to communicate data trends and findings, developers often create data-driven dashboards. Depending on the information the analyst must convey, they will often create click-through dashboards that first display high-level, often aggregated data upon which the user can click in order to drill deeper into the underlying specifics, as shown in **FIGURE 1.1**.

For years, analytic charts consisted primarily of scatter charts, bar charts, line charts, and pie charts, as shown in **FIGURE 1.2**.

Although analysts still use such traditional charts, commonly used charts now include:

- Time-based comparison charts, which represent how one or more sets of values change over time.
- Category-based comparison charts, which represent how two or more categories of values compare.
- Composition charts, which represent how one or more values relate to a larger whole.
- Correlation charts, which represent how two or more variables relate.
- **Dashboard** charts, which represent key performance indicators that companies use to track initiatives.

Data Visualization 5

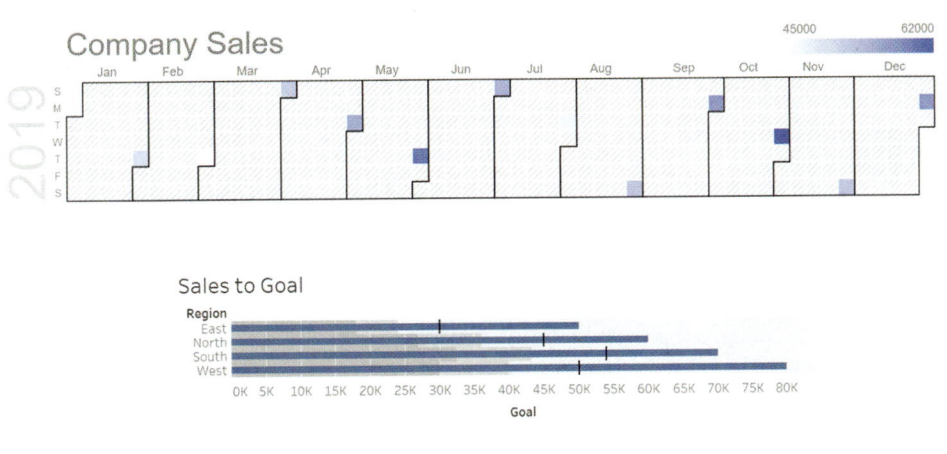

**FIGURE 1.1** Using a click-through dashboard to drill into greater levels of data specifics.
Used with permission of TABLEAU SOFTWARE

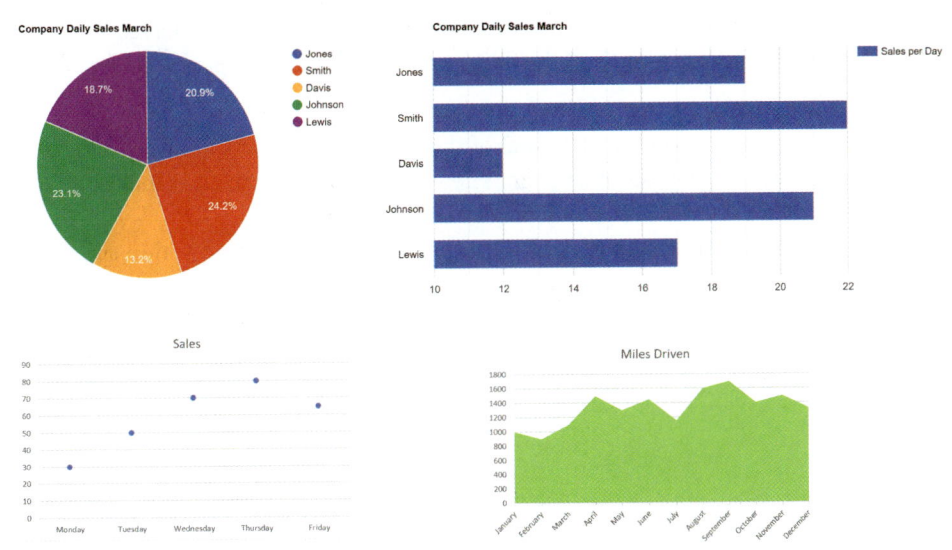

**FIGURE 1.2** The traditional "mainstay" of analytics charts.
Used with permission of Google

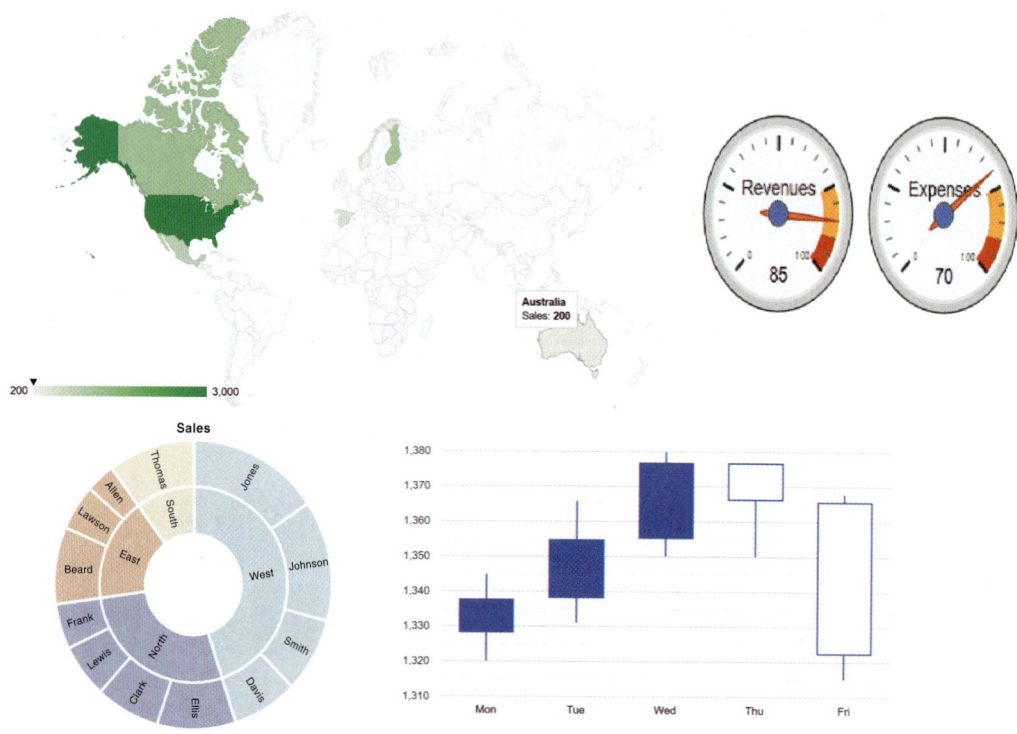

**FIGURE 1.3 Expanding the number of charts available to data analysts.**
Used with permission of Google

- Distribution charts, which represent the frequency of values within a data set.
- Geocharts, which represent how the values from one location compare to values in a different location.

**FIGURE 1.3** illustrates the use of several of these additional charts. As you will learn, the first step to successful data visualization is not knowing how to use each chart, but rather when. Chapter 4, "Data Visualization," examines various data charts in detail.

In the past, analysts created charts using Excel, which they embedded within spreadsheets. Today, in contrast, analysts use Tableau, Sisense, and other tools such as Microsoft Power BI to create web-based dashboards. In a similar way, programmers often embed charts and graphs into the web pages they create using tools such as Google Charts. The following HTML file, SalesByCountry.html, uses Google Charts to create the visual dashboard shown in **FIGURE 1.4**:

```
<html>
  <head>
    <script type="text/javascript" src="https://www.gstatic.com/charts/loader.js"></script>
    <script type="text/javascript">
      google.charts.load('current', {
        'packages':['geochart'],
        // Note: you will need to get a mapsApiKey for your project.
```

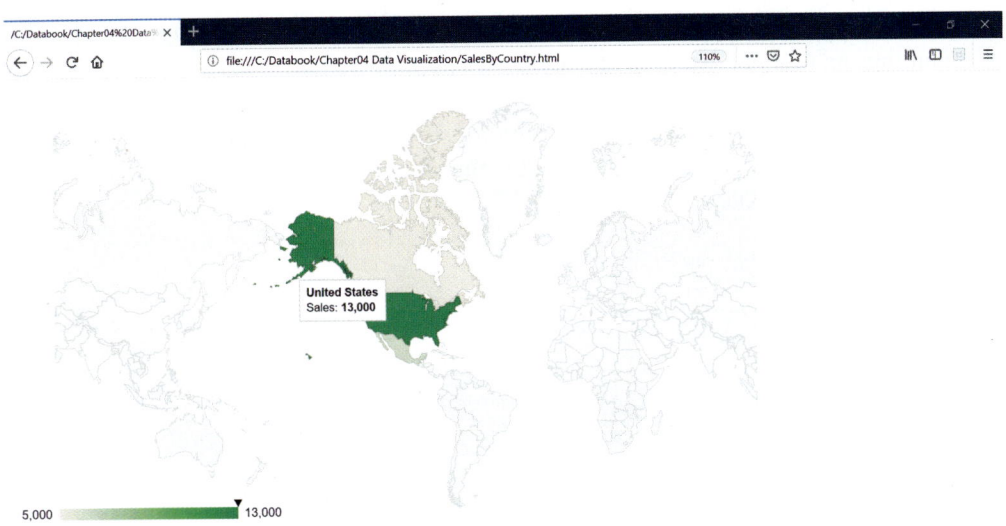

**FIGURE 1.4** Using Google Charts to embed graphics within an HTML page.

Used with permission of Google

```
        // See: https://developers.google.com/chart/interactive/
docs/basic_load_libs#load-settings
        'mapsApiKey': 'AIzaSyD-9tSrke72PouQMnMX-a7eZSW0jkFMBWY'
      });
      google.charts.setOnLoadCallback(drawRegionsMap);

      function drawRegionsMap() {
        var data = google.visualization.arrayToDataTable([
          ['Country', 'Sales'],
          ['United States', 13000],
          ['Canada', 5000],
          ['Mexico', 6000],
        ]);

        var options = { region: '019' };

        var chart = new google.visualization.GeoChart(document.
getElementById('regions_div'));

        chart.draw(data, options);
      }
    </script>
  </head>
  <body>
    <div id="regions_div" style="width: 900px; height: 500px;"></div>
  </body>
</html>
```

Data analysts often leverage the Python and R programming languages to perform data-mining and machine-learning operations. Often, they will create charts to visualize their findings. The following Python script, TitanicCharts.py, opens the Titanic data set, which contains information about the passengers who survived and died on the *Titanic*, and uses the data to create three different pie charts showing the passenger assignments by class, survivors by class, and deaths by class:

```
import matplotlib.pyplot as plt
import pandas as pd
data = pd.read_csv('titanic.csv')

Class = data[['Pclass']].values
Survived = data[['Survived']].values

FirstClass = 0
SecondClass = 0
ThirdClass = 0
FirstClassSurvived = 0
FirstClassDied = 0
SecondClassSurvived = 0
SecondClassDied = 0
ThirdClassSurvived = 0
ThirdClassDied = 0

for i in range(0, len(Class)):
  if Class[i] == 1:
    FirstClass += 1
    if Survived[i] == 1:
       FirstClassSurvived += 1
    else:
       FirstClassDied += 1

  elif Class[i] == 2:
    SecondClass += 1
    if Survived[i] == 1:
       SecondClassSurvived += 1
    else:
       SecondClassDied += 1

  elif Class[i] == 3:
    ThirdClass += 1
    if Survived[i] == 1:
       ThirdClassSurvived += 1
    else:
       ThirdClassDied += 1


# Data to plot
labels = '1st Class', '2nd Class', '3rd Class'
```

```python
sizes = [FirstClass, SecondClass, ThirdClass]
colors = ['gold', 'yellowgreen', 'lightcoral']
explode = (0.1, 0, 0)  # explode 1st slice
plt.title("Passenger Class Assignment")
# Plot
plt.pie(sizes, explode=explode, labels=labels, colors=colors,
autopct='%1.1f%%', shadow=True, startangle=140)

plt.show()

sizes = [FirstClassSurvived, SecondClassSurvived,
ThirdClassSurvived]
colors = ['gold', 'yellowgreen', 'lightcoral']
explode = (0.1, 0, 0)  # explode 1st slice
plt.title("Surviving Passengers by Class Assignment")
# Plot
plt.pie(sizes, explode=explode, labels=labels, colors=colors,
autopct='%1.1f%%', shadow=True, startangle=140)

plt.show()

sizes = [FirstClassDied, SecondClassDied, ThirdClassDied]
colors = ['gold', 'yellowgreen', 'lightcoral']
explode = (0.1, 0, 0)  # explode 1st slice
plt.title("Passenger Deaths by Class Assignment")
# Plot
plt.pie(sizes, explode=explode, labels=labels, colors=colors,
autopct='%1.1f%%', shadow=True, startangle=140)

plt.show()
```

You can download the data set from this text's catalog page at go.jblearning.com/DataMining. The data set contains over 1,300 passenger records that provide age, gender, class of travel, and so on. When you run this script, it will display the charts shown in **FIGURE 1.5**.

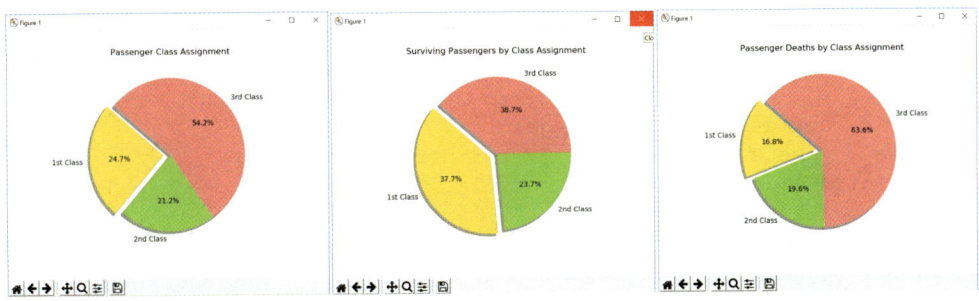

**FIGURE 1.5 Using Python to chart data.**

Used with permission of Python Software Foundation

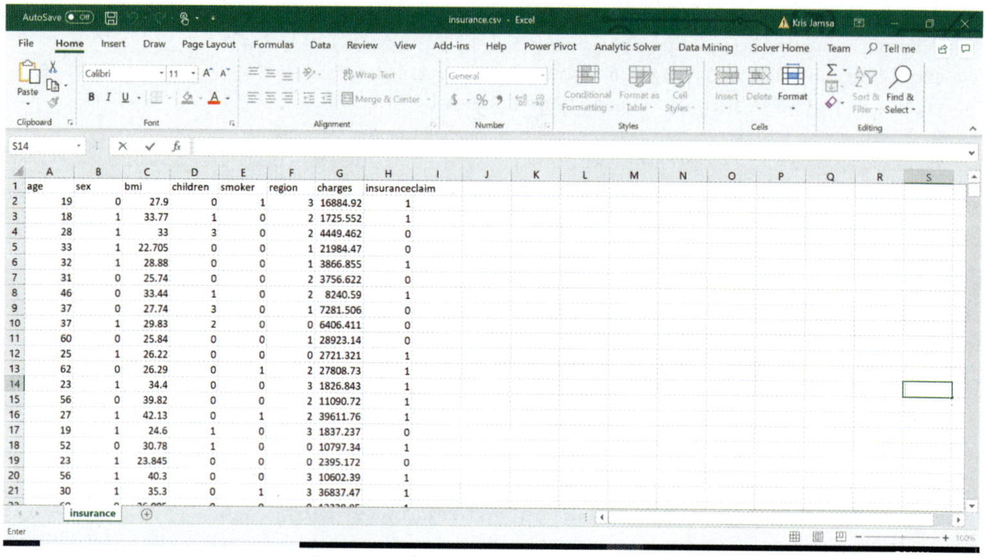

| age | sex | bmi | children | smoker | region | charges | insuranceclaim |
|---|---|---|---|---|---|---|---|
| 19 | 0 | 27.9 | 0 | 1 | 3 | 16884.92 | 1 |
| 18 | 1 | 33.77 | 1 | 0 | 2 | 1725.552 | 1 |
| 28 | 1 | 33 | 3 | 0 | 2 | 4449.462 | 0 |
| 33 | 1 | 22.705 | 0 | 0 | 1 | 21984.47 | 0 |
| 32 | 1 | 28.88 | 0 | 0 | 1 | 3866.855 | 1 |
| 31 | 0 | 25.74 | 0 | 0 | 2 | 3756.622 | 0 |
| 46 | 0 | 33.44 | 1 | 0 | 2 | 8240.59 | 1 |
| 37 | 0 | 27.74 | 3 | 0 | 1 | 7281.506 | 0 |
| 37 | 1 | 29.83 | 2 | 0 | 0 | 6406.411 | 0 |
| 60 | 0 | 25.84 | 0 | 0 | 1 | 28923.14 | 0 |
| 25 | 1 | 26.22 | 0 | 0 | 0 | 2721.321 | 1 |
| 62 | 0 | 26.29 | 0 | 1 | 2 | 27808.73 | 1 |
| 23 | 1 | 34.4 | 0 | 0 | 3 | 1826.843 | 1 |
| 56 | 0 | 39.82 | 0 | 0 | 2 | 11090.72 | 1 |
| 27 | 1 | 42.13 | 0 | 1 | 2 | 39611.76 | 1 |
| 19 | 1 | 24.6 | 1 | 0 | 3 | 1837.237 | 0 |
| 52 | 0 | 30.78 | 1 | 0 | 0 | 10797.34 | 1 |
| 23 | 1 | 23.845 | 0 | 0 | 0 | 2395.172 | 0 |
| 56 | 1 | 40.3 | 0 | 0 | 3 | 10602.39 | 1 |
| 30 | 1 | 35.3 | 0 | 1 | 3 | 36837.47 | 1 |

**FIGURE 1.6 The Insurance.csv data set.**

Used with permission from Microsoft

To create charts using Python, programmers make extensive use of the matplotlib plot library. If you plan to program in Python, you should take time to examine the functions the library provides. Having the ability to quickly plot your data may save you considerable time and effort as you create and troubleshoot your code.

The following R program, ChartData.R, uses the Insurance.csv data set, which contains over 1,300 insurance customer records that contain age, gender, number of children, smoker or nonsmoker, region of the country, body mass index (BMI), and healthcare costs to the insurer, as shown in **FIGURE 1.6**. You can download the data set from this text's catalog page at go.jblearning.com/DataMining. Using the data set, analysts can perform predictive analytics to predict a customer's healthcare costs. The ChartData.R program uses the data set to identify and chart the correlation between each field and the costs.

```
df <- read.csv(file='insurance.csv')

plots <- par(mfrow=c(2, 2))

corr <- cor(df$charges, df$age)
title <- paste("Charges Age ", sprintf("%s", corr))
plot(df$charges, df$bmi, main=title,
   xlab="Charges ", ylab="Age ")

corr <- cor(df$charges, df$bmi)
title <- paste("Charges BMI ", sprintf("%s", corr))
plot(df$charges, df$bmi, main=title,
   xlab="Charges ", ylab="BMI ")
```

```
corr <- cor(df$charges, df$children)
title <- paste("Charges Children ", sprintf("%s", corr))
plot(df$charges, df$children, main=title,
   xlab="Charges ", ylab="Children ")

corr <- cor(df$charges, df$smoker)
title <- paste("Charges Smoker ", sprintf("%s", corr))
plot(df$charges, df$smoker, main=title,
   xlab="Charges ", ylab="Smoker ")


par(plots)
```

When you run the program, it will display the chart shown in **FIGURE 1.7**.

A correlation value approaching one indicates a meaningful relationship. In this case, smokers have higher charges than nonsmokers. The other variables (age, BMI, and number of children) do not have a correlation to the charges.

## Visual Programming

For years, programmers have made extensive use of the Python and R programming languages to create data-mining and machine-learning solutions. Throughout this text, you will do the same. The problem with creating programs to perform data-mining and machine-learning tasks is that someone must know the programming languages and know how to code.

To eliminate the need for such statement-based programming, visual-programming environments are emerging, such as RapidMiner and Orange, which this text presents. The following

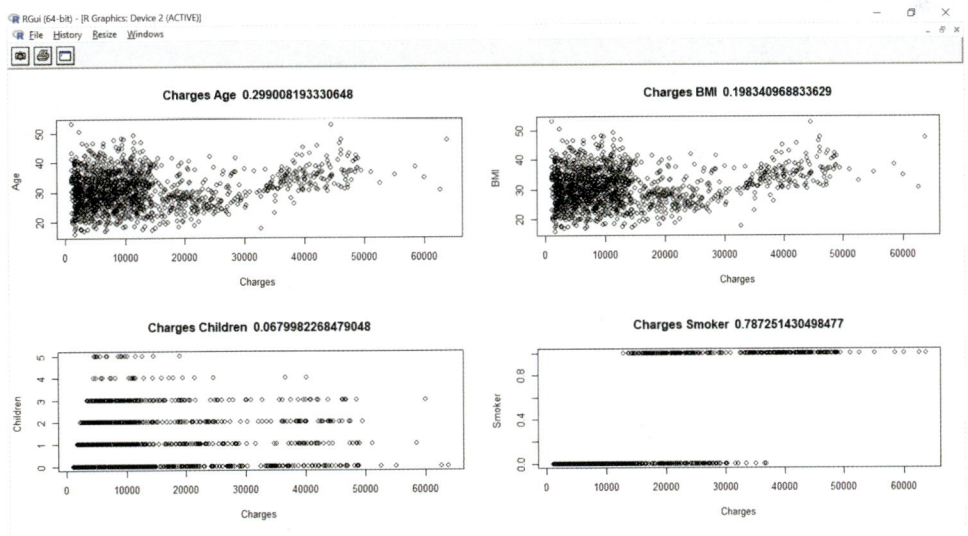

**FIGURE 1.7** Using R to chart correlation data.

Used with permission of The R Foundation

Python script, Titanic.py, for example, opens the TitanicFields data set, which you can download from this text's catalog page at go.jblearning.com/DataMining. It contains data about many of the passengers, such as age, gender, and class of travel. The data set eliminates several of the columns that are not used in the prediction, deletes records with missing data, and converts the text strings "male" and "female" to the values 1 and 0. The script uses random forest classification to predict, based on age, gender, and class of travel, whether a passenger would have survived or died. Chapter 11, "Data Classification," discusses random forest classification in more detail.

```python
import pandas as pd
import numpy as np
from sklearn.model_selection import train_test_split
from sklearn.metrics import accuracy_score
from sklearn.neural_network import MLPClassifier
import sklearn.tree as tree
from sklearn.metrics import confusion_matrix
from sklearn.ensemble import RandomForestClassifier

names = ['Pclass','Sex','Age','Survived']

df = pd.read_csv('TitanicFields.csv', header=None, names=names)
X = np.array(df.iloc[:, 0:2])
y = np.array(df['Survived'])

# split the data into train and test sets
X_train, X_test, y_train, y_test = train_test_split(X, y, test_size=0.30)

model = RandomForestClassifier()
model.fit(X_train, y_train)
pred = model.predict(X_test)
print ('Accuracy Score: ', accuracy_score(y_test, pred))
print('\nConfusion Matrix\n', confusion_matrix(y_test, pred))
```

The script loads the data set and specifies the columns to be used as predictors and the column (Survived) that will be predicted. The script then allocates 70% of the data set as the training set and 30% for the test set. When you execute this script, it will display the following output:

```
Accuracy Score:   0.8407643312101911

Confusion Matrix
 [[164  19]
 [ 31 100]]
```

In this case, the model predicted survival and death with 84% accuracy. The confusion matrix shows that the model correctly predicted 164 of the 183 survivors (missing 19) and 100 of the 131 deaths (missing 31).

RapidMiner provides a visual-programming environment that lets you specify processing steps by dragging and dropping processing widget components into a workflow, as shown in **FIGURE 1.8**. Chapter 12, "Predictive Analytics," discusses RapidMiner in more detail.

# Visual Programming

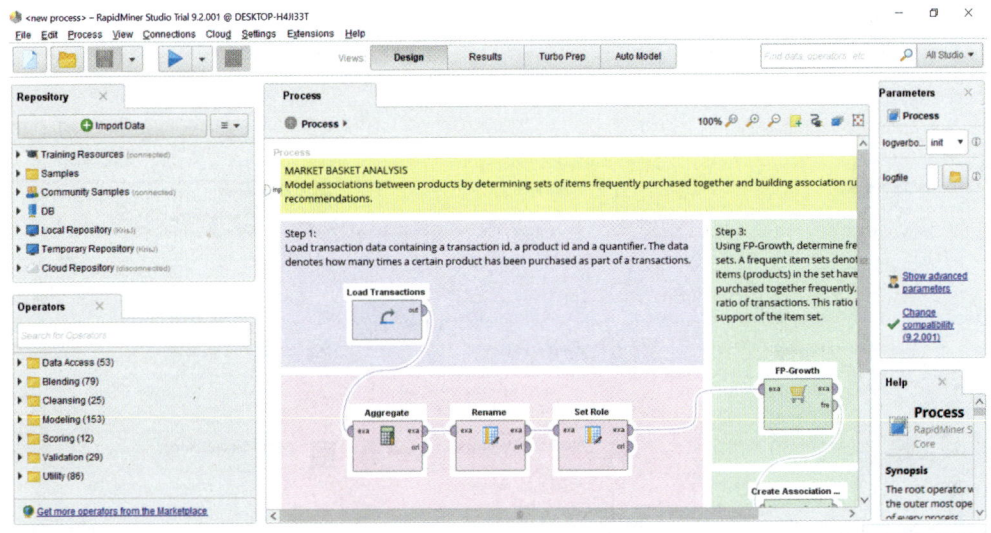

**FIGURE 1.8** Dragging and dropping widgets within a visual-programming environment.
Used with permission of RapidMiner

To perform similar classification using RapidMiner, you would perform these steps:

1. Start RapidMiner. RapidMiner will display its Start a New Project window, as shown in **FIGURE 1.9**.
2. Click Auto Model. RapidMiner will launch a wizard to guide you through the process, as shown in **FIGURE 1.10**.
3. Click Import Data. RapidMiner will use a wizard to load your data. Use the wizard to load the data file Titanic.csv. RapidMiner will load and display the data, as shown in **FIGURE 1.11**.
4. Click the Predict button. RapidMiner will prompt you to click on the column you want to predict. Click on the Survived column and then click Next. RapidMiner will display bar charts representing the number of passengers in the data set who survived or died. Click Next. RapidMiner will prompt you to specify the columns you want it to use in the prediction, as shown in **FIGURE 1.12**.
5. Use the default column selections and click Next. RapidMiner will display a window prompting you for the predictive models you want it to use, as shown in **FIGURE 1.13**.
6. Use the default setting of all models and click Run. RapidMiner will perform its predictions, displaying summary information about each model, as shown in **FIGURE 1.14**.
7. Within the left-hand side of the window, click on the Prediction entry for each model. RapidMiner will display the actual data versus its predicted result, as shown in **FIGURE 1.15**.

As you can see, using a visual-programming tool, an analyst who does not program can perform data-mining and machine-learning operations that before required a programmer.

# CHAPTER 1 Data Mining and Analytics

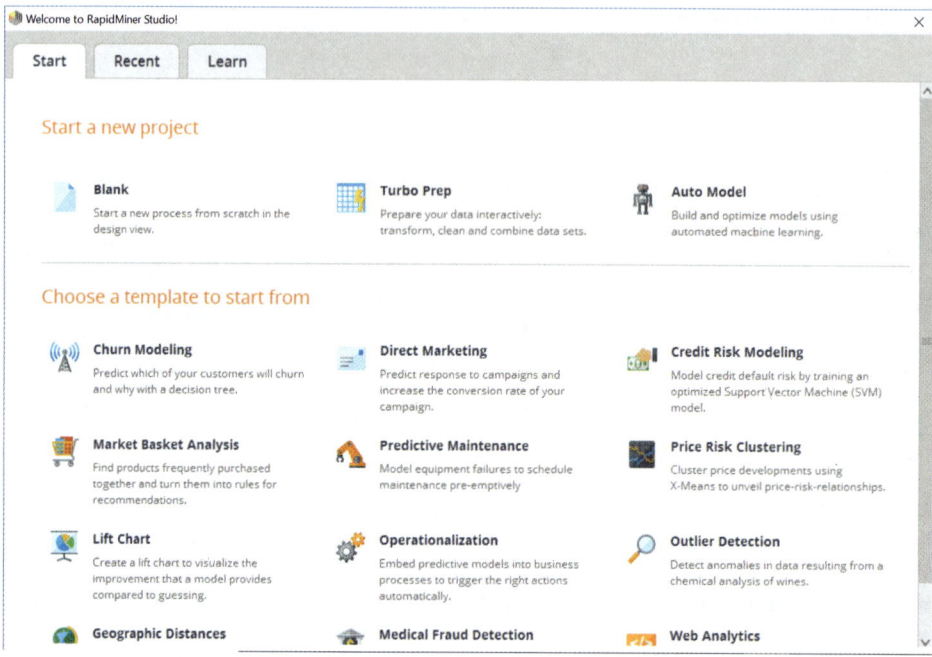

**FIGURE 1.9** The RapidMiner Start a New Project window.

Used with permission of RapidMiner

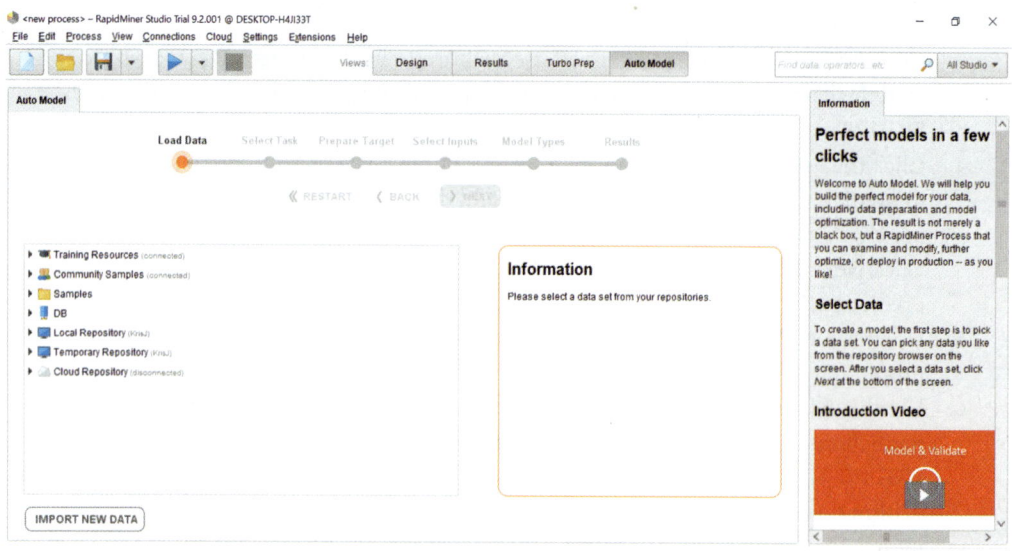

**FIGURE 1.10** Using the RapidMiner Auto Model wizard.

Used with permission of RapidMiner

# Business Intelligence

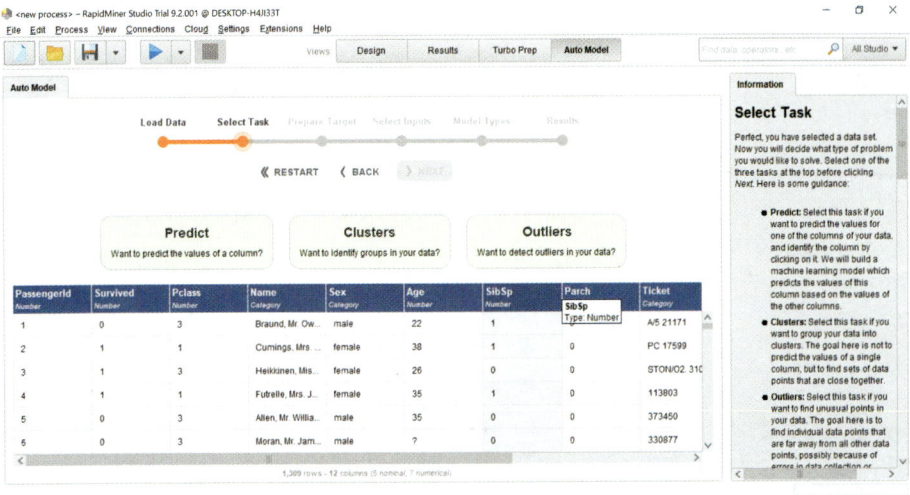

**FIGURE 1.11** Loading the Titanic data set into RapidMiner.
Used with permission of RapidMiner

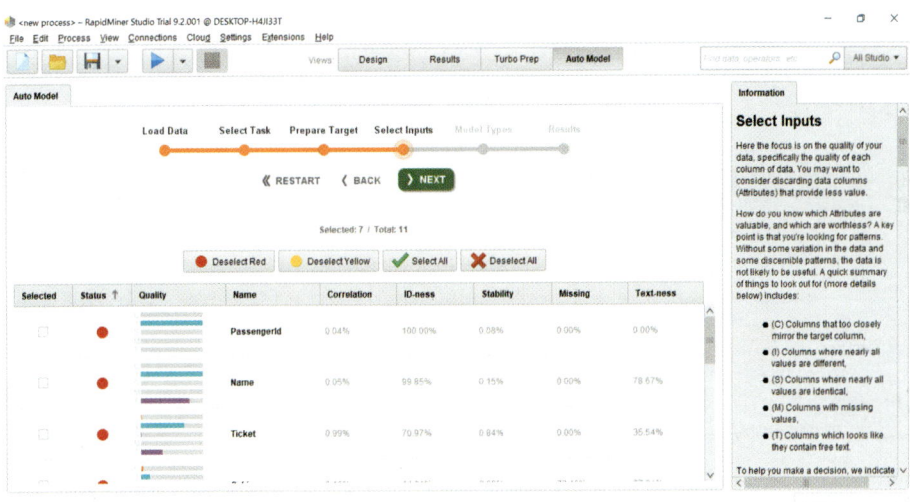

**FIGURE 1.12** Selecting columns for use in the data prediction.
Used with permission of RapidMiner

# Business Intelligence

Business intelligence is the use of tools (data mining, machine learning, and visualization) to convert data into actionable business insights and recommendations. Business intelligence often leverages click-through dashboards, and users can click on items to display greater levels of detail.

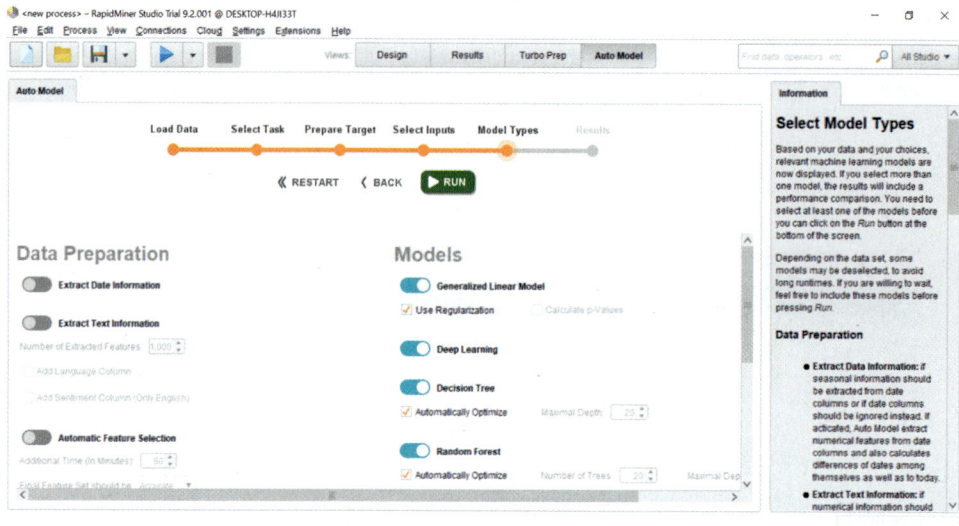

**FIGURE 1.13** Selecting predictive models in RapidMiner.
Used with permission of RapidMiner

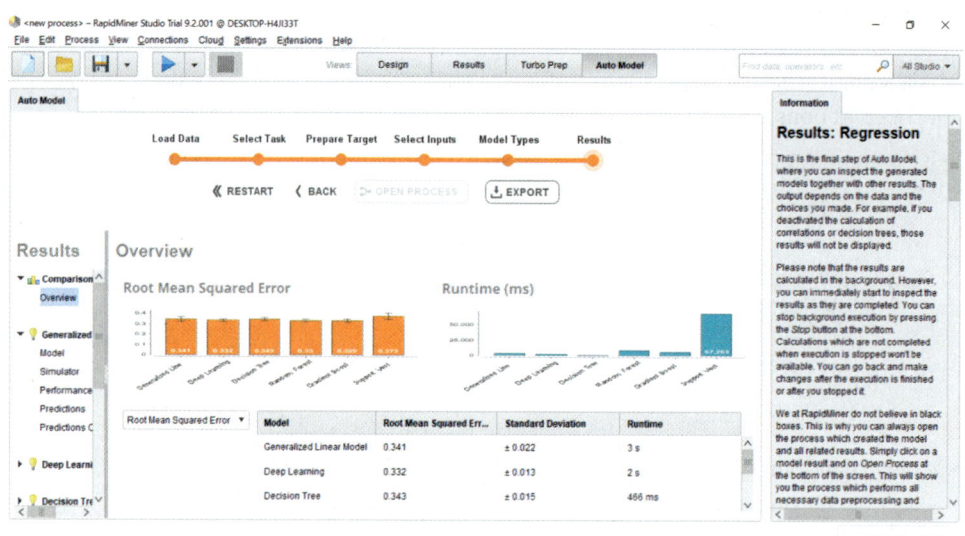

**FIGURE 1.14** Displaying summary information about each prediction model's processing.
Used with permission of RapidMiner

Business intelligence systems often include decision support tools that help users make better decisions. Using historical data, such tools can describe what has happened and potentially why. Using predictive analytics, such tools can predict what should happen in the future, and they may possibly prescribe choices the user should make.

# Understanding the Role of Databases

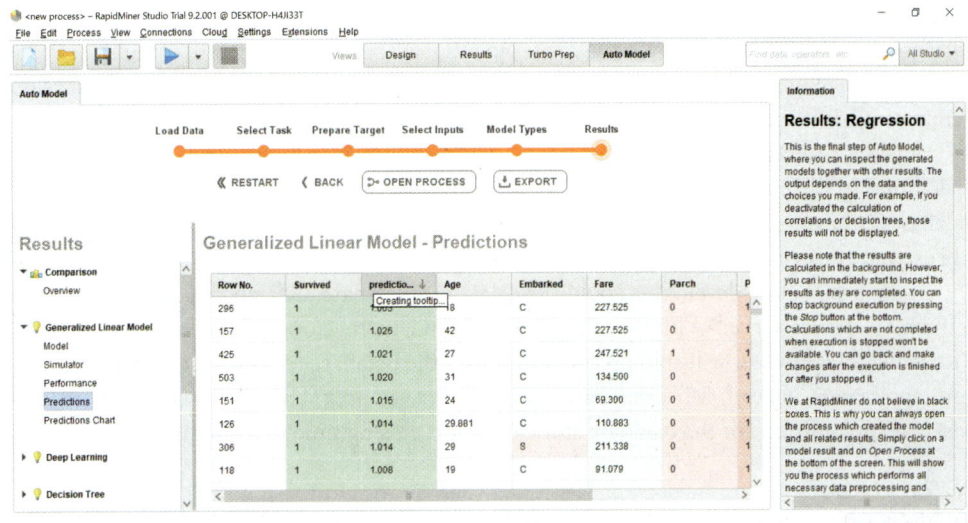

**FIGURE 1.15** Displaying predictions about *Titanic* passenger survival within RapidMiner.
Used with permission of RapidMiner

Business intelligence software normally provides extensive visualization (charting) capabilities. Beyond visualization, the tools will normally include the ability to perform many of the data-mining and machine-learning capabilities this text presents. Throughout this text, you will examine and perform operations using the following business intelligence tools:

- Microsoft Power BI
- Tableau
- Orange
- Solver (previously known as XLMiner)
- RapidMiner
- Excel

# Programming Data Mining and Machine Learning

To perform data-mining and machine-learning operations, programmers often use a programming language to write one or more applications that perform specific processing. Throughout this text, you will make extensive use of the Python and R programming languages to create data-mining and machine-learning applications. That said, such programming is not limited to the use of Python and R. Almost all modern programming languages have libraries you can use for data mining and machine learning. This text uses Python and R based on their popularity and widespread use.

# Understanding the Role of Databases

Before programs and data-mining tools can perform analytic operations, the data must reside within an accessible storage location. As the volume of data applications must process continues to grow, so, too, does the demands on the underlying database. For over five decades, table-based relational databases have been the mainstay for database operations. The explosive growth of highly scaled web and mobile solutions, not to mention the Internet of Things (IoT), has motivated database developers to migrate to different database types, such as graph-based databases and NoSQL databases. Chapter 3, "Databases and Data Warehouses," examines database, data-warehouse, data-mart, and data-lake operations. In Chapter 6, "Keep SQL in Your Toolset," you will examine ways to integrate relational databases into your spreadsheet processing. Finally, in Chapter 7, "NoSQL Data Analytics," you will examine unstructured NoSQL databases, such as MongoDB, CouchDB, Redis, and Cassandra.

In the past, before developers could store data in a database, a database administrator had to spin up a database server. With the advent of the cloud, many cloud providers now offer DBaaS, with which the provider will spin up and administer the database for you, freeing you to focus on your application instead. Most database-managed service providers charge on a pay-as-you-go basis, so you only pay for the database storage and processing time that you use.

## A Word on Data Sets

Throughout this text, you will make extensive use of data sets, which you will need to download and store on your own computer. Often, this text will include a link to the text's catalog page from which you can download a data set. In addition, this text makes extensive use of the UCI data set repository shown in **FIGURE 1.16**.

A second excellent source of data sets is Kaggle.com, shown in **FIGURE 1.17**. In addition to housing a wide range of data sets, the Kaggle site provides access to source code examples, discussions, and more. You should take time to register at the Kaggle site now.

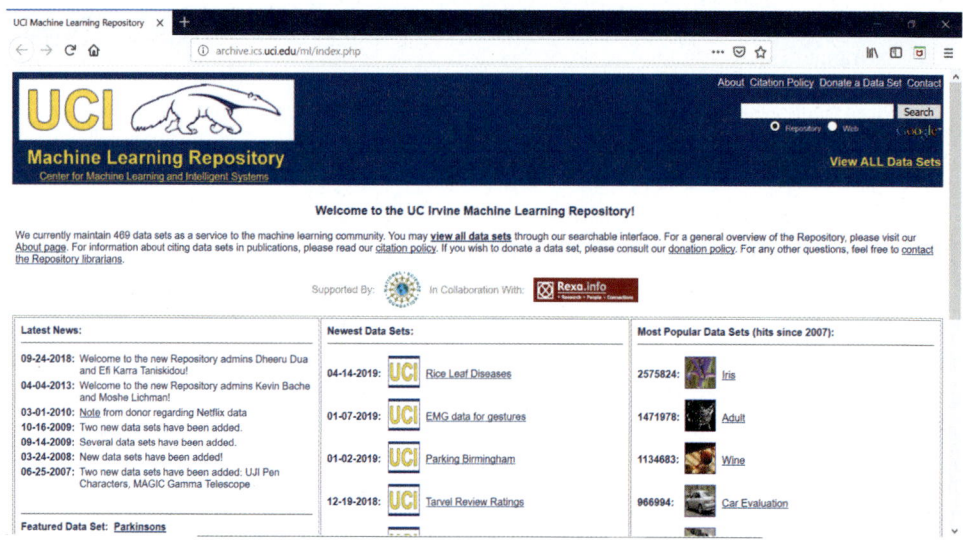

**FIGURE 1.16** The UCI data-set repository.
Used with permission of UC Regents

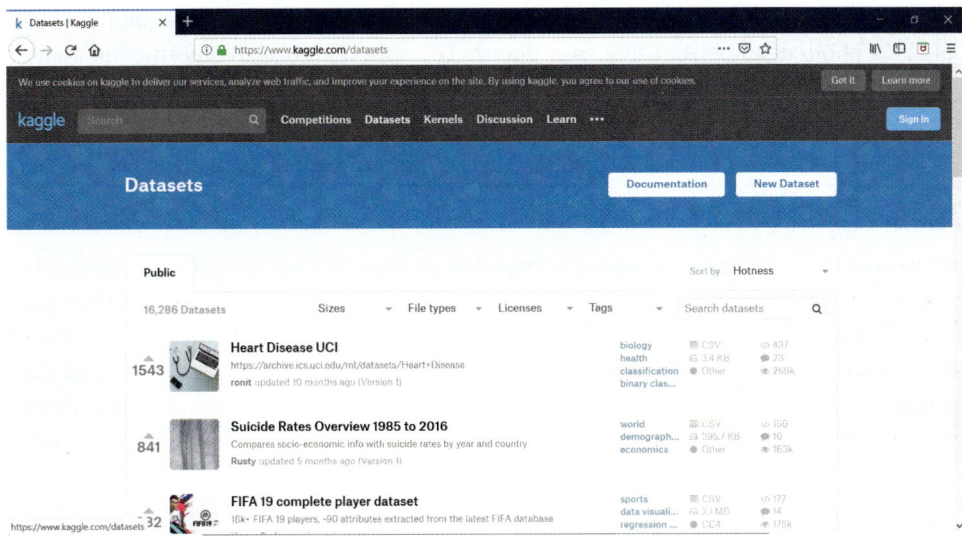

**FIGURE 1.17** The Kaggle website.

Used with permission of RapidMiner

# Data Cleansing and Wrangling

Before a data analyst can start the data-mining process, he or she should determine the quality of the data set and identify any anomalies, such as missing or outlier data, that they will need to resolve. In the simplest sense, data quality is a measure of the data's suitability for use. Data analysts often calculate a data-set's quality based on the following:

- ▸ Accuracy: the degree to which the data correctly represent the underlying real-world values, such as all temperatures from a sensor being in the correct range.
- ▸ Completeness: the degree to which the data represent all required values, such as a data set that should contain an hour of data, for a sensor that reports every second, having 100% of the data values.
- ▸ Consistency: the degree to which similar or related data values align throughout the data set, such as each occurrence of an address having the same ZIP code.
- ▸ Conformity: the degree to which the data values align with the company's business rules, such as the company will measure and store sensor values in 1-second intervals.

# Text and Photo Data Mining

Most people, when they think of data mining, will envision numerical calculations that produce a variety of tables, charts, and graphs. Data mining, however, is not limited to numeric data. In Chapter 14, "Mining Text and Image Data," you will examine the use of data mining and machine learning with text and image data.

For example, using text mining, you can determine the language used to create a document, identify the document's topic, and so on. Using image mining, you can perform facial recognition to identify individuals in a photo and more. There are several popular mobile solutions that let you take a photo of an object using your phone. The apps then display information about the object. Behind the scenes, the applications perform image mining to identify photo matches. In Chapter 14, you will learn how to perform such operations.

## Data Clustering

Data clustering is the process of grouping related data set items into one or more clusters. One of the first tasks a data analyst performs when he or she mines data is to place the data into related groups. Clustering uses an unsupervised machine-learning algorithm, which means the algorithm does not use a training data set. Instead, to group data, the clustering algorithms identify items with similar attributes. As you will learn, there are literally hundreds of clustering algorithms, which differ by:

- Performance
- Memory use
- Hardness or softness
- Data-set size
- Need for the analyst to specify the starting number of clusters
- And more

Chapter 10, "Data Clustering," examines cluster operations in detail. As shown in **FIGURE 1.18**, a common use of clustering is infectious disease control. Through cluster analysis, doctors and researchers can often isolate the source of an infectious disease.

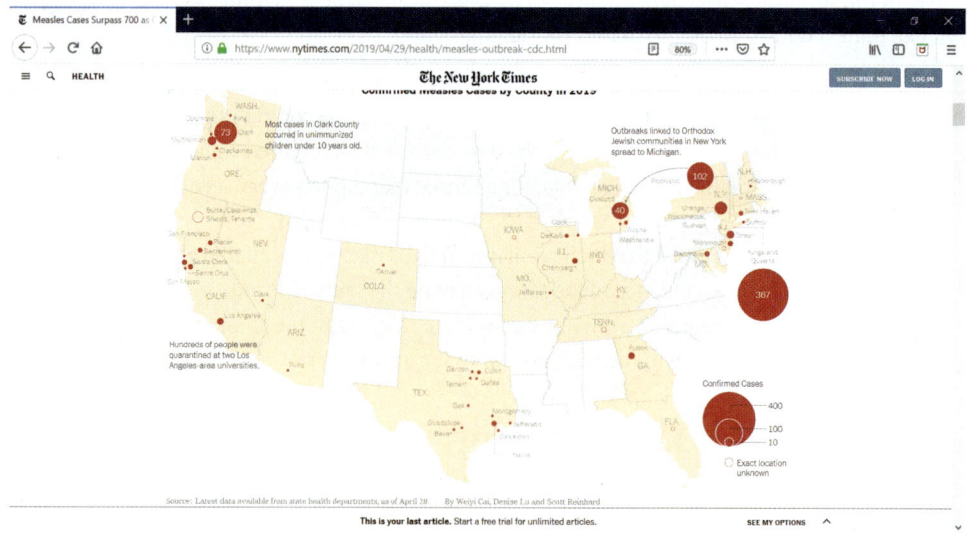

**FIGURE 1.18** Using data clustering to identify the source of an infectious disease.

Used with permission of RapidMiner

Consider the Iris data set, which is a well-known data-mining and machine-learning data set used to introduce the clustering and classification processes. The data set (discussed in detail in Chapter 10) contains sepal and petal lengths for three varieties of iris flowers:

- *Iris setosa*
- *Iris vergenica*
- *Iris versicolor*

The data set has 50 records for each variety.

Using clustering, you can collect the data into groups for further analysis. The following Python script, IrisCluster.py, uses the common k-means clustering algorithm to identify related groups within the data set:

```
import matplotlib.pyplot as plt
from sklearn.cluster import KMeans
import pandas as pd
import numpy as np

names = ['sepal_length', 'sepal_width', 'petal_length', 'petal_width', 'class']

df = pd.read_csv('iris.data.csv', header=None, names=names)
from pandas import DataFrame
from sklearn.decomposition import PCA

df = df.drop('class', axis=1)
pca = PCA(n_components=2).fit(df)
data_2d = pca.transform(df)

kmeans = KMeans(n_clusters=3).fit(data_2d)
centroids = kmeans.cluster_centers_

for i in range(0, data_2d.shape[0]):
  if kmeans.labels_[i] == 0:
    plt.scatter(data_2d[i,0], data_2d[i,1], c='green')
  elif kmeans.labels_[i] == 1:
    plt.scatter(data_2d[i,0], data_2d[i,1], c='yellow')
  elif kmeans.labels_[i] == 2:
    plt.scatter(data_2d[i,0], data_2d[i,1], c='blue')

plt.scatter(centroids[:, 0], centroids[:, 1], c='black', marker='X')
plt.title("Clusters")
plt.show()
```

The Iris data set contains multiple columns of data. To start, the script loads the data set and then transforms the columns into a two-dimensional array of values that represent the original four columns. The script then uses the k-means function to determine the clusters, plotting each cluster in a different color. The script also plots the center of each cluster (called the centroid). When you run this script, it will display a chart, as shown in **FIGURE 1.19**, that identifies the clusters.

Hierarchical clustering algorithms create clusters based on the distance between data-set points (Chapter 10 explains this in more detail.). Hierarchical clustering solutions will often represent the clusters using a graph called a dendrogram, like that shown in **FIGURE 1.20**.

Using the dendrogram, you can see how the algorithm combined nearby points to create the desired number of clusters.

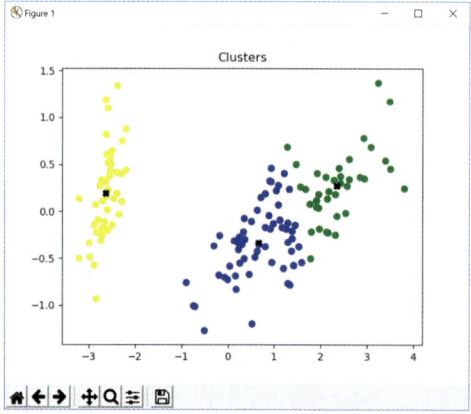

**FIGURE 1.19** Using clustering to identify related groups within the Iris data set.

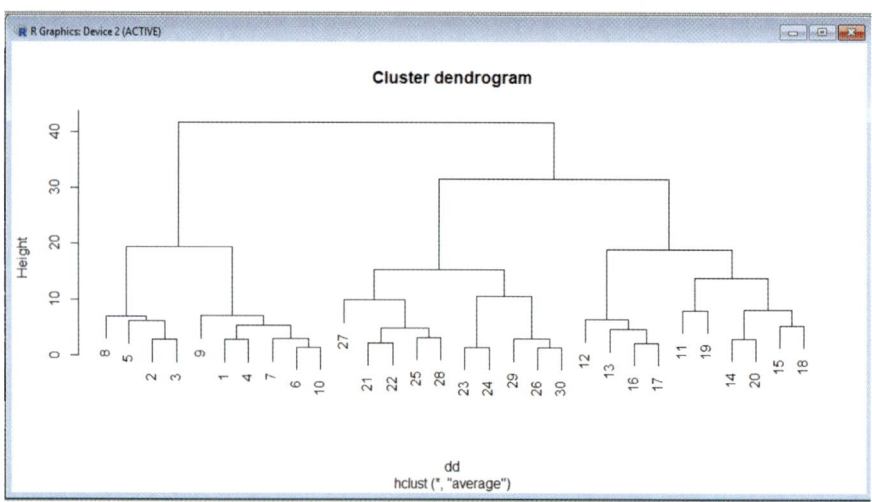

**FIGURE 1.20** Using a dendrogram to illustrate cluster groupings.

The following R program, HierarchicalCluster.R, performs hierarchical clustering on a data set to produce the dendrogram previously shown in Figure 1.20:

```
library(factoextra)
libary(cluster)
library(fpc)

df = data.frame(
     x =  c(35,34,32,37,33,33,31,27,35,34,62,54,57,47,50,57,59,
            52,61,47,50,48,39,40,45,47,39,44,50,48),
     y =  c(79,54,52,77,59,74,73,57,69,75,51,32,40,47,53,36,35,5
            8,59,50,23,22,13,14,22,7,29,25,9,8)
     )

dd <- dist(df, method = "euclidean")

hc <- hclust(dd, method = "average")
plot(hc, labels = NULL, hang = 0.1,
     main = "Cluster dendrogram", sub = NULL,
     xlab = NULL, ylab = "Height")
```

Beyond clustering using Python and R, in Chapter 10, you will learn how to use Solver to cluster data within Excel. Likewise, Chapter 13, "Data Association," shows you how to cluster data using visual programming within Orange.

# Data Classification

Data classification is the process of assigning data to matching groups. There are many different uses for data classification. For example, a bank might examine a customer's attributes to determine if the customer is a high- or low-risk loan candidate. Similarly, airport security teams might examine passenger data to determine if a passenger is a potential threat. Doctors might examine a tumor biopsy to determine if the tumor is malignant or benign. Lastly, security software might use classification to categorize an email message as valid or spam.

Data classification uses supervised machine learning, meaning the classification algorithm will use a training data set to teach the algorithm the common attributes for each category. There are many different data classification algorithms, which differ by memory use and central processing unit (CPU) performance.

Chapter 11, "Data Classification," examines several of the commonly used algorithms. Consider, for example, the Census data set at the UCI that contains census data on individuals such as age, gender, race, and marital status. You can download a subset of the data set from this text's catalog page at go.jblearning.com/DataMining, which has reduced the number of records to 500 and reduced the number of columns. For simplicity, the data set has also converted text fields, such as male and female, to the numeric values 1 and 0 and marital status to 0 not married, 1 married, 2 never married, 3 divorced, and 4 widowed. The data set represents individuals living in the United States as 1 and outside of the United States as 0.

The data set also represents incomes less than $50,000 with the numeric value 0 and incomes greater than or equal to $50,000 as 1.

Although such substitutions accomplish the goal of getting numeric values, this presents the problem of introducing ordinal values, which imply a numeric order such that male is greater than female and black has a more significant value than white. As you will learn in Chapter 2, to avoid such ordered implications, developers use a technique called **hot encoding** that, rather than assigning ordinal numbers, assign binary vector values. In the case of male and female, you might use the following vectors:

```
male    [1 0]
female  [0 1]
```

Likewise, for black, white, and other, you would use:

```
black  [1 0 0]
white  [0 1 0]
other  [0 0 1]
```

The following Python program, PredictIncome.py, uses the Census data set to classify an individual as likely to fall within one of two income levels:

- Earns less than $50,000
- Earns $50,000 or more

```
import pandas as pd
import numpy as np
from sklearn.model_selection import train_test_split
from sklearn.metrics import accuracy_score
from sklearn.neighbors import KNeighborsClassifier
from sklearn.metrics import confusion_matrix

names = ['Married', 'Race', 'Gender', 'Age', 'Country',
'Income']

df = pd.read_csv('census.csv', header=1, names=names)
X = np.array(df.iloc[:, 0:4])
y = np.array(df['Income'])

# split into train and test
X_train, X_test, y_train, y_test = train_test_split(X, y,
test_size=0.30)

knn = KNeighborsClassifier(n_neighbors=3)
knn.fit(X_train, y_train)
pred = knn.predict(X_test)

print ('\nModel accuracy score: ', accuracy_score(y_test, pred))
print (confusion_matrix(y_test, pred))
```

As you can see, the script loads the data set and then splits it into training (70%) and testing data (30%) and calls the KNearestNeighbors function to categorize the data. When you run this program, it will display the following output:

```
C:\> python PredictIncome.py
Model accuracy score:  0.7333333333333333
[[102    9]
 [ 31    8]]
```

In this case, the model has an accuracy of 73%, which would increase with a larger data set. The Confusion Matrix states that the model correctly predicted 102 out of 111 individuals making less than $50K (missing 9) and 31 out of 39 individuals making more than $50K (missing 8).

Chapter 11 examines KNearestNeighbors and other classification algorithms in detail.

# Predictive Analytics

For decades, businesses have used data analytics to explain their performance during the previous quarter or year. Analysts refer to this as **descriptive analytics**—the analysts use data to describe what happened in the past. Predictive analytics, in contrast, uses data to predict what will happen in the future.

A simple form of predictive analytics is linear regression, which creates a linear expression that best models a given data set, as shown in **FIGURE 1.21**.

In simple linear regression, analysts predict a result based on the value of one variable, such as the value of y, using the familiar equation for a line:

$$y = mx + b$$

In multivariate regression, analysts predict a result based on two or more variables:

$$y = ax_0 + bx_1 + cx_2 + dx_3$$

When you perform a multivariate regression, the solutions will provide you with the coefficient values, in this case, for a, b, c, and d shown earlier, which you can then use to predict results. As you might guess, data are not always linear, as shown in **FIGURE 1.22**.

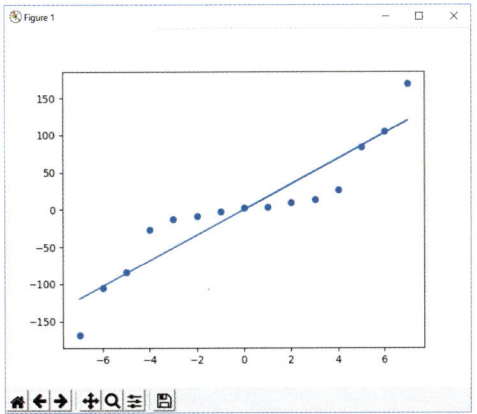

**FIGURE 1.21** Using linear regression to model data points.

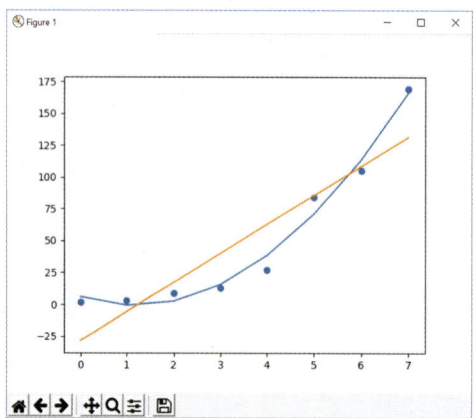

**FIGURE 1.22** Most real-world data sets are not linear.

To help you better map your predicted data to actual data, Chapter 12 presents a variety of regression techniques beyond linear regression.

Consider the Insurance.csv data set previously discussed in this chapter that contains over 1,300 records regarding insurance customers and their insurance charges. The following Python script, PredictInsuranceCosts.py, uses the data set to create a predictive model that analysts can then use to predict a customer's health costs:

```
import pandas as pd
import numpy as np
from sklearn.ensemble import RandomForestRegressor

data = pd.read_csv('insurance.csv')

X = data[['age', 'sex', 'bmi', 'children','smoker', 'region']].values
y = data['charges']

model = RandomForestRegressor(n_estimators=100)
model.fit(X, y)
predictions = model.predict(X)

print(model.feature_importances_)

predictions = model.predict(X)
for index in range(len(predictions)):
  print('Actual: ', y[index], 'Predicted: ', predictions[index])
```

The script uses a random-forest predictive model, discussed in Chapter 12, to calculate the coefficients. Then the script applies the model to the variables, comparing its predicted results to the actual results. When you execute this script, it will display the following output:

```
C:\> python PredictInsuranceCosts.py
[0.13151069 0.00604639 0.2125544  0.02005577 0.61601542
 0.01381734]
Actual:   16884.924 Predicted:   16924.434139000023
Actual:   1725.5523 Predicted:   1966.1617585000026
Actual:   4449.462 Predicted:    5521.289733900003
Actual:   21984.47061 Predicted: 15565.129127299988
Actual:   3866.8552 Predicted:   4084.818179299997
Actual:   3756.6216 Predicted:   3761.8876185000054
Actual:   8240.5896 Predicted:   8626.95272619999
Actual:   7281.5056 Predicted:   7132.781463000001
   :         :           :            :
Actual:   1629.8335 Predicted:   2175.7635584166674
Actual:   2007.945 Predicted:    2020.7115740000029
Actual:   29141.3603 Predicted:  28959.47406849998
```

As you can see, the script first displays the coefficient value and then displays the applied results. Throughout this text, you will examine tools such as RapidMiner that let you perform predictive analysis without the need for Python or R programming.

## Data Association

Data association is the process of identifying relationships between variables for which the presence or absence of a first variable (called the antecedent) influences a second variable (called the consequent). One of the best-known data association problems is market-basket analysis, which examines the items in a shopper's basket to identify associations between them. Using market-basket analysis, for example, analysts found that shoppers who purchased diapers are highly likely to also purchase beer. With such product insights in hand, a store might advertise a sale on diapers, while also increasing the price of beer. Or the store may place beer and diapers far away from one another, so that customers needing both must walk past many other items.

Assume, for example, a popular e-commerce site wants to know how other product sales are driven by their key items: books, videos, and music. The data set for the e-commerce sales contains transactions in the form shown in **FIGURE 1.23**. You can download the data set from this text's catalog page at go.jblearning.com/DataMining.

As you can see, each transaction lists items purchased. The following Python script, EcommerceAssociation.py, uses the apriori algorithm to determine the associations between products:

```
import pandas as pd
from apyori import apriori

data = pd.read_csv('ecommerce.csv', header=None)

records = []
```

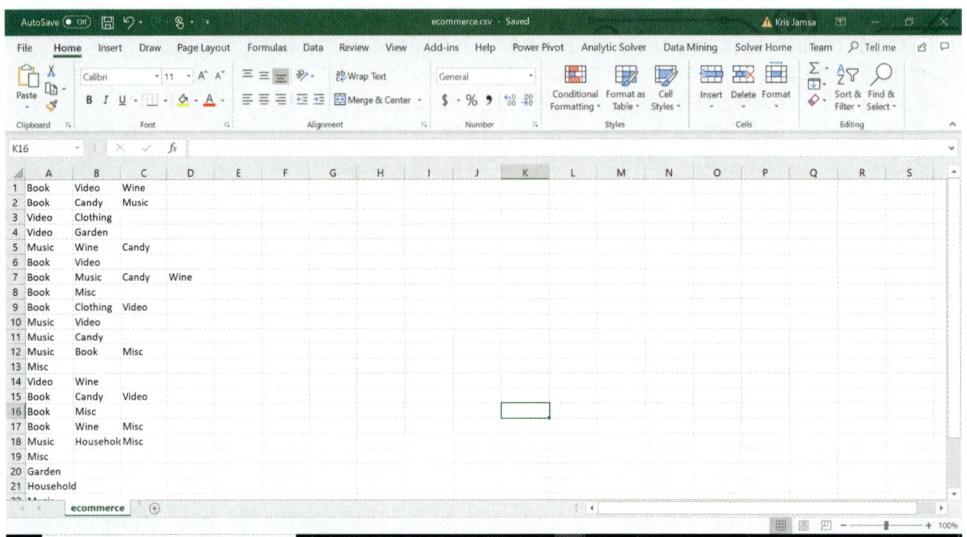

**FIGURE 1.23** Transactions within the e-commerce data set.

Used with permission from Microsoft

```
for i in range(0, len(data)):
    records.append([str(data.values[i,j]) for j in range(0,
len(data.columns))])

rules = apriori(records, min_length=2, min_lift=1.1,
min_support=0.15)
results = list(rules)

for item in results:
  if not 'nan' in str(item):
    print()
    print(item)
    print()
    print("-----------------------")
```

The program opens the data set and then uses a for loop to append the data to a list of lists, which the apriori function requires. The script then calls the apriori function with the data, specifying minimum support and lift values to reduce the output of meaningless associations. When you execute the script, it will display the following output:

```
C:\> python EcommerceAssociation.py
RelationRecord(items=frozenset({'Book', 'Misc'}),
support=0.16, ordered_statistics=[OrderedStatistic(items_
base=frozenset({'Book'}), items_add=frozenset({'Misc'}),
confidence=0.39999999999999997, lift=1.4285714285714284),
OrderedStatistic(items_base=frozenset({'Misc'}),
```

```
    items_add=frozenset({'Book'}), confidence=0.5714285714285714,
    lift=1.4285714285714284)])


    ----------------------

    RelationRecord(items=frozenset({'Book', 'Video'}),
    support=0.16, ordered_statistics=[OrderedStatistic(items_
    base=frozenset({'Book'}), items_add=frozenset({'Video'}),
    confidence=0.39999999999999997, lift=1.1111111111111112),
    OrderedStatistic(items_base=frozenset({'Video'}), items_
    add=frozenset({'Book'}), confidence=0.4444444444444445,
    lift=1.1111111111111112)])


    ----------------------

    RelationRecord(items=frozenset({'Music', 'Candy'}),
    support=0.16, ordered_statistics=[OrderedStatistic(items_
    base=frozenset({'Candy'}), items_add=frozenset({'Music'}),
    confidence=0.7999999999999999, lift=2.2222222222222223),
    OrderedStatistic(items_base=frozenset({'Music'}), items_
    add=frozenset({'Candy'}), confidence=0.4444444444444445,
    lift=2.2222222222222223)])


    ----------------------
```

Within the output you will see one item defined as the base item, which means for the association, it is the antecedent that drives the purchase of the other item (the consequent). With respect to data association, support is a measure that specifies the frequency of the items in the cart. Lift is a measure that indicates the level of influence of the antecedent item on the consequent. A lift value of 1 indicates coincidence. A lift value greater than 1 starts to become meaningful. In this case, from the program's output, you can determine that when a customer purchases music, they will often purchase candy as well.

Chapter 13, "Data Association," examines association and market-based analysis in detail.

## Big Data Mining and Analytics

Across the internet, we are accumulating data at exponential rates and expect to double the amount of data in the world every 2 years. With the advent of the IoT, that rate is expected to increase. That's a lot of data, with a lot more coming! The question many analysts ask is: When does "a lot of data" become "big data"?

In the simplest sense, an application becomes a big data application when we can no longer manipulate the data using traditional databases and data-analytic tools. This means the big data volume exceeds the size of data that tools can support.

To store potentially massive amounts of data, big data solutions often use distributed file systems and databases. In Chapter 7, "NoSQL Data Analytics," you will use the MongoDB NoSQL database. As you will learn, to support big data solutions, database developers will often distribute a database across multiple MongoDB nodes, called shards. For an e-commerce site, for example, the database developers might shard the data by customer region, product type, and so on. **FIGURE 1.24** illustrates the process of sharding a MongoDB database. Behind the scenes, MongoDB will route database requests to the correct shard.

In Chapter 15, "Big Data Mining," you will learn that to process big data, developers often use a model called MapReduce, which allows solutions to leverage data that reside across multiple servers.

# Excel Still Matters

Despite new data-analytic and data-mining tools, Excel remains one of the most widely used analytic tools. Using Excel, you can preview data, cleanse data, search and sort data, visualize data using Excel's built-in charts, and even perform many data-mining and machine-learning operations by leveraging third-party tools, such as Solver. Chapter 5, "Keep Excel in Your Toolset," provides more information on the use of Excel, and Chapter 10, "Data Clustering," provides more detail on Solver.

Throughout this text, you will use many different comma-separated values (CSV) files to store various data sets. Often, you will use Excel to preview such files. **FIGURE 1.25**, for example, shows

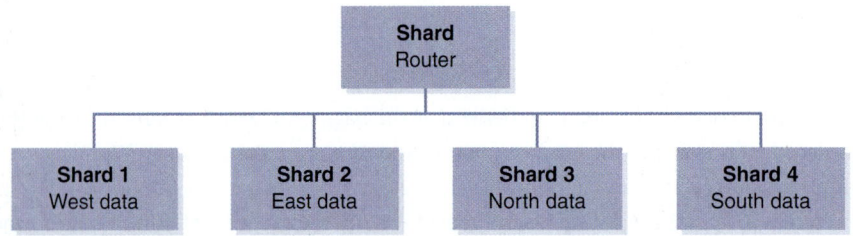

**FIGURE 1.24** Sharding a big data solution.

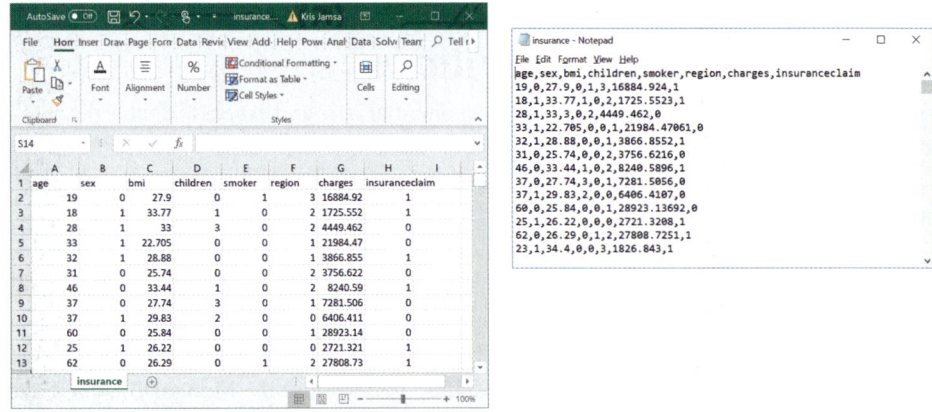

**FIGURE 1.25** Viewing a CSV data set in Windows Notepad and Excel.
Used with permission from Microsoft

the same CSV data set in Windows Notepad and Excel. Not only is the Excel representation of the data set easier to view and interact with but Excel makes it easy to delete data, sort data, or even quickly chart the data.

## Future of Data Mining and Analytics

Despite the explosive growth of data that we are currently experiencing, there are no indications that creation, mining, and analysis will slow down anytime soon. In fact, given data creators such as the billions of devices connected to the IoT, we can only assume continued exponential data growth.

Today, most companies rely on dashboards created by data scientists using the techniques presented throughout this text. Many such dashboards integrate data-mining and machine-learning solutions that were created using a programming language, such as Python or R. As previously discussed, such solutions required one or more programmers to implement the underlying code. As you learned in this chapter, many of the once programmer-required capabilities are now available to nonprogrammers using visual-programming tools.

In Chapter 6, "Keep SQL in Your Toolset," and Chapter 7, "NoSQL Data Analytics," you will learn how to perform database operations. Over the next few years, query operations will evolve from complex, developer-created code solutions into natural language-based queries well suited for nonprogrammers. This means that when a user wants to query a database, he or she will simply ask a question (either through speech or by typing), and the natural language processor will create the underlying query.

## Hands-on Data Mining and Analytics with Weka

Throughout this chapter, you will perform common data-mining operations using Python and R and visual-programming operations using RapidMiner. In this section, you will use Weka, a data-mining tool created at the University of Waikato in New Zealand. Weka stands for Waikato Environment for Knowledge Analysis. A weka is also a bird native to New Zealand.

The purpose of this section is not to drill deep into the data-mining operations it presents—each is the subject of a chapter within this text. Instead, this section's goal is to introduce Weka's functionality. As you later read the specifics about a data-mining technique (such as clustering), you should try the operation using Weka.

To start, download and install Weka from the Weka website at https://www.cs.waikato.ac.nz/ml/weka/, as shown in **FIGURE 1.26**.

When you run Weka, it will display the window shown in **FIGURE 1.27**.

Weka provides many features beyond what this chapter presents. This chapter will focus on the Weka Explorer. The Weka website provides documentation on the remaining operations.

### Cleansing Data with Weka

The first step in data mining is often data cleansing, during which the data analyst removes duplicate records and unnecessary columns, resolves missing values, identifies outliers, and more. The Weka Explorer Preprocess tab helps you perform such operations.

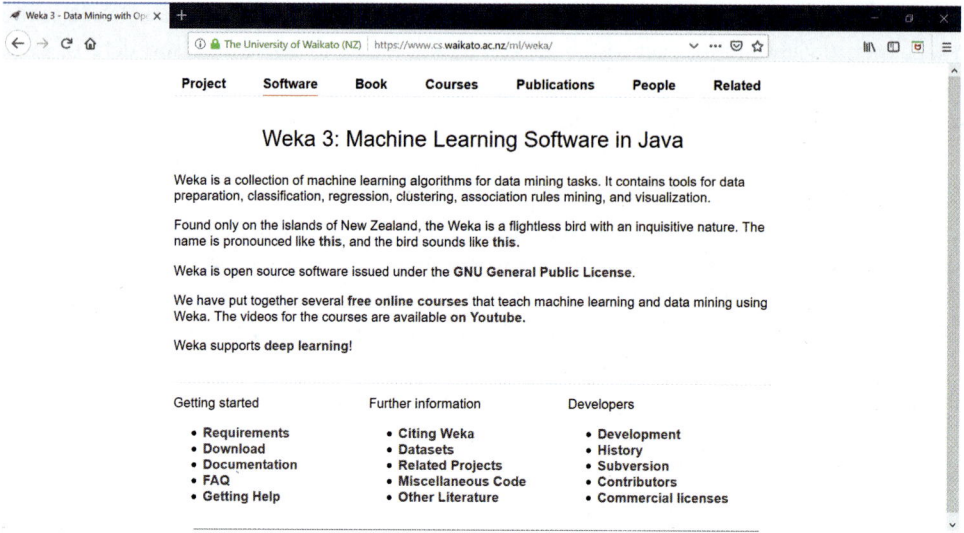

**FIGURE 1.26** The Weka website.
Used with permission from The University of Waikato

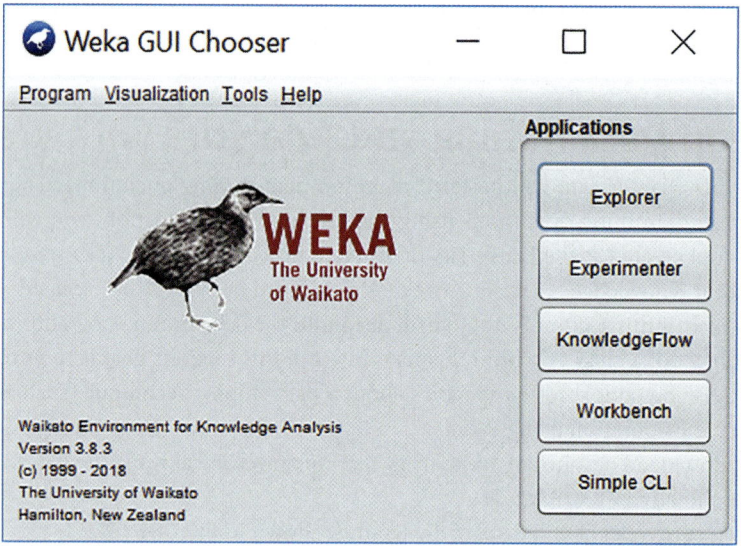

**FIGURE 1.27** Running Weka.
Used with permission from The University of Waikato

To start, download the data set file Seattle.csv from this text's catalog page at go.jblearning.com/DataMining. The data set contains data from the Seattle housing market that relate to the price of homes sold (such as square footage, number of bedrooms, lot size, and so on). Save the file to a

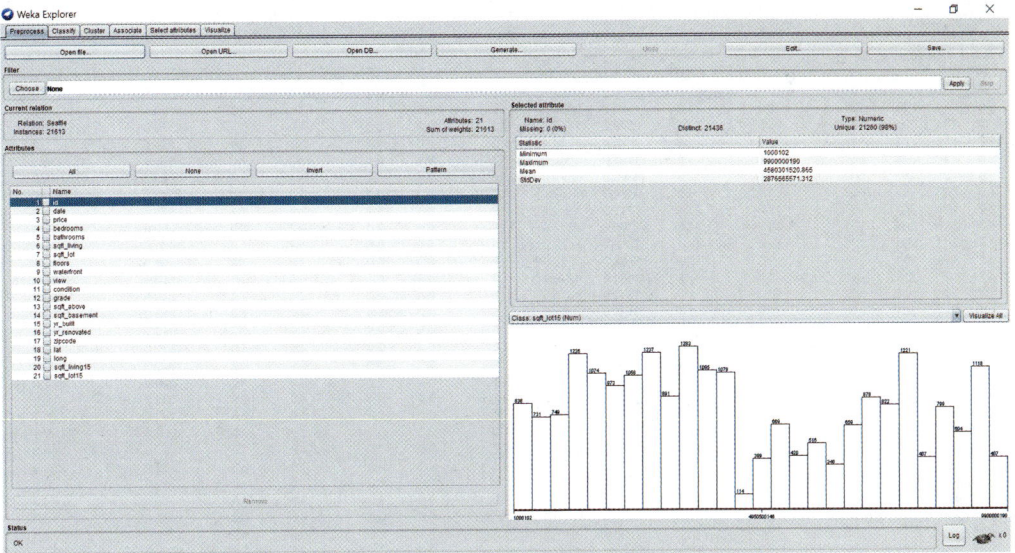

**FIGURE 1.28** Displaying data set columns and statistics within Weka.

Used with permission from The University of Waikato

folder on your disk. Then, using the Weka Open File button, open the Seattle.csv data set file. Weka will display the file's fields, as well as statistics about the current field, as shown in **FIGURE 1.28**.

As you click on different fields, Weka will display statistics specific to that field. From within the Preprocess tab, you can remove unnecessary columns from the data set. Click Edit, and Weka will display an Edit window, as shown in **FIGURE 1.29**, within which you can edit individual field values.

Chapter 9 examines data-cleansing operations in detail.

## Visualizing Data within Weka

Using the Seattle housing market data set that you loaded into Weka in the previous section, click the Weka Explorer Visualize tab. Weka will display many small charts that correspond to the variables charted against one another, as shown in **FIGURE 1.30**.

Within the charts, locate and click on the price versus sqft-living chart. Weka will expand the chart, displaying it as shown in **FIGURE 1.31**.

## Identifying Prediction Variables with Weka

Predictive analytics is the use of statistics, data mining, and machine learning to analyze historical data to predict what will happen in the future. One of the first steps a data analyst performs to create such predictions is to identify the variables that most accurately influence the predicted results. Using the Seattle housing data set, click the Weka Explorer Select Attribute tab. Within

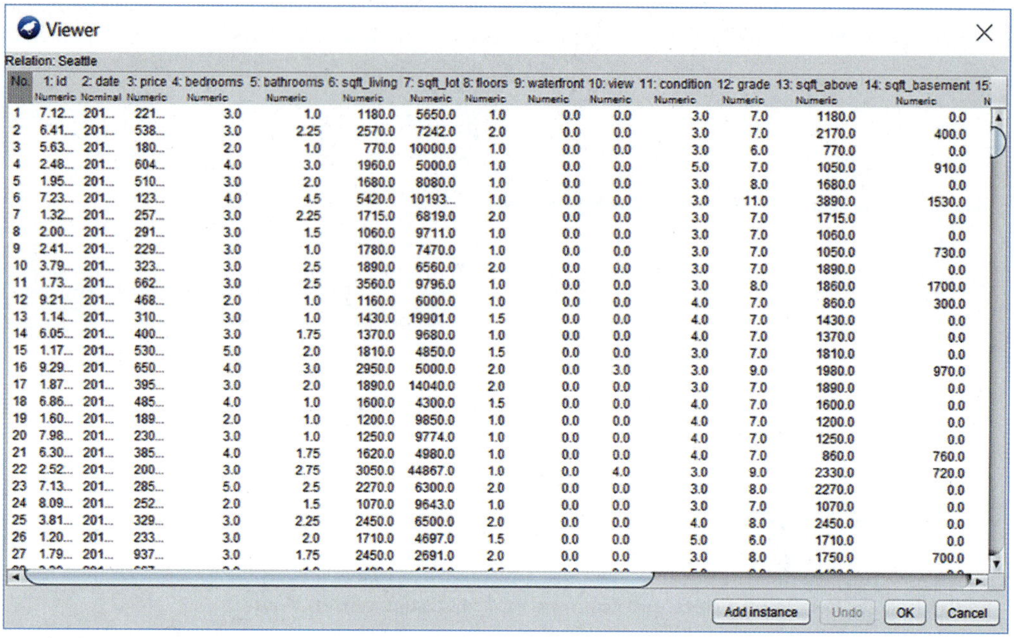

**CHAPTER 1** Data Mining and Analytics

**FIGURE 1.29** Editing data set values in Weka.

Used with permission from The University of Waikato

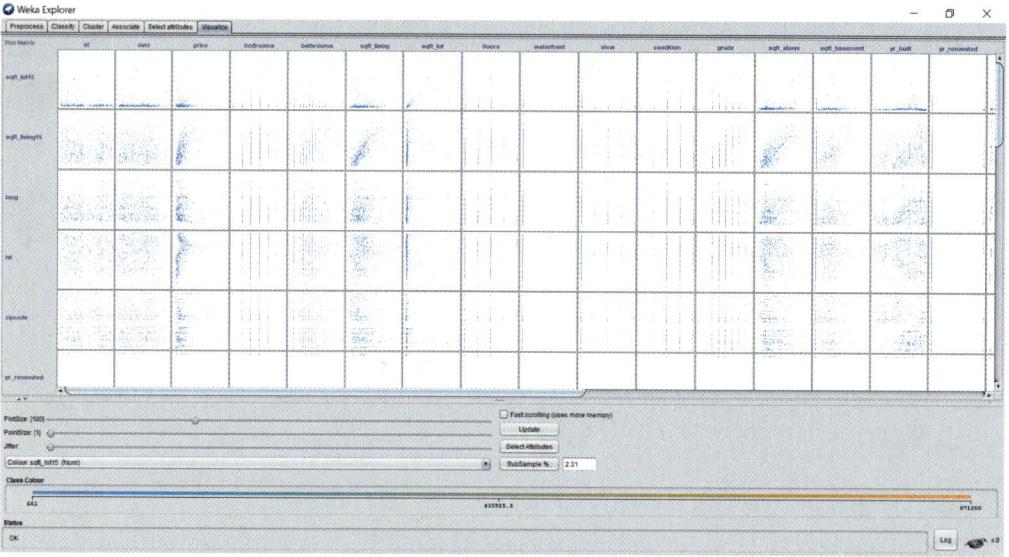

**FIGURE 1.30** Displaying data set variable charts.

Used with permission from The University of Waikato

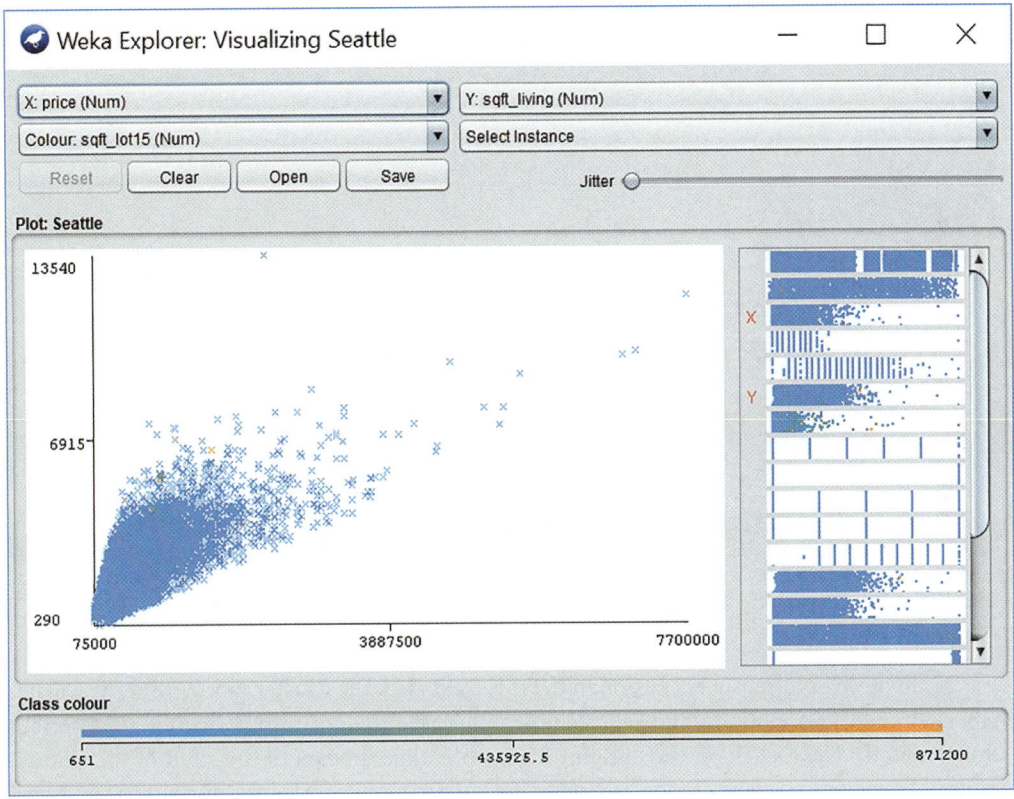

**FIGURE 1.31 Expanding a chart visualization in Weka.**
Used with permission from The University of Waikato

the pull-down list, select the Price attribute. Within the tab, click Start. Weka will analyze the data, displaying the most influential variables affecting price, as shown in **FIGURE 1.32**.

## Clustering Data with Weka

Clustering is the process of grouping related data. To start clustering in Weka, first download the file Iris.data.csv from this text's catalog page at go.jblearning.com/DataMining. The Iris data set is a well-known data-mining and machine-learning data set used to introduce the clustering and classification processes. As mentioned earlier, the data set (discussed in detail in Chapter 10) contains sepal and petal lengths for three varieties of iris flowers:

- *Iris setosa*
- *Iris vergenica*
- *Iris versicolor*

The data set has 50 records for each variety.

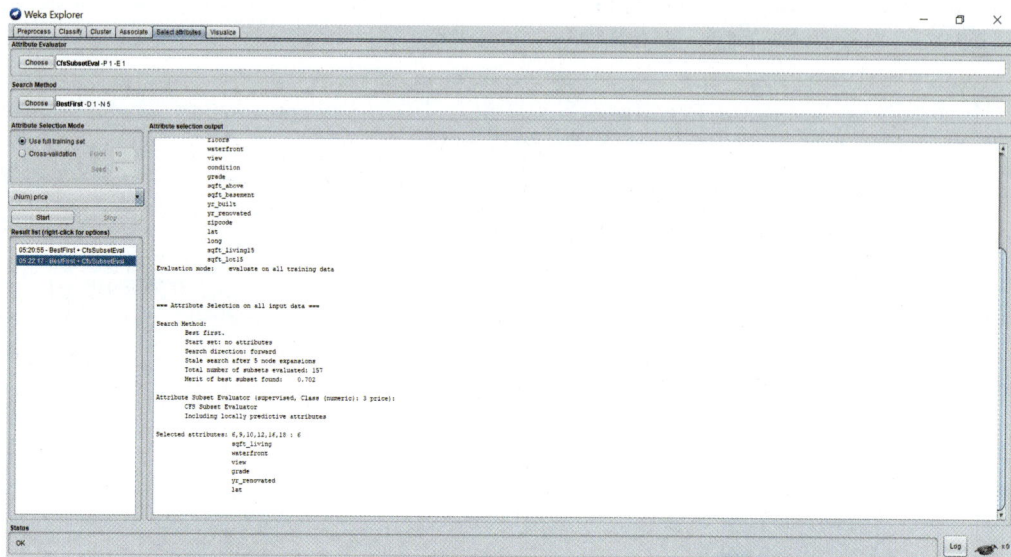

**FIGURE 1.32** Displaying predictive variables in Weka.
Used with permission from The University of Waikato

From the Weka Preprocess tab, open the file. Next click the Cluster tab. Within the Cluster tab, click the Choose button and select the SimpleKMeans algorithm (Chapter 10 describes this in detail). Next, click on the SimpleKMeans box that appears to the right of the Choose button. Weka will display a dialog box that you can use to customize the algorithm, as shown in **FIGURE 1.33**.

Within the dialog box numCluster field, type 3 and choose OK. Then, within the Cluster tab, click Start. Weka will perform its calculations, displaying its results, as shown in **FIGURE 1.34**.

Within the Results list, right-click on the results and select Visualize Cluster Assignments. Weka will display a chart with each cluster uniquely colored, as shown in **FIGURE 1.35**.

## Classifying Data with Weka

**Classification** is the process of assigning data to matching groups. Classification uses **supervised learning**, meaning it will allocate part of a data set for training the algorithm and part for testing how well the model performs. To train and test the algorithm, the training and test data must know (must contain) the correct category assignment.

Using the Iris data set, click on the Classify tab. Within the tab, click Choose, and select the Trees folder random-forest algorithm ( which Chapter 11 describes in detail), as shown in **FIGURE 1.36**.

Within the Test Options field, select a 66% split that directs the algorithm to use 66% of the data set for training and the rest for testing. Click Start. Weka will perform the classification operations, displaying its results as shown in **FIGURE 1.37**.

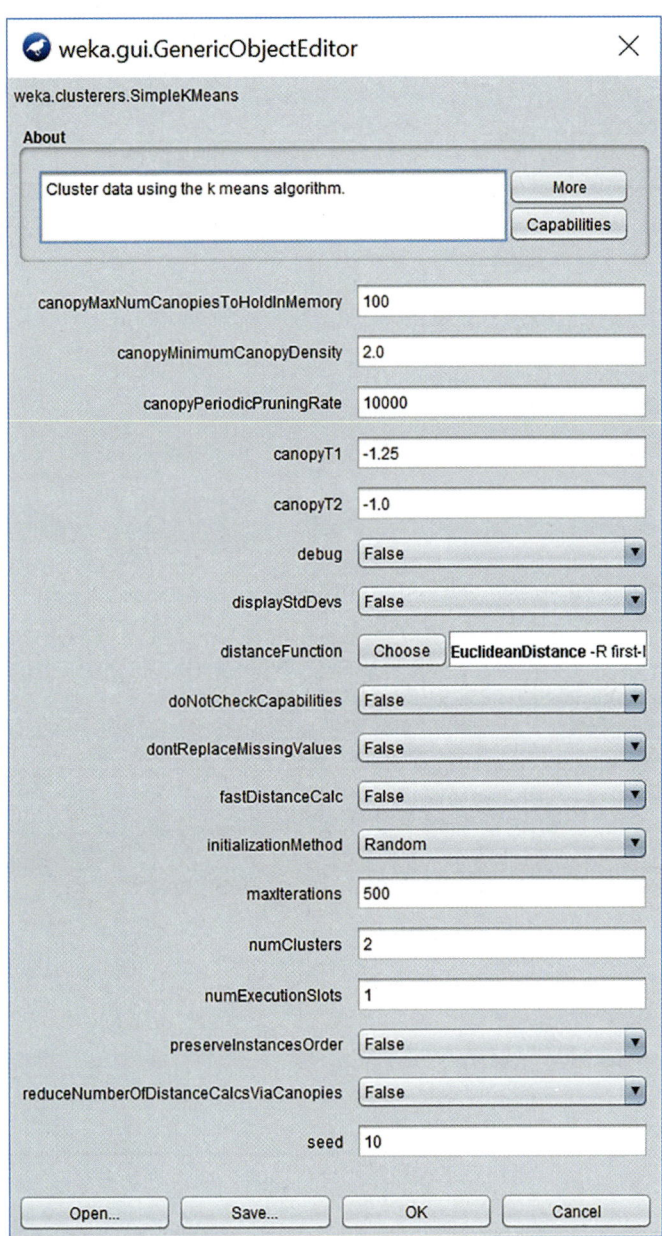

**FIGURE 1.33** Customizing the SimpleKMeans algorithm.
Used with permission from The University of Waikato

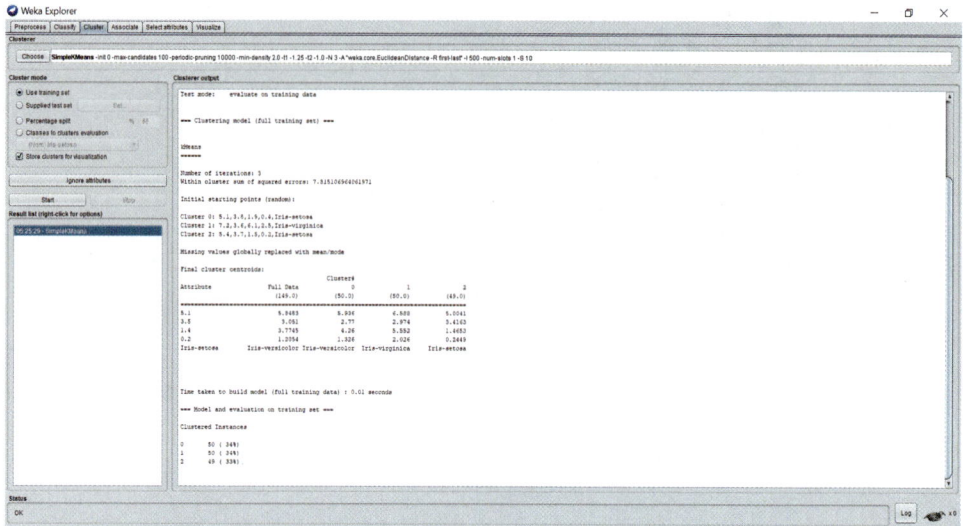

**FIGURE 1.34** Displaying cluster calculation results.
Used with permission from The University of Waikato

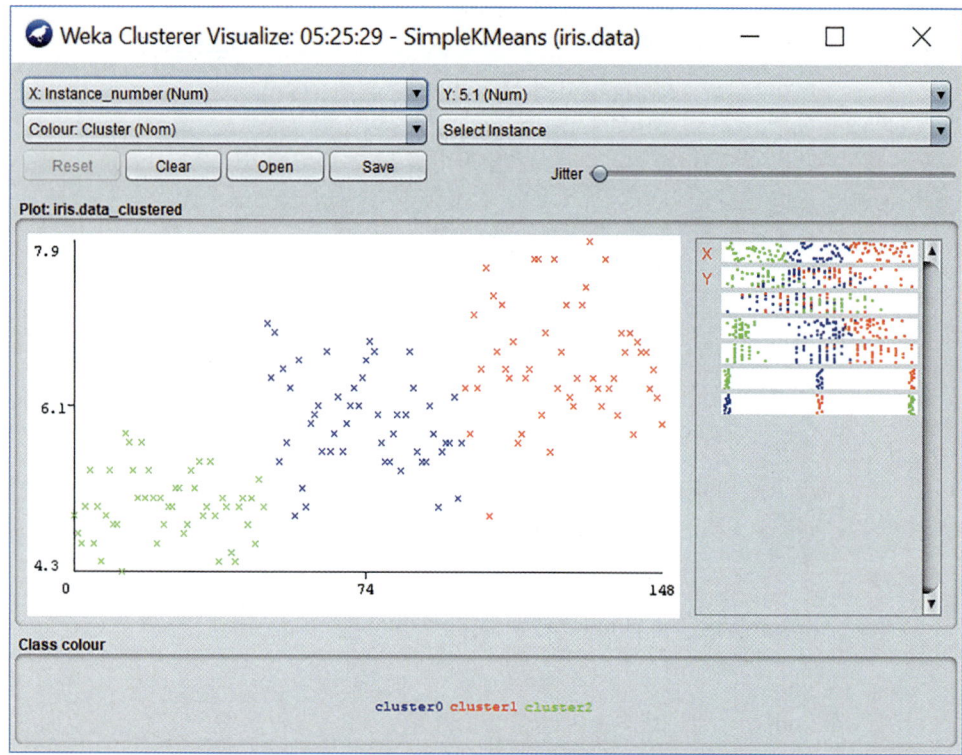

**FIGURE 1.35** Displaying cluster assignments within Weka.
Used with permission from The University of Waikato

**FIGURE 1.36** Selecting random forest classification.
Used with permission from The University of Waikato

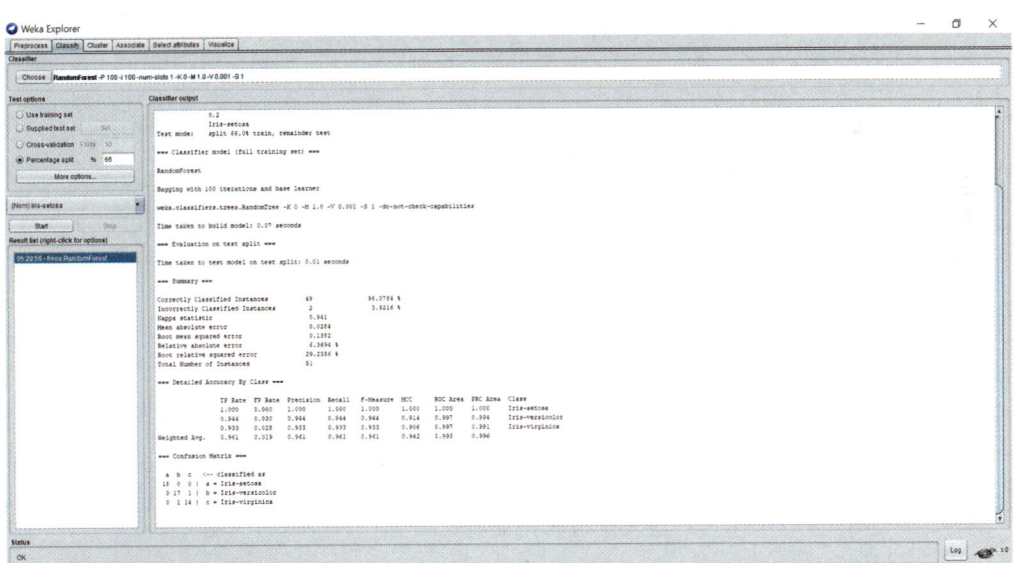

**FIGURE 1.37** Displaying classification results in Weka.
Used with permission from The University of Waikato

In this case, the random-forest algorithm classified data with a 96% accuracy. Within the output, you will find a confusion matrix that shows which assignments the model got right and wrong. Within the confusion matrix, you will learn that the model correctly categorized all *Iris setosa* records but miscategorized one *Iris versicolor* as *Iris vergenica* and one *Iris vergenica* as *Iris versicolor*.

## Performing Data Association within Weka

Data association is the process of identifying relationships between variables. As mentioned, a well-known data association problem is market-basket analysis, for which the items in a customer's shopping cart are examined in order to determine relationships between the items that influence the shopper's behavior. To start, download the file DiapersAndBeer.csv from this text's catalog page at go.jblearning.com/DataMining. From the Weka Preprocess tab, open the file. The data set, as shown in **FIGURE 1.38**, contains records that correspond to shopping cart items for different transactions.

Click on the Associate tab and click Start. Weka will display a list of items, as shown in **FIGURE 1.39**, that most closely associate.

Chapter 13, "Data Association," examines the association values, such as lift and conviction, in detail.

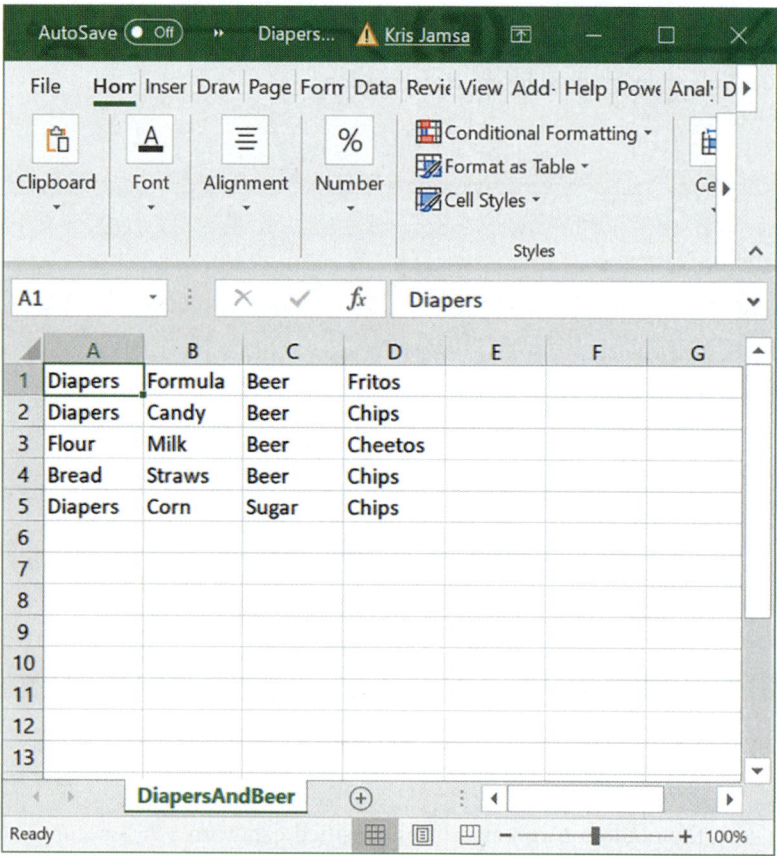

**FIGURE 1.38** The DiapersAndBeer data set contains items purchased in different shopping transactions.

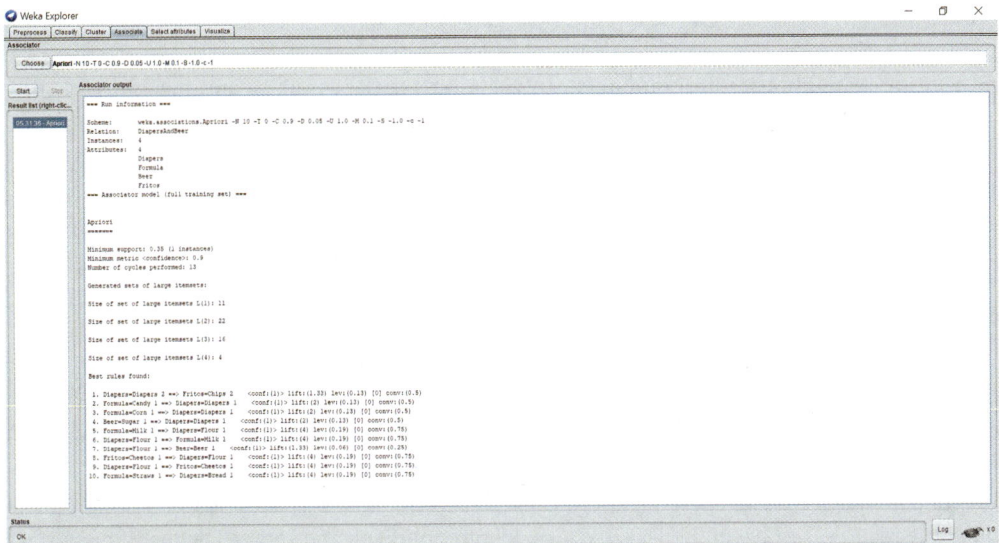

**FIGURE 1.39** Displaying data associations within Weka.
Used with permission from The University of Waikato

# Summary

This chapter introduced data mining, the process of identifying patterns within data. Data mining often involves the use of statistics, database queries, visualization tools, traditional programming, and machine learning. Machine learning is the use of data pattern-recognition algorithms to solve problems. There are two primary forms of machine learning: supervised and unsupervised. In supervised machine learning, the algorithm examines a training data set to learn how to identify patterns. Unsupervised learning, in contrast, does not use a training set.

Data visualization is the use of charts and graphs to represent data. Analysts use many different charts to represent data. The key is knowing which chart to use when. To create visual charts, analysts leverage tools such as Excel and Tableau, as well as the charting and graphing capabilities provided by the Python and R programming languages. In this chapter, you also examined web-based graphics created using Google Charts.

The data-mining and machine-learning programs this text presents make extensive use of a variety of data sets. To provide sample data sets you can use with data-mining and machine-learning algorithms, many sites on the web provide downloadable files. Two of the most commonly used data set repositories are the UCI data set repository and the Kaggle website.

Throughout this text, you will make use of the Python and R programming languages to implement data-mining and machine-learning applications. Most modern programming languages provide software libraries programmers can use to create data-mining and machine-learning solutions. Due to their popularity and common use, this text makes extensive use of Python and R. In addition to using Python and R, analysts now leverage visual-programming tools such as RapidMiner and Orange. Visual programming is the process of specifying processing by dragging and dropping different objects on to a workspace, as opposed to using programming-language statements. This text presents the RapidMiner and Orange visual-programming environments.

Business intelligence is the use of tools (data mining, machine learning, and visualization) to convert data into actionable insights and recommendations.

Vast volumes of data are not only leading database developers to NoSQL databases, they also have them thinking about who should administer databases. One of the cloud's newest key capabilities is DBaaS with which a managed service provider spins up and administers the database so that the customer need only worry about their applications.

The first step that data analysts perform with new data is to cleanse the data to eliminate duplicate records, resolve null or NaN values, identify outliers, and more. There are many ways an analyst can clean data, which may include the use of Excel, a programming language, or even a third-party tool. Data quality is a measure of the data's suitability for use. Data analysts calculate quality by considering factors such as:

- Accuracy: the degree to which the data correctly represent the underlying real-world values, such as all temperatures from a sensor being in the correct range.
- Completeness: the degree to which the data represent all required values, such as a data set that should contain an hour of data, for a sensor that reports every second, having 100% of the data values.
- Consistency: the degree to which similar or related data values align throughout the data set, such as each occurrence of an address having the same ZIP code.
- Conformity: the degree to which the data values align with the company's business rules, such as the company will measure and store sensor values in 1-second intervals.

Data analysts can perform a wide range of data-mining operations. In general, the key operations include:

- Data clustering
- Data classification
- Predictive analytics
- Data association

Data clustering is the process of grouping related data set items into one or more clusters. Clustering uses unsupervised machine learning for which the underlying algorithm does not use a training data set. Data classification is the process of assigning data to matching groups (categories), such as a tumor being benign or malignant, email being valid or spam, or a transaction being legitimate or fraudulent. Predictive analytics is the use of data to predict what will happen in the future. Data association is the process of identifying key relationships between variables.

One of the best-known data association problems is market-basket analysis, which examines items in a customer's shopping cart to determine if the presence of one item in the cart (called the antecedent) influences the addition of a second item (called the consequent). Data analysts still make extensive use of Excel. By installing add-ins, such as Solver, analysts can perform many data-mining operations from within Excel. Weka (Waikato Environment for Knowledge Analysis) is a data-mining tool created at the University of Waikato in New Zealand. Using Weka, you can perform data cleansing, clustering, classification, prediction, and visualization.

## Key Terms

Business intelligence
Classification
Clustering
Dashboard
Data association
Data cleansing
Data quality

Data visualization
Data wrangling
Descriptive analytics
Machine learning
Natural language processing
Predictive analytics
Prescriptive analytics

Supervised learning
Test data set
Training data set
Unsupervised learning
Visual programming

## Review

1. Compare and contrast data mining and machine learning.
2. Using Python, complete the Python examples this chapter presents.
3. Using R, complete the R examples this chapter presents.
4. Using RapidMiner, complete the activity this chapter presents.
5. Describe data clustering.
6. Describe data classification.
7. Describe data association.
8. Using Weka, perform the operations this chapter presented.
9. Compare and contrast descriptive, predictive, and prescriptive analysis.

# CHAPTER 2

# Machine Learning

## Chapter Goals and Objectives

- Perform key data-mining and machine-learning operations.
- Compare and contrast supervised and unsupervised learning.
- Compare and contrast training and testing data sets.
- Define and describe dimensionality reduction.
- Define and describe primary-component analysis.
- Know when and how to apply data-set standard scaling.

As the amount of data with which data analysts must work with continues to grow at exponential rates, so, too, does the need to automate the data analytics and data mining they perform. For the first 50 years of computing, programmers would work with data analysts to create application-specific programs that performed data-analytic operations. In 1959, the concept of machine learning began to emerge; however, it was not until the past few years that the use of machine learning has experienced explosive growth.

**Machine learning** is the use of data pattern-recognition algorithms to solve problems. Today, most popular programming languages provide libraries that contain functions programmers can use to perform machine-learning operations:

- Data classification
- Data clustering
- Predictive analysis
- Data association

Because of their widespread use and popularity, this chapter examines machine learning using the Python and R programming languages. If you are new to Python or R, Chapter 8, "Programming Data Mining and Analytic Solutions," introduces the key concepts you must know to understand the programs this text presents. Further, as discussed in Chapter 1, many visual-programming environments, such as RapidMiner and Orange, exist that let you create machine-learning solutions by dragging and dropping data-mining and machine-learning widgets within a visual workspace.

This chapter introduces machine learning. By the time you finish this chapter, you will understand the following key concepts:

- Machine learning is the use of data pattern-recognition algorithms to solve problems.
- Machine-learning solutions are classified as supervised, unsupervised, reinforced, and deep learning.
- **Supervised learning** is the use of an algorithm that uses labeled data to produce a training data set, from which the algorithm can learn.
- Machine-learning solutions that use supervised learning include **classification** algorithms that determine the correct category for a data item, such as an approved or disapproved loan, a valid email or spam, or a tumor being malignant or benign.
- **Unsupervised learning** does not use labeled data or a training data set. Unsupervised machine-learning solutions identify data patterns by discovery, without training. Common unsupervised machine-learning solutions include **clustering** and data association.
- Reinforced learning is the use of feedback loops to reward correct predictions and to punish mistakes.
- **Deep learning** is a hierarchically structured process that can leverage layers of machine learning, for which the output of one layer becomes the input to the next.
- In supervised learning, one of the first steps most programs perform is to divide a source data set into training and testing components for which the training data set normally contains 70–80% of the data and the test data set contains the rest.
- A **training data set** contains data for the independent variables, which influence the dependent variable, as well as correct results for the dependent variable. By examining the independent-variable values that lead to specific results (dependent-variable values), the machine-learning algorithm can learn.
- After training a machine-learning model, most programs will test the model's accuracy by having the model use a test data set for which the correct result is known. In other words, to test the model, the algorithm will use the test data set to predict results, which it can compare to the known correct values.
- When choosing a data set, the key is not to have a larger number of independent variables (many may not correlate to the dependent variable), but rather, to have a larger number of data records for the key dependent variables.
- After testing a model, most programs will display the model's accuracy, which it calculates by dividing the number of predictions it got correct by the total number of predictions.
- In addition to displaying an accuracy value, many machine-learning programs will display a confusion matrix, which shows the predictions the model got right and the ones the model got wrong—meaning the prediction for which the model was confused.

- Data clustering is the assignment of data items to a related group. Data clustering uses unsupervised learning.
- Data sets are often very large and may contain columns that do not influence the result being explored—meaning the independent variable does not correlate to the dependent variable. To improve processing time and to reduce the amount of memory (random-access memory [RAM]) a solution requires, analysts will delete such columns—a process they call dimensionality reduction.
- To determine which columns to keep and which to remove when performing dimensionality reduction, analysts often use primary component analysis (PCA), an unsupervised dimensionality-reduction approach, and linear determinant analysis (LDA), a supervised-learning approach.
- Most data-mining and machine-learning algorithms require numeric data throughout the data set. Unfortunately, real-world data sets often contain text-based categorical data, such as "male" and "female" for gender data. Before the analysts can use such data sets, they must edit the text fields and replace the values with numeric equivalents.
- Depending on the data set, there may be times when one variable uses a different underlying scale than another, such as a speed-of-service rating being based on a scale of 1–5 and a quality-of-service rating being based on a scale of 1–10. In such cases, the data analyst should align the variable scales before performing his or her machine-learning or data-mining operations.

## Machine Learning Versus Artificial Intelligence

If you are new to machine learning, you may wonder how machine learning is different from **artificial intelligence** (AI). AI is the science of making intelligent machines that can perceive visual items, recognize voices, make decisions, and more. Machine learning is an application of AI. In other words, as shown in **FIGURE 2.1**, there are many different applications of AI, of which machine learning is one.

## Types of Machine Learning

As discussed, machine learning is the use of data pattern-recognition algorithms to solve problems. Developers classify machine-learning algorithms using the following:

- Supervised learning
- Unsupervised learning
- Reinforced learning
- Deep learning

Supervised learning is the use of an algorithm that uses labeled data to produce a training data set an algorithm can use to learn how to identify patterns. Common solutions that use supervised learning include data classification (Chapter 11, "Data Classification," examines this in detail).

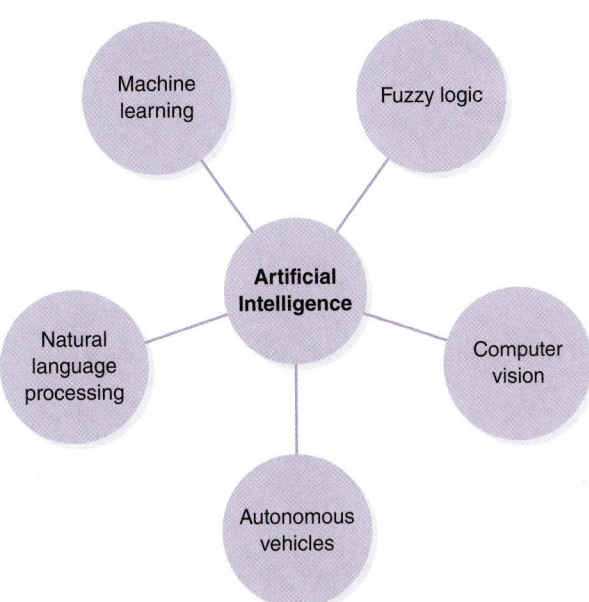

**FIGURE 2.1** Machine learning is an application of artificial intelligence.

Unsupervised learning is the use of an algorithm to identify patterns within data that do not have labels that can be used to create a training data set. Common solutions that use unsupervised learning include:

- Data clustering
- Data association

Chapter 10, "Data Clustering," examines cluster operations in detail. Chapter 13, "Data Association," examines data association.

Reinforced learning is the use of feedback loops to reward correct predictions and to punish mistakes, as shown in **FIGURE 2.2**.

Finally, deep learning is a hierarchically structured process that leverages layers of machine-learning, for which the output of one layer becomes the input to the next in order to drill into a lower-level result.

# Underlying Machine-Learning Algorithms

Throughout this text, you will examine a wide range of machine-learning algorithms. In general, these algorithms use either supervised or unsupervised machine learning. Many of the most commonly used clustering algorithms use unsupervised learning (which is discussed further in Chapter 10). As you will learn, there are hundreds of clustering algorithms, which differ by:

- Performance
- Memory use

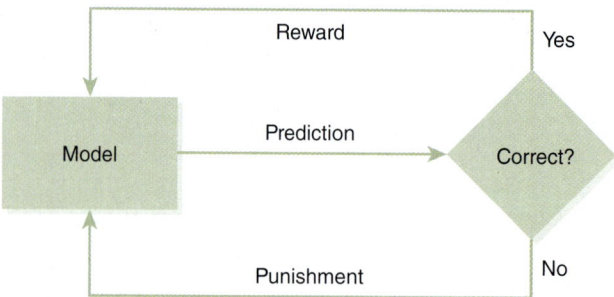

**FIGURE 2.2** Reinforced learning uses a feedback loop to reward correct predictions and to punish mistakes.

- Hardness or softness
- Data set size
- Need for the analyst to specify the starting number of clusters

The clustering algorithms are unsupervised in that they do not use labeled data for which a result is known and can be used to train the algorithm.

In contrast, data classification uses supervised machine learning. As discussed, in supervised machine learning, the data are labeled (meaning a correct result is known), which can be used to create training and testing data sets. Chapter 11 examines data classification and presents several commonly used algorithms. As you will learn, there are hundreds of classification algorithms.

**TABLE 2.1** summarizes the algorithms you will use throughout this text.

# Understanding the Supervised Learning Process

Supervised learning is the use of an algorithm that uses labeled data to produce a training data set an algorithm can use to learn how to identify patterns. A solution that uses a supervised machine-learning approach will perform the following steps:

1. Specify a training data set from which the model can learn to match patterns. The training data set must have values for the independent variables, which will be analyzed, as well as the correct result for the dependent variable. Developers normally use 70–80% of a data set as the training data set.
2. Specify a **testing data set** that the model can use to test its accuracy. Like the training data set, the testing data set must have values for the independent variables with which it will perform its analysis and the dependent variable, which the model will compare to its result. The training data set normally consists of 20–30% of the data set.
3. Use the model with new data to classify data or predict results.

**FIGURE 2.3** illustrates the supervised machine-learning process.

### TABLE 2.1 Supervised and Unsupervised Algorithms Used Throughout This Text

| Algorithm | Purpose | Category |
| --- | --- | --- |
| Agglomerative clustering | Data clustering | Unsupervised |
| Apriori | Data association | Unsupervised |
| DBSCAN | Data clustering | Unsupervised |
| Decision tree classification | Data classification | Supervised |
| Decision tree regression | Predictive analysis | Unsupervised |
| Hierarchical clustering | Data clustering | Unsupervised |
| KMeans | Data clustering | Unsupervised |
| K-nearest-neighbor | Data classification | Supervised |
| Linear regression | Predictive analysis | Unsupervised |
| Logistical regression | Predictive analysis | Unsupervised |
| Multilayer perceptron | Data classification | Supervised |
| Naïve Bayes | Data classification | Supervised |
| Polynomial regression | Predictive analytics | Unsupervised |
| Primary component analysis | Dimensionality reduction | Unsupervised |
| Linear discriminant analysis | Dimensionality reduction | Supervised |
| Random forest classification | Data classification | Supervised |
| Random forest regression | Predictive analysis | Unsupervised |
| Support vector machines | Data classification | Supervised |

## Specifying Training and Testing Data Sets

The purpose of a training data set within supervised machine learning is to teach (train) the model how to correctly recognize data patterns. Assume, for example, your goal is to identify incoming email as valid or spam. To start, your training data set, as shown in **FIGURE 2.4**, would contain various email attributes and, for each record, whether the message was valid or spam.

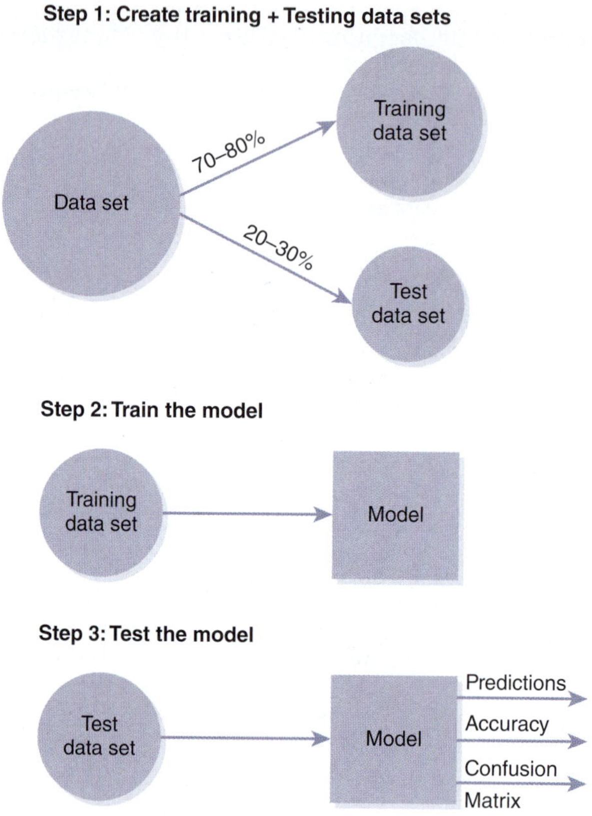

**FIGURE 2.3** The supervised machine-learning process.

In general, the more data that a machine-learning algorithm can evaluate, the better the accuracy of the model the algorithm creates. The key is not having many different attribute variables (some attributes may have nothing in this case to do with detecting spam), but rather, having more records that have meaningful attributes. If your process has a way to identify whether the model's predictions were correct or wrong (reinforced learning), the model will improve (learn) over time.

As you examine the supervised machine-learning solutions presented throughout this text, you will find that developers will normally divide a given data set into training and testing data sets such that the training data set contains 70–80% of the data and the testing data set the remainder.

The following Python program, TrainTest.py, reads the Breast.data.csv file, which contains attributes with which a machine-learning program can classify breast cancer tumor data as malignant or benign into a dataframe object. You can download the data set from this text's catalog page at go.jblearning.com/DataMining. The script first displays the number of rows in

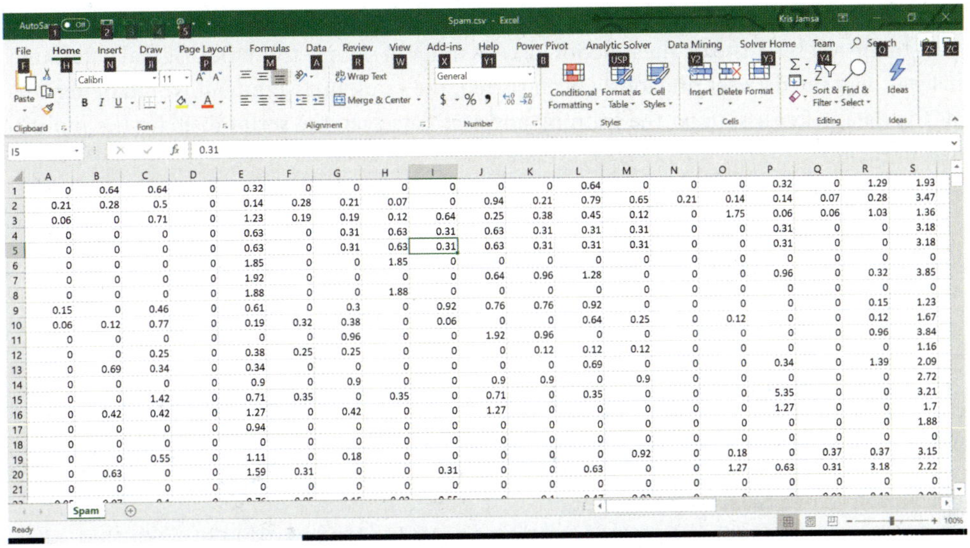

## Understanding the Supervised Learning Process

**FIGURE 2.4** The training data set for a spam email detection application.
Used with permission from Microsoft

the data set. Then, the script assigns 70% of the data to the training dataframe and 30% to the training dataframe:

```
import pandas as pd
import numpy as np
from sklearn.model_selection import train_test_split

names = ['Sample', 'Clump Thickness','Uniformity of Cell
Size','Uniformity of Cell Shape','Marginal Adhesion','Single
Epithelial Cell Size','Bare Nuclei','Bland Chromatin', 'Normal
Nucleoli', 'Mitoses', 'class']

df = pd.read_csv('breast.data.csv', header=None, names=names)
X = np.array(df.iloc[:, 0:9])
y = np.array(df['class'])

# split into train and test
X_train, X_test, y_train, y_test = train_test_split(X, y,
test_size=0.30)

print("Total rows: ", len(df))
print("Training rows: ", len(X_train))
print("Testing rows: ", len(X_test))
```

Note that the train_test function does not allocate the first 70% to the training set and the last 30% to the test set. Instead, the function takes a random sample from the original dataframe. In this way, had the data set previously been sorted, the random assignment would better represent the data. After assigning the training and test data sets, the script displays the number of rows in each.

When you run this script, it will display the following output:

```
C:\Python>python TrainTest.py
Total rows:   683
Training rows:   478
Testing rows:   205
```

The following R program, TrainTest.R, performs similar processing:

```
df <- read.csv(file='breast.data.csv')

## Split in train + test set
indexes <- sample(1:nrow(df),as.integer(0.7*nrow(df)))

trainData <- df[indexes,1:7]
testData <- df[-indexes,1:7]

print("Total rows")
print(nrow(df))
print("Training rows")
print(nrow(trainData))
print("Testing rows")
print(nrow(testData))
```

## Testing Your Machine-Learning Model

After a supervised machine-learning program trains a model, the program should use a test data set to determine the model's accuracy. Like the training data set, the test data set contains attribute values for the independent variables, which the model will examine, as well as correct values for the dependent variable, which the model can compare to its result.

To test a model, a supervised machine-learning program uses the test attributes to determine a result, which it then compares to the known result. By comparing the number of correct predictions to the total number of records in the test data set, you can determine the model's accuracy:

$$\text{Accuracy} = \frac{\text{Number of correct predictions}}{\text{Total number of predictions}}$$

Assume, for example, a solution correctly predicts 192 out of 200 test records. You would calculate the model's accuracy as follows:

$$\text{Accuracy} = \frac{\text{Number of correct predictions}}{\text{Total number of predictions}}$$
$$= \frac{192}{200}$$
$$= 96\%$$

To help you better understand the predictions the model got correct, as well as the predictions that were wrong, you can display a confusion matrix, so named because the matrix summarizes the model's predictions that were correct and wrong (confused). Consider, for example, the confusion matrix

```
[[764  68]
 [ 77 472]]
```

In this case, for the first variable, the model got 784 predictions correct and missed 68. Likewise, for the second variable, the model got 472 predictions correct and missed 77. Note that the number of items in the confusion matrix should equal that in the test data set. The classification programs presented throughout this text normally display the model's accuracy and confusion matrix.

## Classifying Email as Valid or Spam

As you have learned, data classification is the process of assigning data to matching groups. Chapter 11, "Data Classification," examines several commonly used data-classification algorithms in detail. Consider, for example, the Spam data set that contains attributes that correspond to valid email, as well as attribute values that correspond to spam. When you display the data set's values, the attribute values will appear as previously shown in Figure 2.4.

The data set contains 57 attributes and the dependent variable (spam or not spam). The variables include factors such as counts of words that are common in spam. You can view a complete list of the variables at the University of California, Irvine (UCI) data set repository, as shown in **FIGURE 2.5**.

The following Python script, ClassifySpam.py, uses the data set to classify emails as valid or spam:

```
import pandas as pd
import numpy as np
from sklearn.model_selection import train_test_split
from sklearn.metrics import accuracy_score
```

```
spambase - Notepad
File Edit Format View Help
SPAM E-MAIL DATABASE ATTRIBUTES (in .names format)

48 continuous real [0,100] attributes of type word_freq_WORD
= percentage of words in the e-mail that match WORD,
i.e. 100 * (number of times the WORD appears in the e-mail) /
total number of words in e-mail.  A "word" in this case is any
string of alphanumeric characters bounded by non-alphanumeric
characters or end-of-string.

6 continuous real [0,100] attributes of type char_freq_CHAR
= percentage of characters in the e-mail that match CHAR,
i.e. 100 * (number of CHAR occurences) / total characters in e-mail

1 continuous real [1,...] attribute of type capital_run_length_average
= average length of uninterrupted sequences of capital letters

1 continuous integer [1,...] attribute of type capital_run_length_longest
= length of longest uninterrupted sequence of capital letters

1 continuous integer [1,...] attribute of type capital_run_length_total
= sum of length of uninterrupted sequences of capital letters
= total number of capital letters in the e-mail

1 nominal {0,1} class attribute of type spam
= denotes whether the e-mail was considered spam (1) or not (0),
i.e. unsolicited commercial e-mail.

For more information, see file 'spambase.DOCUMENTATION' at the
UCI Machine Learning Repository: http://www.ics.uci.edu/~mlearn/MLRepository.html

1, 0.    | spam, non-spam classes

word_freq_make:         continuous.
word_freq_address:      continuous.
word_freq_all:          continuous.
```

**FIGURE 2.5** The attribute values in the Spam data set.

Used with permission from Microsoft

```python
from sklearn.neighbors import KNeighborsClassifier
from sklearn.metrics import confusion_matrix

df = pd.read_csv('Spam.csv', header=None)
X = np.array(df.iloc[:, 0:56])
y = np.array(df[57])

# split the data into the train and test sets
X_train, X_test, y_train, y_test = train_test_split(X, y,
test_size=0.30)

knn = KNeighborsClassifier(n_neighbors=3)
knn.fit(X_train, y_train)
pred = knn.predict(X_test)

print ('\nModel accuracy score: ', accuracy_score(y_test, pred))

print ('\nConfusion Matrix\n', confusion_matrix(y_test, pred))
```

In this case, the script uses the read_csv to read the spam.csv into a data frame. The script then assigns the independent variables to the X array and the dependent values to the y array. Next, the script assigns the training and test data sets using the K-nearest-neighbors algorithm to classify the data. After classifying the data, the script displays its accuracy and confusion matrix.

When you execute this script, it will display the following output:

```
C:\Python> python ClassifySpam.py
Model accuracy score:   0.8950036205648081
Confusion Matrix
 [[764  68]
 [ 77 472]]
```

In this case, the model had an accuracy of 89.5%. If you examine the confusion matrix, you will find that the algorithm correctly predicted 764 emails as valid and missed 68. Likewise, the model correctly predicted 472 emails as spam and missed 77.

The following R program, ClassifySpam.R, performs similar processing:

```
library (class)
library (datasets)

Spam <- read.csv(file='/python/spam.csv')

## Split in train + test set
indexes <- sample(1:nrow(Spam),as.integer(0.7*nrow(Spam)))

trainData <- Spam[indexes,]
testData <- Spam[-indexes,]

## A 3-nearest neighbors model with no normalization
pred <- knn(train = trainData, test = testData, cl = trainData[,58], k=3)

confusionmatrix = as.matrix(table(Actual = testData[,58],
Predicted = pred))
accuracy = sum(diag(confusionmatrix))/length(testData[,58])

print('Confusion Matrix')
print(confusionmatrix)
print(accuracy)
```

When you execute this program, it will display the following output:

```
Confusion Matrix
       Predicted
Actual   0    1
     0 701  127
     1 139  413
[1] 0.8072464
```

As you can see, the R K-nearest-neighbors algorithm had an accuracy of 81%. Using the confusion matrix, you can see the predictions the model got right and wrong.

## Clustering Stock Data

Data clustering is the process of assigning data items into related groups. Clustering uses unsupervised learning, meaning it does not have correctly labeled data from which training and testing data sets can be used. Consider the Dow Jones Stocks data set that contains stock prices (open, high, low, and close) and trading volume for many stocks. You can download the data set from this text's catalog page at go.jblearning.com/DataMining. When you view the data set, it will appear as shown in **FIGURE 2.6**.

The following Python script, ClusterStocks.py, loads the data set and then uses K-means clustering to group the stocks into three related clusters. Chapter 10 discusses K-means clustering in more detail.

```
import matplotlib.pyplot as plt
from sklearn.cluster import KMeans
import pandas as pd
import numpy as np
from pandas import DataFrame
from sklearn.decomposition import PCA

df = pd.read_csv('DowJones.csv')

df = df.drop('stock', axis=1)
df = df.drop('date', axis=1)
df = df.dropna()
```

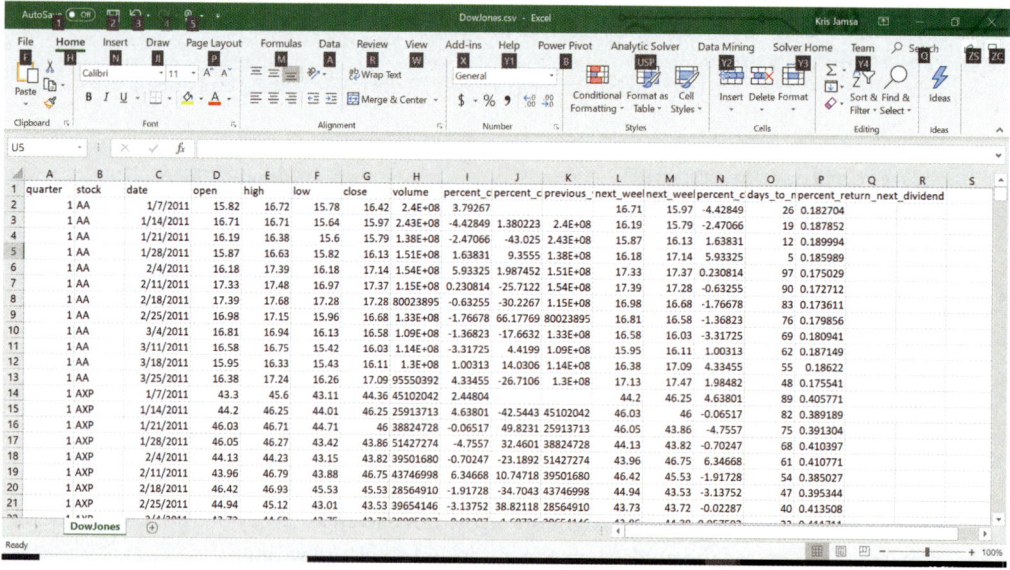

**FIGURE 2.6** The Dow Jones Stocks data set.

Used with permission from Microsoft

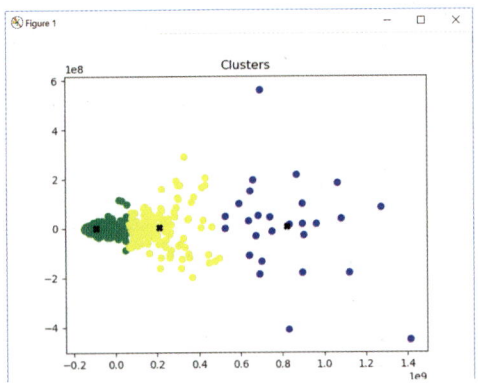

**FIGURE 2.7** Clustering Dow Jones Stocks data.
Used with permission of Python Software Foundation

```
pca = PCA(n_components=2).fit(df)
data_2d = pca.transform(df)

kmeans = KMeans(n_clusters=3).fit(data_2d)
centroids = kmeans.cluster_centers_

for i in range(0, data_2d.shape[0]):
  if kmeans.labels_[i] == 0:
    plt.scatter(data_2d[i,0], data_2d[i,1], c='green')
  elif kmeans.labels_[i] == 1:
    plt.scatter(data_2d[i,0], data_2d[i,1], c='yellow')
  elif kmeans.labels_[i] == 2:
    plt.scatter(data_2d[i,0], data_2d[i,1], c='blue')

plt.scatter(centroids[:, 0], centroids[:, 1], c='black',
marker='X')
plt.title("Clusters")
plt.show()
```

The Stock Prices data set contains many different attributes, which are not well suited for clustering or plotting using a scatter plot. The script therefore uses the PCA library to transform the values into a two-dimensional array, the values of which are representative of the original data and which can be clustered and graphed. Within the cluster chart, the script marks the center of each cluster (called the centroid) with a black X.

When you execute this program, it will display the cluster chart shown in **FIGURE 2.7**.

# Scaling Data-Set Values

Depending on your data set, there may be times when different attributes have different underlying scales. For example, a quality attribute may be based on the values 1–5, whereas a satisfaction attribute, the values 1–10. To improve the results of your machine-learning and data-mining operations, you should align the attribute scales. The following Python script, Scale.py, uses the StandardScaler function to do just that. Behind the scenes, the StandardScaler function will scale column values such that values have a mean of 0 and a standard deviation of 1. The script scales the values of a dataframe, showing the value before and after scaling:

```
from pandas import DataFrame
from sklearn.preprocessing import StandardScaler

Data = {
        'x': [1, 2, 3, 4, 5, 6, 7, 8, 9],
        'y': [10, 20, 30, 40, 50, 60, 70, 80, 90]
       }

df = DataFrame(Data, columns=['x','y'])

print('Original Dataset')
print(df)

sc = StandardScaler()
scaled = sc.fit_transform(df)

print('Scaled Dataset')
print(scaled)
print('Mean:', scaled.mean())
print('Standard deviation:', scaled.std())
```

When you run this script, it will display the following output:

```
C:\> python Scale.py
Original Dataset
   x   y
0  1  10
1  2  20
2  3  30
3  4  40
4  5  50
5  6  60
6  7  70
7  8  80
8  9  90
Scaled Dataset
[[-1.54919334 -1.54919334]
 [-1.161895   -1.161895  ]
 [-0.77459667 -0.77459667]
 [-0.38729833 -0.38729833]
 [ 0.          0.        ]
 [ 0.38729833  0.38729833]
 [ 0.77459667  0.77459667]
```

```
[ 1.161895    1.161895  ]
[ 1.54919334  1.54919334]]
Mean: -2.4671622769447922e-17
Standard deviation: 1.0
```

The StandardScaler function changes the data such that they have a mean of 0 and a standard deviation of 1.

# Understanding Dimensionality Reduction

As the size of data sets increase, so, too, does the time required to process the data, as well as the amount of RAM required to hold it. Depending on the data set with which you are working, there will often be times when one or more of the independent variables within the data set do not influence the dependent variable. In such cases, you can delete the corresponding columns—a process data analysts refer to as dimensionality reduction.

You can download the Breast Cancer data set that contains attributes a machine-learning algorithm can use to predict whether a breast cancer tumor is malignant or benign from this text's catalog page at go.jblearning.com/DataMining. (This data set is used again in Chapter 11, "Data Classification.") When you view the data set contents, you will see the attribute values shown in **FIGURE 2.8**.

As you can see, the data set contains many different variables that include a wide range of values.

A simple way to determine the relationship between variables is to determine the correlation value between them. Variables with a correlation value near 1 have a high correlation—as the

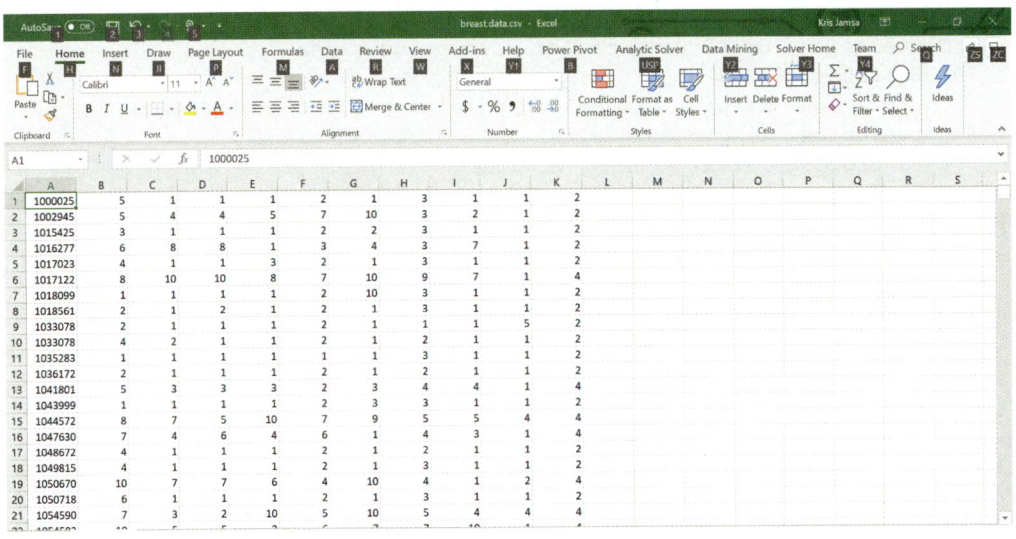

**FIGURE 2.8** The Breast Cancer data set.
Used with permission from Microsoft

value of one variable increases or decreases, so, too, will the value of the second. Variables with a correlation value of –1 have a strong negative correlation, meaning if you increase the value of one variable, the value of the second will decrease proportionally. Variables with a correlation value near 0 have no correlation—therefore, increasing or decreasing one variable's value will have no impact on the second.

The following Python script, BreastCancerCorrelations.py, examines the correlation between the independent variables and the dependent variable class, which specifies whether a tumor is malignant or benign:

```
import pandas as pd
import numpy as np

names = ['Sample', 'Clump Thickness','Uniformity of Cell
Size','Uniformity of Cell Shape', 'Marginal Adhesion','Single
Epithelial Cell Size','Bare Nuclei','Bland Chromatin', 'Normal
Nucleoli', 'Mitoses', 'class']

data = pd.read_csv('breast.data.csv', names=names)

for i in range(1,9):
  print('Correlation ', names[i], 'and class',
np.corrcoef(data[names[i]], data['class'])[0,1])
```

When you run this script, it will display the following output:

```
C:\> python BreastCancerCorrelations.py
Correlation  Clump Thickness and class 0.7147899263221593
Correlation  Uniformity of Cell Size and class
0.8208014428258755
Correlation  Uniformity of Cell Shape and class
0.821890947688868
Correlation  Marginal Adhesion and class 0.7062941354660844
Correlation  Single Epithelial Cell Size and class
0.6909581590873208
Correlation  Bare Nuclei and class 0.8226958729964606
Correlation  Bland Chromatin and class 0.7582275545334305
Correlation  Normal Nucleoli and class 0.7186771878756352
```

As you can see, three of the variables have a higher correlation than the rest. In this case, before you perform your machine-learning operations, you might consider reducing your data set to those three columns. That said, a more accurate approach would be to use PCA or LDA, discussed next.

## Primary Component Analysis

To perform data set dimensionality reduction, analysts will often use a technique called PCA to determine (and select) the key independent variables. PCA is an unsupervised machine-learning algorithm. The following Python script, PCA.py, illustrates the use of PCA. In this case, the script does not reduce the data set, but rather, displays the variance attribute value for each variable:

```python
import pandas as pd
import numpy as np
from sklearn.model_selection import train_test_split
from sklearn.model_selection import train_test_split
from sklearn.preprocessing import StandardScaler
from sklearn.decomposition import PCA

names = ['Sample', 'Clump Thickness','Uniformity of Cell
Size','Uniformity of Cell Shape', 'Marginal Adhesion','Single
Epithelial Cell Size','Bare Nuclei','Bland Chromatin', 'Normal
Nucleoli', 'Mitoses', 'class']

df = pd.read_csv('breast.data.csv', header=None, names=names)
X = np.array(df.iloc[:, 1:9])
y = np.array(df['class'])

X_train, X_test, y_train, y_test = train_test_split(X, y,
test_size=0.3)

sc = StandardScaler()
X_train = sc.fit_transform(X_train)
X_test = sc.transform(X_test)

pca = PCA()
X_train = pca.fit_transform(X_train)
X_test = pca.transform(X_test)
variance = pca.explained_variance_ratio_

for i in range(0, 8):
  print(names[i+1], variance[i])
```

As you can see, the script opens the Breast Cancer data set, assigning it a dataframe. The script then scales the data, as previously discussed, using the StandardScaler function. The code then uses PCA to produce the variance values. When you execute this script, it will display the following output:

```
C:\> python PCA.py
Clump Thickness 0.7064035554940435
Uniformity of Cell Size 0.0669613661433311
Uniformity of Cell Shape 0.06302115143435666
Marginal Adhesion 0.04504714573870766
Single Epithelial Cell Size 0.03859964599913781
Bare Nuclei 0.03464615871617751
Bland Chromatin 0.033703995871346884
Normal Nucleoli 0.01161698060289868
```

In this case, the analysis shows that the primary variables are clump thickness, uniformity of cell size, and uniformity of cell shape.

The following Python script, BreastCancerPCA.py, uses the K-nearest-neighbor classification method to determine if a breast cancer tumor is malignant or benign. The script first uses all the independent variables to determine a result and then uses the first three variables identified by PCA:

```python
import pandas as pd
import numpy as np
from sklearn.model_selection import train_test_split
from sklearn.metrics import accuracy_score
from sklearn.neighbors import KNeighborsClassifier
from sklearn.metrics import confusion_matrix

names = ['Sample', 'Clump Thickness','Uniformity of Cell
Size','Uniformity of Cell Shape', 'Marginal Adhesion','Single
Epithelial Cell Size','Bare Nuclei','Bland Chromatin', 'Normal
Nucleoli', 'Mitoses', 'class']

df = pd.read_csv('breast.data.csv', header=None, names=names)
X = np.array(df.iloc[:, 1:9])
y = np.array(df['class'])

# split into train and test
X_train, X_test, y_train, y_test = train_test_split(X, y,
test_size=0.30)

knn = KNeighborsClassifier(n_neighbors=3)
knn.fit(X_train, y_train)
pred = knn.predict(X_test)

print ('\nModel accuracy score: ', accuracy_score(y_test, pred))
print(confusion_matrix(y_test, pred))

X = np.array(df.iloc[:, 2:4])
y = np.array(df['class'])

# split into train and test
X_train, X_test, y_train, y_test = train_test_split(X, y,
test_size=0.30)

knn = KNeighborsClassifier(n_neighbors=3)
knn.fit(X_train, y_train)
pred = knn.predict(X_test)

print ('\nModel accuracy score: ', accuracy_score(y_test, pred))
print(confusion_matrix(y_test, pred))
```

When you execute this script, it will display the following output:

```
C:\Python> python BreastCancerPCA.py
```

```
Model accuracy score:   0.9609756097560975
[[130    4]
 [  4   67]]

Model accuracy score:   0.9317073170731708
[[129    8]
 [  6   62]]
```

As you can see, by reducing the number of independent variables to the three primary components, the model's accuracy changes only slightly. In this case, the data set is small, but if the data set were very large, you could save considerable processing time by performing such a reduction.

## Linear Discriminant Analysis

To reduce the dimensionality of data sets, analysts often perform PCA, an unsupervised machine-learning algorithm. Like most machine-learning concepts, there are many algorithms (approaches) to performing dimensionality reduction. LDA is a second approach that uses supervised machine learning. The following Python script, LDA.py, illustrates the use of LDA. Again, the script will use the Breast Cancer data set.

```
import pandas as pd
import numpy as np
from sklearn.model_selection import train_test_split
from sklearn.metrics import accuracy_score
from sklearn.neighbors import KNeighborsClassifier
from sklearn.metrics import confusion_matrix
from sklearn.model_selection import train_test_split
from sklearn.model_selection import train_test_split
from sklearn.preprocessing import StandardScaler

names = ['Sample', 'Clump Thickness','Uniformity of Cell
Size','Uniformity of Cell Shape', 'Marginal Adhesion','Single
Epithelial Cell Size','Bare Nuclei','Bland Chromatin', 'Normal
Nucleoli', 'Mitoses', 'class']
df = pd.read_csv('breast.data.csv', header=None, names=names)
X = np.array(df.iloc[:, 1:9])
y = np.array(df['class'])
X_train, X_test, y_train, y_test = train_test_split(X, y,
test_size=0.3)

sc = StandardScaler()
X_train = sc.fit_transform(X_train)
X_test = sc.transform(X_test)

from sklearn.discriminant_analysis import
LinearDiscriminantAnalysis
lda = LinearDiscriminantAnalysis(n_components=3)
```

# CHAPTER 2 Machine Learning

```
X_train = lda.fit_transform(X_train, y_train)
X_test = lda.transform(X_test)

knn = KNeighborsClassifier(n_neighbors=3)
knn.fit(X_train, y_train)
pred = knn.predict(X_test)

print("Accuracy", accuracy_score(y_test, pred))
print(confusion_matrix(y_test, pred))
```

When you run this script, it will display the following output:

```
C:\> python lda.py
Accuracy 0.9707317073170731
[[136    4]
 [  2   63]]
```

In this case, the script applies the LDA results to the dataframe. As you can see, using only the three independent variables, the script has a 97% accuracy.

## Mapping Categorical Variables

As you perform machine-learning operations, you will find that many algorithms require that the data set values are numeric. Unfortunately, many data sets contain text-based categorical data. Consider, for example, the Census data set, shown in **FIGURE 2.9**, that contains attributes a

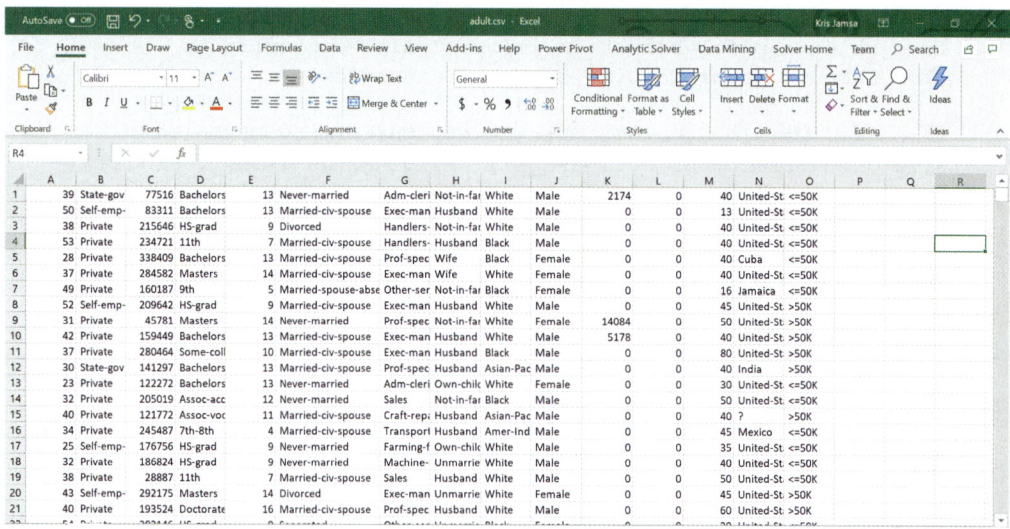

**FIGURE 2.9** The Census data set.

Used with permission from Microsoft

machine-learning algorithm can use to determine whether an individual will make less or more than $50,000 a year. You can download the Census data set from this text's catalog page at go.jblearning.com/DataMining.

One way to change the text values to numeric is to edit the data set using Microsoft Excel. You can also use a programming language such as Python or R to make the changes. At first glance, you might be tempted to perform simple changes, such as converting the text values "male" and "female" to the values 1 and 0 and values such as "black," "white," and "other" to values such as 3, 2, and 1. Although such substitutions accomplish the goal of getting numeric values, this presents the problem of introducing ordinal values, which imply a numeric order such that male is greater than female and black has a more significant value than white.

To avoid such ordered implications, developers use a technique called hot encoding that, rather than assigning ordinal numbers, assigns binary vector values. In the case of male and female, you might use the following vectors:

```
male    [1 0]
female  [0 1]
```

Likewise, for black, white, and other, you would use:

```
black   [1 0 0]
white   [0 1 0]
other   [0 0 1]
```

The following Python script, OneHotEncoding.py, illustrates the process to encode categorical data:

```
from sklearn import preprocessing

data = ['black', 'white', 'other']
print(data)
lb = preprocessing.LabelBinarizer()
encodedvalues = lb.fit_transform(data)
print(encodedvalues)
```

As you can see, the script creates a dataframe with a categorical column. The script then uses the LabelBinarizer function to encode the values, displaying the result. When you run this script, it will display the following output:

```
C:\Python>python OneHotEncoding.py
['black', 'white', 'other']
[[1 0 0]
 [0 0 1]
 [0 1 0]]
```

The script in this case has created a unique binary vector for each value.

The following Python script, OneHotEncodeCensus.py, illustrates the use of hot encoding to update a dataframe that contains the census data:

```python
import pandas as pd
import numpy as np
from sklearn import preprocessing

df = pd.read_csv('adult.csv')

print(df.head())

lb = preprocessing.LabelBinarizer()
encodedvalues = lb.fit_transform(df.iloc[:,8:9])
print('Race')
print(encodedvalues)

dfOneHot = pd.DataFrame(encodedvalues, columns =
["A"+str(int(i)) for i in range(encodedvalues.shape[1])])
df = pd.concat([df, dfOneHot], axis=1)

encodedvalues = lb.fit_transform(df.iloc[:,9:10])
print('Gender')
print(encodedvalues)

dfOneHot = pd.DataFrame(encodedvalues, columns =
["B"+str(int(i)) for i in range(encodedvalues.shape[1])])
df = pd.concat([df, dfOneHot], axis=1)

encodedvalues = lb.fit_transform(df.iloc[:,13:14])
print('Country')
print(encodedvalues)

dfOneHot = pd.DataFrame(encodedvalues, columns =
["C"+str(int(i)) for i in range(encodedvalues.shape[1])])
df = pd.concat([df, dfOneHot], axis=1)

# delete the categorical column just replaced
df.drop(df.columns[13], axis=1)
df.drop(df.columns[8], axis=1)
df.drop(df.columns[9], axis=1)

print(df.head())
```

The script starts by loading the Adult.csv data set into a dataframe and then using the head function to display the first five rows. The script then encodes the race values, creating the corresponding binary vectors. The script then appends those vectors as individual columns within the data set. The script repeats this processing for the gender and country columns. The script then deletes the original (categorical) columns and displays the data set's contents. Before you perform your machine-learning and data-mining operations, you would repeat the steps for the remaining categorical fields.

When you run this script, it will display the following output:

```
C:\> python OneHotEncodingCensus.py
        39           State-gov    77516    Bachelors  ...    0    40
United-States    <=50K
0    50    Self-emp-not-inc    83311    Bachelors  ...    0    13
United-States    <=50K
1    38           Private     215646       HS-grad  ...    0    40
United-States    <=50K
2    53           Private     234721          11th  ...    0    40
United-States    <=50K
3    28           Private     338409    Bachelors  ...    0    40
Cuba       <=50K
4    37           Private     284582       Masters  ...    0    40
United-States    <=50K

[5 rows x 15 columns]
Race
[[0 0 0 0 1]
 [0 0 0 0 1]
 [0 0 1 0 0]
 ...
 [0 0 0 0 1]
 [0 0 0 0 1]
 [0 0 0 0 1]]
Gender
[[1]
 [1]
 [1]
 ...
 [0]
 [1]
 [0]]
Country
[[0 0 0 ... 1 0 0]
 [0 0 0 ... 1 0 0]
 [0 0 0 ... 1 0 0]
 ...
 [0 0 0 ... 1 0 0]
 [0 0 0 ... 1 0 0]
 [0 0 0 ... 1 0 0]]
        39           State-gov    77516    Bachelors    13  ... C37 C38
C39 C40 C41
```

# CHAPTER 2 Machine Learning

```
0    50          Self-emp-not-inc  83311    Bachelors  13  ...  0  0
1     0     0
1    38                    Private  215646    HS-grad    9  ...  0  0
1     0     0
2    53                    Private  234721       11th    7  ...  0  0
1     0     0
3    28                    Private  338409   Bachelors  13  ...  0  0
0     0     0
4    37                    Private  284582     Masters  14  ...  0  0
1     0     0

[5 rows x 63 columns]
```

As you can see, following the encoding operations, the dataframe contains new columns, the names of which begin with the letters A, B, or C, as specified by the script during the data append operation.

## Google Crash Course in Machine Learning

Google is obviously one of the leaders in the field of machine learning, with different Google applications using machine learning in a myriad of ways. To help you get started with machine learning, Google offers a "crash course" in machine learning, which you can take at https://developers.google.com/machine-learning/crash-course/ as shown in **FIGURE A**. You should take time to check out the course.

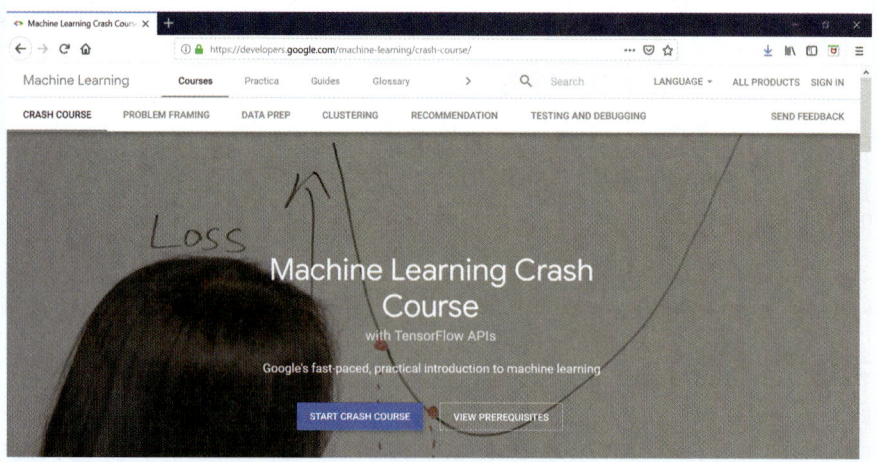

**FIGURE A** The Google crash course in machine learning.

Used with permission of Google

# Hands-on Google TensorFlow Programming Library

Throughout this text, you will use a variety of different programming libraries to accomplish specific data-mining and machine-learning tasks. In this section, you will examine TensorFlow, a very popular open-source machine-learning platform developed by Google. TensorFlow includes many libraries that make it easy to create, build, and test machine-learning solutions. Developers use TensorFlow to create not only desktop operations but also web (cloud) solutions that access the libraries using JavaScript and mobile solutions, as shown in **FIGURE 2.10**.

One way to get started with TensorFlow is to use PIP to install the library, as discussed on the TensorFlow website at http://www.Tensorflow.org, as shown in **FIGURE 2.11**.

Depending on the version of Python you are running, identifying the correct version of TensorFlow to install can be a little challenging. As such, this section will leverage Google Colab to learn about and to run TensorFlow examples. Colab is a Jupyter Notebook implementation that provides an interactive document experience. Within a Colab notebook, you can read text, run Python scripts, and more. In this section, you will learn how to use an existing document. Chapter 16, "Planning and Launching a Data Mining and Data Analytics Project," examines the steps you must perform to create a Jupyter Notebook document.

To start, use a browser—ideally Chrome—to connect to go.jblearning.com/DataMining. There, click on the link titled Colab Tutorial which, as shown in **FIGURE 2.12**, has a tutorial for those getting started with TensorFlow.

As discussed, within a Jupyter Notebook document, you can add, edit, and run code. Behind the scenes the document resides on a server for which all the needed software (in this case, including TensorFlow) is installed. Within the Notebook window, use the pull-down list to connect to a hosted server.

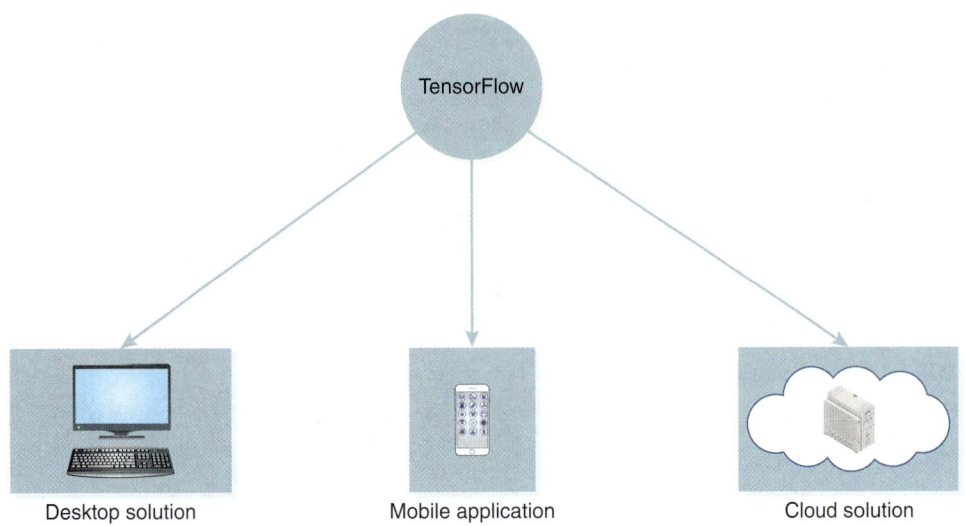

**FIGURE 2.10** Using TensorFlow for desktop, web, and mobile solutions.

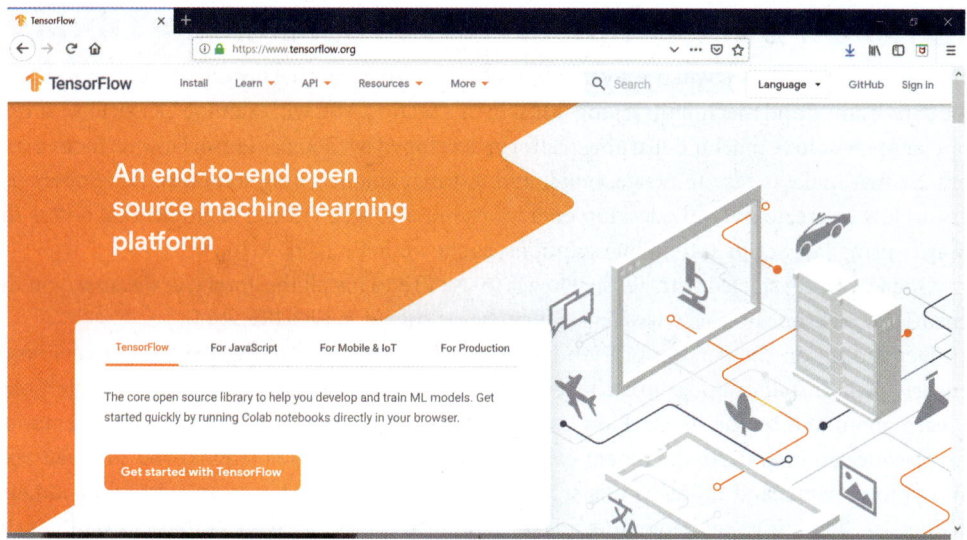

**FIGURE 2.11** The TensorFlow website has downloadable software and detailed documentation.

Used with permission of TensorFlow

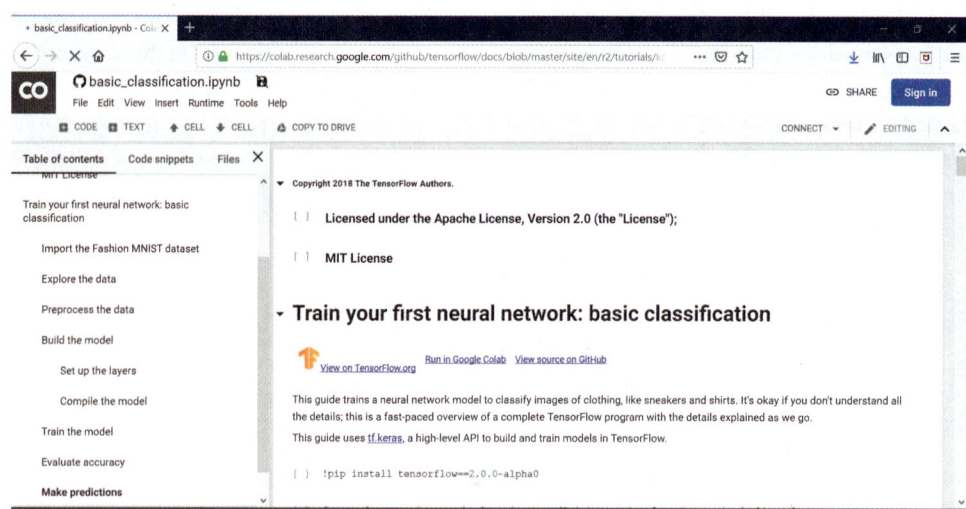

**FIGURE 2.12** A Google Colab tutorial on TensorFlow.

Used with permission of TensorFlow

For this example, you will use TensorFlow to classify clothing images (pants, shoes, skirts, and so on) from the Fashion-mnist data set, which as shown in **FIGURE 2.13**, contains 70,000 clothing images. In Chapter 14, "Text and Image Data Mining," you will examine image-recognition algorithms in detail.

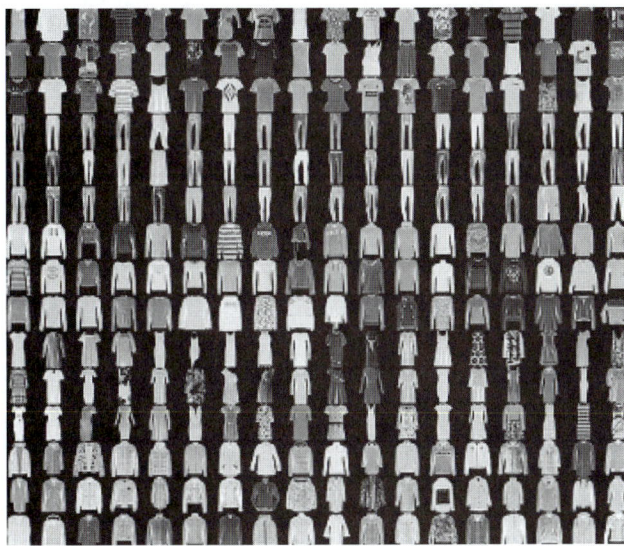

**FIGURE 2.13** Clothing images in the Fashion-mnist data set.
Used with permission of ZALANDO RESEARCH

The TensorFlow document will walk you through the processing that the code performs, letting you focus on one section of code at a time. Within the document, next to the code block, you will see a pair of left and right brackets []. When you hover your mouse over the brackets, the document will change them into a Play button that directs Colab to execute the statements. As you read through the document, you should run each section of code.

This section's goal was simply to introduce you to TensorFlow. Across the web, you can find many examples of TensorFlow source code. Rather than examine the code now, you should continue reading this book to examine the machine-learning processes, such as clustering, regression, and predictive analysis. Then, with that knowledge in hand, you can circle back and examine how developers perform the operations using TensorFlow. As you will find, the TensorFlow implementations will normally require fewer lines of code and create a compact solution. For now, keep in mind that with TensorFlow, you not only receive a library of powerful machine-learning tools, but one that scales and can run on any device.

## Summary

This chapter introduced machine learning, which is the use of data pattern-recognition algorithms to solve problems. As you learned, machine-learning solutions are classified as supervised, unsupervised, reinforced, and deep learning. Supervised learning is the use of an algorithm that uses labeled data to produce a training data set, from which the algorithm can learn. Machine-learning solutions that use supervised learning include classification algorithms that determine the correct category for a data item, such as an approved or disapproved loan, a valid email or spam, or a tumor being malignant or benign.

Unsupervised learning does not use labeled data or a training data set. Unsupervised machine-learning solutions identify data patterns by discovery, without training. Common unsupervised machine-learning solutions include clustering and data association. Reinforced learning is the use of feedback loops to reward correct predictions and to punish mistakes. Deep learning is a hierarchically structured process that leverages layers of machine learning, for which the output of one layer becomes the input to the next. AI is the science of making intelligent machines that can perceive visual items, recognize voices, make decisions, and more. Machine learning is an application of AI.

In supervised learning, one of the first steps most programs perform is to divide a source data set into training and testing components for which the training data set normally contains 70–80% of the data and the test data set the rest. A training data set contains data for the independent variables, which influence the dependent variable, as well as correct results for the dependent variable. By examining the independent-variable values that lead to specific results (dependent-variable values), the machine-learning algorithm can learn. After training a machine-learning model, most programs will test the model's accuracy by having the model use a test data set for which the correct result is known. In other words, to test the model, the algorithm will use the test data set to predict results, which it can compare to the known correct values.

When choosing a data set, the key is not to have a larger number of independent variables (many may not correlate to the dependent variable), but rather, to have a larger number of data records for the key dependent variables. After testing a model, most programs will display the model's accuracy, which it calculates by dividing the number of predictions it got correct by the total number of predictions. In addition to displaying an accuracy value, many machine-learning programs will display a confusion matrix, which shows the predictions the model got right and the ones the model got wrong—meaning the prediction for which the model was confused.

Data clustering is the assignment of data items to a related group. Data clustering uses unsupervised learning.

Data sets are often very large and may contain columns that do not influence the result being explored—meaning the independent variable does not correlate to the dependent variable. To improve processing time and to reduce the amount of memory (RAM) a solution requires, analysts will delete such columns—a process they call dimensionality reduction. To determine which columns to keep and which to remove when performing dimensionality reduction, analysts often use PCA, an unsupervised dimensionality-reduction approach, and LDA, a supervised-learning approach.

Most data-mining and machine-learning algorithms require numeric data throughout the data set. Unfortunately, real-world data sets often contain text-based categorical data, such as "male" and "female" for gender data. Before the analysts can use such data sets, they must edit the text fields and replace the values with numeric equivalents. Depending on the data set, there may be times when one variable uses a different underlying scale than another, such as a speed-of-service rating being based on a scale of 1–5 and a quality-of-service rating being based on a scale of 1–10. In such cases, the data analyst should align the variable scales before performing his or her machine-learning or data-mining operations.

Finally, this chapter introduced you to TensorFlow, a powerful, open-source machine-learning platform developed by Google. Because of its powerful features and the fact that it can run on all devices, developers make extensive use of the TensorFlow library. This chapter also gave you a first-glance look at a Jupyter Notebook that developers use to create interactive documents that not only describe code but also let the reader interact with the code.

## Key Terms

Artificial intelligence
Classification
Clustering
Deep learning
Machine learning
Supervised learning
Testing data set
Training data set
Unsupervised learning

## Review

1. Define and describe machine learning.
2. Compare and contrast supervised and unsupervised machine learning.
3. Define and describe reinforced learning.
4. Compare and contrast machine learning and data mining.
5. Compare and contrast machine learning and artificial intelligence.
6. Explain the purpose of the training and test data sets within a supervised machine-learning solution.
7. Using Python, load the Breast Cancer data set, which you can download from this text's catalog page at go.jblearning.com/DataMining, into a dataframe and display the number of rows the dataframe contains. Then create a training data set with 70% of the data and a test data set with the rest. Display the number of rows in the training and test dataframes.
8. Using R, load the Breast Cancer data set, which you can download from this text's catalog page at go.jblearning.com/DataMining, into a dataframe and display the number of rows the dataframe contains. Then create a training data set with 70% of the data and a test data set with the rest. Display the number of rows in the training and test dataframes.
9. Perform the Python examples this chapter presents.
10. Perform the R examples this chapter presents.
11. Using Python, load the Breast Cancer data set into a dataframe object. Use the head function to display the dataframe contents. Then drop the first column that contains the case identifier. Use head to show the dataframe's new contents.

12. Using R, load the Breast Cancer data set into a dataframe object. Use the head function to display the dataframe contents. Then drop the case identifier column—the first column. Use head to show the dataframe's new contents.
13. Using Python, load the Titanic data set, which you can download from this text's catalog page at go.jblearning.com/DataMining. Use hot coding to convert several of the categorical attributes (the text-based attributes) to numeric representations.

# CHAPTER 3

# Databases and Data Warehouses

## Chapter Goals and Objectives

- Define database and describe the role of databases in data analytics.
- Create an entity relationship diagram (ERD) that represents entities and their relationships.
- Compare and contrast the conceptual, logical, and physical data models.
- Compare and contrast databases, data warehouses, data marts, and data lakes.
- Explain the purpose of data normalization and understand the processing required to achieve third-normal form (3NF).
- Compare and contrast relational, NoSQL, object-oriented, and graph databases.

At the heart of most data applications are databases. Whether an application analyzes big data, mines data using machine learning, or drives real-time dashboards, data are at the center of the processing performed. For the past 50 years, relational (table-based) databases have been the mainstay of data operations. Because developers normally use SQL, the Structured Query Language, to interact with relational databases, developers generally refer to relational databases as SQL databases. Chapter 6, "Keep SQL in Your Toolset," examines relational databases and SQL queries in detail.

With the advent of mobile and web applications that frequently deal with documents, videos, audio files, and other unstructured data, developers today often turn to **NoSQL** databases, such as MongoDB—so named because it can handle humungous amounts of data. Chapter 7, "NoSQL Data Analytics," examines NoSQL database operations in detail.

To align **database** operations with object-oriented programming practices, database developers have implemented object-oriented database management systems (**OODBMS**). Although such databases have not yet achieved popular market adoption, key database solutions, such as Oracle, now integrate object-oriented concepts into their query language.

Finally, real-world objects have a wide range of relationships that traditional databases cannot readily represent. As such, developers are starting to migrate to graph databases, which are designed to handle such numerous relationships. This chapter introduces object-oriented and graph databases.

Databases are normally ideal for transactional operations, such as storing e-commerce sales, inventory levels, employee time-card processing or payroll operations, and other read and write operations. Business dashboards and decision-support tools, in contrast, typically require only a subset of a company's data, normally perform read-only operations, and must provide fast answers to analytic queries. To drive such operations, developers normally use a **data warehouse**.

Depending on the business requirements and the data-warehouse size and complexity, developers often decompose the data warehouse into smaller, specialized data marts.

Recently, big data applications bypass databases and instead connect to data files directly, a process for which developers refer to the file as a **data lake**. Such processing is well suited for interacting with large binary objects (which developers call blobs), as well as audio and video data.

This chapter examines databases, data warehouses, data marts, and data lakes. By the time you finish this chapter, you will understand the following key concepts:

- A database is a collection of data organized for fast storage and retrieval.
- Databases reside within a special software application called a DBMS.
- All systems are composed of things, which database developers call entities. An **entity relationship diagram (ERD)** is a visual representation of things that make up a system, along with the relationships that exist between them.
- The two most common ERDs are the Chen diagram and crow's-foot diagram. Both designs represent entities, their attributes, and their relationships.
- Database developers describe the relationship type that exists between entities in terms of **cardinality**. Common cardinalities include one-to-one, one-to-many, and many-to-many.
- To represent a database design, database developers create the following database models:
  - Conceptual database model
  - Logical database model
  - Physical database model
- A conceptual database model provides a high-level view of the entities that make up a database system. The **conceptual model** does not include specifics about each entity, such as its attributes, and is often used to introduce the database to stakeholders.
- A **logical model** provides greater description of the database entities to include attribute names. The logical model, like the conceptual model, should be independent of hardware and software that will implement the system.
- A physical database model adds entity-attribute data types to the logical model to make it appropriate for a database developer to implement a database. To create a physical data model, a database designer should first select the underlying hardware and DBMS.

- Tables in a **relational database** often have a **primary key** that uniquely identifies each record. Examples of primary keys include a CUSTOMER_ID field or an ORDER_ID field. Databases impose specific rules for primary-key values, such as the primary-key value must be unique and cannot be NULL.
- To create relationships between tables in a relational database, two or more tables will have a common field. When that common field is a primary key in one table, it is called a **foreign key** in the related table. Foreign keys exist to enforce **referential integrity** rules, and as such, databases impose rules on foreign-key values, such that a foreign key cannot be NULL.
- A **schema** is a representation of something in a model or outline form. Database designers visually represent database schemas using an ERD. Similarly, database developers often provide their CREATE TABLE and other queries to provide a schema for a database.
- To reduce the possibility of **data anomalies** (errors) due to INSERT, UPDATE, and DELETE queries, database developers normalize their table designs to achieve specific normal forms, such as first-normal form (1NF), second-normal form (2NF), and third-normal form (3NF). To achieve each level of normal form, the designers must satisfy specific design constraints. As they normalize tables to comply with each normal form, the designers will often decompose one table into two or more tables. Later, when database developers query the database, they will temporarily combine the tables using a JOIN query.
- Relational databases are table-based databases for which the table rows represent records and the table columns represent the attributes (fields) for each record.
- A NoSQL database stores data in a less structured way than a relational database (often in a JavaScript Object Notation [**JSON**] file) and does not use SQL as its primary query language.
- An **object-oriented database** allows developers to store and retrieve objects, which makes them well suited for video and audio objects. Although most object-oriented databases are research based, DBMSs, such as Oracle, now provide support for object-based operations.
- A **graph database** is a NoSQL database designed to store the many different relationships an entity may have. The graph database represents entities as nodes and the relationships between entities as edges of a graph.
- Online Transaction Processing (**OLTP**) describes traditional database operations that store and retrieve data for a transaction, such as an e-commerce sale, a student registration for a course, and so on.
- Online Analytical Processing (**OLAP**) describes database operations that support reporting, decision support operations, and other analytic operations. A data warehouse often uses OLAP.
- A data warehouse is a database optimized for reporting and other analytical processing. Because a data warehouse does not perform transactional processing (with insert, delete, and update operations), data warehouses are not normalized.

- To describe and implement a data warehouse, data-warehouse designers normally use a star (or snowflake) schema that is based on fact tables that contain key-metric values and dimension tables that contain supporting data.
- A data warehouse normally contains data for an entire company. A **data mart** contains a subset of that data specific to a group within the organization, such as sales or manufacturing.
- With the growth of big data applications, many systems support data lakes, which store data in a native format, such as an XML, JSON, or text file.

## Databases Store Things (aka Entities)

Regardless of the processing a system performs, the system itself is made up of "things." An e-commerce site, for example, has products to sell, customers, orders, returns, payments, and so on. In a similar way, an airline reservation system has flights, passengers, pilots, baggage, reservations, planes, and so on. In other words, each system consists of things.

Database developers refer to such "things" as entities. To visually represent such systems, the developers use an ERD that not only describes entities that make up the system but also how the entities relate to one another. For example, within the e-commerce site, each customer may have many orders. Each order, in turn, may include many products. A customer, in turn, may have multiple ship-to addresses, as well as one billing address. Within the airline system, each flight has one origin location and one destination location. A flight will have many passengers, each of which may have several pieces of luggage.

Database designers refer to the relationship types that exist between entities in the system as the relationship's cardinality. Common cardinalities include one-to-one, one-to-many, and many-to-many. Within the ERD that they create to represent a system, database developers will use the cardinality symbols shown in **FIGURE 3.1**.

Using the cardinality symbols, **FIGURE 3.2** illustrates several relationships that will exist within an e-commerce application.

Depending on the database designers who created the ERD, you may see labels that describe the relationships, as shown in **FIGURE 3.3**.

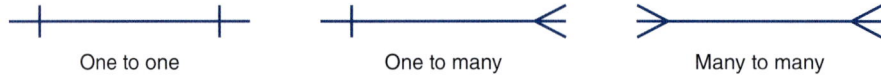

FIGURE 3.1 Cardinality symbols that represent a relationship type.

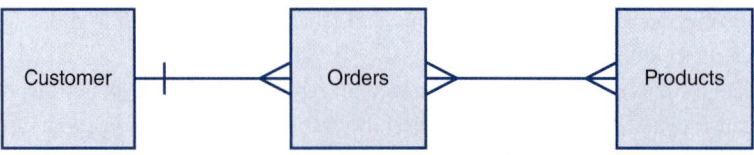

FIGURE 3.2 Relationships between entities in an e-commerce application.

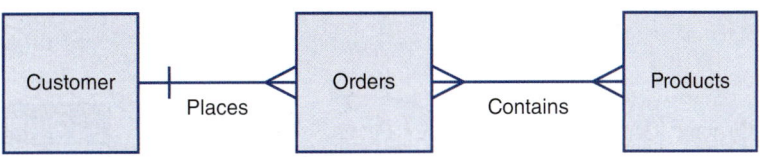

**FIGURE 3.3** Labeling relationships within an ERD.

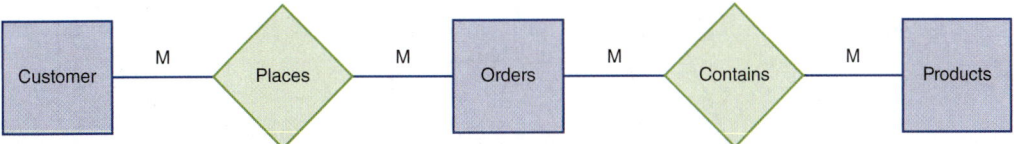

**FIGURE 3.4** An ERD using the Chen format.

## Entity Relationship Diagrams

As discussed, to visually represent the components that make up a database, database designers use ERDs. There are two types of ERDs that differ by how they represent the things that make up a system. As you examine data models, you may encounter ERDs in each form.

The first type of ERD, the crow's-foot ERD, uses the cardinality symbols previously presented in Figure 3.1. The ERD type is so named because the ends of some of the cardinality symbols resemble the tracks that might be left in the dirt by a **crow's foot**.

The second type of ERD is called a Chen diagram, named after its creator, Peter Chen. Entities and relationships using the Chen format take the form shown in **FIGURE 3.4**.

As you can see, within a Chen diagram, the cardinality is expressed using numbers, and the relationship is described within a diamond.

## Entities Have Attributes

As discussed, an **entity** is a "thing" within a system. All entities have attributes. A customer, for example, has a name, phone number, bill-to address, ship-to address, and credit card information. Within a database, such attributes are stored as fields (table columns). **FIGURE 3.5** illustrates how a Chen ERD and a crow's foot ERD represent entity attributes.

As you can see, both the Chen ERD and the crow's-foot ERD make it easy to see the attributes that make up an entity.

## Database Models

A model is a representation of a person or thing. A database model represents the things that will make up a database. As you have learned, database designers use ERDs to visually represent such

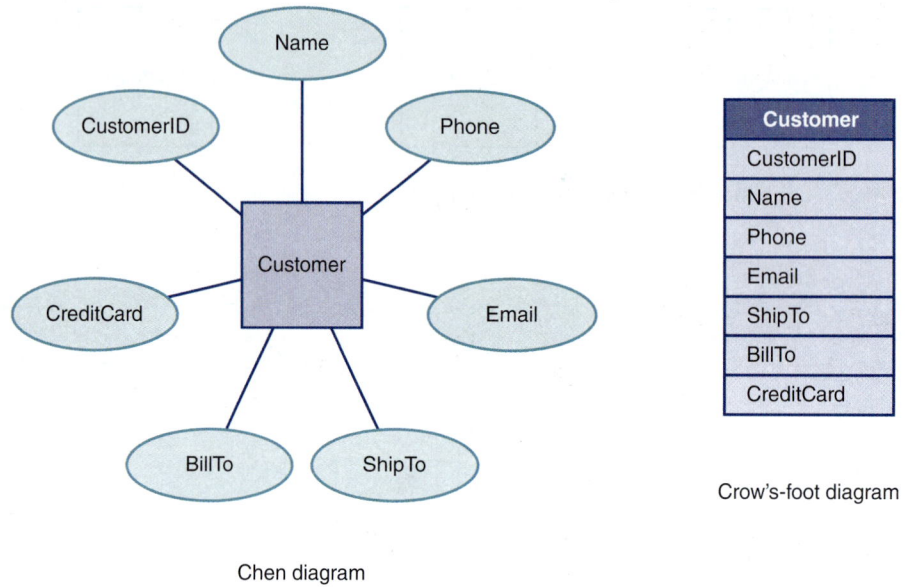

**FIGURE 3.5** Representing attributes within a Chen ERD and crow's-foot ERD.

a model. As they design a database, database designers use three levels of database models that differ in the level of detail they provide:

- Conceptual database model
- Logical database model
- Physical database model

## Conceptual Database Model

When a database designer first starts a database design, he or she will create a conceptual database model that represents the things (entities) that will make up the system. You might think of the conceptual model as a 10,000-foot view of the database—a big picture. The conceptual database model includes the entities and their general relationships, but does not include entity attributes. Depending on the database designer, the conceptual model may include cardinality. **FIGURE 3.6**, for example, illustrates a conceptual view of the e-commerce system.

Database designers often use the conceptual model to present the database design to stakeholders, who may not care about the underlying details.

The conceptual model exists to represent the entities that make up the database system. At the conceptual level, the database designer does not care about the underlying hardware or software that developers will later use to implement the database. In fact, the conceptual model should be independent of the database type (relational, NoSQL, or graph).

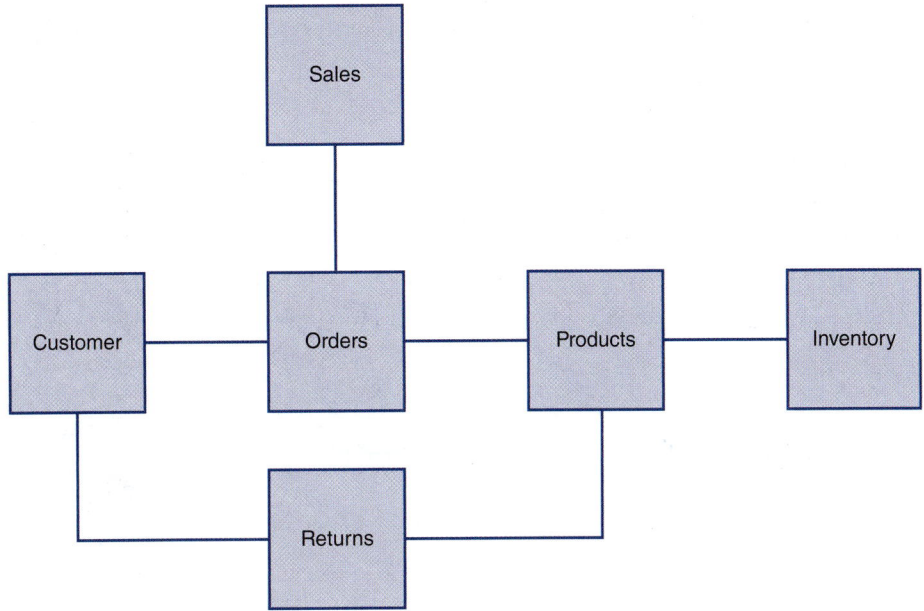

**FIGURE 3.6** A conceptual view of an e-commerce system.

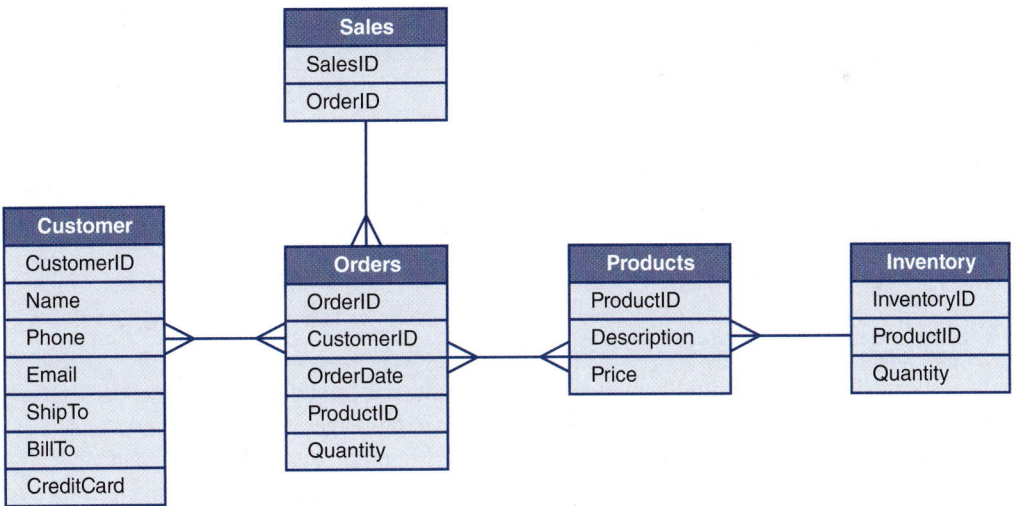

**FIGURE 3.7** A logical view of an e-commerce system.

# Logical Database Model

After the database designer creates the conceptual database model, he or she will provide the next level of detail using the logical model that includes entity attributes. **FIGURE 3.7** illustrates a logical model using a crow's-foot ERD.

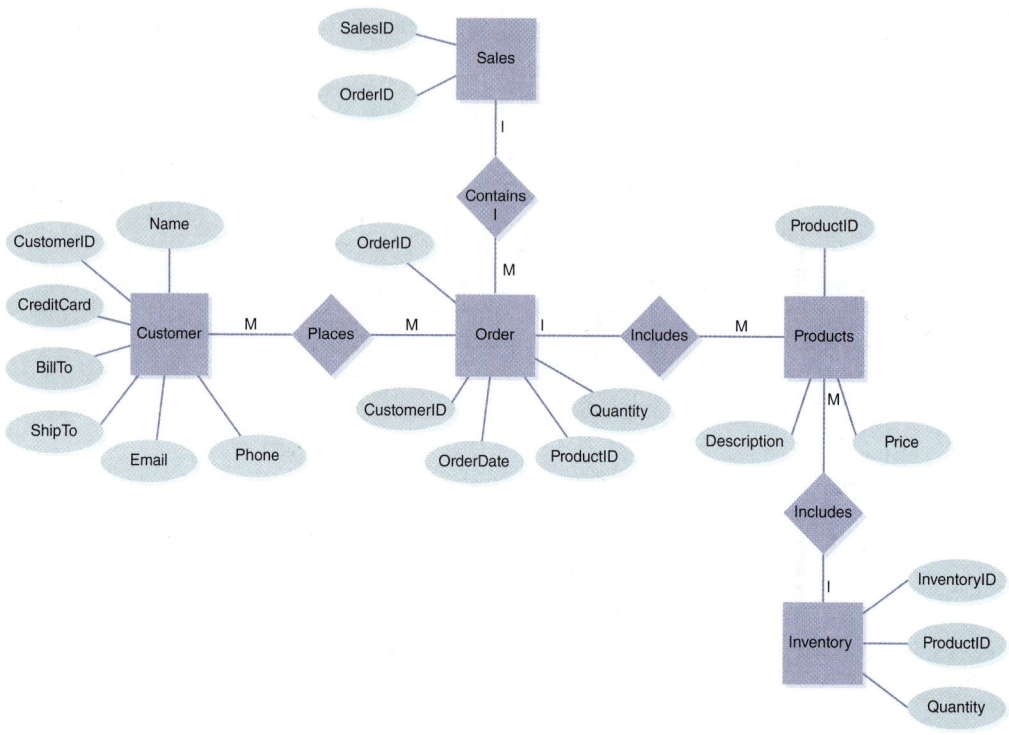

**FIGURE 3.8** A logical view of an e-commerce system using a Chen diagram.

Likewise, **FIGURE 3.8** illustrates a logical model of the e-commerce system using a Chen ERD.

The goal of the logical model is to represent entities and their attributes. The logical model, like the conceptual model, is independent of hardware and software.

## Physical Database Model

The physical database model provides the greatest level of detail about a database system. Within the physical model, the database designer specifies each attribute's data type (such as integer, floating point, or string) used to store each attribute, as well as the fields that will be the primary and foreign keys that create the relationships between entities. **FIGURE 3.9** illustrates a physical model.

The **physical model** is so named because, to create the model, the database developer has selected the hardware and software that developers will use to implement the database system.

As shown in **FIGURE 3.10**, using the physical model, the database developer has all the information he or she needs to perform the query. Chapter 5, "Keep SQL in Your Toolkit," examines SQL and relational database processing. Within the chapter, you will examine the CREATE TABLE query that developers use to create the table to store an entity.

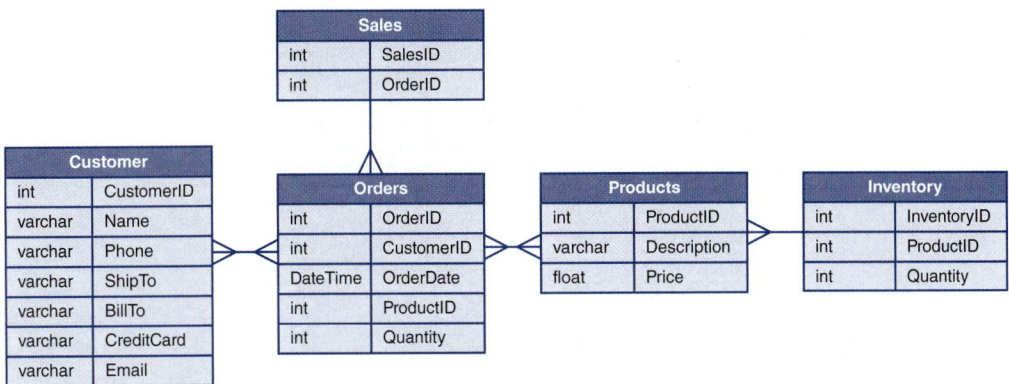

**FIGURE 3.9** A physical model of an e-commerce system.

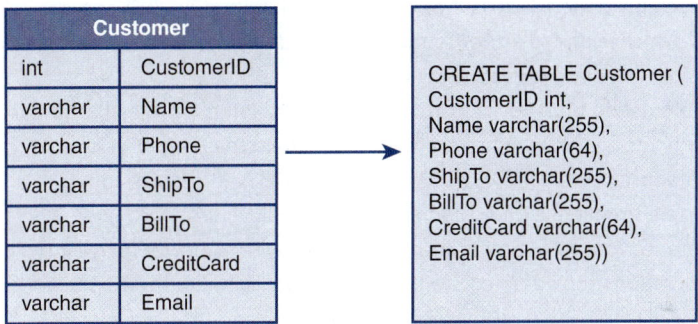

**FIGURE 3.10** Using the physical model to specify a CREATE TABLE query.

## Primary and Foreign Keys

Within a relational database, entities will have a primary key that uniquely identifies each record. A CUSTOMER table, for example, might use a CUSTOMER_ID field to uniquely identify a customer. Likewise, within an airline system, the FLIGHT table might use a FLIGHT_ID field as the primary key.

Because the primary key must uniquely identify a record within the table, the database imposes specific rules for primary keys, the most important of which are that the primary-key value must be unique and cannot be NULL.

Relational databases are so named because, within the database, entities have relationships with one another—flights have passengers, customers have orders, and so on. To implement such relationships, the related tables have common fields. **FIGURE A**, for example, shows how the CUSTOMERS table relates to the ORDERS table using a common CUSTOMER_ID field.

Within the CUSTOMER table, the CUSTOMER_ID field is the primary key. Within the ORDERS table, the ORDER_ID field will be that table's primary key, which uniquely

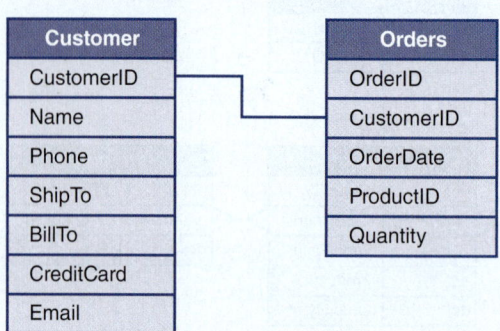

FIGURE A  Relationships between tables are based on a common field.

identifies each order. The CUSTOMER_ID field within the ORDERS table is called a foreign key, which is a field attribute that tells the database that the field is a primary key in a different table—in this case, the CUSTOMERS table.

Databases use foreign keys to provide referential integrity rules that prevent the database from assigning a value to a foreign-key field that would be invalid for a primary key. The database, for example, would not let a NULL value be assigned to a foreign-key field because a primary-key field cannot have a NULL value.

In Chapter 5, you will examine the JOIN query, which lets you combine tables to perform operations such as "Tell me the orders that John Smith has placed." Such queries typically "join" two tables using the primary- and foreign-key fields:

```
SELECT O.OrderID, C.CustomerName, O.OrderDate
FROM Orders O
INNER JOIN Customers C ON O.CustomerID=C.CustomerID;
```

Within the physical model, the ERD will identify the primary- and foreign-key fields using the letters PK and FK as shown in **FIGURE B**.

| Customer | |
|---|---|
| int, PK | CustomerID |
| varchar | Name |
| varchar | Phone |
| varchar | ShipTo |
| varchar | BillTo |
| varchar | CreditCard |
| varchar | Email |

| Orders | |
|---|---|
| int, PK | OrderID |
| int, FK | CustomerID |
| Date Time | OrderDate |
| int, FK | ProductID |
| int | Quantity |

FIGURE B  **Identifying the primary- and foreign-key fields.**

# Database Schemas

A schema is a representation of something in an outline or model form. Database developers use a database schema to describe the collection of things that make up the database, which may include:

- Tables
- Fields
- Views
- Indexes
- Relationships
- Stored procedures and functions
- And more

The ERDs previously shown visually represent several schema components (tables, fields, relationships, and primary and foreign keys). SQL developers, when asked to provide a database schema, will often provide the CREATE TABLE queries used to create tables, the query code for stored procedures, functions, and views, as well as index definitions, and so on.

When you hear the term "schema," think structure as opposed to data.

# A Word on Normalization

As you work with database data, a term you will encounter is database normalization. Although the task of **normalization** is performed by the database designer, you should have a general understanding of the process. As you will learn, to normalize data, the designer will decompose a table into one or more related tables. When developers later perform query operations, they will use the SQL JOIN to temporarily join tables together. Chapter 5 examines JOIN operations in detail.

The database normalization process exists to reduce possible errors during insert, update, and delete operations. To normalize data, the database designer achieves specific table criteria that place a table into a specific normal form. There are many types of normal forms. For simplicity, this section will cover only the first three.

Achieving 1NF is relatively easy. Achieving successive normal forms becomes increasingly more difficult. At a minimum, developers strive to achieve at least 3NF.

Consider the table shown in **FIGURE 3.11**.

As you can see, the table data provide information about a university course. 1NF requires that each attribute (column) in the table be atomic—in other words, the table has no array-like

| Class title | School | Hours | Format 1 | Format 2 | Format 3 |
|---|---|---|---|---|---|
| Advanced SQL | IT | 3 | Face to Face | Online | |
| Data Mining | IT | 3 | Face to Face | Online | Hybrid |
| Calculus | Math | 3 | Face to Face | | |
| Biology | Science | 4 | | Online | |

**FIGURE 3.11** A table not yet in 1NF.

data. In the case of the university table shown in Figure 3.11, the three format attributes are not atomic and are thus problematic. A record might have values for all three fields. A second record may have values for two of the fields and not one. Yet another record may have a value for only one of the fields or possibly none of the fields. To resolve this issue and to place the table into 1NF, we can decompose the table into two tables, removing the format fields from the first table and placing them into their own table, as shown in **FIGURE 3.12**.

2NF requires that a table be in 1NF and that all attributes are dependent only on the candidate key. Consider the table shown in **FIGURE 3.13**, for which the table's candidate key is the class title.

In this case, the school attribute depends on the class title. Likewise, the instructor attribute depends on the class title, as do the topic, format, and grade-level attributes. The instructor and time attributes, however, depend on the class title and format. To place the table into 2NF, you would decompose the table into the two tables shown in **FIGURE 3.14**.

| Class title | School | Hours |
|---|---|---|
| Advanced SQL | IT | 3 |
| Data Mining | IT | 3 |
| Calculus | Math | 3 |
| Biology | Science | 4 |

| Class title | Format |
|---|---|
| Advanced SQL | Face to Face |
| Advanced SQL | Online |
| Data Mining | Face to Face |
| Data Mining | Online |
| Data Mining | Hybrid |
| Calculus | Face to Face |
| Biology | Online |

**FIGURE 3.12** Placing a table into 1NF.

| Class title | School | Topic | Format | Instructor | Time | Grade level |
|---|---|---|---|---|---|---|
| Advanced SQL | IT | SQL | Face to Face | Jones | M - W 12:30 | 6 |
| Advanced SQL | IT | SQL | Online | Smith | T - TH 5:30 | 6 |
| Math 400 | Math | Calculus | Face to Face | Davis | M - W 5:30 | 4 |
| Science 350 | Science | Biology | Face to Face | Allen | T - TH 3:30 | 4 |
| Science 350 | Science | Biology | Online | Williams | M - W 6:00 | 4 |

**FIGURE 3.13** A table with attribute dependencies.

| Class title | School | Topic | Grade level |
|---|---|---|---|
| Advanced SQL | IT | SQL | 6 |
| Math 400 | Math | Calculus | 4 |
| Science 350 | Science | Biology | 4 |

| Class title | Format | Instructor | Time |
|---|---|---|---|
| Advanced SQL | Face to Face | Jones | M - W 12:30 |
| Advanced SQL | Online | Smith | T - TH 5:30 |
| Math 400 | Face to Face | Davis | M - W 5:30 |
| Science 350 | Face to Face | Allen | T - TH 3:30 |
| Science 350 | Online | Williams | M - W 6:00 |

**FIGURE 3.14** Placing a table into 2NF.

| Class title | School | Topic | Grade level | Grade level descriptions |
|---|---|---|---|---|
| Advanced SQL | IT | SQL | 4 | Undergraduate |
| Data Mining | IT | Data Mining | 6 | Graduate |
| Science 350 | Science | Biology | 4 | Undergraduate |
| Math 400 | Math | Calculus | 4 | Undergraduate |
| Math 510 | Math | Geometry | 6 | Graduate |

**FIGURE 3.15** A table with transitive dependencies.

| Class title | School | Topic | Grade level |
|---|---|---|---|
| Advanced SQL | IT | SQL | 4 |
| Data Mining | IT | Data Mining | 6 |
| Science 350 | Science | Biology | 4 |
| Math 400 | Math | Calculus | 4 |
| Math 510 | Math | Geometry | 6 |

| Grade level | Grade level descriptions |
|---|---|
| 4 | Undergraduate |
| 6 | Graduate |

**FIGURE 3.16** Placing a table into 3NF.

Finally, to place a table into 3NF, the table must first be in 2NF and have no transitive dependencies. Consider the table shown in **FIGURE 3.15**.

As you examine the table attributes, you will find that the grade-level title is dependent on the grade-level attribute. To place the table into 3NF, you would decompose it into the two tables shown in **FIGURE 3.16**.

Admittedly, the normalization scenarios shown here were quite simple. The key point for you to understand is that as a database designer normalizes database tables, he or she will wind up with a greater number of tables as the level of normalization increases. The benefit gained by normalizing tables (improved data integrity and less risk of insert, update, and delete anomalies) is worth the increased number of tables and overhead incurred when developers must later join the tables back together as they query the database.

# Common Database Types

Throughout this text, you will make extensive use of relational (SQL) and NoSQL databases. In addition to these database types, the use of object-oriented and graph databases is starting to emerge. The sections that follow introduce each of these database types.

## Relational Database Management Systems

A relational database is a table-based database that stores entities within individual tables. Relational databases are so named because they also store information about the relationships

| | Class title | School | Topic | Grade level |
|---|---|---|---|---|
| | Advanced SQL | IT | SQL | 4 |
| | Data Mining | IT | Data Mining | 6 |
| Records | Science 350 | Science | Biology | 4 |
| | Math 400 | Math | Calculus | 4 |
| | Math 510 | Math | Geometry | 6 |

(Columns = Attributes)

**FIGURE 3.17** Within a relational database table, rows represent records and columns represent the attributes (fields) that make up each record.

between tables, such as the customers who have placed an order or the products that make up an order.

As shown in **FIGURE 3.17**, within a table, the rows correspond to records and the columns to the attributes (fields) that make up the records. Relational databases are often called SQL databases because database developers make extensive use of the SQL language to manipulate them. Chapter 6, "Keep SQL in Your Toolkit," examines relational database operations in detail.

## NoSQL Database Management Systems

Unlike relational databases that store data within tables and that use SQL as the primary query language, a NoSQL (not only SQL) database stores data within files, normally using XML or JSON format, and uses a primary query language other than SQL for database manipulation. Chapter 7, "NoSQL Data Analytics," examines NoSQL database operations in detail.

## Object-Oriented Database Management Systems

Much of the previous discussion relates to relational or table-based databases. In contrast, to support the widespread use of object-oriented programming languages, such as Java, C++, C#, and Python, database researchers have developed object-oriented database management systems (OODBMSs) that allow programmers to store and retrieve objects in one step, as opposed to having to store and retrieve attribute values individually by assigning each to columns in a table. Common uses of object-oriented databases include audio and video storage.

Within an object-oriented database, developers can declare classes and even build upon existing classes using inheritance. Although many of the object-oriented databases are research based, Oracle now includes support for objects within its PL/SQL query language.

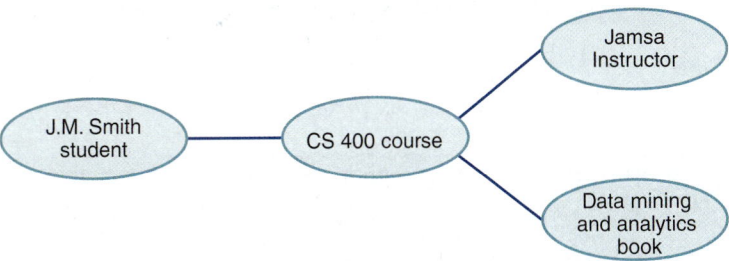

**FIGURE 3.18** Expressing entities and relationships as nodes and edges.

# Graph Database Management Systems

Relational databases are so named because they store related data within tables, keeping track of relationships between tables and normally expressing such relationships in terms of primary and foreign keys.

In the real world, things have many different relationships. Assume, for example, a student is taking CS400, a database management course. The course instructor is Jamsa, and the course book is *Data Mining and Analytics*, which happens to be written by Jamsa. **FIGURE 3.18** illustrates the entities and relationships that exist in this simple example. The entities are nodes within the graph, and the relationships are edges.

Assume that beyond this simple example, the student is taking additional courses, which also have books and instructors. Further, Jamsa is the author of 114 additional books, many of which are used by students taking a variety of courses. As you can imagine, the number of nodes (entities) and edges (relationships) can grow very large quickly.

Graph databases were designed to store such entities and relationships. Some of the more common graph databases include:

- Neo4j
- OrientedDB
- Amazon Neptune
- GraphDB

Graph databases are NoSQL databases, in that they do not store data using relational tables and do not use SQL as their query language. Many graph databases store entities and their relationships using JSON. Other graph databases use the Resource Description Framework (RDF), which is a standard on the web. Chapter 7 examines JavaScript in detail.

To take a graph database for a test drive, visit the Neo4j website, as shown in **FIGURE 3.19**, and download and install the system. As you will learn, Neo4j uses a language called Cypher.

# CHAPTER 3 Databases and Data Warehouses

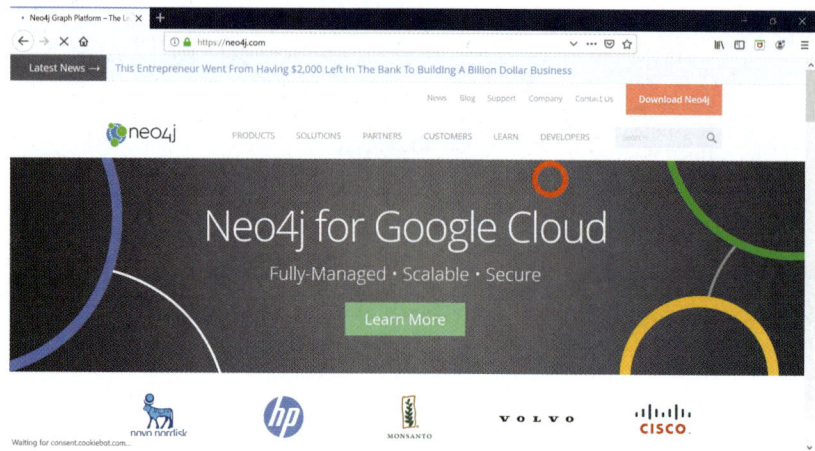

**FIGURE 3.19** Download and install a graph database from the Neo4j website.

Used with the permission of Neo4j, Inc

## Online Transaction Processing Versus Online Analytical Processing

As you read about database operations, you will encounter the terms OLTP and OLAP. OLTP relates to applications that perform database transactions, such as the e-commerce site that tracks product sales and the airline reservation system that tracks flights, passengers, and so on. OLAP, in contrast, includes the reporting, dashboards, and decision support tools. Normally, an OLTP database is the data source for OLAP operations. **FIGURE A** illustrates OLTP and OLAP systems.

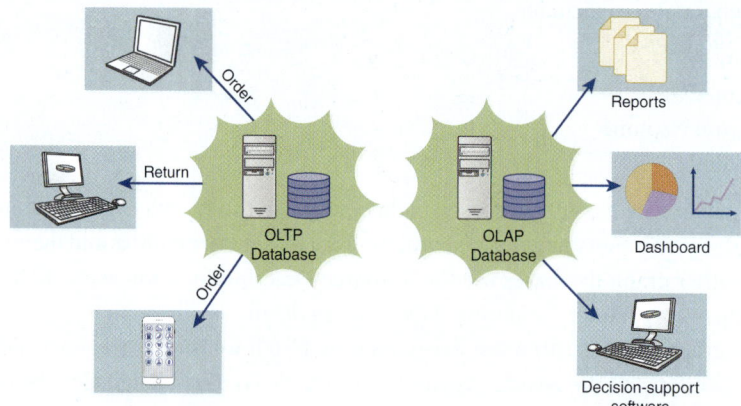

**FIGURE A** OLTP and OLAP systems.

# Data Warehouses

Most companies have databases that store transactional data, such as product sales, shipments, or inventory levels. Although such databases could be used for analytics, their design and structure are not optimized for high-performance data analytic operations, decision support, and dashboard operations. In addition, database developers would not want to add the overhead of such analytic operations to their transactional databases.

Furthermore, it is common to have databases at many locations, possibly across the country. Consider, for example, a large retail company that has sales and inventory databases at store locations across the country. To analyze their company-wide operations, the company must gather data from each of their databases. In this case, to perform analytics, the company needs only sales and inventory data, but not the customer and vendor records.

To hold such analytic data, companies use a data warehouse, which is a database for which the tables are designed to optimize analytic operations. The data warehouse will store a subset of the company data that are required for analytics and reporting. As shown in **FIGURE 3.20**, in the case of the retail companies, the database developers (or an automated process) will load the analytics data from each location into the data warehouse, probably on a daily basis.

Unlike transactional data, which are normalized to prevent insert, update, and delete anomalies, a data warehouse, for performance reasons, does not require normalization. To start a data-warehouse design, data-warehouse designers will normally ask the following questions:

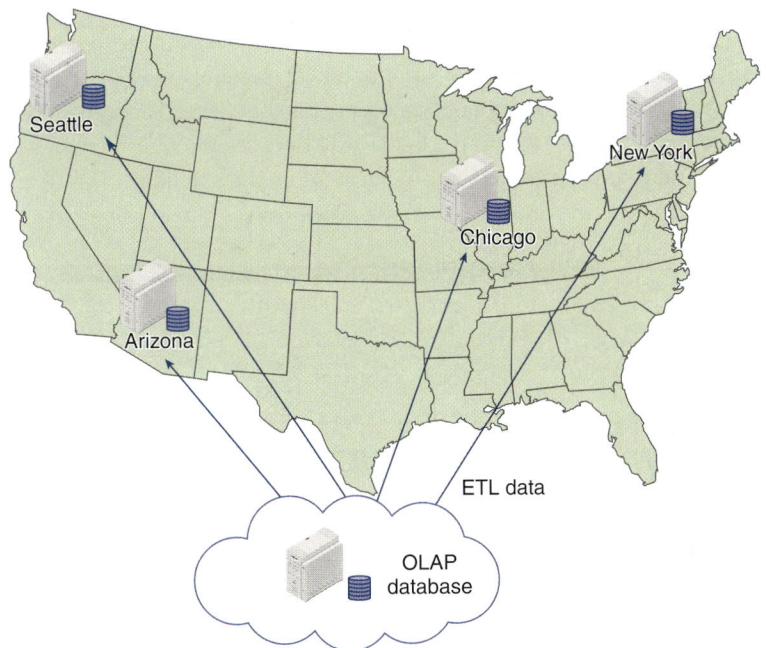

**FIGURE 3.20** Loading analytics data into a data warehouse.

- What reports are required?
- What and where are the sources of data?
- How frequently will new data be collected and loaded into the data warehouse?
- How many users will simultaneously access the data warehouse?
- To what data will different user types (such as finance, sales, and operations) have access?
- How will the extract, transform, and load (ETL) operations be performed?
- What data marts are required?
- How are the reporting, analytics, decision support tools, and dashboard needs expected to change in the future?
- How will the data warehouse be backed up and with what frequency?
- What factors influence the data quality?
- Who owns the data, and who are the primary stakeholders?
- Who will test the reports, analytics, and dashboards to ensure quality assurance?

## Virtual Data Warehouses

For years, data-warehouse developers implemented data warehouses within on-premise database servers. With the advent of the cloud, most data-warehouse developers have moved their data warehouses to the cloud.

The recent trend in data warehousing is to host the data warehouse using a cloud-based managed service provider (MSP). In general, the data-warehouse MSP will not only provide the underlying scalable-on-demand hardware (central processing units [CPUs] and disk space) and software (the DBMS and operating system) but will also administer all the database software, performing updates and patches. In addition, the MSP can be responsible for backups and replication. In this way, because the MSP manages the day-to-day administrative tasks, the developers can focus on the solution.

**FIGURE A** illustrates the Snowflake website. Snowflake is a data-warehouse MSP.

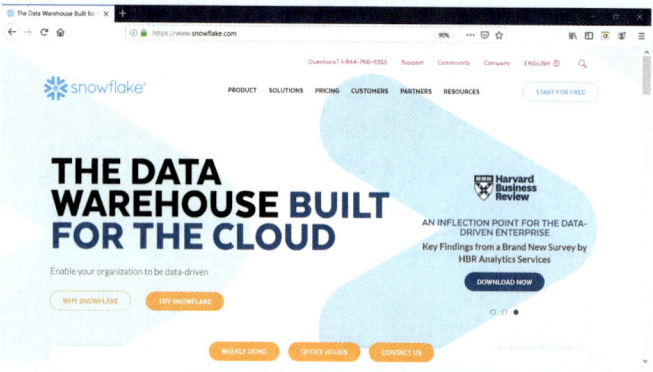

**FIGURE A** The Snowflake cloud-based data-warehouse MSP.

Used with permission of Snowflake Inc

## Data Marts

A data warehouse consists of company-wide data used to represent the company as a whole. As you know, companies consist of organizations, such as sales, manufacturing, and transportation (logistics). A data mart is a simplified component of a data warehouse that focuses on such individual business groups. **FIGURE 3.21**, for example, illustrates how a company might implement data marts.

Internally, the data-warehouse designer will design the data warehouse and data marts using fact and dimension tables, as discussed next.

## Revisiting Schemas

As database designers design databases, they will often create a relational schema that represents the database by showing the tables and their relationships. As the designers normalize the tables, the relational schema may become quite large, consisting of many tables. As you have learned, although the normalization increases the number of tables and creates overhead, when developers must later join tables to perform queries, the reduced risk of errors due to insert, update, and delete anomalies justifies the process.

Although the normalization process is required to support transactional processing, it is normally not required for data-warehouse operations. As such, data-warehouse designers will normally use a different schema design that uses fact and dimension tables. A fact table is a compact table that describes a transaction or aggregation (combination) of transaction totals. In the e-commerce example, a fact table might describe Orders, as shown in **FIGURE 3.22**.

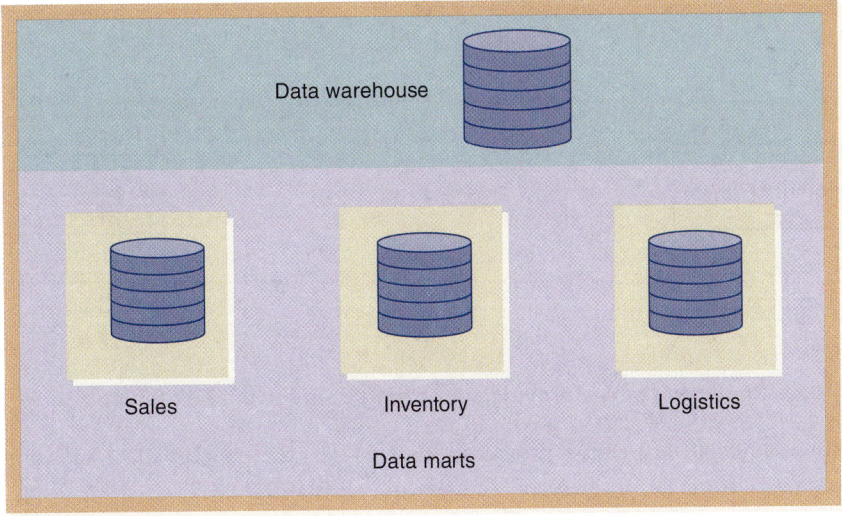

**FIGURE 3.21** A data mart contains data for a specific business group.

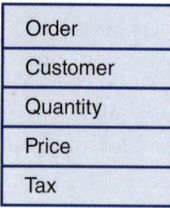

**FIGURE 3.22** A fact table that describes orders in an e-commerce solution.

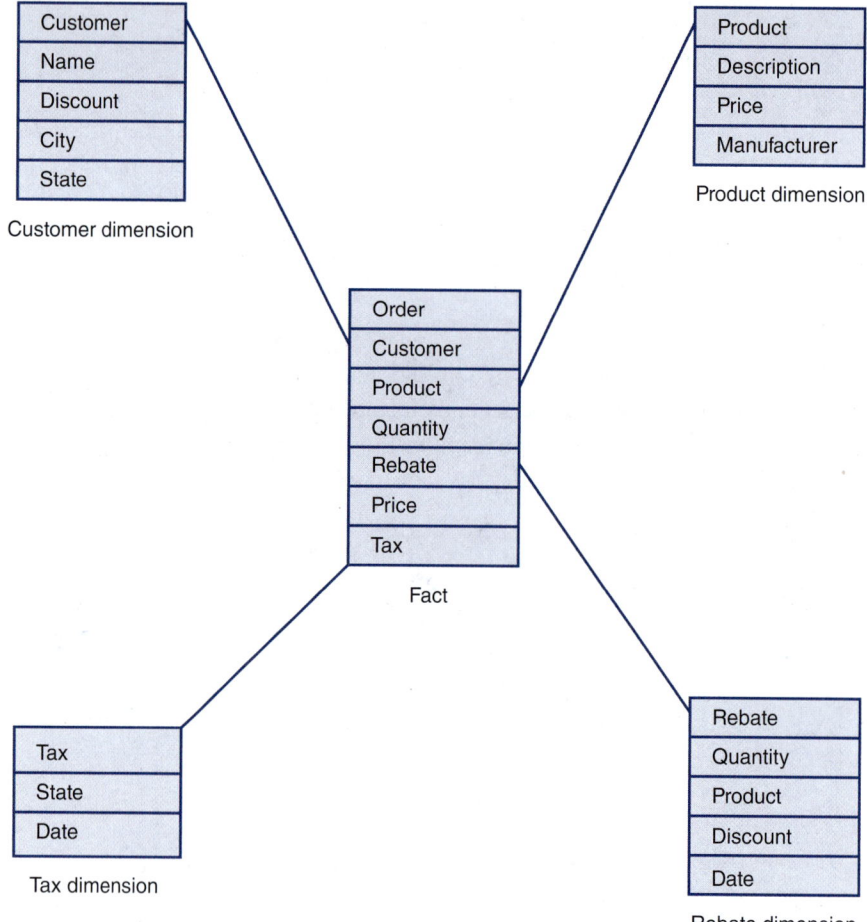

**FIGURE 3.23** Dimension tables provide supporting data for the fact table.

A dimension table, in contrast, provides additional data that support a fact, such as specifics about products, customers, or salespeople, as shown in **FIGURE 3.23**.

To specify facts and dimensions, a data-warehouse designer typically uses the **star schema**, so named because it produces a star-like shape, with the fact table in the center surrounded

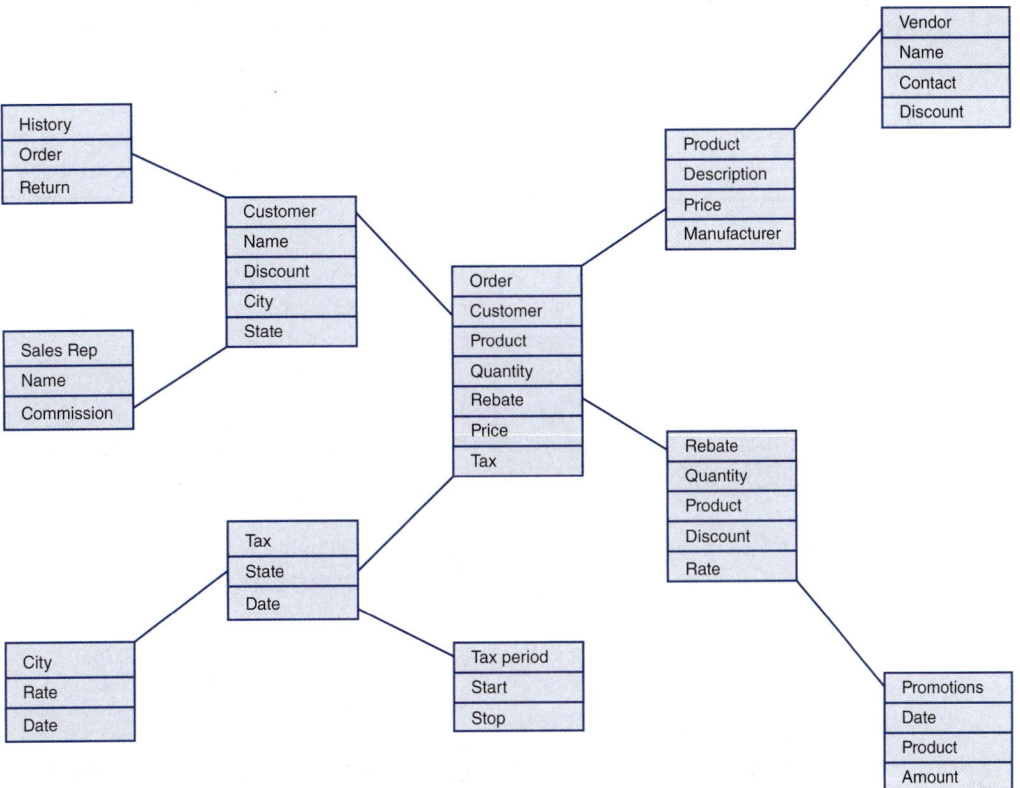

**FIGURE 3.24** A snowflake schema.

by dimension tables. A complex data warehouse may contain multiple fact tables. Depending on the data, the dimension tables themselves may have additional supporting dimensions, which the developers represent using the snowflake schema, as shown in **FIGURE 3.24**. The **snowflake schema** is so named because it produces a visual representation of the model that resembles a snowflake.

## Data Lakes

As you discuss data, you may encounter the term data lake. A data lake stores data outside of a database, normally in a file. The file that implements a data lake can use a structured format, such as XML or JSON, or it can be unstructured using a large binary object (blob) or a text file.

Because of their large size, data lake files often reside on specialized file systems such as Hadoop, Amazon S3, or a Microsoft Azure Data Lake. Chapter 15, "Big Data Analytics," discusses big data operations that may use very large files, which are examples of data lakes.

# Hands On—Creating Entity Relationship Diagrams Using Lucidchart

As you design database and data-warehouse solutions, there may be times when you must draw an ERD to represent a database or a star or snowflake schema to represent a data warehouse. To draw such diagrams, you should consider Lucidchart, a cloud-based software as a service (SaaS) drawing tool.

To get started with Lucidchart, visit the site www.LucidChart.com and sign up for a free account. After you register and log in, Lucidchart will display its workspace, as shown in **FIGURE 3.25**.

Assume, for example, that you must create the ERD shown in **FIGURE 3.26**.

To start, click the ERD template button and then click Blank ERD and Data Flow to create a blank document. From the Lucidchart shapes palette that appears on the left-hand side of your screen, drag an Entity box onto the workspace. Label the box Student. Within the menu bar Fields option, select the value 5. Then fill in the entity fields shown in **FIGURE 3.27**.

Repeat this process to add the entities shown in **FIGURE 3.28**.

Next, to connect the entities and show the relationship cardinality, drag a line between two entities. Then, using the endpoint pull-down list, shown in **FIGURE 3.29**, select the appropriate cardinality types.

Repeat this process to update the line endpoints, as previously shown in Figure 3.26.

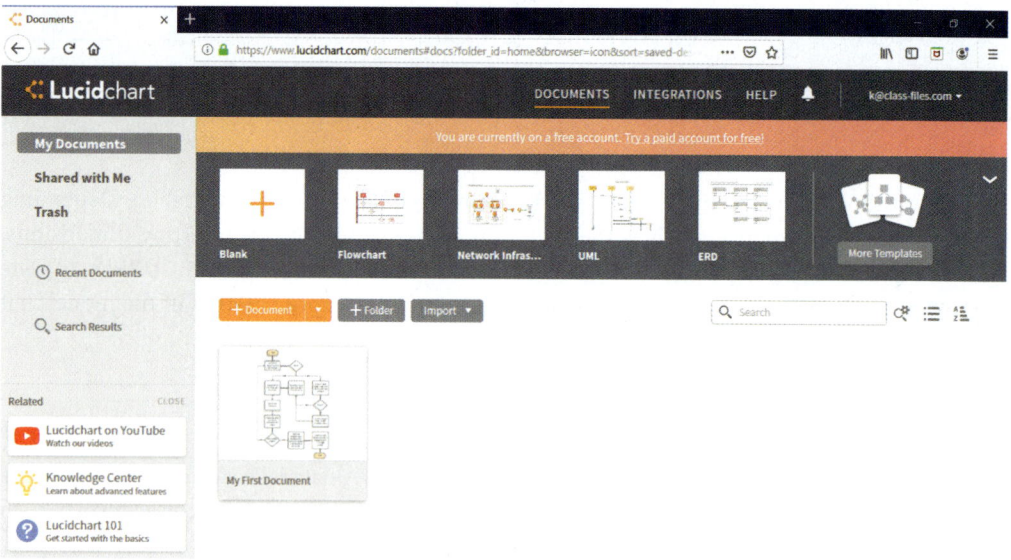

**FIGURE 3.25** The Lucidchart drawing environment.

Used with the permission of Lucid Software Inc

Hands On—Creating Entity Relationship Diagrams Using Lucidchart

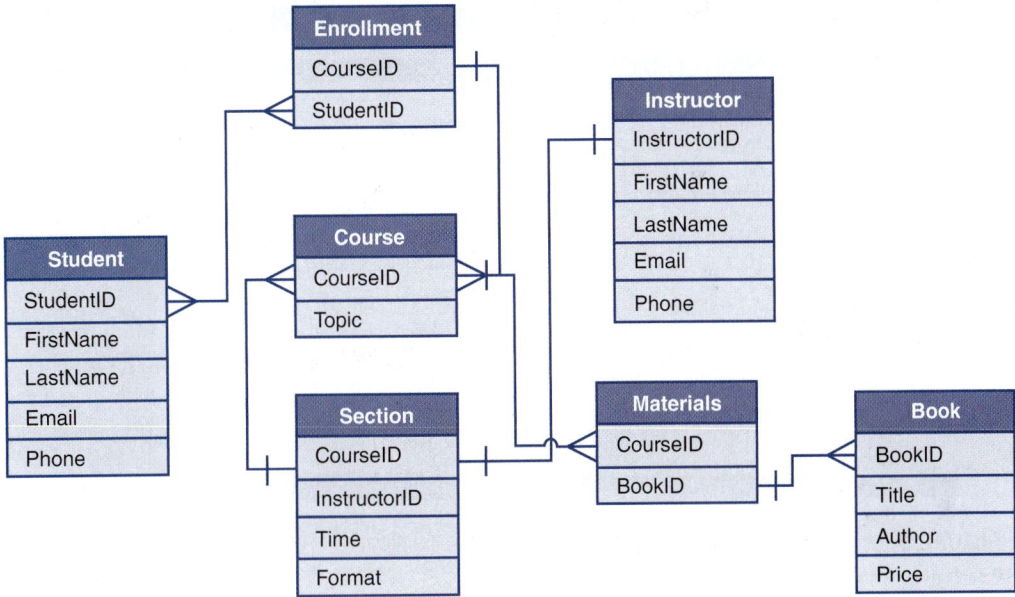

FIGURE 3.26 An ERD for a school's registration system.

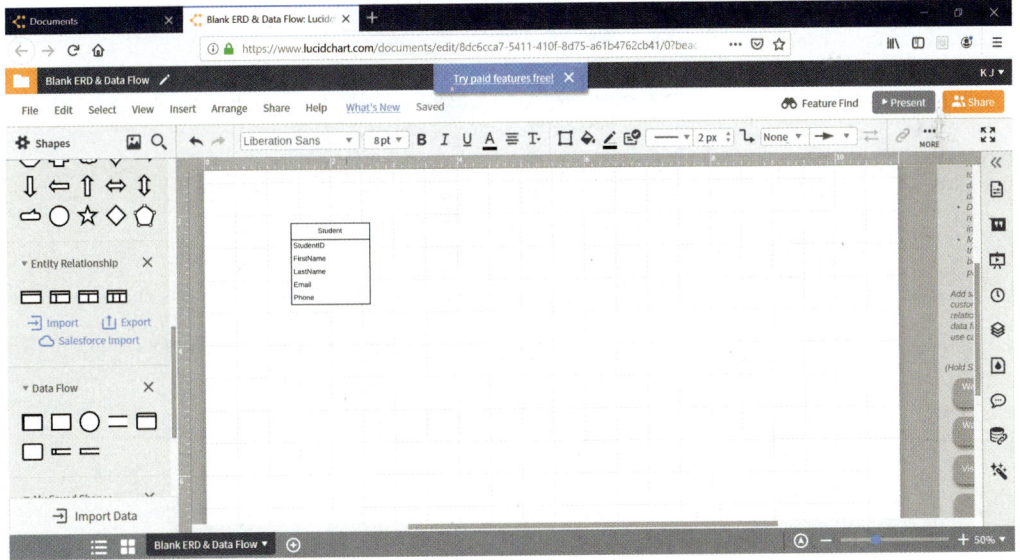

FIGURE 3.27 Assigning attributes to the student entity.

Used with the permission of Lucid Software Inc

## 98 CHAPTER 3 Databases and Data Warehouses

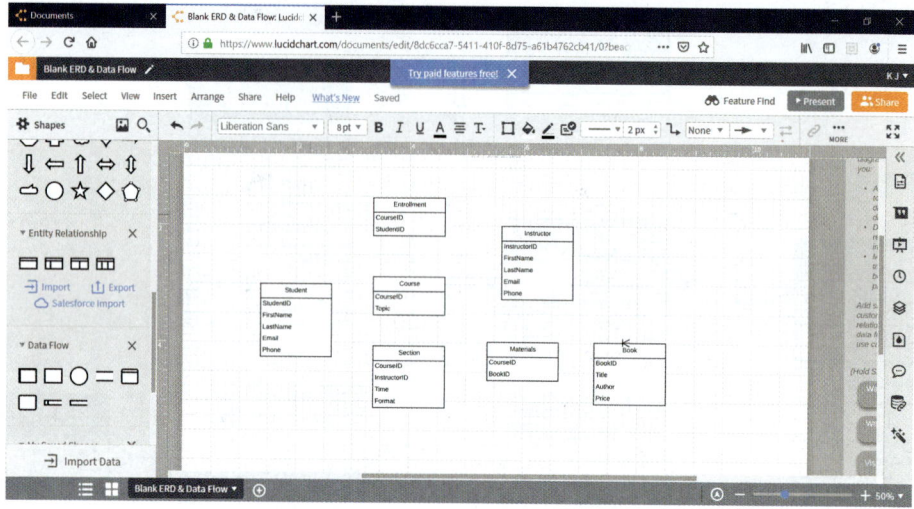

**FIGURE 3.28** Entities within the school ERD.
Used with the permission of Lucid Software Inc

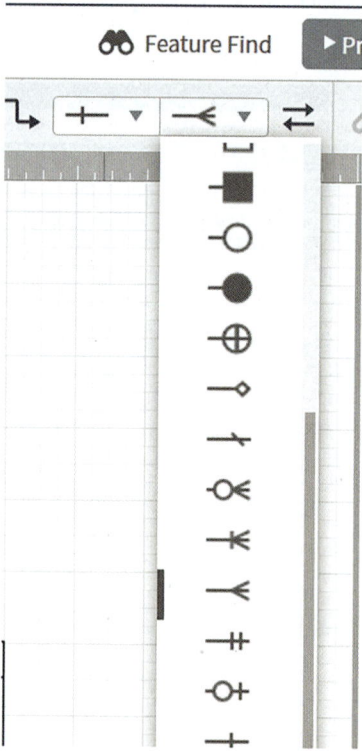

**FIGURE 3.29** Selecting a cardinality symbol using the endpoint pull-down list.
Used with the permission of Lucid Software Inc

# Summary

A database is a collection of data organized for fast storage and retrieval. Databases reside within a special software application called a DBMS.

All systems are composed of things, which database developers call entities. An ERD is a visual representation of things that make up a system along with the relationships that exist between them. The two most common ERDs are the Chen diagram and crow's-foot diagram. Both diagram types represent entities, their attributes, and their relationships. Database developers describe the relationship type that exists between entities in terms of cardinality. Common cardinalities include one-to-one, one-to-many, and many-to-many.

To model a database design, database developers create the following database models:

- Conceptual database model
- Logical database model
- Physical database model

A conceptual database model provides a high-level view of the entities that make up a database system. The conceptual model does not include specifics about each entity, such as attributes, and is often used to introduce the database to stakeholders. A logical model provides greater description of the database entities to include attribute names. The logical model, like the conceptual model, should be independent of the hardware and software that will implement the system. A physical database model adds entity-attribute data types to the logical model to make it appropriate for a database developer to implement a database.

Tables in a relational database often have a primary key that uniquely identifies each record. Examples of primary keys include a CUSTOMER_ID field or an ORDER_ID field. Databases impose specific rules for primary-key values, such as the primary-key value must be unique and cannot be NULL. To create relationships between tables in a relational database, two or more tables will have a common field. When that common field is a primary key in one table, it is called a foreign key in the related table. Foreign keys exist to enforce referential integrity rules, and as such, databases impose rules on foreign-key values, such as that foreign key cannot be NULL.

A schema is a representation of something in a model or outline form. Database designers visually represent database schemas using an ERD. Similarly, database developers often provide their CREATE TABLE and other queries to provide a schema for a database.

To reduce the possibility of data anomalies (errors) due to insert, update, and delete queries, database developers normalize their table designs to achieve specific normal forms, such as 1NF, 2NF, and 3NF. To achieve each level of normal form, the designers must satisfy specific design constraints. As they normalize tables to comply with each normal form, the designers will often decompose one table into two or more tables. Later, when database developers query the database, they will temporarily combine the tables using a JOIN query.

Relational databases are table-based databases for which the table rows represent records and the table columns represent attributes (fields) for each record. A NoSQL database stores data in a less structured way than a relational database (often in a JSON file) and does not use SQL as its primary query language. An object-oriented database allows developers to store and retrieve objects, which makes them well suited for video and audio objects. Although most object-oriented databases are research based, DBMSs, such as Oracle, now provide support for object-based operations. A graph database is a NoSQL database designed to store the many different relationships an entity may have. The graph database represents entities as nodes and the relationships between entities as edges of a graph.

OLTP describes traditional database operations that store and retrieve data for a transaction, such as an e-commerce sale, a student registration for a course, and so on. OLAP describes database operations that support reporting, decision support operations, and other analytic operations. A data warehouse uses OLAP.

A data warehouse is a database optimized for reporting and other analytical processing. Because a data warehouse does not perform transactional processing (with insert, delete, and update operations), data warehouses are not normalized.

To describe and implement a data warehouse, data-warehouse designers normally use a star (or snowflake) schema that is based on a fact table that contains key-metric values and dimension tables that contain supporting data. A data warehouse normally contains data for an entire company. A data mart contains a subset of that data specific to a group within the organization, such as sales or manufacturing. With the growth of big data applications, many systems support data lakes, which store data in a native format, such as an XML, JSON, or text file.

## Key Terms

Cardinality
Conceptual model
Crow's foot
Data anomalies
Database
Data lake
Data mart
Data warehouse
Database Management System (DBMS)
Entity
Entity relationship diagram (ERD)

Foreign key
Graph database
JavaScript Object Notation (JSON)
Logical model
Normalization
NoSQL
Object-oriented database
Object-Oriented Database Management System (OODBMS)
Online Analytical Processing (OLAP)

Online Transaction Processing (OLTP)
Physical model
Primary key
Relational Database Management System (RDBMS)
Referential integrity
Relational database
Schema
Snowflake schema
Star schema

## Review

1. Compare and contrast a database, data warehouse, data mart, and data lake.
2. Compare and contrast a relational, object-oriented, and graph database.

3. Select a system with which you are familiar. Then construct a conceptual, logical, and physical database model for the system, which you represent using an entity relationship diagram.
4. Place the table shown in **FIGURE 3.30** into first-normal form.
5. Place the table shown in **FIGURE 3.31** into second-normal form.
6. Place the table shown in **FIGURE 3.32** into third-normal form.
7. Define and describe cardinality showing the common cardinality symbols.
8. Compare and contrast OLTP and OLAP.
9. Define and describe the term schema.
10. Describe the role of a data-warehouse managed service provider.

| Clinic | Phone | Hours | Pets 1 | Pets 2 | Pets 3 |
|---|---|---|---|---|---|
| Petland | 555 - 1111 | 8 - 5 | Dogs | Cats | Birds |
| Zoo stop | 555 - 1212 | 9 - 3 | Exotics | Birds | |
| Az equine | 555 - 1415 | 8 - 5 | Horses | | |
| Dr K | 555 - 1515 | 9 - 6 | Dogs | Cats | |

**FIGURE 3.30** A table not in first normal form.

| Clinic | Pharmacy | Surgery | Day | Vet |
|---|---|---|---|---|
| Petland | Y | N | M - F | Smith |
| Zoo stop | Y | Y | M - W | Davis |
| Zoo stop | Y | Y | TH - S | Swanson |
| Az Equine | Y | Y | M - Tu | Jones |
| Az Equine | Y | Y | W - F | Lawson |
| Az Equine | Y | Y | Sa | Lewis |

**FIGURE 3.31** A table not in 2NF.

| Clinic | Phone | Hours | Description |
|---|---|---|---|
| Petland | 555 - 1111 | 8 | Business hours |
| Zoo stop | 555 - 1212 | 6 | Afternoon hours |
| Az Enquine | 555 - 1415 | 12 | Evening hours |
| Dr K | 555 - 1515 | 24 | Emergency hours |

**FIGURE 3.32** A table not in 3NF.

# CHAPTER 4

# Data Visualization

## Chapter Goals and Objectives

- Define and describe data visualization.
- Compare and contrast chart types and the appropriate use of each.
- Create a variety of charts using Excel.
- Create HTML-based charts on the web.
- Use best practices when creating charts.

Data analysts are dealing with more data today than ever before; conservatively, that amount of data will continue to double every 2 years for many years to come. With ever-growing amounts of data come many opportunities for discovery. However, as the volume of data increases, so, too, do the challenges of discovering trends and patterns, as well as expressing such findings in a meaningful way to others. In the simplest sense, data visualization is the visual representation of data with the goal of improving communication.

Data analysts have a wide range of communication tools available, from tables, to charts and graphs, to the display of a big number, to represent data. Throughout this chapter, you will examine many of these tools in detail and learn when the use of each is appropriate. You will examine many different visualization tools, which include Excel, Tableau, and Google Charts. By the time you complete this chapter, you will understand the following key concepts:

- A **visualization** is a representation of an object. A chart, for example, is a visualization of a data set. A goal of visualizing data is to improve communication.
- To create a visualization, data analysts have many chart types from which they can choose. Each chart type is well suited to represent a particular type of data.

- To help analysts select the correct chart type, analysts often group charts by the following:
  - **Time-based comparison charts** that represent how a variable's value changes over time.
  - **Category-based comparison charts** that represent one or more categories of values.
  - **Composition charts** that represent how a value relates to the whole.
  - **Distribution charts** that represent the distribution frequency of values within a data set.
  - **Correlation charts** that represent how two or more variables relate.
  - **Dashboard charts** that represent key performance indicators (KPIs), normally on a company dashboard.
  - **Geocharts** that chart data against a map.
- Regardless of the chart type you are creating, you should follow best-practice guidelines to improve the effectiveness of your chart.
- Analysts have a wide variety of visualization tools they can use to create charts, ranging from Excel to Tableau and beyond. Factors to consider when selecting a visualization toolset include price, learning curve, support for web-based charts, and dashboard support.
- To integrate charts into a Hypertext Markup Language (HTML) web page, developers can leverage tools such as Google Charts.

## Visualization Tools

Analysts employ a wide range of tools to create visualizations, from Excel to the widely used Tableau. Across the web, you can find a wide range of visualization tools, most of which provide a trial version you can test-drive for free. **TABLE A** briefly lists the commonly used visualization tools. Factors to consider when selecting a visualization toolset include price, learning curve, support for web-based charts, and dashboard support.

**TABLE A** Common Visualization Tools

| Visualization Tool | Website |
| --- | --- |
| Domo | www.domo.com |
| Microsoft Power BI | powerbi.microsoft.com |
| Sisense | www.sisense.com |
| Tableau | www.tableau.com |
| Qlik | www.qlik.com |
| Tibco SpotfireX | www.tibco.com/products/tibco-spotfire |
| Yellowfin | www.yellowfinbi.com |

## Visualization Best Practices

Creating quality visualizations is both an art and a science. A quality chart uses color effectively, integrates complementary fonts, and highlights points of interest to communicate a message—the art of visualization. Likewise, quality visualizations use the correct chart for the right purpose—the science of visualization. Creating quality charts takes time and effort. Be prepared to make revisions to your charts based on feedback you receive from others. Over time, you will learn your audience preferences.

That said, use the following list of best practices as you create your visualizations:

- Begin with your end goal in mind. In other words, know what you want to show before you begin.
- Keep your audience in mind. If you are presenting to a group of stakeholders with knowledge of your data set, you may only need to present a detailed summary chart. If your audience, in contrast, is new to the data, you may want to use a series of drill-down charts that tell the data story.
- Use the correct chart for the right purpose. This chapter groups charts by the type of data they are well suited to represent. Use the chapter's chart groupings as your guide as you select your chart type.
- Use color effectively. Users often find colors that differ only slightly within a chart confusing. Users normally prefer the use of high-contrast colors instead.
- Use text labels to meaningfully describe your data. Use a legend to define the meanings of colors used within the chart.
- Use axis values consistently. Users are used to seeing axis values that begin with zero. Using a non-zero-based axis may lead to confusion.
- Avoid clutter. Displaying too much information on a chart (or dashboard) may distract the viewer from the message you are trying to convey.
- Focus on actionable content. A good chart informs. A great chart is a call to action.
- Keep it simple. The adage "less is more" applies well to visualization. Complexity and clutter can distract and confuse viewers.
- Build user trust. Do not misrepresent data. Avoid practices that may be perceived as distorting data, such as the use of non-zero-based axes or 3D pie charts.
- Make sure your chart's axis labels are easy to read.
- Use a meaningful chart title that begins to tell a story.
- Sort data appropriately. For example, alphabetize category-based data and display dates in order.
- Draw the viewer's focus to key points. If your chart's goal is to highlight a key value, use a different color to highlight the value's bar or **marker** within the chart.
- Consider using a graphics artist. Depending on the chart's importance, you may want to leverage the skills of a graphics artist to improve the chart's appearance and messaging.

# Selecting the Correct Chart for the Right Purpose

As you will learn in this chapter, there are many different chart types, each of which represents data differently. Your first task in visualizing data is to determine the correct chart type that best corresponds to the message you must communicate. To help you do so, this chapter groups charts into the following categories:

- Time-based comparison charts, which represent how one or more sets of values change over time.
- Category-based comparison charts, which represent how two or more categories of values compare.
- Composition charts, which represent how one or more values relate to a larger whole.
- Correlation charts, which represent how two or more variables relate.
- Dashboard charts, which represent KPIs that companies use to track initiatives.
- Distribution charts, which represent the frequency of values within a data set.
- Geocharts, which represent how the values from one location compare to values in a different location.

## The "Correct" Chart Is More Than Opinion

As you will learn, many analysts criticize the use of pie charts because it can be difficult for viewers to determine the area of each slice. Likewise, those same analysts will often state that a 3D pie chart distorts the data representation. Such criticisms are more than opinions.

For years, researchers have examined how factors, such as the use of different chart types and the use of colors and fonts within a chart, affect the viewer's accurate understanding of the chart's presentation. The research has shown that statements, such as **pie chart** criticisms, often have a factual basis.

This chapter presents a list of charting best practices, which are based upon more than opinion. The practices have emerged based on years of learning from the mistakes and successes of others.

## A Word on Excel

Despite the many visualization tools available on the market, Excel likely remains the most commonly used charting tool. Most of the charts presented in this chapter are readily available in Excel. In fact, many of this chapter's sample visualizations were created in Excel. In Chapter 7, "Keep Excel in Your Toolset," you will examine the steps you must perform to create a chart within Excel.

# Integrating Data Visualizations into Web Solutions

Throughout this chapter, you will examine a wide range of visualization types that you can create using a variety of tools. Data analysts often share the visualizations they create with internal and external users. To do so, they often turn to some type of web-based dashboard, such as one created by Tableau, which this chapter presents, or Microsoft Power BI, discussed in Chapter 6, "Keep SQL in Your Toolset."

Beyond using a dashboard, there are many times when analysts will integrate visualizations into web and mobile solutions. Depending on the rate at which the underlying data change, the analyst may simply create a graphic that contains a **static chart** image, which they can insert into an HTML page. Unfortunately, such an approach would require a web developer to update the page on a regular basis as the chart's underlying values change. A better solution is to let web-based software create the chart in real time.

This section examines Google Charts, which provides a very large collection of customizable visualizations, as shown in **FIGURE 4.1**, that you can easily integrate into a web page.

There are many charting tools developers can use to integrate charts into the web pages they create. The advantages of using Google Charts include:

- It's free to use
- It supports web and mobile solutions
- It's easy to integrate

To use Google Charts, you should register at the Google website to receive your own application programming interface (**API**) key, which you will use within the JavaScript code you create that calls the Google Charts services.

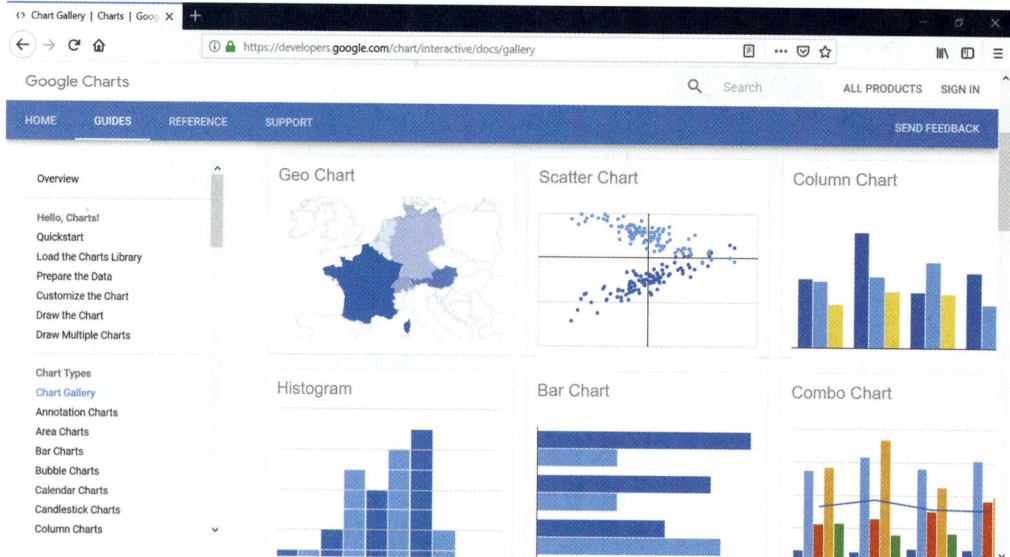

**FIGURE 4.1** The Google Charts gallery of visualizations.
Used with permission of Google

## Creating a Simple Static Chart

The easiest way to create a Google Chart visualization within a web page is to place static data for the chart into the web page. The data values you want to chart will appear hardcoded within the HTML and JavaScript. When you use such static data, you will need to edit the underlying HTML page each time you must update the chart data.

The following HTML file, ShowSales.html, uses Google Charts to display the static pie chart shown in **FIGURE 4.2**.

```
<html>
  <head>
    <script type="text/javascript" src="https://www.gstatic.com/charts/loader.js"></script>
    <script type="text/javascript">
      google.charts.load('current', {'packages':['corechart']});
      google.charts.setOnLoadCallback(drawChart);

      function drawChart() {

        var data = google.visualization.arrayToDataTable([
          ['Sales', 'Sales per Day'],
          ['Jones',    19],
          ['Smith',       22],
          ['Davis',   12],
          ['Johnson', 21],
          ['Lewis',     17]
        ]);
```

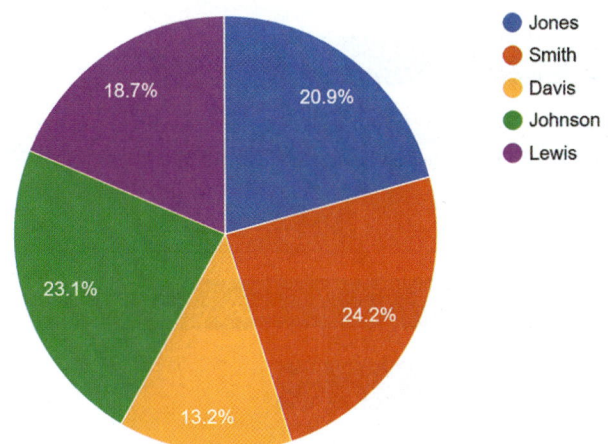

**FIGURE 4.2** Creating a static pie chart within a web page using Google Charts.
Used with permission of Google

```
      var options = {
        title: 'Company Daily Sales March'
      };

      var chart = new google.visualization.PieChart(document.
getElementById('piechart'));

      chart.draw(data, options);
    }
    </script>
  </head>
  <body>
    <div id="piechart" style="width: 900px; height: 500px;"></
div>
  </body>
</html>
```

The HTML code—in this case, the JavaScript—assigns the data to an array, which contains the employee names and their sales amounts. The JavaScript also assigns the chart title to an option and then renders the chart.

The HTML file, BarShowSales.html, changes the previous example slightly to use a **bar chart**, as opposed to a pie chart, as shown in **FIGURE 4.3**.

```
<html>
  <head>
    <script type="text/javascript" src="https://www.gstatic.com/
charts/loader.js"></script>
    <script type="text/javascript">
```

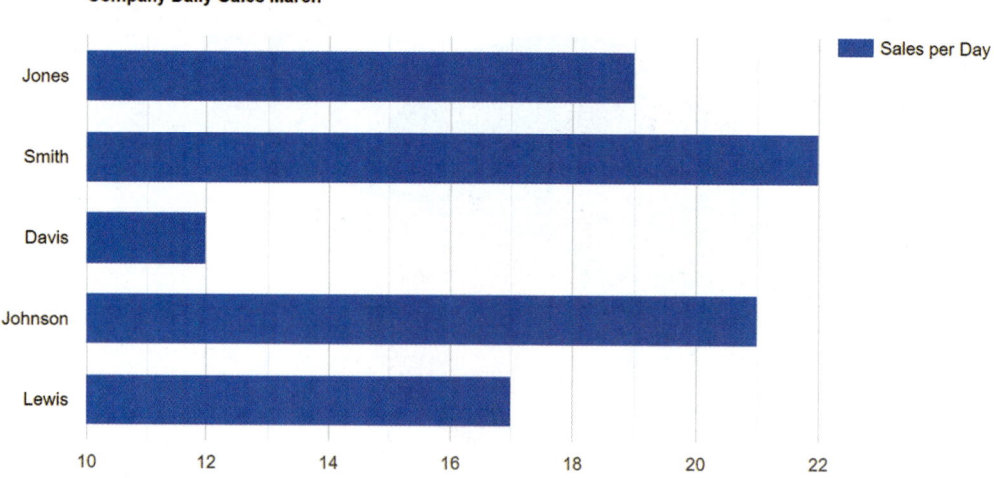

**FIGURE 4.3** Using Google Charts to create a bar chart.
Used with permission of Google

```
      google.charts.load('current', {'packages':['corechart']});
      google.charts.setOnLoadCallback(drawChart);

      function drawChart() {

        var data = google.visualization.arrayToDataTable([
          ['Sales', 'Sales per Day'],
          ['Jones',     19],
          ['Smith',     22],
          ['Davis',   12],
          ['Johnson', 21],
          ['Lewis',     17]
        ]);

        var options = {
          title: 'Company Daily Sales March'
        };

        var chart = new google.visualization.BarChart(document.
  getElementById('piechart'));

        chart.draw(data, options);
      }
    </script>
  </head>
  <body>
    <div id="piechart" style="width: 900px; height: 500px;"></
  div>
  </body>
</html>
```

As you can see, the code to create the bar chart is nearly identical to that of the pie chart, with the one-line difference in the call to the BarChart function.

Finally, the HTML file, SalesByCountry.html, maps information about a company's sales onto a map. As the user hovers his or her mouse over points on the map, the chart will display popup specifics about the data point, as shown in **FIGURE 4.4**.

```
    <html>
      <head>
        <script type="text/javascript" src="https://www.gstatic.com/
  charts/loader.js"></script>
        <script type="text/javascript">
          google.charts.load('current', {
            'packages':['geochart'],
            // Note: you will need to get a mapsApiKey for your
  project.
            // See: https://developers.google.com/chart/interactive/
  docs/basic_load_libs#load-settings
            'mapsApiKey': 'AIzaSyD-9tSrke72PouQMnMX-a7eZSW0jkFMBWY'
```

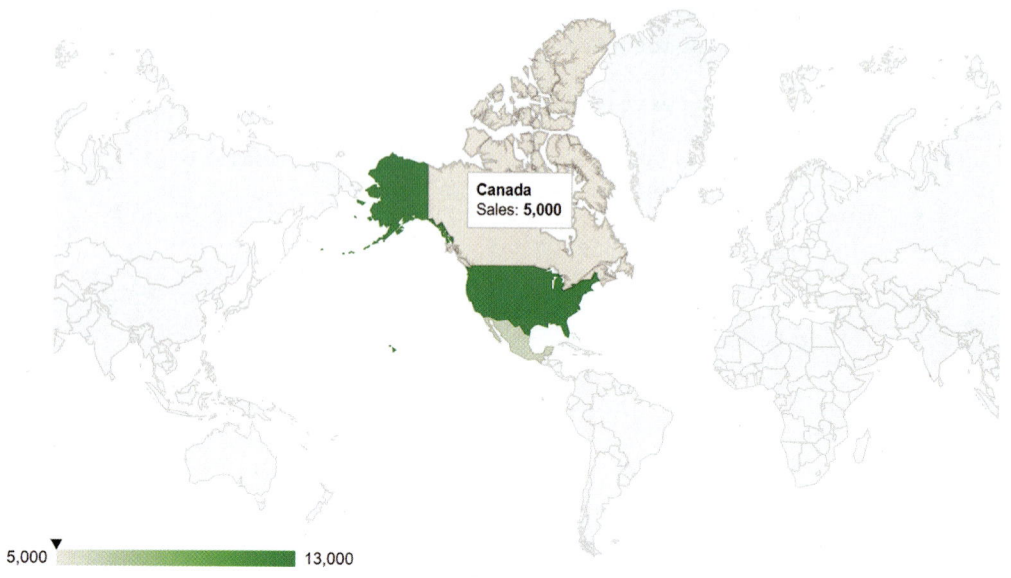

**FIGURE 4.4** Displaying a data-point popup on map data.

Used with permission of Google

```
    });
    google.charts.setOnLoadCallback(drawRegionsMap);

    function drawRegionsMap() {
      var data = google.visualization.arrayToDataTable([
        ['Country', 'Sales'],
        ['United States', 13000],
        ['Canada', 5000],
        ['Mexico', 6000],
      ]);

      var options = { region: '019' };

      var chart = new google.visualization.GeoChart(document.getElementById('regions_div'));

      chart.draw(data, options);
    }
    </script>
  </head>
  <body>
    <div id="regions_div" style="width: 900px; height: 500px;"></div>
  </body>
</html>
```

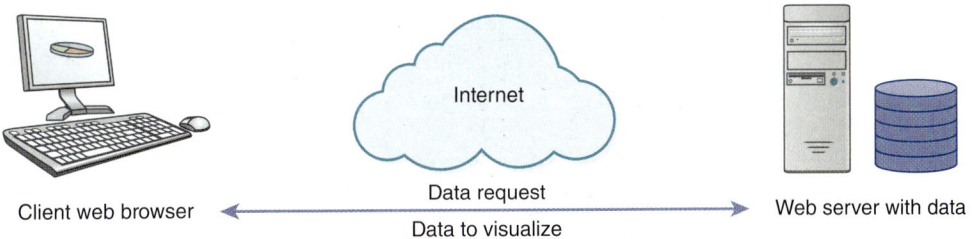

**FIGURE 4.5** Displaying a dynamic chart, **the content of which changes each time the page is displayed.**

In this case, the code assigns the region code of 019 for North America and then specifies data for the countries of interest.

## Creating a Real-Time Dynamic Chart

When you use a static chart within an HTML page, someone, or some program, must update the chart each time the chart's underlying data change. In contrast, a real-time chart connects to a data source to receive and display the chart data in real time, that is, on demand. To create a real-time chart, your HTML file can use asynchronous JavaScript (AJAX) to connect to a web server and request the data that the chart is to display, as shown in **FIGURE 4.5**.

## Time-Based Comparison Charts

As discussed, analysts use time-based comparison charts to represent how one or more sets of values change over time. Common time-based comparison charts include:

- Line chart
- Multiline chart
- Area chart

## Line Chart

When analysts chart how a variable's value changes over time, they will often chart the data as a set of points, as shown in **FIGURE 4.6**. The analysts refer to each point's location on the chart as a marker.

A **line chart** uses line segments to connect the markers, ideally making it easier for viewers to visualize trends, as shown in **FIGURE 4.7**.

The data set shown in **FIGURE 4.8** specifies the markers for the line chart previously shown in Figure 4.7.

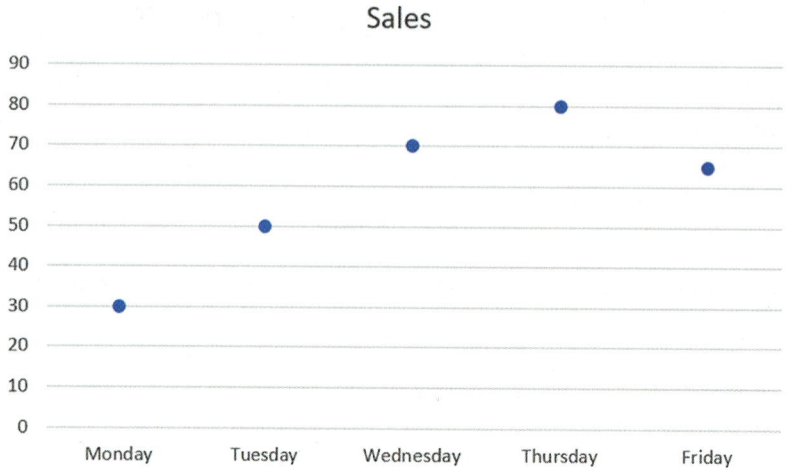

**FIGURE 4.6** Charting data-set points.

Used with permission of Google

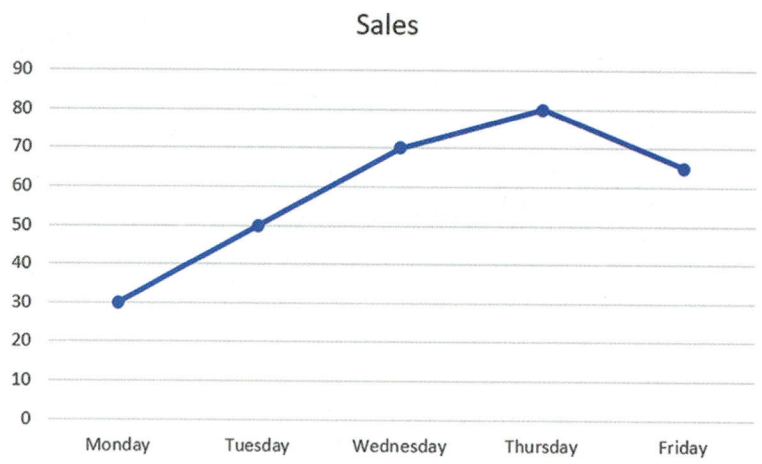

**FIGURE 4.7** A line chart connects data points to better represent trends.

Used with permission of Google

| 1 | Monday | 30 |
| 2 | Tuesday | 50 |
| 3 | Wednesday | 70 |
| 4 | Thursday | 80 |
| 5 | Friday | 65 |

**FIGURE 4.8** A data set representing daily sales.

## Multiline Charts

A line chart is ideal for representing a single data set. Often, data analysts will chart multiple data sets on the same chart using different line types (dashed or dotted, for example) or different colors so they can compare related data sets, creating a multiline chart, as shown in **FIGURE 4.9**. The figure also includes the data set used to create this chart.

## Top *x*-Axis Line Chart

Normally, within a line chart, the *x*-axis will appear at the bottom of the chart. Depending on the height of the *x*-axis data you are charting, you may want to move the axis to the top of the chart, as shown in **FIGURE 4.10**.

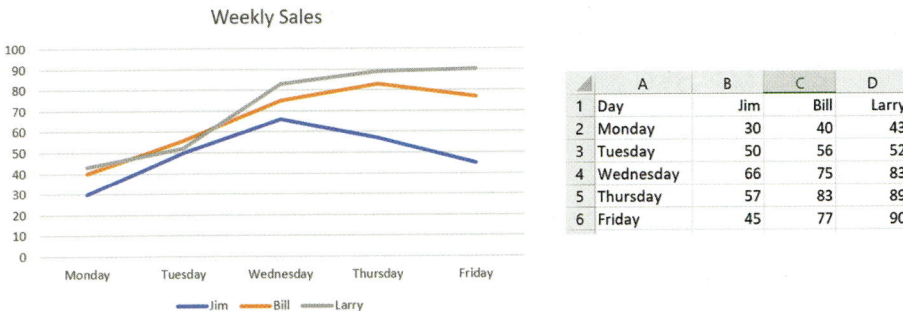

**FIGURE 4.9** A multiline chart.

Used with permission of Google

**FIGURE 4.10** Moving the *x*-axis to the top of a line chart.

Used with permission of Google

The following HTML file, ShowTopXaxis.html, uses Google Charts to create the line chart previously shown in Figure 4.10:

```html
<html>
<head>
  <script type="text/javascript" src="https://www.gstatic.com/charts/loader.js"></script>
    <script type="text/javascript">
      google.charts.load('current', {'packages':['line']});
      google.charts.setOnLoadCallback(drawChart);

    function drawChart() {

      var data = new google.visualization.DataTable();
      data.addColumn('number', 'Day');
      data.addColumn('number', 'E-Commmerce Sales');

      data.addRows([
        [1, 38.8],
        [2, 33.9],
        [3, 35.4],
        [4, 31.7],
        [5, 36.9],
        [6, 30.8],
        [7, 29.6]]);

      var options = {
        chart: {
          title: 'E-Commerce Sales Week 1',
          subtitle: 'in millions of dollars (USD)'
        },
        width: 900,
        height: 500,
        axes: {
          x: {
            0: {side: 'top'}
          }
        }
      };

      var chart = new google.charts.Line(document.getElementById('line_top_x'));

      chart.draw(data, google.charts.Line.convertOptions(options));
    }
    </script>
</head>
<body>
  <div id="line_top_x"></div>
</body>
</html>
```

In this case, the JavaScript defines the data points as an array. For a multiline chart, you would comma-separate values in the array. Then, the code specifies that the *x*-axis should appear at the top.

## Smoothing Line Chart Data

Depending on the data and line segment size, you may find that the line chart creates a distorted (choppy) representation of the data. In such cases, you may want to smooth the line segments, as shown in **FIGURE 4.11**.

The following HTML file, SmoothLineChart.html, uses Google Charts to smooth the line chart segments, as previously shown in Figure 4.11:

```
<html>
<head>
   <script type="text/javascript" src="https://www.gstatic.com/charts/loader.js"></script>
   <script type="text/javascript">
     google.charts.load('current', {'packages':['corechart']});
     google.charts.setOnLoadCallback(drawChart);

     function drawChart() {
       var data = google.visualization.arrayToDataTable([
         ['Year', 'Sales', 'Expenses'],
         ['2016',   2000,      700],
         ['2017',   2170,      860],
         ['2018',   1660,     1210],
         ['2019',   1330,      740]
       ]);
```

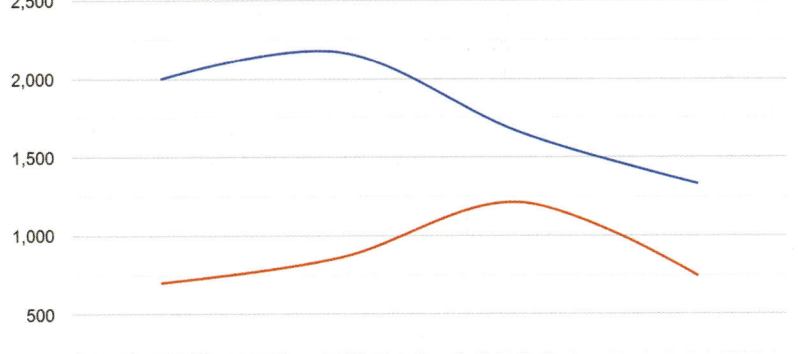

**FIGURE 4.11** Smoothing (curving) line segments within a line chart.

Used with permission of Google

```
          var options = {
            title: 'Sales versus Expenses',
            curveType: 'function',
            legend: { position: 'bottom' }
          };

          var chart = new google.visualization.LineChart(document.
getElementById('curve_chart'));

          chart.draw(data, options);
        }
    </script>
  </head>
  <body>
    <div id="curve_chart" style="width: 900px; height: 500px"></
div>
  </body>
</html>
```

As you can see, to curve the line, the JavaScript directs Google Charts to use a function for the curve type.

## Dual y-Axis Chart

Depending on the data you must visualize, there may be times when you want to show the relationship between two values for which the data sets have *y*-axis values that are in different ranges. In such cases, you can use a dual *y*-axis chart, as shown in **FIGURE 4.12**.

The following HTML file, DualYChart.html, creates the chart previously shown in Figure 4.12:

```
<html>
<head>
  <script type="text/javascript" src="https://www.gstatic.com/
charts/loader.js"></script>
    <script type="text/javascript">
      google.charts.load('current', {'packages':['line']});
      google.charts.setOnLoadCallback(drawChart);
      google.charts.load('current', {'packages':['line',
'corechart']});
      google.charts.setOnLoadCallback(drawChart);

    function drawChart() {
      var chartDiv = document.getElementById('chartDiv');
      var data = new google.visualization.DataTable();
      data.addColumn('date', 'Month');
      data.addColumn('number', "Revenues");
      data.addColumn('number', "Expenses");
```

# Time-Based Comparison Charts 117

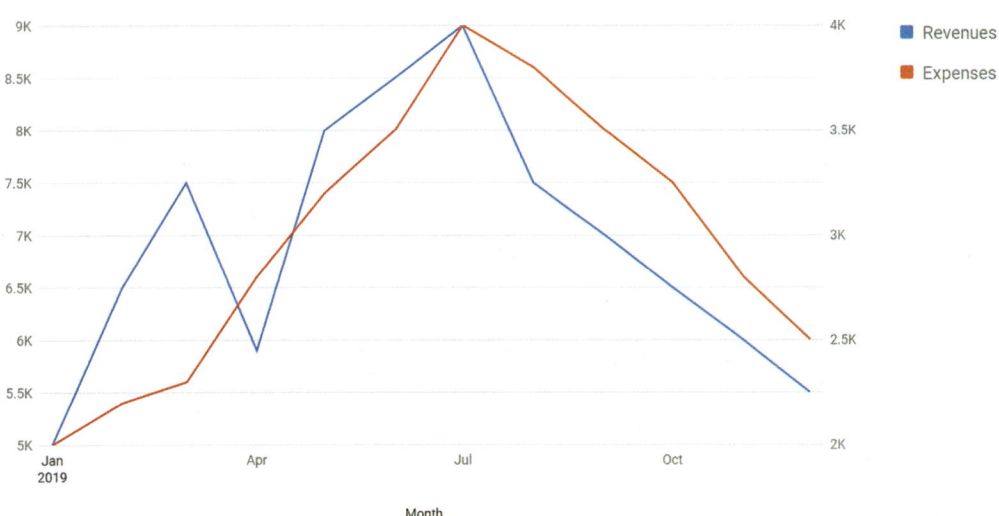

**FIGURE 4.12** A dual y-axis chart.

Used with permission of Google

```
            data.addRows([
              [new Date(2019, 0),   5000, 2000],
              [new Date(2019, 1),   6500, 2200],
              [new Date(2019, 2),   7500, 2300],
              [new Date(2019, 3),   5900, 2800],
              [new Date(2019, 4),   8000, 3200],
              [new Date(2019, 5),   8500, 3500],
              [new Date(2019, 6),   9000, 4000],
              [new Date(2019, 7),   7500, 3800],
              [new Date(2019, 8),   7000, 3500],
              [new Date(2019, 9),   6500, 3250],
              [new Date(2019, 10),  6000, 2800],
              [new Date(2019, 11),  5500, 2500]
            ]);

            var materialOptions = {
              chart: {
                title: 'Revenues versus Expenses'
              },
              width: 900,
              height: 500,
              series: {
                // Gives each series an axis name that matches the
  Y-axis below.
                0: {axis: 'Revenues'},
                1: {axis: 'Expenses'}
              },
```

```
        axes: {
           // Adds labels to each axis; they don't have to match the axis names.
           y: {
              Temps: {label: 'Revenues'},
              Daylight: {label: 'Expenses'}
           }
        }
     };

     function drawMaterialChart() {
       var materialChart = new google.charts.Line(chartDiv);
       materialChart.draw(data, materialOptions);
     }

     drawMaterialChart();
   }
  </script>
</head>
<body>
  <div id="chartDiv"></div>
</body>
</html>
```

## Area Chart

An **area chart** is like a line graph, in that analysts often use it to display data trends over time. As shown in **FIGURE 4.13**, area charts are so named because they shade the area under the line.

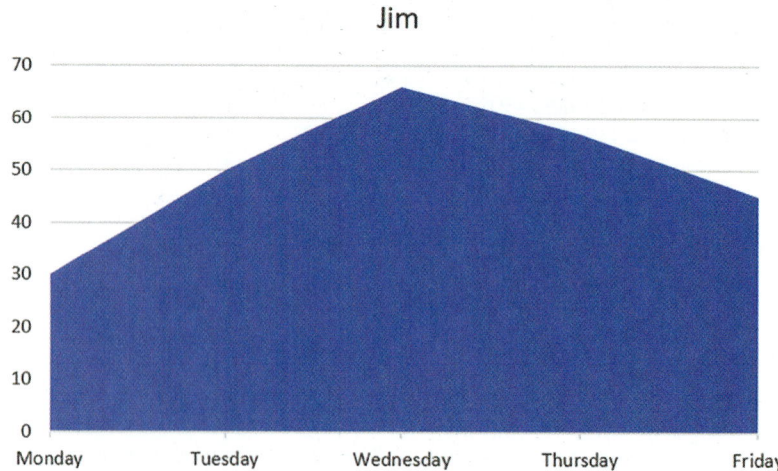

**FIGURE 4.13** An area chart often represents data values over time.
Used with permission of Google

| | B | C |
|---|---|---|
| 1 | Month | Miles Driven |
| 2 | January | 1000 |
| 3 | February | 900 |
| 4 | March | 1100 |
| 5 | April | 1500 |
| 6 | May | 1300 |
| 7 | June | 1450 |
| 8 | July | 1150 |
| 9 | August | 1600 |
| 10 | September | 1700 |
| 11 | October | 1400 |
| 12 | November | 1500 |
| 13 | December | 1325 |

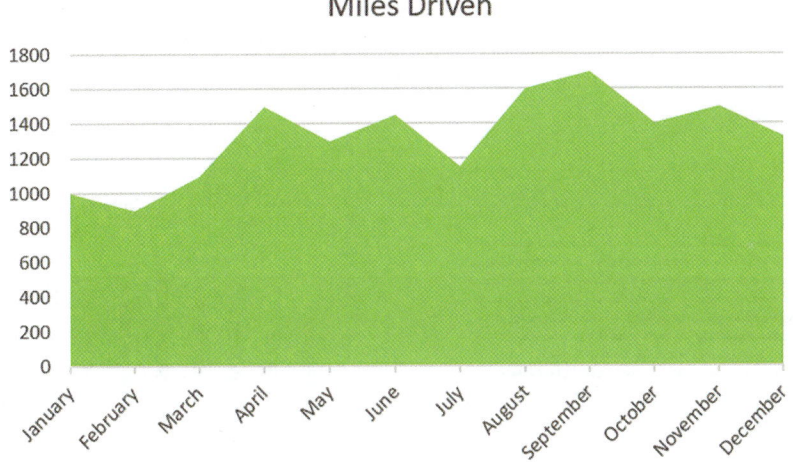

**FIGURE 4.14** **A data set representing miles driven by the delivery team by month.**

**FIGURE 4.15** **Creating an area chart.**

Used with permission of Google

Area charts are best suited for cases where you want to focus the viewer's attention on the trend as opposed to specific values. Assume that you have the data set shown in **FIGURE 4.14**.

If you chart the data set using an area chart, the visualization will appear as shown in **FIGURE 4.15**.

# Category-Based Comparison Charts

Analysts use category-based comparison charts to represent how one or more categories of values compare. Common category-based comparison charts include:

- Bar chart
- Column chart

- Clustered/grouped bar or column chart
- Radar chart
- Combo chart
- Diff chart
- Waterfall chart

## Bar and Column Charts

A bar chart represents data values as rectangular bars, the lengths of which correspond to the underlying data value. As shown in **FIGURE 4.16**, you can display a bar chart using horizontal or vertical bars. Analysts refer to the vertical bar chart as a **column chart**.

Bar and column charts are ideal for displaying data that correspond to categories, such as sales by month or revenues by customer. Often, your choice of whether to use a bar or column chart is based upon the length of labels you want to display for the data. Displaying long labels beside horizontal bars often appears less cluttered than trying to squeeze the labels under the corresponding columns.

Assume you are given the data set shown in **FIGURE 4.17**.

If you chart the data set using a bar and column chart, the visualizations will appear as shown in **FIGURE 4.18**.

**FIGURE 4.16 A bar chart uses horizontal bars, whereas a column chart uses vertical bars.**

Used with permission of Google

| | A | B |
|---|---|---|
| 1 | Quarter | Profit |
| 2 | Q1 | 25000 |
| 3 | Q2 | 15000 |
| 4 | Q3 | -5000 |
| 5 | Q4 | 12500 |

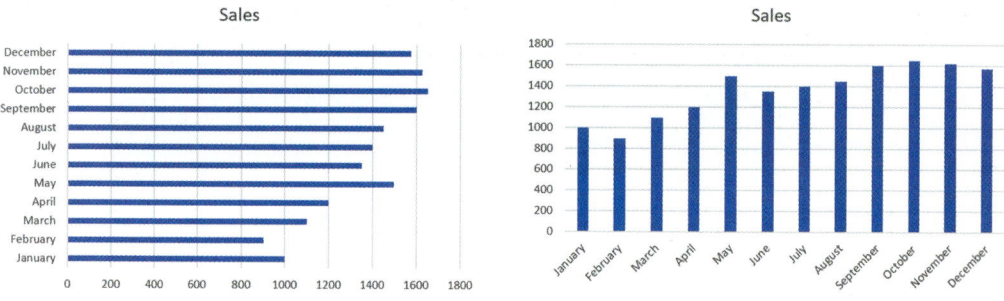

**FIGURE 4.17 A data set representing quarterly profit and loss.**

## Category-Based Comparison Charts

 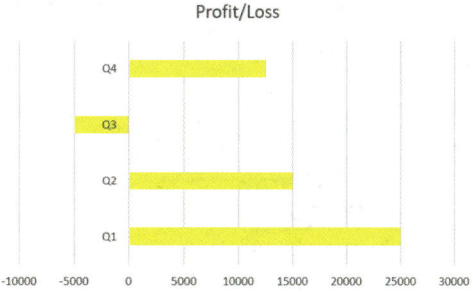

**FIGURE 4.18** Creating a bar and column chart.
Used with permission of Google

 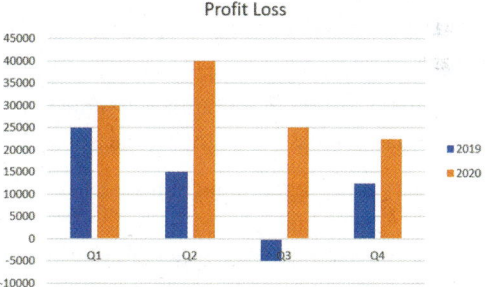

**FIGURE 4.19** Clustered bar and clustered column charts group related data for comparison.
Used with permission of Google

|   | A | B | C |
|---|---|---|---|
| 1 | Expenses | 2019 | 2020 |
| 2 | Travel | 25000 | 30000 |
| 3 | Payroll | 27500 | 40000 |
| 4 | Rent | 45000 | 50000 |
| 5 | Supplies | 5000 | 7500 |

**FIGURE 4.20** A data set representing year-over-year quarterly profit and loss.

## Clustered Bar and Column Charts

Assume you want to illustrate your sales data by month and compare that data to the previous year's sales, as shown in **FIGURE 4.19**. In such a case, you can use a grouped bar or column chart, often called a clustered bar or clustered column chart.

Assume that you have the data set shown in **FIGURE 4.20**.

If you chart the data using clustered bar and clustered column charts, the visualizations will appear as shown in **FIGURE 4.21**. In this case, the chart rendered the visualizations in 3D.

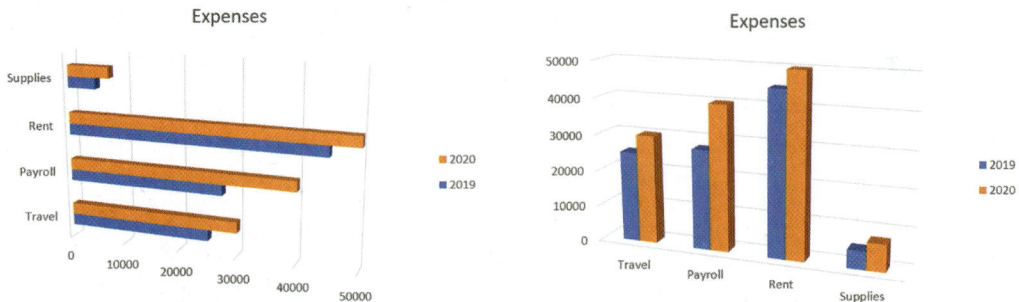

**FIGURE 4.21** **Creating clustered bar and clustered column charts.**
Used with permission of Google

## Radar Chart

Often, analysts must visually represent the differences between multiple data sets across several specific measures. For example, assume that you need to compare the skills of three programmer candidates across the following measures:

- Java programming skills
- SQL skills
- Object-oriented programming knowledge
- Testing capabilities
- Team fit

To start, you can create a data set, similar to that shown in **FIGURE 4.22**, that aggregates each candidate's interview feedback.

If you chart the data set using a **radar chart**, the visualization will appear as shown in **FIGURE 4.23**.

The radar chart in this case uses five axes, the angles of which have no significance. The origin of each axis is the center of the chart.

## Combo Chart

Depending on the data you need to visualize, there may be times when you want to combine different chart types. For example, **FIGURE 4.24** shows a **combo chart** that displays monthly sales for the previous year as a column chart and sales for the current year as a line chart. The figure includes the data set used to create the chart.

## Diff Chart

Analysts often use charts to compare similar values, such as year-over-year monthly revenues or year-over-year monthly expenses. The **diff chart**, as shown in **FIGURE 4.25**, is designed to represent such differences between data sets.

Category-Based Comparison Charts  **123**

|   | A | B | C | D |
|---|---|---|---|---|
| 1 |   | A | B | C |
| 2 | Java | 66 | 57 | 83 |
| 3 | SQL | 40 | 98 | 55 |
| 4 | OOP | 55 | 68 | 85 |
| 5 | Testing | 75 | 96 | 86 |
| 6 | Team Fit | 98 | 77 | 80 |

**FIGURE 4.22** A data set representing interview candidate skill sets.

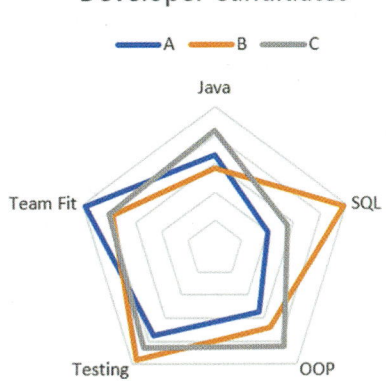

**FIGURE 4.23** Using a radar chart to compare interview candidate skill sets.
Used with permission of Google

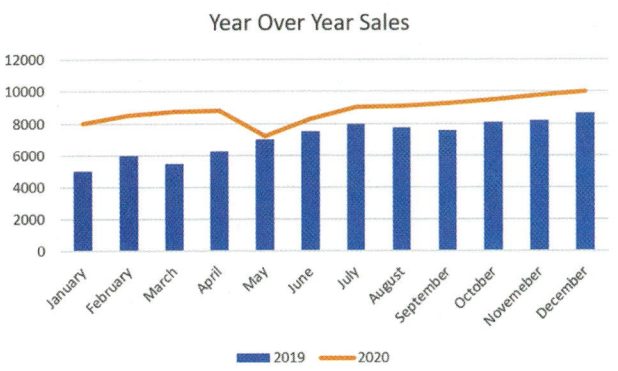

| 1 | Month | 2019 | 2020 |
|---|---|---|---|
| 2 | January | 5000 | 8000 |
| 3 | February | 6000 | 8500 |
| 4 | March | 5500 | 8750 |
| 5 | April | 6250 | 8800 |
| 6 | May | 7000 | 7200 |
| 7 | June | 7500 | 8300 |
| 8 | July | 8000 | 9000 |
| 9 | August | 7750 | 9100 |
| 10 | September | 7600 | 9250 |
| 11 | October | 8100 | 9500 |
| 12 | Novemeber | 8200 | 9750 |
| 13 | December | 8650 | 10000 |

**FIGURE 4.24** Using a combo chart to compare year-over-year sales data.
Used with permission of Google

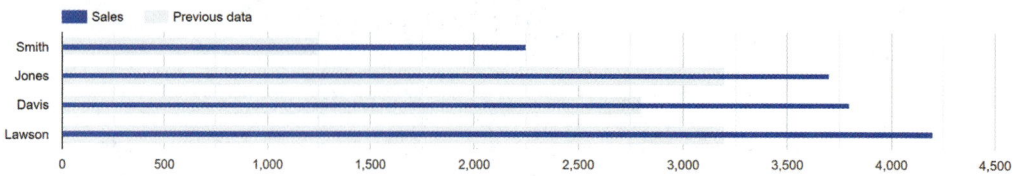

**FIGURE 4.25** Using a diff chart to compare year-over-year monthly revenues.

Used with permission of Google

The following HTML file, ShowDiffChart.html, uses Google Charts to create the diff chart previously shown in Figure 4.25:

```
<html>
<head>
  <script type="text/javascript" src="https://www.gstatic.com/
charts/loader.js"></script>
  <script type="text/javascript">
    google.charts.load('current', {packages:['corechart']});
    google.charts.setOnLoadCallback(drawChart);

  function drawChart() {
    var Sales2018Data = google.visualization.arrayToDataTable([
      ['Name', 'Sales'],
      ['Smith', 1250],
      ['Jones', 3200],
      ['Davis', 2800],
      ['Lawson', 3200]
    ]);

    var Sales2019Data = google.visualization.arrayToDataTable([
      ['Name', 'Sales'],
      ['Smith', 2250],
      ['Jones', 3700],
      ['Davis', 3800],
      ['Lawson', 4200]
    ]);

    var barChartDiff = new google.visualization.
BarChart(document.getElementById('chartDiv'));
    var diffData = barChartDiff.computeDiff(Sales2018Data,
Sales2019Data);

    var options = { legend: { position: 'top' } };

    barChartDiff.draw(diffData, options);
  }
</script></head>
<body>
```

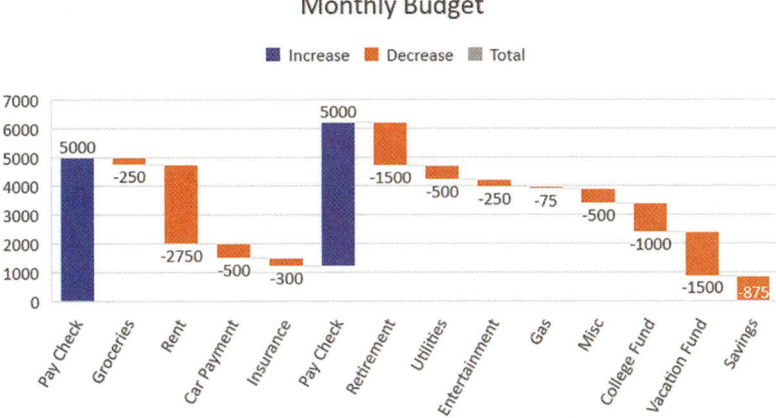

**FIGURE 4.26** A waterfall chart illustrating decrements and increments to a family budget.
Used with permission of Google

```
    <div id="chartDiv"></div>
  </body>
</html>
```

As you can see, the JavaScript creates the new and old data and then creates an array that contains the value differences.

## Waterfall Chart

A **waterfall chart** is so named because it represents how a series of values increment and decrement, flowing from left to right, affect a starting value. The waterfall chart normally represents negative values (decrements) in orange and positive values (increments) in blue. The waterfall chart shown in **FIGURE 4.26** illustrates how increments and decrements over the course of a month affect a family's bank account.

The data set shown in **FIGURE 4.27** was used to create the family budget waterfall chart shown in Figure 4.26.

## Composition Charts

Analysts use composition charts to represent how one or more values relate to a larger whole. Common composition charts include:

- Pie chart
- Donut chart
- Sunburst chart
- Stacked bar or column chart
- Stacked area chart

|   | A | B |
|---|---|---|
| 1 | Pay Check | 5000 |
| 2 | Groceries | -250 |
| 3 | Rent | -2750 |
| 4 | Car Payment | -500 |
| 5 | Insurance | -300 |
| 6 | Pay Check | 5000 |
| 7 | Retirement | -1500 |
| 8 | Utilities | -500 |
| 9 | Entertainment | -250 |
| 10 | Gas | -75 |
| 11 | Misc | -500 |
| 12 | College Fund | -1000 |
| 13 | Vacation Fund | -1500 |
| 14 | Savings | -875 |

**FIGURE 4.27** A data set representing increments and decrements to a family budget.

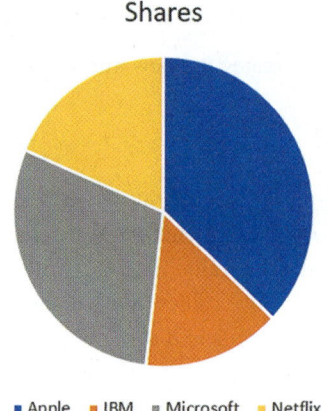

**FIGURE 4.28** Using a pie chart to show component values.

Used with permission of Google

- Treemap chart
- Funnel chart
- Pyramid chart

# Pie Chart

For years, analysts have used pie charts to represent related quantities, such as sales by customer, stocks in a portfolio, and expenses by product, as shown in **FIGURE 4.28**.

The pie chart is so named because the circular chart resembles a pie and the individual components, slices of the pie. The proportional area of each slice represents its percentage of the entire pie. Visually, it is easy to determine in general the related values of the components based upon the area of the slices. As shown in **FIGURE 4.29**, pie charts can be two- or three-dimensional.

Assume you are given the data set shown in **FIGURE 4.30**.

If you chart the data set using pie charts, the visualization will appear as shown in **FIGURE 4.31**. As you can see, this chart includes the data values within the pie slices.

To focus the viewer's attention on a specific slice of the pie, analysts can explode one or more slices from the pie, as shown in **FIGURE 4.32**.

Finally, depending on the value you want to highlight, there may be times when you can combine a simple pie chart with a big number to produce a meaningful visual, as shown in **FIGURE 4.33**.

Despite the pie chart's simplicity, the criticism that perceiving the underlying value can be difficult has led analysts to move away from the pie chart to the donut chart, discussed in the next session. Analysts using 3D pie charts often experience a similar criticism that the charts can sometimes distort the area that represents the underlying value.

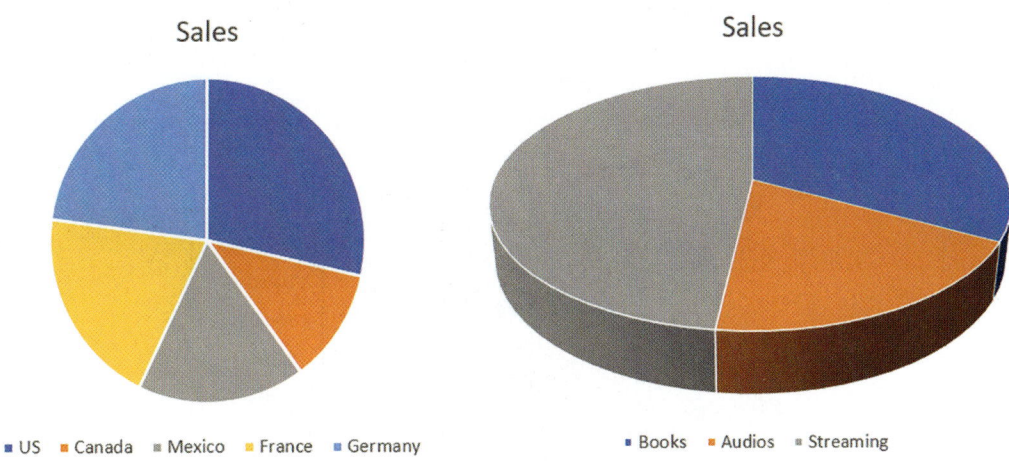

**FIGURE 4.29** Representing values using pie charts.
Used with permission of Google

| | A | B |
|---|---|---|
| 1 | Day | Calls |
| 2 | Monday | 50 |
| 3 | Tuesday | 35 |
| 4 | Wednesday | 45 |
| 5 | Thursday | 39 |
| 6 | Friday | 25 |

**FIGURE 4.30** A data set representing the number of calls to a call center by day.

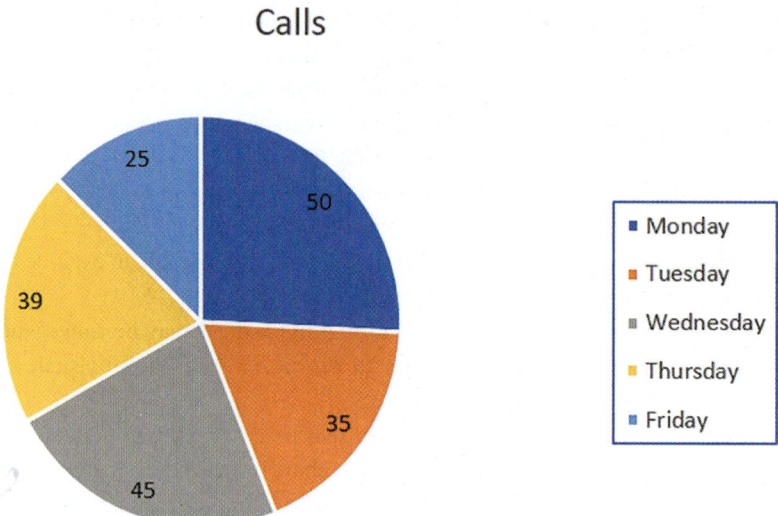

**FIGURE 4.31** A pie chart representing calls to a call center by day.
Used with permission of Google

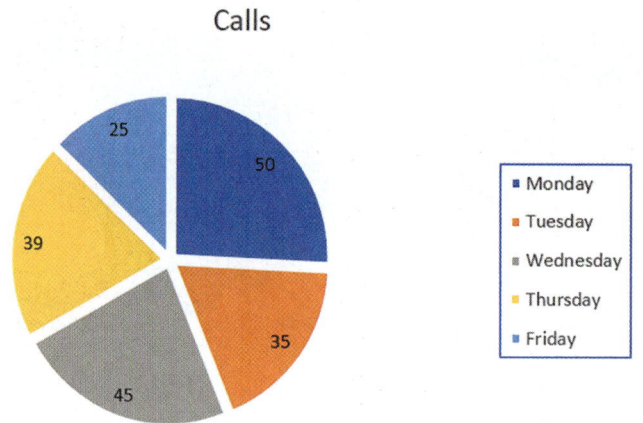

**FIGURE 4.32** Exploding pie slices to focus the viewer's attention.
Used with permission of Google

A further complexity of pie charts occurs when analysts use them to represent too many categories. As a general rule, the appropriateness of a pie chart's representation and visual at-a-glance use decrease when more than six categories are present, as shown in **FIGURE 4.34**.

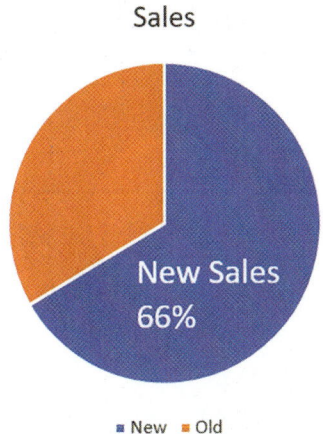

**FIGURE 4.33** Combining a pie chart with a big number to produce a meaningful visual.
Used with permission of Google

**FIGURE 4.34** Displaying too many categories on a pie chart reduces the pie chart's effectiveness.
Used with permission of Google

## Donut Chart

As you have learned, analysts often criticize the use of the pie chart based on the fact that it can be hard for viewers to determine the area of the slices. The donut chart solves this shortcoming by removing the center of the pie chart, as shown in **FIGURE 4.35**. In so doing, donut chart viewers are more likely to focus their attention on each slice's length of the outer arc.

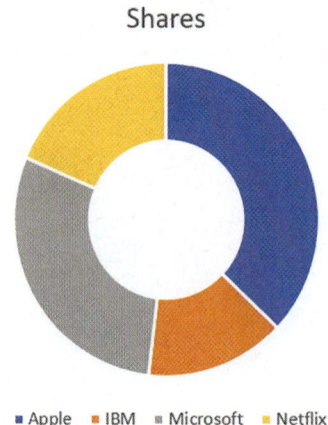

**FIGURE 4.35** A donut chart removes the center of a pie chart to focus the user's attention on the length of each slice's outer arc.

Used with permission of Google

|   | A | B |
|---|---|---|
| 1 | Skill | Rating |
| 2 | Machine Learning | 30 |
| 3 | Data Mining | 25 |
| 4 | Visualization | 20 |

**FIGURE 4.36** A data set representing the number of votes for desired new hire skills.

To improve the effectiveness of your donut chart, you should limit the number of values you display on the chart to five or six. Assume you are given the data set shown in **FIGURE 4.36**.

If you chart the data using a donut chart, the visualization will appear as shown in **FIGURE 4.37**. As you can see, this chart moves the legend, includes data values for each slice, and applies a shaded background.

## Sunburst Chart

A **sunburst chart**, as shown in **FIGURE 4.38**, appears as a multilayer pie or donut chart. The sunburst chart is well suited for hierarchically related data, such as sales by quarter, month, and week, or inventory by product by customer segment.

Assume you are given the data set shown in **FIGURE 4.39**.

## Stacked Bar and Column Charts

Depending on your data, you may want to show the composition of the data the bar represents. For example, if your sales come from e-commerce, in-store, and phone-based orders,

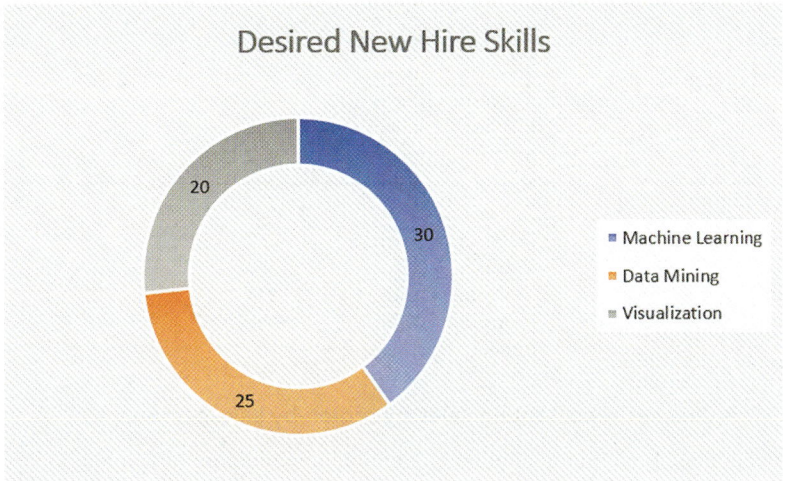

**FIGURE 4.37** Using a donut chart to represent new hire skills.
Used with permission of Google

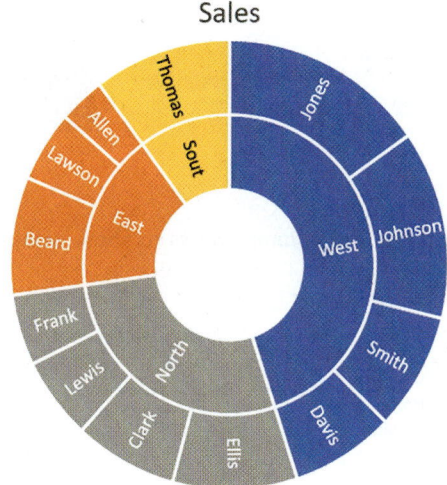

**FIGURE 4.38** Using a sunburst chart to visualize hierarchically related data.
Used with permission of Google

you might represent your monthly revenues using a stacked bar or column chart, as shown in **FIGURE 4.40**.

Assume you have the data set shown in **FIGURE 4.41** that provides a breakdown of where a company's employees worked during the previous quarters.

If you chart the data using stacked bar and column charts, the visualizations will appear as shown in **FIGURE 4.42**. In this case, the 3D **stacked bar chart** is drawn at an angle.

|   | A | B | C |
|---|---|---|---|
| 1 | West | Smith | 500 |
| 2 | West | Davis | 450 |
| 3 | West | Jones | 900 |
| 4 | West | Johnson | 800 |
| 5 | East | Lawson | 300 |
| 6 | East | Allen | 200 |
| 7 | East | Beard | 500 |
| 8 | North | Lewis | 350 |
| 9 | North | Clark | 450 |
| 10 | North | Ellis | 544 |
| 11 | North | Frank | 300 |
| 12 | Sout | Thomas | 600 |

**FIGURE 4.39** A data set representing sales by region by salesperson.

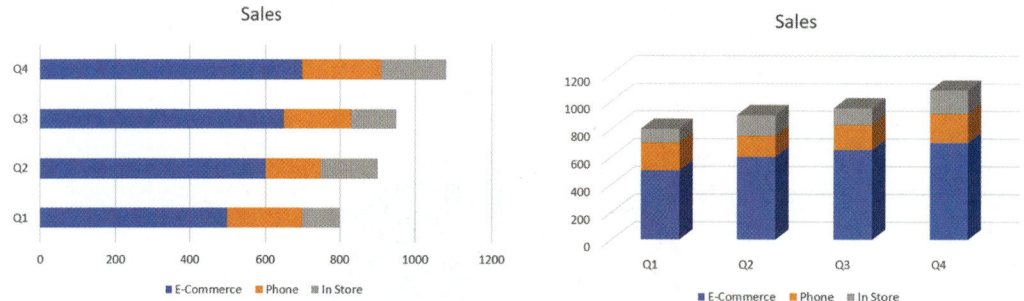

**FIGURE 4.40** Using stacked bar and column charts to show composition.

Used with permission of Google

| 1 | Location | Q1 | Q2 | Q3 | Q4 |
|---|----------|----|----|----|----|
| 2 | Offshore | 30 | 30 | 35 | 40 |
| 3 | Home | 10 | 13 | 15 | 12 |
| 4 | On Site | 25 | 20 | 15 | 20 |

**FIGURE 4.41** A data set representing employee work locations by quarter.

## Stacked Area Chart

The area chart is appropriate to display trending information for one data set. Often, you will use area charts to compare two or more trends. The area chart shown in **FIGURE 4.43**, for example, compares the trend of sales revenues versus expenses.

There will be many times when you want to compare the trends of several related values, such as the sales of your entire sales team. In such cases, you can use a stacked area chart similar to that shown in **FIGURE 4.44**. In this case, the visualization includes both a graphic and the underlying data.

Composition Charts

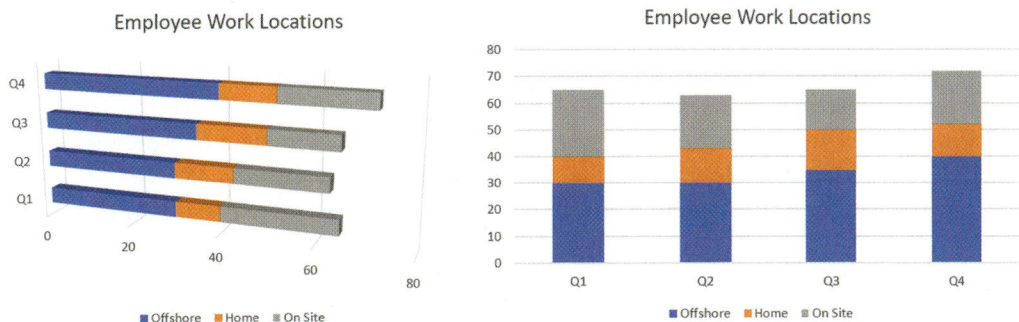

**FIGURE 4.42 Creating stacked bar and column charts.**
Used with permission of Google

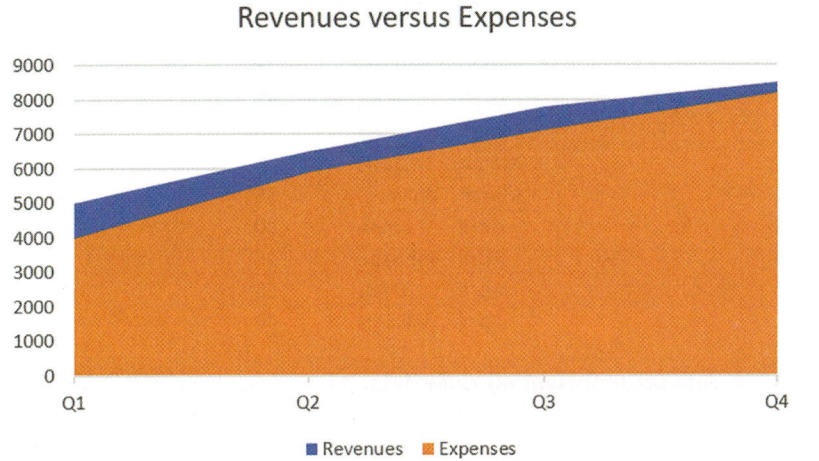

**FIGURE 4.43 Using a stacked area chart to compare revenues and expenses over time.**
Used with permission of Google

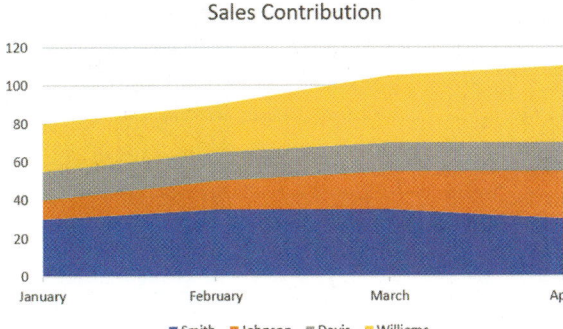

|  | January | February | March | April |
|---|---|---|---|---|
| Smith | 30 | 35 | 35 | 30 |
| Johnson | 10 | 15 | 20 | 25 |
| Davis | 15 | 15 | 15 | 15 |
| Williams | 25 | 25 | 35 | 40 |

**FIGURE 4.44 Using a stacked area chart to trend multiple related values.**
Used with permission of Google

## Treemap Chart

A **treemap chart** is designed to represent hierarchically related data through the use of boxes, the sizes of which represent the underlying value. The treemap is so named because it maps hierarchically related data, well suited for representation as nodes within a tree data structure, to two-dimensional shapes. Assume, for example, you have the sales data set shown in **FIGURE 4.45**.

If you chart the data using a treemap, the visualization will appear as shown in **FIGURE 4.46**.

| | | |
|---|---|---|
| January | Smith | 30 |
| January | Johnson | 10 |
| January | Davis | 15 |
| January | Williams | 25 |
| February | Smith | 35 |
| February | Johnson | 15 |
| February | Davis | 15 |
| February | Williams | 25 |
| March | Smith | 35 |
| March | Johnson | 20 |
| March | Davis | 15 |
| March | Williams | 35 |
| April | Smith | 30 |
| April | Johnson | 25 |
| April | Davis | 15 |
| April | Williams | 40 |

**FIGURE 4.45** A data set representing sales data.

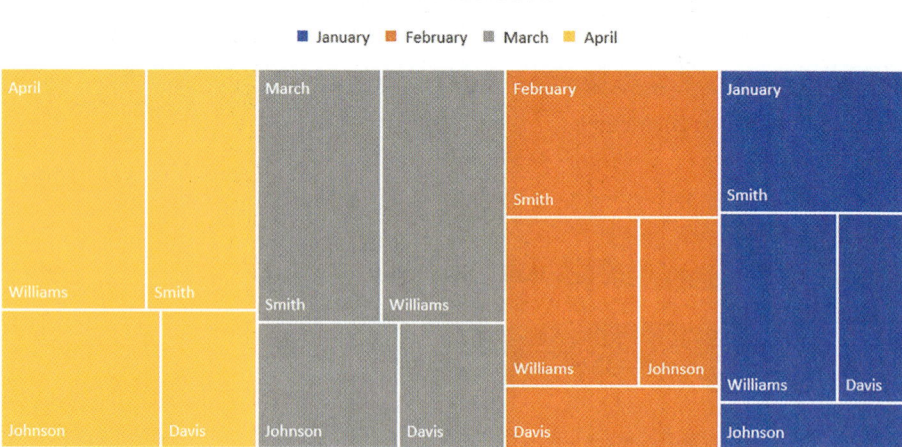

**FIGURE 4.46** A treemap representing sales data.

Used with permission of Google

Composition Charts  **135**

# Funnel Chart

The **funnel chart**, so named because the chart's shape takes on the form of a funnel, represents cumulative values, such as sales by salesperson, revenues by product, or customer service calls by call center. Within the funnel chart, the area of each segment represents the underlying value. The funnel chart shown in **FIGURE 4.47** represents the company sales by salesperson.

**FIGURE 4.48**, for example, uses a funnel chart to represent visitors by age group to a theme park.

**FIGURE 4.47** A funnel chart representing the cumulative sales by product.
Used with permission of Google

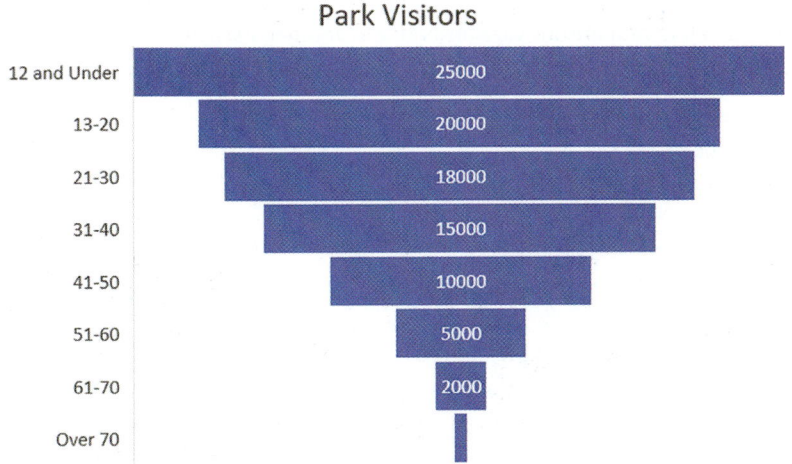

**FIGURE 4.48** A funnel chart that represents visitors by age group to an amusement park.
Used with permission of Google

# CHAPTER 4 Data Visualization

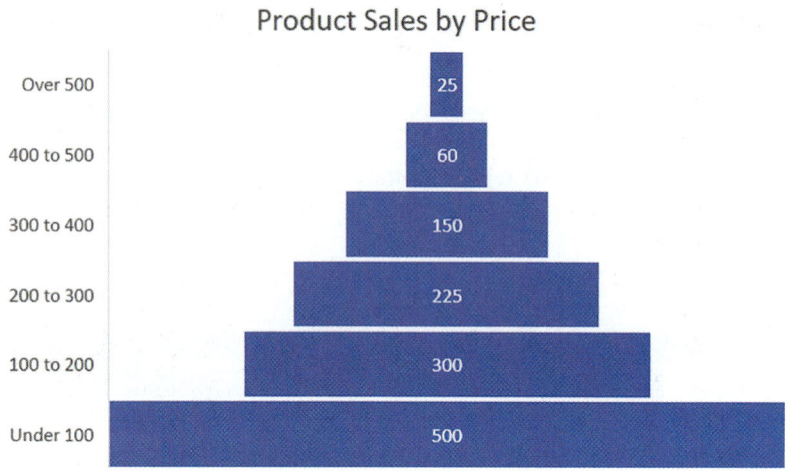

**FIGURE 4.49** A pyramid chart representing orders by price for the day.
Used with permission of Google

## Pyramid Chart

The **pyramid chart** is so named because its triangular shape is similar to that of a pyramid. The chart's proportional segments represent the underlying values. Analysts often refer to the pyramid chart as an upside-down funnel chart. **FIGURE 4.49**, for example, uses a pyramid chart to represent orders by price for the day.

## Correlation Charts

Data analysts will often compare one variable's value to another. In such cases, they will leverage correlation charts, which represent how two or more variables relate. Common correlation charts include:

- Scatter chart
- Bubble chart

## Scatter Chart

Often during data exploration, analysts will compare one variable to another to determine if a relationship exists. To visualize the data, analysts will plot the values on a Cartesian coordinate plane to create a **scatter chart**, as shown in **FIGURE 4.50**.

As discussed in Chapter 10, "Data Clustering," using a scatter chart is an effective way to visually represent clusters and to identify outliers. Assume, for example, you are given the data set shown in **FIGURE 4.51** that represents call center data.

By analyzing clusters within the scatter chart, you might decide to create scripts for the operators based on the caller's age in order to try to reduce the corresponding call duration.

Correlation Charts    **137**

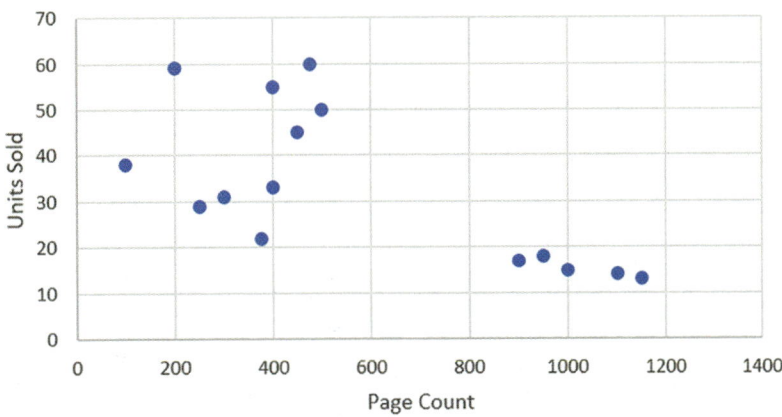

**FIGURE 4.50** A scatter chart based on two variables.

Used with permission of Google

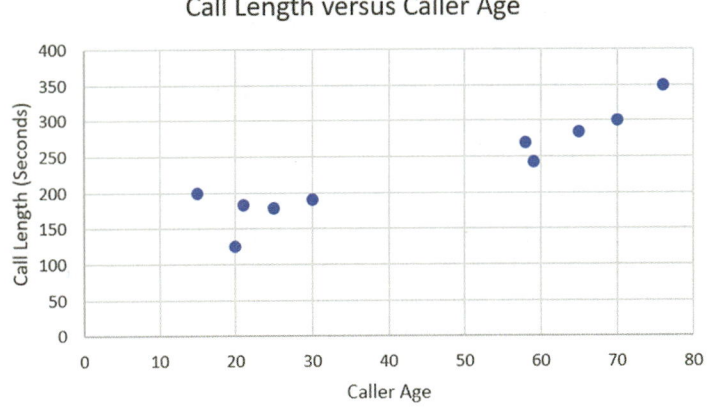

| | A | B |
|---|---|---|
| 1 | Caller Age | Length |
| 2 | 20 | 125 |
| 3 | 21 | 183 |
| 4 | 30 | 190 |
| 5 | 25 | 179 |
| 6 | 70 | 300 |
| 7 | 65 | 285 |
| 8 | 59 | 243 |
| 9 | 58 | 270 |
| 10 | 15 | 200 |
| 11 | 76 | 350 |

**FIGURE 4.51** A data set representing call center data that chart the caller age versus the length of the call.

Used with permission of Google

## Bubble Chart

A **bubble chart** represents data using circles (bubbles) based upon three (and sometimes four) dimensions:

- *x*-coordinate
- *y*-coordinate
- size
- color

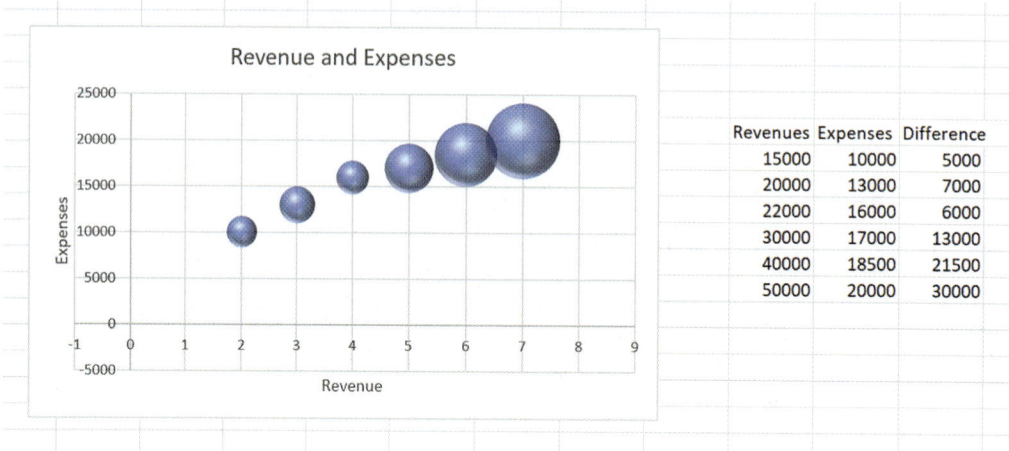

**FIGURE 4.52** A bubble chart that compares revenues and expenses.

**FIGURE 4.52** shows a bubble chart that charts a company's revenues versus expense data. In this case, the size of each bubble corresponds to the revenues minus expenses. Excel does not support a negative bubble size (meaning a profit loss). Depending on the charting software you are using, you may be able to use color to represent a profit (green) or a loss (red).

## Dashboard Charts

As discussed, data analysts often leverage dashboards to organize and display data visualizations. The following dashboard charts are well suited to represent KPIs that companies use to track initiatives.

### Gauge Chart

A **gauge chart** resembles a dial that might appear on an automobile dashboard. As shown in **FIGURE 4.53**, a gauge chart typically uses a needle to represent where the data value falls within the gauge's range of values. Because gauge charts provide an at-a-glance representation of a value, analysts often use them within a KPI dashboard.

The following HTML file, ShowGauge.html, uses Google Charts to create the gauge chart previously shown in Figure 4.53:

```
<html>
  <head>
    <script type="text/javascript" src="https://www.gstatic.com/charts/loader.js"></script>
    <script type="text/javascript">
      google.charts.load('current', {'packages':['gauge']});
      google.charts.setOnLoadCallback(drawChart);
```

Dashboard Charts

**FIGURE 4.53** A gauge chart uses a needle to indicate the current value within the gauge's range of values.
Used with permission of Google

```
      function drawChart() {

        var data = google.visualization.arrayToDataTable([
          ['Label', 'Value'],
          ['Revenues', 80],
          ['Expenses', 55]
        ]);

        var options = {
          width: 400, height: 120,
          redFrom: 90, redTo: 100,
          yellowFrom:75, yellowTo: 90,
          minorTicks: 5
        };

        var chart = new google.visualization.Gauge(document.
getElementById('chartDiv'));
        data.setValue(0, 1, 85);
        data.setValue(1, 1, 70);
        chart.draw(data, options);
      }
    </script>
  </head>
  <body>
    <div id="chartDiv" style="width: 400px; height: 120px;"></
div>
  </body>
</html>
```

## Calendar Chart

In business, analysts often visualize data based upon a past or projected calendar day, such as sales per day for October. To display such data in a meaningful way, you can use a calendar

## CHAPTER 4 Data Visualization

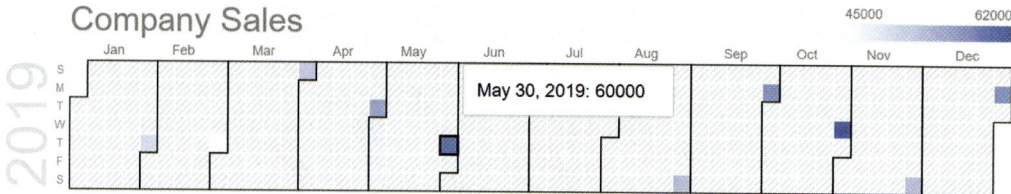

**FIGURE 4.54** Using a calendar chart to show annual sales by day.
Used with permission of Google

chart, similar to that shown in **FIGURE 4.54**. For simplicity, the calendar shows data for only 1 day per month. When you hover your mouse over a day, the calendar will display the corresponding sales.

The following HTML file, SalesCalendar.html, uses Google Charts to display the chart previously shown in Figure 4.54:

```
<html>
  <head>
    <script type="text/javascript" src="https://www.gstatic.com/charts/loader.js"></script>
    <script type="text/javascript">
      google.charts.load("current", {packages:["calendar"]});
      google.charts.setOnLoadCallback(drawChart);

  function drawChart() {
     var dataTable = new google.visualization.DataTable();
     dataTable.addColumn({ type: 'date', id: 'Date' });
     dataTable.addColumn({ type: 'number', id: 'Sales' });
     dataTable.addRows([
        [ new Date(2019, 0, 31), 50000 ],
        [ new Date(2019, 1, 28), 45000 ],
        [ new Date(2019, 2, 31), 52000 ],
        [ new Date(2019, 3, 30), 55500 ],
        [ new Date(2019, 4, 30), 60000 ],
        [ new Date(2019, 5, 30), 55000 ],
        [ new Date(2019, 6, 30), 47000 ],
        [ new Date(2019, 7, 31), 53000 ],
        [ new Date(2019, 8, 30), 57500 ],
        [ new Date(2019, 9, 30), 62000 ],
        [ new Date(2019, 10, 30), 53000 ],
        [ new Date(2019, 11, 30), 57500 ],
     ]);

     var chart = new google.visualization.Calendar(document.getElementById('chartDiv'));

     var options = {
```

```
      title: "Company Sales",
      height: 350,
    };

      chart.draw(dataTable, options);
   }
    </script>
  </head>
  <body>
    <div id="chartDiv" style="width: 1000px; height: 350px;"></div>
  </body>
</html>
```

## Candlestick Chart

A **candlestick chart**, as shown in **FIGURE 4.55**, is often used for financial data to represent a stock's opening, closing, high, and low values. By assigning colors to the corresponding boxes, the chart indicates whether the stock closed up or down for the day.

The following HTML file, StockPrices.html, uses Google Charts to display Amazon's stock prices for a week, as previously shown in Figure 4.55:

```
<html>
  <head>
    <script type="text/javascript" src="https://www.gstatic.com/charts/loader.js"></script>
    <script type="text/javascript">
      google.charts.load('current', {'packages':['corechart']});
      google.charts.setOnLoadCallback(drawChart);
```

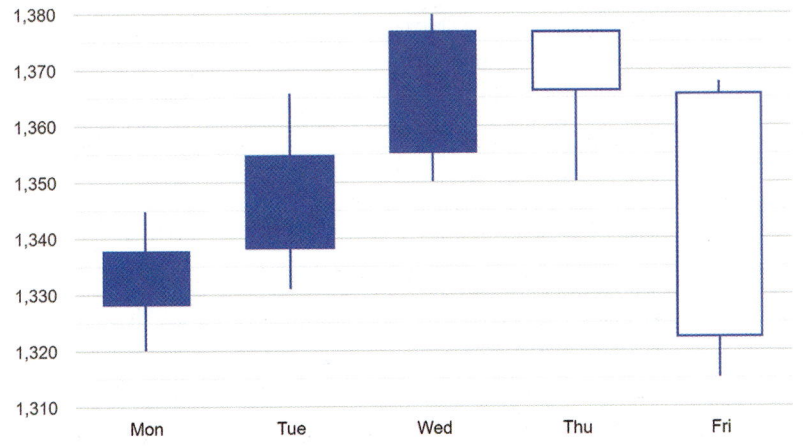

**FIGURE 4.55** Using a candlestick chart to represent stock prices.

Used with permission of Google

```
    function drawChart() {
      var data = google.visualization.arrayToDataTable([
        ['Mon', 1320, 1328, 1338, 1345],
        ['Tue', 1331, 1338, 1355, 1366],
        ['Wed', 1350, 1355, 1377, 1380],
        ['Thu', 1377, 1377, 1366, 1350],
        ['Fri', 1368, 1366, 1322, 1315]
      ], true);

      var options = {
        legend:'none'
      };

      var chart = new google.visualization.CandlestickChart(document.getElementById('chartDiv'));

      chart.draw(data, options);
    }
    </script>
  </head>
  <body>
    <div id="chartDiv" style="width: 900px; height: 500px;"></div>
  </body>
</html>
```

## Distribution Charts

Often, analysts are interested in the number of times an event occurs, such as the number of visits to a website, the number of customer product returns, or the number of calls into a call center. In such cases, the analyst can use distribution charts, which represent the frequency of values within a data set. Common distribution charts include:

- Histogram chart
- Box and whisker chart

### Histogram Chart

Analysts often track the frequency of occurrence of values over time, such as the number of website visits by time of day, orders per day, and so on. A histogram, which looks like a bar chart in that it uses rectangular bars, charts such distributions of values. Using the histogram's frequency counts (or percentages), analysts can estimate future events based on the chart's probability distribution. In other words, the histogram shows the probability of an event's future occurrence. The histogram groups values into bins, such as the number of sales orders for 1–5 products, 6–10 products, and so on.

**FIGURE 4.56** illustrates a histogram that shows the frequency of order sizes based on a bin width of 33.

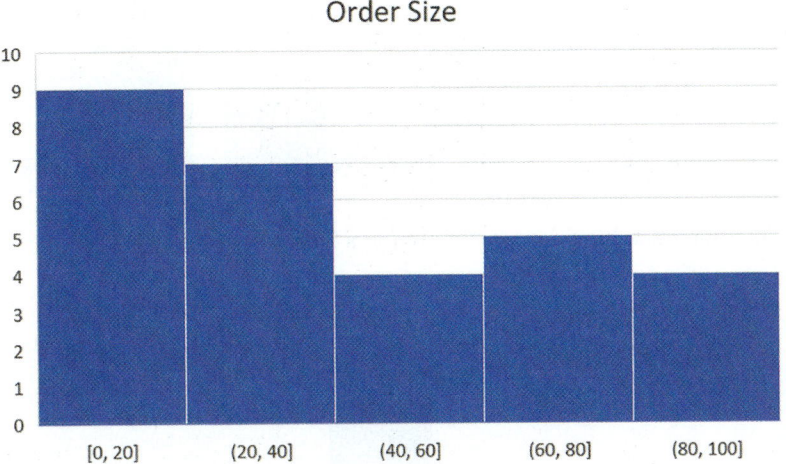

**FIGURE 4.56** A histogram representing the frequency of order sizes.

Used with permission of Google

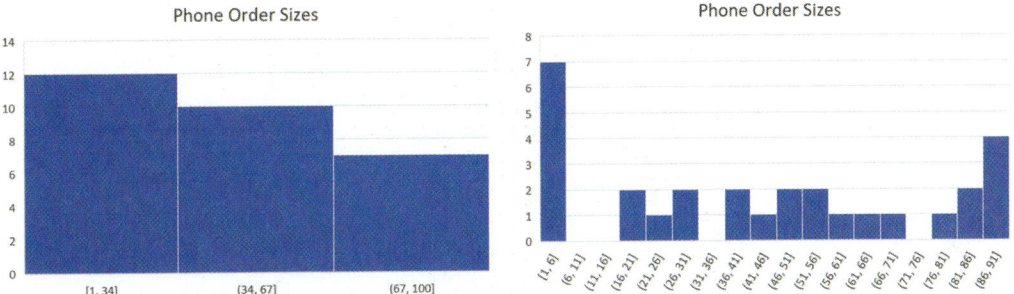

**FIGURE 4.57** Using different histogram bin sizes.

Used with permission of Google

When creating a histogram, you must choose the bin size carefully. By selecting too large of a bin size, the chart may hide meaningful information. Likewise, too small of a bin size will clutter the chart. **FIGURE 4.57** shows the same chart using different bin sizes (33 and 5). As you can see, decreasing the bin size in this case provides greater insight into high- and low-value frequencies. As you chart data with a histogram, you should experiment with different bin sizes. As it turns out, data analysts use several different algorithms to determine the suggested number of bins based on characteristics of the data set. A simple approach is to take the square root of the number of data samples. For example, if you have 25 data samples, you would use 5 bins; likewise, for 100 data samples, you would use 10 bins.

Number of bins = Square root (Number of samples)

Data analysts use the number of histogram peaks to categorize the chart as unimodal, bimodal, or multimodal, as shown in **FIGURE 4.58**.

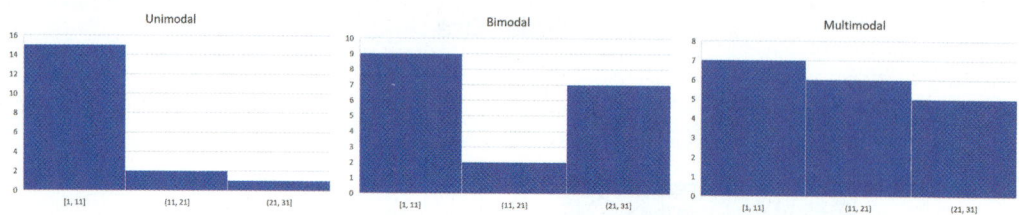

**FIGURE 4.58** Unimodal, bimodal, and multimodal histograms.

Used with permission of Google

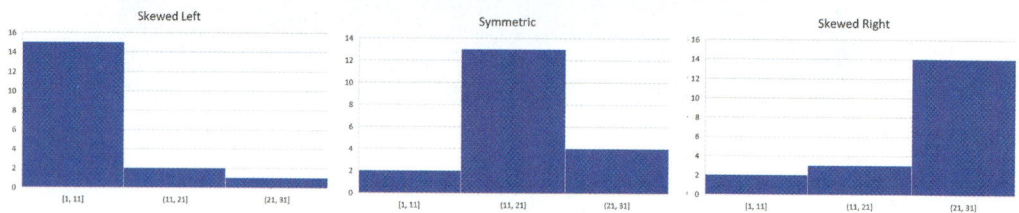

**FIGURE 4.59** A skewed right, skewed left, and symmetric histogram.

Used with permission of Google

| | A |
|---|---|
| 1 | Visitor Age |
| 2 | 12 |
| 3 | 82 |
| 4 | 12 |
| 5 | 13 |
| 6 | 44 |
| 7 | 33 |
| 8 | 25 |
| 9 | 99 |
| 10 | 66 |
| 11 | 77 |

**FIGURE 4.60** A data set representing the age of visitors.

Likewise, analysts will use the location of the peaks to describe the histogram as skewed right, skewed left, or symmetric, as shown in **FIGURE 4.59**. By knowing how data are skewing, the analyst gains further insight into the underlying values. A normal distribution is symmetric, taking on the shape of a bell, meaning most values fall near the average.

Assume you are given the data set shown in **FIGURE 4.60**.

If you chart the data using a histogram, the visualization will appear as shown in **FIGURE 4.61**.

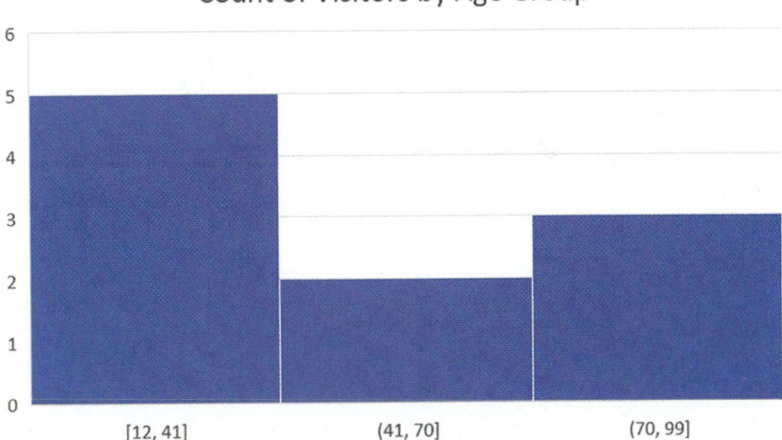

**FIGURE 4.61** A histogram representing count of visitors by age.

Used with permission of Google

## Box and Whisker Charts

When data analysts perform simple statistical analysis, they will often sort data and then determine the median value in the sorted list. The median value is different from the mean value—the median is the middle value in the sorted list, whereas the mean is the list's average value.

Consider, for example, the following list of 17 values that range from 0 to 20:

```
0
2
5
6
7
9
10
11
13    ←  Median value    Mean 12
15
16
16
17
19
19
19
20
```

As shown, the list's median value is 13 and the mean value is 12. By definition, half the values will be less than the median and half will be larger. To gain additional insight into the data, analysts will further group the data in quartiles named $Q_1$, $Q_2$, and $Q_3$, which are defined as follows:

- $Q_1$: the middle value between the smallest value and the median
- $Q_2$: the median value
- $Q_3$: the middle value between the median and the largest value

The following list shows the quartiles:

```
0
2
5
6
            Q₁ is 6.5
7
9
10
11
15    ←   Q₂
16
16
17
            Q₃ is 18
19
19
19
20
```

The **box and whiskers chart** represents the data-set quartiles. Within the chart, the box groups the values between $Q_1$ and $Q_3$. The whiskers (the branches that come off the box), in turn, extend to highlight the majority (normally 96%) of the smallest and largest values, as shown in **FIGURE 4.62**. Normally, the 2% of data at each end of the list that is not represented is composed of potential outliers.

As a second example, assume you are given the data set shown in **FIGURE 4.63**.

If you chart the data using a box and whiskers chart, the visualization would appear as shown in **FIGURE 4.64**.

## Geocharts

Often, analysts want to associate data values with a state, region, country, or even a continent. As shown in **FIGURE 4.65**, a **geochart** provides such visualizations. Within the geochart, analysts often use colors to draw the viewer's attention to specific locations. As the viewer navigates his or her mouse over the chart, he or she can display additional popups that contain more information about the data point. In addition, this chart color shades the regions based upon their sales.

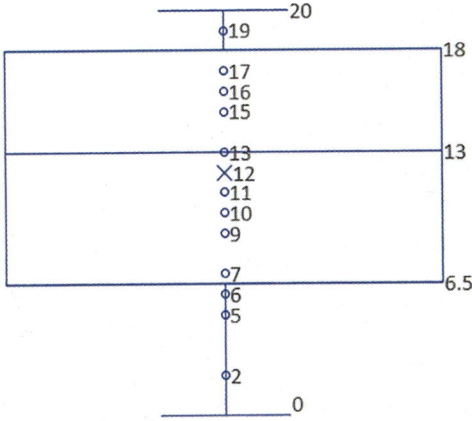

**FIGURE 4.62** **A box and whiskers chart grouping a data-set's quartile values.**

Used with permission of Google

| | A |
|---|---|
| 1 | Fives |
| 2 | 0 |
| 3 | 5 |
| 4 | 10 |
| 5 | 15 |
| 6 | 20 |

**FIGURE 4.63** **A simple data set.**

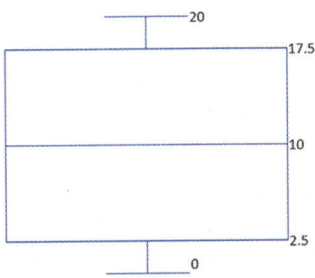

**FIGURE 4.64** **Using a box and whiskers chart to represent a simple data set.**

Used with permission of Google

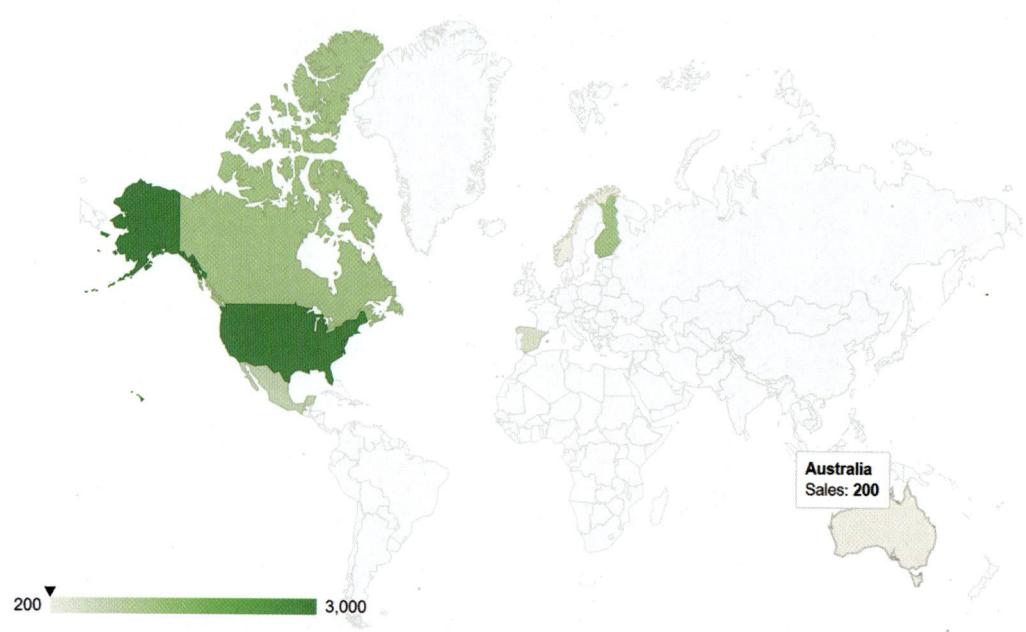

**FIGURE 4.65** A geochart integrates a map with data values.

Used with permission of Google

The following HTML file, ShowWorld.html, creates the geochart previously shown in Figure 4.65:

```
<html>
  <head>
    <script type="text/javascript" src="https://www.gstatic.com/charts/loader.js"></script>
    <script type="text/javascript">
      google.charts.load('current', {
        'packages':['geochart'],
        // Note: you will need to get a mapsApiKey for your project.
        // See: https://developers.google.com/chart/interactive/docs/basic_load_libs#load-settings
        'mapsApiKey': 'AIzaSyD-9tSrke72PouQMnMX-a7eZSW0jkFMBWY'
      });
      google.charts.setOnLoadCallback(drawRegionsMap);

      function drawRegionsMap() {
        var data = google.visualization.arrayToDataTable([
          ['Country', 'Sales'],
          ['Finland', 1200],
          ['United States', 3000],
          ['Mexico', 800],
          ['Canada', 1200],
```

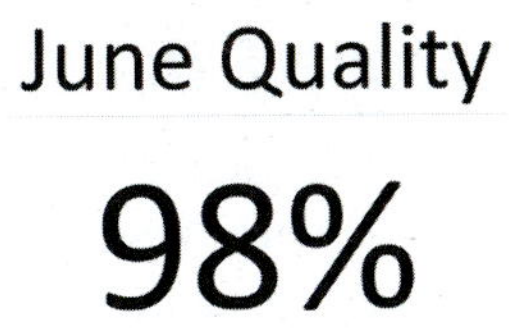

## June Quality
## 98%

**FIGURE 4.66** Using a big number to present a result to viewers.

```
        ['Spain', 500],
        ['Norway', 200],
        ['Australia', 200]
    ]);

    var options = {};

    var chart = new google.visualization.GeoChart(document.getElementById('chartDiv'));

    chart.draw(data, options);
   }
  </script>
 </head>
 <body>
    <div id="chartDiv" style="width: 900px; height: 500px;"></div>
 </body>
</html>
```

## Big Number

Although not a chart, per se, but rather a visualization, the use of a big number is an effective way to communicate a result. When you walk into a restaurant, for example, you will often find that it proudly displays the big letter A it has received from the Department of Health. **FIGURE 4.66** illustrates the use of a big number within a data quality dashboard.

Most dashboard and charting tools provide support for textboxes. To create a big number, use a textbox to position the number and then choose the font and size you desire.

## Plotting Data Using the Python and R Programming Languages

Chapter 8, "Programming Data Mining and Analytic Solutions," examines the use of the Python and R programming languages for data mining and data analytics. As you will learn, developers use the languages to create custom machine-learning and data-mining applications. In Chapter 8, you will examine charting in Python and R.

## Tables Still Communicate Effectively

The adage "if you give a child a hammer, everything becomes a nail" applies to the use of charts and graphs. Not everything requires a chart. Remember, your goal in presenting data and visualizations is to communicate. Often, a table can meaningfully communicate a message to users. In addition, there may be times when you will want to include a table of details next to a chart, as shown in **FIGURE 4.67**.

## Hands-on Data Visualization Using Tableau

Data analysts have many choices when it comes to which tool they will use to create their visualizations. If you only need to create one or two charts, your tool choice may be less critical. However, if you must roll out an operational dashboard with drill-downs across an organization, you should consider an industry-leading tool, such as Tableau. For years, Tableau has been the most widely used visualization tool (possibly following Excel). Data analysts use Tableau not only for creating visualizations and dashboards but also as a discovery tool to identify trends and data patterns. In this section, you will get up and running with Tableau, creating a Sales dashboard.

### Getting Started with Tableau

Visit the Tableau website at www.tableau.com, as shown in **FIGURE 4.68**.

For years, data analysts have made extensive use of the Tableau Desktop tool, which you download, install, and run on their own computers. Tableau also supports a cloud-based, software as a service (SaaS) interface, which you can run from the cloud, making it easy for you to access Tableau from any computer at any time. In this section, you will use the Tableau Desktop. After you download, install, and run the Tableau Desktop, it will appear as shown in **FIGURE 4.69**.

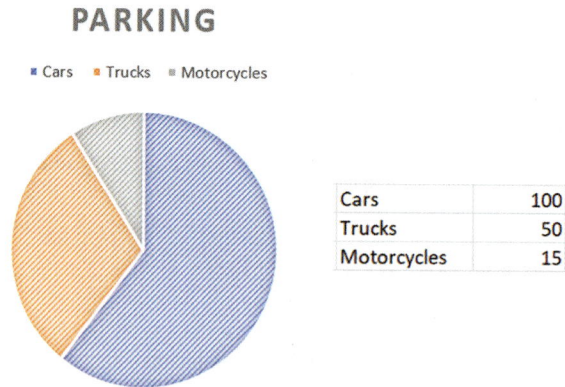

**FIGURE 4.67** Combining a chart and table to better communicate with a viewer.
Used with permission of Google

Hands-on Data Visualization Using Tableau

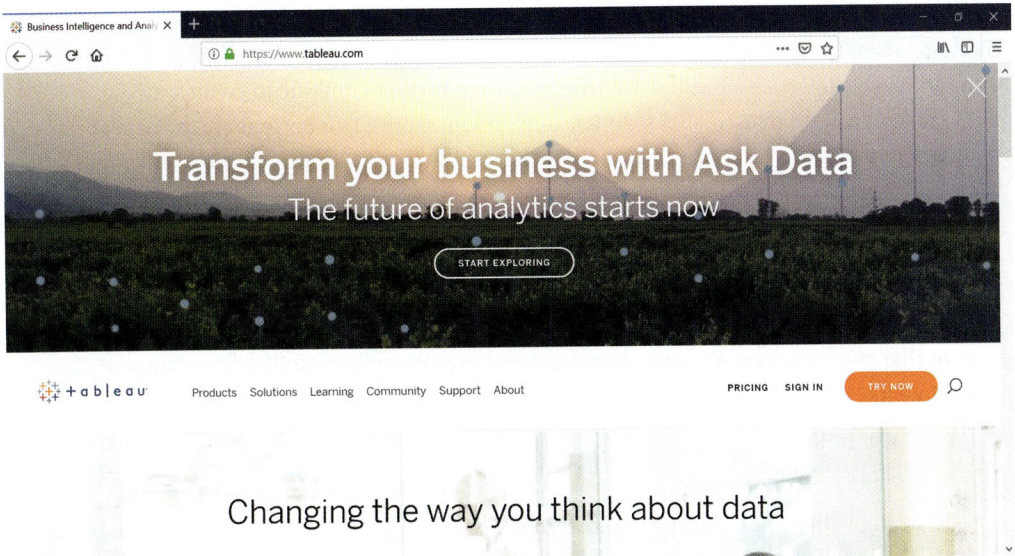

**FIGURE 4.68** The Tableau website.
Used with permission of TABLEAU SOFTWARE

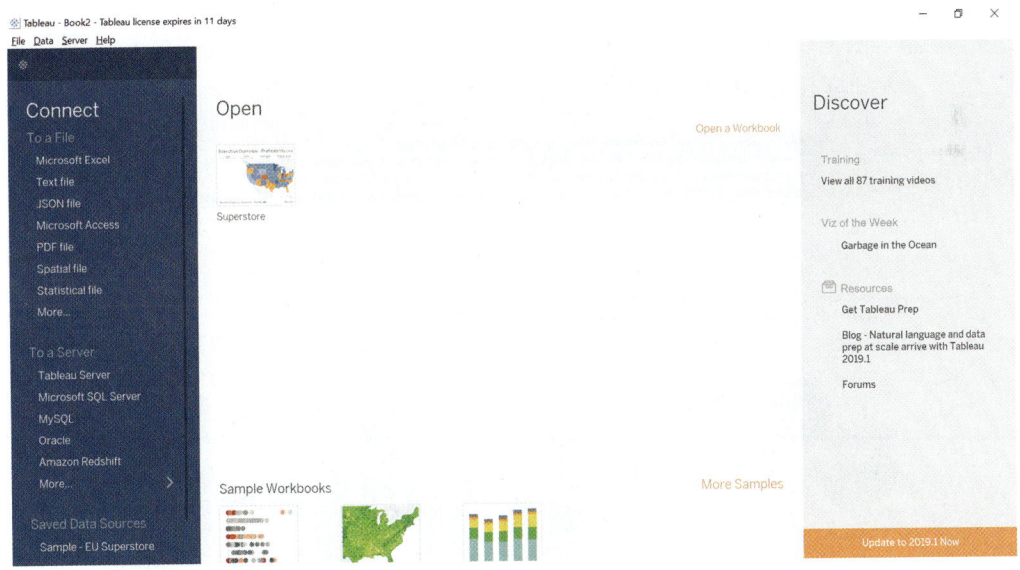

**FIGURE 4.69** The Tableau Desktop.
Used with permission of TABLEAU SOFTWARE

Before you get started, you should understand the following key terms and concepts. Within Tableau, a single visualization is called a sheet (some analysts review to a sheet as a view). You combine sheets to create a dashboard, which you can further combine to create a story.

Tableau makes extensive use of dimensions and measures. Dimensions are the data points you want to chart. A measure is an aggregation, such as a sum, count, average, minimum, or maximum.

## Creating a Sales Dashboard

As discussed, a Tableau dashboard is a collection of views (visualizations). In this section, you will create the sales dashboard shown in **FIGURE 4.70**.

So that you have data to chart, download and save the following files from this text's catalog page at go.jblearning.com/DataMining:

- Sales by Region
- Sales by Person

To begin, within the Tableau Connection field, click Microsoft Excel. Tableau will display an Open dialog box from which you can open the Sales by Region spreadsheet. Tableau will display your new data source, as shown in **FIGURE 4.71**.

Within the bar that appears at the bottom of your Tableau window, click the Sheet 1 button. Tableau will display a blank sheet, which you can use to define your visualization. Within the sheet,

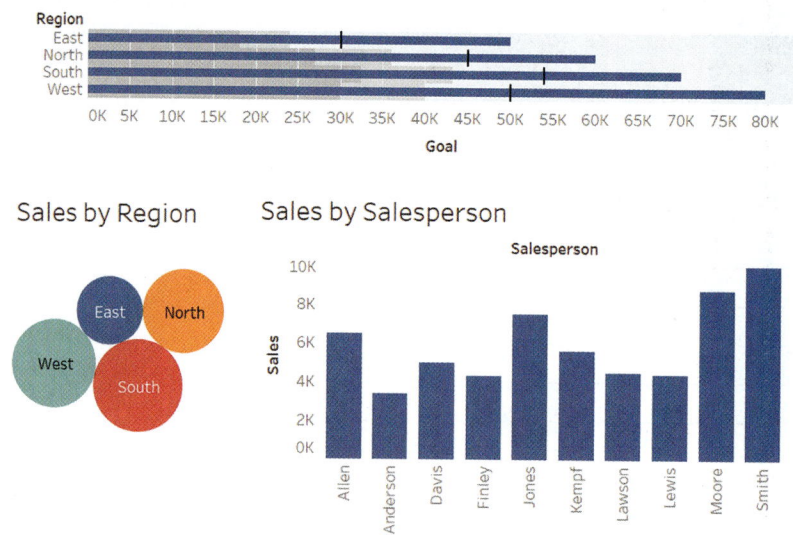

**FIGURE 4.70** A sales dashboard created using Tableau.

Used with permission of TABLEAU SOFTWARE

Hands-on Data Visualization Using Tableau     153

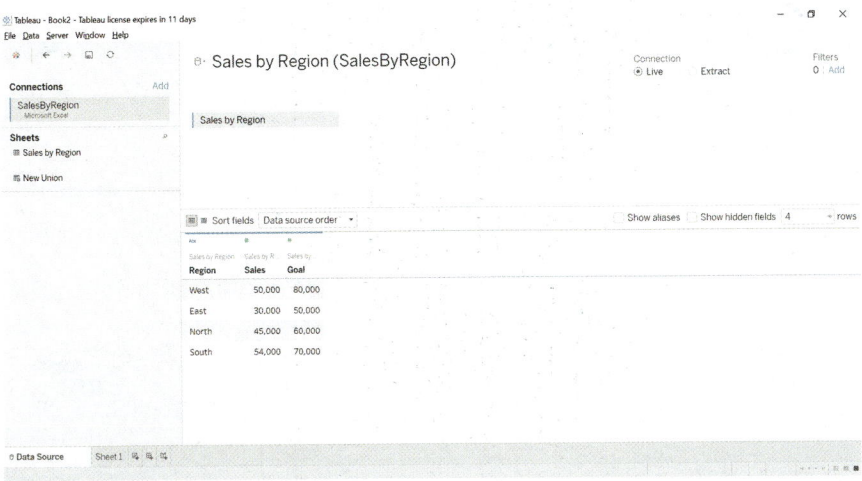

**FIGURE 4.71** Adding a data source.
Used with permission of TABLEAU SOFTWARE

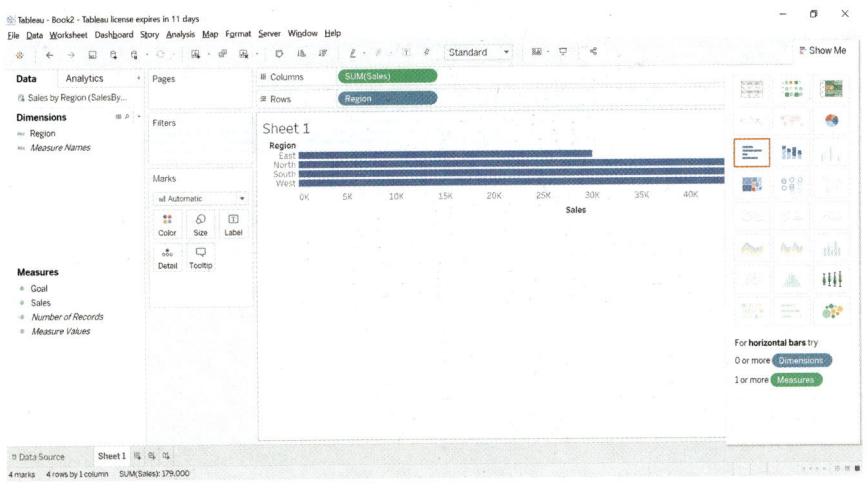

**FIGURE 4.72** Creating a bar chart of sales by region.
Used with permission of TABLEAU SOFTWARE

drag the Region dimension to the Rows field and the Sales measure to the Columns field. Tableau, in turn, will display a bar chart of the data, as shown in **FIGURE 4.72**.

Within the Show Me tab that appears along the right side of your window, click on the different visualizations Tableau provides for this type of data set. Tableau will immediately display each visualization you select. Choose the packed bubbles chart, as shown in **FIGURE 4.73**. Right-click your mouse on the Sheet 1 button and rename the sheet Sales by Region.

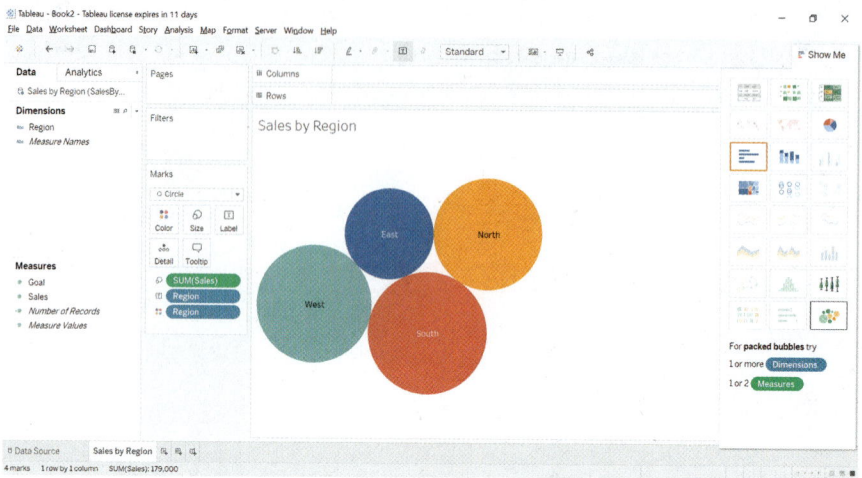

**FIGURE 4.73** Displaying sales by region as a packed bubble chart.
Used with permission of TABLEAU SOFTWARE

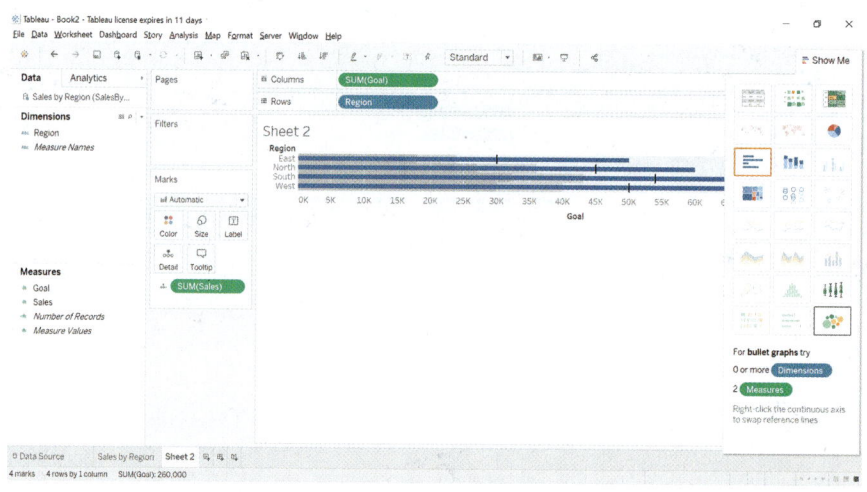

**FIGURE 4.74** Displaying sales to goal as a bullet chart.
Used with permission of TABLEAU SOFTWARE

Within the bar that appears at the bottom of your window, click the New Worksheet button. Tableau will display a blank worksheet. Within the sheet, drag the Regions to the Rows field and Sales and Goals to the Column field. Rename the sheet Sales to Goal. Using the Show Me tab, select a bullet chart, which is well suited for showing actual-to-goal relationships. Tableau will display the bullet chart shown in **FIGURE 4.74**.

Click the Data menu and then the New Data Source option. Tableau will display its Data Source screen. Click Microsoft Excel and open the Sales by Person spreadsheet you previously downloaded. Tableau will display the data, as shown in **FIGURE 4.75**.

**FIGURE 4.75** Loading the sales by person data.

Used with permission of TABLEAU SOFTWARE

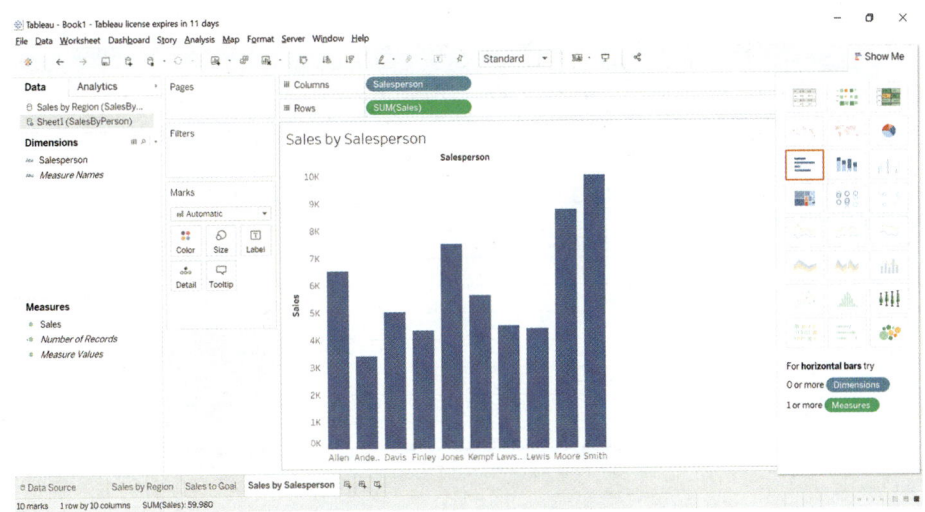

**FIGURE 4.76** Displaying sales by salesperson as a column chart.

Used with permission of TABLEAU SOFTWARE

Within the bar at the bottom of your window, click the New Worksheet button. Drag the Salesperson dimension to the Columns field and Sales to the Rows field. Rename the sheet Sales by Salesperson. Tableau will display a column chart, as shown in **FIGURE 4.76**.

Within the bar at the bottom of your window, click the New Dashboard button. Tableau will display a blank dashboard. Drag the Sales to Goal sheet on to the dashboard. Tableau will display the sheet. Click on the Layout tab that appears on the left side of your window. Within the Layout tab, click the floating check box and then size and position the sheet as shown in **FIGURE 4.77**.

Repeat these steps to size and position the Sales by Region and Sales by Salesperson sheets on to the dashboard, as shown in **FIGURE 4.78**. Rename the dashboard Company Sales Summary.

Tableau is a very powerful tool with capabilities far beyond those presented here. This section's goal was to get you up and running with Tableau. On the Tableau Help menu, you will find a link to videos that present Tableau functionality in detail.

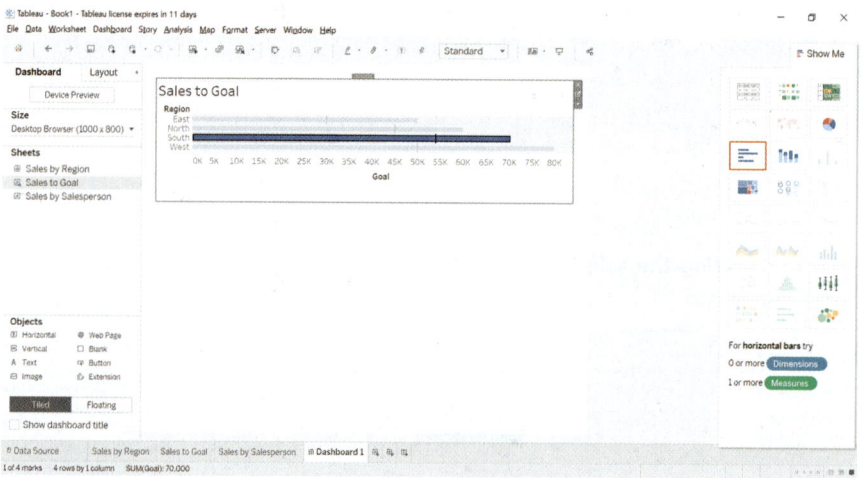

**FIGURE 4.77** Sizing and positioning a sheet on a Tableau dashboard.
Used with permission of TABLEAU SOFTWARE

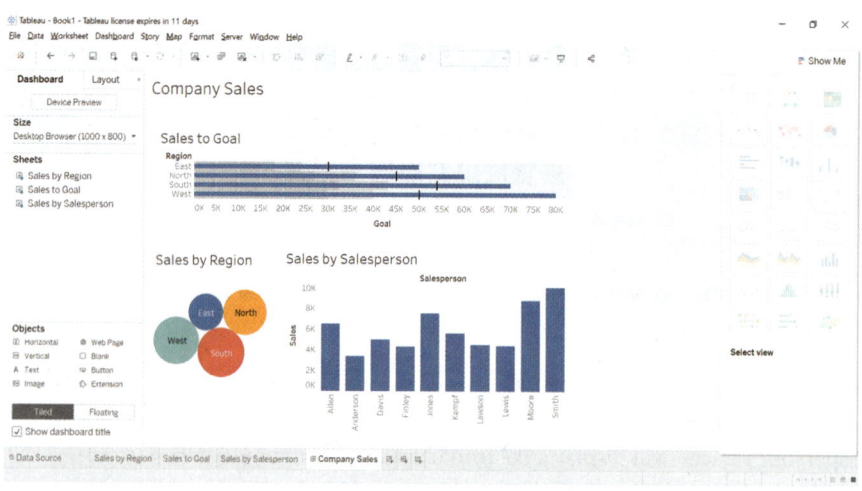

**FIGURE 4.78** Sizing and positioning sheets on a Tableau dashboard.
Used with permission of TABLEAU SOFTWARE

## Summary

Visualization is the visual representation of data, with the goal of improving communication. In this chapter you examined a wide range of visualization tools, from pie charts to geocharts, that let you represent data in a meaningful way. As you learned, each chart is well suited for a specific type of data. To help you select the correct chart for your needs, this chapter organized charts by purpose:

- Time-based comparison charts represent how a variable's value changes over time.
- Category-based comparison charts represent one or more categories of values.
- Composition charts represent how a value relates to the whole.
- Distribution charts represent the distribution frequency of values within a data set.
- Correlation charts represent how two or more variables relate.
- Dashboard charts represent KPIs.
- Geocharts chart data against a map.

Further, to improve the quality of your charts, this chapter examined charting best practices. In this chapter you used Excel, Google Charts, and Tableau to create charts. In upcoming chapters, you will use Python, R, and MongoDB, as well as other visualization and business intelligence tools.

## Key Terms

Application Program Interface (API)
Area chart
Bar chart
Box and whiskers chart
Bubble chart
Candlestick chart
Category-based comparison charts
Column chart
Combo chart
Composition charts
Correlation charts
Dashboard charts
Diff chart
Distribution charts
Dynamic chart
Funnel chart
Gauge chart
Geocharts
Histogram chart
Line chart
Marker
Pie chart
Pyramid chart
Quartile
Radar chart
Scatter chart
Stacked bar chart
Stacked column chart
Static chart
Sunburst chart
Time-based comparison charts
Treemap chart
Visualization
Waterfall chart

## Review

1. List and describe the common chart grouping categories, and for each category, list its common chart types.
2. Discuss the pros and cons of using 2D and 3D pie charts.

3. Download the Excel file, ChartData.xlsx, from this text's catalog page at go.jblearning.com/DataMining. Within the spreadsheet, you will find data sheets with names such as Bar Chart Data, Pie Chart Data, Scatter Chart Data, and so on.

Using the data the Excel file provides, create the following charts:

4. Bar Chart Data Sheet
    a. Create a bar chart
    b. Create a column chart
5. Pie Chart Data Sheet
    a. Create a 2D pie chart
    b. Create a 3D pie chart
    c. Create a donut chart
6. Line Chart Data Sheet
    a. Create a line chart
    b. Create a multiline chart
7. Scatter Chart Sheet
    a. Create a scatter chart
    b. Create a bubble chart
8. Radar Chart Sheet
    a. Create a radar chart
9. Sunburst Chart Sheet
    a. Create a sunburst chart
10. Treemap Chart Sheet
    a. Create a treemap chart
11. Funnel Chart Sheet
    a. Create a funnel chart
12. Stock Chart Sheet
    a. Create a candlestick chart
13. Waterfall Chart Sheet
    a. Create a waterfall chart
14. Histogram Chart Sheet
    a. Create a histogram chart
15. Using Tableau, complete the steps discussed in the Hands-on section of this chapter, creating screen captures of your steps.

# CHAPTER 5

# Keep Excel in Your Toolset

## Chapter Goals and Objectives

- Sort and filter data using Excel.
- Create charts to visualize data using Excel.
- Apply conditional formatting to highlight key values.
- Compare and contrast spreadsheet file formats.
- Use pivot tables to analyze data and to produce reports.
- Perform "what if" processing within Excel.

Despite the recent explosive growth of machine-learning and data-mining tools and solutions, Excel remains the most widely used data analysis program. Using Excel, data analysts model complex data, create visualizations, cleanse data, and more. Often, one of the first steps a data analyst performs when he or she receives a new data set is to open and examine it within Excel. This chapter examines common data operations using Excel, as well as key built-in Excel functions. By the time you finish this chapter, you will understand the following key concepts:

- One of the most common operations data analysts perform when mining data is to sort the data into ascending (lowest to highest) or descending (highest to lowest) order. To sort data in Excel, click in the column by which you want to sort and then click the Data tab A–>Z or Z<–A button. Excel will sort the sheet based on the column selected.
- Excel is one of the most widely used charting solutions. To that end, Excel provides support for many built-in charts. To chart data within Excel, select the data you want to visualize and then choose the Insert tab chart icon that corresponds to the chart type you desire.

- As you work with large data sets, you will often want to view specific data, such as sales by region or sales by a salesperson. Using an Excel filter, you can direct Excel to display only the data you desire.
- As you analyze data, you will often want to highlight data that match a specific condition. In such cases, you can use Excel's **conditional formatting** to highlight the cells matching the condition, using a specific font or color.
- Data analysts must work with data that arrive in one of many file formats, such as comma-separated values (CSV), Extended Markup Language (XML), or JavaScript Object Notation (JSON). Excel makes it very easy to import data in such formats and to export data to such formats.
- To support data analytics, Excel provides a wide range of built-in statistical functions analysts can use to calculate average values, standard deviations, variances, correlations, and more.
- What-if processing allows data analysts to quickly answer questions such as the following: What if we increase our price? or What if we could sell more products? Using Excel's built-in Goal Seek tool, analysts can quickly perform such calculations.
- Often, analysts must forecast future performance based on current data trends. To support such operations, Excel provides the forecast sheet.
- One of Excel's most powerful and underused tools is the **pivot table**. Using a pivot table, you can quickly group data, identify data relationships, and create reports.

## Sorting Data Values

As you analyze data, a common operation you will perform is to sort data in ascending (lowest to highest) or descending (highest to lowest) value based on the values in a specific column. To sort data within Excel, click your mouse on any cell within the column by which you want to sort. Then, click Excel's Data tab and locate the Sort Options field, as shown in **FIGURE 5.1**.

Using the A->Z button, you can sort data in ascending order. Likewise, the Z->A button sorts data in descending order. When you click one of the buttons, Excel will sort the records in your spreadsheet based on the column values. The large Sort button within the Sort Options lets you sort the spreadsheet contents based upon multiple columns. When you click the button, Excel will display the Sort dialog box, shown in **FIGURE 5.2**, which lets you specify two or more columns by which you want to sort. When you sort by multiple columns, you specify the primary column by which Excel will sort and then a secondary column by which Excel will further sort the first result and so on.

Assume, for example, you have opened the Auto-MGP.csv data set, which you can download from this text's catalog page at go.jblearning.com/DataMining, that contains automobile makes, years, and engine attributes that produce each car's miles per gallon. To sort the data by year and make, you would use the Sort dialog box shown in **FIGURE 5.3**.

Excel, in turn, will display the sorted data as shown in **FIGURE 5.4**.

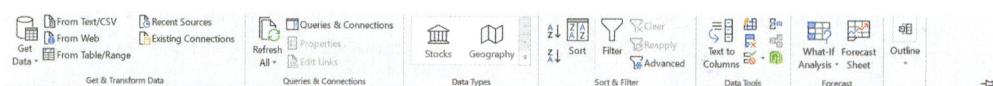

**FIGURE 5.1** The Sort Options field.

Used with permission from Microsoft

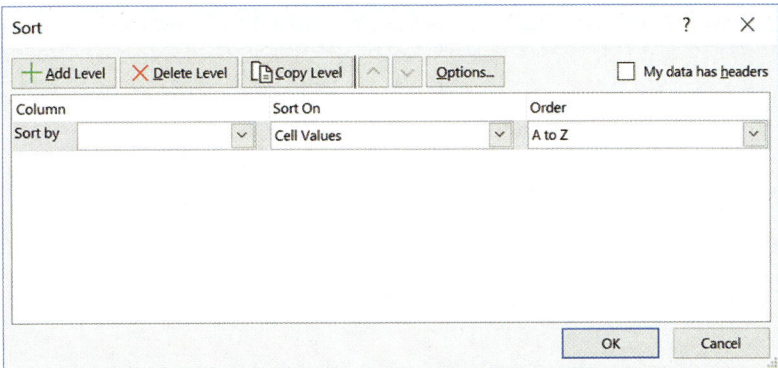

**FIGURE 5.2** Using the Sort dialog box to sort a spreadsheet by multiple columns.
Used with permission from Microsoft

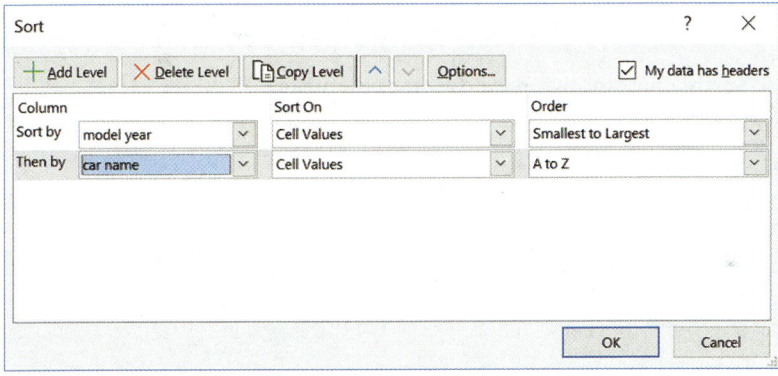

**FIGURE 5.3** Sorting auto data by year and make.
Used with permission from Microsoft

# Filtering Data

As you mine data, there will be times when you will want to work with subsets of data. In the case of the automotive data just discussed, you might want to view cars for a specific year or with an MPG greater than 20 miles per gallon. Excel users refer to the process of selecting subsets of data as **filtering**.

To filter data within Excel, select the Data tab Filter button. Excel, in turn, will display arrows in each header column you can use to open a pull-down list that lets you select the data you desire, as shown in **FIGURE 5.5**. Within the pull-down list, you can use the checkbox to enable or disable the display of data.

Assume, for example, you have the sales data spreadsheet shown in **FIGURE 5.6**. You can download the spreadsheet from this text's catalog page at go.jblearning.com/DataMining.

To view data for a specific region, select the Region column and click the Data tab Filter button. Excel will add a pull-down menu, as shown in **FIGURE 5.7**, you can use to select the region you desire.

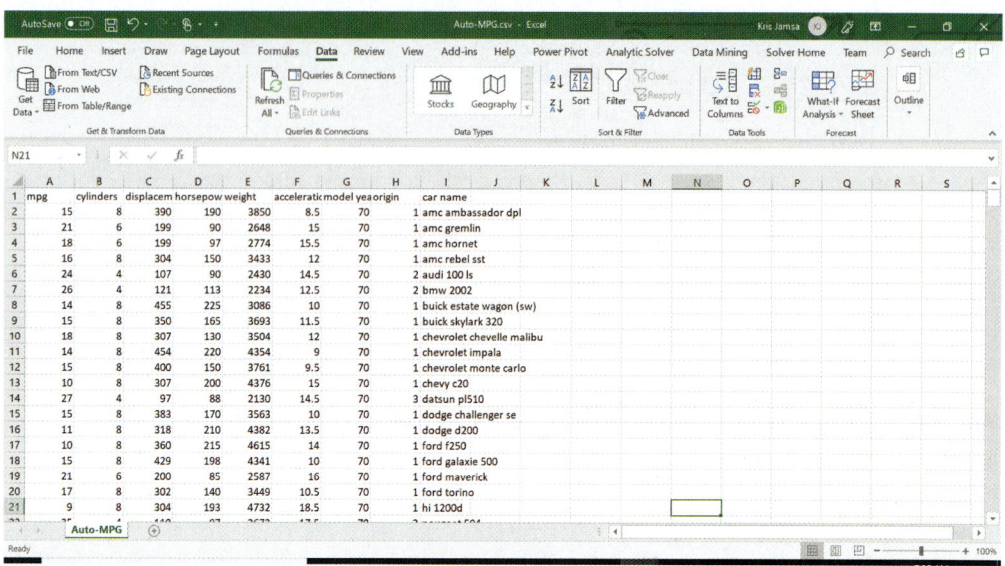

**FIGURE 5.4** Sorting automotive data by year and make.

Used with permission from Microsoft

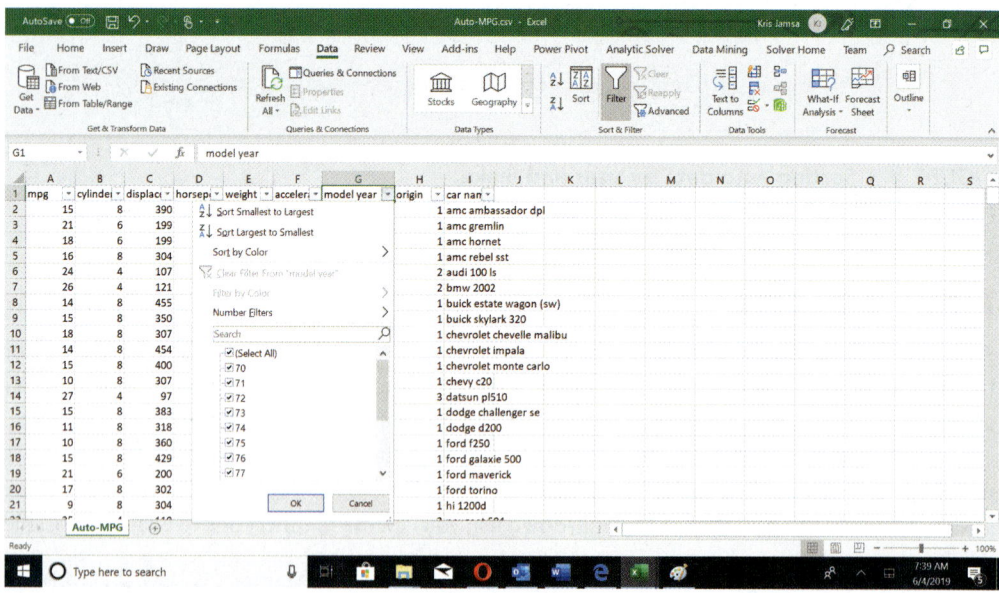

**FIGURE 5.5** Using filters to view subsets of data.

Used with permission from Microsoft

Filtering Data    163

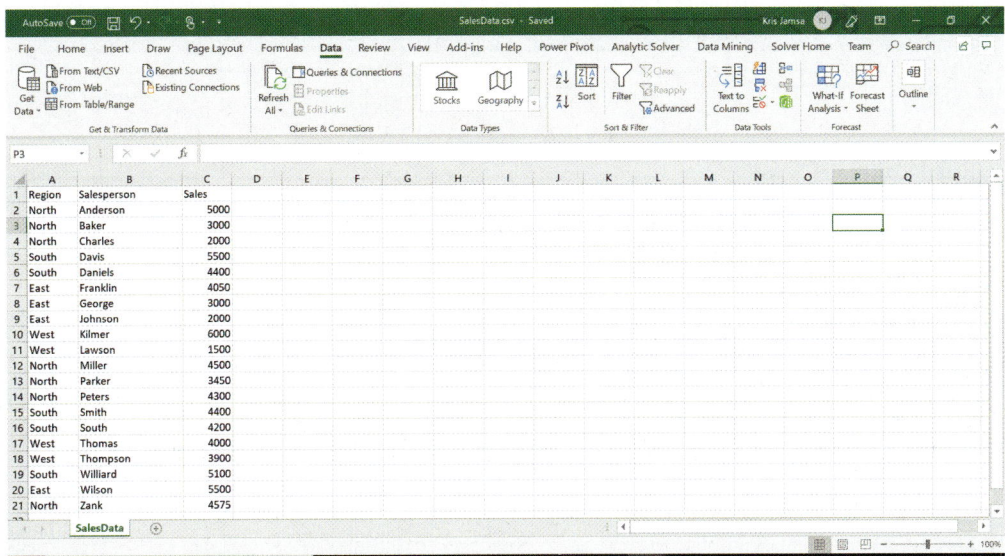

**FIGURE 5.6** A sales data spreadsheet containing sales data by region.
Used with permission from Microsoft

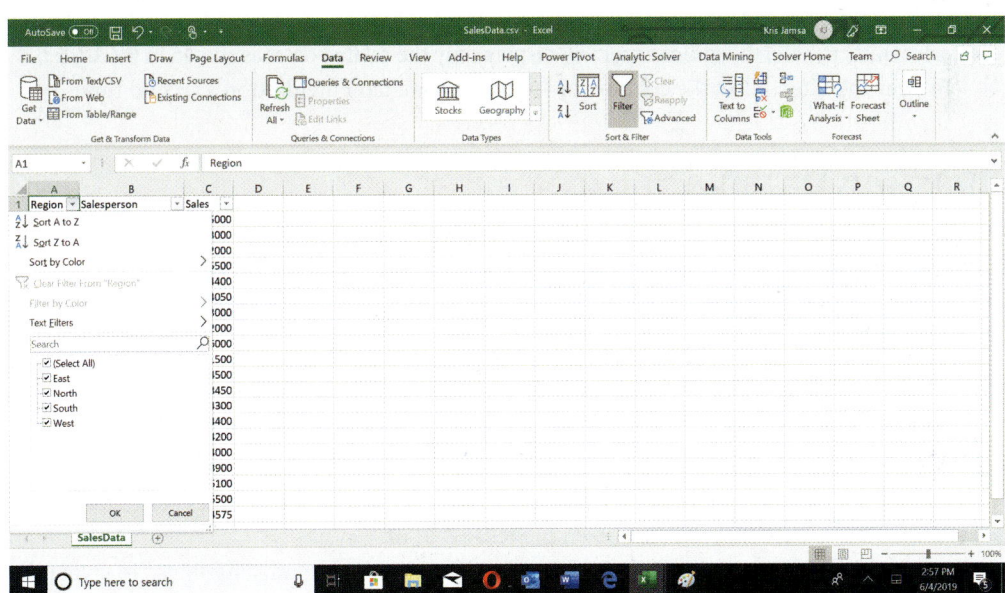

**FIGURE 5.7** Adding a column filter to a spreadsheet.
Used with permission from Microsoft

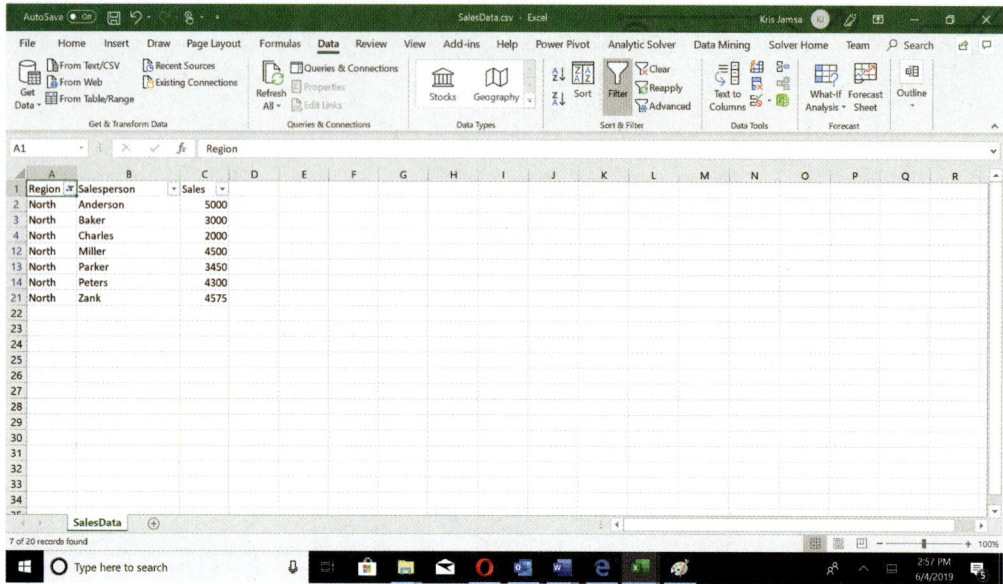

**FIGURE 5.8** Filtering sales data by region.

Used with permission from Microsoft

Within the pull-down list, place a checkmark in front of the region, or regions, you desire. In this case, select only the North region. Excel will display only the related data, as shown in **FIGURE 5.8**.

To clear the filter, select the column and click the Data tab Filter button a second time.

## Charting Data with Excel

As shown in **FIGURE 5.9**, Excel provides many chart types. Chapter 4, "Data Visualization," examines data visualization in detail, discussing different chart types and their use.

Regardless of the type of chart you want to create, the steps you will perform to create the charts are quite similar:

1. Select the cells that you want to chart.
2. From the Excel Insert tab, click the chart type you desire.
3. Assign the chart and axis titles and select any options you require.

Assume, for example, you want to know how many cars have different miles per gallon. To do so, you would create a histogram, as shown in **FIGURE 5.10**.

As you can see, to organize the results, the histogram groups counts into bins. To create the chart, perform these steps:

1. Select the miles per gallon column by clicking your mouse on the cell letter above the column.
2. Select the Insert tab and choose the histogram chart.

Charting Data with Excel    **165**

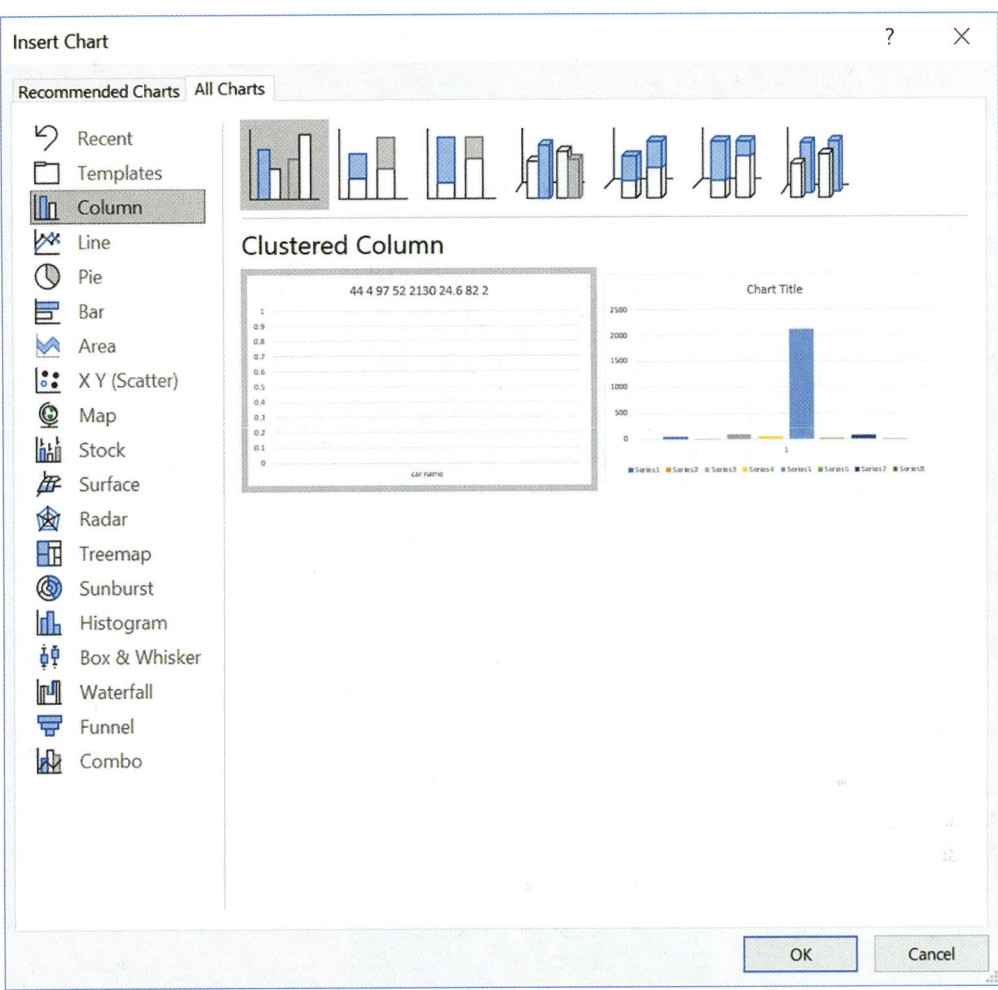

**FIGURE 5.9** Excel chart types.

Used with permission from Microsoft

Click your mouse on the paint-brush icon that appears to the right of the chart. Excel will display chart styles from which you can pick. As you select a style, Excel will display your chart using the style, as shown in **FIGURE 5.11**.

Within the chart-style popup, click the Color tab. Excel will display predefined color groups you can apply to your chart. Again, as you click on different color groups, Excel will apply the colors to your chart.

Assume that you want to chart miles per gallon against car horsepower. To do so, perform these steps:

1. Select the miles per gallon and horsepower columns by holding down your Ctrl key and clicking the letter above each column.

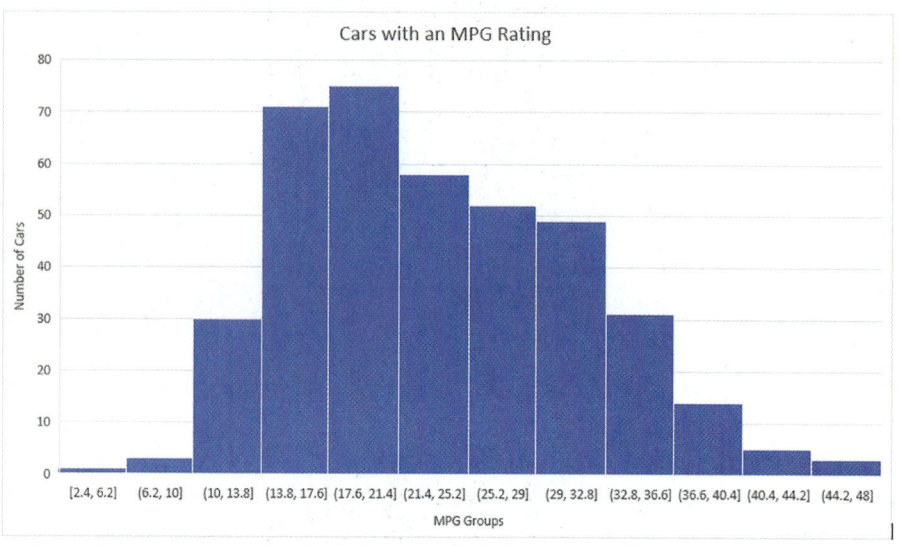

**FIGURE 5.10** **A histogram of miles per gallon.**

Used with permission from Microsoft

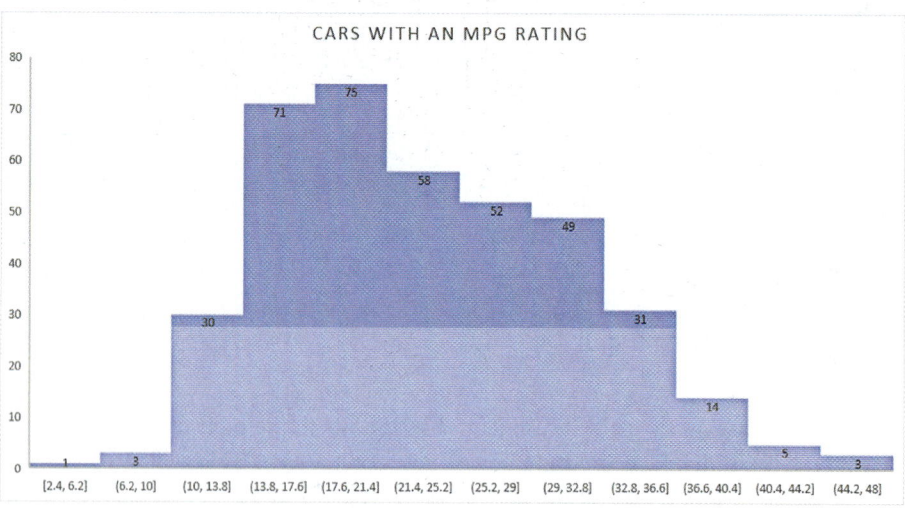

**FIGURE 5.11** **Styling an Excel chart.**

Used with permission from Microsoft

2. Select the Insert tab Scatter chart. Excel will chart the data.
3. Click on the chart and then click on the plus sign that appears to the right of the chart. Excel will display the chart's elements list. Within this list, select Axis, Axis Title, Chart Title, and Gridlines.
4. Edit the title and axis titles as shown in **FIGURE 5.12**.

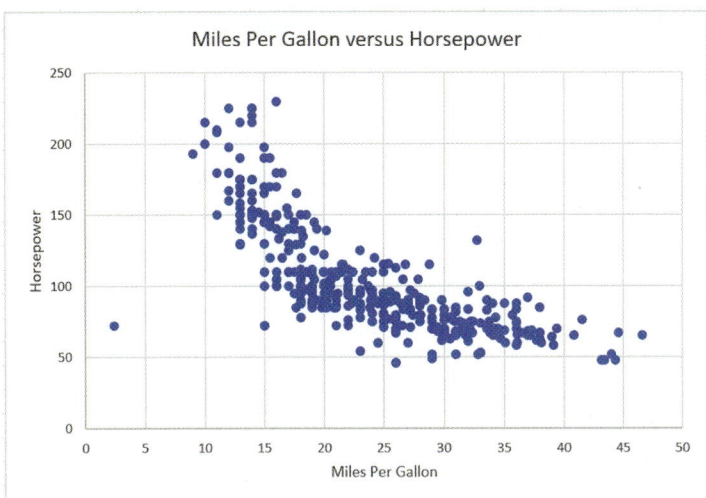

**FIGURE 5.12** Charting miles per gallon and horsepower.

Used with permission from Microsoft

# Conditional Formatting

Depending on the size of your data set, it may be difficult at a glance to detect specific values, such as data outliers. In addition, if you are sharing a spreadsheet with others, there will often be times when you will want to highlight specific values. To support such processing, Excel provides conditional formatting, which lets you assign different formatting (font, color, background color, and so on) to cells based on the values each contains.

Using conditional formatting, you can highlight values (cells) based on:

- A cell's value being less than, greater than, or equal to a specified value
- A cell's value being between a range of values
- A cell containing specific text
- A cell's content having a duplicate value
- A cell value following at the top (or bottom) percent of values
- And more

**FIGURE 5.13** illustrates a spreadsheet that uses conditional formatting.

To apply conditional formatting, perform these steps:

1. Select the desired cell range you want to consider.
2. Click on the Home tab Conditional Formatting button. Excel will display a pull-down list of conditional formatting options, as shown in **FIGURE 5.14**.
3. Click New Rule. Excel will display the New Formatting Rule dialog box shown in **FIGURE 5.15**.
4. Within the dialog box, select the rule that you desire, specify the needed values, and choose the formatting you desire.

Should you later want to turn off specific conditional formatting, you can use the Clear Rules menu option shown in **FIGURE 5.16**.

# CHAPTER 5 Keep Excel in Your Toolset

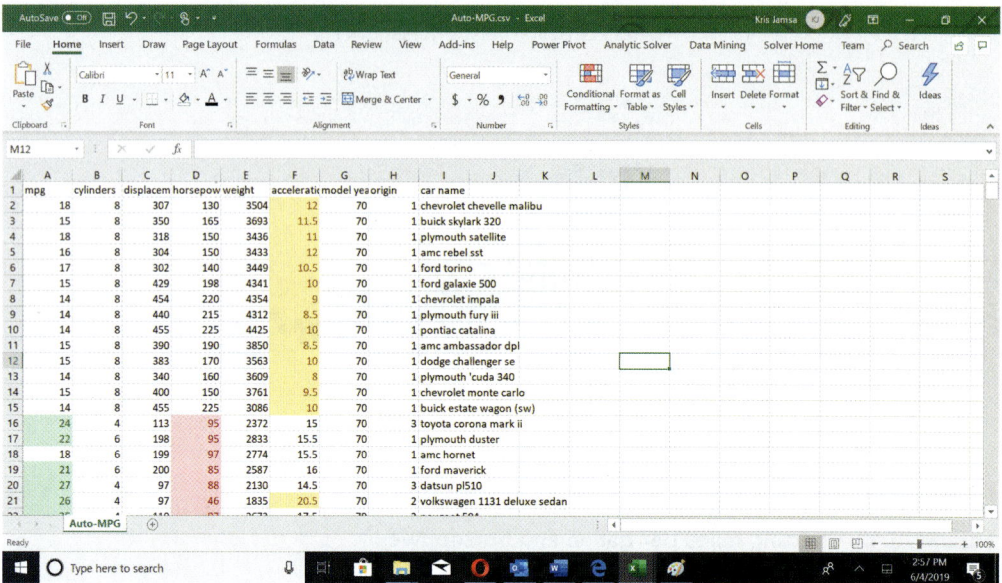

**FIGURE 5.13** Using conditional formatting to highlight specific cells.
Used with permission from Microsoft

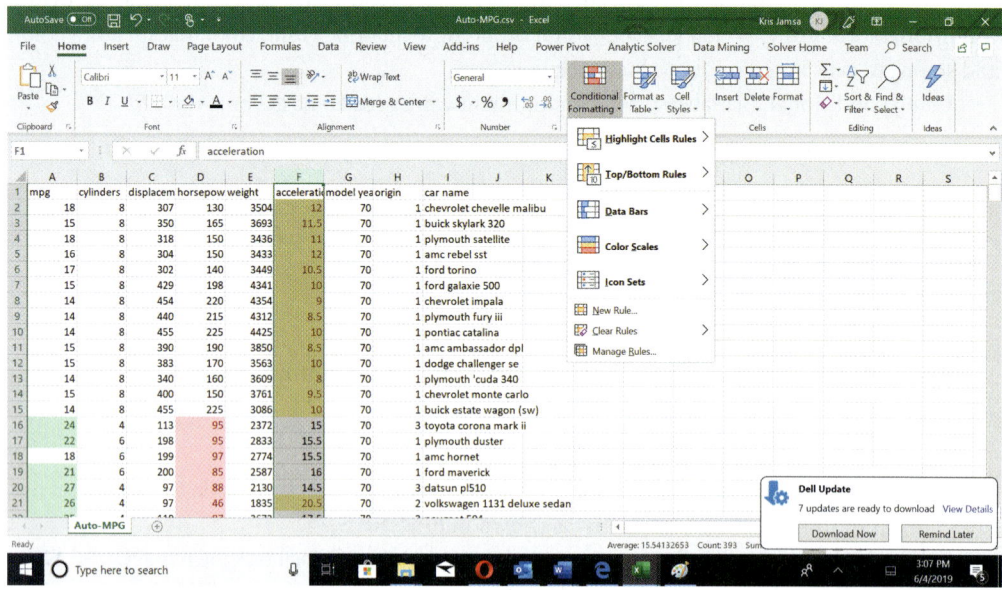

**FIGURE 5.14** Conditional formatting options in Excel.
Used with permission from Microsoft

## Conditional Formatting

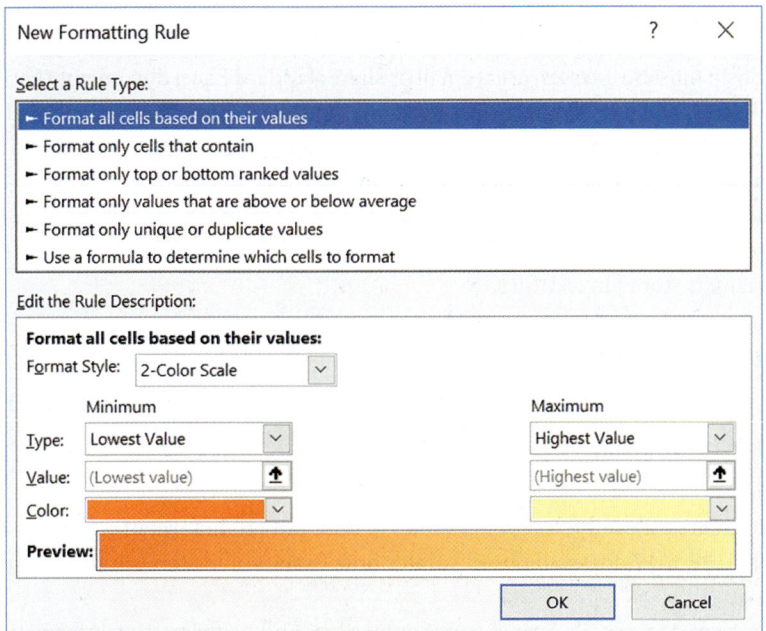

**FIGURE 5.15** The New Formatting Rule dialog box.

Used with permission from Microsoft

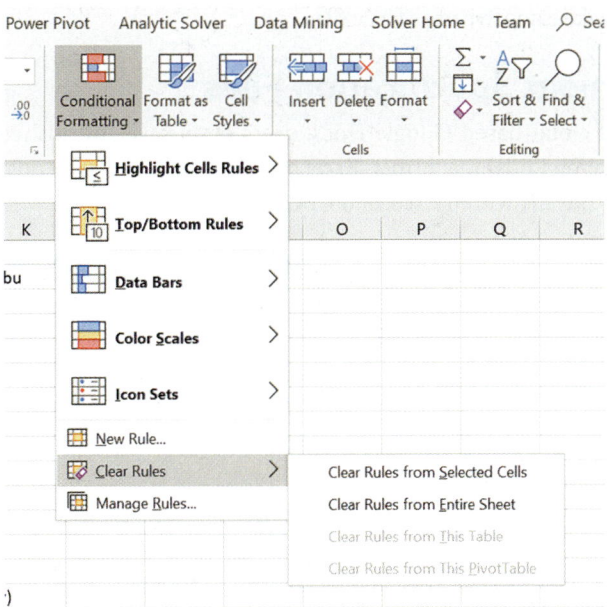

**FIGURE 5.16** The Clear Rules menu.

Used with permission from Microsoft

## Understanding File Formats

Every day, within most businesses, users email or share standard Excel documents that contain one or more worksheets and have the .xlsx file extension. Working with such standard Excel documents is easy—by default, Excel stores spreadsheets using this format, and when users double-click their mouse upon one, Excel will start, displaying the document's contents.

That said, users do not always use the standard Excel file format. Depending on the data source, you may receive spreadsheets in one of several forms. For example, throughout this text, you will download data sets stored in .csv files.

### Comma-Separated Value Files

The .csv file format stores data as text values, each separated from one another with a comma:

```
value1, value2, value3,
value4, value5, value6
```

A .csv-formatted file only stores data values; it does not retain formatting information (color, font, etc.). **FIGURE 5.17**, for example, illustrates how Excel would store spreadsheet values using the .csv format.

As you can see, the .csv file format stores only values and no formatting information. Further, if an Excel document contains multiple worksheets, you must save each individually within their own .csv file. The advantage of using .csv files is that most data-mining applications can read them. Using Excel, you can open a .csv file or save a spreadsheet using the .csv file format. Throughout this text, you will make extensive use of .csv files.

### Open Document Specification Files

With the advent of cloud-based Google Docs, users often save spreadsheets using the Open Document Specification (.ods) file format. Excel can both open and save .ods files. **FIGURE 5.18** illustrates the same .ods file within Excel and Google Docs.

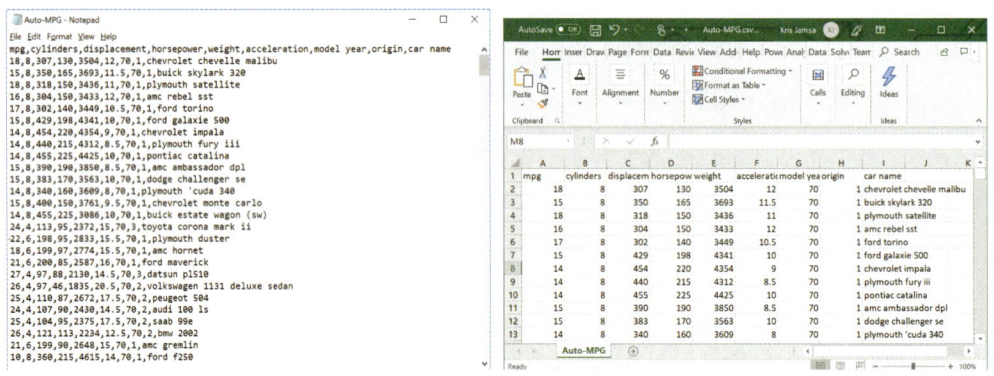

**FIGURE 5.17** Storing data using a .csv file.

Used with permission from Microsoft

# Understanding File Formats

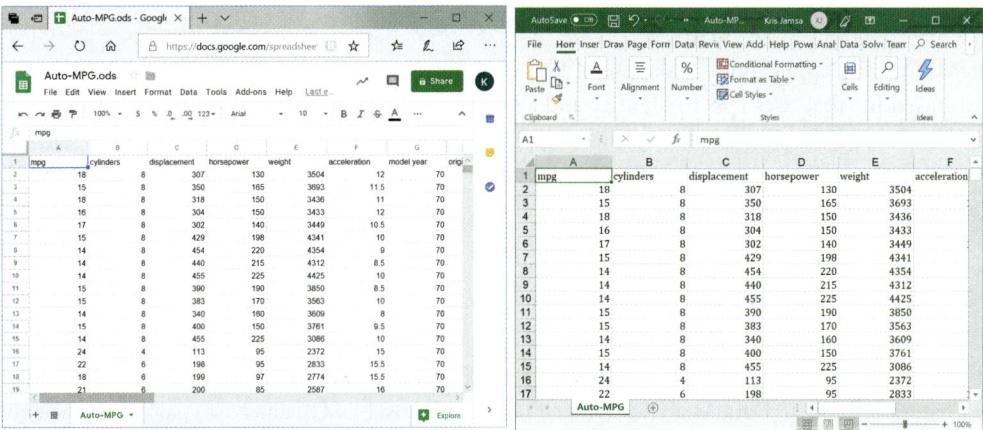

**FIGURE 5.18** Using an .ods file to exchange documents between Excel and Google Docs.
Used with permission from Microsoft

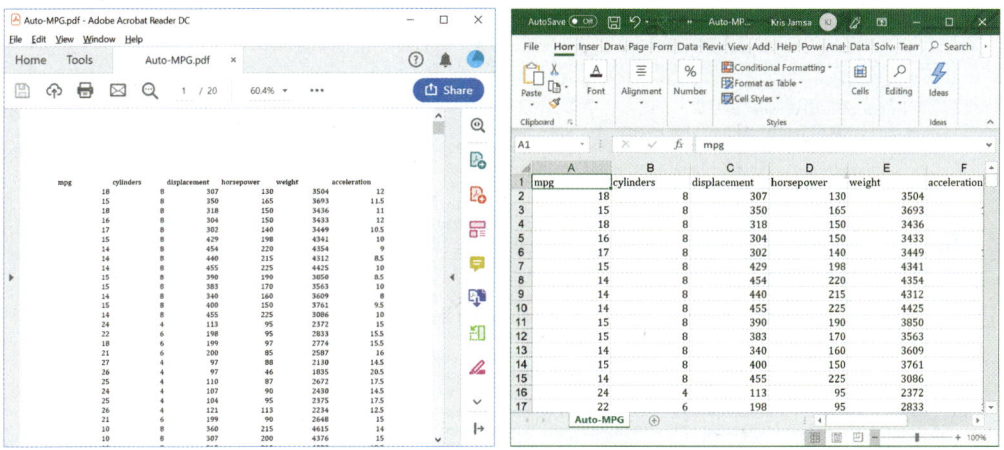

**FIGURE 5.19** A spreadsheet document within Excel and as a .pdf file.
Used with permission from Microsoft

## Portable Document Format Files

Often, Excel users want to provide other users with a "final" uneditable version of a worksheet, suitable for referencing or printing. In such cases, the user can save his or her worksheet as a Portable Document Format (.pdf). Files in .pdf format are ideal for exchange via email. **FIGURE 5.19** illustrates a spreadsheet within Excel and as a .pdf file. As you can see, the .pdf file maintains all formatting and can include graphics.

## Extensible Markup Language Files

Across the web, applications make use of files stored in XML to exchange data. An XML file is a text-based file that uses tags to identify and group data. **FIGURE 5.20** illustrates the contents of the file Auto-MPG.xml, which uses tags to group automotive data.

Because of widespread use of XML to exchange data, Excel can open and save files in XML format. **FIGURE 5.21** illustrates how Excel will display the XML sales data previously shown.

## JavaScript Object Notation Files

To exchange data, most web applications use either XML or JSON. The JSON file format uses object-grouping symbols from the JavaScript programming language to describe objects (things). In Chapter 7, "NoSQL Data Analytics," you will find that most NoSQL databases (such as the widely used MongoDB) make extensive use of JSON to store data.

Should you need to open an existing JSON file, you can perform these steps:

1. Select the Data tab GetData button and choose the From File option. Excel will display a menu of options that include JSON, as shown in **FIGURE 5.22**.
2. Within the menu, select the JSON option. Excel will display a dialog box prompting you for the JSON file.

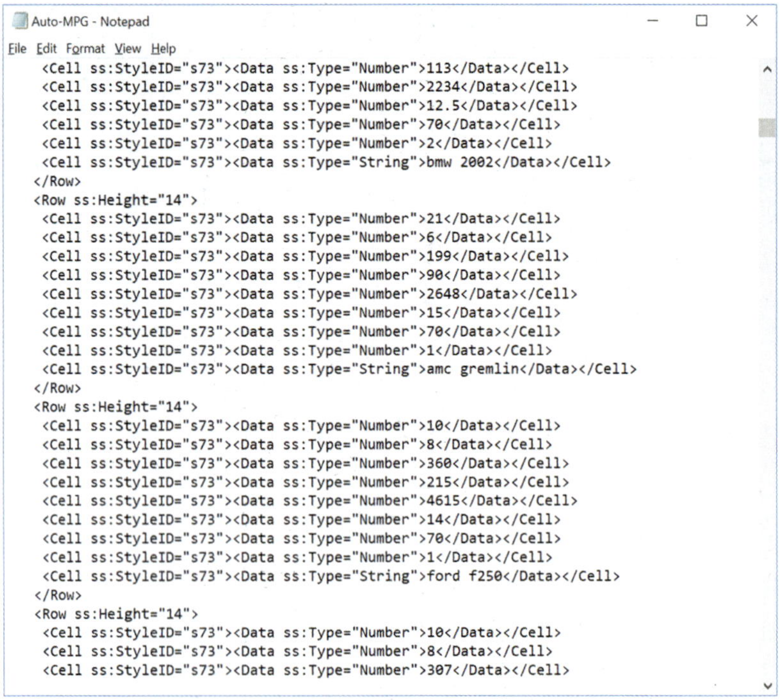


```
 <Cell ss:StyleID="s73"><Data ss:Type="Number">113</Data></Cell>
 <Cell ss:StyleID="s73"><Data ss:Type="Number">2234</Data></Cell>
 <Cell ss:StyleID="s73"><Data ss:Type="Number">12.5</Data></Cell>
 <Cell ss:StyleID="s73"><Data ss:Type="Number">70</Data></Cell>
 <Cell ss:StyleID="s73"><Data ss:Type="Number">2</Data></Cell>
 <Cell ss:StyleID="s73"><Data ss:Type="String">bmw 2002</Data></Cell>
</Row>
<Row ss:Height="14">
 <Cell ss:StyleID="s73"><Data ss:Type="Number">21</Data></Cell>
 <Cell ss:StyleID="s73"><Data ss:Type="Number">6</Data></Cell>
 <Cell ss:StyleID="s73"><Data ss:Type="Number">199</Data></Cell>
 <Cell ss:StyleID="s73"><Data ss:Type="Number">90</Data></Cell>
 <Cell ss:StyleID="s73"><Data ss:Type="Number">2648</Data></Cell>
 <Cell ss:StyleID="s73"><Data ss:Type="Number">15</Data></Cell>
 <Cell ss:StyleID="s73"><Data ss:Type="Number">70</Data></Cell>
 <Cell ss:StyleID="s73"><Data ss:Type="Number">1</Data></Cell>
 <Cell ss:StyleID="s73"><Data ss:Type="String">amc gremlin</Data></Cell>
</Row>
<Row ss:Height="14">
 <Cell ss:StyleID="s73"><Data ss:Type="Number">10</Data></Cell>
 <Cell ss:StyleID="s73"><Data ss:Type="Number">8</Data></Cell>
 <Cell ss:StyleID="s73"><Data ss:Type="Number">360</Data></Cell>
 <Cell ss:StyleID="s73"><Data ss:Type="Number">215</Data></Cell>
 <Cell ss:StyleID="s73"><Data ss:Type="Number">4615</Data></Cell>
 <Cell ss:StyleID="s73"><Data ss:Type="Number">14</Data></Cell>
 <Cell ss:StyleID="s73"><Data ss:Type="Number">70</Data></Cell>
 <Cell ss:StyleID="s73"><Data ss:Type="Number">1</Data></Cell>
 <Cell ss:StyleID="s73"><Data ss:Type="String">ford f250</Data></Cell>
</Row>
<Row ss:Height="14">
 <Cell ss:StyleID="s73"><Data ss:Type="Number">10</Data></Cell>
 <Cell ss:StyleID="s73"><Data ss:Type="Number">8</Data></Cell>
 <Cell ss:StyleID="s73"><Data ss:Type="Number">307</Data></Cell>
```

**FIGURE 5.20** **An XML file grouping automotive data.**

Used with permission from Microsoft

Understanding File Formats 173

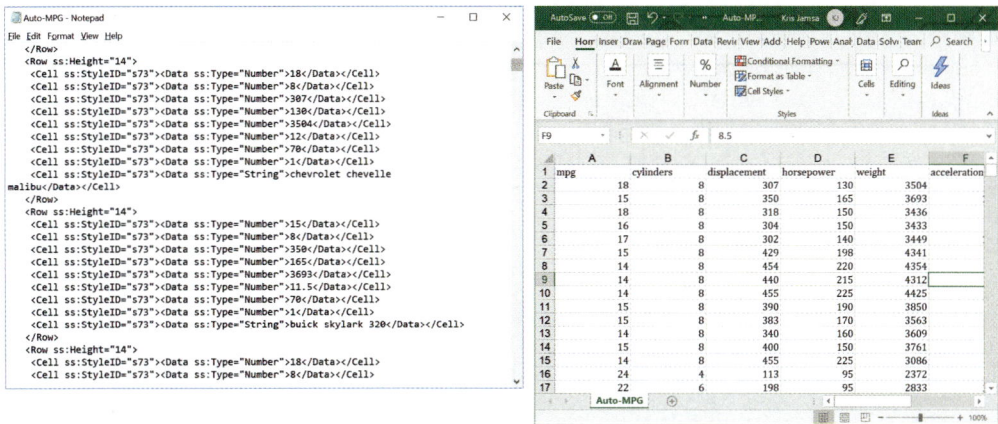

**FIGURE 5.21** Opening an XML file with Excel.

Used with permission from Microsoft

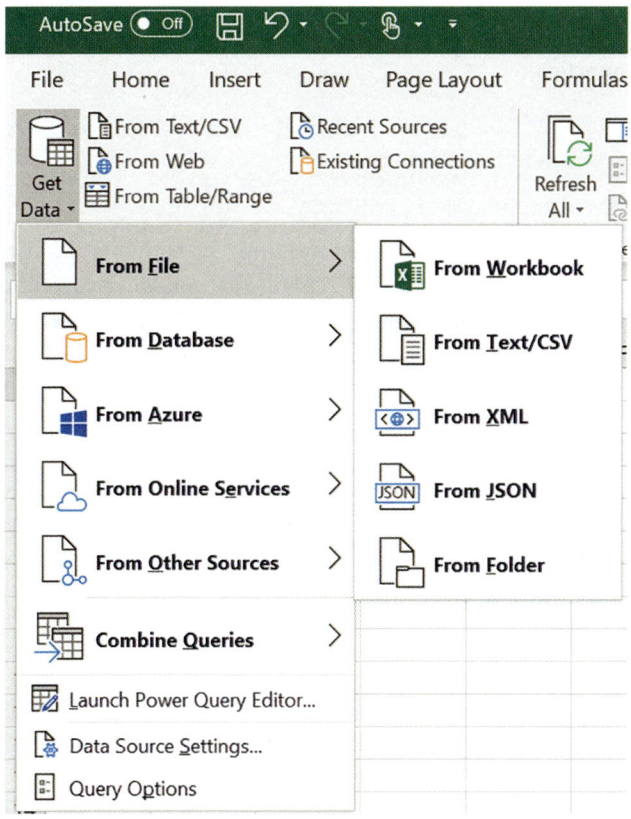

**FIGURE 5.22** Importing a JSON file within Excel.

Used with permission from Microsoft

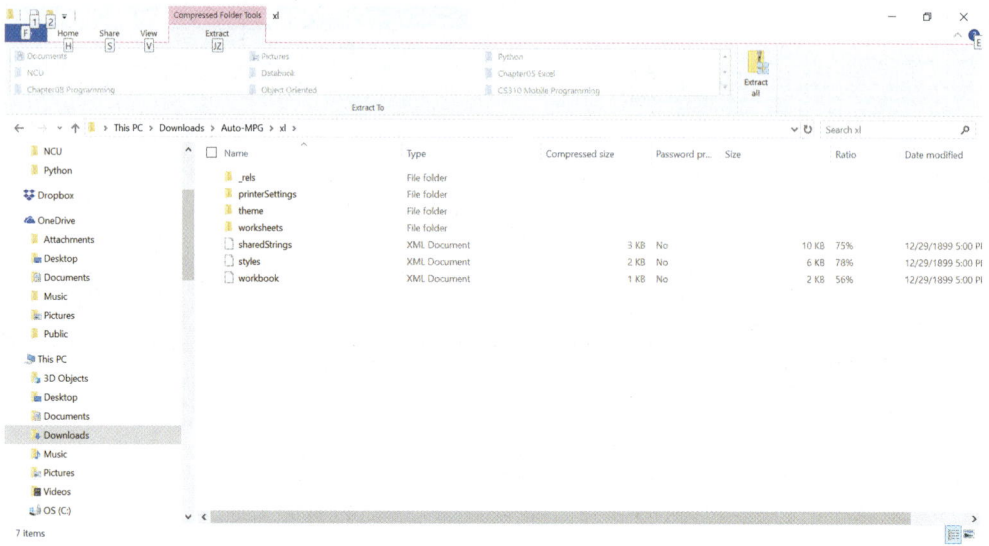

**FIGURE 5.23** An Excel .xlsx file actually zips (compresses) XML files to store spreadsheet data and their properties.

Used with permission from Microsoft

## Excel Files

By default, Excel stores a spreadsheet document within a file with the .xlsx file extension. It turns out that the .xlsx file is actually a compressed (Zip) file that contains many different .xml files that describe the spreadsheet's data values and properties. In fact, if you rename an .xlsx file to .zip, you can view the XML files that describe the spreadsheet, as shown in **FIGURE 5.23**.

## Leveraging Excel Statistical Functions

As discussed, Excel is the most widely used data analysis tool. To that end, Excel provides a collection of built-in functions you can use to perform common (and key) data analysis operations. This section examines many of these functions. You should take the time to try the functions this chapter presents. Using these functions you can quickly:

- Identify duplicate data
- Identify data outliers
- Determine the level of variance between data values
- Determine the correlation measure between two variables
- And more

## Determining the Arithmetic Mean with AVERAGE

To analyze data, analysts will normally use the average value, or mean, in some way. The AVERAGE function returns the **arithmetic mean**:

$$\text{Average} = \frac{\sum_{i=1}^{n} x_i}{n}$$

When you use AVERAGE within a large spreadsheet that may have missing values, AVERAGE will ignore empty cells. **FIGURE 5.24** illustrates the use of the AVERAGE function.

---

### Connecting to a Database

Normally, analysts will open a data set as a .csv file using Excel to explore the data-set values. Depending on the database you are using, you may be able to connect Excel directly to the database by performing these steps:

1. Select the Data tab and click on Get Data. Excel will display a menu of data sources.
2. Select the From Database option. Excel will display a submenu of available databases.
3. From within the list, select the appropriate database type.
4. Excel will display a dialog box that lets you connect to the database you desire.

---

## Determining the Arithmetic Mean for Mixed Data Using AVERAGEA

The AVERAGE function returns the arithmetic mean for numeric data, ignoring empty cells. Depending on the values you must evaluate, there may be times when you want to include the empty cells (included as zero) or cells that contain text, such as True or False. The AVERAGEA function performs such calculations using the following rules:

- Empty cells are 0
- Cells that contain text are 0
- Cells that contain True are 1
- Cells that contain False are 0

**FIGURE 5.25** illustrates the use of the AVERAGEA function.

# CHAPTER 5 Keep Excel in Your Toolset

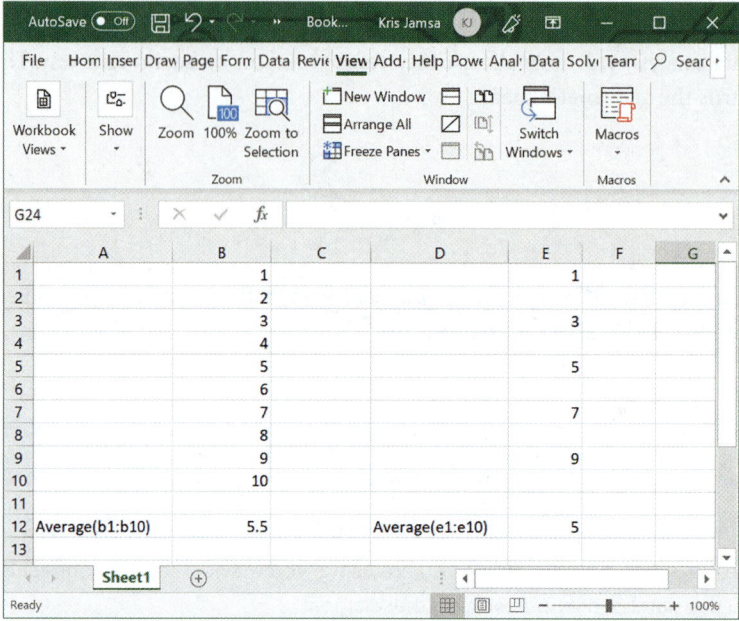

**FIGURE 5.24** Using AVERAGE to calculate the arithmetic mean.

Used with permission from Microsoft

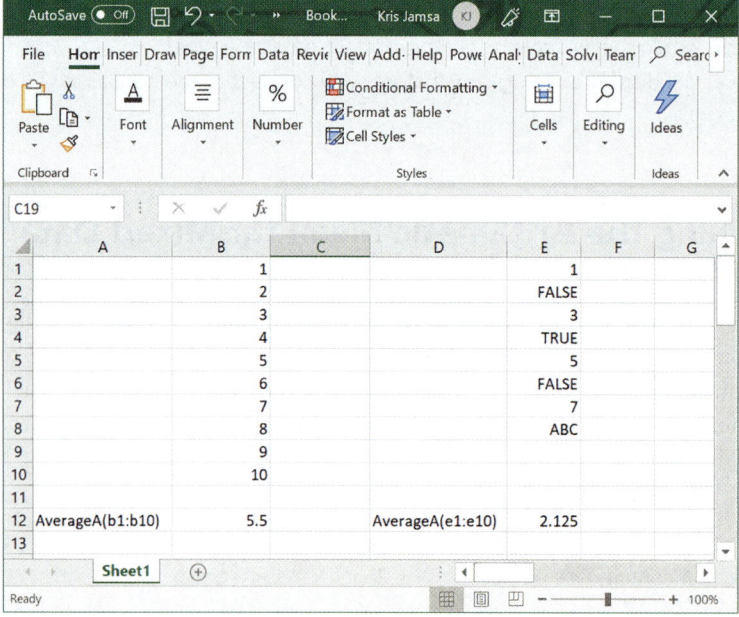

**FIGURE 5.25** Calculating the arithmetic mean for mixed data using AVERAGEA.

Used with permission from Microsoft

## Determining the Arithmetic Mean for Values Meeting a Specific Condition Using AVERAGEIF and AVERAGEIFS

Often, as you analyze data, you will perform operations based on different conditions. For example, assume you have a spreadsheet that contains monthly sales data. Assume you want to know the average by which sales members exceeded their quota or the average price for products that sold in September. The AVERAGEIF function provides the average for values that meet a specific condition. The format of the AVERAGEIF function is:

```
AVERAGEIF(range, "condition"[,second_range])
```

The AVERAGEIF function will calculate the average of the values that satisfy the specified condition. The condition, which you specify in quotes, takes the form "<5" for values less than 5 and ">=0" for values greater than or equal to zero. If the second range parameter is specified, Excel will perform the condition against values in the first range and compute the average using values in the second range.

**FIGURE 5.26** illustrates the use of the AVERAGEIF.

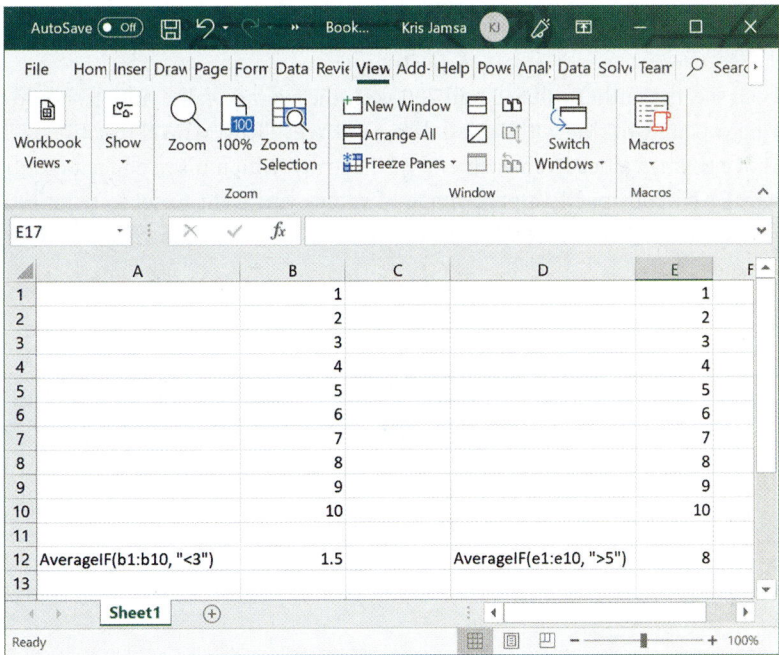

**FIGURE 5.26** Using the AVERAGEIF function to calculate the average of values that satisfy a condition.

Used with permission from Microsoft

The AVERAGEIFS function is similar, but it lets you specify more criteria:

```
AVERAGEIFS(range_to_average, range1, condition1[, range2, condition2])
```

The following formula, for example, would calculate the average value in a1:a10 for which the corresponding values are greater than 0 and less than 5:

```
AVERAGEIFS(A1:A10,A1:A10, ">0", A1:A10, "<5")
```

## Eliminating the Impact of Outliers on the Mean Using TRIMMEAN

One of the first tasks a data analyst performs when he or she receives a new data set is to cleanse the data of outlier values (which, if not deleted, will skew the results of most data-mining solutions). Chapter 9, "Data Cleansing," explains this in more detail. In a similar way, a problem with the arithmetic mean is that outliers can significantly affect the value. Consider, for example, the following test scores:

```
1, 33, 33, 33, 34, 32, 34, 200
Average = 50
```

As you can see, the outlier values 1 and 200 skew the average value, which should be near 33.

Assuming you are working with sorted data, the Excel TRIMMEAN function lets you direct Excel to remove (trim) values from each end of the array, which may reduce potential outliers. Using TRIMMEAN, you specify a percentage of values you want Excel to trim. **FIGURE 5.27** illustrates the use of TRIMMEAN. You do not need to first sort the values—Excel will do so behind the scenes.

### Using SUM, SUMIF, and SUMIFS

As you perform data analysis, there may also be times when you need to sum data. Excel provides the SUM function, which returns the sum of a range of values, as well as SUMIF and SUMIFS, similar to AVERAGEIF and AVERAGEIFS, that let you sum only the values that satisfy a specified condition. The following formula, for example, would sum only those values that are greater than 100:

```
SUMIF(a1:a10, ">100")
```

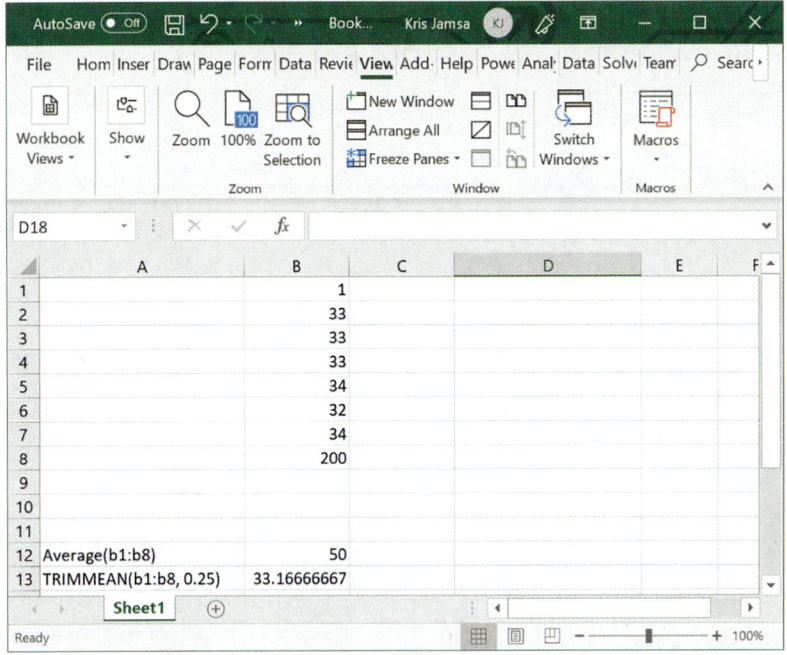

**FIGURE 5.27** Reducing the impact of outliers on the mean using TRIMMEAN.

Used with permission from Microsoft

## Calculating the Geometric Mean with GEOMEAN and the Harmonic Mean with HARMEAN

If you ask most people to calculate the mean (average) value of the numbers 1, 2, 3, 4, and 5, they will quickly calculate the result: 3.

$$\begin{array}{c} 1 \\ 2 \\ \boxed{3} \longleftarrow \text{Mean} \\ 4 \\ 5 \end{array}$$

In statistics, however, there is more than one mean value. The arithmetic mean provides one way to calculate the mean, but there is also the **geometric mean** and the **harmonic mean**. Each type of mean is straightforward to calculate. The challenge is in knowing when to use each. **TABLE 5.1** briefly describes the mean types.

## TABLE 5.1 Summary of Arithmetic, Geometric, and Harmonic Means

| Mean Type | Calculation | Uses |
|---|---|---|
| Arithmetic | $$\text{Average} = \frac{\sum_{i=1}^{n} x_i}{n}$$ | Most often used. Appropriate for positive and negative numbers when the sum of the values is meaningful. Example: Test scores |
| Geometric | $$\text{Geometric Mean} = \sqrt[n]{x_1 x_2 x_3 \ldots x_n}$$ | Only positive numbers for which the product of values is meaningful. Example: Compound interest rates |
| Harmonic | $$\text{Harmonic Mean} = \frac{n}{(1/x_1 + 1/x_2 + 1/x_3 \ldots 1/x_n)}$$ | Good to reduce the impact of outlier values. Only for positive values. Example: Average driving speed for a trip |

Within Excel, you use GEOMEAN to calculate the geometric mean. Likewise, the HARMONIC mean function returns the harmonic mean. **FIGURE 5.28** illustrates the use of each function.

## Determining the Median Value Using MEDIAN

The **median** value for a list of data provides the middle value of the sorted list values:

$$
\begin{array}{l}
2 \\
4 \\
\boxed{6} \longleftarrow \text{Median} \\
8 \\
10
\end{array}
$$

The Excel MEDIAN function returns the median value for a list. You do not need to sort the list to use MEDIAN. Instead, the function will do so behind the scenes, leaving your list unchanged. **FIGURE 5.29** illustrates the use of the MEDIAN function.

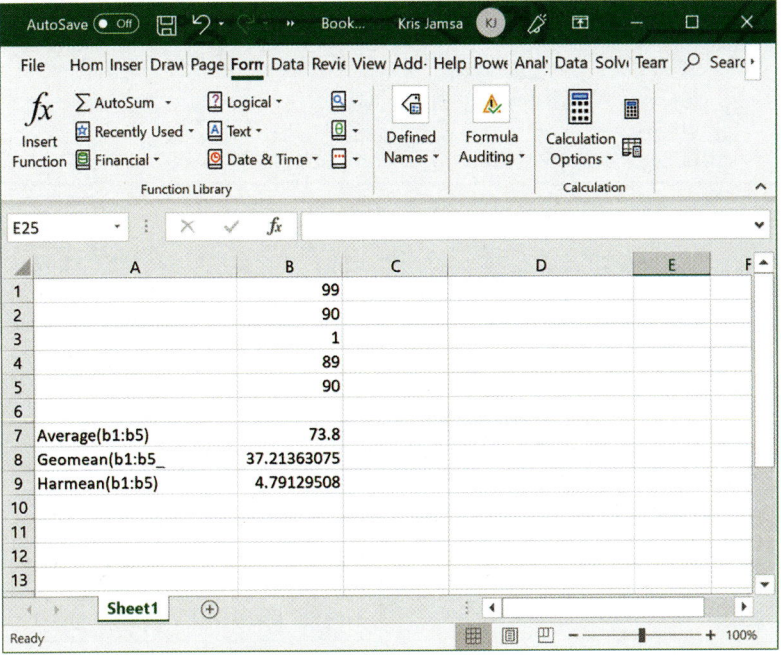

**FIGURE 5.28** Using the Excel mean functions.

Used with permission from Microsoft

# Determining the Maximum and Minimum Values Using MAX and MIN

Often, as you work with a data set, you will want to know the data set's maximum and minimum values, possibly to determine potential outliers. To calculate the maximum and minimum value, you use the MAX and MIN functions. In addition, Excel provides the following related functions:

MINA and MAXA perform their calculations using:

- Empty cells are 0
- Cells that contain text are 0
- Cells that contain True are 1
- Cells that contain False are 0

MINIFS and MAXIFS return the minimum and maximum values that satisfy a given condition. **FIGURE 5.30** illustrates the use of the MAX and MIN functions.

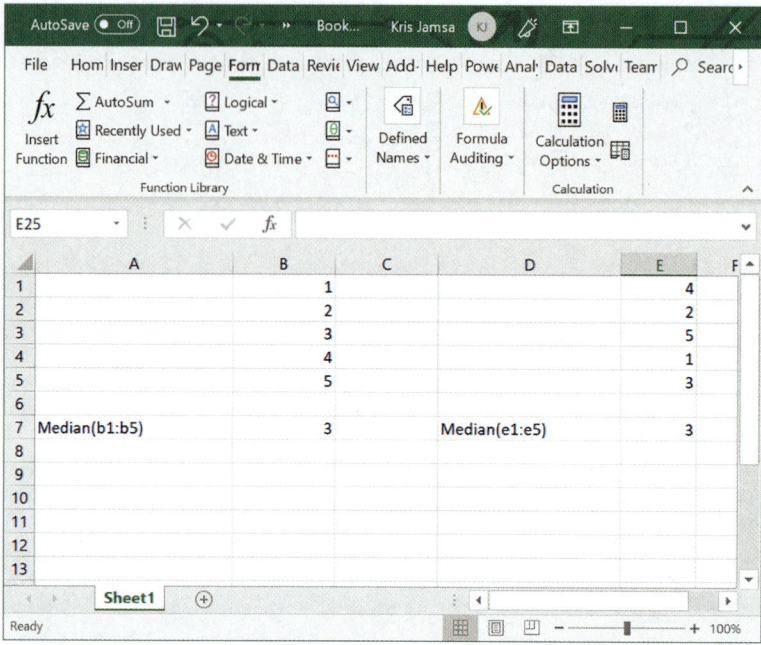

**FIGURE 5.29** Calculating the median value of data lists.

Used with permission from Microsoft

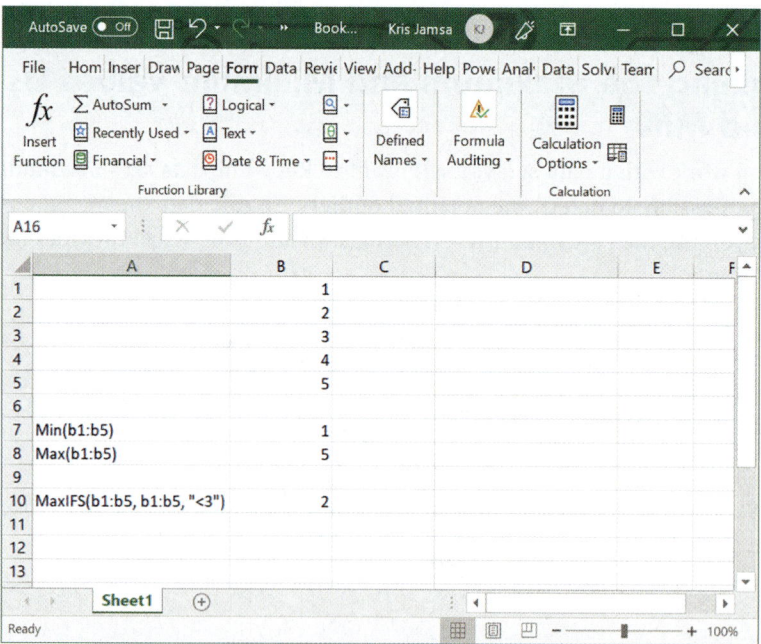

**FIGURE 5.30** Calculating minimum and maximum data-set values.

Used with permission from Microsoft

## Determining the Quartile Values Using QUARTILE

A **quartile** is a number in a sorted list that identifies 25% of the data. The first quartile is the bottom 25%. The second quartile (also the median) identifies the 50% mark. The third quartile identifies 75% of the data and the fourth, 100%.

To calculate the quartile values using Excel, you use the QUARTILE function. Excel provides two forms of the function, the formats of which are:

```
QUARTILE.EXC(range, quartile_desired)
```
or
```
QUARTILE.INC(range, quartile_desired)
```

The quartile desired parameter is an integer value that specifies the desired result:

- 0 minimum data-set value
- 1 first quartile (25th percentile)
- 2 median value (50th percentile)
- 3 third quartile (75th percentile)
- 4 maximum data-set value

When determining the quartile, there are two approaches to dealing with the percentage. The first includes values that are greater than or equal to the percentage (quartile.inc), and the second includes only values that are greater than the percentage (quartile.exc).

**FIGURE 5.31** illustrates the use of the QUARTILE function.

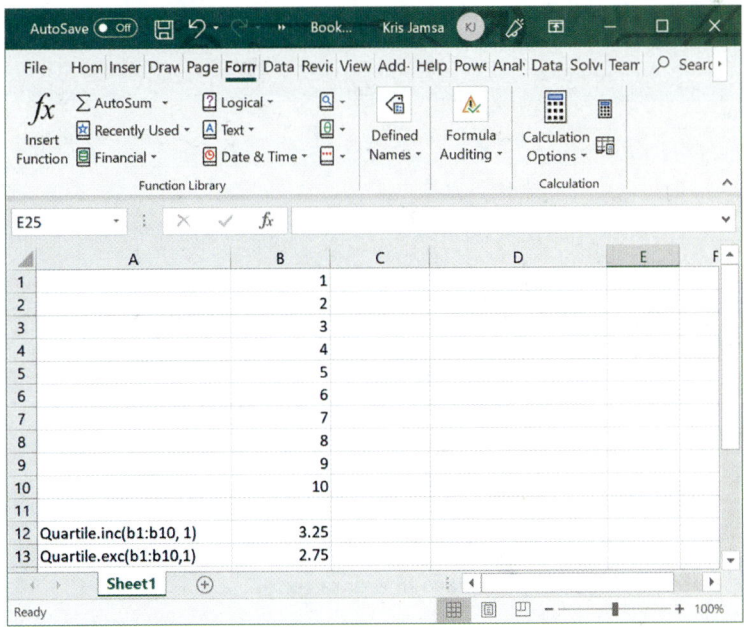

**FIGURE 5.31** Calculating quartile values.

Used with permission from Microsoft

## Determining the *n*th Largest and Smallest Value in a Data Set Using LARGE and SMALL

The Excel MAX and MIN functions return the largest and smallest values in a data range. There may be times when you need to know the second largest (or smallest) value, or the third, fourth, and so on—possibly to identify outliers. To do so, you use the LARGE and SMALL functions:

```
LARGE(range, n)
SMALL(range, n)
```

where *n* specifies the second, third, and fourth value desired, and so on. **FIGURE 5.32** illustrates each function's use.

## Counting the Number of Cells Using COUNT

As you analyze data, there will be many times when you must know the number of cells in a range of values that contain numbers. The COUNT function returns such a count. COUNT will ignore empty cells and cells that contain text but will count quoted numbers such as "777."

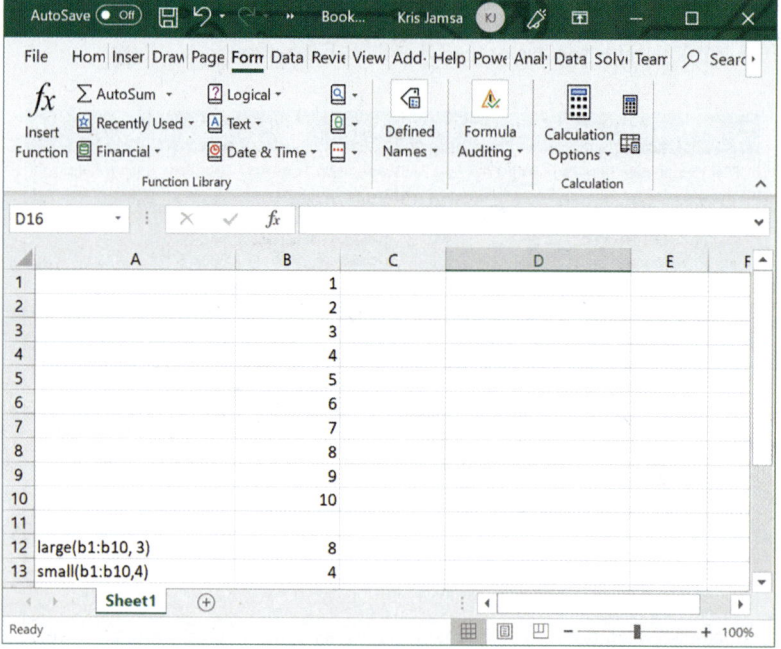

**FIGURE 5.32** Determining specific values in a data range.
Used with permission from Microsoft

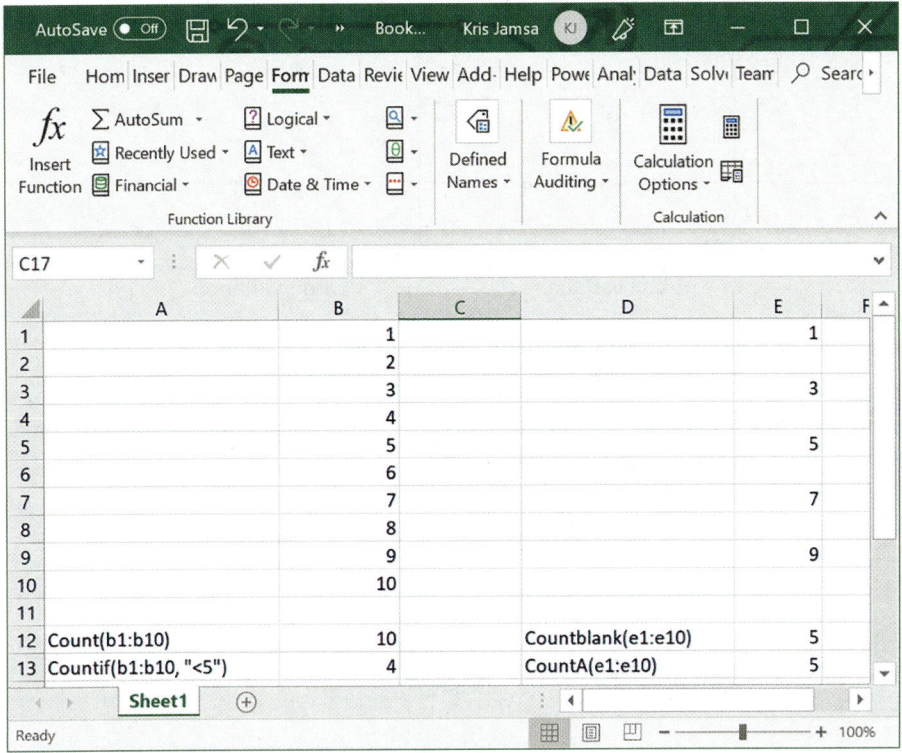

**FIGURE 5.33** Counting cells within an Excel spreadsheet.

Used with permission from Microsoft

To count all nonempty cells, you can use COUNTA, and to count empty cells (a common operation to determine data quality), you use COUNTBLANK. Finally, to count the number of cells that meet a specific condition, you can use the COUNTIF and COUNTIFS functions. **FIGURE 5.33** illustrates the use of the COUNT functions.

Using the COUNT function with a large data set, you may be able to identify missing values.

## Calculating by How Much Data-Set Values Differ from Their Mean Using VAR and STDEV

As you analyze data, one of your first insights into a data set is to determine how close (or far) the data values vary from the mean. **FIGURE 5.34**, for example, illustrates two data sets with the same mean. The first data-set values have a small **variance**, while the variance of the second set is much greater.

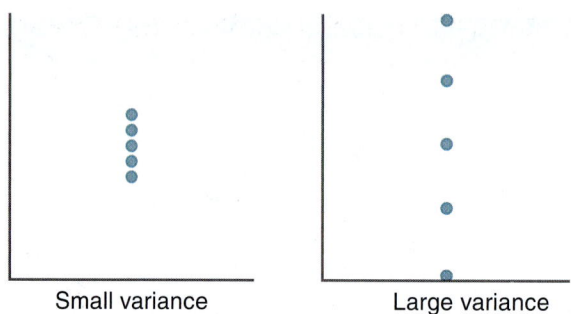

**FIGURE 5.34** Two data sets with the same mean but very different variances.

To measure the distance between values and the mean, you can use the **standard deviation** or variance, which are defined as follows:

$$\text{Standard Deviation} = \sqrt{\frac{1}{n}\sum_{i=1}^{n}(x_i - \bar{x})^2}$$

$$\text{Variance} = \frac{\sum_{i=1}^{n}(x_i - \bar{x})^2}{n}$$

As discussed, to determine how closely data-set values align with the data-set mean, you can use either the standard deviation or variance. Analysts will often use the standard deviation because it is expressed in the same units as the data-set values, whereas the variance is expressed in the units squared. For example, if you are comparing student heights in inches, the standard deviation would be in inches and the variance in inches squared. Excel provides several functions, as listed in **TABLE 5.2**, to calculate the variance.

| TABLE 5.2 Calculate the Variance of Values in a Data Set | |
|---|---|
| **Function** | **Notes** |
| VAR.P | Population |
| VAR.S | Sample (normally n – 1) |
| VARA | Treats True as 1, False as 0, and text as 0 for sample |
| VARPA | Treats True as 1, False as 0, and text as 0 for population |

Likewise, as listed in **TABLE 5.3**, Excel provides a similar set of functions to calculate the standard deviation.

**FIGURE 5.35** illustrates the use of Excel functions to calculate the standard deviation and variance.

**TABLE 5.3** Excel Functions to Calculate the Standard Deviation of Values in a Data Set

| Function | Notes |
| --- | --- |
| STDEV.P | Population |
| STDEV.S | Sample (normally n − 1) |
| STDEVA | Treats True as 1, False as 0, and text as 0 for sample |
| STDEVPA | Treats True as 1, False as 0, and text as 0 for population |

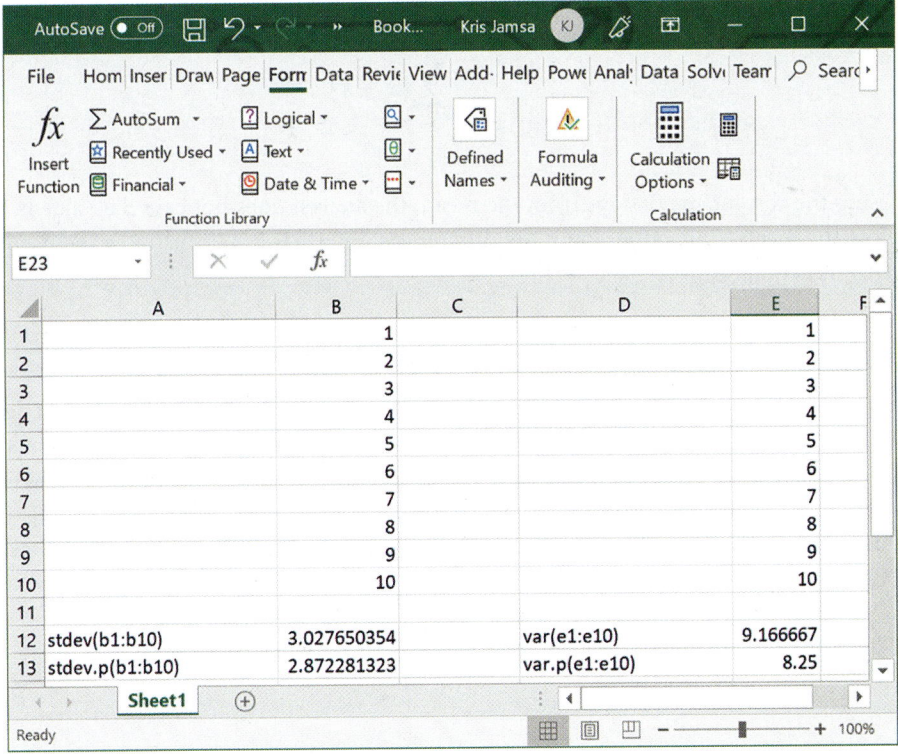

**FIGURE 5.35** Using Excel functions to calculate the standard deviation and variance of data-set values.

Used with permission from Microsoft

## Determining the Sum of Squared Deviations Using DEVSQ

You have learned that data analysts use variance and standard deviation to measure by how much data-set values differ from their mean. In a similar way, the DEVSQ function returns the sum of squared deviations:

$$\text{Dev SQ} = \sum_{i=1}^{n} (x_i - \bar{x})^2$$

**FIGURE 5.36** illustrates the DEVSQ function's use.

## Determining Variability Using AVEDEV

One way an analyst understands a data set is to examine how values differ from the average (mean) value. The data within a data set with low variation from the mean will be more tightly grouped than a data set with high variability. The AVEDEV function returns the average of the absolute deviations of values from the mean:

$$\text{AVEDEV} = \frac{\sum_{i=1}^{n}(x_i - \bar{x})^2}{n}$$

Using the absolute deviations from the mean, the analyst does not care if a value is above or below the mean—but rather, only the differences. **FIGURE 5.37** illustrates the use of the AVEDEV function.

## Determining the Correlation Coefficient Using CORREL

As they perform data-mining operations, analysts often examine how variables within a data set are related. You might, for example, determine how rainfall relates to automobile accidents or to employees being late to work. **Correlation** is a statistical measure of the relationship between two variables. Variables with a correlation approaching 1 have strong correlation—meaning as one variable's value increases or decreases, so, too, will the other's. Variables with a correlation value of −1 are inversely correlated—as one variable's value increases, the other's will decrease and vice versa. Variables with a correlation value approaching zero have no relationship.

The CORREL function returns the correlation coefficient for two variables:

```
CORREL(range1, range2)
```

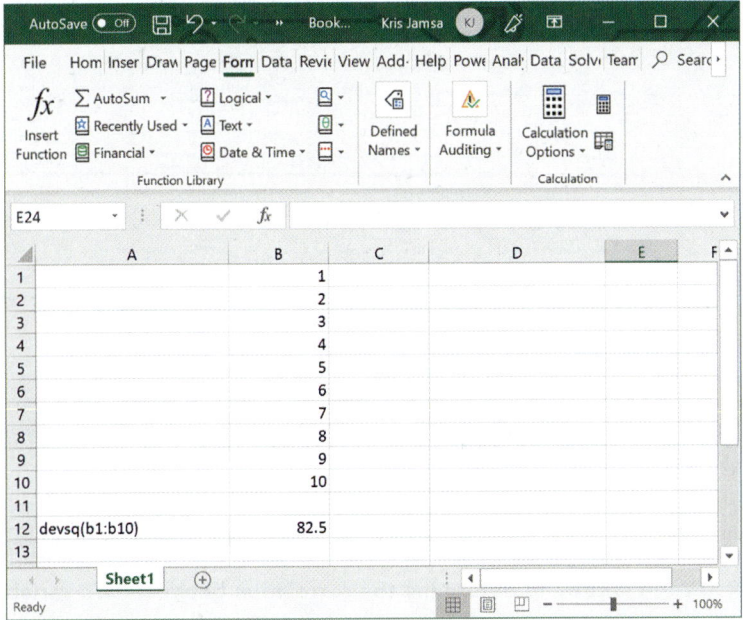

**FIGURE 5.36** Using the DEVSQ function.

Used with permission from Microsoft

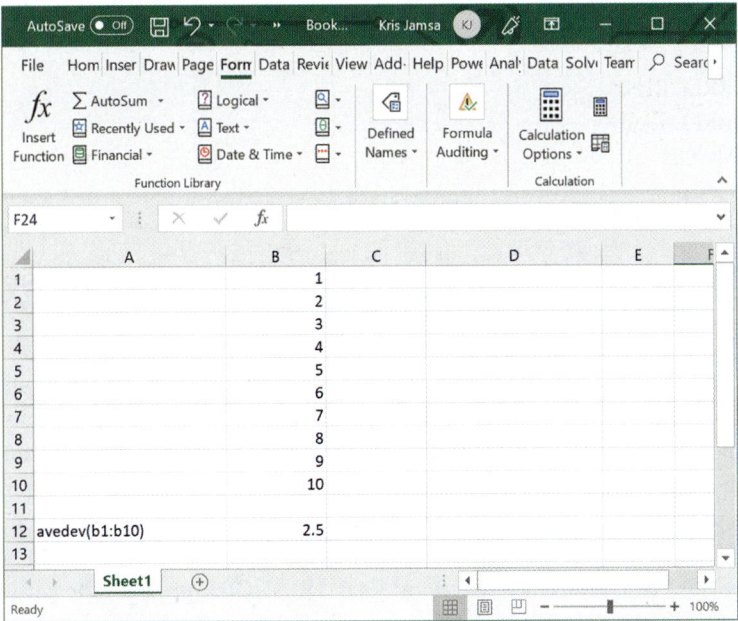

**FIGURE 5.37** Using AVEDEV to determine the average deviation.

Used with permission from Microsoft

# CHAPTER 5 Keep Excel in Your Toolset

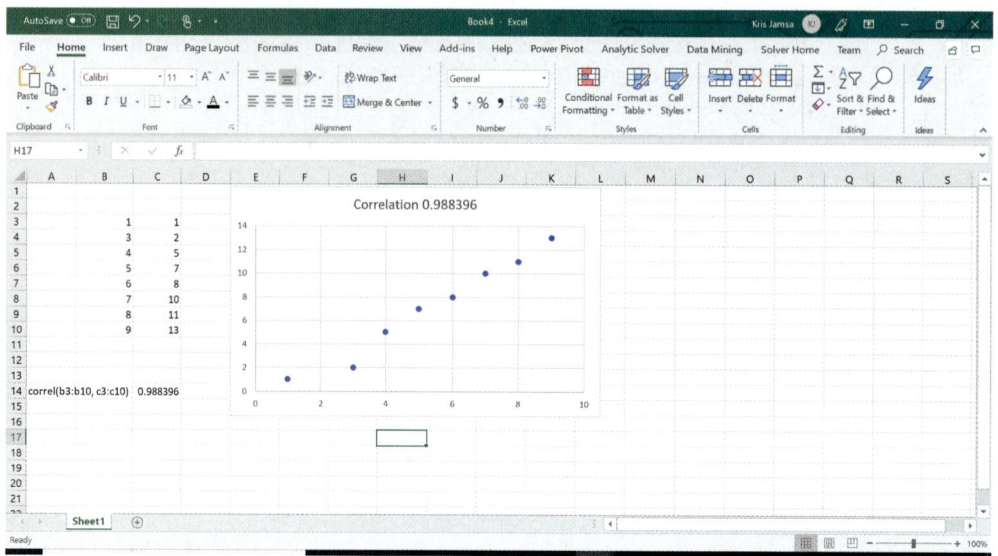

**FIGURE 5.38** Using CORREL to determine the correlation between two variables.

Used with permission from Microsoft

**FIGURE 5.38** illustrates the use of the CORREL function.

In addition to CORREL, Excel provides more functions that calculate the correlation using different underlying algorithms:

- CORREL.RHO
- CORREL.TAO
- PEARSON

**FIGURE 5.39** illustrates the use of these functions.

## Determining the Covariance Using COVARIANCE.S and COVARIANCE.P

As you have learned, variance provides a measure of how much data-set values differ from the mean. **Covariance** is a similar measure, but it examines two variables to determine if there is a relationship between the greater values of one variable and the greater or lesser values of another variable. If the large values of one variable align with the large values of a second variable, the covariance is positive. If, instead, the large values of one variable align with the small values of the other variable, the covariance is negative.

Excel provides two covariance functions. COVARIANCE.P provides the covariance for the entire population, and COVARIANCE.S for a sample (often $n - 1$):

# Leveraging Excel Statistical Functions

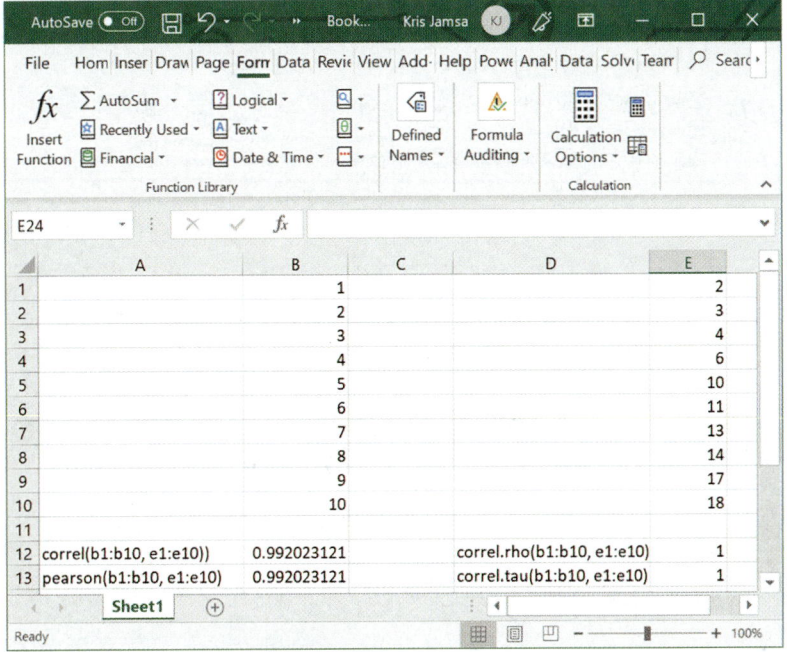

**FIGURE 5.39** Using additional Excel correlation functions.

Used with permission from Microsoft

```
COVARIANCE.P(range1, range2)
```
or
```
COVARIANCE.S(range1, range2)
```

**FIGURE 5.40** illustrates the use of the covariance functions.

## Determining the Slope and Intercept of a Line That Represents a Data Set Using SLOPE and INTERCEPT

Linear regression provides an equation for a line in the form $y = mx + b$ for a given $x$ and $y$, for which $m$ specifies the slope and $b$ the $y$-intercept, as shown in **FIGURE 5.41**. (Chapter 12, "Predictive Analytics," examines linear regression in detail.)

To determine the line's slope and intercept, you use the SLOPE and INTERCEPT functions:

```
SLOPE(y_values, x_values)
INTERCEPT(y_values, x_values)
```

**FIGURE 5.42** illustrates each function's use.

**192** **CHAPTER 5** Keep Excel in Your Toolset

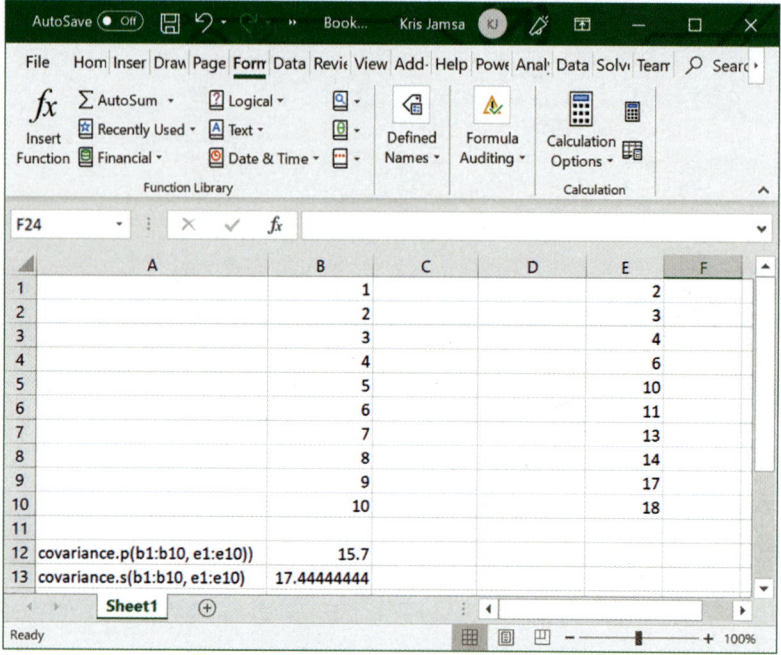

**FIGURE 5.40** Calculating the covariance of a sample and population.

Used with permission from Microsoft

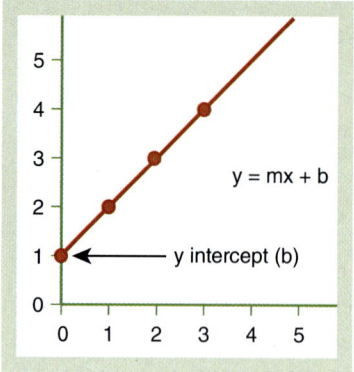

**FIGURE 5.41** Calculating the slope and intercept of a line representing a data set.

Leveraging Excel Statistical Functions

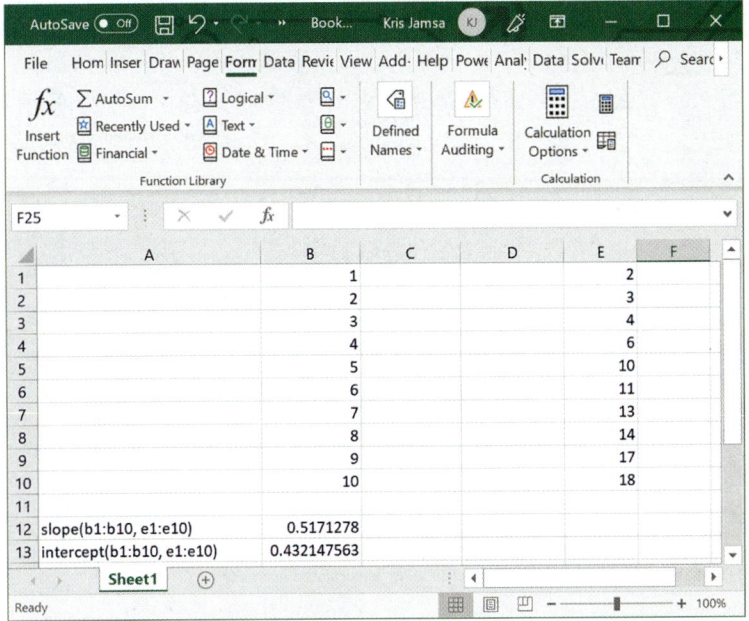

**FIGURE 5.42** Calculating the slope and intercept of a line that represents a data set.
Used with permission from Microsoft

## Determining an Equation for a Line Using LINEST

There are many ways to map a line to a data set. The LINEST function calculates an equation for a line that represents data set values using a least-squares algorithm. For a simple $x$ and $y$ data set, the equation will be in the form $y = mx + b$. The form of the LINEST function is:

    LINEST(y_values, x_values, [constant], [statistics])

where y_values is a set of $y$ values and x_values is the set of $x$ values. The optional constant parameter, when True, directs LINEST to calculate $b$ (the $y$-intercept) and, when False, forces $b$ to zero. The statistics parameter, when True, directs LINEST to return error values and other statistics. **FIGURE 5.43** illustrates the use of LINEST.

## Determining the Equation for a Curve Using LOGEST

Not all data are linear. The Excel LOGEST function calculates an exponential curve that best represents data. For simple data, LOGEST will return an equation in the form $y = mb^\wedge x$. The form of the LOGEST function is:

    LOGEST(y_values, x_values, [constant], [statistics])

## CHAPTER 5 Keep Excel in Your Toolset

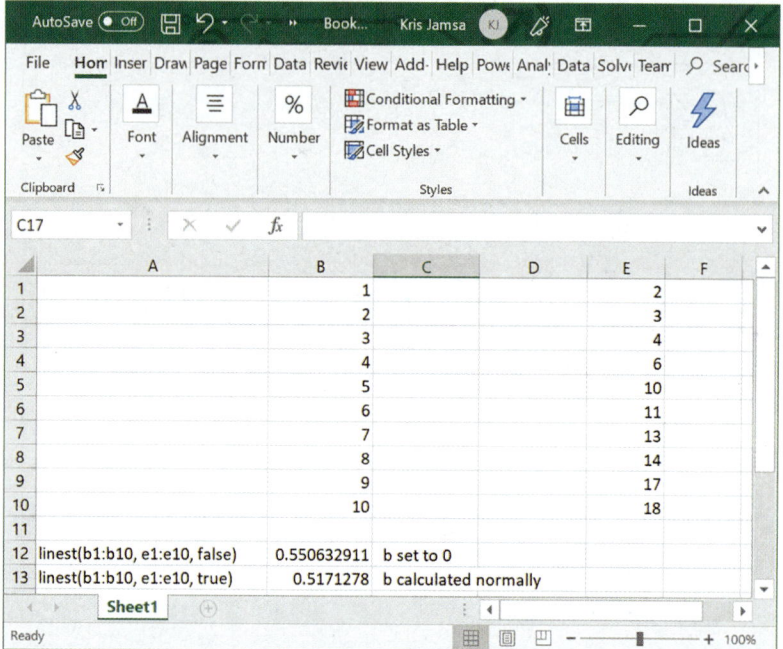

**FIGURE 5.43** Using LINEST to determine the equation of lines that map to data-set values.
Used with permission from Microsoft

where y_values is a set of *y* values and x_values is the set of *x* values. The optional constant parameter, when True, directs LOGEST to calculate *b* (the *y*-intercept) and, when False, forces *b* to 1. The statistics parameter, when True, directs LOGEST to return error values and other statistics. **FIGURE 5.44** illustrates the use of LOGEST.

## Determining Frequency Counts for Data-Set Values Using FREQUENCY

As you mine data, there will be times when you want to know the count (frequency) of values within a data set or possibly the values that occur most often. In Chapter 4, "Data Visualization," you used a histogram to visually represent such counts, as shown in **FIGURE 5.45**.

In a similar way, the Excel FREQUENCY function returns the frequency of data-set value occurrences:

```
FREQUENCY(range, binValue)
```

where binValue specifies a value under which you want to gather and count data values. For example, a binValue of 50 would count the number of values less than 50.

**FIGURE 5.46** illustrates the FREQUENCY function's use.

Leveraging Excel Statistical Functions   195

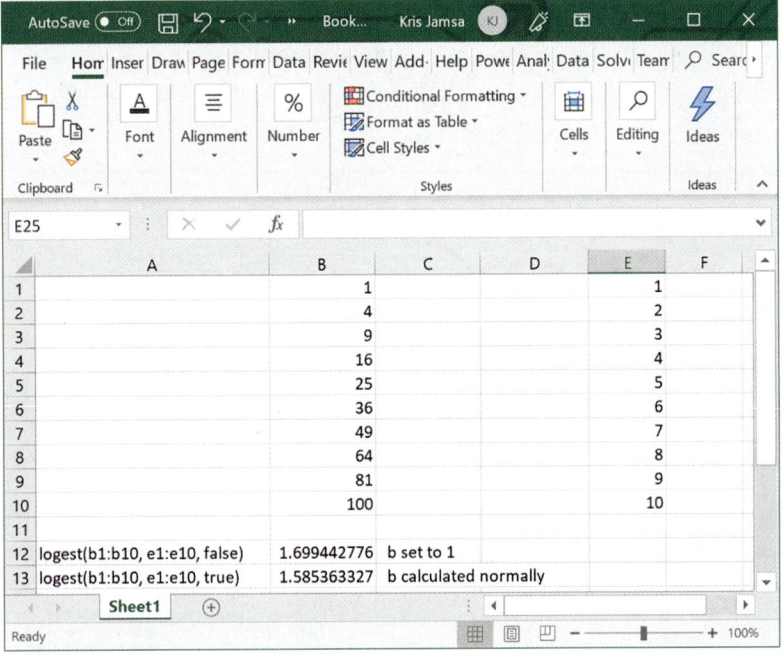

FIGURE 5.44  Using LOGEST to determine the equation of an exponential curve.
Used with permission from Microsoft

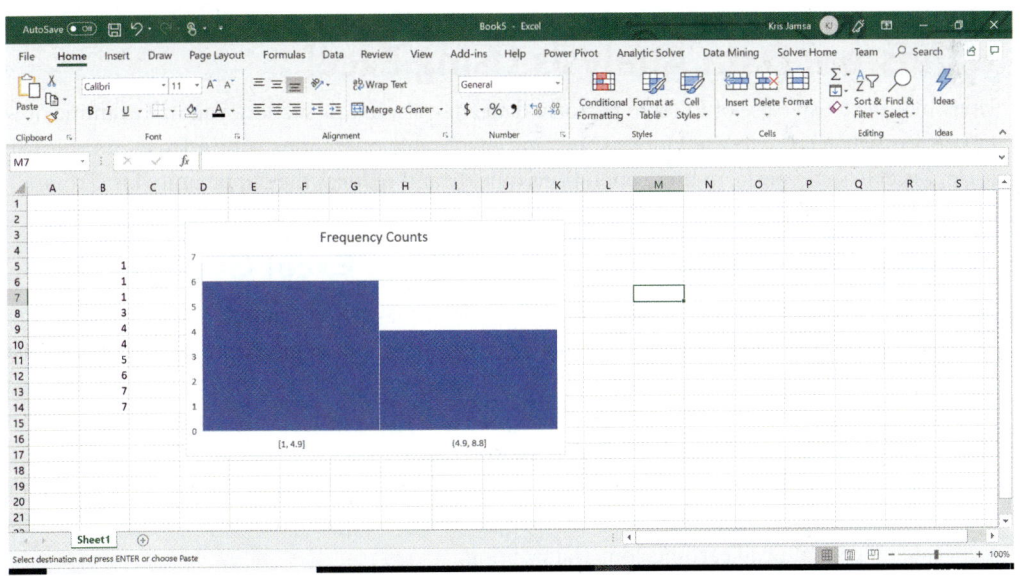

FIGURE 5.45  Using a histogram to display the frequency of data-set values.
Used with permission from Microsoft

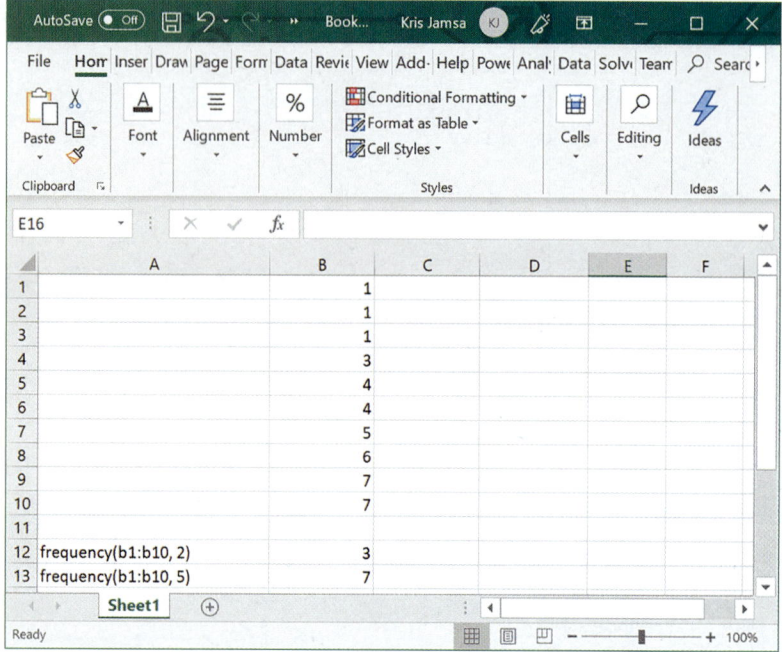

**FIGURE 5.46** Determining data frequency counts using FREQUENCY.

Used with permission from Microsoft

# Hands-on: Data Analysis Using Excel

Users make extensive use of Excel to perform data analysis. In this section, you will examine how to perform what-if processing, forecasting, and pivot table operations within Excel. As you will learn, Excel lets you perform these operations quickly and reduces the opportunity for errors.

## Performing What-If Processing Using Excel Goal Seek

As you analyze different data scenarios, you must often answer questions such as the followings: What if we raised our product price? or What if we sold 10% more product? or By how much must we reduce expenses to achieve a 10% margin? Excel has always been described as a what-if analysis tool. Using Excel, you can manually make changes to your spreadsheet to calculate such results. In addition, you can use Excel's built-in Goal Seek tool.

Assume, for example, you have the spreadsheet shown in **FIGURE 5.47** that shows a company's product sales, price, revenue, expenses, and margin. You can download this spreadsheet from this text's catalog page at go.jblearning.com/DataMining.

Assume your goal is to determine ways the company can achieve a 10% margin. To start, click cell B7 that contains the margin calculation. Then select the Data tab What-If Analysis button.

# Hands-on: Data Analysis Using Excel    197

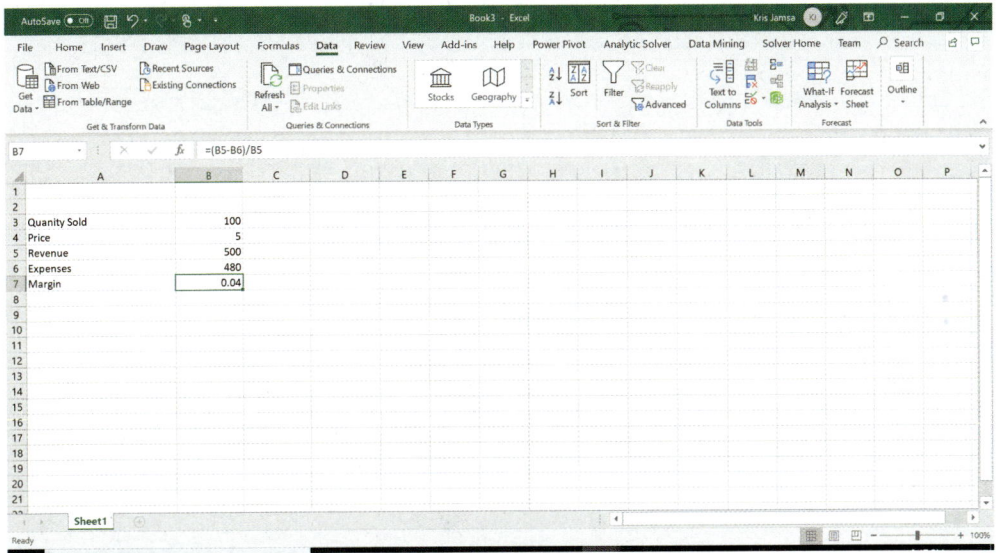

**FIGURE 5.47** Company revenue, expense, and margin data.
Used with permission from Microsoft

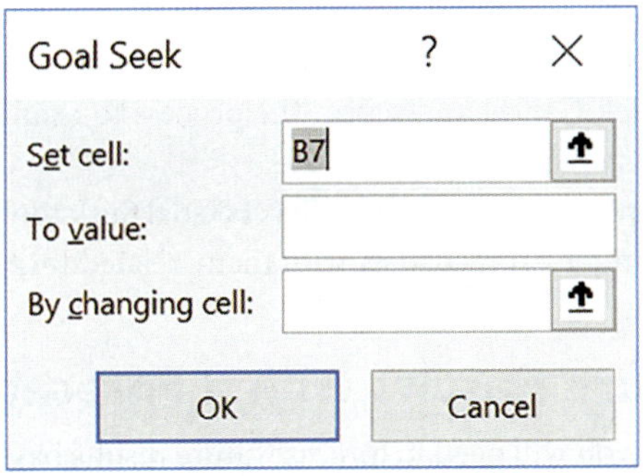

**FIGURE 5.48** The Goal Seek dialog box.
Used with permission from Microsoft

Excel will display the Goal Seek dialog box, shown in **FIGURE 5.48**, that you will use to perform your calculations.

In this case, you can examine price, quantity sold, and expenses to determine their effect on margin. Within the Goal Seek dialog box, enter the cell B7 into the Set Cell field and enter 0.10 in the To Value field. Within the By Changing field, first examine the Price field by entering B4. When you click OK, Excel will display the Goal Seek Status dialog box, as shown in **FIGURE 5.49**.

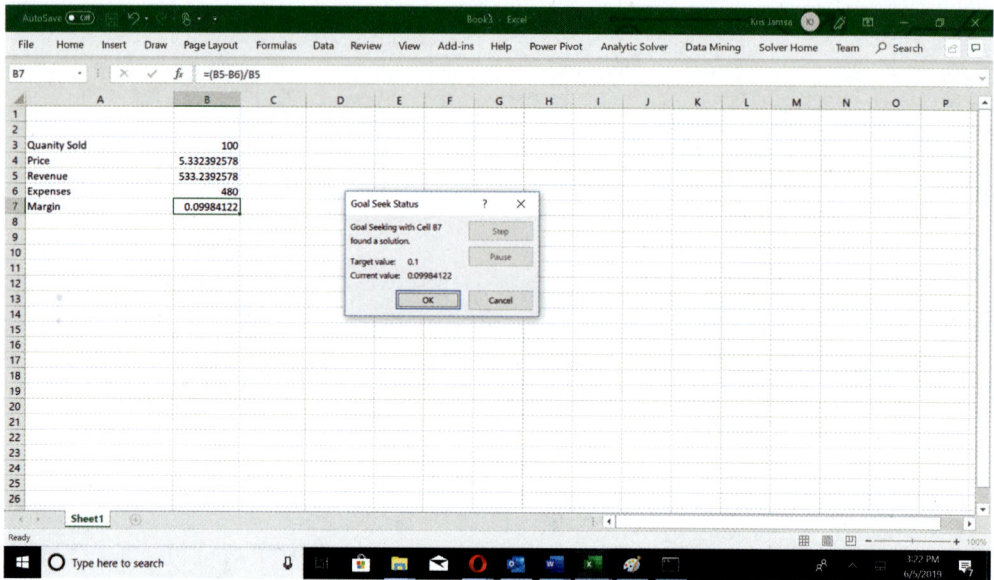

**FIGURE 5.49** Identifying the price needed to obtain a 10% margin.
Used with permission from Microsoft

If you click OK, Excel will change the price value within your spreadsheet and will update the related values. For now, click Cancel and repeat the process to examine the quantity sold. Excel will display the dialog box shown in **FIGURE 5.50**.

Admittedly, this example was quite simple. Excel's Goal Seek tool can perform similar operations with a much more complex spreadsheet with many related formulas.

## Forecasting Future Results with a Forecast Sheet

Often, as you analyze data, you will need to forecast future results based on current data trends. In such cases, you can use an Excel forecast sheet. Assume, for example, you have the sales spreadsheet, shown in **FIGURE 5.51**, that shows daily sales for the past 30 days. You can download this spreadsheet from this text's catalog page at go.jblearning.com/DataMining.

Using the 30-day sales data, your goal is to forecast upcoming sales. To do so, select the dates and sales quantities. Then click the Data tab Forecast Sheet button. Excel will display the Create Forecast Worksheet dialog box, as shown in **FIGURE 5.52**.

Within the dialog box, Excel will forecast upcoming sales using a default **confidence interval** of 95% that means the forecasted values may be correct, low, or high. To illustrate these possibilities, Excel provides a forecasted line, lower-limit forecast, and upper-limit forecast.

If you click the dialog box Options pull-down, Excel will expand the dialog box, as shown in **FIGURE 5.53**, which lets you change several values, such as the confidence interval. As you

Hands-on: Data Analysis Using Excel

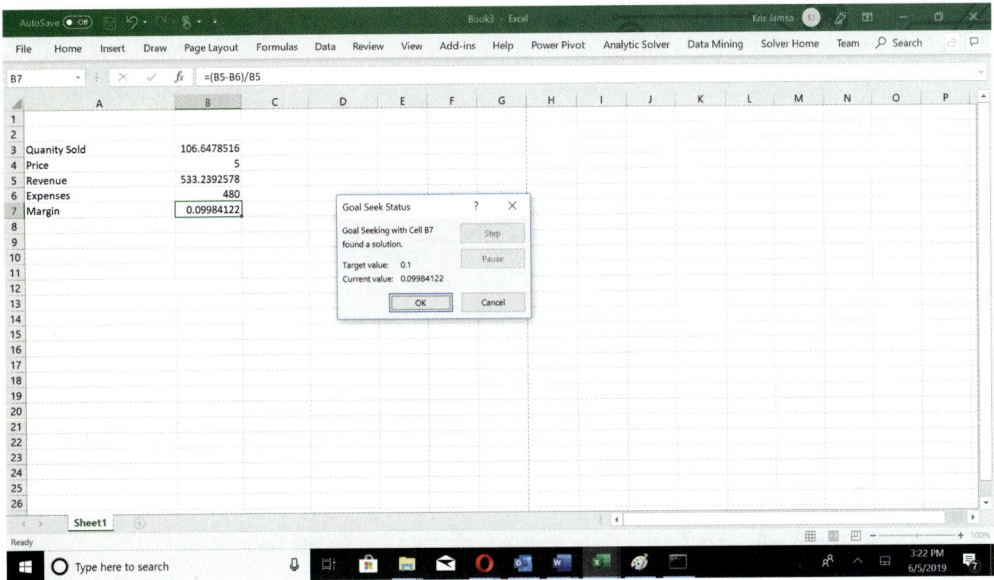

FIGURE 5.50  Identifying the quantity needed to obtain a 10% margin.
Used with permission from Microsoft

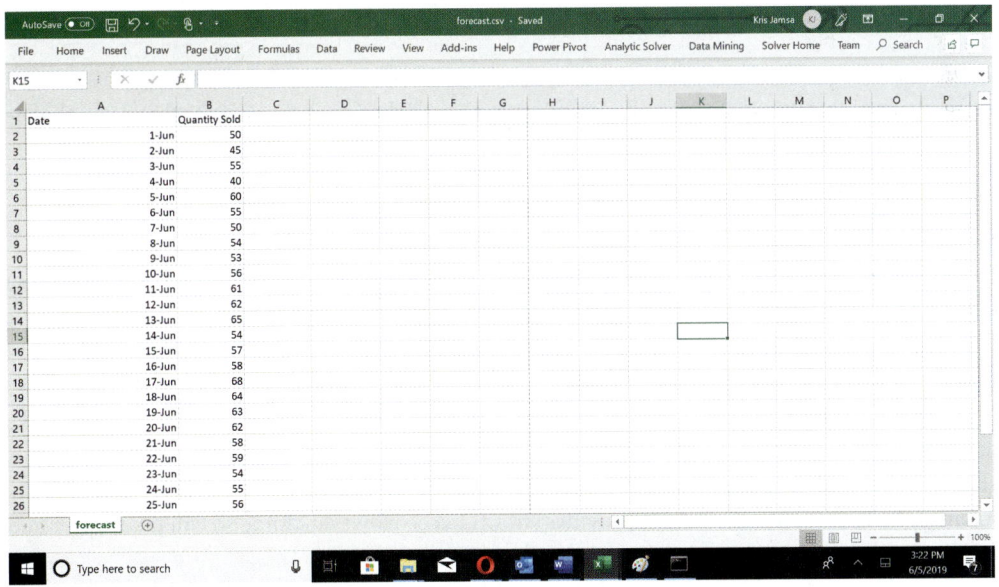

FIGURE 5.51  A company's previous 30-day sales data.
Used with permission from Microsoft

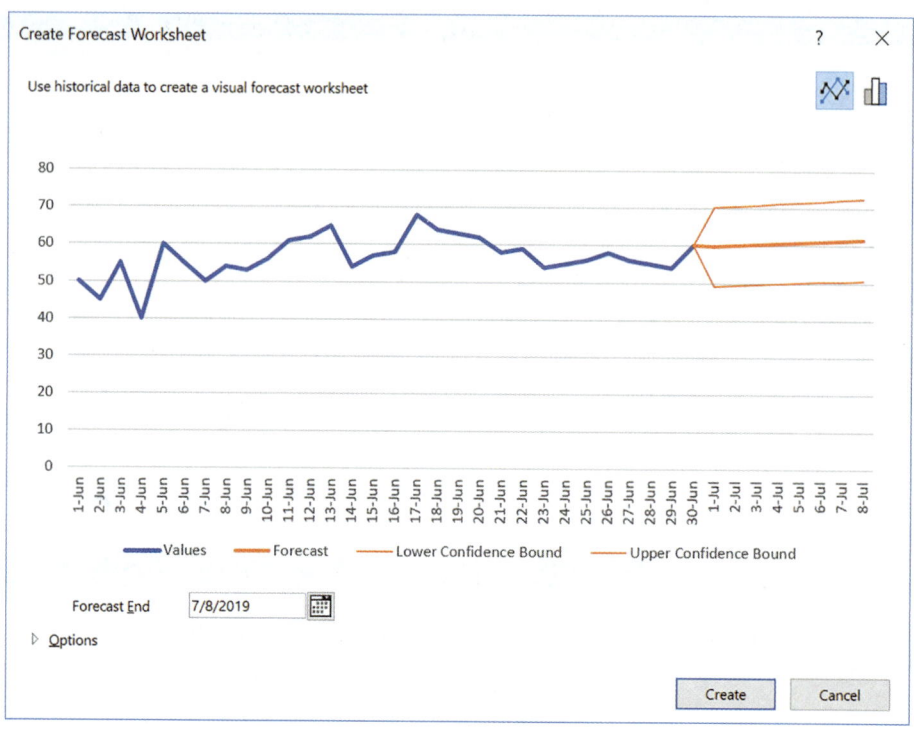

**FIGURE 5.52** The Create Forecast Worksheet dialog box.

Used with permission from Microsoft

make changes to settings, Excel will immediately update the forecast chart. In this case, change the confidence interval to 85%.

## Excel Pivot Tables

Despite Excel's widespread use, most users fail to leverage one of Excel's most powerful reporting and analytic tools: the pivot table. In the simplest sense, a pivot table collects and organizes your data in a way that makes it easy for you to group related data, discover new data relationships, and format your data for reporting.

The pivot table, which has existed for nearly 20 years, is very powerful. In fact, many books have been written on ways users can customize and better leverage pivot table capabilities. This chapter's goal is to introduce you to pivot table processing. Admittedly, you can perform manually many of the operations a pivot table provides within Excel. However, doing so will take longer and be more prone to human error.

To help you get started, download the .csv file PivotDemo.csv from this text's catalog page at go.jblearning.com/DataMining. When you open the file, you will find that it contains regional product sales information by salesperson, as shown in **FIGURE 5.54**.

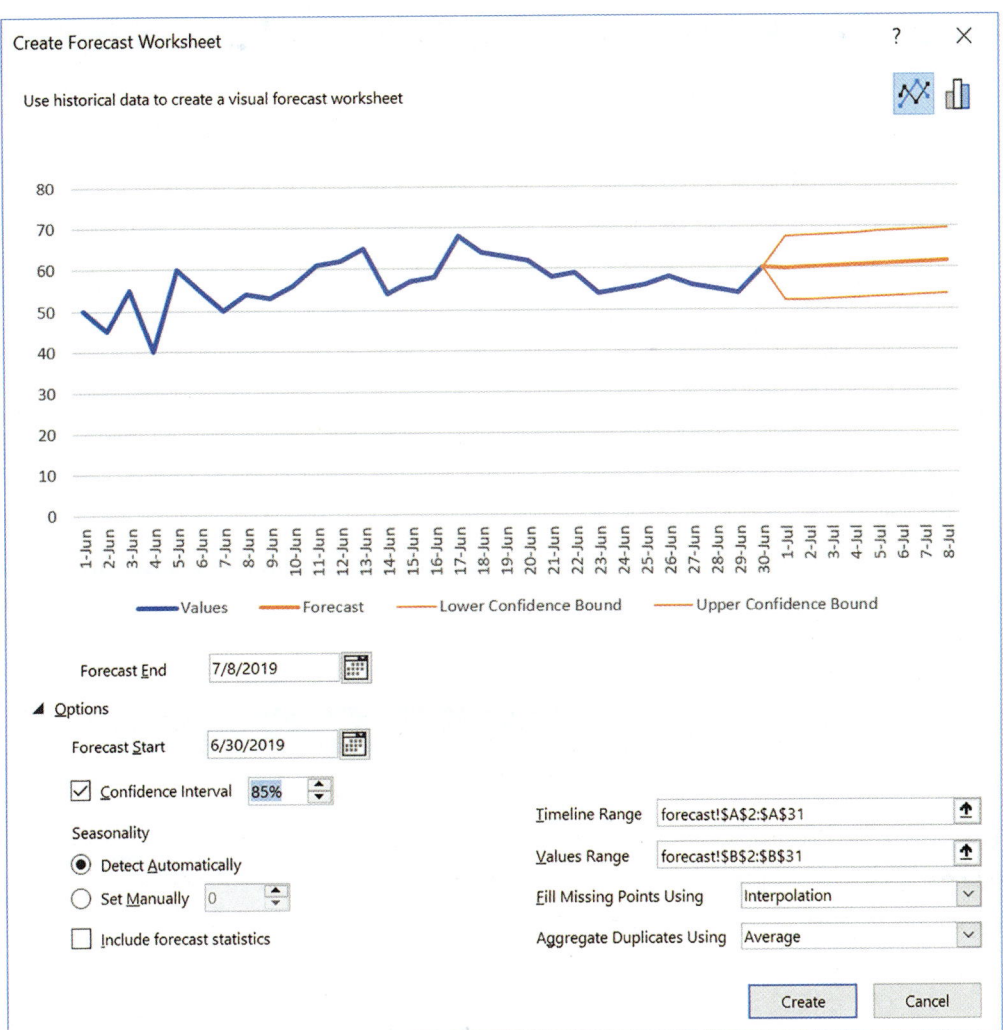

**FIGURE 5.53** Expanding the Create Forecast Worksheet dialog box.
Used with permission from Microsoft

## Preparing Data for Pivot Table Use

Before you create a pivot table, you should perform basic data cleansing, eliminating missing or duplicate data and ensuring that each column has a meaningful header label. As you examine your column labels, make sure you avoid column labels that are also data. Consider the spreadsheet shown in **FIGURE 5.55** that lists product sales by salesperson.

In this case, the spreadsheet has column labels, but those labels also provide data information that identify sales to specific salespeople. In contrast, consider the spreadsheet shown in **FIGURE 5.56** that does not have data in the column labels.

# CHAPTER 5 Keep Excel in Your Toolset

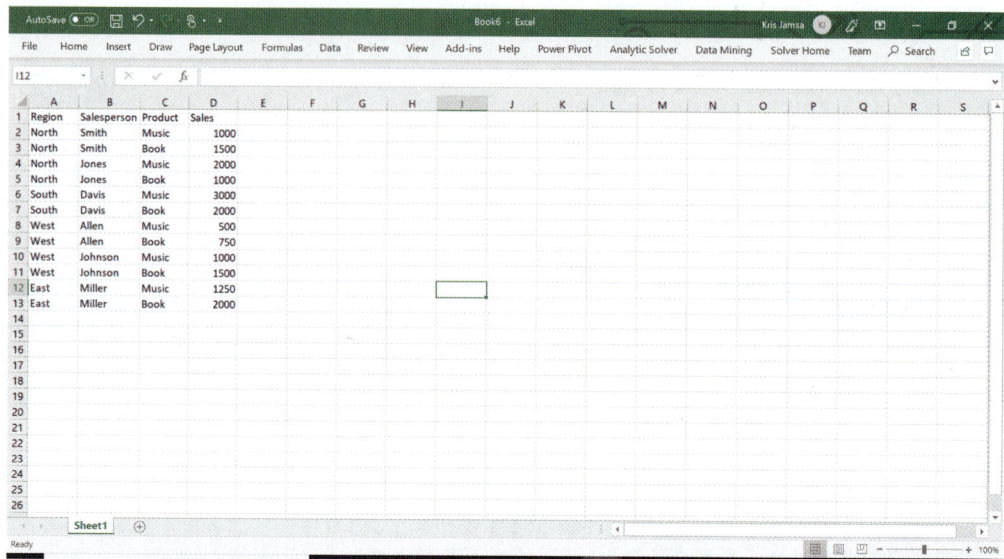

**FIGURE 5.54** Sales information within PivotDemo.csv.
Used with permission from Microsoft

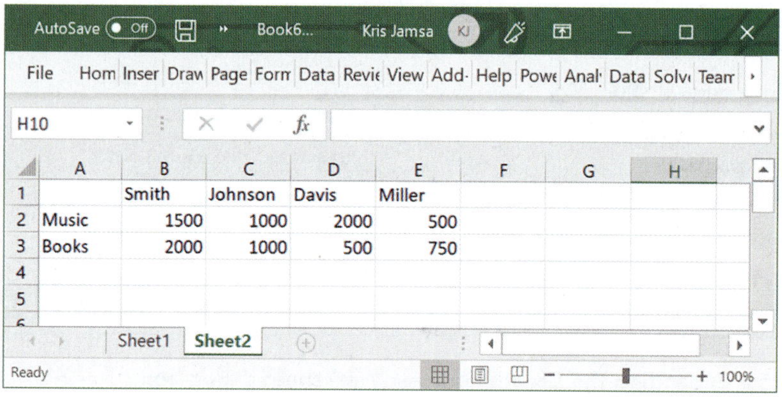

**FIGURE 5.55** A spreadsheet containing product sales by salesperson.
Used with permission from Microsoft

In a similar way, **FIGURE 5.57** shows how you would prepare data that list sales by month for pivot table use.

## Creating a Pivot Table

To create a pivot table, select the data range that you desire and then click the Insert tab Pivot Chart option PivotChart & PivotTable option. Excel will display the Create PivotTable dialog box, as shown in **FIGURE 5.58**.

# Hands-on: Data Analysis Using Excel

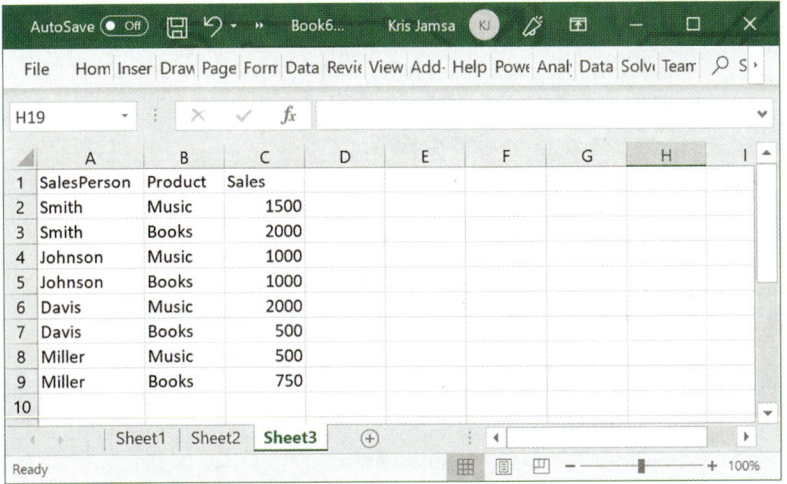

**FIGURE 5.56** Spreadsheet labels that are not part of the data.

Used with permission from Microsoft

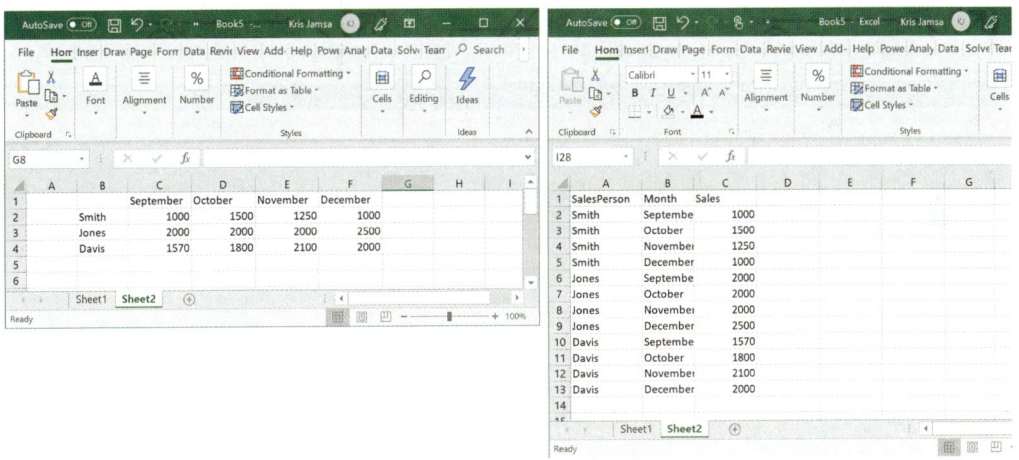

**FIGURE 5.57** Eliminating month labels that are data in preparation for pivot table use.

Used with permission from Microsoft

As you can see in Figure 5.58, Excel lets you place the pivot table within the current worksheet or in a separate worksheet. For now, select New Worksheet and click OK. Excel will display a blank pivot table report to which you can add the fields you desire.

To start, assume that you want to group data by region. To do so, place a checkmark next to the Region field. Excel will add the region to the pivot table Rows section, updating the pivot table, as shown in **FIGURE 5.59**.

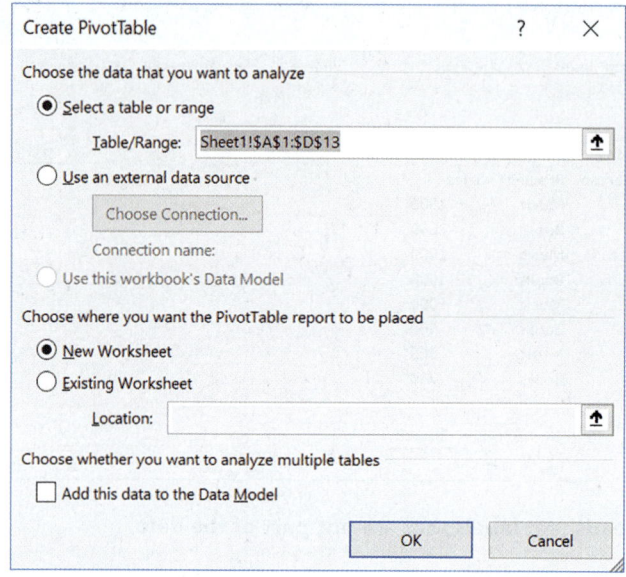

**FIGURE 5.58** The Create PivotTable dialog box.
Used with permission from Microsoft

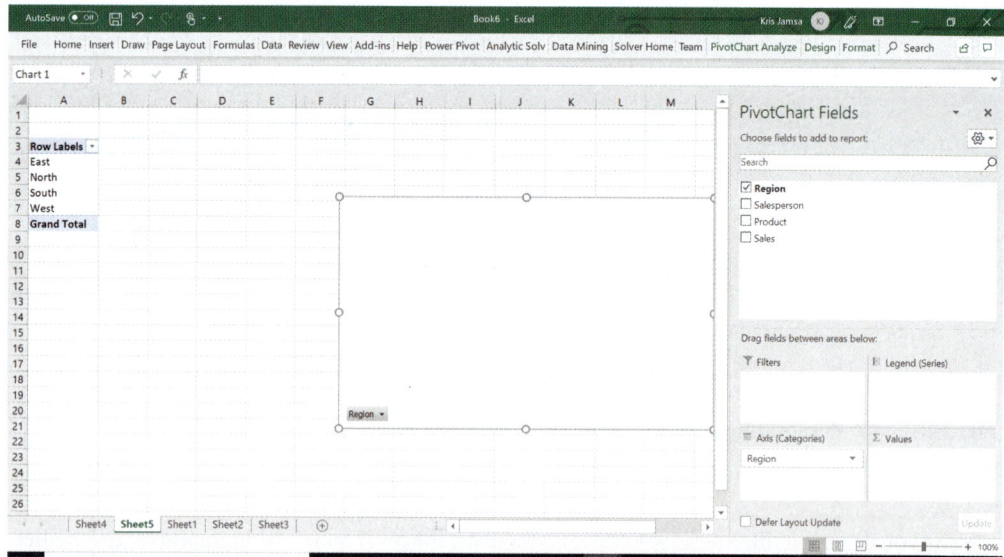

**FIGURE 5.59** Grouping sales data by region.
Used with permission from Microsoft

# Hands-on: Data Analysis Using Excel

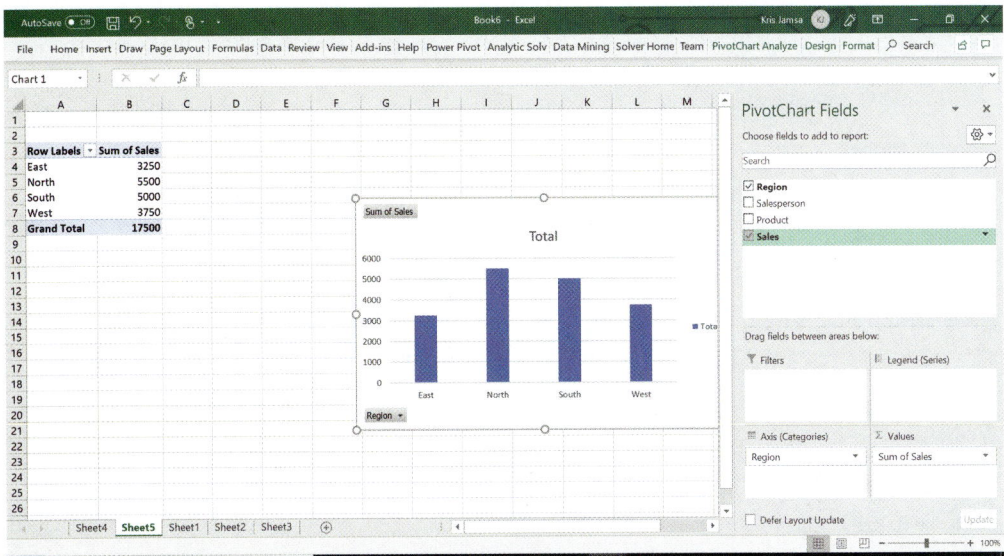

**FIGURE 5.60** Adding sales data to the pivot table.

Used with permission from Microsoft

Next, place a checkmark next to the Sales field. Excel will add the field to the pivot table Values section, updating the pivot table, as shown in **FIGURE 5.60**.

Next, assume you want to group sales data by salesperson. Place a checkmark next to the Salesperson name. Excel will update your pivot table, as shown in **FIGURE 5.61**.

Finally, assume you want to further describe sales by product. To do so, place a checkmark next to the Product field. Excel will update your pivot table, as shown in **FIGURE 5.62**.

## Pivoting Data

Pivot tables are a powerful tool, in that you can quickly move column data to a row or vice versa. For example, using your mouse, drag the Product field from the Row section to the Column section. Excel will update your pivot table, as shown in **FIGURE 5.63**. By moving row and column data in this way, you can quickly produce reports in the form you desire.

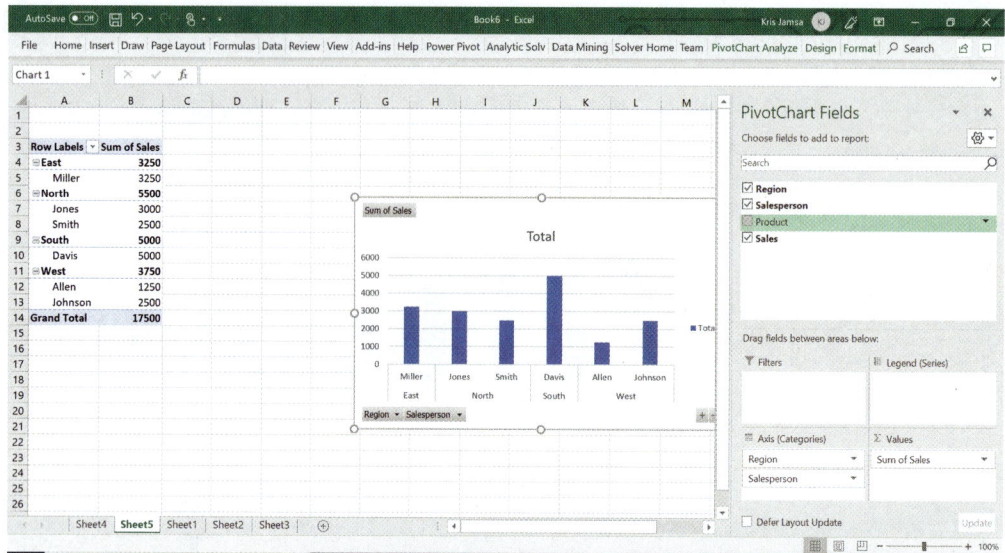

**FIGURE 5.61** Grouping sales data by salesperson.

Used with permission from Microsoft

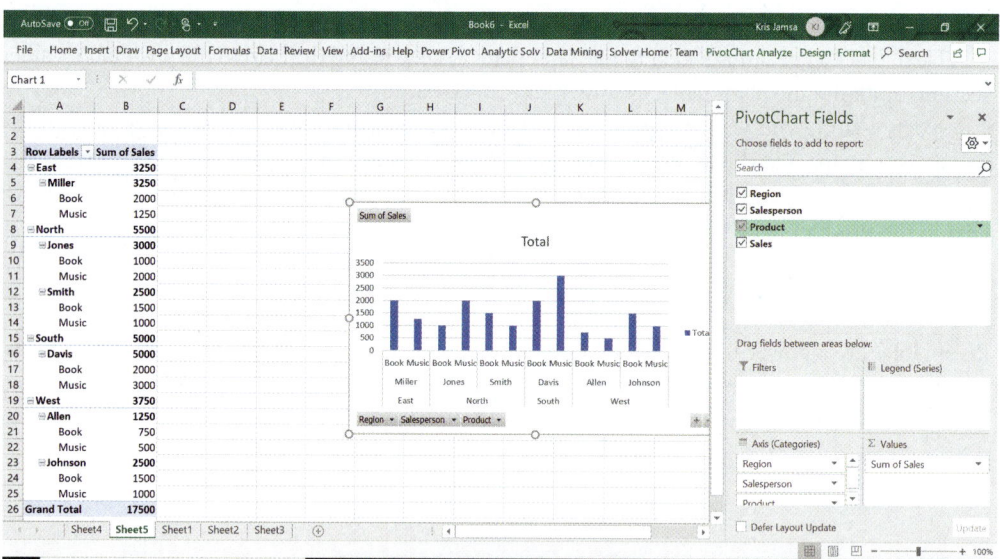

**FIGURE 5.62** Including product details within the sales data.

Used with permission from Microsoft

Hands-on: Data Analysis Using Excel    207

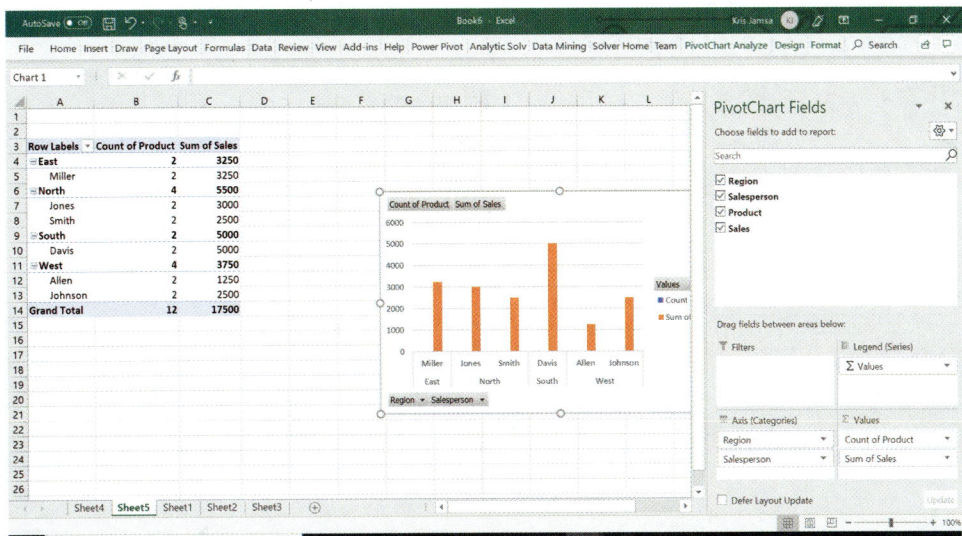

**FIGURE 5.63** Pivoting data within a pivot table.
Used with permission from Microsoft

## Filtering Pivot Table Data Using Slicers

Earlier in this chapter, you learned how to filter data to display only the specific data you desire. A pivot table slicer is similar to a filter. To create a slicer, click your mouse within the pivot table and then click the Insert tab Slicer button. Excel will display the Insert Slicer dialog box, as shown in **FIGURE 5.64**.

Within the dialog box, click the Region and Product fields, placing a checkmark next to each. Excel will add the slicers to your pivot table, as shown in **FIGURE 5.65**.

Within the pivot table, as you click on different slicer options, Excel will enable and disable the display of the corresponding fields. If your pivot table has date-based data, you can create a timeline slicer that lets you group or filter data by date. To create a timeline slicer, use the Insert tab Timeline Slicer button.

**CHAPTER 5** Keep Excel in Your Toolset

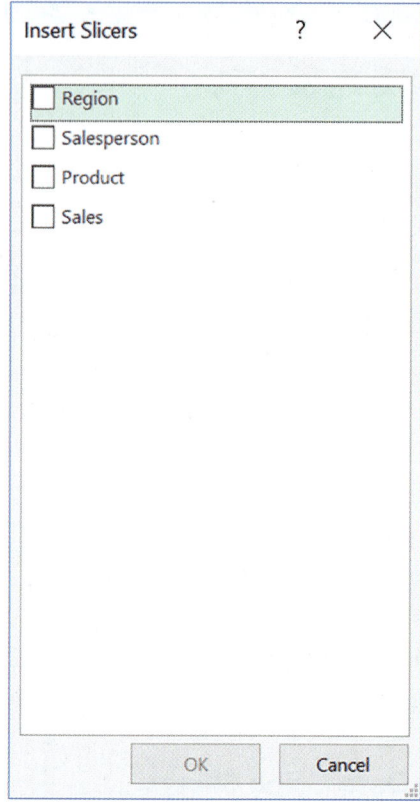

**FIGURE 5.64** The Insert Slicer dialog box.
Used with permission from Microsoft

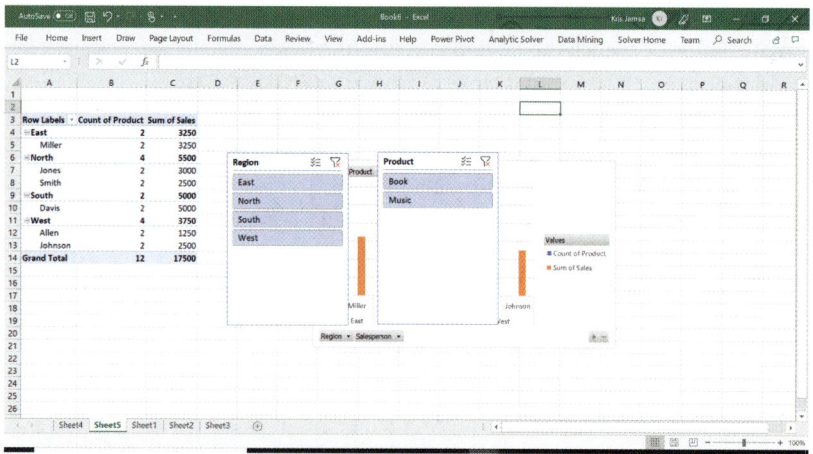

**FIGURE 5.65** Inserting slicers (filters) into a pivot table.
Used with permission from Microsoft

## Summary

Excel is the most widely used data-analysis tool. One of the first steps a data analyst performs when he or she receives a data set is to open and examine it in Excel. In this chapter, you learned how to perform common data-analytic operations using Excel. As you learned, data analysts will often sort data into ascending or descending order. To sort data in Excel, click in the column by which you want to sort and then click the Data tab A–>Z or Z<–A button.

Excel will sort the sheet based on the column. Excel is also one of the most widely used charting solutions. To chart data within Excel, select the data you want to visualize and then choose the Insert tab chart icon that corresponds to the chart type you desire. Chapter 4, "Data Visualization," examined many different charts data analysts use to visualize data.

As you work with large data sets, you will often want to view specific data, such as sales by region or by salesperson. Using a filter, you can direct Excel to display only data you desire.

When you work with large data sets, you will often want to highlight data that match a specific condition. Using Excel's conditional formatting, you can quickly highlight the cells matching the criteria you select using a specific font or color. Using conditional formatting, for example, you can define rules that let you highlight outlier data.

Data analysts must work with data that arrive in one of many file formats, such as CSV, XML, or JSON. Excel makes it very easy to import data in such formats or to export data into such formats.

To support data analytics, Excel provides a wide range of built-in statistical functions analysts can use to calculate average values, standard deviations, variances, correlation, and more.

What-if processing allows data analysts to quickly answer questions such as the following: What if we increase our price? or What if we could sell more products? Using Excel's built-in Goal Seek tool, analysts can quickly perform such calculations. In a similar way, analysts must often forecast future performance based on current data trends. To support such operations, Excel provides the forecast sheet.

One of Excel's most powerful and underused tools is the pivot table. Using a pivot table, you can quickly group data, identify data relationships, and create reports. After you organize data using a pivot table, you can quickly visualize your findings using a pivot chart.

## Key Terms

Arithmetic mean
Conditional formatting
Confidence interval
Correlation
Covariance
Filtering
Geometric mean
Harmonic mean
Median
Pivot table
Quartile
Standard deviation
Variance

## Review

To obtain the data for the following questions, download the Excel spreadsheet Questions.xlsx from this text's catalog page at go.jblearning.com/DataMining.

1. Using the Excel file Questions.xlsx sheet Question 1:
   a. Create a pie chart of the sales by product columns.
   b. Create a bar chart of sales by employee.
   Capture screens showing your results.
2. Using the Excel file Questions.xlsx sheet Question 2, filter the sales data to show only sales for the South region and then sort the sales from highest to lowest. Capture a screen showing your results.
3. Using the Excel file Questions.xlsx sheet Question 3, save the automotive data as a .csv file. Capture a screen showing your results.
4. Using the Excel file Questions.xlsx sheet Question 4, calculate the mean, median, standard deviation, and variance of the data values provided. Capture a screen showing your results.
5. Using the Excel file Questions.xlsx sheet Question 5, use Excel's conditional formatting to highlight the top 10% of values and the bottom 10% of values. Capture a screen showing your results.
6. Using the Excel file Questions.xlsx sheet Question 6, determine the min, max, fourth largest, and fifth largest values. Capture a screen showing your results.
7. Using the Excel file Questions.xlsx sheet Question 7, calculate the equation of the line that best matches the data. Capture a screen showing your results.
8. Using the Excel file Questions.xlsx sheet 8, use Excel's What-If Analysis to determine the price change you would need to make to produce a profit of $1,000. Capture a screen showing your results.
9. Using the Excel file Questions.xlsx sheet 9, forecast sales with a 90% confidence interval.
10. Using the Excel file Questions.xlsx sheet 10, create a pivot table that shows sales by salesperson per month.

# CHAPTER 6

# Keep SQL in Your Toolset

## Chapter Goals and Objectives

- Define and describe the components of a relational database.
- Compare and contrast DCL, DDL, and DML queries.
- Perform complex SQL queries.
- Compare and contrast SQL JOIN operations.
- Use SQL aggregation functions and query techniques to group data for reporting.

For over 50 years, Structured Query Language (SQL) has been the primary way database developers create and manipulate table-based relational databases. In fact, developers often refer to relational databases as SQL databases. This chapter examines SQL operations in detail. As you will learn, SQL is the language you will use to speak (interact) with a database and the tables it contains. SQL provides queries that let you create databases, create tables within the database, and then insert, update, and delete data records within those tables.

Many software companies, such as Oracle, Microsoft, and even Amazon, provide implementations of SQL database systems. Each of these systems provides different capabilities. At their core, you will find that all such systems support the base set of SQL queries, which this chapter presents.

To perform data mining and analytics, it is important that you understand SQL. As you will learn, an SQL database (or data warehouse within a database) is often the source of the data that data-mining and data-analytic tools access. Having the ability to **query** and manipulate underlying data will increase your ability to independently complete your data-mining and data-analytic work. Further, as you will learn, using SQL operations, such as JOINs, GROUP BY with ROLLUPs, and nested SELECTs, you can create query results well suited for immediate analysis. This chapter will provide you with the foundational knowledge you need. By the time you complete this chapter, you will understand the following key concepts:

- Within a relational database, all operations are based upon SQL.
- Developers group SQL queries into three primary categories: Data Definition Language (DDL), Data Manipulation Language (DML), and Data Control Language (DCL) queries.
- DDL queries define the structure of the underlying database, tables, and columns.
- DCL queries define access (authorization) to database components.
- DML queries specify data retrieval, insertion, update, and deletion operations performed on a database.
- A database server may house many different databases. To tell the database system with which database you want to work, you issue the USE query. To display a list of available databases, you issue the SHOW DATABASES query.
- A relational database stores data within tables. To view a list of tables a database contains, you issue the SHOW TABLES query.
- A relational database table stores data within records, which correspond to the table's rows. Each record consists of fields, which correspond to the table columns.
- To retrieve the records a table contains, you use the SELECT query.
- To retrieve only those records that meet a specific criterion, a process that developers refer to as filtering, such as sales for the month of December, you use the SELECT query WHERE clause.
- To help you specify SELECT query filters, SQL provides **relational operators** such as =, >, <= and the **logical operators** NOT, AND, and OR.
- SQL provides a set of **arithmetic operators** you can use to perform mathematical operations within your queries, as well as a set of built-in arithmetic functions you can use to perform advanced mathematical operations.
- To compare field values within your queries, you use the SQL relational operators such as equals (=), greater than (>), and less than (<).
- To create a compound condition within an SQL query that compares two conditions, you use the SQL AND and OR operators.
- To connect to a **remote database**, you must specify the database server's Internet Protocol (IP) address (or domain name), the **network port** the database system monitors for connections, as well as a username and password.
- Throughout this chapter, you will execute queries one query at a time. Database developers often group multiple queries into an SQL script, placing a semicolon (;) at the end of each query to separate one query from the next.
- Importing and exporting data into and from a database to or from a file, spreadsheet, or even another database table are common operations. SQL provides a set of commands to help you perform such operations.
- One of the most common operations database developers perform is to extract data from one table, change the data in some way, and then load the data into a new table. Developers refer to such operations as extract, transform, and load (**ETL**) operations.

- In the past, most companies stored their databases within an **on-premise server** within their own data center. Today, most companies are migrating such servers to the cloud.
- To insert data into a table, you use the SQL INSERT query.
- To change data within a table, you use the SQL UPDATE query.
- To delete records from a table, you use the SQL DELETE query.
- To delete a table or a database, you use the SQL DROP query.
- To group (**aggregate**) related records in your query results, the SELECT query provides the GROUP BY clause.
- To place subtotals and totals within GROUP BY results, you can include ROLLUPs and cubes.
- To sort your query results, you use the ORDER BY clause. To specify the sort order, you include the ASC (for ascending) and DESC (for descending) key words.
- To improve query performance, developers often assign an index to key fields. To create an **index**, you use the SQL CREATE INDEX query.

## Understanding SQL Query Types: DDL, DCL, and DML

Everything that happens within an SQL database is ultimately driven by a query operation. SQL supports many types of queries, the operations of which fall into three primary query subsets:

- DDL queries define the structure of the underlying database, tables, and columns.
- DCL queries define access (authorization) to database components.
- DML queries specify data retrieval, insertion, update, and deletion operations performed on a database.

The SQL DDL queries allow users to create, alter, and delete databases, tables, and other database components, such as views, functions, and stored procedures. **TABLE 6.1** briefly describes the SQL DDL queries.

**TABLE 6.1** The SQL DDL Queries

| Query | Description |
| --- | --- |
| CREATE | Creates a database or table. |
| DROP | Deletes a database or table. |
| ALTER | Changes an object's structure. |
| RENAME | Renames an object. |
| TRUNCATE | Removes all records from a table, freeing up previously consumed disk space. |
| COMMENT | Places a comment within a data dictionary. |

**TABLE 6.2** The SQL DCL Queries

| Query | Description |
|---|---|
| GRANT | Assigns one or more privileges to a user. |
| REVOKE | Removes one or more privileges from a user. |

**TABLE 6.3** The SQL DML Queries

| Query | Description |
|---|---|
| SELECT | Retrieves records from a table. |
| INSERT | Inserts a record into a table. |
| UPDATE | Updates one or more fields with records. |
| DELETE | Deletes one or more records from a table. |
| LOCK | Locks access to an object. |

The SQL DCL queries allow administrators to specify who can access specific database components and how. **TABLE 6.2** briefly describes the common SQL DCL queries.

Lastly, the SQL DML queries perform operations on the database, such as retrieving data from, inserting data into, deleting records from, or updating the contents of a table. **TABLE 6.3** briefly describes the common SQL DML queries.

In addition to the DDL, DCL, and DML queries, database developers often use the terms transactional queries, sometimes called Transaction Control Language (TCL) queries, to group queries that support transaction processing, such as ROLLBACK and COMMIT.

## Understanding Create, Read, Update, and Delete Operations

The most common operations database developers perform are to create databases and tables; insert data into the tables; retrieve values from tables; update table values; and, finally, delete data, tables, and databases. Developers refer to these operations using the **CRUD** acronym, which stands for create, read, update, and delete.

**TABLE A** lists the SQL queries that relate to each CRUD operation.

**TABLE A** The SQL CRUD Queries

| CRUD Query Category | SQL Queries |
| --- | --- |
| Create | CREATE |
| Read | SELECT |
| Update | UPDATE |
| Delete | DELETE, DROP |

## Downloading and Installing MySQL

For nearly 25 years, MySQL has been the most popular and widely used relational database system. In fact, MySQL is the "M" in the LAMP (Linux, Apache, MySQL, Perl/PHP/Python) acronym, which describes the popular open-source developer stack.

Today, MySQL is owned by Oracle Corporation, which offers different software licenses to meet the needs of large and small organizations. The MySQL licenses are normally significantly lower in price than competing database solutions such as Microsoft SQL Server, Oracle, and IBM DB2. Across the web, you will find different implementations of MySQL, the capabilities of which are similar. Two of the best-known MySQL alternatives are MariaDB and Amazon's Aurora. All the MySQL concepts and queries presented in this chapter are fully compatible with these two implementations.

Using MySQL, you can perform the queries this chapter presents as you read. To download and install MySQL on your computer, perform these steps:

1. Within your browser, visit www.mysql.com, as shown in **FIGURE A**.
2. Within the MySQL website, click on the Downloads list. The site will display the Downloads page.
3. Within the Downloads page, locate the MySQL Community Edition and click on the corresponding link. The site will display the MySQL Community Edition Downloads page.
4. Within the MySQL Community Edition Downloads page, locate the MySQL Server installation for your operating system and initiate the installation. The MySQL installation will open a wizard, as shown in **FIGURE B**, that will guide you through the installation.

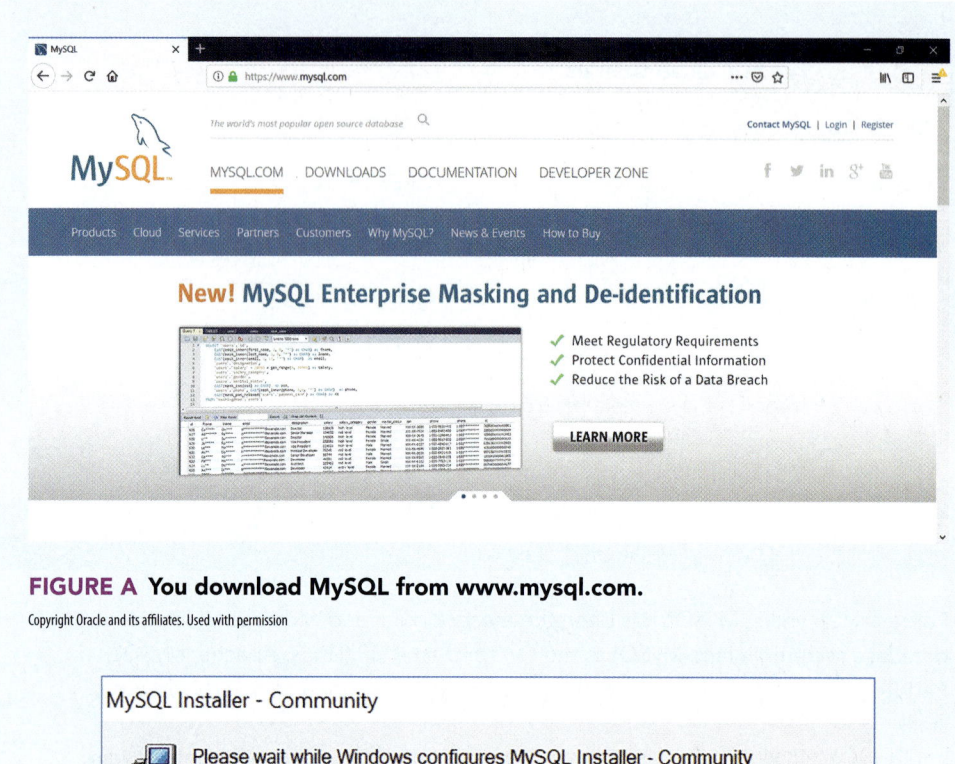

**FIGURE A  You download MySQL from www.mysql.com.**
Copyright Oracle and its affiliates. Used with permission

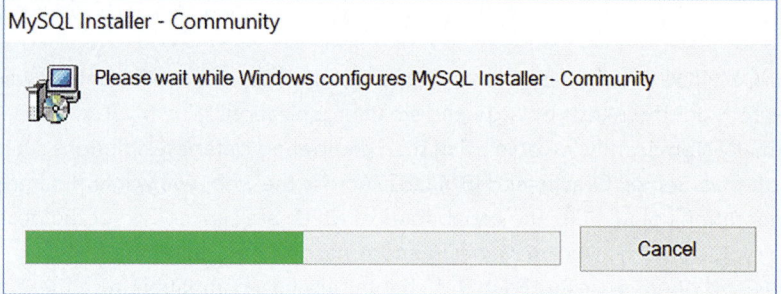

**FIGURE B  Using the MySQL installation wizard to install MySQL on your system.**
Copyright Oracle and its affiliates. Used with permission

When you install MySQL on your own PC, the installation process will place the database server software on your system that you will need to store data, and it will install client software (the MySQL command-line shell and the visual Workbench **graphical user interface**) that you will use to interact with databases. Each time your system starts, it will automatically start the MySQL database server, which will wait in the background for you to connect one of the client programs to a database, as shown in **FIGURE C**.

After the MySQL installation completes, you have two primary ways to interact with MySQL: using the MySQL command-line shell interface shown in **FIGURE D** or using the graphical MySQL Workbench interface shown in **FIGURE E**.

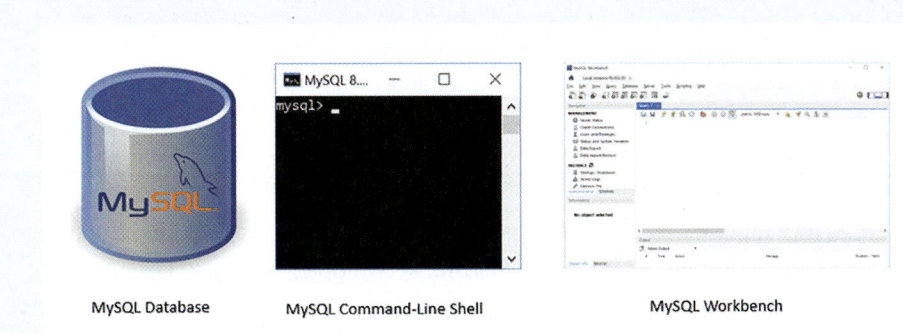

**FIGURE C** MySQL consists of a database server that stores data and client programs that allow a user to interact with databases.

Copyright Oracle and its affiliates. Used with permission

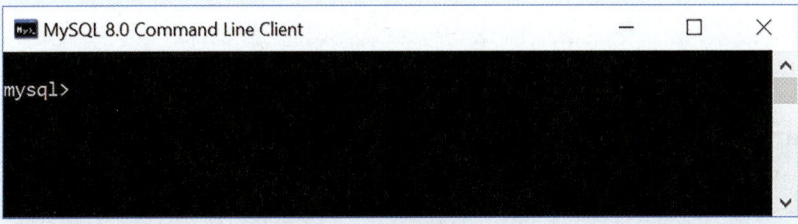

**FIGURE D** Executing SQL queries from within the MySQL command-line shell interface.

Copyright Oracle and its affiliates. Used with permission

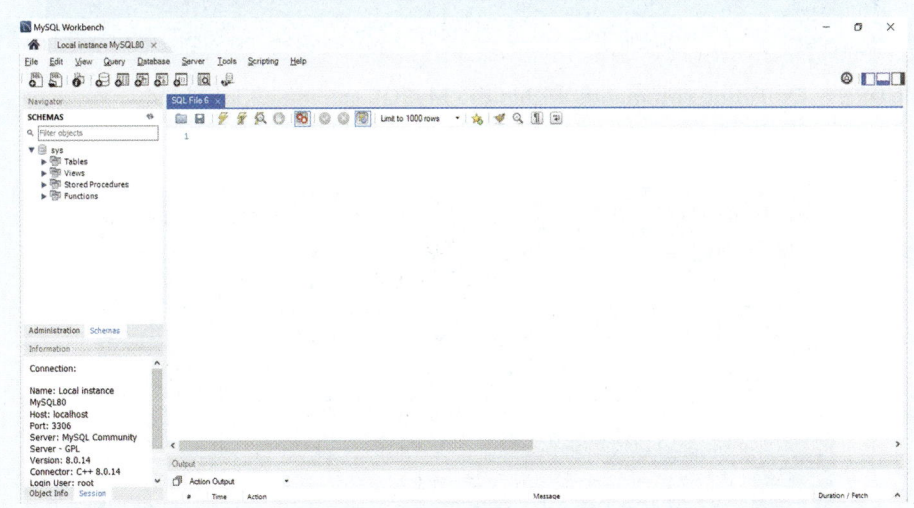

**FIGURE E** Interacting with the MySQL Workbench graphical user interface to execute SQL queries.

Copyright Oracle and its affiliates. Used with permission

### Executing Queries from the MySQL Command-Line Shell

The MySQL command-line shell provided runs within a command-line window, as shown in **FIGURE F**, and displays a prompt at which you can type your SQL queries. MySQL will display the query results within the window.

To execute a query within the MySQL command-line shell, perform these steps:

5. Start the MySQL command-line shell. If you are using Windows, you can start the shell from the Start menu, as shown in **FIGURE G**. Windows, in turn, will launch the shell, which may prompt you to specify the username and password that you entered during the MySQL installation.
6. From the MySQL command-line prompt, type the SHOW DATABASES query and press Enter. MySQL will display the query's results, as shown in **FIGURE H**.

When you are done with the shell, you can type Quit at the MySQL prompt, or you can simply close the window.

*Note*: When you execute an SQL query at the MySQL command-line prompt, you must place a semicolon at the end of the query.

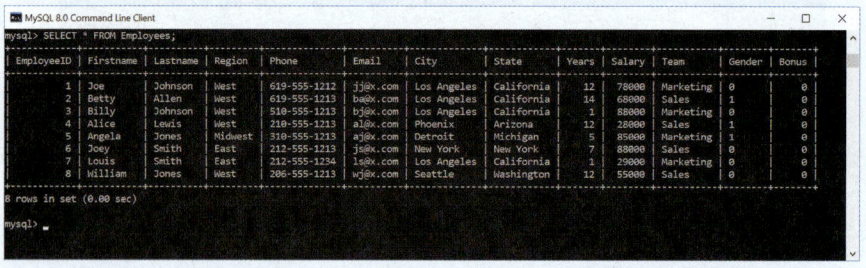

**FIGURE F** Executing commands within the MySQL command-line shell.
Copyright Oracle and its affiliates. Used with permission

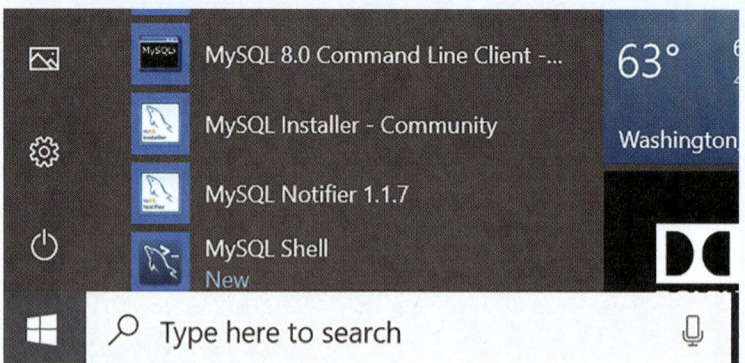

**FIGURE G** Starting MySQL command-line shell from the Windows Start menu.
Copyright Oracle and its affiliates. Used with permission

## Understanding SQL Query Types: DDL, DCL, and DML

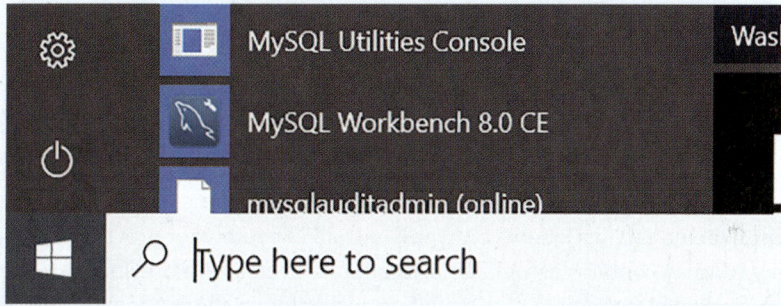

**FIGURE H** Executing a query at the MySQL command-line prompt.
Copyright Oracle and its affiliates. Used with permission

**FIGURE I** Starting MySQL Workbench from the Windows Start menu.
Copyright Oracle and its affiliates. Used with permission

### Executing SQL Queries from Within the MySQL Workbench

The MySQL Workbench provides a graphical user interface within which you can execute queries and view the query results. To execute a query within the MySQL Workbench, perform these steps:

7. Start the MySQL Workbench. If you are using Windows, you can start the Workbench from the Start menu, as shown in **FIGURE I**. Windows will launch the Workbench.
8. Locate the query window and type the SHOW DATABASES query. (You may need to create a new query window by clicking the SQL+ button.)
9. Press the Ctrl+Shift+Enter keyboard combination or click the lightning-bolt icon to execute the query. Workbench will display the query's results, as shown in **FIGURE J**.

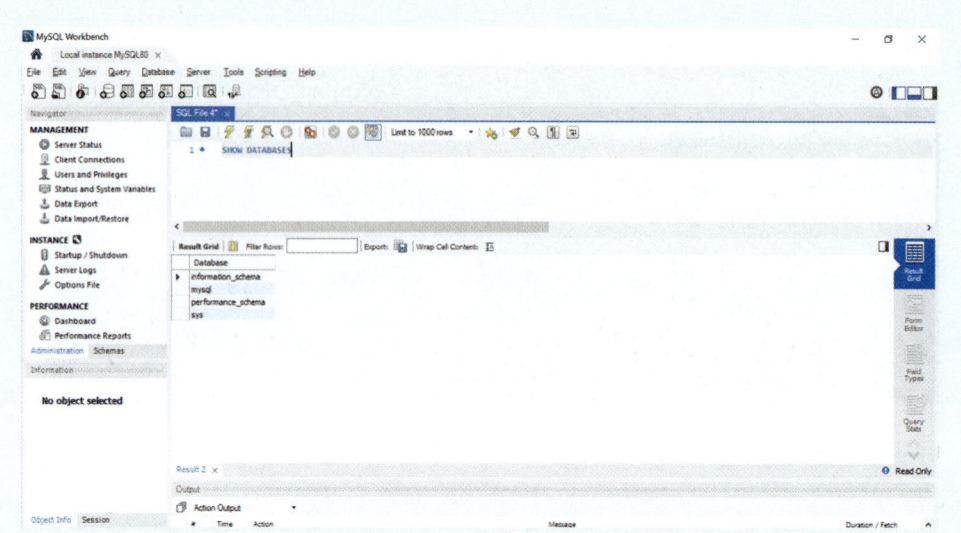

**FIGURE J** **Executing a query within the MySQL Workbench.**

Copyright Oracle and its affiliates. Used with permission

When you execute SQL queries using the Workbench, you press Ctrl+Shift+Enter or click the lightning icon to run the query. By default, the Workbench will execute every query listed in the query window. In other words, the Workbench won't just execute the last query you typed—it will execute your previous queries the query window contains as well. One solution is to clear the previous queries from the window by selecting all the queries and deleting them. Or you can select the query you desire using your keyboard arrow keys and holding down the Shift key or by dragging your mouse over the query. Then you can direct the Workbench to execute only the selected query by pressing Ctrl+Shift+Enter or clicking the lightning icon.

### Using MySQL's Built-in Databases

The MySQL installation provides several built-in databases. To view the available databases from the MySQL command-line shell, execute the SHOW DATABASES query as previously shown in Figure J.

As shown in **FIGURE K**, the MySQL Workbench displays the list of available databases within a pane near the upper-left corner of the window. To display the databases, click on the Schemas tab and then expand the database list by clicking on the right-facing triangle next to Sys.

# Understanding SQL Query Types: DDL, DCL, and DML

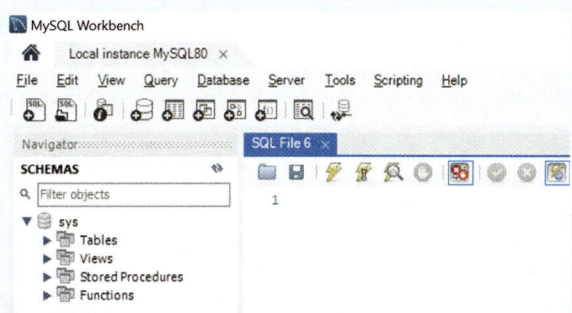

**FIGURE K** MySQL Workbench displays the available databases in its upper-left corner.
Copyright Oracle and its affiliates. Used with permission

## Using the Semicolon (;) at the End of an SQL Query

An SQL query specifies a single operation you want to perform on a database. An SQL server normally performs one query at a time. Throughout this chapter, you have issued a variety of queries, one at a time. There may be times, however, when you will need to execute a group of queries, such as the USE query followed by one or more SELECT queries. In such cases, you place a semicolon (;) after each query to separate one from the next:

```
USE CHAPTER06;
SELECT * FROM Sales;
SELECT * FROM Employees;
```

As you examine SQL queries, you will find that many end with the semicolon. In such cases, if only a single query exists, the semicolon has no impact. If multiple queries exist, SQL will use the semicolon to determine where one query ends and the next begins.

*Note*: When you execute SQL queries at the MySQL command-line prompt, you must place a semicolon at the end of each query.

## Spend Time with the W3Schools SQL Tutorial

Across the web, one of the best learning sites for web developers is the W3Schools site at www.w3schools.com.

Within the W3Schools site, you will find tutorials on Hypertext Markup Language (HTML), Cascading Style Sheets (CSS), JavaScript, and much more. The site provides an outstanding tutorial on SQL.

> If you are new to SQL or simply need a refresher, you should invest time in the W3Schools SQL tutorial. The tutorial is unique in that it lets you edit and execute many queries in a hands-on environment, viewing your query results in real time.

## SQL Database Vendors

SQL is the way users interact with a database. An SQL database, in turn, is a database that supports SQL operations. Many different software companies, such as Oracle, Microsoft, and IBM, offer SQL databases. Many of these solutions offer trial versions, which you can install and try for free. **TABLE 6.4** lists common SQL solutions.

In general, the SQL queries you issue on one system will run on another system. That said, each of the larger SQL database systems provides an extended set of system-specific SQL capabilities. Microsoft SQL, for example, supports TSQL commands (the T is for transactional), and Oracle provides PL/SQL (for Procedural Language/Structured Query Language), which includes additional programming constructs such as loops, conditions, and procedural blocks. Although languages such as PL/SQL and TSQL provide developers with additional functionality, the fact that these languages are vendor specific makes solutions that use them harder to move from one database system to another.

**TABLE 6.4 Common SQL Database Systems**

| Database Solution | Website |
|---|---|
| MySQL | www.mysql.com |
| Oracle | www.oracle.com |
| Microsoft MS SQL Server | www.microsoft.com |
| IBM DB2 | www.ibm.com |
| PostgreSQL (often called Postgres) | www.postgresql.org |
| Amazon Aurora | aws.amazon.com/rds/aurora |
| Microsoft Access | www.microsoft.com |
| SQLite | sqlite.org |
| Firebird | Firebirdsql.org |
| Actian | https://www.actian.com/data-management/actian-x-hybrid-rdbms/ |

## Using Databases Provided on This Text's Catalog Page

Throughout this chapter, you will read about each SQL query and see examples of each query's use. Rather than simply reading about each query, you should instead execute them. To do so, however, you must have the database that contains the tables the queries use on your system. Fortunately, you can quickly download and install the tables by downloading and executing a file of SQL queries that resides on this text's catalog page at go.jblearning.com/DataMining. Use the link to download the file. If you are using Windows, your system will display the file's contents within the Notepad accessory, as shown in **FIGURE A**.

Within your text editor, select all the queries and copy them to the Clipboard. If you are using the Windows Notepad accessory, press the Ctrl+A keyboard combination to select the query text and then press Ctrl+C to copy the selected text to the Windows Clipboard.

Next, start the MySQL Workbench and paste the queries from the Clipboard into the query pane by clicking your mouse in the pane and pressing the Ctrl+V keyboard combination, as shown in **FIGURE B**.

Move your cursor in front of the first query at the front of the list. Then press Ctrl+A to select all the queries. Next, press the Ctrl+Shift+Enter keyboard combination to

**FIGURE A** Downloading the SQL queries that will create the tables used throughout this chapter.

Used with permission from Microsoft

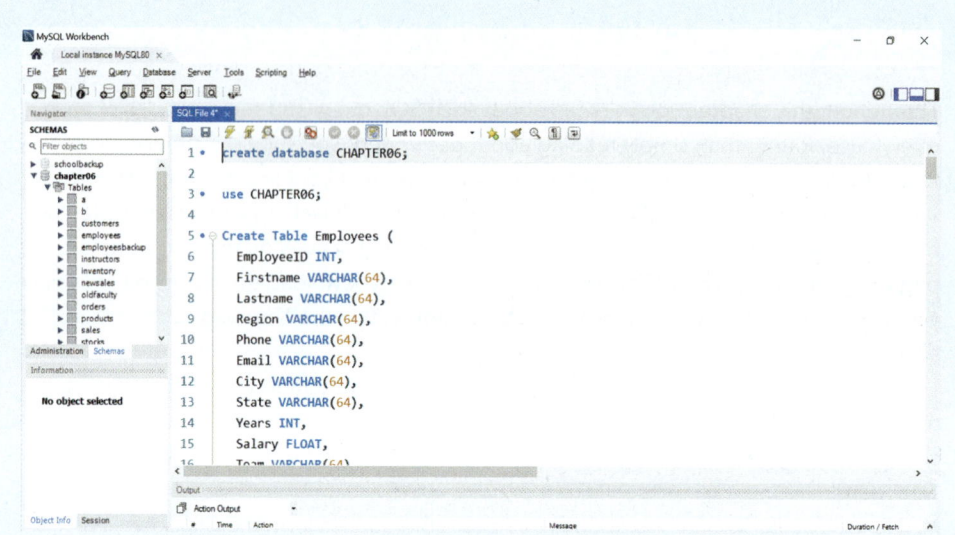

**FIGURE B** Copying the queries into the Workbench query pane.

Copyright Oracle and its affiliates. Used with permission

execute the queries. MySQL will create the corresponding databases and tables and will insert the specified data. Issue the SHOW DATABASES query. MySQL will display the databases the server contains, which includes the new CHAPTER06 database, as shown in **FIGURE C**.

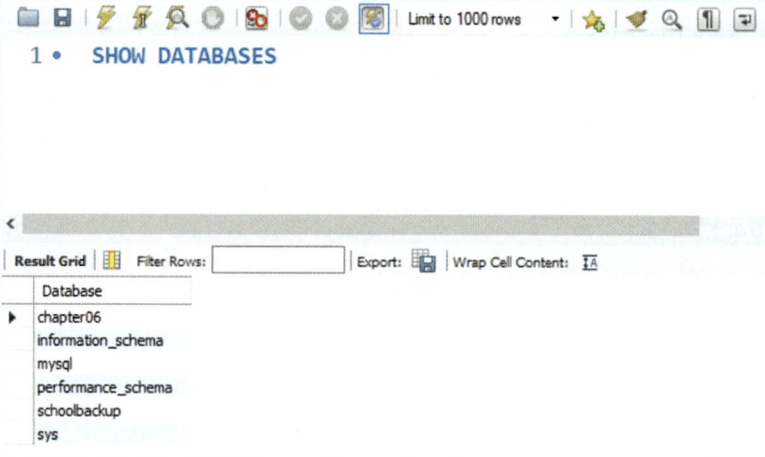

**FIGURE C** Displaying this text's companion databases within the MySQL Workbench.

Copyright Oracle and its affiliates. Used with permission

If you are not using the MySQL Workbench, but rather, the MySQL command-line shell, you can paste the queries into the shell by clicking on the window's Control menu and selecting the Paste option, as shown in **FIGURE D**.

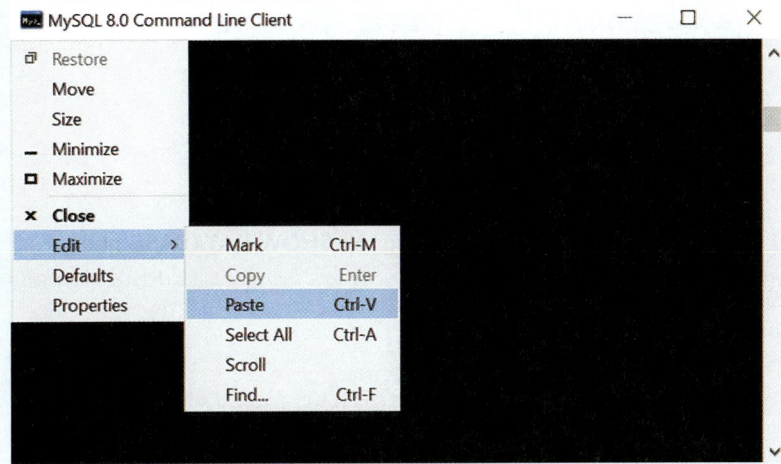

**FIGURE D** Copy the queries to create this chapter's databases and tables to the MySQL command-line prompt.

Copyright Oracle and its affiliates. Used with permission

## Using SELECT to Retrieve Rows (Records) from a Table

The SQL SELECT query, which is likely the most frequently used query, retrieves rows (records) from a table. The general syntax (form) of the SELECT query is:

```
SELECT column[, column …] FROM table [WHERE condition] [ORDER BY field [ASC | DESC]]
```

Within the SELECT query format, the items that appear within brackets [ ] are optional. The ellipses (…) indicate that you can specify more than one comma-separated column name.

Before you can use SELECT to query a table within a database, you must issue the SQL USE query to specify the database you want to use. To view the list of available databases to which you can connect, issue the SHOW DATABASES query:

```
SHOW DATABASES
```

When you execute the query, SQL will display the database list, as shown in **FIGURE 6.1**.

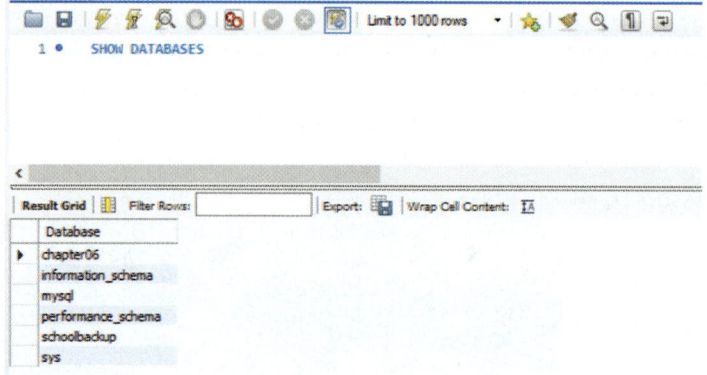

**FIGURE 6.1** Viewing available databases using the SHOW DATABASE query.

*Note:* If your system does not list the CHAPTER06 database, which is used throughout this chapter, download and install the database from this text's catalog page as previously discussed.

Copyright Oracle and its affiliates. Used with permission

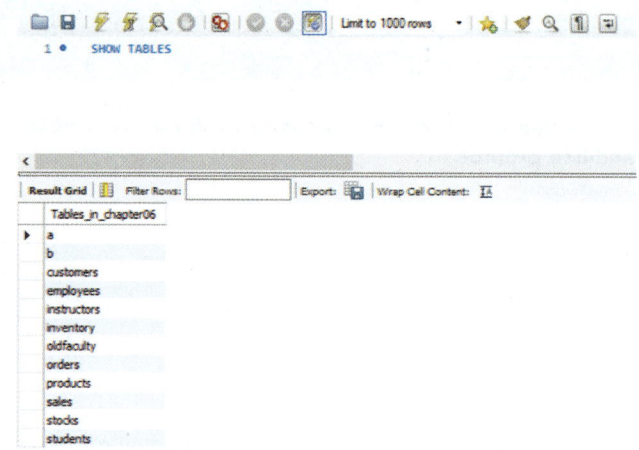

**FIGURE 6.2** Using the SHOW TABLES query to list the tables a database contains.

Copyright Oracle and its affiliates. Used with permission

The following USE command, for example, directs the database server to use the CHAPTER06 database:

```
USE CHAPTER06
```

To view the list of tables the database contains, issue the SHOW TABLES query:

```
SHOW TABLES
```

If you are using the CHAPTER06 database, SQL will display the table list shown in **FIGURE 6.2**.

A relational database consists of tables, which, in turn, consist of records that are made up of fields, as shown in **FIGURE 6.3**. Chapter 5, "Database and Data Warehouse Considerations," discusses relational databases in more detail.

Using the SELECT query, you specify the names of columns you want your database query to return. For example, the following SELECT query returns the Lastname column for all records within the Employees table:

```
SELECT Lastname FROM Employees
```

When you execute this query, SQL will display the single column of fields, with one field for each record in the table, as shown in **FIGURE 6.4**.

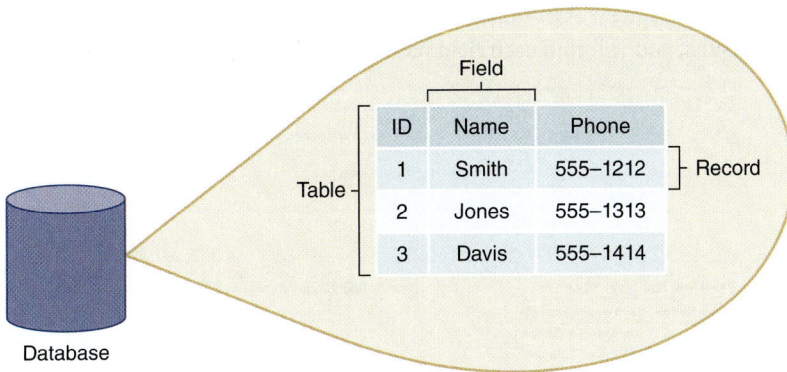

**FIGURE 6.3** The components of a relational database.

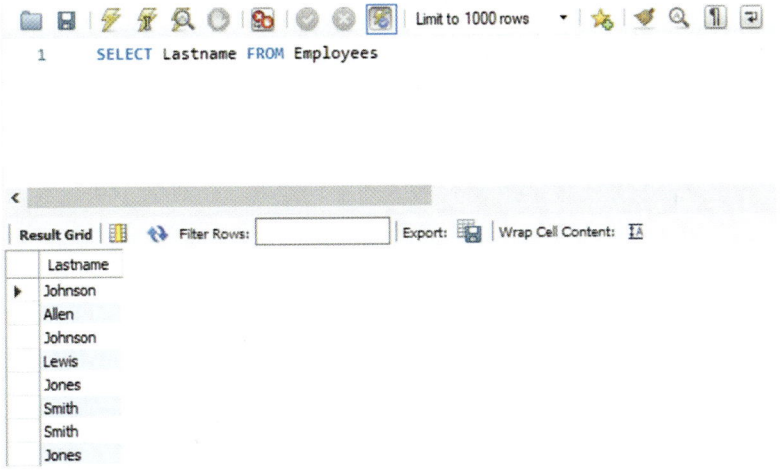

**FIGURE 6.4** Displaying a single field using SELECT.

Copyright Oracle and its affiliates. Used with permission

Often, you will want to retrieve data for more than one field. In such cases, you simply separate the field names with commas. The following SELECT query, for example, displays each employee's first name, last name, and email address:

```
SELECT Firstname, Lastname, Email FROM Employees
```

When you execute the query, SQL will display the fields as shown in **FIGURE 6.5**.

When you first start working with a table, you may not know the names of the table fields and you may want to take a look at the data the table contains. In such cases, use the asterisk (*) **wildcard** character to direct SELECT to return all the fields for each record in the table, as shown here:

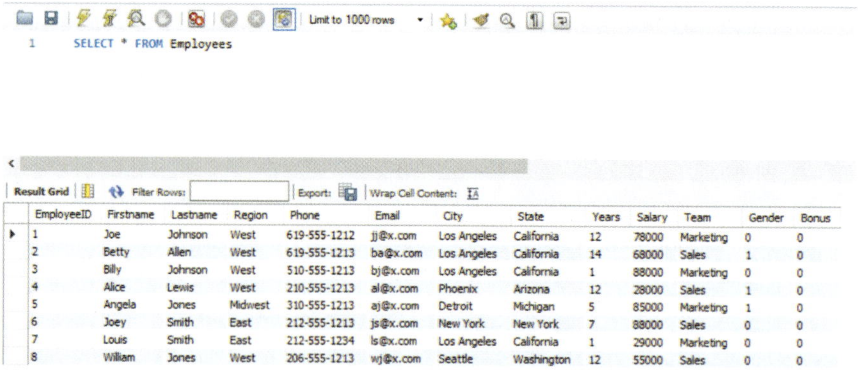

```
SELECT * FROM Employees
```

When you execute this query, SQL will display all the fields, as shown in **FIGURE 6.6**. At the top of your query results, you will find each field name.

**FIGURE 6.5** Using SQL to display multiple field values.

Copyright Oracle and its affiliates. Used with permission

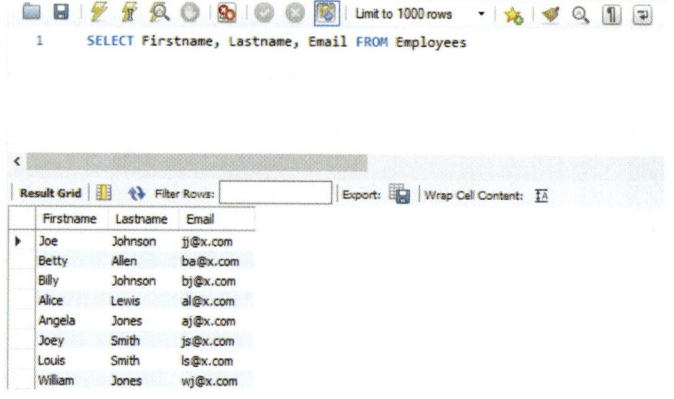

**FIGURE 6.6** Using the asterisk (*) wildcard character to display all fields for all records in a table.

Copyright Oracle and its affiliates. Used with permission

## Limiting the Number of Rows SELECT Returns

When you execute a SELECT query, SQL will display all the matching records. When your tables are small, displaying all the records may not be a problem. As your table size increases, you can limit the number of records SELECT returns using the LIMIT keyword and specifying the number of records you desire. The following SELECT query, for example, uses LIMIT to direct SELECT to display only the first five records in the Employees table:

```
SELECT * FROM Employees LIMIT 5
```

When you execute this query, SQL will display the five records as shown in **FIGURE 6.7**.

## Sorting Your Query Results

Often, the first way database developers analyze data is simply to sort the data from highest to lowest (descending) or lowest to highest (ascending) order based on the value of one or more fields. To sort the results of a SELECT query, you use the ORDER BY clause. The following SELECT query, for example, sorts the Employees table by last name:

```
SELECT * FROM Employees ORDER BY LastName
```

By default, SELECT will sort the values in ascending order, from lowest to highest, as shown in **FIGURE 6.8**.

To sort records in descending order, you include the DESC keyword after your sort-field names. Similarly, to force ascending order, you use the ASC keyword. The following SELECT query displays students by grade point average (GPA) in descending order:

```
SELECT * FROM Students ORDER BY GPA DESC
```

When you execute this query, SQL will display the sorted records as shown in **FIGURE 6.9**.

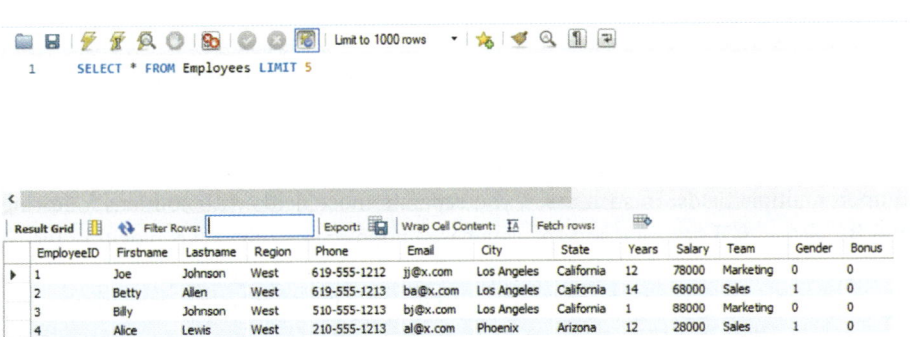

**FIGURE 6.7** Limiting the number of records SELECT returns using the LIMIT keyword.

*Note:* If you are using Microsoft SQL, you will use the TOP keyword instead of LIMIT, such as: SELECT * TOP 5 FROM Employees, and if you are using Oracle, you will use the RowNum variable: SELECT * FROM Employees WHERE RowNum <= 5.

Copyright Oracle and its affiliates. Used with permission

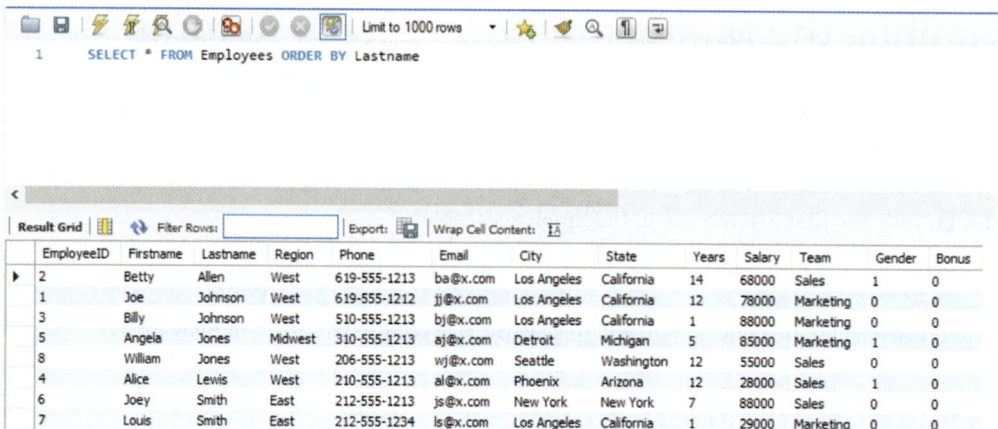

**FIGURE 6.8** Sorting records in the Employees table by last name in ascending order.
Copyright Oracle and its affiliates. Used with permission

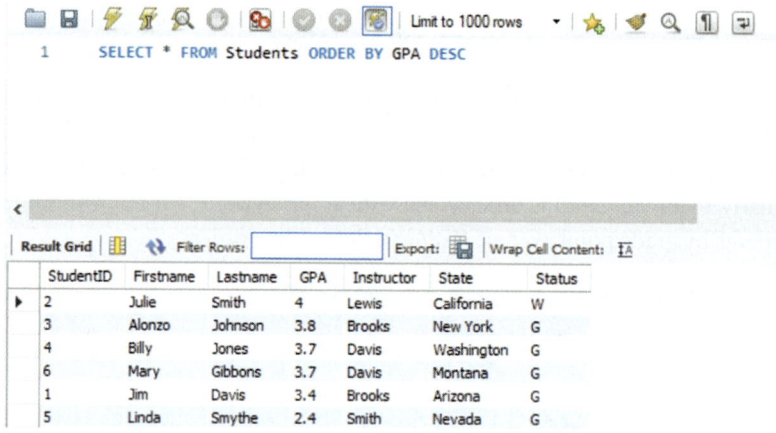

**FIGURE 6.9** Using ORDER BY DESC to sort records in descending order.
Copyright Oracle and its affiliates. Used with permission

Depending on your data, there may be times when you will want to sort your query results based upon multiple fields. In such cases, you separate those fields with commas following the ORDER BY clause. SQL will first sort the data based upon the first field. Then, within the sorted results, SQL will sort related records based upon the second field. SQL will perform similar processing for the remaining fields. For example, the following SELECT query will sort sales data by region and then sort that data by employee last name:

```
SELECT * FROM Employees ORDER BY Region, Lastname
```

When you execute this query, SQL will display the results shown in **FIGURE 6.10**.

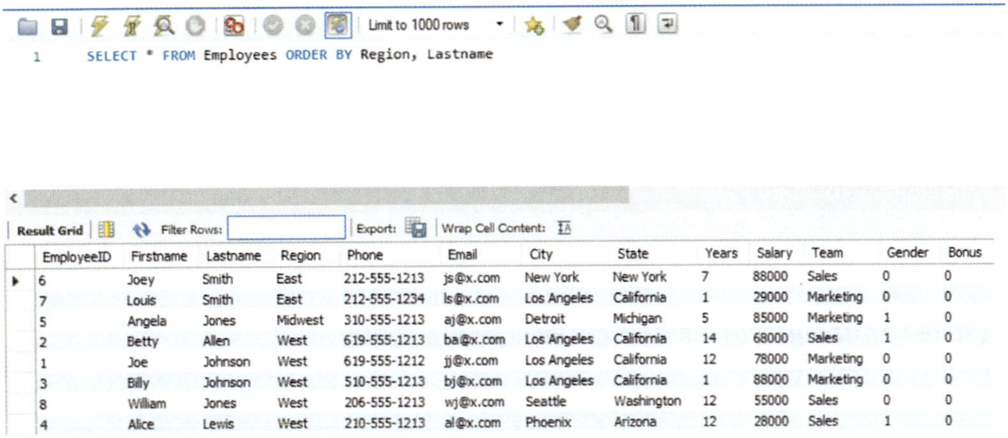

```
SELECT * FROM Employees ORDER BY Region, Lastname
```

| EmployeeID | Firstname | Lastname | Region | Phone | Email | City | State | Years | Salary | Team | Gender | Bonus |
|---|---|---|---|---|---|---|---|---|---|---|---|---|
| 6 | Joey | Smith | East | 212-555-1213 | js@x.com | New York | New York | 7 | 88000 | Sales | 0 | 0 |
| 7 | Louis | Smith | East | 212-555-1234 | ls@x.com | Los Angeles | California | 1 | 29000 | Marketing | 0 | 0 |
| 5 | Angela | Jones | Midwest | 310-555-1213 | aj@x.com | Detroit | Michigan | 5 | 85000 | Marketing | 1 | 0 |
| 2 | Betty | Allen | West | 619-555-1213 | ba@x.com | Los Angeles | California | 14 | 68000 | Sales | 1 | 0 |
| 1 | Joe | Johnson | West | 619-555-1212 | jj@x.com | Los Angeles | California | 12 | 78000 | Marketing | 0 | 0 |
| 3 | Billy | Johnson | West | 510-555-1213 | bj@x.com | Los Angeles | California | 1 | 88000 | Marketing | 0 | 0 |
| 8 | William | Jones | West | 206-555-1213 | wj@x.com | Seattle | Washington | 12 | 55000 | Sales | 0 | 0 |
| 4 | Alice | Lewis | West | 210-555-1213 | al@x.com | Phoenix | Arizona | 12 | 28000 | Sales | 1 | 0 |

**FIGURE 6.10** Sorting query results by multiple fields.

Copyright Oracle and its affiliates. Used with permission

## Selecting Only Records that Meet a Condition

By default, the SELECT query will return every record the specified table contains. When your tables are small, viewing all records may be fine. Normally, however, you want to retrieve only those records that meet a specific condition, such as students with a grade of B or higher, salespeople working on the West Coast, or products with an inventory level greater than 100. Database developers refer to such query operations as filtering the data.

To specify a condition within a SELECT query, you add a WHERE clause:

```
SELECT Field(s) FROM Table WHERE Condition
```

Assume, for example, you are using the Employees table previously shown. The following SELECT query uses a WHERE clause to display only those employees working in New York:

```
SELECT * FROM Employees WHERE City='New York'
```

As you can see, the query uses the asterisk wildcard to display all fields. Within the WHERE clause, the query specifies the City field and desired filter—in this case, 'New York'. Because the City field contains a string value, you must specify the city name within single quotes. When you execute this query, SQL will examine each row in the table to see if the City field contains the value New York, displaying the matching records shown in **FIGURE 6.11**.

In a similar way, the following query uses a WHERE clause to view records for employees with the last name 'Smith':

```
SELECT * FROM Employees WHERE Lastname='Smith'
```

Given the Employees table has records for multiple employees with the last name Smith, the query will return a record for each, as shown in **FIGURE 6.12**.

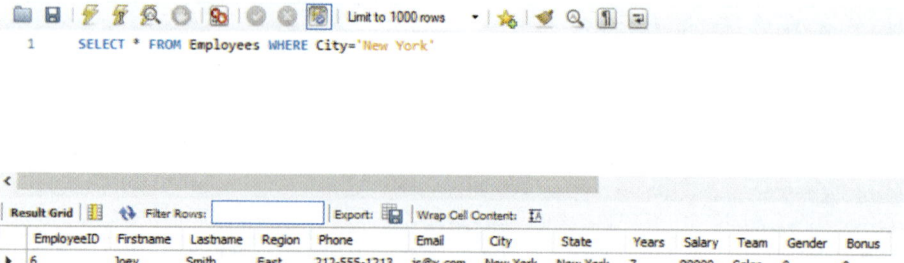

**FIGURE 6.11** Using a WHERE clause to filter records by city.
Copyright Oracle and its affiliates. Used with permission

**FIGURE 6.12** Using a WHERE clause to filter records by last name.
Copyright Oracle and its affiliates. Used with permission

Finally, the following SELECT query will display the first name, last name, and phone number for employees who work in California:

```
SELECT Firstname, Lastname, Phone FROM Employees WHERE
State='California'
```

When you execute this query, SQL will display the results shown in **FIGURE 6.13**.

## Using the SQL Relational Operators

The previous queries have used the SQL equality operator, the equals sign (=), to test for columns whose values are equal to the value specified in the WHERE clause. As described in **TABLE 6.5**, SQL supports several relational operators you can use within a WHERE clause condition.

The following query, for example, uses the greater than or equal to (>=) relational operator to display employees who have worked for the company for 10 or more years:

```
SELECT * FROM Employees WHERE Years >= 10
```

## Selecting Only Records that Meet a Condition

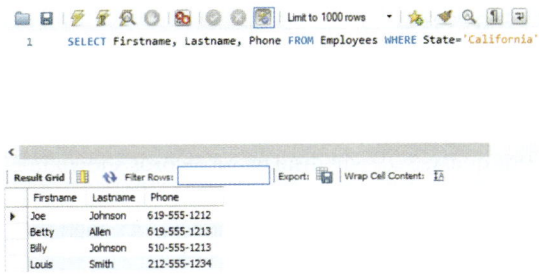

**FIGURE 6.13** Specifying field names and a WHERE clause within a SELECT query to filter specific values.
Copyright Oracle and its affiliates. Used with permission

**TABLE 6.5** The SQL Relational Operators

| Operator | Description | Example |
|---|---|---|
| = | True if the values are equal | WHERE Field=101 |
| <> | True if the values are not equal | WHERE Day <> 'Tuesday' |
| != | True if the values are not equal | WHERE Month != 'January' |
| > | True if the first value is greater than the second | WHERE Age > 13 |
| < | True if the first value is less than the second | WHERE Sales < 5 |
| >= | True if the first value is greater than or equal to the second | WHERE Age >= 21 |
| <= | True if the first value is less than or equal to the second | WHERE Hour <= 12 |
| ANY | True if a value matches any of a subquery's results | WHERE Field = ANY (SELECT column FROM table) |
| BETWEEN | True if a value is between two specified values | WHERE Score BEWEEN 70 AND 100 |
| IN | True if a value is in the list of specified values | WHERE Day IN ('Monday', 'Tuesday', 'Wednesday') |
| LIKE | True if a value matches the specified wildcard characters | WHERE Name LIKE 'Jo%' |
| SOME | True if a value matches any of a subquery's results | WHERE Field = SOME (SELECT column FROM table) |

When you execute this query, SQL will display the records shown in **FIGURE 6.14**. In a similar way, the following query lists employees who make less than $30,000:

```
SELECT * FROM Employees WHERE Salary < 30000
```

When you execute this query, SQL will display the records shown in **FIGURE 6.15**.

The SQL BETWEEN operator lets you compare a range of values. For example, the following query returns the employees who make between $50,000 and $75,000 a year:

```
SELECT * FROM Employees WHERE Salary BETWEEN 50000 AND 75000
```

When you execute this query, SQL will display the employees shown in **FIGURE 6.16**.

The SQL IN operator lets you compare a column's value to a specified set of values. For example, the following query lists the employees who live in New York, Los Angeles, or Seattle:

```
SELECT * FROM Employees WHERE CITY IN ('New York', 'Los Angeles', 'Seattle')
```

**FIGURE 6.14** Using the greater than or equal to (>=) operator to display employees who have worked for the company for 10 or more years.

Copyright Oracle and its affiliates. Used with permission

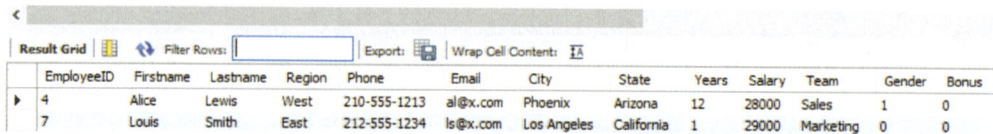

**FIGURE 6.15** Using the less than (<) operator to display employees making less than $30,000.

Copyright Oracle and its affiliates. Used with permission

## Selecting Only Records that Meet a Condition

**FIGURE 6.16** Using the BETWEEN operator to display employees making between $50,000 and $75,000 a year.
Copyright Oracle and its affiliates. Used with permission

**FIGURE 6.17** Using the IN operator to compare a field's value to a set of values.
Copyright Oracle and its affiliates. Used with permission

Again, because the city names are string values, you must enclose the names within quotes. When you execute this query, SQL will display the values shown in **FIGURE 6.17**.

The SQL LIKE operator lets you compare a field's value to a pattern that may contain one or more wildcard characters. The LIKE operator supports the percent sign (%) and underscore (_) wildcards. The percent sign wildcard directs SQL to match zero or more characters. **TABLE 6.6** describes several uses of the percent sign wildcard.

The SQL underscore wildcard, in contrast, matches only one character. **TABLE 6.7** describes several uses of the underscore (_) wildcard.

The following SELECT query uses the percent sign wildcard with the LIKE clause to display employees whose last names begin with the letters 'Jo':

```
SELECT * FROM Employees WHERE Lastname LIKE 'Jo%'
```

## TABLE 6.6 Examples of the SQL Percent Sign (%) Wildcard

| Wildcard Operation | Matches |
|---|---|
| LIKE 'Sm%' | Smith, Smythe, Smothers, Smart |
| LIKE 'J%' | James, Jo, Johnson, Jones, Julie |
| LIKE '212%' | 212, 2120, 2125, 2120222 |
| LIKE '%' | Matches everything |

## TABLE 6.7 Examples of the SQL Underscore (_) Wildcard

| Wildcard Operation | Matches |
|---|---|
| LIKE '_IKE' | Ike, Mike, Nike, Tike |
| LIKE '_arry' | Parry, Harry, Larry |
| LIKE '1_:00' | 1:00, 10:00, 11:00, 12:00 |

```
1  SELECT * FROM Employees WHERE Lastname LIKE 'Jo%'
```

| EmployeeID | Firstname | Lastname | Region | Phone | Email | City | State | Years | Salary | Team | Gender | Bonus |
|---|---|---|---|---|---|---|---|---|---|---|---|---|
| 1 | Joe | Johnson | West | 619-555-1212 | jj@x.com | Los Angeles | California | 12 | 78000 | Marketing | 0 | 0 |
| 3 | Billy | Johnson | West | 510-555-1213 | bj@x.com | Los Angeles | California | 1 | 88000 | Marketing | 0 | 0 |
| 5 | Angela | Jones | Midwest | 310-555-1213 | aj@x.com | Detroit | Michigan | 5 | 85000 | Marketing | 1 | 0 |
| 8 | William | Jones | West | 206-555-1213 | wj@x.com | Seattle | Washington | 12 | 55000 | Sales | 0 | 0 |

**FIGURE 6.18** Using the percent sign wildcard character to display employees whose name begins with the letters 'Jo'.

Copyright Oracle and its affiliates. Used with permission

When you execute this query, SQL will display the records shown in **FIGURE 6.18**.
In a similar way, the following SELECT query displays employees with New York area codes (212):

```
SELECT * FROM Employees WHERE Phone LIKE ('212%')
```

When you execute this query, SQL will display the records shown in **FIGURE 6.19**.

# Selecting Only Records that Meet a Condition

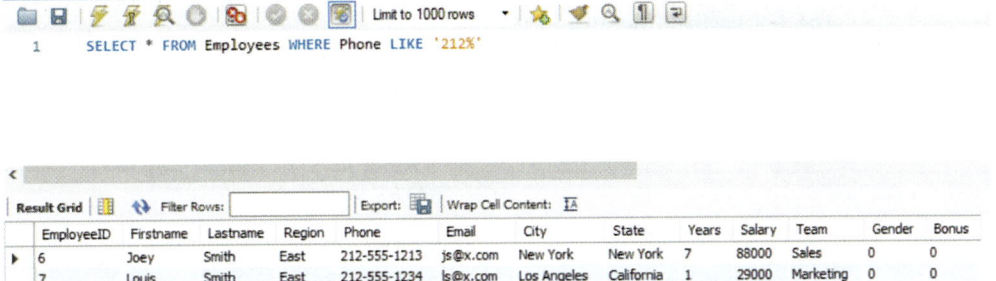

**FIGURE 6.19** Using the SQL percent sign wildcard character to display employees with the 212 area code.

Copyright Oracle and its affiliates. Used with permission

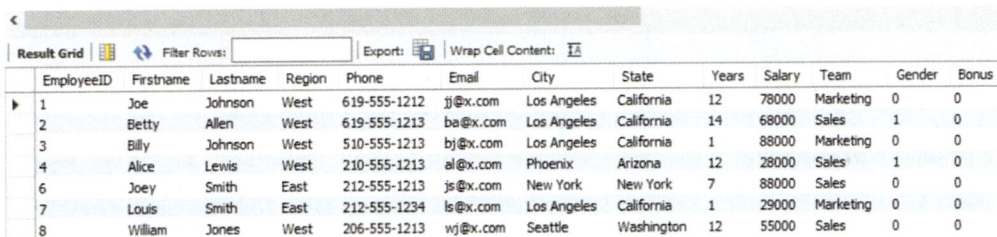

**FIGURE 6.20** Using the SQL underscore character to display employees who work in the east or west regions.

Copyright Oracle and its affiliates. Used with permission

Finally, this query uses two underscore wildcards to display employees who work in the west or east regions:

```
SELECT * FROM Employees WHERE Region LIKE "__ST"
```

When you execute this query, SQL will display the matching records as shown in **FIGURE 6.20**.

## Using Logical Operators for Complex Conditions

The SQL WHERE clause lets you specify a condition that a field must satisfy for the corresponding record to be included in the query results. The previous WHERE clauses have used only one condition, such as City='New York', Sales>=100, or City IN ['Seattle', 'Los Angeles', 'New York']. Often, however, your conditions will be complex, based on two or more conditions. In such cases, you will use the SQL logical operators listed in **TABLE 6.8**.

## TABLE 6.8 The SQL Logical Operators

| Operator | Description | Example |
|---|---|---|
| AND | True if both conditions are true | SELECT * FROM Employees WHERE Region = 'West' AND SALES >= 100,000 |
| OR | True if either or both of the conditions are true | SELECT * FROM Students WHERE GPA >= 3.0 OR Instructor = 'Smith' |
| NOT | Converts a true expression to false and a false condition to true | SELECT * FROM Employees WHERE State NOT IN ('New York', 'Seattle') |

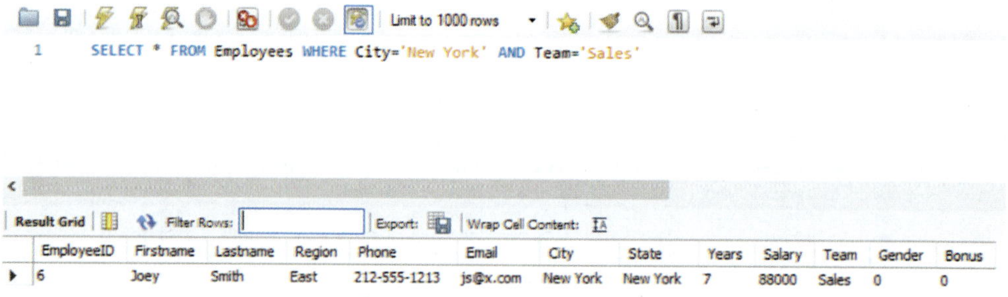

**FIGURE 6.21** Using the SQL AND operator to create a complex query.
Copyright Oracle and its affiliates. Used with permission

The following SELECT query uses the logical AND operator to display the salespeople who live in New York:

```
SELECT * FROM Employees WHERE City='New York' AND Team='Sales'
```

When you execute this query, SQL will display the results shown in **FIGURE 6.21**.

The SQL logical AND operator includes a record only if both conditions are true. In this case, the query only considers a record a match if the City field is 'New York' and the record's Team field is 'Sales'. The SQL logical OR operator, in contrast, includes the record if either condition (or both) is true. The following SELECT query, for example, will list employees who work in either Sales or Marketing:

```
SELECT * FROM Employees WHERE Team='Sales' OR Team='Marketing'
```

When you execute this query, SQL will display the records shown in **FIGURE 6.22**. As you can see, when you use the OR operator, SQL will consider a record a match if either the Team field is 'Sales' or the Team field is 'Marketing'.

The SQL NOT operator directs SQL to include a record if the specified condition is not met. For example, the following query would list employees who do not live in California, New York, or Arizona:

SELECT * FROM Employees WHERE State NOT IN ('California', 'New York', 'Arizona')

When you execute this query, SQL will display the results shown in **FIGURE 6.23**.

**FIGURE 6.22** Using the SQL OR operator to display records meeting either condition or both.

Copyright Oracle and its affiliates. Used with permission

**FIGURE 6.23** Using the SQL NOT operator to display records that do not meet the specified condition.

Copyright Oracle and its affiliates. Used with permission

## SQL and Uppercase and Lowercase Letters

When you include a text field within an SQL WHERE clause, it is very important that you know that SQL will ignore the case of letters when it performs its tests. This means SQL will consider the following conditions the same:

```
WHERE City= 'new york'
WHERE City= 'New York'
WHERE City= 'NEW YORK'
```

**FIGURE A** illustrates a SELECT query that shows SQL text comparisons are not case sensitive. The query will display the employees who reside in the specified states.

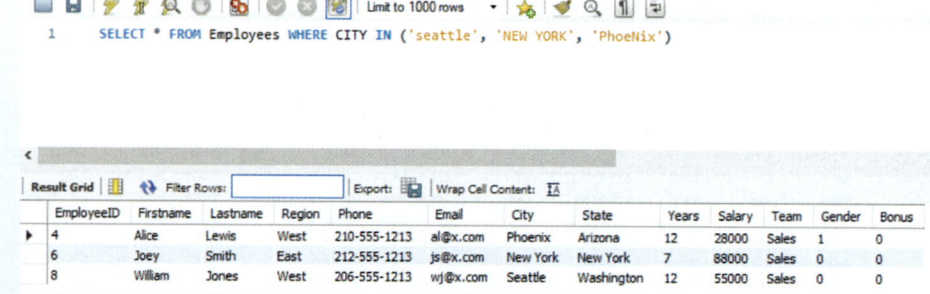

**FIGURE A** When matching text in a condition, SQL ignores the case of letters.

Copyright Oracle and its affiliates. Used with permission

## Connecting to a Remote Database

Before you can use a database to perform operations, you must issue the USE query to tell SQL the name of the database with which you want to work:

```
USE DatabaseName
```

The CHAPTER06 database you have used throughout this chapter resides within a local database (one on your system). Often, you will need to connect to a database that resides on a remote server. To do so, you must provide information about the server's address, the network port on the server that responds to database connections, and username and password authentication data.

To connect to a remote database using the MySQL Workbench, you specify the connection information from the Database Connection dialog box shown in **FIGURE A**.

**FIGURE A** Connecting to a remote database using the MySQL Workbench.

Copyright Oracle and its affiliates. Used with permission

## Specifying Different Field Names with Query Results Using AS

By default, when you perform a SELECT query, SQL displays the table's field name at the top of the query results. For example, the following SELECT query displays all fields from the Employees table:

    SELECT * FROM Employees

When you execute this query, SQL will display the table's field names across the top of its results followed by the field values, as shown in **FIGURE 6.24**.

Depending on how you are using your query results, there may be times when you want to direct SELECT to display specific field names. In such cases, you use the AS keyword. The following query, for example, directs SELECT to use the field names Employee Last Name and Employee Salary within the query results:

    SELECT Lastname AS 'Employee Last Name', Salary As 'Employee
    Salary' FROM Employees

When you execute this query, SQL will display the output shown in **FIGURE 6.25**.

**FIGURE 6.24** By default, SELECT displays the table field names at the top of its results.

Copyright Oracle and its affiliates. Used with permission

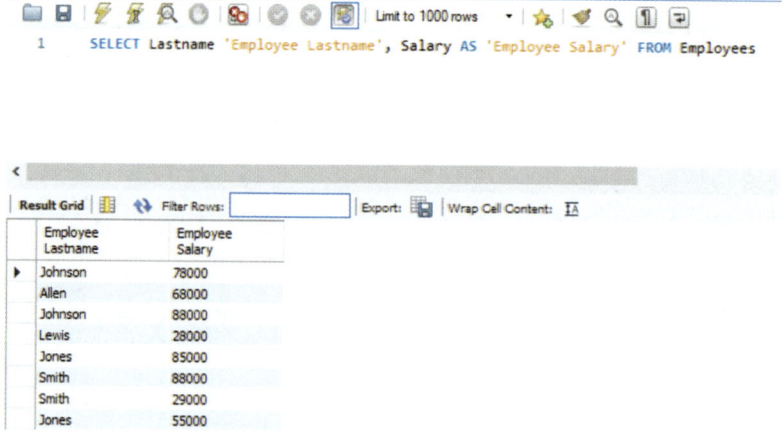

**FIGURE 6.25** Using the AS keyword to specify desired field names.

Copyright Oracle and its affiliates. Used with permission

Later in this chapter, you will examine the SQL COUNT function, which you can use to determine the number of records the query returns. The following SQL query directs SELECT to display a count of the number of records in the Employees table:

```
SELECT COUNT(*) FROM Employees
```

Depending on the database system you are using, the field value that SQL displays for the count result will differ. **FIGURE 6.26**, for example, shows the result in MySQL.

The following query uses the AS keyword to direct SELECT to use the field name 'Number of Records' within the result:

```
SELECT COUNT(*) AS 'Number of Records' FROM Employees
```

When you execute this query, SQL will use the specified field name, as shown in **FIGURE 6.27**.

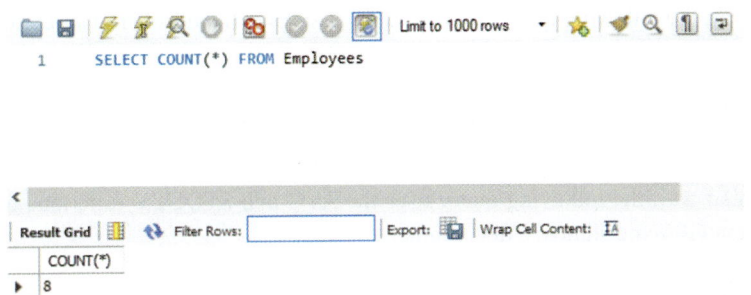

**FIGURE 6.26** The default MySQL field name for a COUNT function's result.
Copyright Oracle and its affiliates. Used with permission

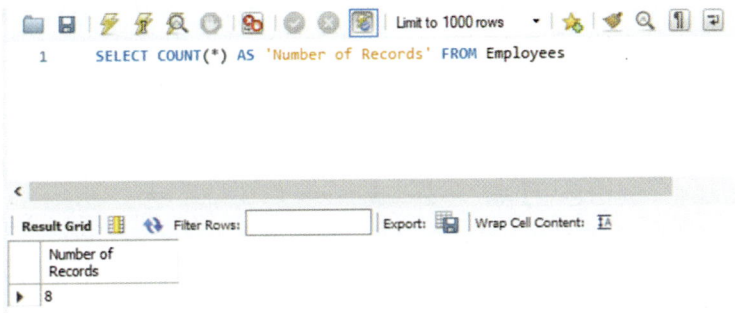

**FIGURE 6.27** Using the AS keyword to specify the field name for a query's COUNT result.
Copyright Oracle and its affiliates. Used with permission

# Using the SQL Built-in Aggregate Functions

As you begin to analyze data using SQL, you will perform common operations, such as summing field values, determining the average field value and its standard deviation, counting the number of records a query returns, and determining the minimum and maximum column values. To help you perform such operations, SQL provides a set of built-in aggregate functions, so named because they work with an aggregate, or group, of records:

- COUNT() returns the number of records a SELECT query returns.
- SUM() returns the sum of the records for the specified column.
- AVG() returns the average record value of the specified column.
- STDDEV() returns the standard deviation of the records for the specified column.
- MAX() returns the maximum column value.
- MIN() returns the minimum column value.

The SQL COUNT function returns the number of records a SELECT query returns. For example, the following query displays the number of records in the Students table:

```
SELECT COUNT(*) FROM Students
```

In a similar way, the following query uses COUNT to display the number of students with a GPA greater than 3.5:

```
SELECT COUNT(*) FROM Students WHERE GPA > 3.5
```

When you execute this query, SQL will display the result shown in **FIGURE 6.28**.

In a similar way, the following query uses the AVG and STDDEV functions to display the average student GPA and standard deviation:

```
SELECT AVG(GPA), STDDEV(GPA) FROM Students
```

When you execute this query, SQL will display the results shown in **FIGURE 6.29**.

Finally, the following query uses the SUM, MIN, and MAX functions to display salary information:

```
SELECT SUM(Salary), MIN(Salary), MAX(Salary) FROM Employees
```

When you execute this query, SQL will display the result shown in **FIGURE 6.30**.

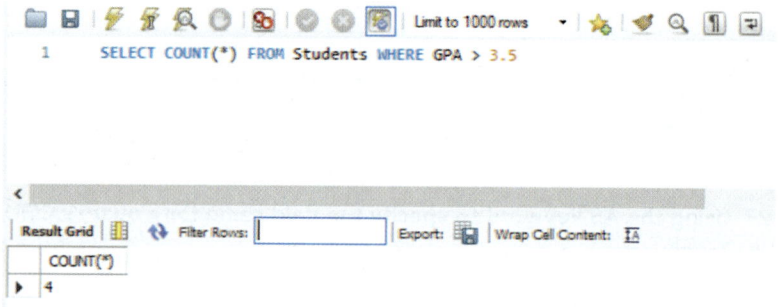

**FIGURE 6.28** Displaying a count of the number of students with a GPA greater than 3.5.

Copyright Oracle and its affiliates. Used with permission

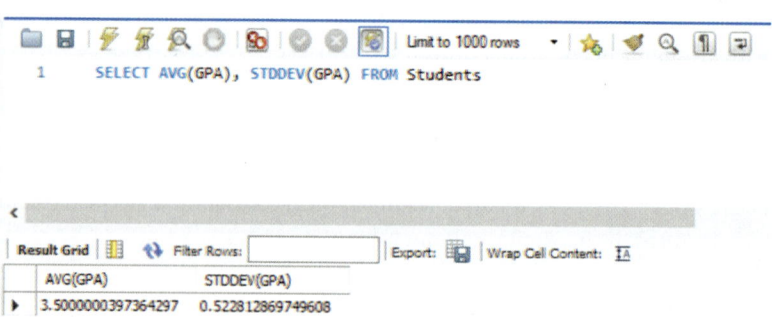

**FIGURE 6.29** Using the AVG and STDDEV functions.

Copyright Oracle and its affiliates. Used with permission

## Performing Arithmetic Operations

When you perform queries, there may be times when you need to perform an arithmetic operation on your query result. For example, you may need to multiply a sales amount by a tax percentage in order to calculate a total price. The following SELECT query multiplies the sales amount by 5% to determine the sales tax amount:

```
SELECT Price, Price*0.05 AS 'Tax Amount' FROM Products WHERE
ProductID=7
```

When you execute this query, SQL will display the result shown in **FIGURE 6.31**.

To display the tax amount for every product, you can use the following query:

```
SELECT Description, Price, Price*0.05 AS 'Tax Amount'
```

**FIGURE 6.30** Displaying salary information using SUM, MIN, and MAX.
Copyright Oracle and its affiliates. Used with permission

**FIGURE 6.31** Using a multiplication operator to calculate the sales tax on a product price.
Copyright Oracle and its affiliates. Used with permission

In this case, when you execute the query, SQL will display the results shown in **FIGURE 6.32**.

To help you perform such arithmetic operations, SQL supports the operators listed in **TABLE 6.9**.

Depending on the data your table contains, there may be times when you need to perform bitwise operations, which operate on individual bits within values. **TABLE 6.10** describes the SQL bitwise operators.

When you create a stored procedure that contains a list of queries that perform a specific operation, there are many times when you will use a field's value within a calculation and then store your result back into the field. For example, the following assignment operator increases the value of the variable Price by 10% by multiplying the variable's current value by 1.1:

```
Price = Price * 1.1;
```

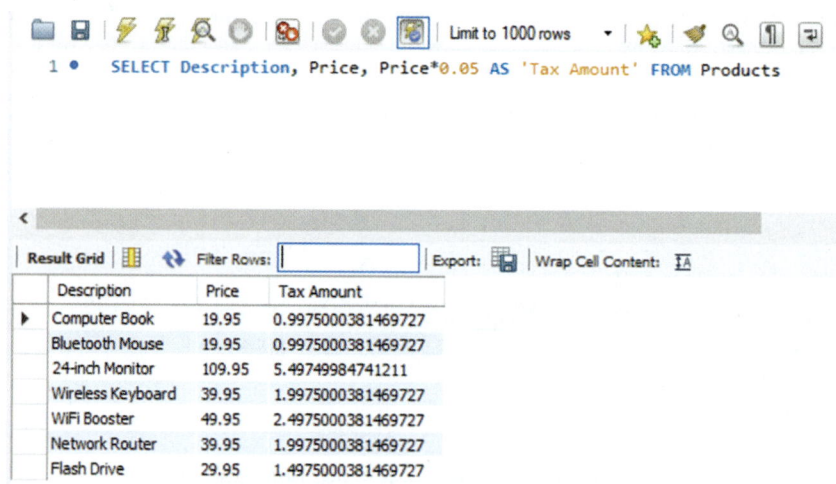

**FIGURE 6.32** Apply an arithmetic operation on all records.

Copyright Oracle and its affiliates. Used with permission

**TABLE 6.9** The SQL Arithmetic Operators

| Arithmetic Operator | Operation |
| --- | --- |
| + | Addition |
| - | Subtraction |
| * | Multiplication |
| / | Division |
| % | Modulo (remainder) |

### TABLE 6.10 The SQL Bitwise Operators

| Bitwise Operator | Operation |
| --- | --- |
| & | Bitwise AND |
| \| | Bitwise OR |
| ^ | Bitwise Exclusive OR |

### TABLE 6.11 The SQL Compound Arithmetic Operators

| Compound Operator | Operation |
| --- | --- |
| =+ | Addition |
| -= | Subtraction |
| *= | Multiplication |
| /= | Division |
| %= | Modulo |
| &= | Bitwise AND |
| \|= | Bitwise OR |
| ^= | Bitwise Exclusive OR |

When you want to assign the result of an arithmetic operation on a field back to the field, you can use the SQL compound operators listed in **TABLE 6.11**. The following assignment operator, for example, uses the compound multiplication operator (*=) to multiply the value of the Price variable by 1.1, similar to the query previously shown:

```
Price *= 1.1;
```

## SQL Arithmetic Functions

When you perform data-analytic operations using SQL, there may be times when you must perform more complex arithmetic operations beyond the SUM, AVG, and STDDEV previously discussed. To help you perform such operations, SQL provides the arithmetic functions listed in **TABLE 6.12**. Chapter 7, "Keep Excel in Your Toolset," defines and describes these arithmetic functions in detail.

Assume, for example, you import the table of stock prices shown in **FIGURE 6.33**. As you can see, the prices contain values beyond a two-digit currency.

**TABLE 6.12** The SQL Arithmetic Functions

| Function | Operation |
|---|---|
| ABS | Returns a value's absolute value |
| ACOS | Returns a value's arc cosine |
| ASIN | Returns a value's arc sine |
| ATAN | Returns a value's arc tangent |
| ATAN2 | Returns the arc tangent of two values |
| CEIL | Returns the smallest integer value that is greater than or equal to the specified number |
| CEILING | Returns the smallest integer value that is greater than or equal to the specified number |
| COS | Returns a value's cosine |
| COT | Returns a value's cotangent |
| DEGREES | Returns the degree equivalent of a value in radians |
| DIV | Returns the integer result of a division operation (not the remainder, as does MOD) |
| EXP | Returns the value of e raised to the power of the specified number |
| FLOOR | Returns the largest integer value that is less than or equal to a value |
| GREATEST | Returns the greatest value in a list of values |
| LEAST | Returns the smallest value in a list of values |
| LN | Returns a value's natural logarithm |
| LOG | Returns a value's natural logarithm or the value's logarithm to a specified base |
| LOG10 | Returns a value's natural logarithm to base 10 |
| LOG2 | Returns a value's natural logarithm to base 2 |
| MAX | Returns the maximum value in a set of values |

| | |
|---|---|
| MIN | Returns the minimum value in a set of values |
| MOD | Returns the remainder (modulo) of a value divided by another number |
| PI | Returns the value of pi |
| POW | Returns the value of a number raised to the power of the specified number |
| POWER | Returns the value raised to the power of the specified number |
| RADIANS | Returns the radian equivalent of a value specified in degrees |
| RAND | Returns a random number |
| ROUND | Returns the value rounded to the specified number of decimal places |
| SIGN | Returns a value's sign |
| SIN | Returns a value's sine |
| SQRT | Returns a value's square root |
| SUM | Returns the sum of a set of values |
| TAN | Returns a value's tangent |
| TRUNCATE | Returns a value truncated to the specified number of decimal places |

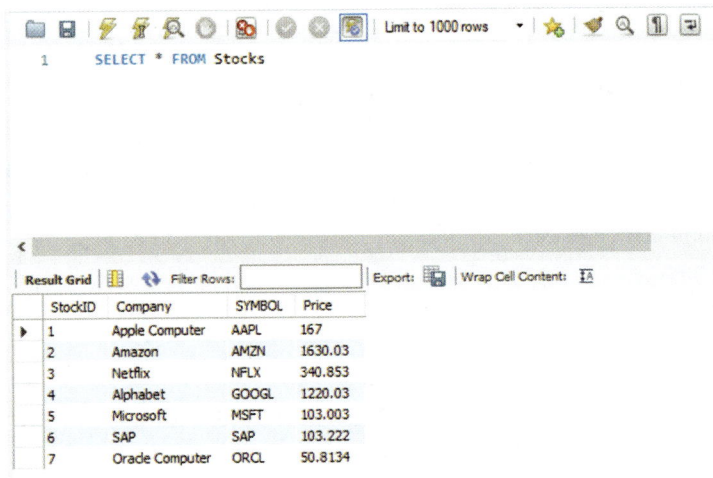

**FIGURE 6.33** A table containing imported stock prices.

Copyright Oracle and its affiliates. Used with permission

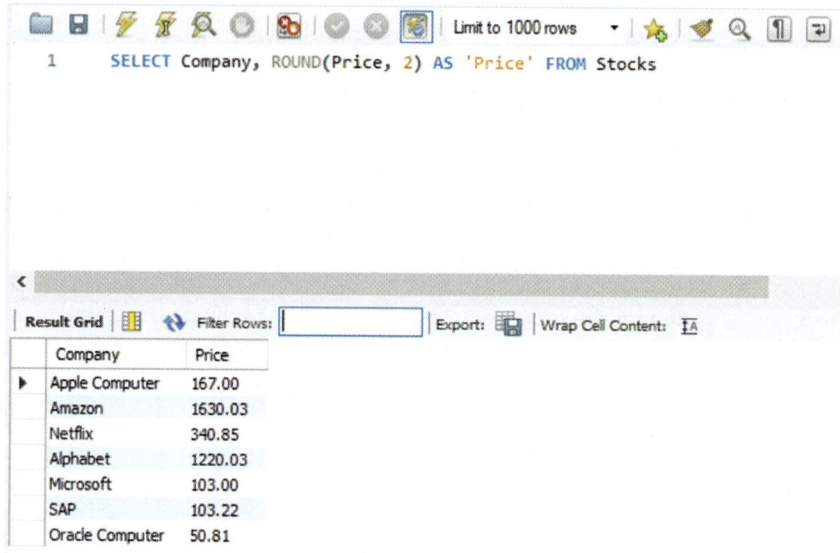

**FIGURE 6.34** Rounding stock price values into a dollars-and-cents form.
Copyright Oracle and its affiliates. Used with permission

The following SELECT query uses the ROUND function to round the values into dollars and cents:

```
SELECT Company, ROUND(Price, 2) AS 'Price' FROM Stocks
```

When you execute this query, SQL will update the records, as shown in **FIGURE 6.34**.

## Grouping Query Results Using GROUP BY

Often, you will perform queries to create reports that summarize key operations. For example, you may produce a monthly sales report that summarizes your sales team results. Depending on the size of your sales team, you may want to group results by division, by region, by sales manager, or even by a combination of each. To perform such operations, you can use the SELECT query GROUP BY clause.

The following query displays current sales data:

```
SELECT * FROM Sales
```

When you execute this query, SQL will display the sales records shown in **FIGURE 6.35**.

To better analyze your sales, you decide to group the data by region, displaying a count of the number of salespeople in each region. To do so, you would use the GROUP BY clause as follows:

```
SELECT Region, COUNT(*) FROM SALES GROUP BY Region
```

When you execute the query, SQL will display the results shown in **FIGURE 6.36**.

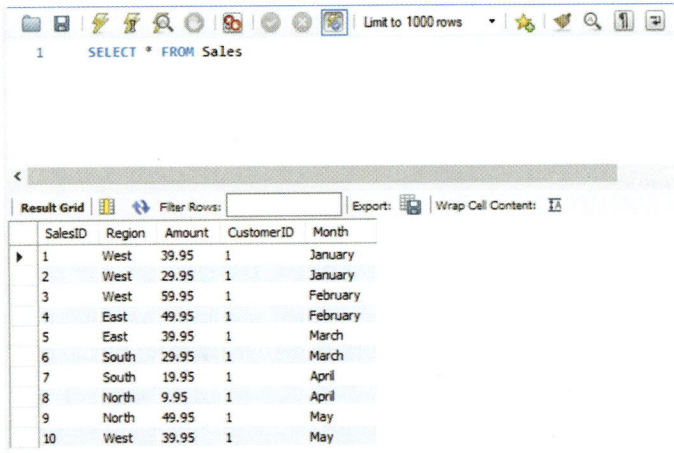

**FIGURE 6.35** Displaying records from the Sales table.
Copyright Oracle and its affiliates. Used with permission

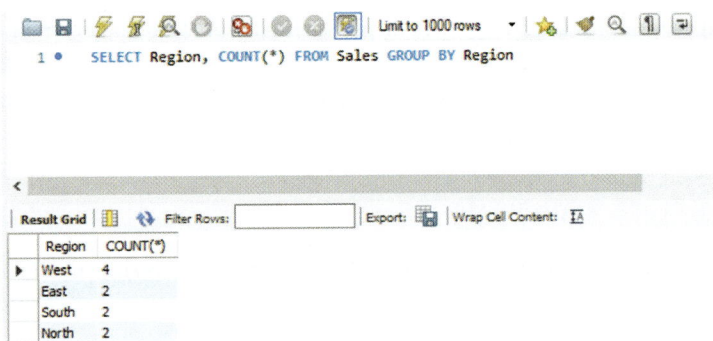

**FIGURE 6.36** Using the SELECT GROUP BY clause to group sales by region.
Copyright Oracle and its affiliates. Used with permission

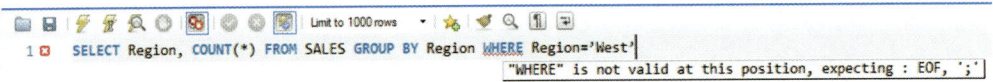

**FIGURE 6.37** SQL will display a syntax error if you try to use a WHERE clause with GROUP BY.
Copyright Oracle and its affiliates. Used with permission

# Using HAVING to Specify a Condition with GROUP BY

As you have learned, to filter queries, you use the WHERE clause to specify a condition:

```
SELECT * FROM Students WHERE Instructor='Jones'
```

When you use a GROUP BY clause within a SELECT query, you do not use the WHERE clause. Instead, you use the HAVING clause. If you try to use a WHERE clause with GROUP BY, SQL will display a syntax error message, as shown in **FIGURE 6.37**.

```
SELECT Region, COUNT(*) FROM Sales GROUP BY Region WHERE
Region='West'
```

To correct this error, execute the command using the HAVING clause:

```
SELECT Region, COUNT(*) FROM Sales GROUP BY Region HAVING
Region='West'
```

## Using GROUP BY ROLLUPs and Cubes

When you group data, there will be many times when you want to create subtotals and a grand total for your groupings. Assume, for example, that your Inventory table contains the records shown in **FIGURE 6.38**.

The following query will display the subtotals for the inventory contained in each state:

```
SELECT State, Product, SUM(Quantity)
FROM Inventory
GROUP BY State
```

When you execute this query, SQL will display the state subtotals, as shown in **FIGURE 6.39**.

Although having state subtotals is valuable, you likely also want to know the total inventory. In such cases, you can use a ROLLUP within the query to direct SQL to "roll up" the subtotals:

```
SELECT State, Product, SUM(Quantity)
FROM Inventory
GROUP BY State WITH ROLLUP
```

When you execute the query, SQL will display the grand total, as shown in **FIGURE 6.40**.

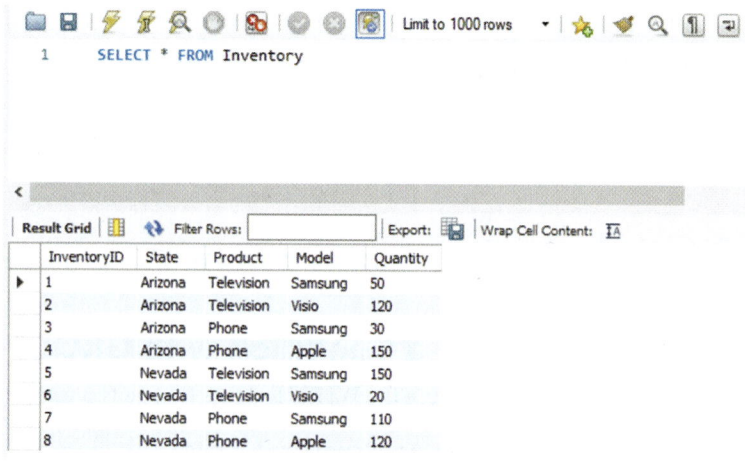

**FIGURE 6.38** The contents of the Inventory table.
Copyright Oracle and its affiliates. Used with permission

## Grouping Query Results Using GROUP BY

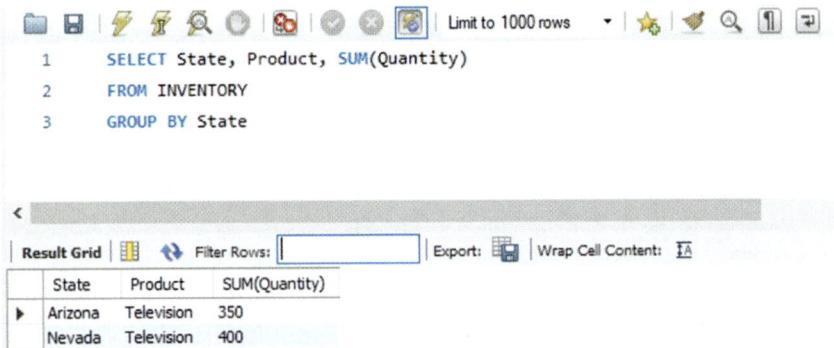

**FIGURE 6.39** Using GROUP BY and SUM() to display the inventory subtotals for each state.
Copyright Oracle and its affiliates. Used with permission

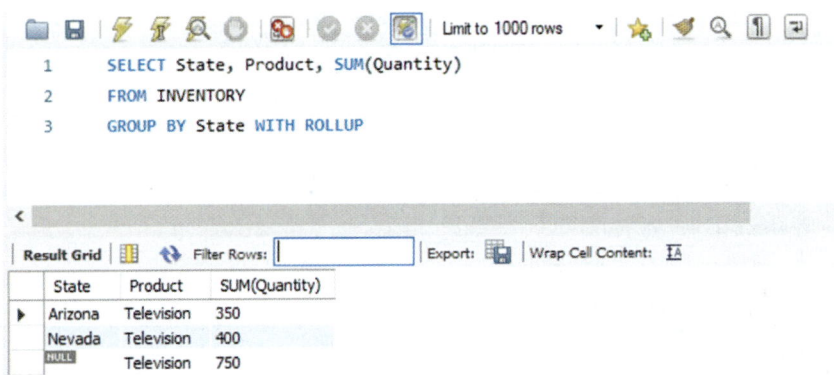

**FIGURE 6.40** Using a ROLLUP to display an inventory grand total.
Copyright Oracle and its affiliates. Used with permission

As you can see in Figure 6.40, SQL does not display a label for the inventory grand total (actually, SQL displays a null). To display a label, you can add a COALESCE statement that directs SQL to substitute the value specified in place of the null, as shown here:

```
SELECT COALESCE(State, 'Total Inventory') State, Product,
 SUM(Quantity)
FROM Inventory
GROUP BY State WITH ROLLUP
```

When you execute this query, SQL will label the result as shown in **FIGURE 6.41**.
The following query uses a ROLLUP to display a summary of products within each state:

```
SELECT State, Product, SUM(Quantity)
FROM Inventory
GROUP BY State, Product WITH ROLLUP
```

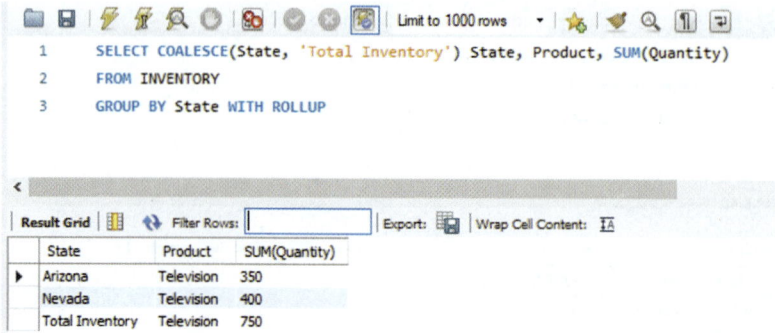

**FIGURE 6.41** Using COALESCE to add a label to a previously null value.
Copyright Oracle and its affiliates. Used with permission

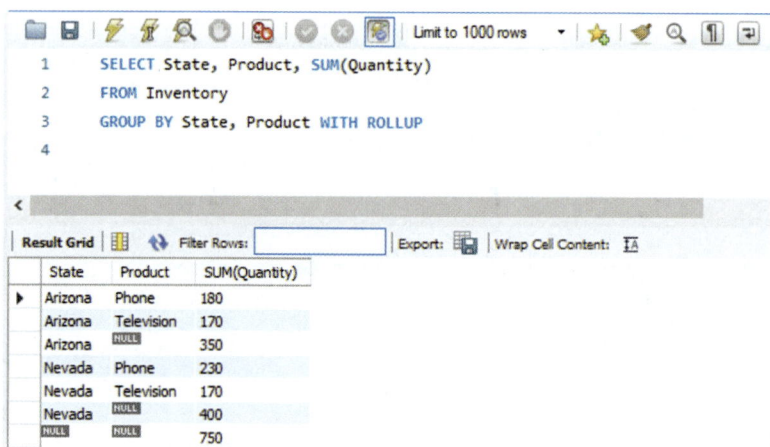

**FIGURE 6.42** Using a ROLLUP to create a product summary, grouped by state.
Copyright Oracle and its affiliates. Used with permission

When you execute this query, SQL will display the product summary, as shown in **FIGURE 6.42**. Finally, the following query produces your complete report:

```
SELECT COALESCE(State, 'Total Inventory') State,
COALESCE(Product, '') Product,
COALESCE(Model, '') Model, SUM(Quantity)
FROM Inventory
GROUP BY State, Product, Model WITH ROLLUP
```

When you execute this query, SQL will display the report shown in **FIGURE 6.43**.

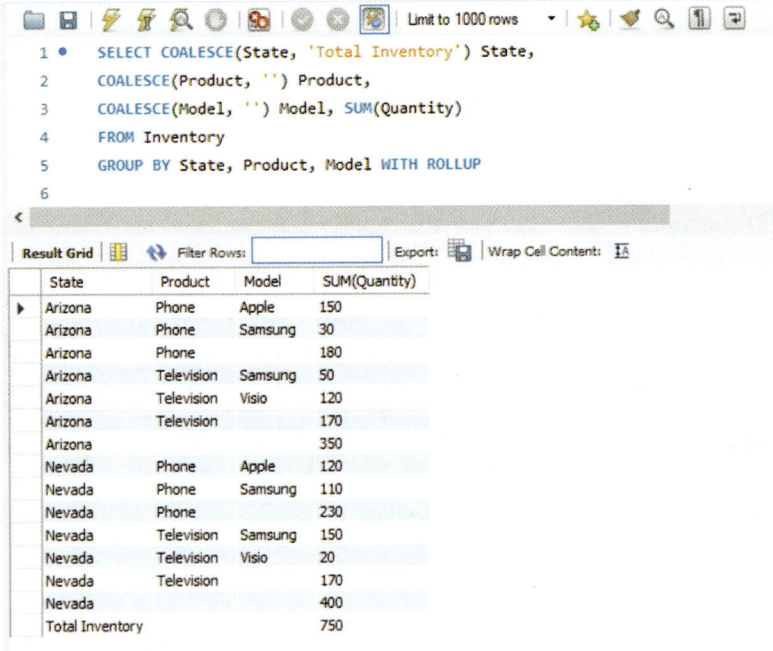

**FIGURE 6.43** Rolling up two fields to create subtotals and a labeled grand total.

*Note:* If you are using a database system other than MySQL, the system may support a CUBE operation, which further extends the ROLLUP capabilities.

Copyright Oracle and its affiliates. Used with permission.

## Joining One Table to Another

When you normalize your data design, you will often break one table into two or more tables to achieve your desired normal form (Chapter 5, "Database and Data Warehouse Considerations," describes this in more detail). When you later need to query the data, you will need to put the tables back together temporarily for the duration of the query's execution. In such cases, you will use a **JOIN** query.

Consider the Orders and Customers tables provided in the CHAPTER06 database from this text's catalog page and shown in **FIGURE 6.44.**

As you can see, both tables have the CustomerID field in common—meaning that the two tables are related on the CustomerID field. As such, you can perform a JOIN operation using that field to combine the tables, as shown in the following query:

```
SELECT Customers.Lastname, Orders.ProductID FROM Customers
JOIN Orders ON Customers.CustomerID = Orders.CustomerID
```

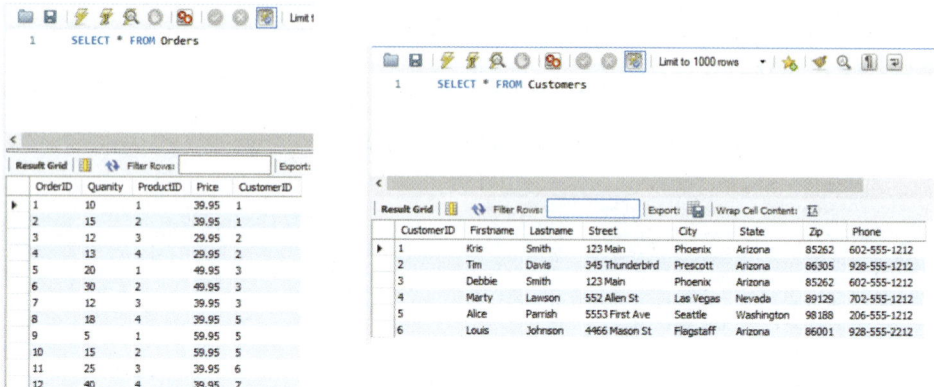

**FIGURE 6.44** The Orders and Customers tables.

Copyright Oracle and its affiliates. Used with permission

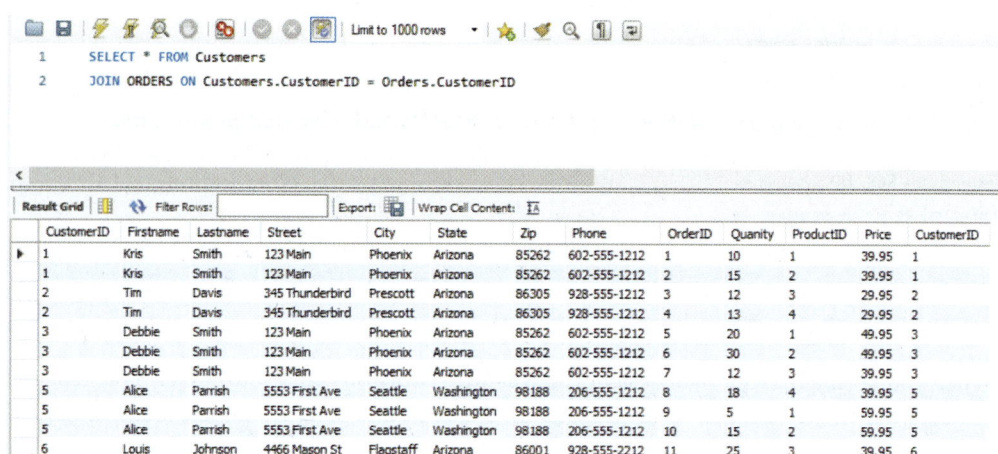

**FIGURE 6.45** JOIN operations create a temporary table based upon matching records in two tables.

Copyright Oracle and its affiliates. Used with permission

There's a lot going on within this query—first, the query precedes the field names with the table names (such as Customers.Lastname). Because JOIN operations use two tables that may each use the same field names, by preceding the field names with the table names, you reduce any chance of confusion as to which field the query references. Next, the JOIN query specifies the name of the second table and the fields within each table upon which the JOIN will be made. As the query executes, SQL will create a temporary table behind the scenes that contains the fields of both tables for the records for which the JOIN fields are equal, as shown in **FIGURE 6.45**.

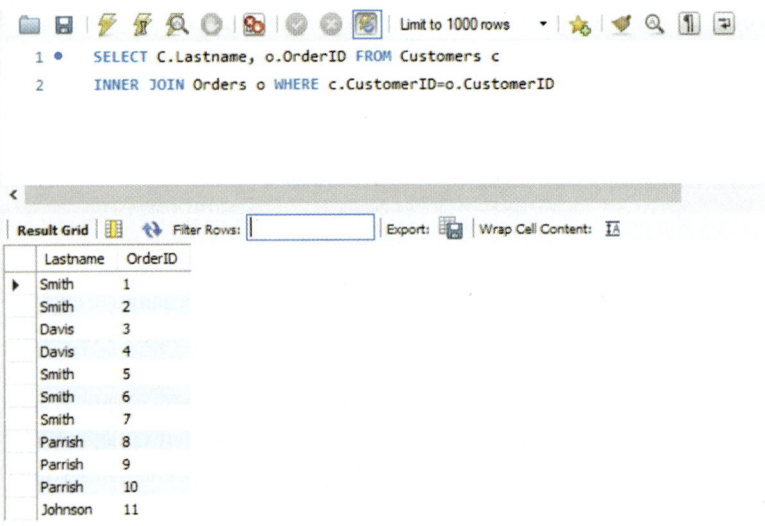

**FIGURE 6.46** Displaying all fields in the temporary table created by a JOIN operation.
Copyright Oracle and its affiliates. Used with permission

The following query extends the previous JOIN operation to display all the fields within the resultant table:

```
SELECT * FROM Customers JOIN Orders WHERE Customers.CustomerID = Orders.CustomerID
```

When you execute this query, SQL will display the results shown in **FIGURE 6.46**.

## Using Table Alias Names

When you perform a JOIN operation, to avoid field name conflicts, you will precede field names with the corresponding table names. To reduce your typing and the length of your queries, SQL lets you create table alias names, to which your query can refer, as a shorthand alternative to the longer table name. The following query uses the table aliases c for Customers and o for Orders. To specify an alias name, you include the alias after the table name reference:

```
SELECT * FROM Customers c JOIN Orders o WHERE c.CustomerID = o.CustomerID
```

## Understanding JOIN Types

When you perform a JOIN operation, you temporarily combine two table's fields for those records for which the fields specified within the operation's ON clause have matching values.

Often, there will be records in one table that do not have a matching record within the other. In the case of the Customers and Orders tables, it is very possible that some customers have not yet placed an order, and as such, do not have a matching entry within the Orders table. Visually, you would represent the JOIN operation as the intersection of the two tables, as shown in **FIGURE 6.47**. Such a JOIN is called an **inner join**.

To direct SQL to perform an inner join, you include the keyword INNER, as shown here:

```
SELECT c.Lastname, o.OrderID FROM Customers c
INNER JOIN Orders o WHERE c.CustomerID = o.CustomerID
```

This query would display the order IDs for each customer's orders.

Given the customers and orders scenario, you may want to know the names of customers who have not yet placed an order. In such cases, you can perform a different type of JOIN operation that directs SQL not only to return the matching records but also the records for customers who do not have a matching orders record. Visually, you would represent this JOIN operation as shown in **FIGURE 6.48**.

Because this JOIN operation includes all the records from the left table, the JOIN operation is called a **left join**. To direct SQL to perform a left join, you include the LEFT keyword within the query, as shown here:

```
SELECT c.Lastname, o.OrderID FROM Customers c
LEFT JOIN Orders o WHERE c.CustomerID = o.CustomerID
```

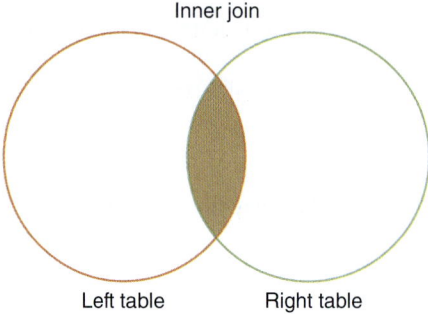

**FIGURE 6.47** An inner join is the intersection of the matching records between two tables.

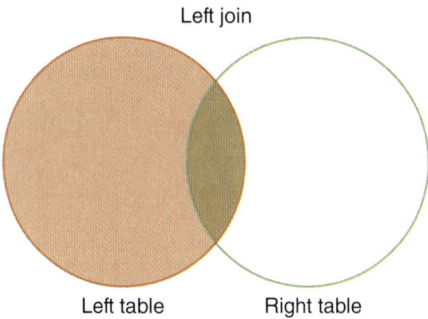

**FIGURE 6.48** A LEFT JOIN operation will include all matching records, plus records from the table specified on the left that do not have matching records.

When you execute this query, SQL will display the records shown in **FIGURE 6.49**.

When SQL creates the resulting left-join table, the Orders table will not have matching CustomerID fields for some of the records, and as such, SQL will not have data to include in the Orders table's side of the JOIN record. When a match does not occur, SQL will assign null values to each field within the Order's side of the table.

Knowing that SQL will assign null values to the missing fields, you can create a query that tests for OrderID is NULL in order to retrieve the customers who have not yet placed an order:

```
SELECT c.Lastname FROM Customers c
LEFT JOIN Orders o WHERE c.CustomerID = o.CustomerID
WHERE OrderID = NULL
```

When you execute this query, SQL will display the names of the customers who have not yet placed an order, as shown in **FIGURE 6.50**.

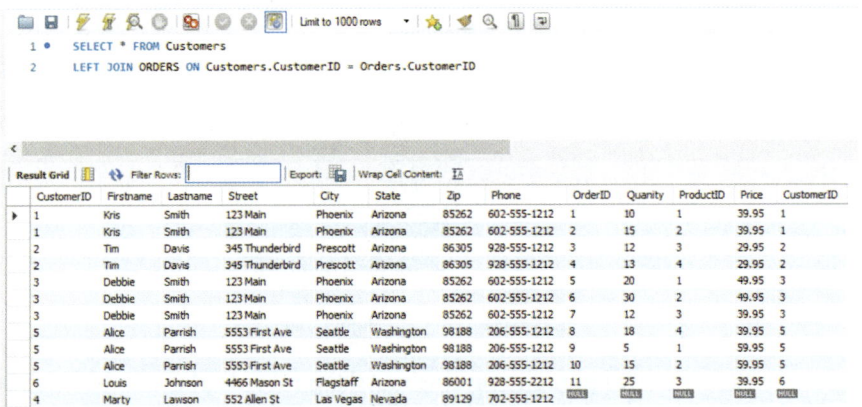

**FIGURE 6.49** Displaying the results of a LEFT JOIN operation.

Copyright Oracle and its affiliates. Used with permission

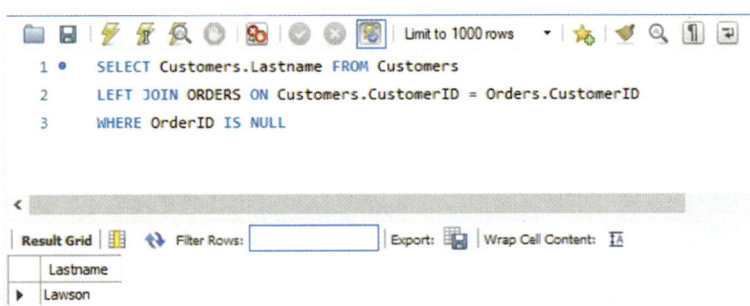

**FIGURE 6.50** Testing for null values in the join table to determine customers who have not yet placed an order.

Copyright Oracle and its affiliates. Used with permission

If you are auditing the company's data, you might want to confirm that every order has an existing customer. In this case, you can perform a right-join operation to retrieve not only the matching records but also every record that appears in the table specified on the right side of the JOIN operation, as shown in **FIGURE 6.51**.

In this case, if SQL cannot find a matching customer for an order, it will assign null values to fields within the temporary JOIN table. The following query performs a **right join** and tests for a null value to determine orders without a customer:

```
SELECT o.OrderID FROM Customers c
RIGHT JOIN Orders o WHERE c.CustomerID = o.CustomerID
WHERE CustomerID = NULL
```

When you execute this query, SQL will return the order IDs of orders that do not have a corresponding customer, as shown in **FIGURE 6.52**.

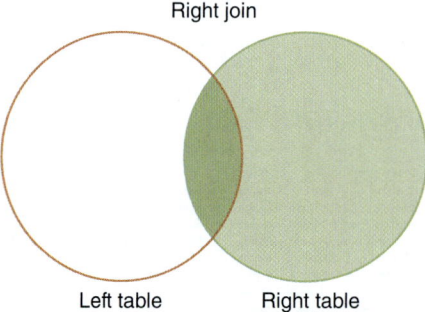

**FIGURE 6.51** A RIGHT JOIN operation returns matching records plus the records within the table that appears on the right side of the JOIN operation.

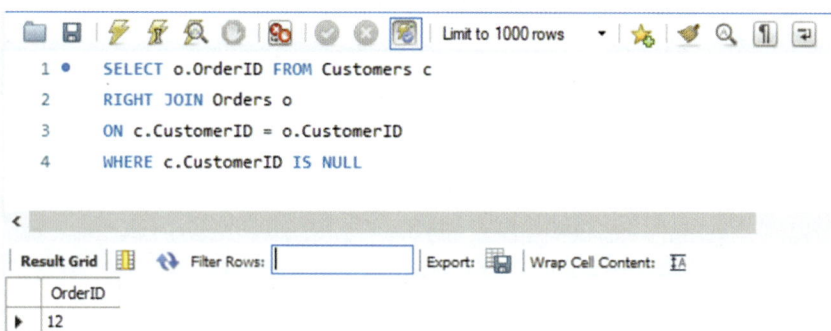

**FIGURE 6.52** Using a RIGHT JOIN to determine orders without a matching customer.

*Note:* MySQL does not support a FULL **OUTER JOIN** operation, which would return matching records, all records from the left table, as well as all records from the right table. Many SQL databases do. To simulate the FULL OUTER JOIN, you can take the UNION of the RIGHT OUTER JOIN with the LEFT OUTER JOIN.

Copyright Oracle and its affiliates. Used with permission

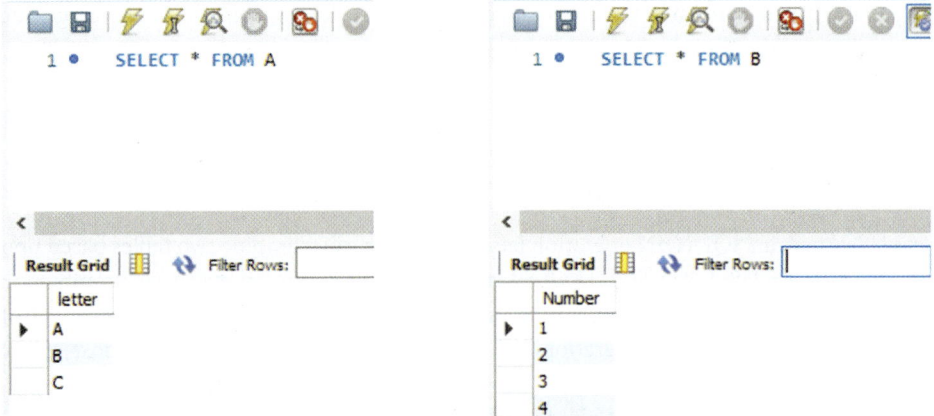

**FIGURE 6.53** The values of the A and B tables.

Copyright Oracle and its affiliates. Used with permission

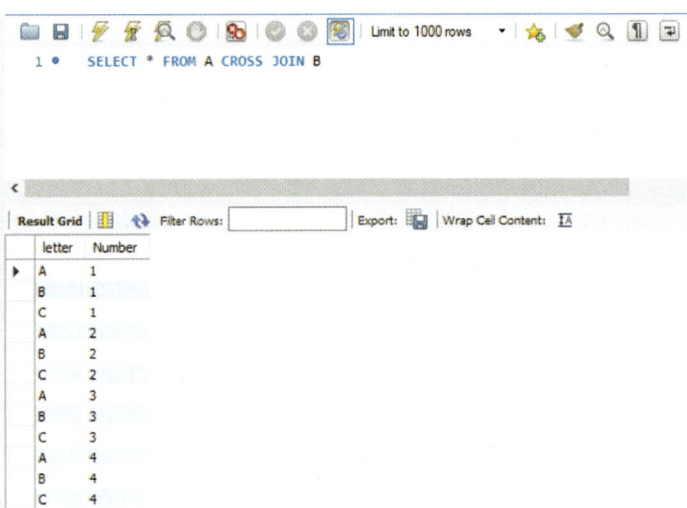

**FIGURE 6.54** The results of a CROSS JOIN operation on two small tables.

Copyright Oracle and its affiliates. Used with permission

The final JOIN, which is not often used, is the **cross join**, so named because SQL will create a record that joins each field in the left table to each field in the right. Assume, for example, the tables contain the values shown in **FIGURE 6.53**.

The following query performs a cross join on table A and B:

```
SELECT * FROM A CROSS JOIN B
```

When you execute this query, SQL will return the records shown in **FIGURE 6.54**.

As you might guess, because the cross join can create a resultant table that is very large, such a query can be very time consuming.

# Understanding SQL Query UNION and INTERSECT Operations

As you just learned, an SQL JOIN operation lets you temporarily combine two tables based upon a related field. In a related way, SQL UNION and INTERSECT operations let you combine the results of two queries. The UNION operation will produce a result that contains all records from the two tables. The INTERSECT operation will produce a result that contains only those records that appear in both queries.

For example, assume you want to know the states for which a university has instructors and students. In such a case, you can use the following UNION query:

```
SELECT State FROM Instructors
UNION
SELECT State FROM Students
```

When you execute this query, SQL will display a list of states for which the university has an instructor or student, as shown in **FIGURE 6.55**.

MySQL does not support an INTERSECT operation. However, you can simulate one using a query similar to the following:

```
SELECT State FROM Instructors WHERE State IN (SELECT State FROM Students)
```

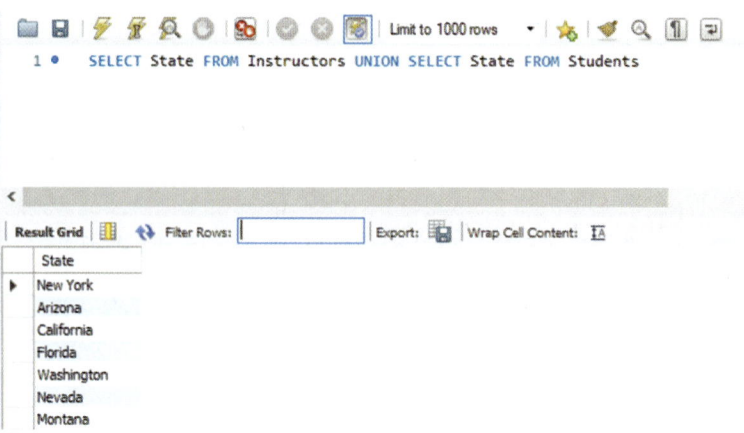

**FIGURE 6.55** Displaying the union of states contained in the Instructors and Students tables.

Copyright Oracle and its affiliates. Used with permission

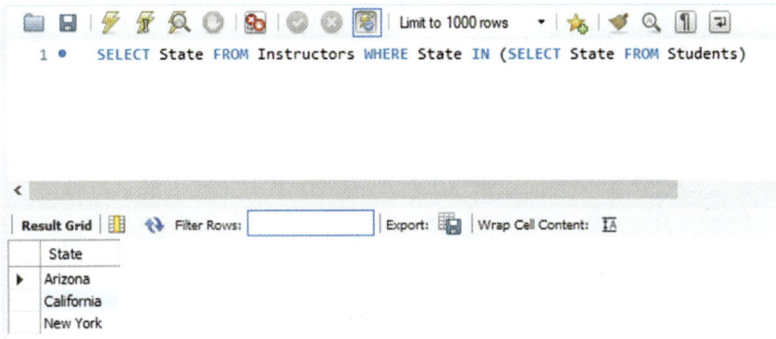

**FIGURE 6.56** Displaying the intersection of states contained in the Instructors and Students tables.

Copyright Oracle and its affiliates. Used with permission

This query uses a nested SELECT query, also called a **subquery**, to select a list of states from the Students table. You will examine nested queries in detail later in this chapter.

When you execute this query, SQL will display the records shown in **FIGURE 6.56**.

# Importing and Exporting Database Data

After a database developer creates a database, they must often next load data into one or more tables from a variety of sources, such as a file, a spreadsheet, or even a different database table.

## Importing Data from a File

Depending on the database system you are using, the commands you must execute to import data from a file will differ. To start, the file that you want to import must separate the field values in some way, normally using a comma or tab character. Database developers refer to such files as comma-separated or tab-delimited files. Assume, for example, you have a comma-separated file containing employee data. (You can download such a file from this text's catalog page at go.jblearning.com/DataMining.) Using MySQL, you can use the following LOAD command to import the data into the Employees table:

```
LOAD DATA INFILE 'C:/ProgramData/MySQL/MySQL Server 8.0/Uploads/
Employees.csv'
INTO TABLE Employees
FIELDS TERMINATED BY ','
ENCLOSED BY '"'
LINES TERMINATED BY '\r\n';
```

When you execute the query, SQL will append the data to the table's contents, as shown in **FIGURE 6.57**.

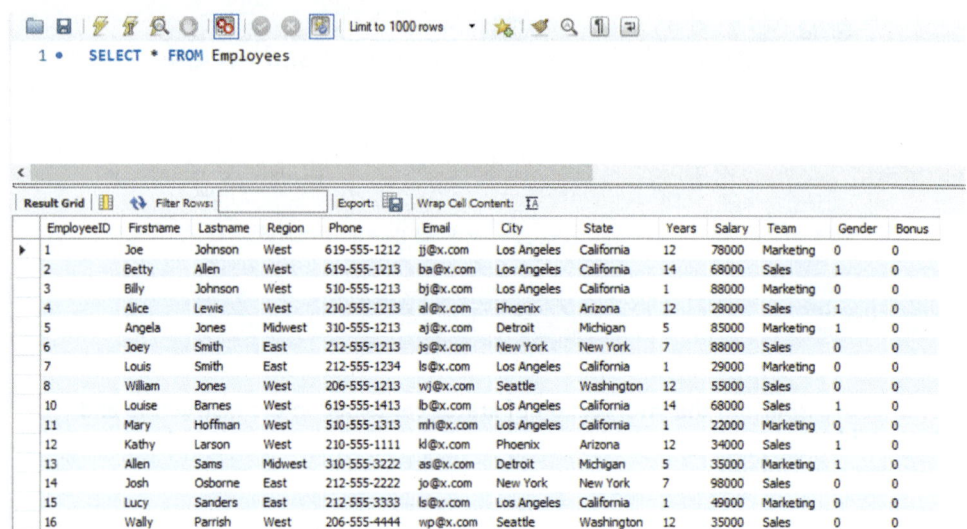

**FIGURE 6.57** Importing a comma-separated file into the MySQL Employees table.

*Note:* This query used the folder shown because, by default, MySQL allows write operations to that folder. To import from a different folder, you will need to change permissions with MySQL.

Copyright Oracle and its affiliates. Used with permission

## Importing Data from a Spreadsheet

Depending on the spreadsheet program you are using, you may have multiple ways to **import** data into a database. First, you can save the spreadsheet as a comma-separated file (a .csv file) and then import the file's contents into the database as just discussed.

Second, because importing spreadsheet data into a database is a common operation, Excel makes the process very easy. Chapter 7, "Keep Excel in Your Toolset," will walk you through the process of connecting Excel to an SQL database and then importing data from a database table into Excel.

## Importing Data from Another Database Table

Often, you may need to move data from one table into another. In such cases, you can use the MySQL INSERT INTO query. The following query copies data from the Sales table into the NewSales table:

```
INSERT INTO NewSales SELECT * FROM Sales
```

Likewise, the following query uses INSERT INTO to copy the contents of the Employees table to a backup table named EmployeesBackup:

```
INSERT INTO EmployeesBackup SELECT * FROM Employees
```

The previous INSERT INTO queries copied all fields from the source table. There may be times, however, when you only want to insert specific fields; in such cases, you specify the desired fields within your SELECT query.

In addition, there may be times when you want to copy the contents of a table that resides in a different database. In such cases, you simply precede the table name with the database name and a period. The following command would display records contained in the Chapter06 database Students table:

```
INSERT INTO StudentsBackup SELECT * From Chapter06.Students
```

*Note:* Before you can insert one table into another, both tables must exist.

## Exporting Data to a File

Just as there will be times when you must import data to a file, there will also be times when you need to **export** a table's data to a file. Again, depending on the database system you are using, the command you execute will differ. The following MySQL command directs MySQL to export the contents of the Employees table to a comma-separated file named EmployeesExport.csv:

```
SELECT * FROM Employees
INTO OUTFILE 'C:/ProgramData/MySQL/MySQL Server 8.0/Uploads/
EmployeesExport.csv'
FIELDS ENCLOSED BY '"'
TERMINATED BY ','
ESCAPED BY '"'
LINES TERMINATED BY '\r\n';
```

After you perform the query, the EmployeeExport.csv file will contain the contents shown in **FIGURE 6.58**.

**FIGURE 6.58** Exporting a table's values to a comma-separated file.

*Note:* This query used the folder shown because, by default, MySQL allows write operations to that folder. To import from a different folder, you will need to change permissions with MySQL.

Used with permission from Microsoft

## Exporting Data to a Spreadsheet

To export data for use by a spreadsheet, you can export the data into a .csv file and then open that file within your spreadsheet program. In addition, if you are using Microsoft Excel, you can connect directly to the database and import the data. Chapter 7, "Keeping Excel in Your Toolset," examines the steps you must perform within Excel to connect directly to an SQL database.

## Performing Extract, Transform, and Load Operations

In the previous sections, you learned how to import and export data into and from a database table. One of the most common operations database developers must perform is to extract data from one or more tables, change that data in some way, and then load the result into a different table. Developers refer to such operations as ETL operations.

Depending on how the data must be changed, the transform operation will differ from one ETL operation to the next. A simple transform operation, for example, might change the numeric values 0 and 1 into character string values such as 'Male' and 'Female.' Similarly, a transform operation might change street addresses into their corresponding geolocation latitude and longitude values.

To perform such ETL operations, database developers can use a programming language such as Python or PHP to read data from one table, update the data as needed, and then write the data to a new table. Chapter 16, "Data Mining Programming Tools," illustrates such operations in detail using the Python programming language. In addition to creating their own applications, database developers can use one of many third-party ETL applications:

- Data Migrator
- Microsoft SQL Server Integration Services (SSIS)
- Oracle Warehouse Builder (OWB)
- Cognos Data Manager
- CloverETL

Finally, the following queries illustrate the use of SQL to perform a simple ETL operation. The SELECT query that follows the USE extracts data from the Employees table into the EmployeeTemp table. Then, using the EmployeeTemp table, the UPDATE queries change the gender value of 1 to male and the gender value of 0 to female. Finally, the fifth query loads the updated data into an EmployeeNew table, and the sixth deletes the temporary table EmployeeTemp, which was used for the transform:

```
USE CHAPTER06;
INSERT INTO EmployeeTemp SELECT * FROM Employee;
UPDATE EmployeeTemp SET Gender='Male' WHEN Gender='1';
UPDATE EmployeeTemp SET Gender='Female' WHEN Gender='0';
INSERT INTO EmployeeNew SELECT * FROM EmployeeTemp;
DROP TABLE EmployeeTemp;
```

*Note:* Remember, if you want to move data to and from a table that resides in a different database, you can precede the table name with the database name and a period: mydata.tablename.

## Using a Cloud-Based Database

To perform simple database operations individually, meaning the data are not shared with other users, you can install the database as a local database on your own notebook or desktop PC. To share data with other users, however, you must install the database on a server that resides at a fixed location in the network, as shown in **FIGURE 6.59**.

Depending on the database you are using, the steps you perform to connect to a remote network database will differ. In any case, you must specify the server's IP address, as well as the network port that listens to database connections. The default MySQL network port is 3306.

Database developers normally refer to database servers that reside within the company's data center as an on-premise database, or on-prem for short. In contrast to using an on-premise database, more companies today are using cloud-based databases that reside in the data center of a cloud provider, such as Amazon AWS, Microsoft Azure, or Google Cloud Platform. To connect to a cloud-based database, you must specify the server's IP address, network port, and authentication information (username and password).

## Using the phpMyAdmin Utility

If you are using a cloud-based MySQL database, many cloud providers include the phpMyAdmin tool, which you can use to connect to the database and to perform database queries. Normally, the cloud provider will include an icon for phpMyAdmin within their tool's dashboard, as shown in **FIGURE 6.60**.

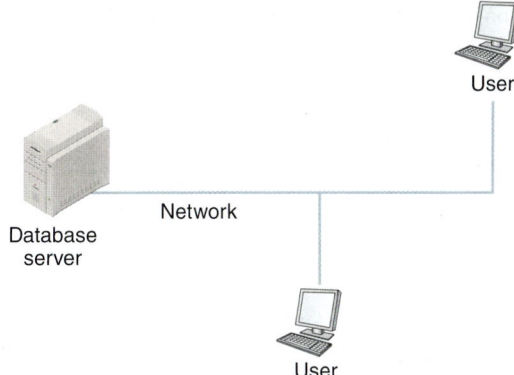

**FIGURE 6.59** For users to share a database, the database must reside on a network-based database server.

**FIGURE 6.60** Many cloud providers include the phpMyAdmin utility for interacting with MySQL databases.

Used with permission of phpMyAdmin

# CHAPTER 6 Keep SQL in Your Toolset

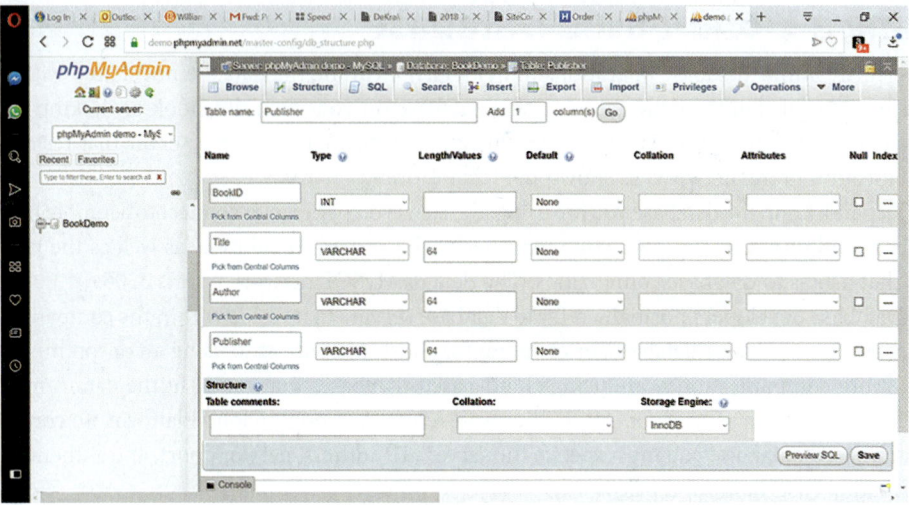

**FIGURE 6.61** Using the phpMyAdmin utility to perform operations on a cloud-based database.

*Note:* You can test drive the phpMyAdmin utility at http://demo.phpmyadmin.net.

Used with permission of phpMyAdmin

After you launch phpMyAdmin, you can use it within a browser to connect to your database and to perform operations. **FIGURE 6.61**, for example, shows the use of the phpMyAdmin editor to create a table.

## Using a Cloud-Based Managed Database Service

With the explosive growth in cloud computing, many companies have moved their databases from their on-premise data center to a cloud-based server. Originally, most companies continued to manage their database server software in the cloud, applying updates and patches, performing their own backups, and so on. Today, in contrast, many companies are moving to cloud-based managed database services, for which the cloud provider takes over such administrative services. In this way, the company's developers can instead concentrate on development, as opposed to administration. Across the web, most cloud providers provide such managed database services. You don't have to be a large company to make use of such services. A developer within a small company, even a one-person shop, may choose to use a **managed database server**, as opposed to spinning up their own database server in the cloud. **FIGURE 6.62** shows information about the MySQL managed service that runs in the Oracle cloud.

## Creating Database Tables

When you create a table, you must specify the names of the fields (columns) the table will store, as well as each field's data type, such as INT, FLOAT, or VARCHAR. A data type specifies the set of values a field can store, as well as the set of operations SQL can perform on the field. A value of type INT, for example, can store positive and negative whole numbers, such as −1, 0, and 1.

**FIGURE 6.62** Using a managed database service to simplify database deployment in the cloud.
Copyright Oracle and its affiliates. Used with permission

A field of type FLOAT can store numbers with a decimal point, such as 3.14, and a field of type VARCHAR(64) can store a variable-length string with up to 64 characters.

As discussed, a data type specifies a set of operations that SQL can perform on a field. It makes sense to add, subtract, multiply, and divide numeric values. It does not make sense, however, to divide or multiply a character string. Depending on the database system you are using (such as MySQL or Microsoft SQL), the data type names may differ. **TABLE 6.13** describes the MySQL data types.

The following CREATE TABLE query creates a table capable of storing book information:

```
CREATE TABLE Book (
     Title VARCHAR(64),
     Author VARCHAR(64),
     PublisherID INT,
     Price FLOAT,
     ISBN VARCHAR(64)
)
```

As you can see, the table creates fields of type VARCHAR to hold string values, a value of type FLOAT to store a price, and a PublisherID of type INT, which can be used later to create a relationship between a publisher in the Publisher table.

In a similar way, this query creates a table capable of storing publisher information:

```
CREATE TABLE Publisher (
      Name VARCHAR(64),
      Website VARCHAR(64),
      Phone VARCHAR(64)
)
```

After you create a table, you can confirm the table's existence by executing the SHOW TABLES query.

### TABLE 6.13 MySQL Data Types

| Data Type | Description |
|---|---|
| BIGINT(size) | Stores an integer value in the range −9,223,372,036,854,775,808 to 9,223,372,036,854,775,807, where size specifies the maximum number of digits |
| BIGINT(size) UNSIGNED | Stores an integer value in the range 0 to 18,446,744,073,709,551,615, where size specifies the maximum number of digits |
| BLOB | Stores a binary large object up to 65,535 bytes |
| BOOLEAN | Stores a true or false value |
| CHAR(size) | Specifies a fixed-size string up to 255 characters, where size specifies the maximum number of characters |
| DATE() | Stores a date in the form YYYY-MM-DD |
| DATETIME() | Stores a date and time in the form YYY-MM-DD HH:MM:SS |
| DECIMAL(size, fractional_digits) | Stores a DOUBLE as a string, where size specifies the number of digits and fractional_digits specifies the number of digits to the right of the decimal point |
| DOUBLE(size, fractional_digits) | Stores a double-precision floating-point number, where size specifies the number of digits and fractional_digits specifies the number of digits to the right of the decimal point |
| ENUM(a, b, c) | Stores a set of up to 65,535 enumerated values |
| FLOAT(size, fractional_digits) | Stores a floating-point number, where size specifies the number of digits and fractional_digits specifies the number of digits to the right of the decimal point |
| INT(size) | Stores an integer value in the range −2,147,483,648 to 2,147,483,647, where size specifies the maximum number of digits |
| INT(size) UNSIGNED | Stores an integer value in the range 0 to 4,294,967,295, where size specifies the maximum number of digits |
| LONGBLOB | Stores binary large object up to 4,294,967,295 bytes |
| LONGTEXT | Stores a string of up to 4,294,967,295 characters |
| MEDIUMBLOB | Stores a binary large object up to 16,777,215 bytes |
| MEDIUMTEXT | Stores a string of up to 16,277,215 characters |

| | |
|---|---|
| SET(a, b, c) | Stores a set of up to 64 enumerated values |
| SMALLINT(size) | Stores an integer value in the range −32,768 to 32,767, where size specifies the maximum number of digits |
| SMALLINT(size) UNSIGNED | Stores an integer value in the range 0 to 65,535, where size specifies the maximum number of digits |
| TEXT | Stores a string of up to 65,535 characters |
| TINYTEXT | Stores a string of up to 255 characters |
| TINYINT(size) | Stores an integer value in the range −128 to 127, where size specifies the maximum number of digits |
| TINYINT(size) UNSIGNED | Stores an integer value in the range 0 to 255, where size specifies the maximum number of digits |
| VARCHAR(size) | Stores a variable-length string of up to 255 characters, where size specifies the maximum number of characters |

## Inserting Data into a Database Table

After you create a database table, you store data in the table using the INSERT query, the format of which is:

```
INSERT INTO Table (Fieldname [, Fieldname …]) VALUES (Value [, Value …])
INSERT INTO Table VALUES (Value [, Value …])
```

As you can see, the SQL INSERT query supports two forms. In the first, you specify the names of each field into which you are inserting the specified values. In the second form, you do not specify the field names.

The following INSERT query, for example, inserts data into the Students table:

```
INSERT INTO Students (StudentID, Firstname, Lastname, GPA,
Instructor, State, Status)
VALUES (8, 'Joe', 'Wilson', 3.8, 'Smith', 'Arizona', 'G');
```

In this case, SQL will insert the specified values into the corresponding fields, as shown in **FIGURE 6.63**.

If the INSERT query does not specify values for every field, SQL will assign the null value to the remaining fields.

When you do not specify field names within an INSERT query, SQL will assign the values you specify to the table fields from left to right. For example, the following INSERT query does not specify field names:

```
INSERT INTO Students VALUES (9, 'Ronald', 'Lewis', 3.6,
'Brooks', 'Nevada', 'W')
```

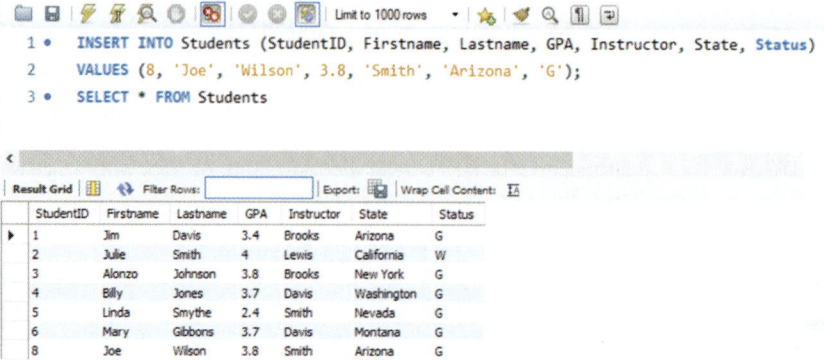

**FIGURE 6.63** Specifying field names within an INSERT query.
Copyright Oracle and its affiliates. Used with permission

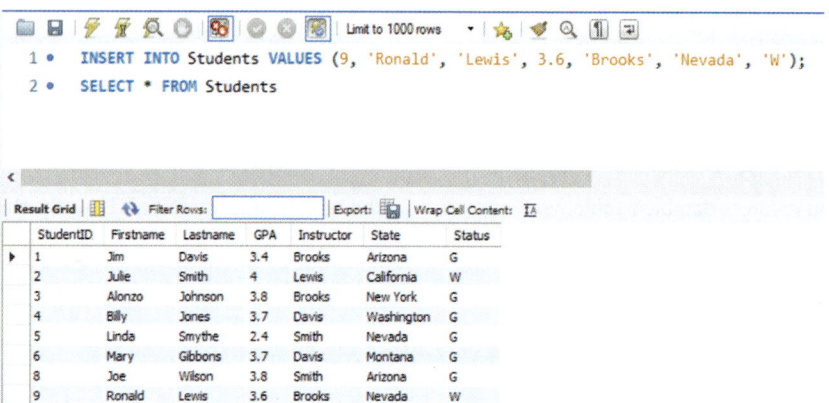

**FIGURE 6.64** When an INSERT query does not specify field names, SQL inserts the values from left to right starting with the table's first column.
Copyright Oracle and its affiliates. Used with permission

When you execute this query, SQL will insert the values into the table from left to right, as shown in **FIGURE 6.64**. Again, if you do not specify a value for every field, SQL will insert the null value.

## Updating Data Within a Database Table

To update the value of one or more records within a database table, you use the SQL UPDATE query, the format of which is:

```
UPDATE Table SET Field=Value[, Field=Value …] [WHERE Condition]
```

The following UPDATE query will change the office number for the instructor John Smith to 1301:

```
UPDATE Instructors SET Office='1301' WHERE Name='Smith'
```

After you execute this query, SQL will update the table, as shown in **FIGURE 6.65**.

## Turning Off Safe Queries in Workbench

If you run an UPDATE or DELETE query within MySQL Workbench and nothing happens, you need to disable Workbench's safe-update operations by performing these steps:

1. Within Workbench, select the Edit menu Preferences option. Workbench will display the Workbench Preferences dialog box.
2. With the Preferences dialog box, select the SQL Query option and clear the Safe Updates check box, as shown in **FIGURE A**, and select Save.

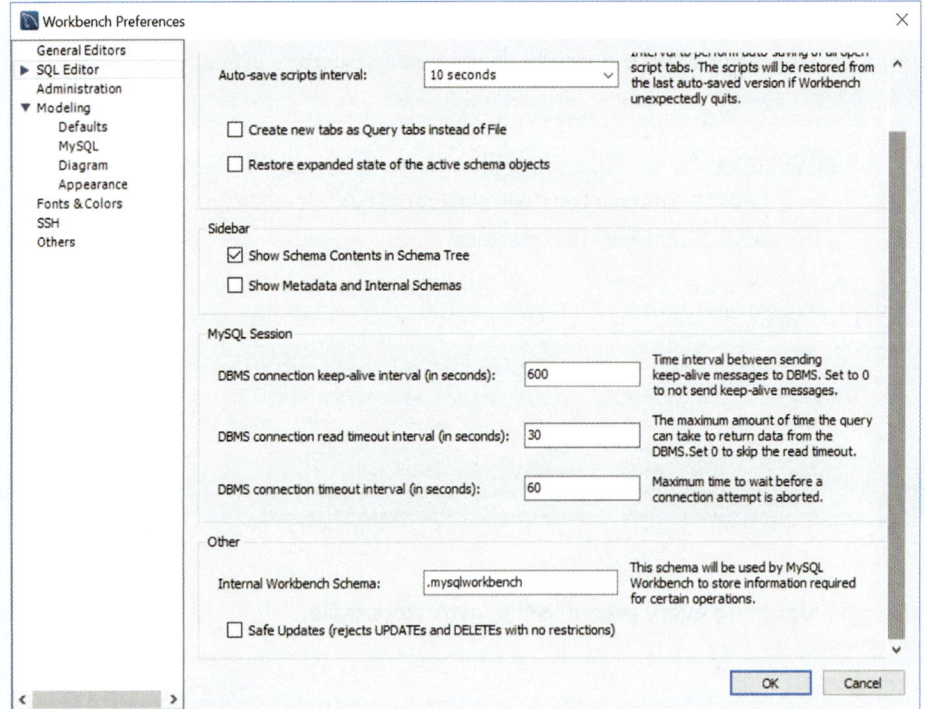

**FIGURE A** To perform UPDATE and DELETE queries within MySQL Workbench, you must disable Safe Updates.

Copyright Oracle and its affiliates. Used with permission

If you don't specify a WHERE clause when you execute an UPDATE query, SQL will update every record to use the specified value. The following query assigns the university name 'Acme University' to the University field for every instructor in the Instructors table:

```
UPDATE Instructors SET University='Acme University'
```

After you execute the query, the Instructors table will contain the data shown in **FIGURE 6.66**.

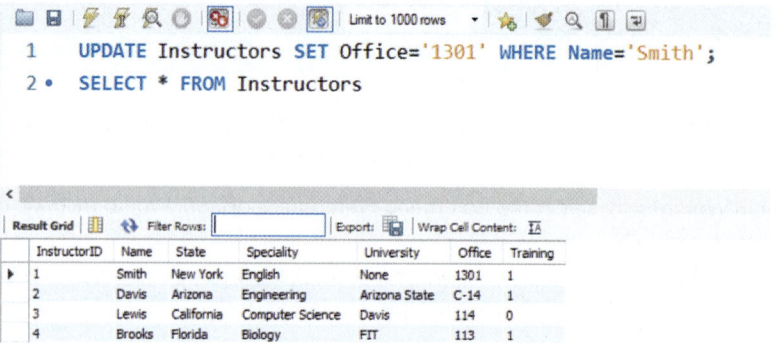

**FIGURE 6.65** Using an UPDATE query to change an instructor's office.
Copyright Oracle and its affiliates. Used with permission.

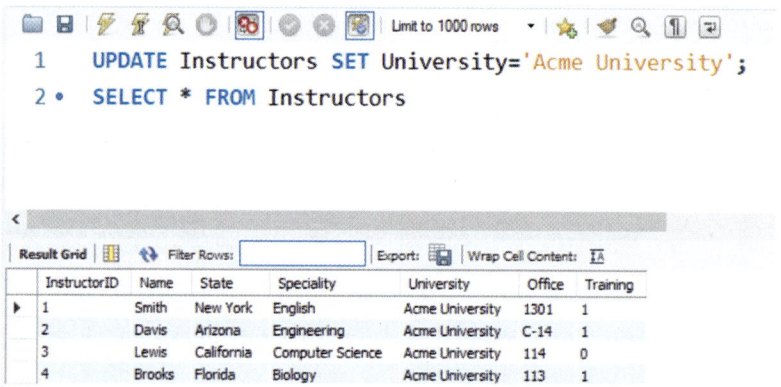

**FIGURE 6.66** Updating every record in the Instructors table.
Copyright Oracle and its affiliates. Used with permission.

## Deleting Records from a Database Table

Just as there will be times when you must insert or update data within a table, there will also be times when you must delete one or more records. To delete records, you use the SQL DELETE query, the format of which is:

```
DELETE FROM Table [Where Condition]
```

The following DELETE query deletes records from the Students table for which the Status field contains the value W for withdrawn:

```
DELETE FROM Students WHERE Status='W'
```

After you execute the query, the Students table will contain the records shown in **FIGURE 6.67**.

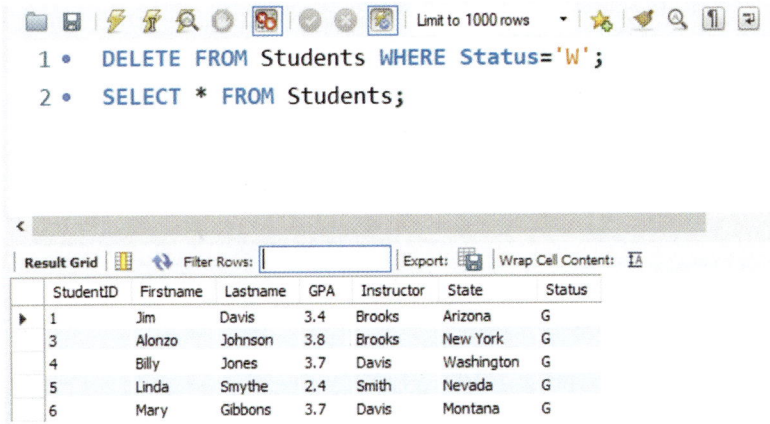

**FIGURE 6.67** Deleting specific records from the Students table.

Copyright Oracle and its affiliates. Used with permission

Be careful when using the DELETE query. For example, if you do not specify the WHERE clause when executing DELETE, SQL will delete every record the table contains:

```
DELETE FROM SomeTable
```

Should you errantly delete records, you will need to restore them from a backup.

## Dropping (Deleting) a Table or Database

Using the SQL DELETE query, you can delete one or more records from a specified table. There may be times when you want to delete a table or even the database itself. In such cases, you use the SQL DROP query, the format of which is:

```
DROP DATABASE DatabaseName
DROP TABLE TableName
```

Use the DROP query with caution. When you drop a table or database, SQL will delete it, regardless of the data it contains. The following DROP query deletes the table OldFaculty:

```
DROP DATABASE OldFaculty
```

When you execute the query, SQL will delete the table, as shown in **FIGURE 6.68**.

Likewise, the following query deletes the database SchoolBackup:

```
DROP DATABASE SchoolBackup
```

Again, when you execute the query, SQL will remove the database, as shown in **FIGURE 6.69**.

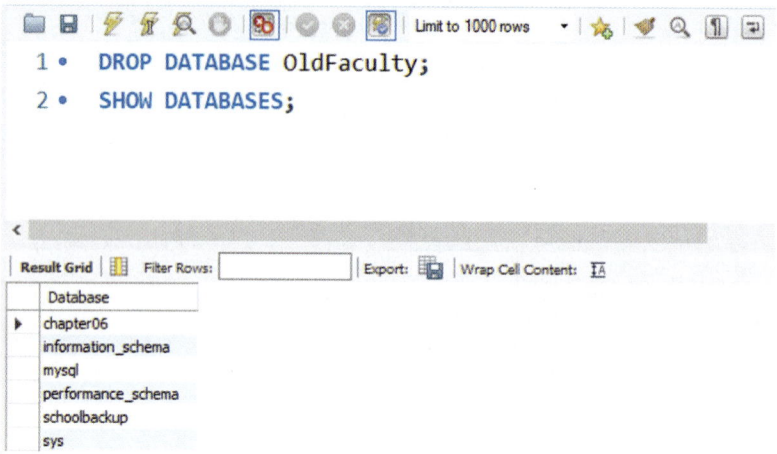

**FIGURE 6.68** Using the SQL DROP query to delete the OldFaculty table.
Copyright Oracle and its affiliates. Used with permission

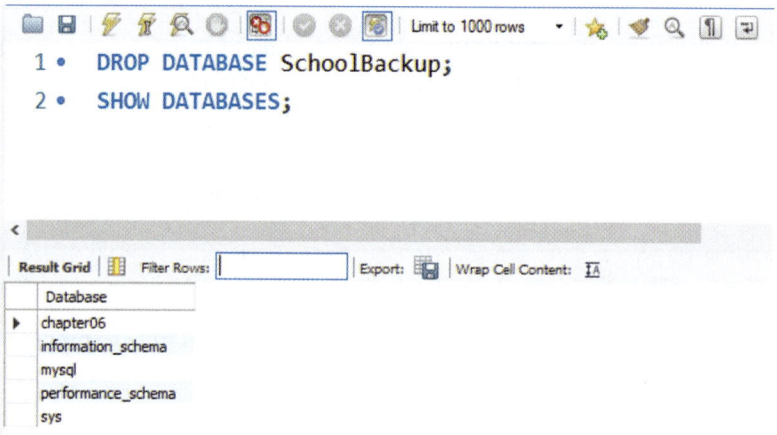

**FIGURE 6.69** Using the SQL DROP query to delete the SchoolBackup database.
Copyright Oracle and its affiliates. Used with permission

## Nesting a SELECT Query

Often, when you perform a query that uses a WHERE clause, you first need to perform a SELECT query to look up specific values in one table, such as an employee ID, before you can perform an operation on another table. In such cases, you can use a nested SELECT query.

Assume, for example, that you want to update the Bonus table AmountDue field for employees who had sales in April. One approach would be to first query the Sales table to get the employee IDs for the employees with sales:

```
SELECT EmployeeID FROM Sales WHERE Month='April'
```

Then, with the employee IDs in hand, you can execute your UPDATE query:

    UPDATE Bonus SET AmountDue = 1000.0 WHERE EmployeeID IN [1, 2]

A second approach to the operation is to use a nested SELECT query. A **nested query** is so named because it appears within an outer query. Some developers refer to nested queries as a subquery. When you nest a SELECT query, you enclose the query within parentheses. The following UPDATE query uses a nested query to select the employees with sales in April:

    UPDATE Bonus SET AmountDue = 1000.0
    WHERE EmployeeID IN  (SELECT EmployeeID FROM Sales WHERE
    Month='April')

In a similar way, the following UPDATE query uses a nested query to set the AtRisk field to true within the StudentWatch table for students who scored less than 70 on the last exam:

    UPDATE StudentWatch SET AtRisk=True StudentID IN (SELECT
    StudentID FROM Grades WHERE TestScore < 70)

Finally, this DELETE query deletes instructors from the Faculty table who have not completed a training course:

    DELETE FROM Faculty WHERE FacultyID IN (SELECT FacultyID FROM
    Training WHERE Present=0)

# Using an Index to Improve Query Performance

If you identify one or more queries that you (or others) will execute on a regular basis in the future, you will want to optimize the query to improve its performance. One way that database developers improve performance is to index key fields within a table. Developers often find that queries that took a long time to complete, or even timed out, will execute quickly after they assign an index.

To understand how an index improves performance, consider the following scenario: A bank's Customer table contains 5 million records, one for each customer. When a user calls the bank, the customer service representative asks the caller to provide his or her Social Security number. The representative then uses that number to retrieve the customer record.

Behind the scenes, if no index exists, the database will retrieve the first record in the table and compare its Social Security number to that provided by the user. If the numbers match, the query will return the record. If the numbers do not match, SQL will repeat this process with the second record, then the third, and so on, as shown in **FIGURE 6.70**. As you might guess, this sequential search process can become a time-consuming process.

An index is a data structure that stores an index value (such as a Social Security number) and a pointer to the record within the table that contains the value. Because the file that contains the indexes is smaller than the database table, SQL can read the index values much faster. In addition, behind the scenes, SQL stores the indexes in a form that optimizes searching.

| SSN | Name | Phone | Account | Balance |
|---|---|---|---|---|
| 011-11-1111 | Jones | 555–1212 | 1 | 103.18 |
| 012-11-2212 | Davis | 555–1414 | 2 | 5013.83 |
| 013-44-1131 | Smith | 555–1431 | 3 | 7012.63 |
| 014-56-7112 | Allen | 555–0123 | 4 | 37.84 |
| ⋮ | | | | |
| 928-11-3311 | Waltor | 555 – 1712 | 4999999 | 1537.16 |
| 937-55-4123 | Lewis | 555 – 1011 | 5000000 | 2173.57 |

**FIGURE 6.70** Without an index, SQL must sequentially search each record's values, a slow process.

| Index | Record |
|---|---|
| 011-11-1111 | 1 |
| 014-56-7112 | 4 |
| 333-12-1152 | 1017014 |
| ⋮ | |
| 012-11-2222 | 3 |
| 762-14-5123 | 400 |

| SSN | Name | Phone | Account | Balance |
|---|---|---|---|---|
| 011-11-1111 | Jones | 555–1212 | 1 | 103.18 |
| 012-11-2722 | Davis | 555–1414 | 2 | 5013.83 |
| 013-44-3131 | Smith | 555–1431 | 3 | 7012.63 |
| 014-56-7112 | Allen | 555–0123 | 4 | 37.84 |
| ⋮ | | | | |
| 333-12-1152 | Barnes | 555 – 7777 | 327103 | 33.77 |
| 367-11-0111 | Williams | 555 – 3333 | 410217 | 771.55 |
| 368-22-1118 | Jones | 555 – 1217 | 432107 | 55.77 |
| 937-55-9153 | Lewis | 555 – 1214 | 5000000 | 7173.57 |

**FIGURE 6.71** Improving database performance using an index.

When the database must retrieve the record that corresponds to a specific value, the database first retrieves the index and then uses the pointer it contains to quickly retrieve the record from the database table, as shown in **FIGURE 6.71**.

It is important to note that although indexes will normally significantly improve performance, they have a small performance and storage impact. To keep the index values up to date, each time you insert a value into an indexed table, SQL must create a corresponding index, which requires some processing time. In addition, SQL must store the index values, which will consume some disk space. That said, the benefits of indexes normally far outweigh the costs.

To create an index on a table, you use the CREATE INDEX query, the format of which is:

```
CREATE INDEX IndexName ON Tablename (ColumnName [, ColumnName ...])
```

As you can see from the CREATE INDEX format, when you create an index, you can index a single field or you can create a combined index based on multiple fields. The following query creates an index on the StudentID field of the Students table:

```
CREATE INDEX StudentIdx ON Students (StudentID)
```

Should you later decide that you no longer need an index, you can delete it using the DROP INDEX query, as shown here:

```
DROP INDEX StudentIdx ON Students
```

## Hands-On: Building a Data Quality Dashboard Using Microsoft Power BI

Microsoft Power BI is a business intelligence (BI) visualization tool you can use to quickly create dashboards and reports from hundreds of different data source types (database systems, spreadsheets, files, and more). As shown in **FIGURE A**, using Power BI, you can quickly create a dashboard with state-of-the-art visualizations that include:

- Bar and column charts (stacked and clustered)
- Line and area charts
- Ribbon charts
- Waterfall charts
- Scatter charts
- Pie and donut charts
- Treemap charts
- Map charts
- Funnel charts
- Gauge charts

Using Power BI, users can display dashboards on their computer screen or mobile device. Chapter 9, "Data Visualization," examines charting and visualization in detail.

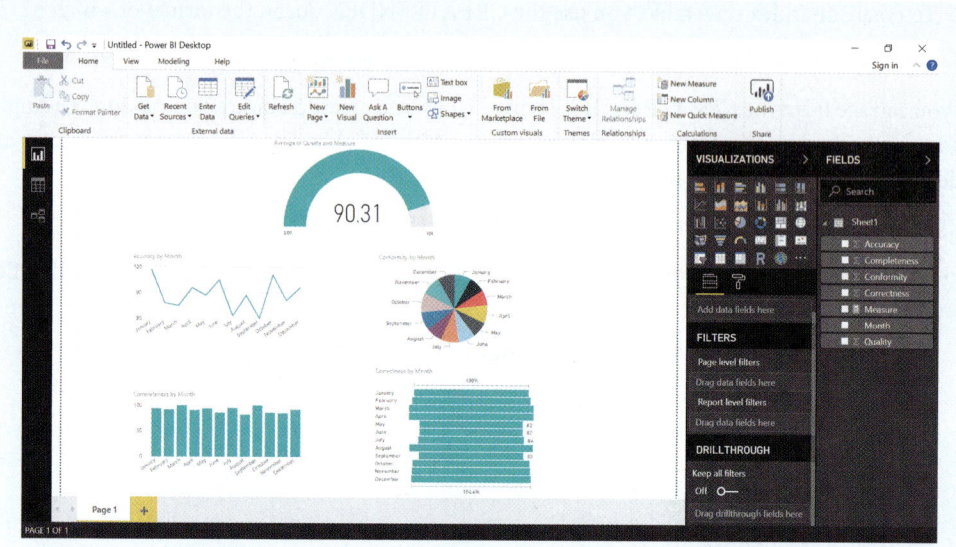

FIGURE A  Using Power BI to create a business intelligence dashboard.

Used with permission from Microsoft

## Getting Started with Power BI

Microsoft allows users to test drive a trial version of Power BI. Download and install Power BI from http://powerbi.microsoft.com, as shown in **FIGURE B**.

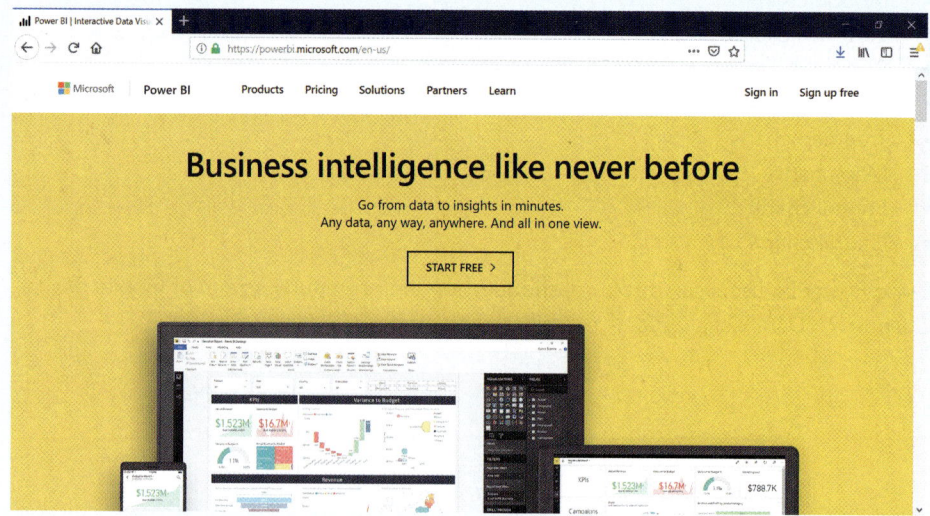

FIGURE B  The Microsoft Power BI website.

Used with permission from Microsoft

## Creating a Data-Quality Dashboard

Database analysts often create key performance indicator (KPI) values to track the quality of their data. (Chapter 9, "Data Preprocessing and Cleansing," discusses this in more detail.) The analysts often express quality in terms of the following metrics:

- Accuracy: the degree to which the data correctly represent the underlying real-world values, such as all temperatures from a sensor in the correct range
- Completeness: the degree to which the data represent all required values, such as a data set containing an hour of data for a sensor that reports every second having 100% of the data values
- Consistency: the degree to which similar or related data values align throughout the data set, such as each occurrence of an address having the same ZIP code
- Conformity: the degree to which the data values align with business rules, such as the company will measure sensor values in 1-second intervals

To share the data-quality KPIs with others, such as the data governance board, developers will create a data-quality dashboard, similar to that previously shown in Figure A. In this section, you will use Power BI to create that dashboard.

To help you get started, this text's catalog page provides the Quality.csv file, which you can download and save from go.jblearning.com/DataMining.

Next, start Power BI from the Windows Start menu. Windows will open Power BI, as shown in **FIGURE C**.

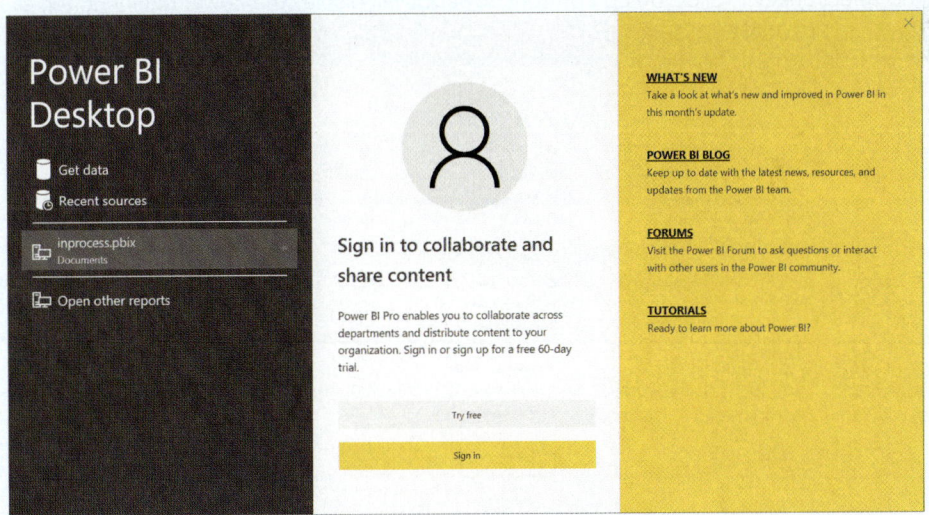

**FIGURE C** Microsoft Power BI.

Used with permission from Microsoft

Within Power BI, click Get Data. Power BI will display a window, as shown in **FIGURE D**, within which you can select your data source.

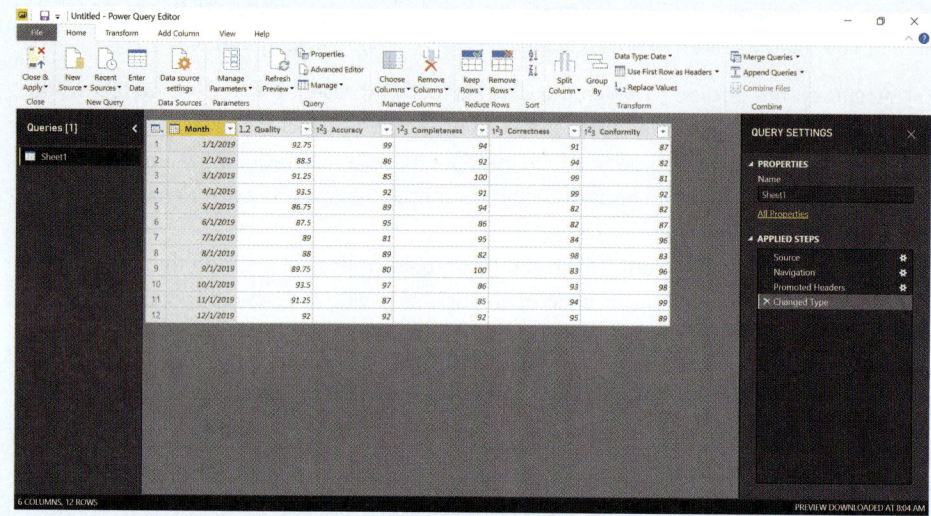

**FIGURE D** Selecting a data source within Power BI.
Used with permission from Microsoft

Select the Excel option and then connect to the Quality.csv file that you just downloaded and select Sheet 1. Click the Edit button. Power BI will display the Power Query Editor, as shown in **FIGURE E**.

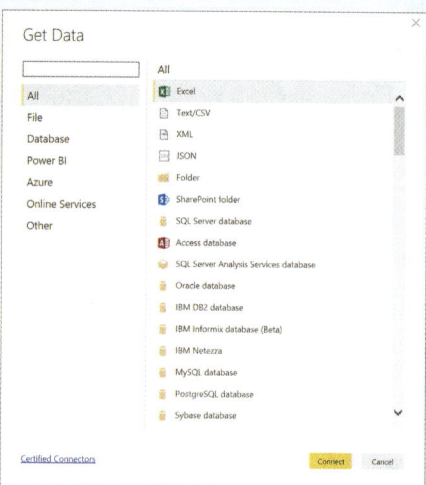

**FIGURE E** The Power Query Editor.
Used with permission from Microsoft

Using the Power Query Editor, you can add or delete columns, change column data types, and more. For now, click the toolbar Apply & Close button. Power BI will display its visualization canvas, which you will use to lay out your dashboard and reports. First, click the data icon, which looks like a table and appears in the upper-left corner of the window. Power BI will display the data window, as shown in **FIGURE F**.

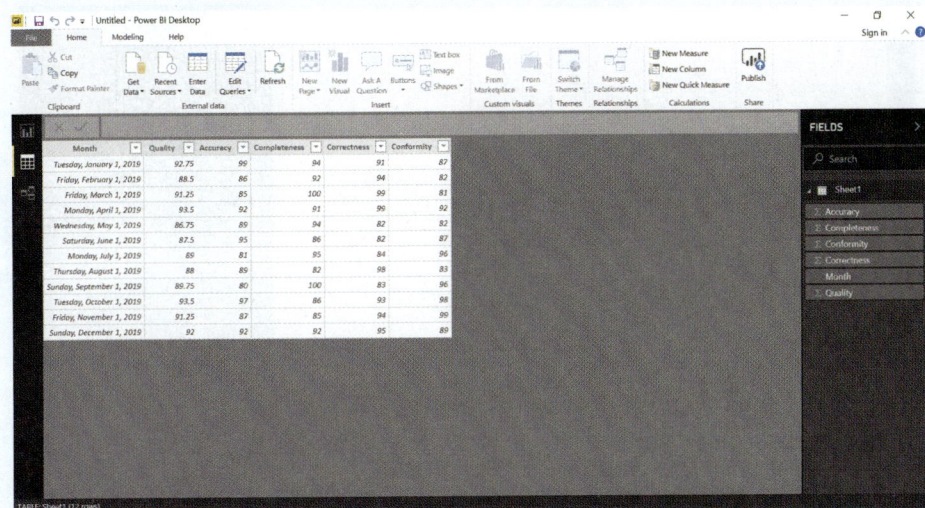

**FIGURE F** The Power BI data window.

Used with permission from Microsoft

Select the Month column by clicking the Month header. Then select the Modeling tab and choose the Date Time format Mar 14 (mmmm d), as shown in **FIGURE G**.

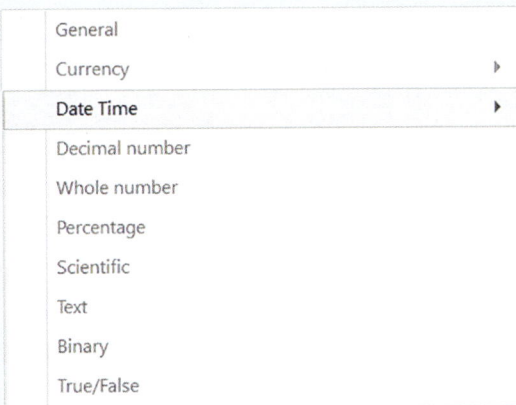

**FIGURE G** Changing the Date Time format.

Used with permission from Microsoft

Click the Report icon that appears along the left side of the window. Power BI will display its canvas, as shown in **FIGURE H**.

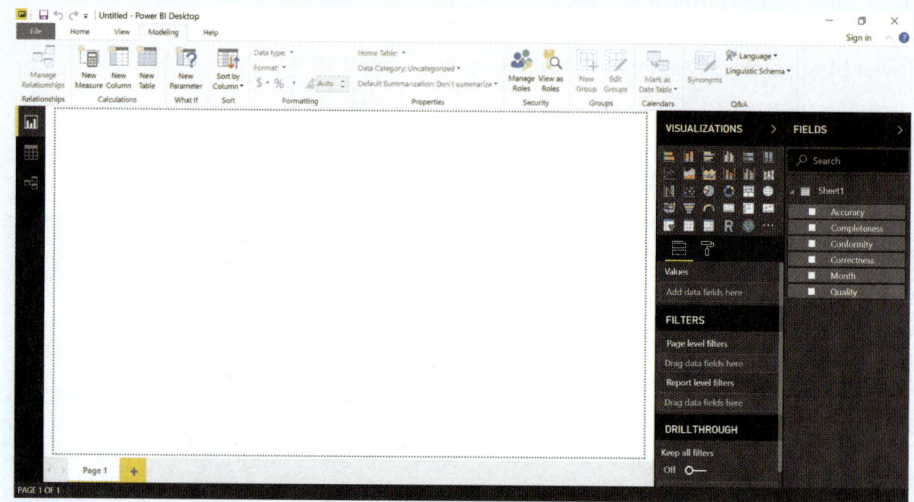

**FIGURE H** The Power BI canvas.

Used with permission from Microsoft

Within the Fields section, click your mouse on the Accuracy and Month field, placing a checkmark in front of each. Then, from the chart palette, drag a line chart onto the canvas. Power BI will display its starting line chart canvas, as shown in **FIGURE I**.

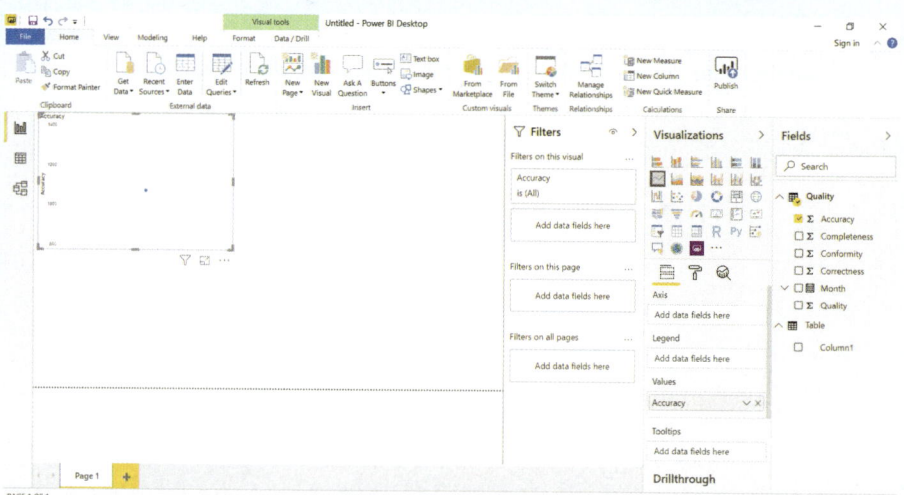

**FIGURE I** The starting line chart on the Power BI canvas.

Used with permission from Microsoft

Within the Axis section, click the X that appears before Year, Quarter and Day. Power BI will update the line chart to show each month's accuracy value, as shown in **FIGURE J**.

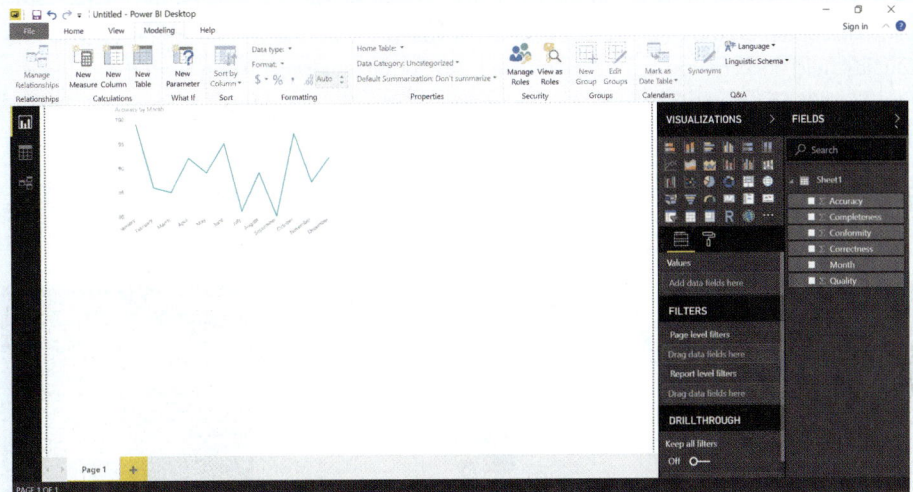

**FIGURE J** Charting data accuracy by month.

Used with permission from Microsoft

Repeat these steps to create a bar chart that presents completeness by month, a pie chart and an area chart for conformity by month, and a funnel chart for correctness by month. Position the charts as shown in **FIGURE K**.

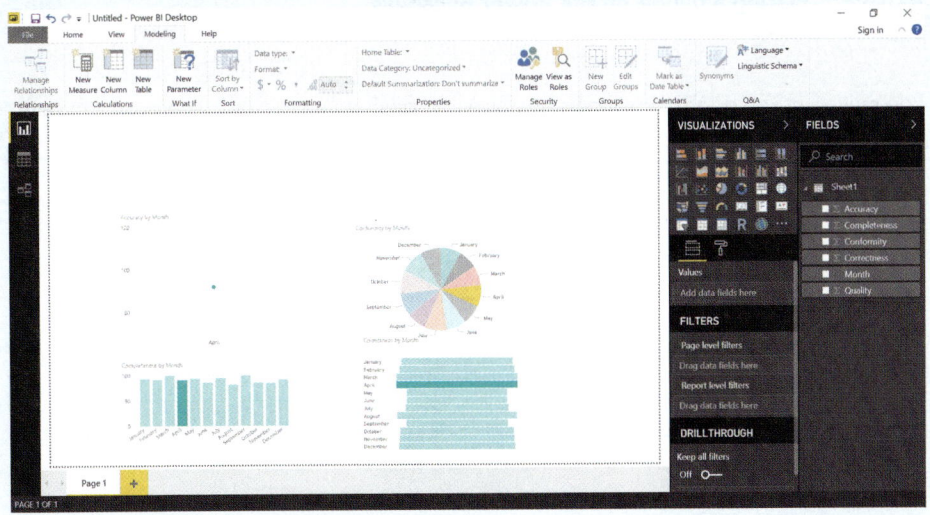

**FIGURE K** Displaying data-quality charts on the Power BI canvas.

Used with permission from Microsoft

Lastly, click on the Quality field only. Then drag a gauge chart to the top of the canvas. Then click the ellipses (…) that appear near Sheet 1 above the field names and create a new column. Assign the column the value 100. Power BI will add the column to the field list. Click again on the gauge chart on the canvas. Beneath the visualizations, click on the Quality field and change the aggregation from Sum to Average. Then drag the column into the Maximum value field for the chart. Power BI will display the gauge on the chart, as shown in **FIGURE L**.

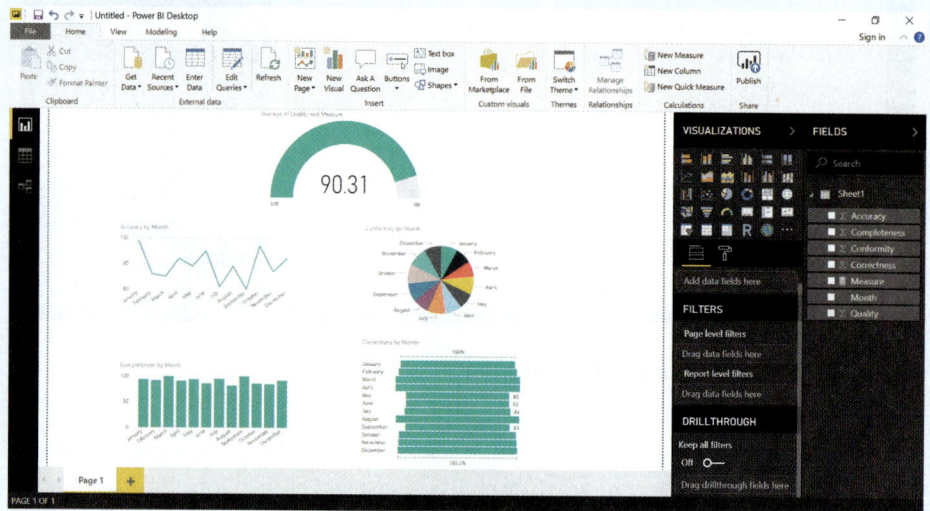

**FIGURE L** Placing a gauge on the Power BI canvas.

Used with permission from Microsoft

You may want to add textbox labels and size and position each chart. Then you can save, print, or share your dashboard.

## Summary

Despite the rapid growth in the use of NoSQL databases, relational databases remain the most widely used way to store and retrieve data. To manipulate a relational database, you use SQL. Software companies such as Oracle, Microsoft, IBM, and Amazon offer SQL database solutions. Each system provides different capabilities. All of these systems, however, support the base SQL queries that this chapter presents. In Chapter 7, "Data Mining and NoSQL," you will examine NoSQL databases, so named because their query operations do not use SQL.

In the past, companies stored databases on a database server that resided in the company's on-premise data center. Today, in contrast, most companies are moving their servers to the cloud, using a provider such as Microsoft Azure or Amazon AWS.

Most database systems provide two types of solutions—a database server that stores data and a user interface that lets users connect to and query a database. Most users will not need their own database system, but rather, they will use a client program, such as MySQL Workbench, to connect to and query a company-provided database.

Throughout this chapter, you have examined a wide range of SQL queries. **TABLE 6.14** briefly summarizes the queries you have examined.

**TABLE 6.14** SQL Queries Examined Throughout This Chapter

| Query | Description |
| --- | --- |
| SHOW DATABASES | Lists the databases the database server contains. |
| SHOW TABLES | Lists the tables within a database. |
| USE database | Selects a database for use. |
| SELECT | Retrieves records from a table. |
| UPDATE | Changes field values within a table. |
| DELETE | Deletes records from a table. |
| CREATE DATABASE database | Creates the specified database. |
| CREATE TABLE | Creates a table within a database. |
| INSERT | Inserts a record into a table. |
| DROP DATABASE database | Deletes the specified database. |
| DROP TABLE table | Deletes the specified table. |
| CREATE INDEX | Creates an index on the specified field. |

## Key Terms

Aggregate
Arithmetic operators
Comma-delimited file
Cross join
CRUD
Delimiter
Extract Transform and Load (ETL)
Export
Graphical user interface
Import
Index
Inner join
JOIN
Left join
Logical operators
Managed database server
Nested query
Network port
On-premise server
Outer join
Query
Relational operators
Remote database
Right join
Subquery
Wildcard

## Review

1. Define and describe the components of an SQL database.
2. Complete the SQL Quiz at the w3schools.com website with a score of 85% or higher and submit a screen capture of your quiz score.
3. Compare and contrast DDL, DML, and DCL.
4. Compare and contrast database server and database client software.
5. Provide SQL queries to perform the following operations:
   a. Display the list of databases on a server.
   b. Display the list of tables within a database.
   c. Select the database CHAPTER06 for use.
6. Describe the purpose of a semicolon within an SQL query.
7. Provide SQL queries to perform the following:
   a. Display all records within the Students table.
   b. Display the first and last names of all instructors in the Instructors table.
   c. Display all students with a GPA in the range 3.0–4.0.
   d. Sort the contents of the Students table by name in descending order.
   e. Display the female employees (gender = '1') in the Employees table.
   f. Display the first three records in the Instructors table.
   g. Compare and contrast inner, right, left, and cross joins.
   h. Display a count of the number of records in the Products table.
   i. Display the average and standard deviation of student GPAs.
   j. Display the minimum and maximum student GPA.
   k. Display a list of those students with a GPA greater than the average GPA.
   l. Sort students by GPA and then by name.
   m. Use a query with GROUP BY and ROLLUP to produce the result shown in **FIGURE 6.72**.

| State | Product | Model | SUM(Quantity) |
|---|---|---|---|
| Arizona | Phone | Apple | 150 |
| Arizona | Phone | Samsung | 30 |
| Arizona | Phone | | 180 |
| Arizona | Television | Samsung | 50 |
| Arizona | Television | Visio | 120 |
| Arizona | Television | | 170 |
| Arizona | | | 350 |
| Nevada | Phone | Apple | 120 |
| Nevada | Phone | Samsung | 110 |
| Nevada | Phone | | 230 |
| Nevada | Television | Samsung | 150 |
| Nevada | Television | Visio | 20 |
| Nevada | Television | | 170 |
| Nevada | | | 400 |
| Total Inventory | | | 750 |

**FIGURE 6.72** Using the GROUP BY with ROLLUP.

    n. Delete instructors who teach English from the Instructors table.
    o. Update all students from Arizona to have a GPA of 4.0.
    p. Create an index on the Employees table EmployeeID field.
8. Provide SQL queries to perform the following options:
    a. Create a database named Entertainment.
    b. Create a Movie table with the following fields:
        i. Name
        ii. Producer
        iii. Starring
        iv. DateReleased
    c. Create a TVShows table with the following fields
        i. Name
        ii. Station
        iii. Starring
        iv. DayOf
        v. Week
        vi. Time
    d. Insert data of your choice into each table.
    e. Use an UPDATE query to change a record in each table.
    f. Use a DELETE query to delete one or more records from each table.

9. Using the Customers and Orders tables presented in this chapter, create a JOIN query that displays the name of customers who have not placed an order.
10. Export the contents of the Students table to a comma-separated file named Students.csv.
11. Import the contents of the Students.csv file you created in Question 10 into the StudentsBackup file.
12. Create a SELECT query that displays the prices of stocks in the Stocks table to dollars only.
13. Download and install Microsoft Power BI and follow the steps performed in the Hands-On section of this chapter to create the Quality dashboard shown in Figure A in the previous summary.

# CHAPTER 7

# NoSQL Data Analytics

## Chapter Goals and Objectives

- Compare and contrast relational and NoSQL databases.
- Compare and contrast NoSQL database management systems.
- Perform NoSQL query operations.
- Understand the role of JSON within NoSQL solutions.
- Define and describe managed database services.

For the first 50+ years of computing, database developers have made extensive use of SQL relational (table-based) databases. The explosive growth of web- and mobile-based applications, however, has introduced challenges to traditional databases:

- The need to store documents, videos, and less "structured" data
- The need to scale database storage and processing power up and down based upon demand
- The continued need for high performance and reliability

In response to these demands, **NoSQL** databases have emerged, so named because they do not use Structured Query Language (SQL). Instead, NoSQL databases use query mechanisms that are not SQL. Further, unlike relational databases that store data with tables, NoSQL databases store data in a less structured way, often using JavaScript Object Notation (**JSON**) to store objects. This chapter examines NoSQL database processing through the popular MongoDB database and briefly introduces additional NoSQL databases, which include Redis, CouchDB, Cassandra, and others.

As you will learn, the cloud makes it very easy for you to set up and run these databases. By the time you finish this chapter, you will understand the following key concepts:

- A NoSQL database is so named because it does not use SQL as its primary query mechanism.
- Many NoSQL databases are starting to introduce support for SQL, and many third-party tools that provide SQL support for NoSQL databases are emerging. As such, the term NoSQL is evolving from meaning "no SQL" to "not only SQL."
- Commonly used NoSQL databases include MongoDB, Redis, CouchDB, Cassandra, HBase, RocksDB, and DynamoDB.
- Unlike relational databases that store data within tables, NoSQL databases store data in a less structured way—often using JSON objects behind the scenes to store data objects.
- JSON was originally created to represent, store, and transmit JavaScript objects.
- JSON stores objects using name–value pairs, which it groups, separated by commas, between left and right braces { }.
- JSON objects have advantages in that they are human readable (text based), **lightweight**, **self-describing**, and language independent.
- Developers store JSON objects in text-based files, normally using the .json file extension.
- A MongoDB database consists of named collections (similar to a table) that store documents (similar to records).
- MongoDB provides queries you will use to create and manage databases and collections and to perform create, read, update, and delete (**CRUD**) operations on documents.
- To scale a database, you can scale vertically by adding random-access memory (RAM) and central processing unit (CPU) processing power to a server, or you can scale horizontally by adding servers.
- The process of **scaling** a MongoDB horizontally is known as sharding.
- To replicate a MongoDB in real time, database developers deploy additional MongoDB servers, which reside within replication sets.
- To interact with a MongoDB database, you can use the Mongo command-line shell, Compass; the Mongo graphical user interface (**GUI**); or third-party GUIs.

# Understanding JSON

As you will learn, many NoSQL databases use JSON behind the scenes to store data. JSON was originally developed in the early 2000s to represent JavaScript objects, not only for storage but also as a way to send and receive data between applications—normally a browser-based web application and a web server, as shown in **FIGURE 7.1**.

A JSON object looks like a JavaScript object, in that it is grouped by left and right braces { } and consists of comma-separated name–value pairs. The following JSON object, for example, contains employee data:

```
{"name": "Bill Smith", "age": 50, "ID": 123456, "Salary":
105000, "Email": "BSmith@Company.com"}
```

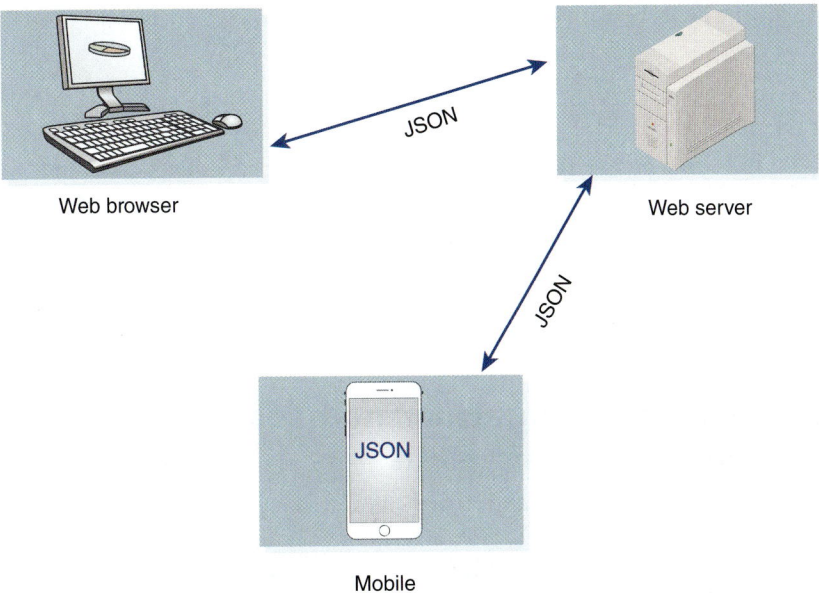

**FIGURE 7.1** Exchanging JSON data between a web application and server.

Within a JSON object, you group each field name within quotes, separating the name from its value with a colon (:). The previous object consists of four fields. Within a JSON object, you separate name–value pairs with commas. JSON supports a variety of value types. In this case, the object uses numbers and strings.

The following JSON object represents a student:

```
{"name": "Laurie Jones", "GPA": 3.5, "Grade": 97}
```

As you can see, the student object contains three name–value pairs. The first, name, uses a string value. The second and third, GPA and Grade, use numeric values.

## JSON Field Data Types

JSON objects consist of name–value pairs. Each pair has a unique quoted name and a value. Each value must be one of the following data types:

- String: Contains a value within quotes
- Number: An integer or floating-point value
- Object: A nested object enclosed in left and right braces { }
- Array: A collection of values grouped in left and right brackets [ ]
- Boolean: A true or false value
- Null: Represented by the keyword null

The following JSON book object represents the use of each JSON data type:

```
{
   "Title": "Data Mining and Analytics",
   "Chapters": 16,
   "Author": {"Last": "Jamsa", "First": "Kris", "ID": 1983},
  "OtherBooks": true,
   "Universities": [ "ASU", "UNLV", "San Diego State University"],
    "NextBook": null
  }
```

## JSON Is Self-Describing, Human Readable, Language Independent, and Lightweight

A key feature of JSON is that JSON objects are self-describing, meaning there is not an overall schema that describes what each object looks like, but rather, the object structure is described by the groupings of name–value pairs found within the object itself.

JSON objects are also human readable, which means (after a little practice) that you can look at an object and identify the object's name–value pairs. In addition, JSON objects are language independent, which means you can create and use JSON objects in Java, C#, Python, and more.

Extensible Markup Language (XML) is also self-describing, human readable, and language independent. As such, developers must often choose whether they will use JSON or XML to represent objects. **FIGURE 7.2** shows the same employee object represented using JSON and XML.

As you can see within Figure 7.2, JSON groups objects with braces and brackets, whereas XML uses start and end tags to group objects and their name–value pairs. Because JSON objects are smaller and faster to create, developers refer to JSON objects as lightweight, meaning the syntax developers use to describe objects lets them to do so efficiently, with minimal overhead.

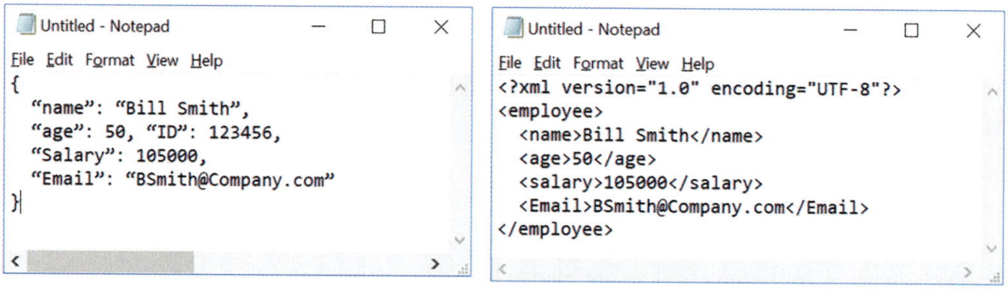

**FIGURE 7.2** Representing an employee object using JSON and XML.

Used with permission from Microsoft

## Storing Multiple Values Using a JSON Array

An array is a data structure that stores multiple values of the same type. To represent an array in JSON, you group comma-separated values within left and right brackets [ ]. The following JSON array represents multiple test scores:

```
{"scores": [88, 90, 77, 93]}
```

Similarly, the following JSON array groups employee names:

```
{"employees" : ["Lee Adams", "Bill Davis", "Alice Smith"]}
```

Finally, the following JSON object specifies the IDs of employees participating in a particular insurance plan:

```
{
  "Company": "Super Software",
  "Policy": "ABC Healthcare",
  "Employees": [103, 115, 99, 87]
}
```

In this case, the object contains three fields, two of which are strings, and one (Employees) is an array.

## Nesting JSON Objects

Nesting an object is the process of storing one object within another and is a common JSON practice. The following JSON object uses nested objects to represent my dogs and cat:

```
{
    "Veterinarian": "Dr. Jim Smith",
    "Dogs": [ {"name": "Bently", "Age": 10, "Breed": "Black Lab"},
              {"name": "Bo", "Age": 8, "Breed": "German Shepherd"},
              {"name": "Blue Sky", "Age": 8, "Breed": "Mixed"} ],
    "Cat":   {"name": "Frisco", "Age": 13, "Breed": "Feral"}
}
```

As you can see, the object uses an array to store three dog objects and an object to represent a cat.

## JSON Is Self-Describing

As discussed, a self-describing object brings with it all the information a database or an application must know about the object's structure. In the case of an SQL database, which is not self-describing, a table schema specifies the layout, name, and structure of the underlying object. In contrast, a

JSON object specifies its own fields and field values without such a schema. If you consider the following JSON object, for example:

```
{
    "Name": "Billy Smith",
    "ID": 1234,
    "Position": "Supervisor",
    "Salary": 35000,
    "Age": 34,
    "Office": "A114"
}
```

through observation, you know the object consists of six fields, you know the field names, and you can determine the field values. When an application uses this object, it will parse the object's content to determine the same.

## Storing JSON Objects

Developers store JSON objects within text files that you can edit using a text editor, such as the Windows Notepad accessory. **FIGURE 7.3** illustrates a JSON object within Notepad.

JSON files normally have the .json file extension, such as Pets.json. A JSON database, therefore, is simply a text file that contains one or more JSON objects. **FIGURE 7.4** illustrates how you might store a **relational database** table of records as a JSON object within a text file.

## Validating JSON Content

As the complexity of the JSON objects you create increases, so, too, will the difficulty of correctly typing and editing each object's JSON. To help you quickly identify missing commas, colons, and braces, several sites on the web provide JSON validators. **FIGURE 7.5**, for example, illustrates the JSON validator at json-validator.com. As you can see, using the validator, you can quickly identify JSON syntax errors or confirm that your JSON is correct.

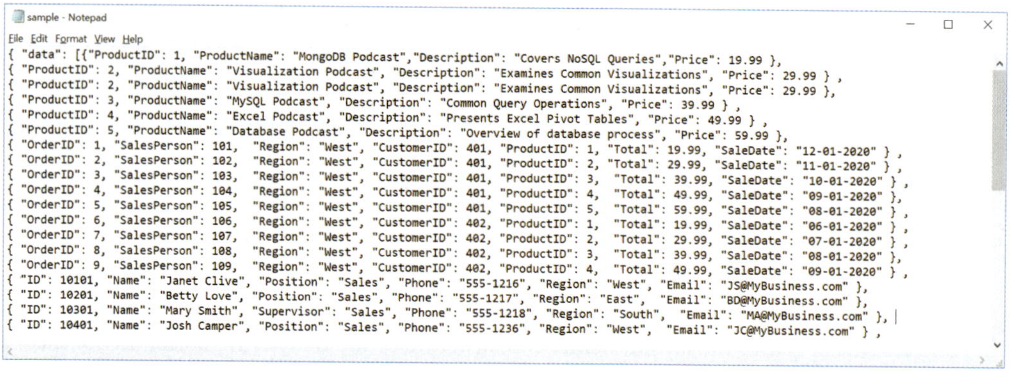

**FIGURE 7.3** Developers create and edit text-based JSON files using a text editor, such as Windows Notepad.

Used with permission from Microsoft

# Understanding JSON

| ID | Category | Price | Sales |
|----|----------|-------|-------|
| 1 | MongoDB Podcast | 19.99 | 50 |
| 2 | Visualization Podcast | 29.99 | 30 |
| 3 | MySQL Podcast | 39.99 | 20 |

```
{ "_id": 1, "Category": "MongoDB Podcast", "Price": 19.99, "Sales": 50 } );
{ "_id": 2, "Category": "Visualization Podcast", "Price": 29.99, "Sales": 30 } );
{ "_id": 3, "Category": "MySQL Podcast", "Price": 39.99, "Sales": 20 } );
```

**FIGURE 7.4** A JSON database is a text file containing JSON objects.

Used with permission of JSONLint.com

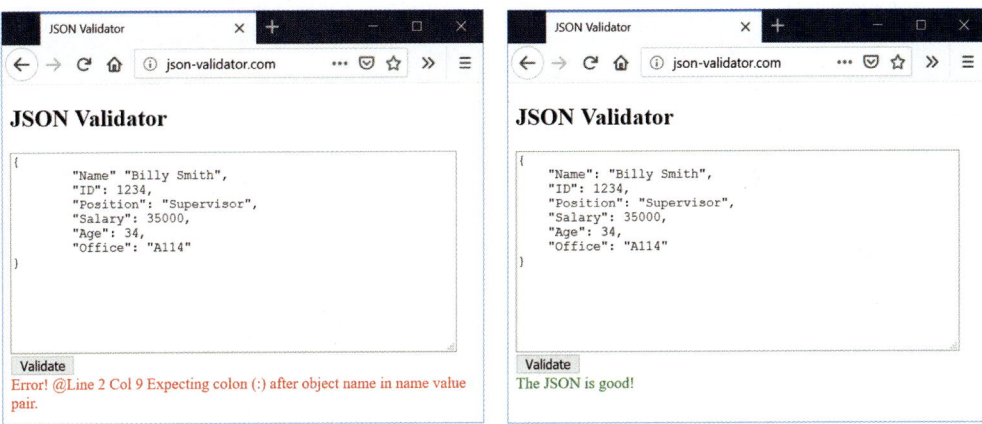

**FIGURE 7.5** Using a JSON validator to validate JSON content.

Used with permission of JSONLint.com

## JavaScript Object Notation (JSON)

JSON provides developers with a way to represent and store objects. The advantages of JSON include:

- Self-describing
- Human readable
- Language independent
- Lightweight

**FIGURE A** illustrates the component of a JSON object.

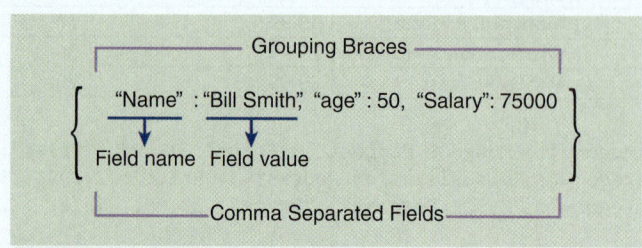

**FIGURE A** The components of a JSON object.

Behind the scenes, many NoSQL databases store their content as JSON objects.

# Getting Started with MongoDB

MongoDB is an open-source, object-oriented database created to provide a fast, scalable solution for web applications. MongoDB stores data as JSON objects. The three primary components of a MongoDB database include:

- Database: stores data within named collections
- **Collection**: similar to a relational table, in that it groups or collects objects
- **Document**: similar to a record, in that it contains name–value pairs

**FIGURE 7.6** represents a MongoDB, and collections within the database store documents within which you will find the name–value pairs.

MongoDB supports many platforms, meaning you can install it on Windows, Linux, and macOS. To install MongoDB, visit the MongoDB site, as shown in **FIGURE 7.7**.

After you install MongoDB, you can use its command-line shell (Mongo) to interact with your databases, as shown in **FIGURE 7.8**.

As you can see in Figure 7.8, the show databases command lists the available databases. To select a specific database for use, you issue the use command. If you specify a database that does not exist, MongoDB will create it. (Although your newly created database will not appear in the show databases list until you add a collection to it.)

To list the collections a database contains, you use the show collections command. **FIGURE 7.9** selects the MyBusiness database and then displays the collections it contains.

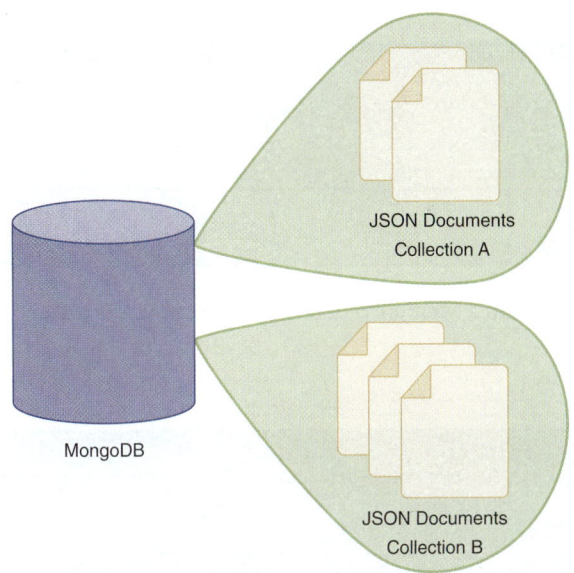

**FIGURE 7.6** A MongoDB database consists of collections of documents.

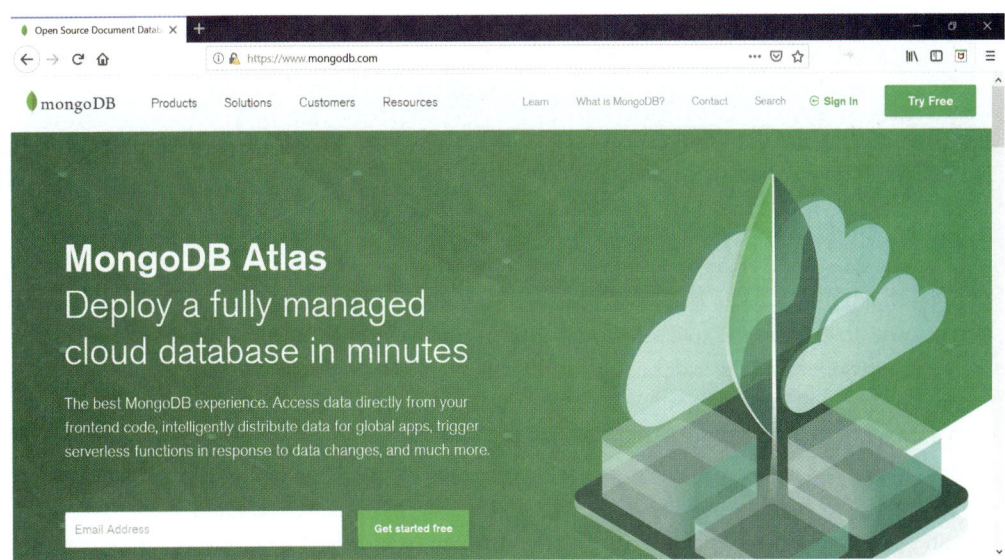

**FIGURE 7.7** Download and install MongoDB from the MongoDB site.

Used with permission of MongoDB, Inc.

**FIGURE 7.8** To interact with a MongoDB database, you can use the Mongo command-line shell.
Used with permission from Microsoft

**FIGURE 7.9** Listing the collections within a MongoDB database.
Used with permission from Microsoft

## Using the MongoDB Databases Provided on This Text's Catalog Page

Throughout this chapter, you will read about each MongoDB query and see examples of the query's use. Rather than simply reading about each query, you should instead execute them. To do so, however, you must have the database that contains the database collections the queries use on your system. Fortunately, you can quickly download and install the database and collections by downloading and executing a file of MongoDB queries that resides on this text's catalog page at go.jblearning.com/DataMining. Use the link to download the file. If you are using Windows, your system will display the file's contents within the Notepad accessory, as shown in **FIGURE A**.

Within your text editor, select the queries and copy them to the clipboard. If you are using the Windows Notepad accessory, press the Ctrl+A keyboard combination to select the query text and then press Ctrl+C to copy the selected text to the Windows Clipboard.

Using the Mongo command-line shell, you can paste the queries into the shell by clicking your mouse on the window's Control menu and choosing Edit, followed by Paste, as shown in **FIGURE B**.

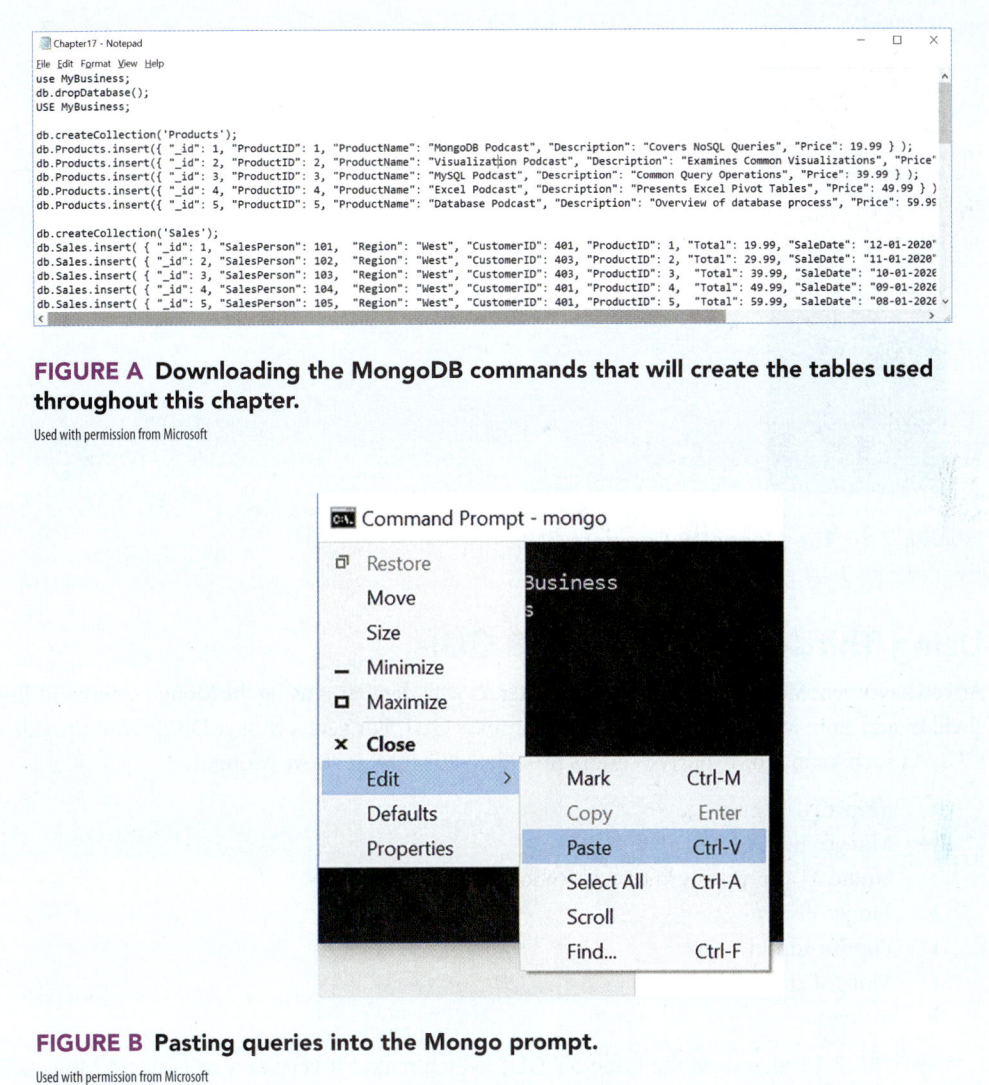

**FIGURE A** Downloading the MongoDB commands that will create the tables used throughout this chapter.

Used with permission from Microsoft

**FIGURE B** Pasting queries into the Mongo prompt.

Used with permission from Microsoft

# Using the MongoDB Graphical User Interface

To perform the queries this chapter presents, you will make extensive use of the Mongo command shell. In addition to the command shell, MongoDB provides a GUI, called Compass, as shown in **FIGURE 7.10**.

Within Compass, you can create databases, collections within a database, and documents within a collection. In addition, Compass lets you perform common data retrieval operations.

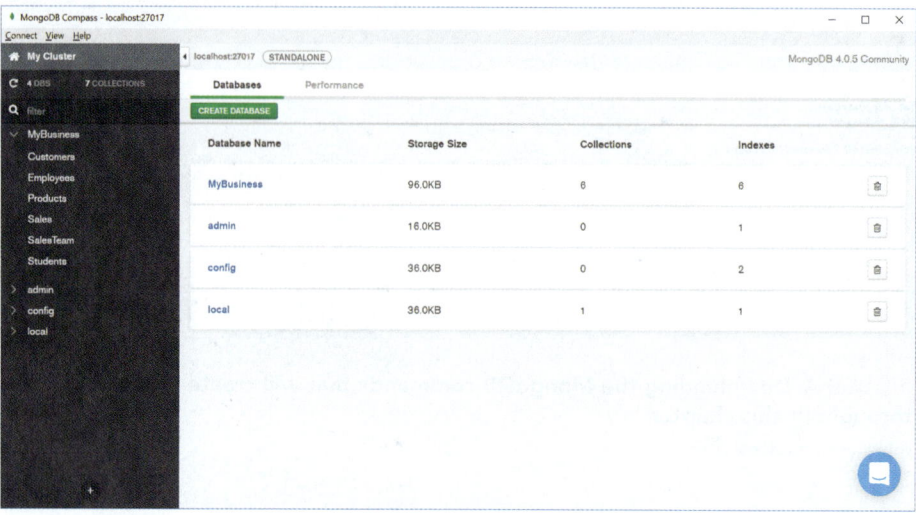

**FIGURE 7.10  The MongoDB Compass GUI.**
Used with permission of MongoDB, Inc.

## Using Third-Party MongoDB GUIs

As you have seen, MongoDB developers can interact with databases using the Mongo command-line shell. In addition, MongoDB provides the Compass GUI. For years, MongoDB did not provide a GUI. As such, many third-party vendors provide GUIs that sit above MongoDB:

- MongoDBManager
- MongoVue
- Studio 3T (previously known as Robo 3T and RoboMongo)
- MongoVision
- PhpMoAdmin
- MongoExplorer
- mViewer

**FIGURE 7.11** illustrates the Robo 3T GUI, which makes it very easy to issue all MongoDB query types within a visual environment.

## Querying a MongoDB Collection

A MongoDB collection is similar to a table within a relational database, in that it groups data objects—which MongoDB refers to as documents. A MongoDB database may store many different collections, such as Customers, Products, and Orders. To refer to a specific collection within the current database, you use the notation db.collectionName, where db represents the current database. For example, the statement db.Employees.find() displays all the documents (records) within the Employees collection, as shown in **FIGURE 7.12**.

*Note:* When you issue MongoDB queries, keep in mind that the statements are case dependent—meaning db.collection.find(), with a lowercase f for find, is correct and db.collection.Find() is not.

## Using the MongoDB Graphical User Interface

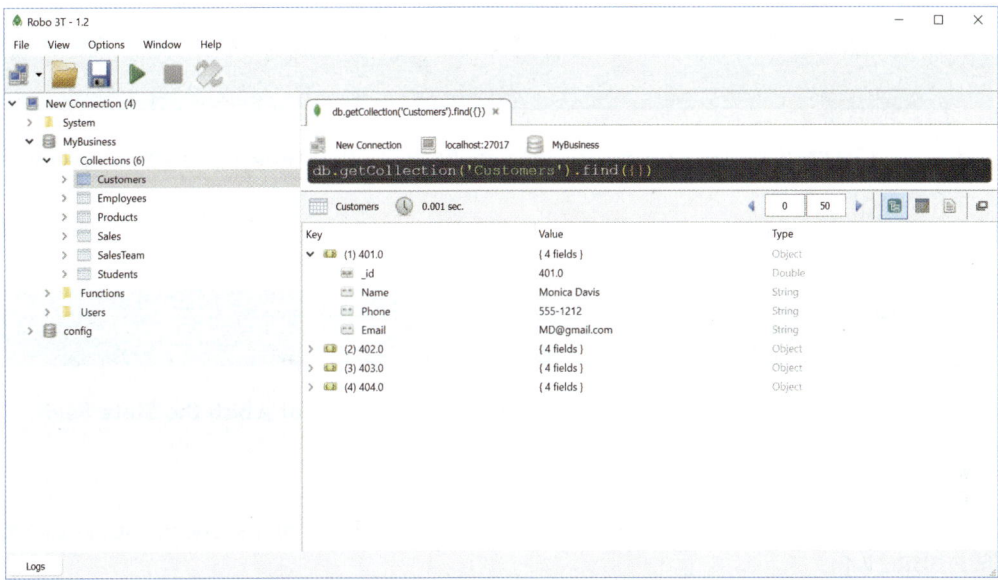

**FIGURE 7.11** Using the Robo 3T GUI to interact with MongoDB.
Used with permission of 3T Software Labs

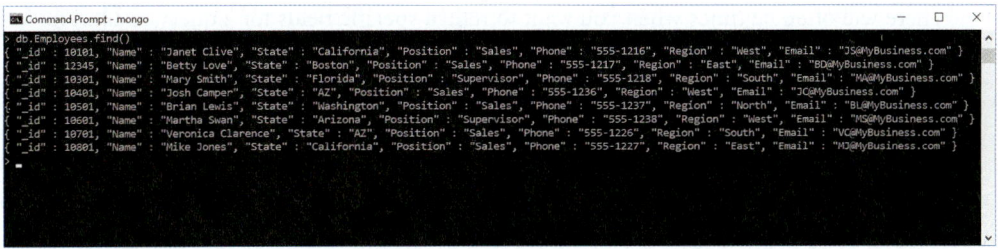

**FIGURE 7.12** Displaying all the documents within the Employees collection.
Used with permission from Microsoft

The query shown in Figure 7.14 returns all the records within the collection. To display documents that contain specific values, you specify your desired **filter** as JSON within the find method call. For example, the following query will display only those documents for which the value of the Position field is Supervisor:

```
db.Employees.find({"Position": "Supervisor"})
```

When you execute the query, MongoDB will display the documents, as shown in **FIGURE 7.13**. Likewise, the following query would list only those documents with the field value State equal to Arizona:

```
db.Employees.find({"State": "Arizona"})
```

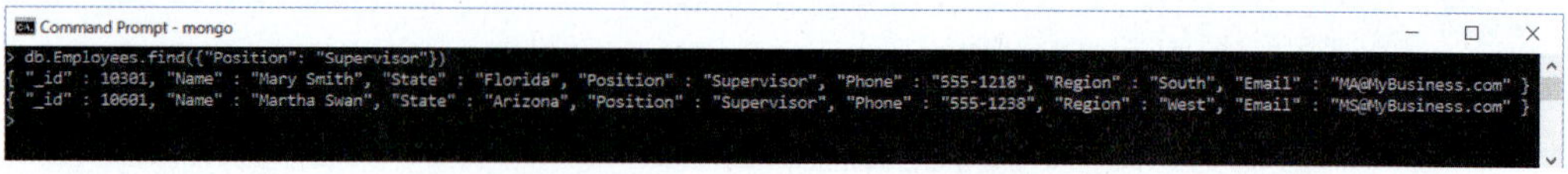

**FIGURE 7.13** Filtering query results for documents with the Position field value equal to Supervisor.
Used with permission from Microsoft

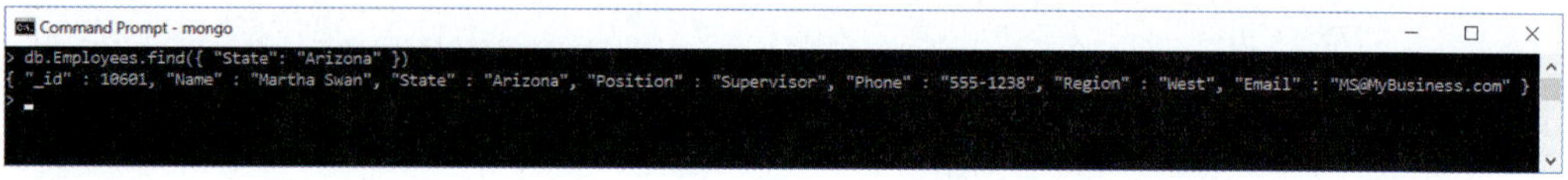

**FIGURE 7.14** Filtering query results for employee documents for which the State field value is Arizona.
Used with permission from Microsoft

Again, when you execute this query, MongoDB will list the employee documents, as shown in **FIGURE 7.14**.

If the field that you want to find or update is part of a nested object, you use dot notation to refer to the field:

```
db.collection.find({"Somefield.NestedField": value})
```

There will often be times when you want to return specific fields for a query result. The following query uses find to display only employee names:

```
db.Employees.find({}, {"Name": 1, "_id": 0})
```

To direct MongoDB to return a field, you follow the field name with a 1. By default, MongoDB will always return the _id field. By assigning it the value 0, you remove it from the result. When you execute this query, MongoDB will display the results shown in **FIGURE 7.15**.

Likewise, the following query displays student names and phone numbers:

```
db.Students.find({}, {"Name": 1, "Phone": 1, "_id": 0})
```

When you execute this query, MongoDB will display the results shown in **FIGURE 7.16**.

## Using Relational Operators Within a Query

As you perform MongoDB queries, there will be times when you want to retrieve documents for which the field values are equal to, greater than or equal to, less than or equal (and so on) a specified value. In such cases, you will use the MongoDB relational operators described in **TABLE 7.1**. **Relational operators** are so named because they compare how two values or expressions relate, based upon the specified operator, and return a true or false result.

The following query uses $ne to list employees who do not live in Arizona:

```
db.Employees.find({"State": {$ne: "Arizona"}})
```

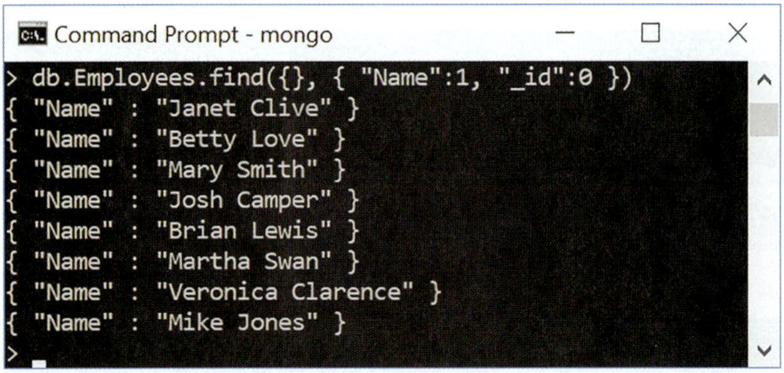

Using the MongoDB Graphical User Interface

**FIGURE 7.15** Displaying specific fields in a query result.
Used with permission from Microsoft

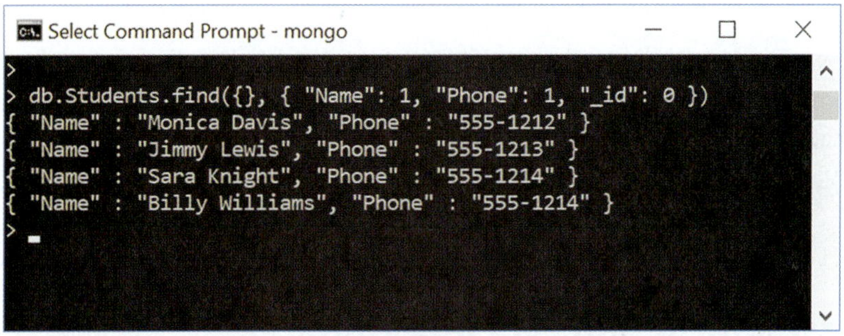

**FIGURE 7.16** Displaying student names and phone numbers.
Used with permission from Microsoft

**TABLE 7.1** The MongoDB Relational Operators

| Relational Operator | Meaning |
| --- | --- |
| $eq | Equality |
| $lt | Less than |
| $gt | Greater than |
| $lte | Less than or equal to |
| $gte | Greater than or equal to |
| $ne | Not equal |

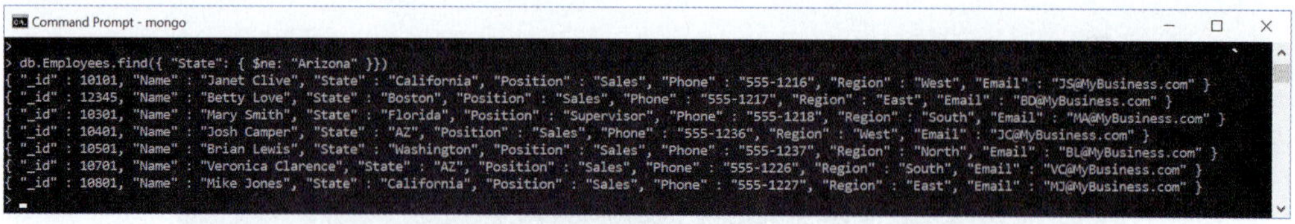

```
> db.Employees.find({ "State": { $ne: "Arizona" }})
{ "_id" : 10101, "Name" : "Janet Clive", "State" : "California", "Position" : "Sales", "Phone" : "555-1216", "Region" : "West", "Email" : "JC@MyBusiness.com" }
{ "_id" : 12345, "Name" : "Betty Love", "State" : "Boston", "Position" : "Sales", "Phone" : "555-1217", "Region" : "East", "Email" : "BD@MyBusiness.com" }
{ "_id" : 10301, "Name" : "Mary Smith", "State" : "Florida", "Position" : "Supervisor", "Phone" : "555-1218", "Region" : "South", "Email" : "MA@MyBusiness.com" }
{ "_id" : 10401, "Name" : "Josh Camper", "State" : "AZ", "Position" : "Sales", "Phone" : "555-1236", "Region" : "West", "Email" : "JC@MyBusiness.com" }
{ "_id" : 10501, "Name" : "Brian Lewis", "State" : "Washington", "Position" : "Sales", "Phone" : "555-1237", "Region" : "North", "Email" : "BL@MyBusiness.com" }
{ "_id" : 10701, "Name" : "Veronica Clarence", "State" : "AZ", "Position" : "Sales", "Phone" : "555-1226", "Region" : "South", "Email" : "VC@MyBusiness.com" }
{ "_id" : 10801, "Name" : "Mike Jones", "State" : "California", "Position" : "Sales", "Phone" : "555-1227", "Region" : "East", "Email" : "MJ@MyBusiness.com" }
```

**FIGURE 7.17** Using the MongoDB $ne relational operator.

Used with permission from Microsoft

```
> db.Sales.find({ "Total": { $gte: 39.99 }})
{ "_id" : 3, "SalesPerson" : 103, "Region" : "West", "CustomerID" : 403, "ProductID" : 3, "Total" : 39.99, "SaleDate" : "10-01-2020" }
{ "_id" : 4, "SalesPerson" : 104, "Region" : "West", "CustomerID" : 401, "ProductID" : 4, "Total" : 49.99, "SaleDate" : "09-01-2020" }
{ "_id" : 5, "SalesPerson" : 105, "Region" : "West", "CustomerID" : 401, "ProductID" : 5, "Total" : 59.99, "SaleDate" : "08-01-2020" }
{ "_id" : 8, "SalesPerson" : 108, "Region" : "West", "CustomerID" : 402, "ProductID" : 3, "Total" : 39.99, "SaleDate" : "08-01-2020" }
{ "_id" : 9, "SalesPerson" : 109, "Region" : "West", "CustomerID" : 402, "ProductID" : 4, "Total" : 49.99, "SaleDate" : "09-01-2020" }
```

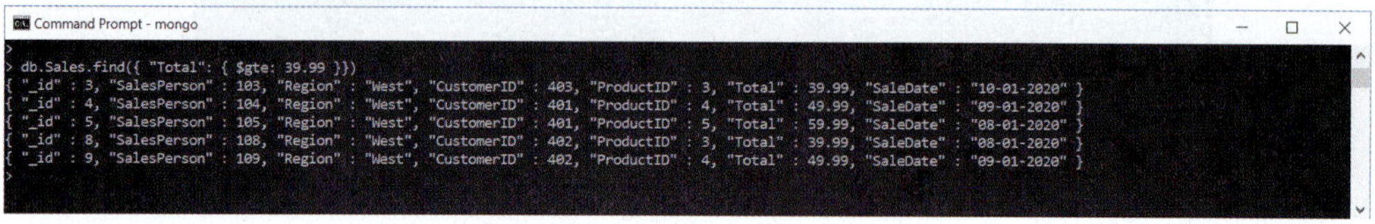

**FIGURE 7.18** Using the MongoDB $gte operator.

Used with permission from Microsoft

When you execute this query, MongoDB will display the results shown in **FIGURE 7.17**.

In a similar way, the following query uses the $gte operator to display orders for which the price is greater than or equal to $39.99:

```
db.Sales.find({"Total": {$gte: 39.99}})
```

When you execute this query, MongoDB will display the results shown in **FIGURE 7.18**.

## Using MongoDB Logical Operators

As your MongoDB queries become more complex, there will be many times when you must specify multiple conditions, such as the students who are taking a specific course and who have a grade point average (GPA) greater than 3.0. To specify compound conditions, you use the MongoDB **logical operators** listed in **TABLE 7.2**.

The following query uses the logical $or operator to display employees who work in Arizona or AZ:

```
db.Employees.find({$or: [{"State": "Arizona"},
{"State": "AZ"}]})
```

When you execute this query, MongoDB will display the results shown in **FIGURE 7.19**.

To display the names and phone numbers for such employees, you can modify the query as follows:

```
db.Employees.find({$or: [{"State": "Arizona"},
{"State": "AZ"}]}, {Name:1, Phone:1, _id:0})
```

When you execute this query, MongoDB will display the results shown in **FIGURE 7.20**.

The following query lists supervisors who live in Arizona:

```
db.Employees.find({$and: [{"State": "Arizona"},
{"Position": "Supervisor"}]}, {Name:1, Phone:1, _id:0})
```

**TABLE 7.2** The MongoDB Logical Operators

| Logical Operator | Meaning | Example |
| --- | --- | --- |
| $and | And | db.Employees.find({ $and: [{ "State": "Arizona"} , { "City": "Prescott" }]}) |
| $or | Or | db.Employees.find({ $or: [{ "State": "Arizona"} , { "State": "AZ" }]}) |
| $not | Not | db.students.find( { gpa: { $not: { $gt: 3.0 } } } ) |

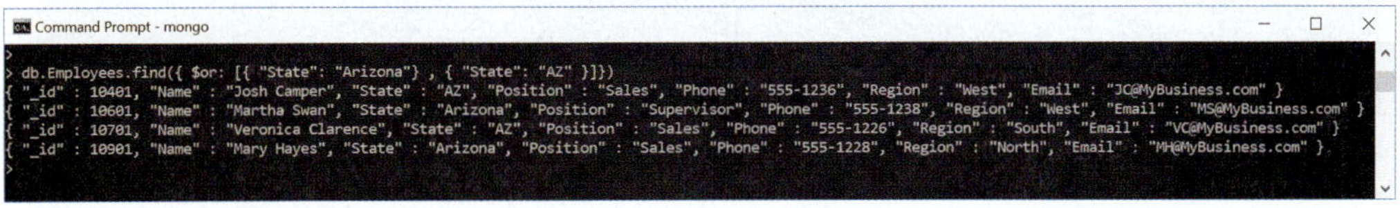

**FIGURE 7.19** Using the $or operator to display employees who work in Arizona or AZ.
Used with permission from Microsoft

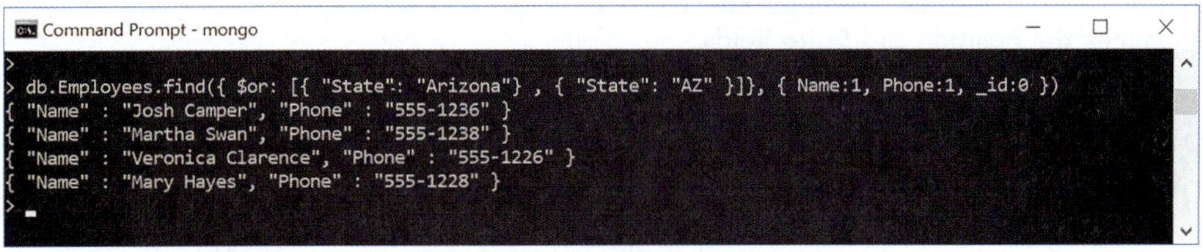

**FIGURE 7.20** Displaying specific fields for matching documents.
Used with permission from Microsoft

When you execute this query, MongoDB will display the results shown in **FIGURE 7.21**. Finally, this query lists sales team members who do not live in California:

```
db.Employees.find({$and: [{"State": {$ne: "California"}},
{"Position": "Sales"}]}, {Name:1, State:1, _id:0})
```

When you execute this query, MongoDB will display the results shown in **FIGURE 7.22**. The following complex query selects supervisors who work in Arizona:

```
db.Employees.find({$and: [{"State": "Arizona",
"Position": "Supervisor"}]}, {Name:1, Phone:1, _id:0})
```

When you execute this query, MongoDB will display the results shown in **FIGURE 7.23**.

```
> db.Employees.find({ $and: [{ "State": "Arizona"} , { "Position": "Supervisor" }]}, { Name:1, Phone:1, _id:0 })
{ "Name" : "Martha Swan", "Phone" : "555-1238" }
>
```

**FIGURE 7.21** Using the $and operator to list supervisors who live in Arizona.

Used with permission from Microsoft

```
> db.Employees.find({ $and: [{"State": { $ne: "California"}} , { "Position": "Sales" }]}, { Name:1, State:1, _id:0})
{ "Name" : "Betty Love", "State" : "Boston" }
{ "Name" : "Josh Camper", "State" : "AZ" }
{ "Name" : "Brian Lewis", "State" : "Washington" }
{ "Name" : "Veronica Clarence", "State" : "AZ" }
{ "Name" : "Mary Hayes", "State" : "Arizona" }
>
```

**FIGURE 7.22** Displaying sales members who do not live in California.

Used with permission from Microsoft

```
> db.Employees.find({ $and: [{ "State": "Arizona" , "Position": "Supervisor" }]}, { Name:1, Phone:1, _id:0 })
{ "Name" : "Martha Swan", "Phone" : "555-1238" }
>
```

**FIGURE 7.23** Using the $and operator to create a complex MongoDB query that examines the Position and State fields.

Used with permission from Microsoft

## Sorting Your Query Results

Often, when you perform a database query, you want to sort your results based on a specific field in ascending (lowest to highest) or descending (highest to lowest) order. To sort your MongoDB query results, you use the sort method, using JSON to specify the field upon which you want to sort, as well as the sort order. For example, the following query would sort the Employees collection based on the State field:

```
db.Employees.find().sort({"State": 1})
```

The value 1 within the JSON specifies that you want to sort the data in ascending order. To sort in descending order, specify the value −1:

```
db.Employees.find({}, {Name:1, State:1, _id:0}).sort({"State": -1})
```

When you execute this query, MongoDB will display the sorted content, as shown in **FIGURE 7.24**.
The previous query sorted the documents based on a single field. Often there will be times when you want to sort documents based on two or more fields. In such cases, you comma-separate the fields. The following query will sort the Employees collection by State and then by Position:

```
db.Employees.find().sort({"State": 1, "Position": 1})
```

When you execute this query, MongoDB will display the sorted results, as shown in **FIGURE 7.25**.

```
> db.Employees.find({}, { Name:1, State:1, _id:0 }).sort({ "State": -1 })
{ "Name" : "Brian Lewis", "State" : "Washington" }
{ "Name" : "Mary Smith", "State" : "Florida" }
{ "Name" : "Janet Clive", "State" : "California" }
{ "Name" : "Mike Jones", "State" : "California" }
{ "Name" : "Betty Love", "State" : "Boston" }
{ "Name" : "Martha Swan", "State" : "Arizona" }
{ "Name" : "Mary Hayes", "State" : "Arizona" }
{ "Name" : "Josh Camper", "State" : "AZ" }
{ "Name" : "Veronica Clarence", "State" : "AZ" }
>
```

**FIGURE 7.24** To sort MongoDB query results, you use the sort method.
Used with permission from Microsoft

```
> db.Employees.find().sort({ "State":1, "Position":1 })
{ "_id" : 10401, "Name" : "Josh Camper", "State" : "AZ", "Position" : "Sales", "Phone" : "555-1236", "Region" : "West", "Email" : "JC@MyBusiness.com" }
{ "_id" : 10701, "Name" : "Veronica Clarence", "State" : "AZ", "Position" : "Sales", "Phone" : "555-1226", "Region" : "South", "Email" : "VC@MyBusiness.com" }
{ "_id" : 10901, "Name" : "Mary Hayes", "State" : "Arizona", "Position" : "Sales", "Phone" : "555-1228", "Region" : "North", "Email" : "MH@MyBusiness.com" }
{ "_id" : 10601, "Name" : "Martha Swan", "State" : "Arizona", "Position" : "Supervisor", "Phone" : "555-1238", "Region" : "West", "Email" : "MS@MyBusiness.com" }
{ "_id" : 12345, "Name" : "Betty Love", "State" : "Boston", "Position" : "Sales", "Phone" : "555-1217", "Region" : "East", "Email" : "BD@MyBusiness.com" }
{ "_id" : 10101, "Name" : "Janet Clive", "State" : "California", "Position" : "Sales", "Phone" : "555-1216", "Region" : "West", "Email" : "JS@MyBusiness.com" }
{ "_id" : 10801, "Name" : "Mike Jones", "State" : "California", "Position" : "Sales", "Phone" : "555-1227", "Region" : "East", "Email" : "MJ@MyBusiness.com" }
{ "_id" : 10301, "Name" : "Mary Smith", "State" : "Florida", "Position" : "Supervisor", "Phone" : "555-1218", "Region" : "South", "Email" : "MA@MyBusiness.com" }
{ "_id" : 10501, "Name" : "Brian Lewis", "State" : "Washington", "Position" : "Sales", "Phone" : "555-1237", "Region" : "North", "Email" : "BL@MyBusiness.com" }
```

**FIGURE 7.25** Sorting documents by State and then by Position.
Used with permission from Microsoft

## Using MongoDB Arithmetic Operators

MongoDB supports the **arithmetic operators** listed in **TABLE 7.3**.

This chapter will illustrate the use of these operators in the section that examines field updates.

## Using MongoDB Arithmetic Functions

As you analyze MongoDB data, there will be times when you must perform arithmetic operations, such as summing products sold, multiplying a sales price times a state tax, and so on. To help you perform such operations, MongoDB provides the arithmetic functions shown in **TABLE 7.4**.

## Limiting the Number of Documents a Query Returns

If you are working with a large collection, there will be times when you want to limit the number of documents your query returns. You may, for example, only want to quickly view a collection's general format, as opposed to waiting for all the records to display. To limit the number of documents a query displays, you use the limit method. The following query limits the results to output to three documents:

```
db.Students.find().limit(3)
```

When you execute this query, MongoDB will display the results shown in **FIGURE 7.26**.

**TABLE 7.3** The MongoDB Arithmetic Operators

| Arithmetic Operator | Operation |
| --- | --- |
| + | Addition |
| − | Subtraction |
| * | Multiplication |
| / | Division |

**TABLE 7.4** The MongoDB Arithmetic Functions

| Function | Purpose |
| --- | --- |
| $abs | Returns the absolute value of an expression. |
| $add | Returns the sum of the specified expressions. Or adds numbers and a date and returns a new date, treating the numbers specified as milliseconds. |
| $ceil | Returns the smallest integer greater than or equal to the specified expression. |
| $divide | Returns the result of dividing the first expression by the second. |
| $exp | Returns e raised to the specified exponent. |
| $floor | Returns the largest integer less than or equal to the specified expression. |
| $ln | Returns the natural log of an expression. |
| $log | Returns the log of a number in the specified base. |
| $log10 | Returns the log base 10 of a number. |
| $mod | Returns the remainder of the first expression divided by the second. |
| $multiply | Returns the product of the specified expressions. |
| $pow | Returns the result of an expression raised to the specified exponent. |
| $sqrt | Returns the square root of an expression. |
| $subtract | Returns the difference of the specified expressions. Or subtracts numbers from a date and returns a new date, treating the numbers specified as milliseconds. |
| $trunc | Returns the truncation of an expression to an integer. |

```
> db.Students.find().limit(3)
{ "_id" : ObjectId("5c70c45a1d67aecd75554346"), "StudentID" : 501, "Name" : "Monica Davis", "Year" : "F", "Phone" : "555-1212", "Email" : "MD@gmail.com" }
{ "_id" : ObjectId("5c70c45a1d67aecd75554347"), "StudentID" : 502, "Name" : "Jimmy Lewis", "Year" : "So", "Phone" : "555-1213", "Email" : "JL@gmail.com" }
{ "_id" : ObjectId("5c70c45a1d67aecd75554348"), "StudentID" : 503, "Name" : "Sara Knight", "Year" : "J", "Phone" : "555-1214", "Email" : "SK@gmail.com" }
>
```

**FIGURE 7.26** To limit the number of documents a query displays, you use the limit method.
Used with permission from Microsoft

## Grouping MongoDB Query Results

Often, to analyze data, you need to perform operations on groups of data, such as grouping sales by region, students by year, and so on. To help you perform such grouping operations, MongoDB provides the $group operator. The following query uses $group to display a count of the number of documents in the SalesTeam collection:

```
db.SalesTeam.aggregate(
   [
      {
         $group : {
            _id : null,
            count: {$sum: 1}
         }
      }
   ]
)
```

To create an aggregation in MongoDB, you use the aggregate method, which will process the documents in a collection as an array, moving through each to perform your calculation. Within the method call, the $group operator specifies the field upon which you want to group and the operation, in this case, $sum, which simply adds 1 to the accumulated value for each document—counting the records.

When you execute this query, MongoDB will display the results shown in **FIGURE 7.27**.

As you analyze MongoDB data, there will be many times when you need to perform aggregation operations, such as summing and averaging data, determining the minimum or maximum value, or calculating a standard deviation. To help you perform such operations, MongoDB provides the following operators:

- $avg
- $sum
- $max
- $min
- $stdDevPop
- $stdDevSamp

```
> db.SalesTeam.aggregate(
...     [
...         {
...             $group : {
...                 _id : null,
...                 count: { $sum: 1 }
...             }
...         }
...     ]
... )
{ "_id" : null, "count" : 9 }
>
```

**FIGURE 7.27** Using $group to display a count of the number of documents in a collection.

Used with permission from Microsoft

The following query uses $avg to calculate the average product price:

```
db.Products.aggregate(
    [
        {
            $group:
            {
                _id: "1",
                avgPrice: {$avg: "$Price"}
            }
        }
    ]
)
```

Again, the aggregate method will create an array containing the documents and will move through each document, grouping on the _id field to create the average.

When you execute this query, MongoDB will display the results shown in **FIGURE 7.28**.

In a similar way, the following queries display the maximum product price:

```
db.Products.aggregate(
    [
        {
            $group:
            {
                _id: "1",
                MaxPrice: {$max: "$Price"}
            }
        }
    ]
)
```

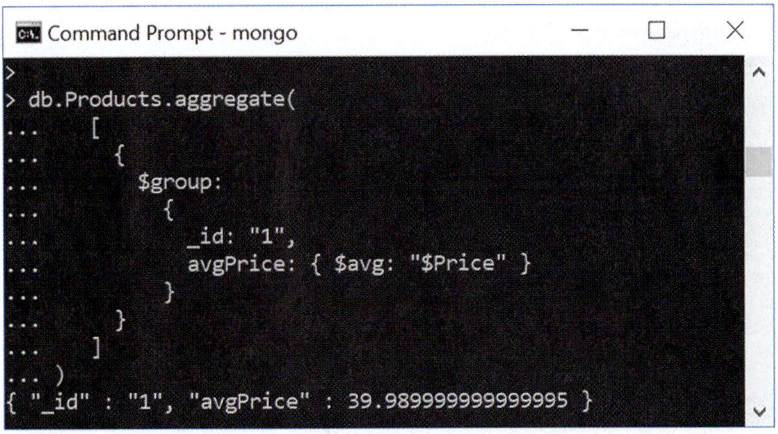

```
> db.Products.aggregate(
...   [
...     {
...       $group:
...         {
...           _id: "1",
...           avgPrice: { $avg: "$Price" }
...         }
...     }
...   ]
... )
{ "_id" : "1", "avgPrice" : 39.989999999999995 }
```

**FIGURE 7.28** Using $avg to calculate the average product price.

Used with permission from Microsoft

```
> db.Products.aggregate(
...   [
...     {
...       $group:
...         {
...           _id: "1",
...           MaxPrice: { $max: "$Price" }
...         }
...     }
...   ]
... )
{ "_id" : "1", "MaxPrice" : 59.99 }
```

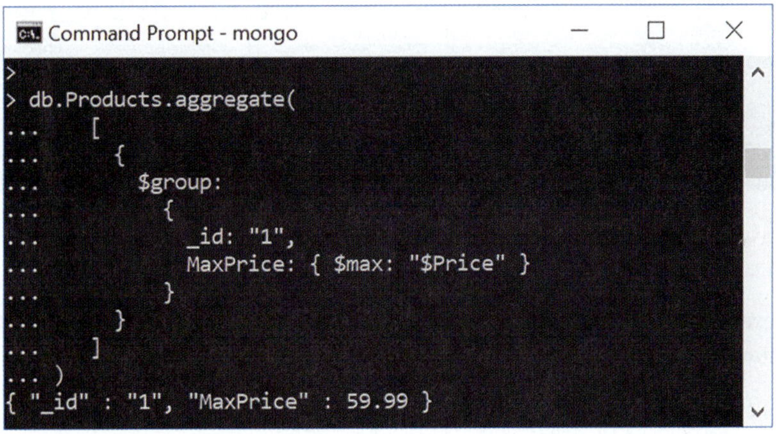

**FIGURE 7.29** Displaying the maximum price.

Used with permission from Microsoft

When you execute these queries, MongoDB will display the results shown in **FIGURE 7.29**.

Finally, this query sums the company's sales:

```
db.Products.aggregate(
  [
    {
      $group:
        {
          _id: "1",
          TotalSales: {$sum: "$Price"}
        }
    }
  ]
)
```

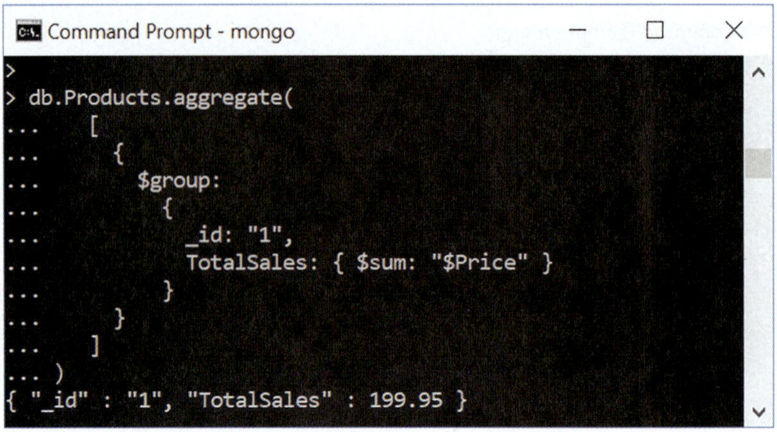

**CHAPTER 7** NoSQL Data Analytics

```
> db.Products.aggregate(
...   [
...     {
...       $group:
...         {
...           _id: "1",
...           TotalSales: { $sum: "$Price" }
...         }
...     }
...   ]
... )
{ "_id" : "1", "TotalSales" : 199.95 }
```

**FIGURE 7.30** Using the MongoDB $sum operator.
Used with permission from Microsoft

```
> db.Sales.aggregate([{ $group: { _id: "$CustomerID", total: { $sum: "$Total" }}}, { $sort: { total: -1 } }])
{ "_id" : 402, "total" : 139.96 }
{ "_id" : 401, "total" : 129.97 }
{ "_id" : 403, "total" : 69.98 }
>
```

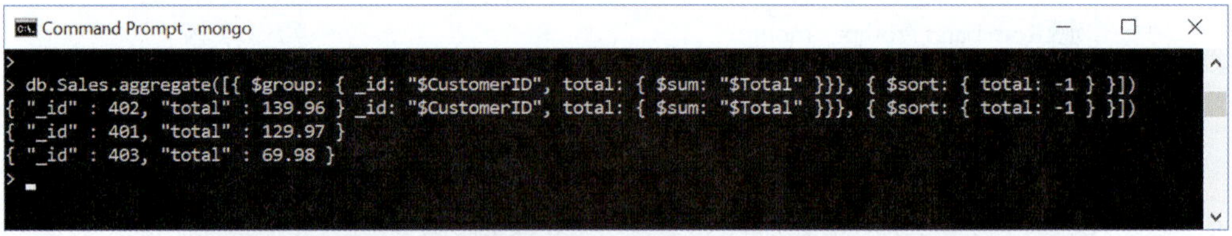

**FIGURE 7.31** Grouping sales by customers.
Used with permission from Microsoft

When you execute this query, MongoDB will display the results shown in **FIGURE 7.30**.

The following query uses $group to group sales by customer:

```
db.Sales.aggregate([{$group: {_id: "$CustomerID", total:
{$sum: "$Total"}}}, {$sort: {total: -1}}])
```

When you execute this query, MongoDB will display the results shown in **FIGURE 7.31**.

## Inserting Data into a MongoDB Collection

MongoDB databases store data as documents within a collection. To insert a document (record) into a collection, you use the insert method, specifying the object's name–value pairs using JSON. The following query will insert a document into the Students collection:

```
db.Students.insert({"StudentID": 601, "Name": "Alvin Dawson",
"Year": "F", "Phone": "555-1232", "Email": "AD@gmail.com"});
```

When you insert document values, the order in which you specify the JSON name–value pairs does not matter. The following queries, with the order of the name–value pairs changed, are all valid:

```
db.Students.insert({"StudentID": 601, "Year": "F", "Phone":
"555-1312", "Email": "MR@gmail.com", "Name": "Manny Reece"});
```

```
db.Students.insert({"Name": "Ben Salmon", "StudentID": 701,
"Year": "F", "Phone": "555-1362", "Email": "BS@gmail.com"});
```

After you execute these queries, the Students collection will contain the documents shown in **FIGURE 7.32**.

MongoDB is often described as "less structured" than a traditional relational database. As such, when you insert a document within a collection, you do not need to provide a fixed number of name–value pairs. Instead, you can specify name–value pairs for all the collection fields, for some of the fields, or for even more fields than you thought the collection contained. For example, the following queries will each create documents within the Employees collection:

```
db.Employees.insert({"_id": 50101, "Name": "Julie Adams",
"Position": "Sales", "Phone": "555-1316", "Region": "West"});

db.Employees.insert({"_id": 52345, "Name": "Bobby Lewis",
"Phone": "555-1217", "Region": "East"});

db.Employees.insert({"_id": 50301, "Name": "Marvin Train",
"Position": "Supervisor", "Phone": "555-3218"});
```

As you can see, each insert operation specifies a different number of name–value pairs. One even specifies extra fields. MongoDB will insert each of these documents into the collection. After you execute these queries, the Employees collection will contain the documents shown in **FIGURE 7.33**.

Remember, MongoDB objects are said to be self-describing. In this way, the number of fields may differ within each document in a collection. When MongoDB (or a different application) retrieves each document, it will parse the self-describing JSON to determine which name–value pairs the document contains and handle the data appropriately.

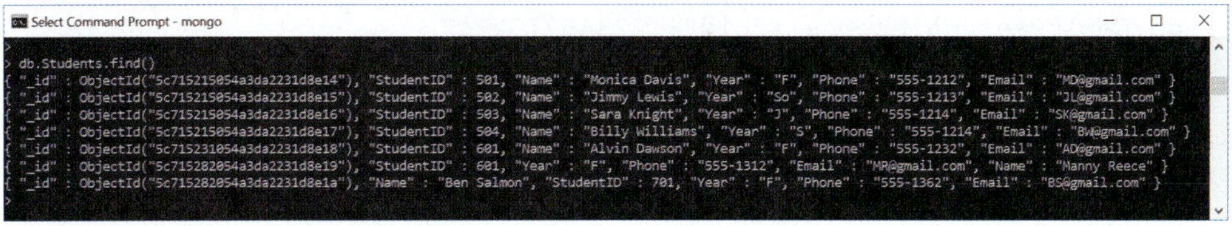

**FIGURE 7.32** The Students collection.

Used with permission from Microsoft

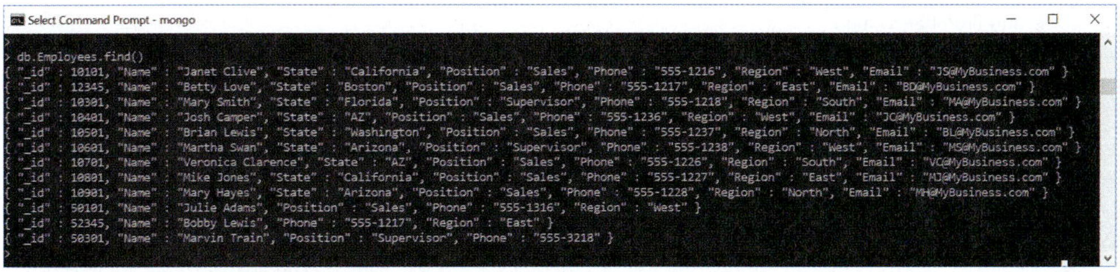

**FIGURE 7.33** The Employees collection.

Used with permission from Microsoft

## Updating a MongoDB Document

Just as there will be times when you must insert new documents into a collection, there will also be times when you must update an existing document. To update a MongoDB document, you use the update method, using JSON to specify the fields and values you desire. The following query updates the employee with the ID 12345 to the position of supervisor:

```
db.Employees.update({"_id": 12345}, {$set: {"Position":
"Supervisor"}} )
```

The query uses $set to specify the field to set. If you do not specify $set, MongoDB would delete the remaining fields.

In a similar way, the following query updates employees who have the abbreviation AZ within the State field to use instead of the complete state name:

```
db.Employees.update({"State": "AZ"}, {$set: {"State":
"Arizona"}} )
```

When you execute this query, MongoDB will display the results shown in **FIGURE 7.34**.

Finally, this query uses $set to update multiple fields for employee 10301:

```
db.Employees.update({"_id": 10301}, {$set: {"State": "Montana",
"Phone": "777-3333"}} )
```

## Deleting MongoDB Documents

Just as there will be times when you insert or update documents within a collection, there will also be times when you must delete documents. To delete one or more documents, you use the deleteOne or deleteMany method. The following query deletes the employee with the ID 12345:

```
db.Employees.deleteOne({"_id": 12345})
```

When you execute this query, MongoDB will display the results shown in **FIGURE 7.35**.

Likewise, this query will delete all employees who work in California:

```
db.Employees.deleteMany({"State": "California"})
```

When you execute this query, MongoDB will display the results shown in **FIGURE 7.36**.

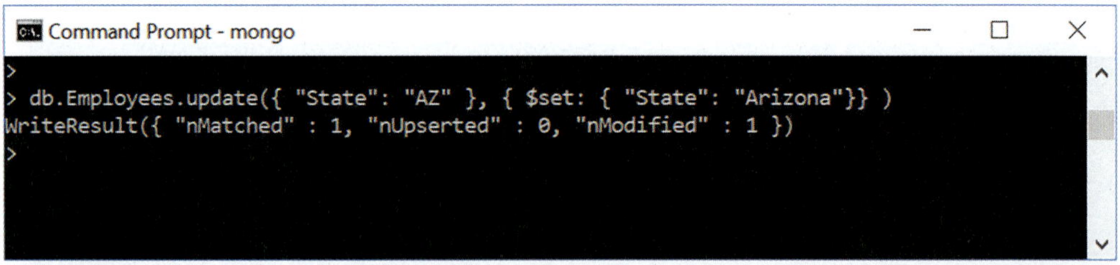

**FIGURE 7.34** To update existing documents within a collection, you use the update method.
Used with permission from Microsoft

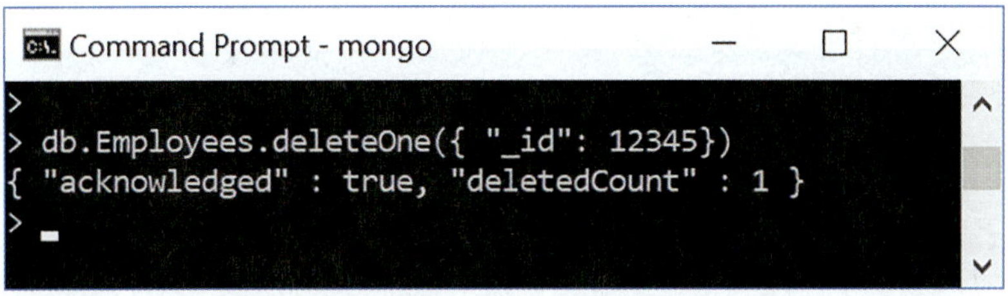
Command Prompt - mongo
>
> db.Employees.deleteOne({ "_id": 12345})
{ "acknowledged" : true, "deletedCount" : 1 }
>

**FIGURE 7.35 Deleting a document from the Employees collection.**

Used with permission from Microsoft

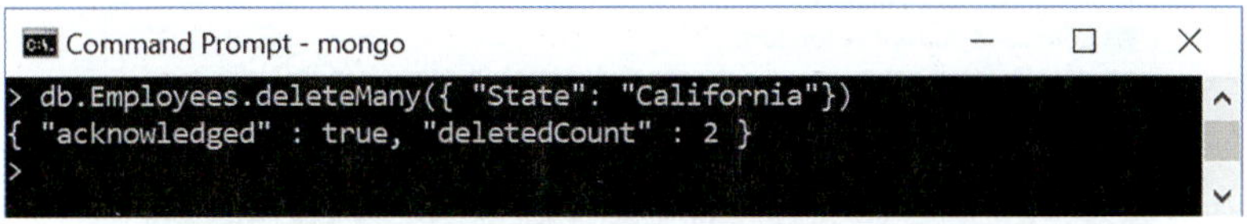
Command Prompt - mongo
> db.Employees.deleteMany({ "State": "California"})
{ "acknowledged" : true, "deletedCount" : 2 }
>

**FIGURE 7.36 Deleting a group of employees from the Employees collection.**

Used with permission from Microsoft

Be careful when you use the deleteMany method. If you specify delete without any parameter, it will delete all records within the collection:

```
db.Employees.deleteMany({ })
```

## Creating and Dropping MongoDB Collections and Databases

As you have learned, a MongoDB database stores objects within a named collection. To create a collection, you use the db.createCollection("collection name") query. For example, to create a collection named PartTimeEmployees, you would use the following query:

```
db.createCollection("PartTimeEmployees")
```

**FIGURE 7.37** shows the steps to create a Students collection within a database named School. As discussed, if the database you specify within a use command does not exist, MongoDB will create it.

To delete (drop) a collection, you use the drop method. The following query drops the Students collection:

```
db.Students.drop()
```

Likewise, to delete the current database, you use the db.dropDatabase() method. Be careful when you execute the db.dropDatabase() method, as MongoDB will delete the database even if it contains collections. **FIGURE 7.38** illustrates the process of dropping a collection and a database.

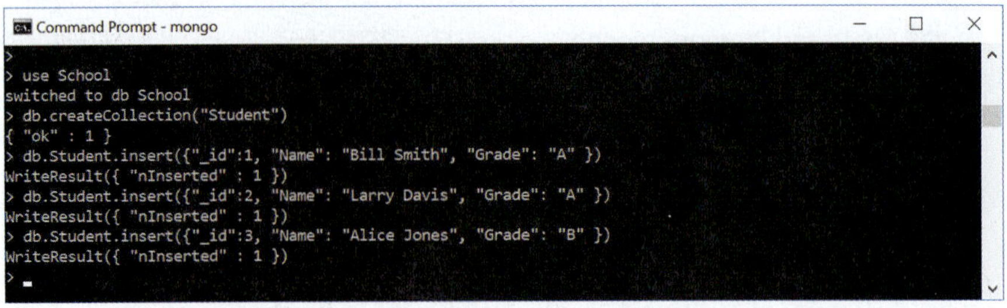
Command Prompt - mongo
>
> use School
switched to db School
> db.createCollection("Student")
{ "ok" : 1 }
> db.Student.insert({"_id":1, "Name": "Bill Smith", "Grade": "A" })
WriteResult({ "nInserted" : 1 })
> db.Student.insert({"_id":2, "Name": "Larry Davis", "Grade": "A" })
WriteResult({ "nInserted" : 1 })
> db.Student.insert({"_id":3, "Name": "Alice Jones", "Grade": "B" })
WriteResult({ "nInserted" : 1 })
>

**FIGURE 7.37 Creating a School database and a Student collection within that database.**

Used with permission from Microsoft

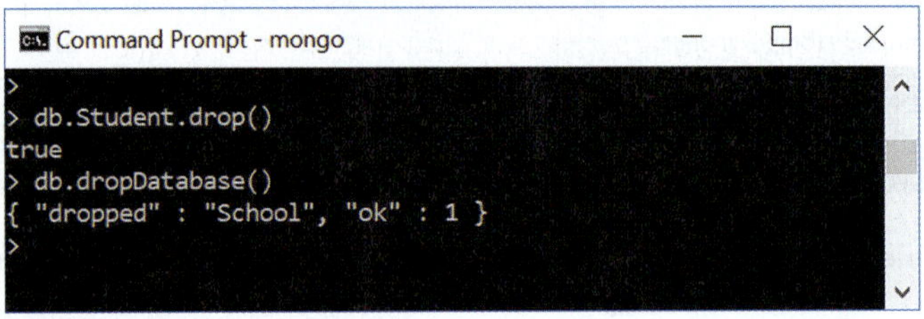
Command Prompt - mongo
>
> db.Student.drop()
true
> db.dropDatabase()
{ "dropped" : "School", "ok" : 1 }
>

**FIGURE 7.38 To delete a MongoDB collection, you use the drop() method, and to delete a database, you use the dropDatabase query.**

Used with permission from Microsoft

## MongoDB and CRUD

Database developers often describe query operations using the CRUD acronym:

- Create
- Read
- Update
- Delete

In this chapter, you have learned that MongoDB provides commands and query methods you can use to perform CRUD operations. **TABLE A** lists the MongoDB CRUD methods.

**TABLE A MongoDB Methods that Perform Crud Operations**

| Operation | MongoDB Query |
|---|---|
| Create | createCollection(), insert() |
| Read | find() |
| Update | update() |
| Delete | delete() |

## Revisiting MySQL and JSON

As you learned in Chapter 6, "Keep SQL in Your Toolset," MySQL is a SQL-based relational database. Because of the widespread use of JSON, MySQL has expanded its query capabilities to support a JSON data type that you can use to store a JSON object. In addition, MySQL provides functions you can use to query and manipulate JSON data. For example, if a record contains a JSON Students field, using MySQL's JSON capabilities, you can construct queries that manipulate specific items within that field. For specifics on the MySQL JSON functions, refer to the MySQL documentation, as shown in **FIGURE 7.39**.

## Using an Index to Improve MongoDB Query Performance

If you identify one or more queries that you (or others) will execute on a regular basis in the future, you should optimize the query to improve its performance. One way database developers improve performance is to index key fields within a MongoDB collection.

To understand how indexes improve performance, consider the following scenario: A bank's Customer collection contains 5 million documents, one for each customer. When a user calls the bank, the customer service representative asks the caller to provide his or her Social Security number. The representative then uses that number to retrieve the customer's document.

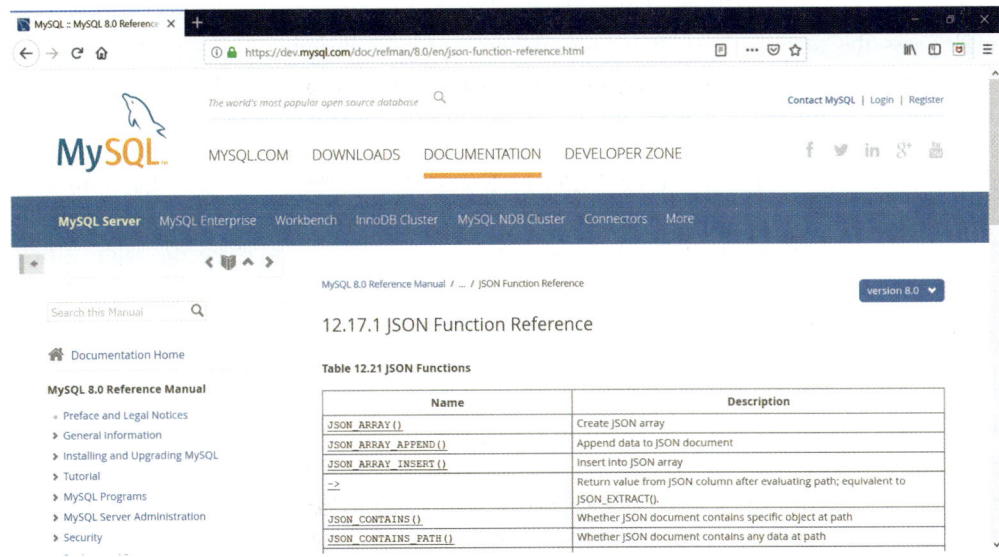

**FIGURE 7.39** The MySQL JSON functions.
Copyright Oracle and its affiliates. Used with permission

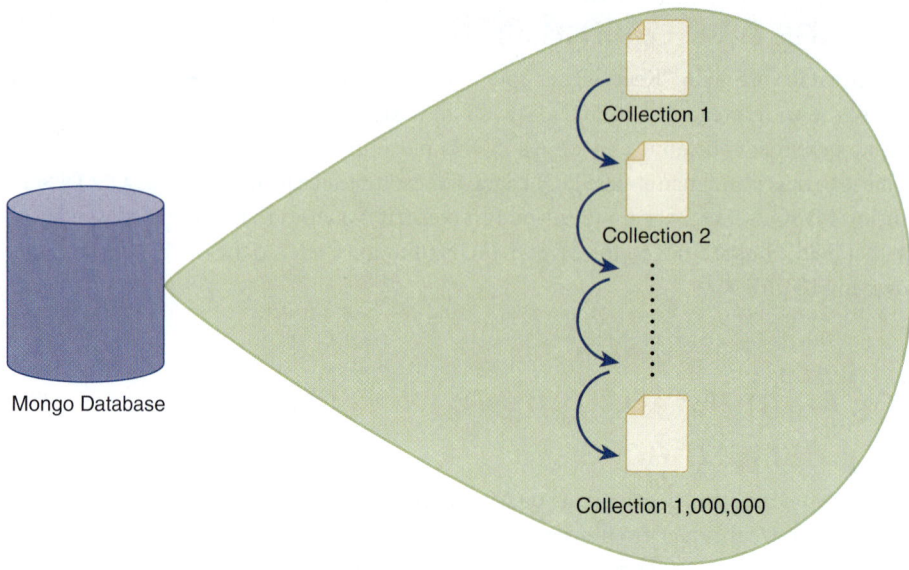

**FIGURE 7.40** Without an index, MongoDB must sequentially search each record's values—a slow process.

Behind the scenes, if no index exists, the database will retrieve the first document in the collection and compare its Social Security number to that provided by the user. If the numbers match, the query will return the document. If the numbers do not match, MongoDB will repeat this process with the second record, then the third, and so on, as shown in **FIGURE 7.40**. As you might guess, this sequential search process can become time consuming.

An **index** is a data structure that stores an index value (such as a Social Security number) and a pointer to the document within the collection that contains the value. Because the file that contains the index is smaller than the collection, MongoDB can read the index values much faster. In addition, behind the scenes, MongoDB stores the indexes in a form that optimizes searching.

When MongoDB must retrieve the document that corresponds to a specific value, it first retrieves the index and then uses the pointer it contains to quickly retrieve the document from the collection.

It is important to note that although indexes will normally significantly improve performance, they have a small performance and storage impact. To keep the index values up to date, each time you insert a value into an indexed table, MongoDB must create a corresponding index, which requires some processing time. In addition, MongoDB must store the index values, which will consume some disk space. That said, the benefits of indexes normally far outweigh the costs.

To create an index on a collection, you use the createIndex method:

```
db.collection.createIndex({"field": 1})
```

In this case, the 1 within the createIndex method call directs MongoDB to create the index based upon the values sorted in ascending order. To create the index based on descending values, use -1.

When you create an index, you can index a single field or you can create a combined index based on multiple fields. The following query creates an index on the StudentID and Name fields of the Students collection:

```
db.Students.createIndex({"StudentID": 1, "Name": 1})
```

Should you later decide that you no longer need an index, you can delete it using the dropIndex method, as shown here:

```
db.collection.dropIndex({"field": 1})
```

The following query would delete the multifield index previously created:

```
db.Students.dropIndex({"StudentID": 1, "Name": 1})
```

## Importing and Exporting Data to and from a MongoDB Database

One of the most common operations a database developer must perform is to **import** data from a different source, such as an Excel spreadsheet or a JSON file. To help developers perform such operations, MongoDB provides the mongoimport and mongoexport commands.

The following mongoimport command, for example, loads the contents of the Excel file Students.csv into the Students collection:

```
mongoimport -d MyBusiness -c Students --type csv --file \Data\students.csv --headerline
```

In this case, the -d specifies that the database, in this case MyBusiness follows, and -c specifies the collection, Students. The --headerline specifies that the .csv file has a header row that specifies the field names. When you execute this query, MongoDB will display the results shown in **FIGURE 7.41**.

The following mongoimport command imports the contents of the JSON file Students.json into the Students collection:

```
mongoimport -d School -c Students --file students.json
```

**FIGURE 7.41** Importing a .csv file's contents into a MongoDB collection.

Used with permission from Microsoft

# CHAPTER 7 NoSQL Data Analytics

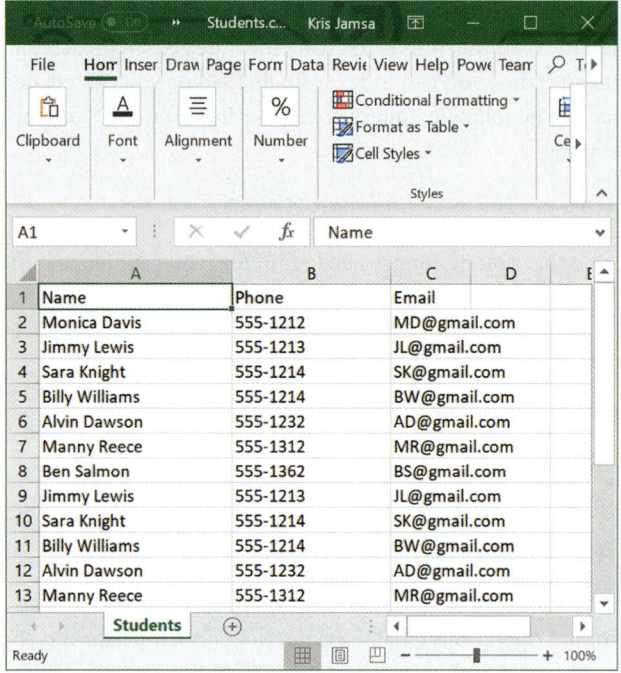

**FIGURE 7.42 Exporting documents into a .csv file.**
Used with permission from Microsoft

Just as developers frequently import data into a MongoDB collection, they also must often export data. To perform such **export** operations, developers use the mongoexport command. For example, the following mongoexport command exports all the documents in the Students collection into the Excel file Students.csv:

```
mongoexport -d MyBusiness -c Students --out Students.csv --type
csv --fields Name,Phone,Email
```

When you execute this query, MongoDB will create the comma-separated file, which you can open in Excel, as shown in **FIGURE 7.42**.

Similarly, this mongoexport command exports data into the JSON file StudentsBackup.json:

```
mongoexport -d MyBusiness -c Students --out StudentsBackup.json
```

## Performing SQL Queries on a MongoDB Database

As discussed, third-party tools are emerging that let database developers perform SQL queries on NoSQL databases. MongoDB is no exception. The following third-party tools support SQL queries on MongoDB:

- Studio 3T
- NoSQLBooster

- Stich Query Translator
- Enhanced PolyBase

**FIGURE 7.43** illustrates the use of Studio 3T for MongoDB to perform SQL queries.

Because of MongoDB's widespread use, the number of applications that support SQL operations for NoSQL databases will continue to grow. In fact, developers have been working on prototype versions of SQL, called SQL++, that extend SQL capabilities to support NoSQL databases.

## Distributing a MongoDB Database Using Shards

Scalability describes an application's ability to increase or decrease its processing capabilities based on demand. In general, there are two ways to scale a database: vertically and horizontally. With **vertical scaling**, you increase the processing capabilities of a single database server by adding processing power, RAM, and disk space. With horizonal scaling, you increase processing power and storage by spreading the solution across multiple servers.

Assume, for example, that the use and size of your MongoDB database are doubling. As shown in **FIGURE 7.44**, you can scale the database server by doubling the number of processor cores, RAM, and, if necessary, disk space.

Next, assume that your MongoDB database's use and size are growing by a factor of 10 or even a factor of 100. As you might guess, it would be hard to vertically scale a single server to meet this demand. Instead, you would scale the database horizontally by spreading the database across multiple servers, which MongoDB refers to as shards, as shown in **FIGURE 7.45**.

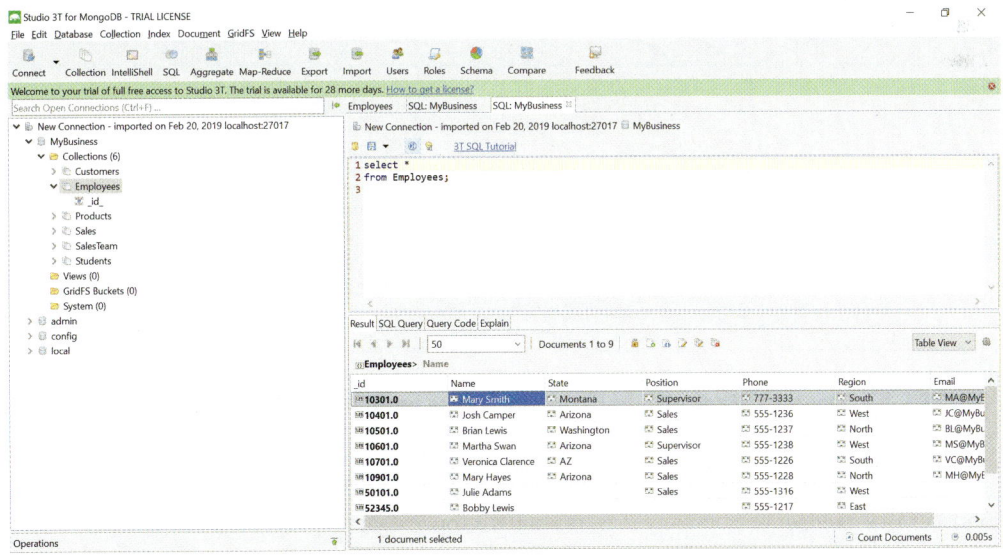

**FIGURE 7.43** Performing SQL queries on a MongoDB database using Studio 3T.

Used with permission of 3T Software Labs

## CHAPTER 7 NoSQL Data Analytics

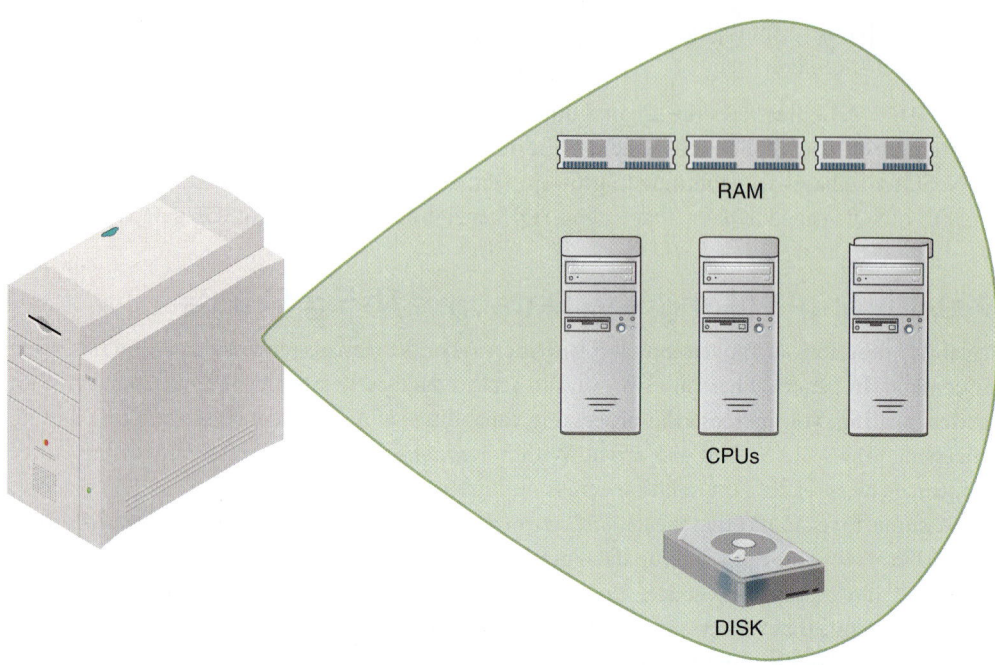

**FIGURE 7.44** Vertical scaling increases a single server's processing capabilities.

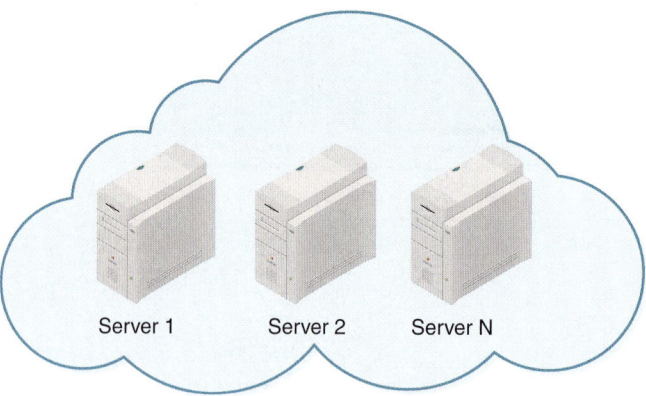

**FIGURE 7.45** Scaling a MongoDB horizontally across multiple shards.

To use the sharded data, the Mongo shell, or an application that uses the database, would connect to a server (or one of many servers) called a router that maps requests for data to the correct **shard**. Depending on the data's contents and use, how data are assigned and organized across shards will differ. One database might shard by customer ID, another by an order's state of origin, and so on. After the database developers start the shards, the process of routing data is automatic.

By scaling horizontally, the database developers can add or remove shards to best align the resource costs with the needed performance. As such, sharding is the mechanism through which MongoDB is a **distributed database** system.

## Replicating a MongoDB Database Using Replica Sets

As the size of a database increases, backing up the database can become more challenging, time consuming, and expensive. For systems that cannot afford downtime in the event of a database failure, developers turn to real-time replication. To implement such replication, the database developers use two or more identical databases, ideally residing in different parts of the country, to prevent a single disaster from damaging both servers. As shown in **FIGURE 7.46**, when one database inserts, updates, or deletes data, the replication process immediately updates the other database automatically. Should one of the two systems fail, processing can immediately fall over to the other, without downtime.

MongoDB provides replication through the use of distributed systems called replication sets, or **replica sets** for short.

A replication set groups MongoDB databases with one or more backup databases. Assume, for example, that you have a five-node MongoDB cluster. To replicate the nodes in such a way to prevent a single failure from bringing down the system, you might create the replication sets shown in **FIGURE 7.47**.

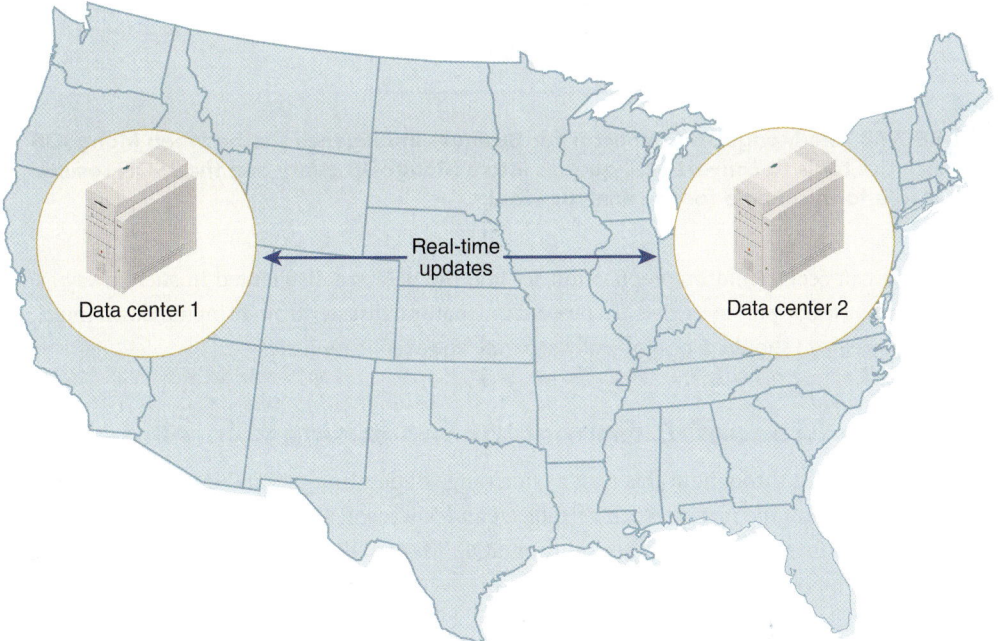

**FIGURE 7.46** Replicating a database provides a real-time backup or load-sharing environment.

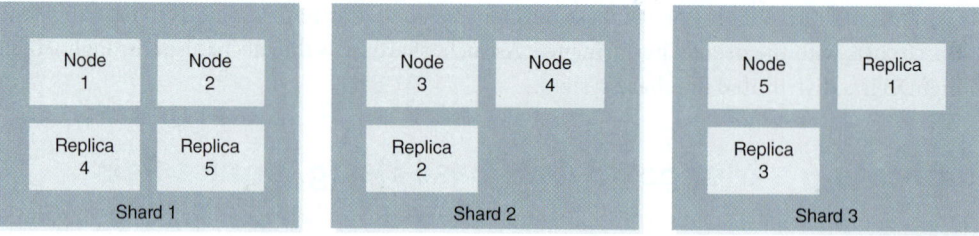

**FIGURE 7.47** Creating replication sets to prevent a single failure from bringing down the system.

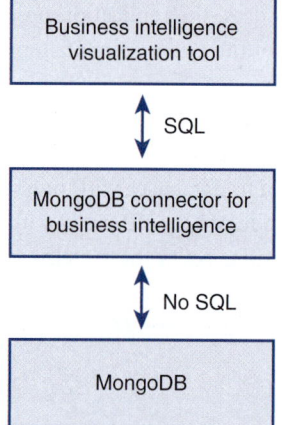

**FIGURE 7.48** The MongoDB Connector for Business Intelligence sits between MongoDB and analytics tools to convert SQL queries into a MongoDB query and the JSON results into a table form suitable for the analytics tool.

As you can see, should one replication set fail, the data are distributed in such a way as to ensure a database copy always exists. To prevent one natural disaster from bringing down multiple replication sets, you should geographically separate your replication sets.

## Using the MongoDB Connector for Business Intelligence

As you have learned throughout this text, a wide range of data analysis and business-intelligence tools are available on the market, such as Tableau and Microsoft Power BI. These tools normally connect to a database or data warehouse using SQL. MongoDB, however, is a NoSQL database that does not support SQL.

To allow these tools to use a MongoDB database, the MongoDB developers created the MongoDB Connector for Business Intelligence. As shown in **FIGURE 7.48**, The MongoDB Connector for Business Intelligence sits between the MongoDB database and the data-analytics tool to convert the tool's SQL queries and results into forms suitable for a MongoDB query and for display by the tool.

Because of the growth of NoSQL databases, many business intelligence and visualization tools now include their own connectors, which allow them to connect to and use NoSQL data.

## Other Popular NoSQL Databases

Because of its widespread adoption, ease of use, and suitability to illustrate the storage of JSON objects, MongoDB is presented in depth within this chapter. That said, **TABLE 7.5** describes several popular NoSQL databases, any one of which could have been used in this chapter to represent NoSQL solutions. Table 7.5 intends only to provide you with a brief overview of each database. In most cases, you can find complete tutorials and books that drill deep into the particular database's features and functionality. The following sections will introduce you to several popular NoSQL databases.

### CouchDB

CouchDB is an open-source NoSQL database that stores data using JSON as collections and documents. CouchDB is unique in that its primary interface is application programming interface (API) driven—making it well suited for programmers creating applications that interact with a NoSQL database. CouchDB is used by companies such as Grubhub.

Although front-end user-interface programs, such as Fauxton, exist that you can use to interact with CouchDB, developers normally interact with CouchDB using HTTP GET, PUT, UPDATE and DELETE operations.

To install CouchDB on your system, visit the CouchDB website at couchdb.apache.org, as shown in **FIGURE 7.49**.

After you install CouchDB on your system, use the cURL program to issue Hypertext Transfer Protocol (HTTP) requests to the database server. cURL is an open-source command-line program (it's built into Windows, and you can install it on others like Linux) that will transfer data to and

**TABLE 7.5** Commonly Used NoSQL Databases

| Database | Companies Using | Website |
| --- | --- | --- |
| CouchDB | Grubhub | couchdb.apache.org |
| Redis | Twitter, Craigslist | redis.io |
| HBase | Facebook, LinkedIn | hbase.apache.org |
| RocksDB | Facebook, LinkedIn | rocksdb.org |
| Cassandra | Netflix | Cassandra.apache.org |
| DynamoDB | Apple, Netflix | Aws.amazon.com/dynamodb |

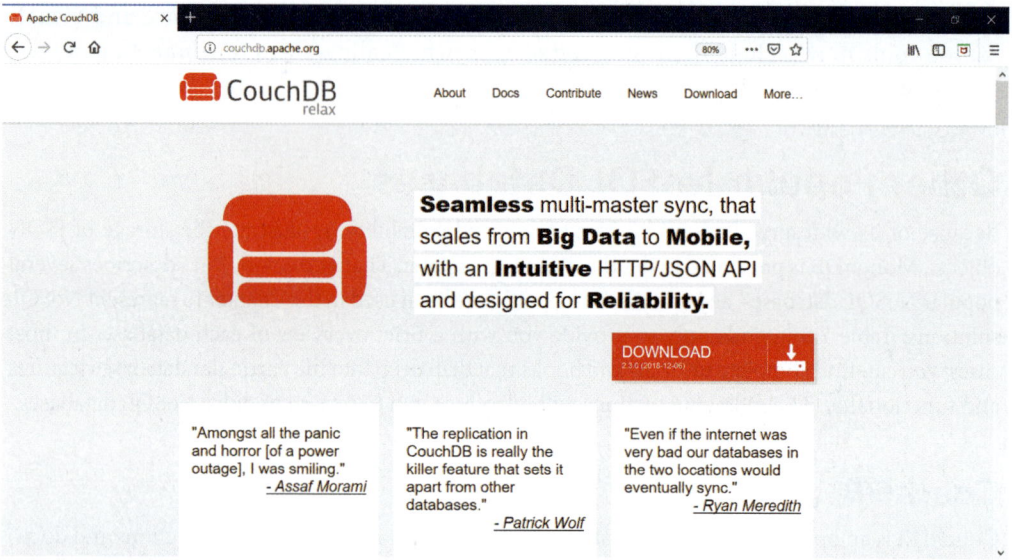

**FIGURE 7.49** Install CouchDB from the CouchDB website.

Used with permission of The Apache Software Foundation

**FIGURE 7.50** Using HTTP to request version information from CouchDB.

Used with permission of The Apache Software Foundation

from servers using different network protocols. The following curl command, for example, will display the CouchDB version number:

```
curl http://127.0.0.1:5984
```

As you can see, the cURL command specifies the CouchDB server's Internet Protocol (IP) address and port number. When you execute this query, your system will display a result similar to that shown in **FIGURE 7.50**.

The following command will create a database named book:

```
curl -X PUT http://127.0.0.1:5984/book
```

When you execute the command, CouchDB will respond, as shown in **FIGURE 7.51**. To display the list of databases, execute this query:

```
curl -X GET http://127.0.0.1:5984/_all_dbs
```

CouchDB will display the database list, as shown in **FIGURE 7.52**.

**FIGURE 7.51** Using HTTP to create the book database in CouchDB.
Used with permission from Microsoft

**FIGURE 7.52** Displaying CouchDB databases.
Used with permission from Microsoft

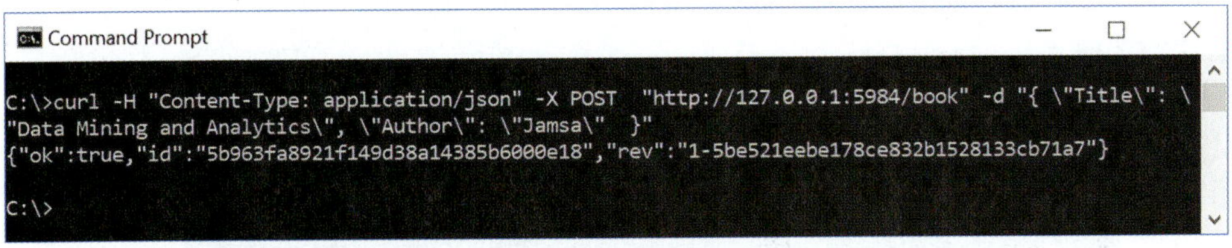

**FIGURE 7.53** Storing a document within a CouchDB database.
Used with permission from Microsoft

The following command will create a document within the book database:

```
curl -H "Content-Type: application/json" -X POST
"http://127.0.0.1:5984/book" -d "{\"Title\": \"Data Mining and
Analytics\", \"Author\": \"Jamsa\" }"
```

In this case, within the Windows environment, the command escapes the double quotes within the JSON using \". When you execute this command, your screen will display output similar to that shown in **FIGURE 7.53**.

As you can see, CouchDB returns an ID field for the document, which you can then use to query the database:

```
curl -X GET http://127.0.0.1:5984/
book/5b963fa8921f149d38a14385b6000e18
```

In this case, CouchDB will return the record, as shown in **FIGURE 7.54**.
To direct CouchDB to return all documents, issue the following query:

```
curl -X GET http://127.0.0.1:5984/
book/_all_docs?include_docs=true
```

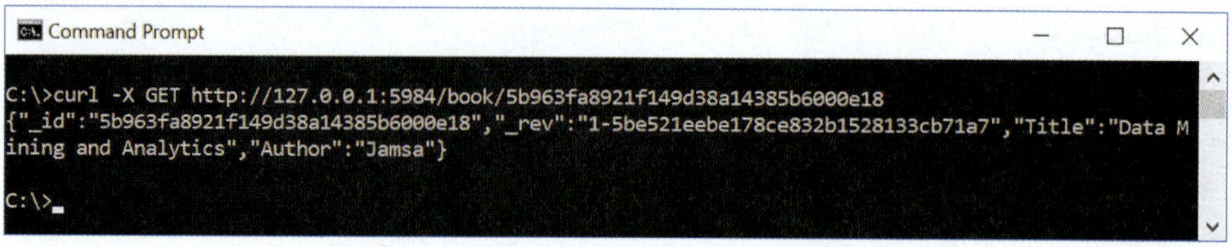

**FIGURE 7.54** Querying a CouchDB database for a specific record.
Used with permission from Microsoft

**FIGURE 7.55** Displaying all documents in a CouchDB database.
Used with permission from Microsoft

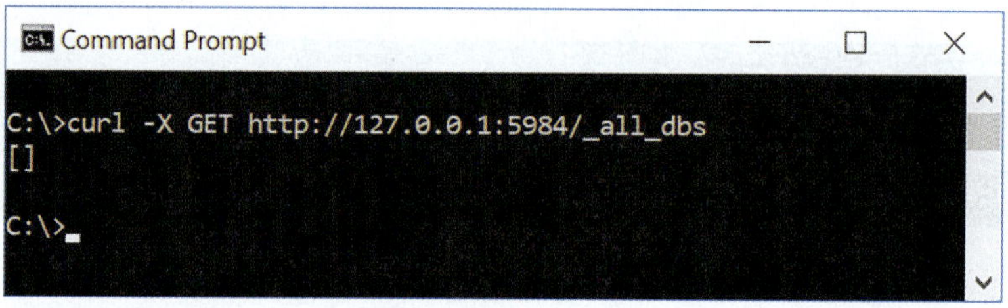

**FIGURE 7.56** Deleting a CouchDB database.
Used with permission from Microsoft

CouchDB will display your document list, as shown in **FIGURE 7.55**.

To delete your book database, you can use the following query:

```
curl -X DELETE http://127.0.0.1:5984/book
```

When you execute this query, CouchDB will delete the database, which you can confirm by viewing all databases, as shown in **FIGURE 7.56**.

This chapter's goal is to introduce you to CouchDB and its HTTP-based API. For more specifics on CouchDB queries, visit the tutorial at http://docs.couchdb.org/en/stable/intro/tour.html, as shown in **FIGURE 7.57**.

Lastly, as discussed, you can use Fauxton as a user interface for CouchDB, as shown in **FIGURE 7.58**. To run Fauxton, use http://127.0.0.1:5984/_utils.

## Redis

Redis, which stands for Remote Dictionary Server, is an open-source, high-performance, in-memory NoSQL database. Although Redis can be used for a wide range of operations, it is often used as a cache (fast memory-based database) that sits in front of web applications to store data and session

Other Popular NoSQL Databases    **331**

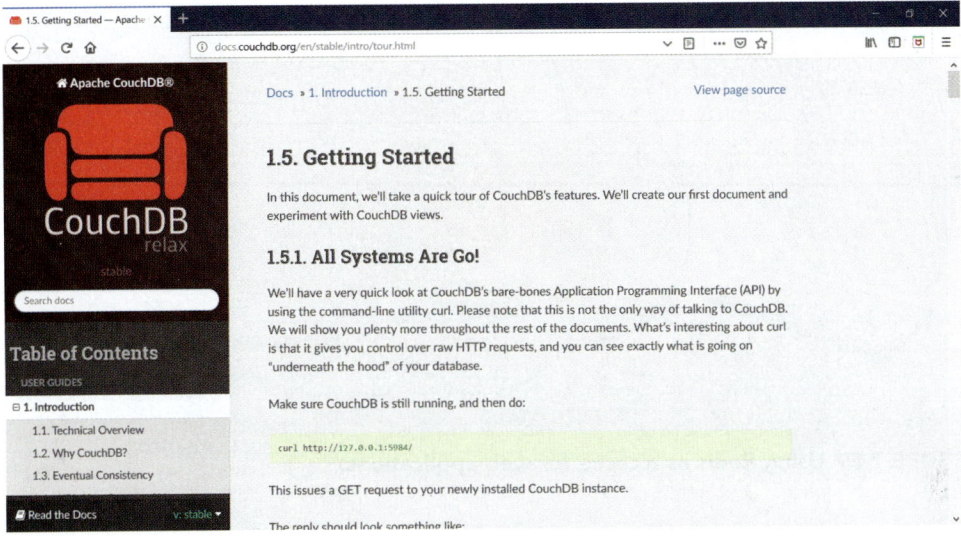

**FIGURE 7.57** A CouchDB tutorial.
Used with permission of The Apache Software Foundation

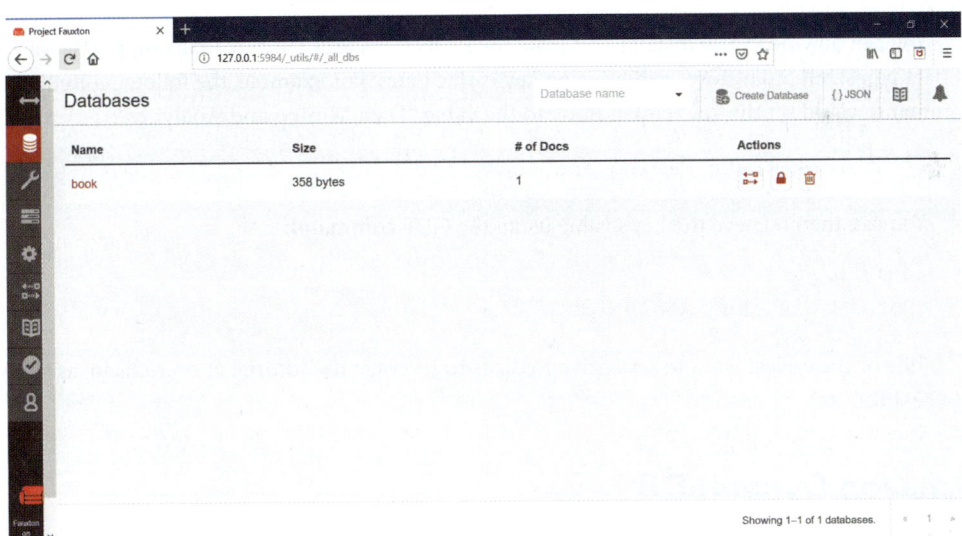

**FIGURE 7.58** Using Fauxton as a CouchDB user interface.
Used with permission of The Apache Software Foundation

information. As shown in **FIGURE 7.59**, to improve performance and redundancy, developers can deploy multiple Redis clusters that synchronize their content automatically.

Redis is an in-memory database—which makes it very fast. Redis will perform queries in a few milliseconds, as opposed to slower disk-based databases. Because it is in RAM, its contents

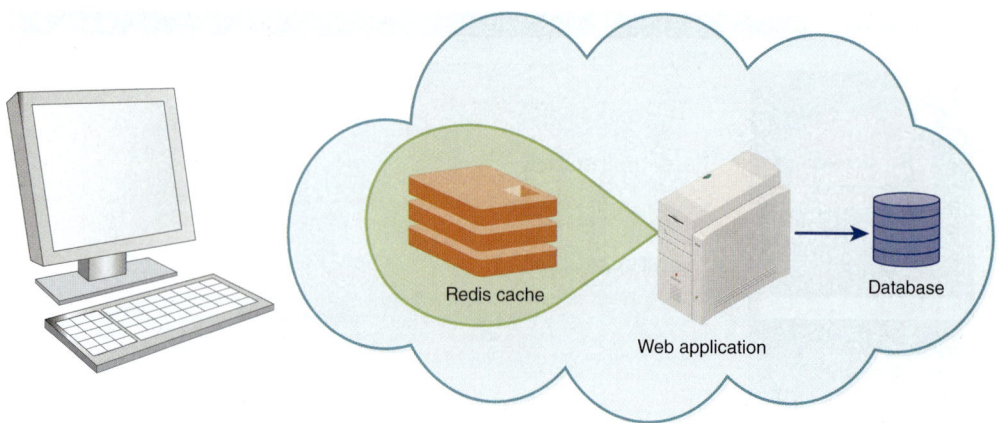

**FIGURE 7.59** Using Redis as a cache for web applications.

are lost should the system fail. To achieve data persistence, developers will use multiple Redis databases within a **cluster**. Should one database fail, the others will take over. Using the clusters, Redis can also load balance requests. In addition, the developers can periodically write the database contents to disk.

You can download and install Redis from the Redis website at redis.io. Redis supports a variety of data types, but often stores values using key–value pairs. For example, the following Redis SET command would set the key named Book to the value "Data Mining and Analytics":

```
> SET Book "Data Mining and Analytics"
```

You can then retrieve the key's value using the GET command:

```
> GET Book
"Data Mining and Analytics"
```

One of the easiest ways to test-drive Redis is to leverage the tutorial at try.redis.io, as shown in **FIGURE 7.60**.

## Amazon DynamoDB

Amazon is obviously one of the largest sites on the web. To drive performance, Amazon created the scalable DynamoDB database, which stores key–value pairs. Amazon makes DynamoDB available to developers through Amazon Web Services (AWS) as a managed database service. DynamoDB is used by companies such as Snap, Nike, and Samsung. By scaling on demand, AmazonDB handles over a trillion requests a day—over 20 million per second!

AmazonDB is well suited for caching, as well as local storage for microservices, mobile applications, and more. For specifics on DynamoDB, visit the aws.amazon.com/dynamodb.

## Other Popular NoSQL Databases

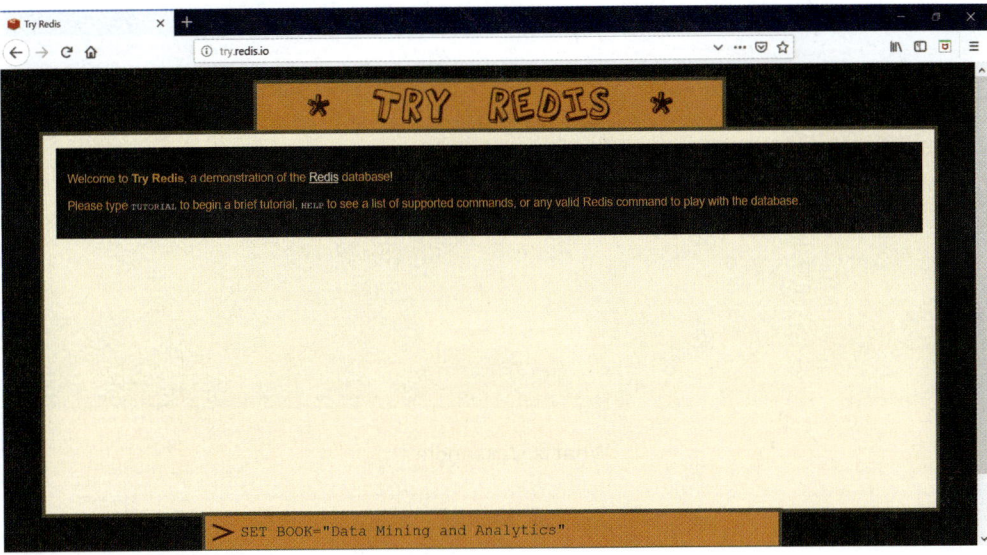

**FIGURE 7.60 Testing Redis through the interactive tutorial at try.redis.io.**
Used with permission of GitHub, Inc.

| Customer ID | Name | Address 01 | Address 02 | City | State | Z.P | Product 01 | Product 02 | Product 03 |
|---|---|---|---|---|---|---|---|---|---|
| 10001 | Smith | 123 Main | | Dallas | TX | 75201 | Book | Video | |
| 10002 | Jones | 563 Cloud | APZ 452 | Prescott | AZ | 86305 | Book | Video | Song |

**FIGURE 7.61 Cassandra is a wide-column NoSQL database.**

## Cassandra

Cassandra is an open-source NoSQL database originally developed at Facebook and designed for high performance and high reliability through distributed clustered database nodes. Cassandra is a wide-column database for which the number of columns and even the column names and values can differ for each row, as shown in **FIGURE 7.61**. Cassandra uses a custom SQL-like query language called CQL—the Cassandra Query Language.

As a wide-column database, Cassandra does not support join operations. Instead, all the data are stored within columns. Cassandra is used by companies such as Apple and Netflix to process trillions of queries per day. To download Cassandra, visit the Cassandra website at cassandra.apache.org, as shown in **FIGURE 7.62**.

## HBase

HBase is an open-source NoSQL database originally developed at Facebook for big data (billions of rows with millions of columns) operations in a high-performance, fault-tolerant environment. HBase is written in Java and supports the Java Database Connectivity (JDBC) and REST APIs. HBase sits on top of the Hadoop Distributed File System (HDFS) and is well suited for MapReduce

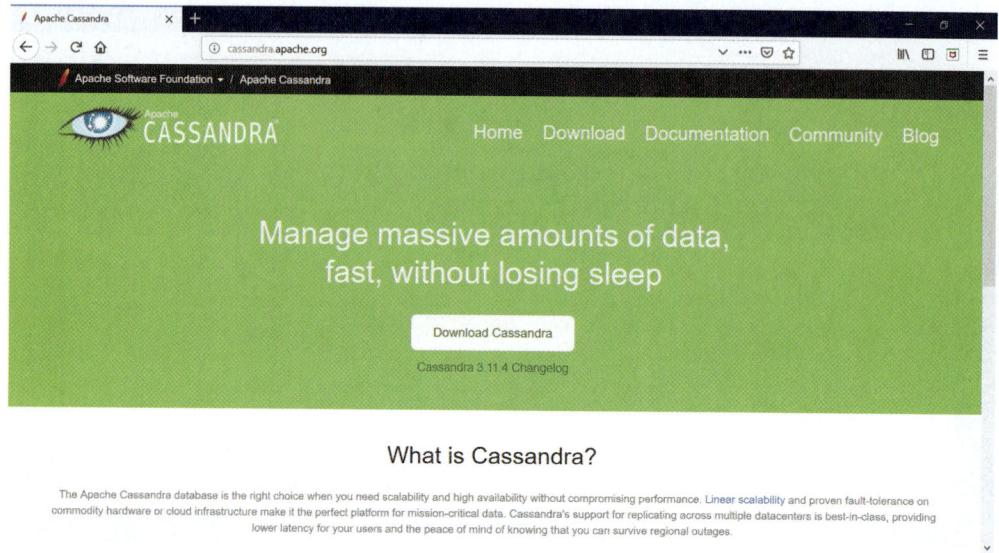

**FIGURE 7.62** Downloading the Cassandra NoSQL database.
Used with permission of The Apache Software Foundation

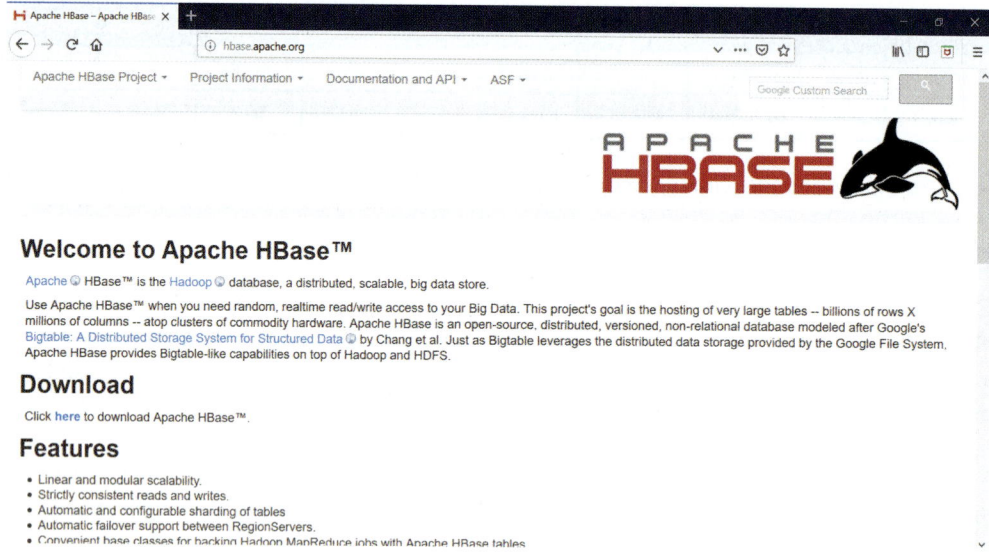

**FIGURE 7.63** The HBase NoSQL big data database.
Used with permission of The Apache Software Foundation

operations, which are discussed in Chapter 13, "Big Data Tools." Companies using HBase include Facebook and LinkedIn. For more information on HBase, visit the HBase website at hbase.apache.org, as shown in **FIGURE 7.63**.

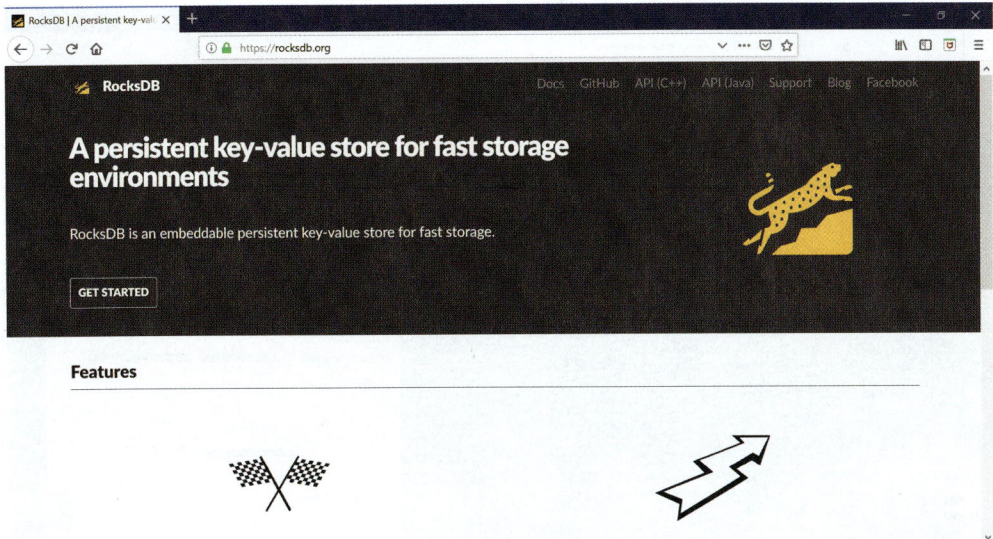

**FIGURE 7.64** The RocksDB key–value NoSQL database.
Used with permission of Rocksdb

## RocksDB

RocksDB, like Redis and DynamoDB, is a key–value database. Originally developed by Facebook, RocksDB is used for caches and application data storage. It is well suited for servers with a large number of processor cores (vertical scaling). Companies using RocksDB include Facebook and LinkedIn. RocksDB is an open-source database. For more information on RocksDB, visit its website at rocksdb.org, as shown in **FIGURE 7.64**.

# Hands-on: MongoDB Managed Service and MongoDB Charts

With the explosive growth in cloud computing, many companies have moved their databases from their on-premise data center to a cloud-based server. Originally, most companies continued to manage their database server software in the cloud, applying updates and patches, performing their own backups, and so on. Today, in contrast, many companies are moving to cloud-based managed database services, for which the cloud provider takes over such administrative services. In this way, the company's developers can instead concentrate on development, as opposed to administration. Across the web, most cloud providers provide such managed database services. You don't have to be a large company to make use of such services. A developer within a small company, even a one-person shop, may choose to use a **managed database server**, as opposed to spinning up their own database server in the cloud. **FIGURE 7.65** shows information about the MongoDB managed service called Atlas, which runs in AWS, Azure, or Google Cloud Platform. Using the MongoDB Atlas managed service, you don't have to worry about spinning up and managing your

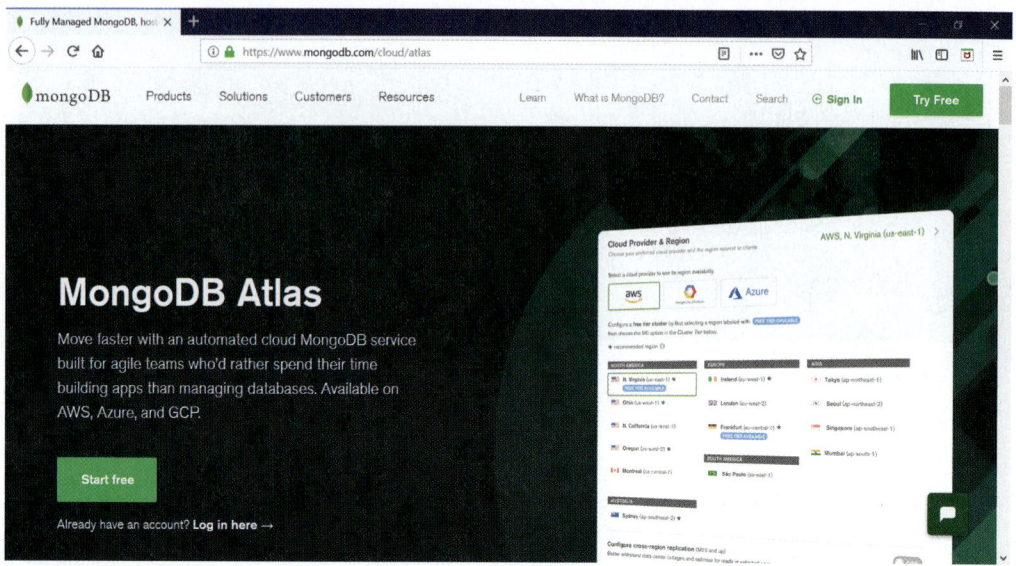

**FIGURE 7.65** Using a managed database service to simplify database deployment in the cloud.

Used with permission of MongoDB, Inc.

own MongoDB server. Instead, you just connect to Atlas, spin up the server or servers you need, and then pay as you go for what you use. To get started, you can use Atlas for free. Within Atlas, you can create as many databases as you need. Atlas will group your databases within a cluster.

To create a free account within the MongoDB managed service environment Atlas, you first register at the MongoDB.com website. Then you use the username and registration you created to log in to Atlas. After you log in, Atlas will display a page within which you can connect to your managed database cluster. To interact with your Atlas databases, you will run the Mongo command shell or the Compass GUI on your own computer. Within that software, you will specify a connection string that connects you to your Atlas database.

To get started, within your web browser, click the Connect button within the Atlas page. Atlas will display a window similar to that shown in **FIGURE 7.66**, which you can use to get the connection string you must use to connect to your Atlas cluster. For now, click the Mongo command-shell option and choose the standard connection string option. Atlas will display a window showing you the connection string you will use.

Within the window, click the Copy button to copy the connection string to the Clipboard. Then start the Mongo command shell, and within the command-shell window, click on the Control menu and select the Edit menu Paste option, shown in **FIGURE 7.67**, to paste the connection string into your command line. Within your connect string, replace the <PASSWORD> field with your password, or omit the field and Atlas will prompt you for your password.

After you connect to Atlas, interacting with Mongo is no different than issuing the queries you have performed throughout this chapter. To help you get started, download the file Atlas.txt from

# Hands-on: MongoDB Managed Service and MongoDB Charts 337

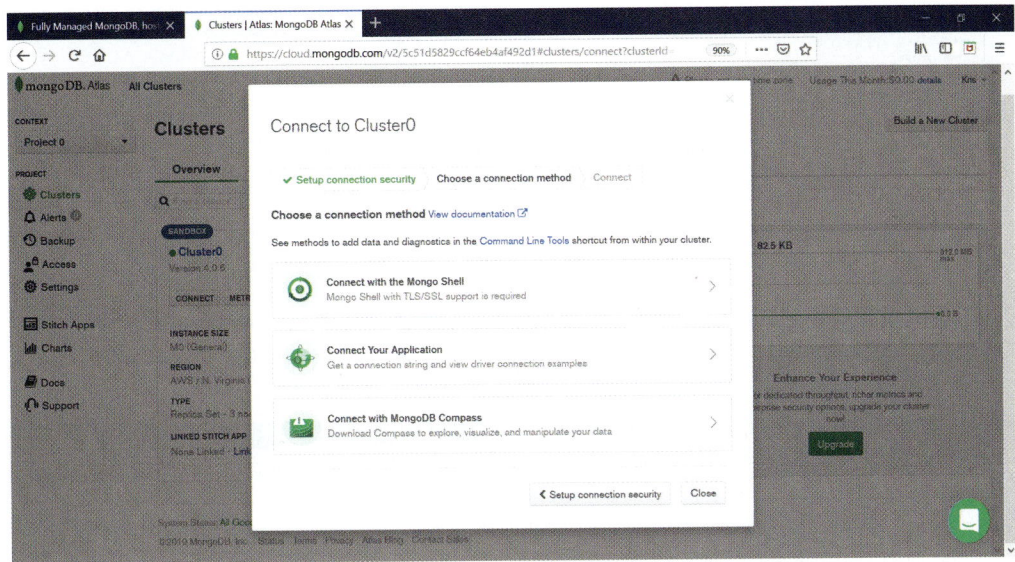

**FIGURE 7.66** Displaying the connection string you will use to connect to the Atlas managed service database cluster.

Used with permission of MongoDB, Inc.

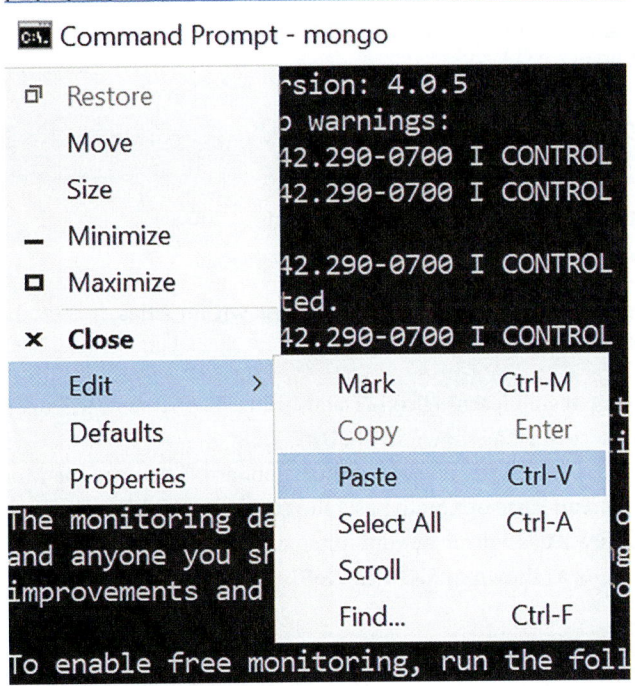

**FIGURE 7.67** Copy the connection string to the Mongo command prompt.

Used with permission from Microsoft

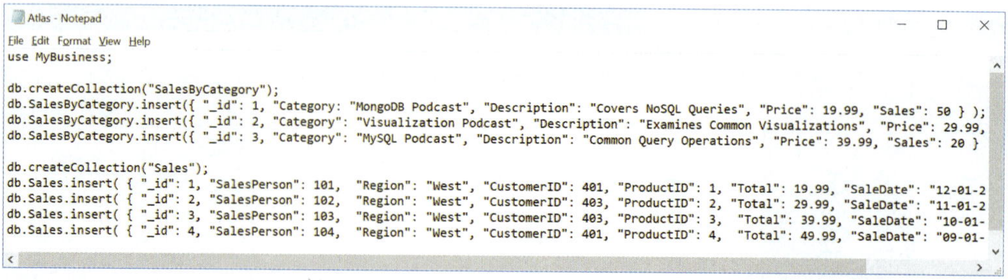

**338** CHAPTER 7 NoSQL Data Analytics

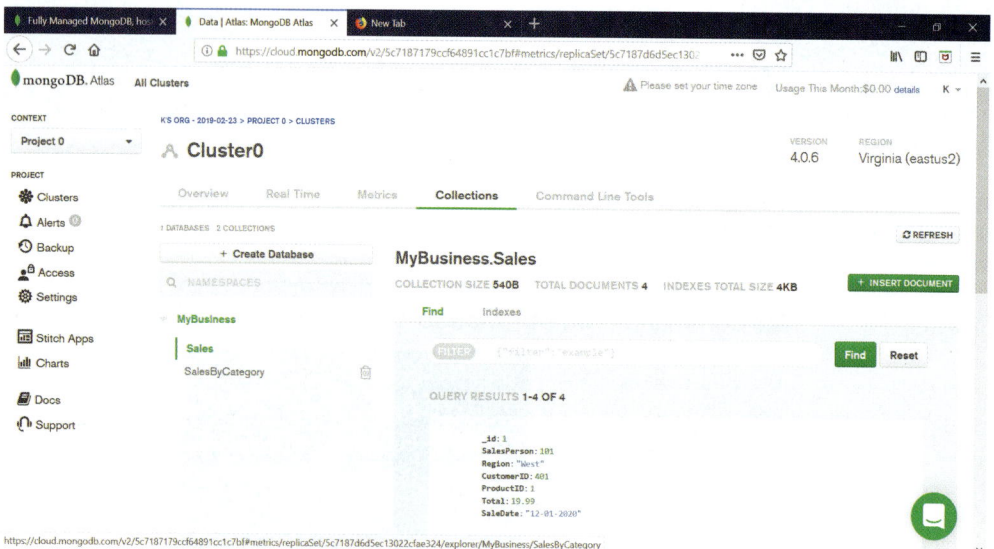

**FIGURE 7.68** Downloading queries to create your initial databases within the Atlas managed service.
Used with permission from Microsoft

**FIGURE 7.69** Displaying databases and collections within Atlas.
Used with permission of MongoDB, Inc.

this text's catalog page at go.jblearning.com/DataMining. Your system will open the file within the Windows Notepad accessory, as shown in **FIGURE 7.68**.

Within Notepad, copy all the queries to the Clipboard. Then use the Mongo shell window's Control menu Edit menu Paste option to paste the queries to the Mongo command prompt. After you execute the queries, Atlas will create your initial databases and collections. Click the Collections button to display them, as shown in **FIGURE 7.69**.

## Using Charts Within Atlas

MongoDB Charts is a visualization tool that lets you create a variety of charts directly from MongoDB data. There are two ways to use MongoDB charts. First, you can download and install

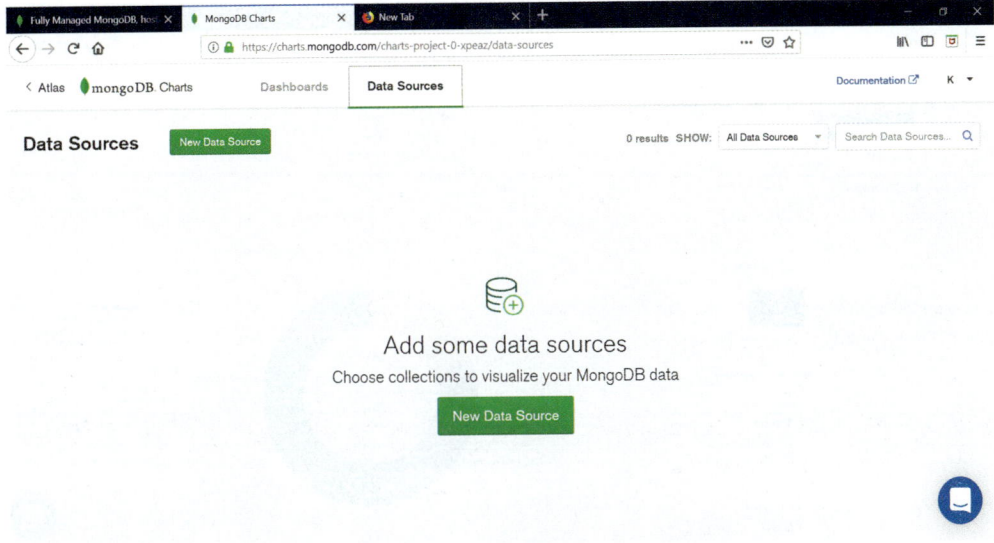

**FIGURE 7.70** Selecting the data source to visualize within Charts.
Used with permission of MongoDB, Inc.

the software locally on your own system, and second, you can run Charts from the MongoDB Atlas managed service environment. This section examines the use of Charts from within the Atlas environment.

To run MongoDB Charts within Atlas, click the Charts button within the Atlas website. Atlas will display a page within which you can create a dashboard. To start, you must define a data source for the charts. Click the Data Sources tab. Atlas will then display a page prompting you to add some charts to the dashboard. Click the Add a Chart button. Atlas will display the screen shown in **FIGURE 7.70** from which you can identify the chart's data source.

Click on your project. Atlas will display a wizard that walks you through selecting the data source. Use the wizard to select the following collections:

- SalesByCategory
- SalesByMonth

Set the permission for each data source to Reader and then publish each data source. Click the Dashboard tab and create a new dashboard. From the pull-down data source list, choose SalesByCategory. Atlas will display the collection's field names. Using your mouse, drag the Category name to the label field that appears beneath the chart type. Then drag the Sales field to the arc. Charts will display your donut chart, as shown in **FIGURE 7.71**.

Size the donut chart on the dashboard, and then click the Add Chart button and select a bar chart.

Using the data source pull-down list, choose the Mybusiness.Sales data source. Then select a column chart. Using your mouse, drag the ProductID data to the Y axis and the SalesDate data to the X axis. Charts will display your chart. Click Save and Close. Charts will display your dashboard, as shown in **FIGURE 7.72**.

**340** CHAPTER 7 NoSQL Data Analytics

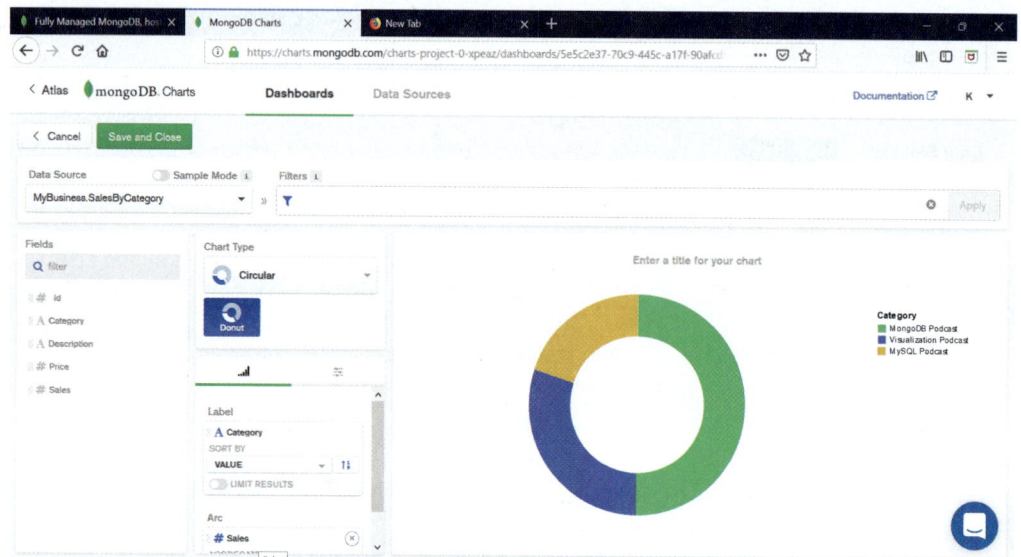

**FIGURE 7.71** Displaying a donut chart within a Charts dashboard.
Used with permission of MongoDB, Inc.

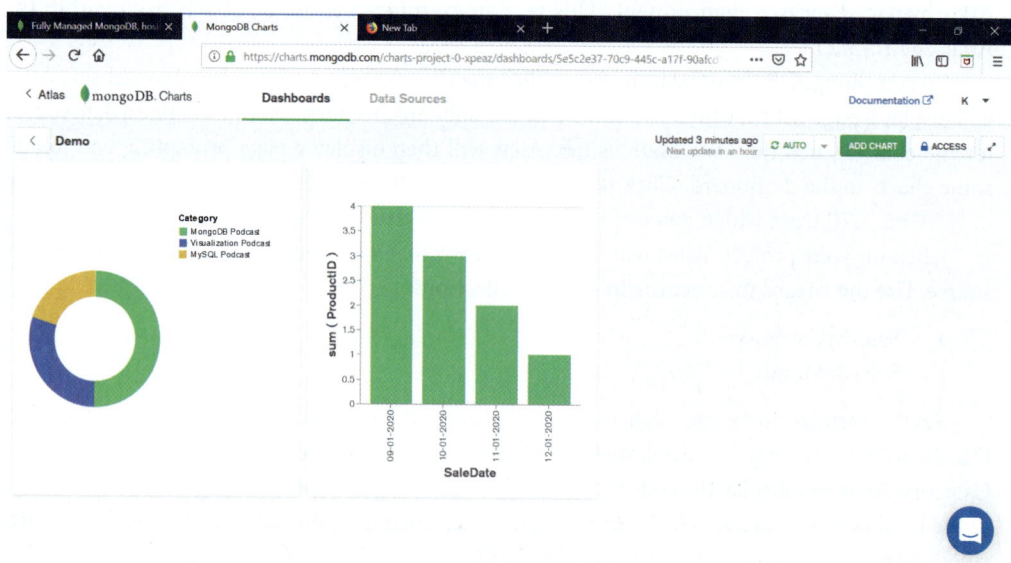

**FIGURE 7.72** Creating a simple dashboard with MongoDB Charts.
Used with permission of MongoDB, Inc.

## Summary

Database developers have made extensive use of table-based relational databases for more than 50 years, and today, such databases remain widely used. Because such relational databases make extensive use of SQL, developers refer to relational databases as SQL databases.

The explosive growth of web and mobile applications has driven requirements such as greater scalability, support for less structured data (documents and videos), and greater performance and reliability, which have driven equally explosive growth of NoSQL databases such as MongoDB, CouchDB, Cassandra, Redis, and Amazon DynamoDB.

NoSQL databases are so named because they do not use SQL for their primary query mechanism. In addition, NoSQL databases are not table based (meaning they are not relational). Behind the scenes, many NoSQL databases use JSON to represent data. JSON uses a JavaScript-like syntax to group objects as comma-separated name–value pairs within braces { }. JSON is well suited to store data because it is self-describing, lightweight, language independent, and human readable. Because of its widespread use, this chapter focused on MongoDB, which stores data within a database as documents (similar to a record), which the database groups into collections (similar to a table).

To help data analysts visualize NoSQL data, you learned that MongoDB provides the MongoDB Connector for Business Intelligence that allows SQL-based tools such Tableau and Microsoft Power BI to interact with the NoSQL data. You also learned how to chart NoSQL data directly using MongoDB charts. Finally, you learned how to use Atlas, the MongoDB managed service provider, to create pay-as-you-go MongoDB databases in the cloud.

## Key Terms

| | | |
|---|---|---|
| Arithmetic operators | GUI | Relational database |
| Cluster | Horizontal scaling | Relational operator |
| Collection | Import | Replica sets |
| Create, Read, Update, Delete (CRUD) | Index | Scaling |
| | JSON | Self-describing |
| Distributed database | Lightweight | Shard |
| Document | Logical operator | Vertical scaling |
| Export | Managed database server | |
| Filter | NoSQL | |

## Review

1. Define and describe the term NoSQL database.
2. Compare and contrast common NoSQL databases.

3. Using MongoDB (either by downloading or by using the Atlas managed service):
   a. Create a database named ToDo.
   b. Show the list of current databases.
   c. Select the ToDo database for use.
   d. Create a collection named List.
   e. Show the list of current collections.
   f. Create documents for the following:
      i. Bill—Register the company cars.
      ii. Jim—Buy office supplies.
      iii. Betty—Provide year-to-date sales data.
      iv. Joe—Wash the company cars.
      v. Sharon—Put together the board of directors' books
      vi. Jim—Hire new salespeople.
   g. List all documents in the List collection.
   h. Display the list sorted by employee name.
   i. Change Joe's task to Wash the company cars and trucks.
   j. Delete Sharon's task.
   k. Display all tasks sorted by task.
   l. Display Bill and Betty's tasks.
   m. Display Jim's tasks.
   n. Delete the List collection.
   o. Show the remaining collections.
   p. Delete the ToDo database.
4. Describe the Atlas managed service.
5. Use Charts to create a donut chart based on:
   a. Sales 20%
   b. Products 30%
   c. HR 50%
6. Use CouchDB to perform the operations shown in this chapter.
7. Discuss the role of the MongoDB Connector for Business Intelligence.
8. Define and describe JSON.
9. Create a JSON object to store the following objects. Validate your JSON with a web-based validator.
   a. Name: Larry Ellison
      Company: Oracle
      Year: 1977
   b. Name: Bill Gates
      Company: Microsoft
      Year: 1975

    c. Mark Zuckerberg
       Company: Facebook
       Year: 2004
10. Define and describe a key–value database.
11. Describe the advantages of JSON.
12. Describe the components of a MongoDB database.
13. Describe the role of MongoDB shards.
14. Describe the role of MongoDB replica sets and illustrate a replica set for a seven-node MongoDB cluster.
15. Define scaling. Compare and contrast **vertical** and **horizontal scaling**.

# CHAPTER 8

# Programming Data Mining and Analytic Solutions

## Chapter Goals and Objectives

- Use Python to perform common machine-learning and data-mining operations.
- Use R to perform common machine-learning and data-mining operations.
- Compare and contrast Python and R solutions.

Throughout this text, you will make extensive use of the Python and R programming languages to perform data-mining and machine-learning operations. Both Python and R are very powerful programming languages with a wide range of capabilities and features. This chapter introduces the fundamental concepts you need to know in order to understand the programs this text presents. The chapter's goal is to get you up and running with each quickly. By the time you finish this chapter, you will understand the following key concepts:

- Python is one of the world's most popular programming languages and is used to create solutions that range from websites, data mining, machine learning, visualization, and more.
- Python is open-source software that users can download, install, and use for free.
- Python is an interpreted language, as opposed to a compiled language, for which the Python **interpreter** executes one statement at a time.

- Developers can interactively execute one statement at a time via the Python interpreter's prompt, or developers can group statements into a text file, called a Python script, which they then direct Python to execute.
- Programmers use variables to store information as a program executes. In Python, a **script** creates a variable simply by assigning a value to the variable's name, using the equals sign (=), which is the Python assignment operator.
- Python variable names must start with a letter or underscore and cannot be the same as a Python reserved word.
- Data-mining programs often assign large amounts of data to a variable. In Python, when you are done using a variable, you can delete it to free up the memory the variable contained.
- Python recognizes the pound sign (#) as the start of a comment. When Python encounters the #, it will ignore any remaining text on that line.
- Python provides **arithmetic operators** similar to those found in other programming languages, such as + for addition, – for subtraction, * for multiplication, and / for division.
- To allow scripts to make comparisons, Python provides a set of **relational operators**, such as < for less than, > for greater than, and so on.
- Often, scripts must test multiple conditions. As such, Python provides the AND **logical operator** and the OR logical operator. In addition, Python provides a NOT operator.
- An array is a data structure that can store multiple values of the same type. Python implements arrays using lists. A list can be one-dimensional (a vector) or multidimensional. To access the values within a list, developers specify an index that corresponds to the location they desire. Python uses **zero-based indexing**, which means the first item in the list resides at the index location 0 (someList[0]).
- To allow scripts to evaluate a condition and perform statements accordingly, Python provides the if-elif-else statements.
- Unlike other programming languages that use braces {} to group related statements, Python relies on statement indentation to group statements.
- Python provides a **ternary operator**, which is like a shorthand notation for an if-else statement, which takes the form (falseResult, trueResult)[condition].
- To allow programs to repeat a set of statements until a condition is met, Python supports the for and while statements.
- Python is a procedural programming language, in that it supports functions. A function is a named (related) group of statements that perform processing that solves a specific task. Python provides built-in functions, such as print, which you call by specifying the function name and parameter values within parentheses.
- Python developers use the def keyword to specify a function name and statements the function performs to accomplish its task. Within the function, developers indent the function statements to indicate their relationship to the function.

- Parameters are values passed to a function. Python supports default parameter values. If a function call does not include values for all parameters, Python will use the default values (if they exist, or it will display an error otherwise).
- Python is an object-oriented language in that it supports class definitions and object instances. To define an object class, developers use the Python def statement.
- To perform data-mining operations, Python scripts make extensive use of dataframe objects. You can think of a dataframe as a two-dimensional table that holds a data-set's values.
- Since Python's release in 1990, developers have created over 170,000 libraries, each of which holds code that performs specific tasks, which you may be able to use within the scripts you create. To use a Python library, the code must exist on your system. To download and install a Python library, developers use the **PIP** command. Then you use the import statement to include the library code within your script.
- To perform data-mining and machine-learning operations in this chapter, you will make extensive use of the following Python libraries:
  - **pandas**, which defines the dataframe object
  - numpy, which provides functions and data structures for numeric operations
  - matplotlib for plotting charts
  - **sklearn**, which defines data structures and functions that support machine-learning and data-mining operations such as clustering, classification, and regression
- R has become one of the most popular programming languages for data mining and machine learning.
- R is open-source software that users can download, install, and use for free.
- R is an interpreted language, as opposed to a compiled language, for which the R interpreter executes one statement at a time.
- Developers can interactively execute one statement at a time via the R interpreter's prompt, or developers can group statements into a text file, called an R program or script, which they then direct R to execute.
- Programmers use variables to store information as a program executes. In R, a script creates a variable simply by assigning a value to the variable's name, using <–, which is the R assignment operator.
- R variable names must start with a letter or dot and cannot be the same as an R reserved word.
- To view a list of variables you have created in the current session, you use the R ls function.
- R recognizes the pound sign (#) as the start of a comment. When R encounters a #, it will ignore any remaining text on that line.
- R provides arithmetic operators, like those found in other programming languages, such as + for addition, – for subtraction, * for multiplication, and / for division.
- To allow scripts to make comparisons, R provides a set of relational operators, such as < for less than, > for greater than, and so on.

- Often, scripts must test multiple conditions. As such, R provides the AND (&&) and OR (||) logical operators. In addition, R provides a NOT operator (!).
- An array is a data structure that can store multiple values of the same type. An array can be one-dimensional (a vector) or multidimensional. To access the values within a list, developers specify an index that corresponds to the location they desire. R does not use zero-based indexing, which means the first item in the list resides at the index location 1 (someList[1]).
- To allow scripts to evaluate a condition and perform statements accordingly, R provides the if-else statements.
- R uses left and right braces {} to group related statements.
- To allow programs to repeat a set of statements until a condition is met, R supports the for, repeat, and while statements.
- R is a procedural programming language, in that it supports functions. A function is a named (related) group of statements that perform processing to solve a specific task. R provides built-in functions, such as print, which you call by specifying the function name and parameter values within parentheses.
- Using the function keyword, R developers specify the name of and the statements the function performs to accomplish its task. Within the function, developers group the function statements using left and right braces ({}) to indicate the statements' relationship to the function.
- Parameters are values passed to a function. R supports default parameter values. If a function call does not include values for all parameters, R will use the default values (if they exist, or it will display an error otherwise).
- To perform data-mining operations, R scripts make extensive use of dataframe objects. You can think of a dataframe as a two-dimensional table that holds a data-set's values.
- R developers have created thousands of libraries, each of which holds code that performs specific tasks, which you may be able to use within the scripts you create. To use an R library, the library code must exist on your system. To download and install an R library, developers use the install.packages function. Then you use the import statement to include the library code within your script.

# Getting Started with Python

Python is an open-source programming language, widely used for web applications, data mining, and machine learning. Depending on the category (most in demand, most popular, best to know, and so on), Python is one of the top programming languages. It is an interpreted programming language for which the Python interpreter processes the code one statement at a time, as opposed to a compiled language (such as Java or C#), for which the language **compiler** converts the program's source code into an executable file. An advantage of Python's interpreted environment is that you can execute Python statements one at a time, interactively, using the interpreter.

*Note:* This chapter will help you install Python, R, and many libraries for each. If you are using this text's Cloud Desktop, you do not need to perform the installations. Instead, the lab has preinstalled all the software you will need.

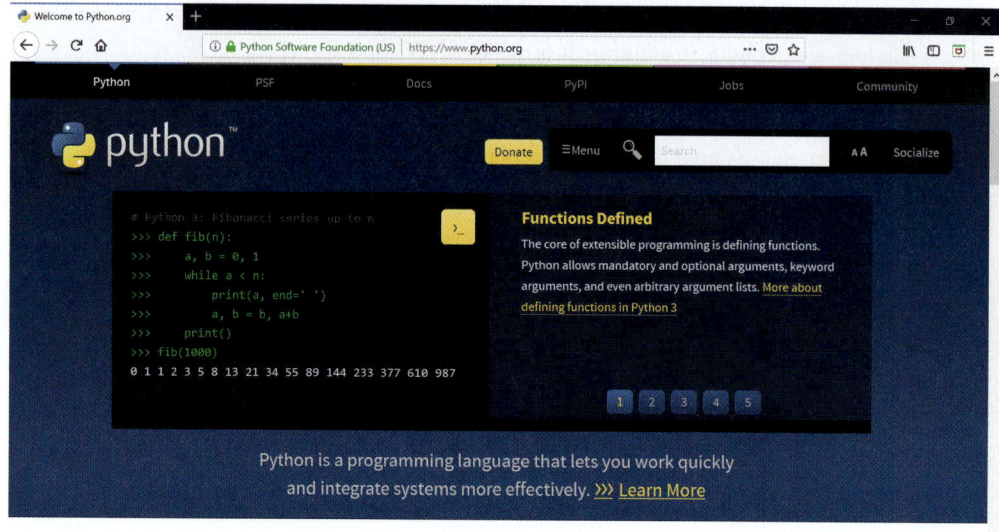

**FIGURE 8.1** The Python website.

Used with permission of Python Software Foundation

Before you can execute Python programs (which programmers call scripts), you must download and install Python on your system. To do so, visit the Python website at www.python.org, as shown in **FIGURE 8.1**.

From the site's Download page, locate and download the Python version that corresponds to your operating system. After the installation completes, you will run Python from a command-line prompt:

```
C:\> python   <Enter>
>>> print("Hello, world!")
Hello, World!
>>>
```

The triple greater-than symbol (>>>) is the Python interpreter's prompt. If, when you try to run Python, you receive a bad command error message, make sure you include the Python folder within your system's command PATH. If you are using Windows, you can launch Python from the Start menu, as shown in **FIGURE 8.2**.

From the Python prompt, type the following print statement:

```
>>> print("Hello, Data Mining!")
```

Python is a case-dependent programming language that considers uppercase and lowercase characters as different. Therefore, you must match the case of the examples shown throughout

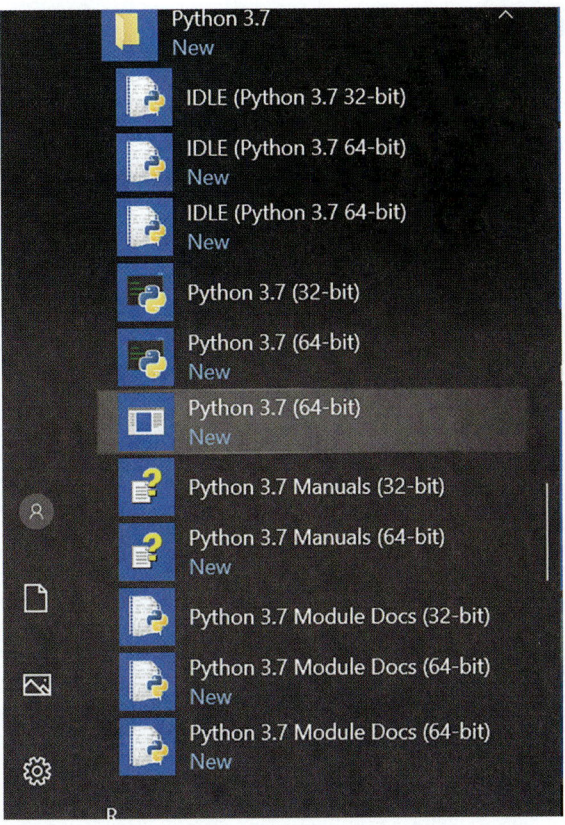

**FIGURE 8.2 Launching Python from the Windows Start menu.**
Used with permission of Python Software Foundation

this chapter. When you press Enter to execute the statement, Python will display the Hello, Data Mining! message, as shown here:

```
>>> print("Hello, Data Mining!")
Hello, Data Mining!
```

From the Python system prompt, execute the following statements:

```
>>> print(1 + 2)
3
>>> import datetime as dt
>>> print('Today is: ', dt.datetime.now())
Today is: 2019-09-02 20:03:48.942513
>>> name = input('What is your name?')
What is your name? Kris
>>> print("Hello," name)
Hello, Kris
```

## Leverage the Many Python Tutorials

This chapter's goal is to get you up and running with Python so that you can successfully understand and execute the Python scripts this text presents. The Python programming language has many powerful capabilities, which may require reading one or more books for you to fully understand. As you get started with Python, you should leverage documentation on the Python website, as well as tutorials, such as that provided on the W3Schools website.

## Python Assignment Operator

To assign a value to a variable in Python, you use the equals-sign assignment operator. Unlike other programming languages, you do not need to declare a Python variable before you use it:

```
age = 21
name = "John Davis"
email = "jd@somesite.com"
```

Often, you will need to initialize many variables at the start of your scripts:

```
a = 0
b = 0
c = 0
```

Python also provides a shorthand notation you can use to initialize multiple variables at one time:

```
a = b = c = 0
```

In addition, Python supports the following:

```
a, b, c = 1, 2, 3
```

In this case, Python will assign the value 1 to a, 2 to b, and 3 to c, as shown here:

```
>>> a, b, c = 1, 2, 3
>>> print(a, b, c)
1 2 3
```

## Python Variable Names

Python variable names must start with a letter or underscore. Remember, Python is a case-dependent programming language, which means it considers the variable names *age* and *Age* to be different.

As you assign names to Python variables, you cannot use the Python keywords (words that have special meaning to Python), which are listed in **TABLE 8.1**.

## Deleting Unneeded Variables

A variable is a name that Python associates with a region in memory that holds the variable's value. Just as you can create variables as you need them within Python, you can also delete variables. When

## TABLE 8.1 Python Reserved Words

| and | As | asset | break |
|---|---|---|---|
| class | Continue | def | del |
| elif | Else | except | False |
| finally | For | from | global |
| if | Import | in | is |
| lambda | None | nonlocal | not |
| pass | Raise | return | True |
| try | Which | with | yield |

you are done using a large dataframe, for example, you can direct Python to delete the variable to free up the memory. To delete a variable, you use the del statement:

```
del variableName
```

The following statements illustrate the use of del:

```
df = pd.read_csv('iris.data.csv', header=None, names=names)
X = np.array(df.iloc[:, 0:4])
y = np.array(df['class'])
del df
# split the data into train and test sets
X_train, X_test, y_train, y_test = train_test_split(X, y,
test_size=0.30)
del X
del y
```

## Creating and Executing Python Scripts

Using the Python interpreter, you can execute one statement at time, interactively:

```
>>> import numpy as np
>>> import matplotlib.pyplot as plt
>>>
>>> X = np.array([[0],[1],[2],[3]])
>>> y = np.array([2,3,4,5])
>>>
>>> plt.plot(X, y)
>>> plt.show()
```

Working with Python interactively in this way can be very convenient when you are testing functions or troubleshooting code. However, as your number of statements increases, you will

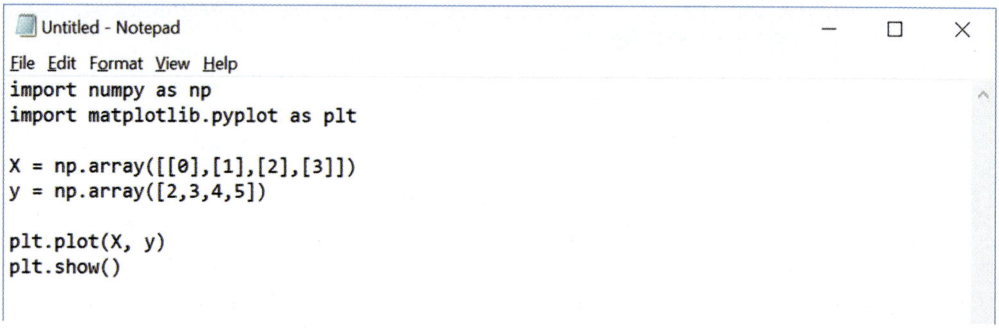

```
Untitled - Notepad
File Edit Format View Help
import numpy as np
import matplotlib.pyplot as plt

X = np.array([[0],[1],[2],[3]])
y = np.array([2,3,4,5])

plt.plot(X, y)
plt.show()
```

**FIGURE 8.3** Using the Windows Notepad to create a Python script.

Used with permission of Microsoft

want to create a file that contains your statements. Python developers refer to a file of Python statements as a script.

To create a script, you can use any text editor, such as the Windows Notepad accessory, shown in **FIGURE 8.3**.

Developers store scripts in files with the .py extension, such as HelloName.py, shown here:

```
name = input("Enter your name: ")
print("Hello, " + name + "!")
```

To execute a script, you include the script filename within the command line when you run Python, as shown here:

```
C:\python> python HelloName.py    <Enter>
Enter your name: Kris
Hello, Kris!
```

Throughout this text, you will make extensive use of Python scripts.

## Commenting a Python Script

In Python, the pound sign (#) indicates the start of a comment. When the Python interpreter encounters a comment symbol, it will ignore the text that follows through the end of the line. The following code fragment illustrates the use of comments within a Python script:

```
# prompt the user for his or name
name = input("Enter your name: ")
# display hello message
print("Hello, " + name + "!")
```

## Python Variables Are Dynamic

Unlike strongly typed programming languages, such as Java and C#, for which you must declare a variable before you use it, specifying the variable's data type and name, Python variables are dynamic, meaning you simply refer to a variable's name in order to use it. The following statements illustrate the use of variables within Python:

```
value = 1001
print(value)
value = "Hello, world!"
print(value)
value = 3.14
print("Area equals: ", 5*5*value)
```

As you can see, the statements use a variable named value in three different ways. If you execute these statements, Python will display the following output:

```
>>> value = 1001
>>> print(value)
1001
>>> value = "Hello, world!"
>>> print(value)
Hello, world!
>>> value = 3.14
>>> print("Area equals: ", 5*5*value)
Area equals:  78.5
>>>
```

## Python Operators

Python supports many of the same operators you will find in other programming languages, as shown in **TABLE 8.2**.

Table 8.2 presents the operators in their order of precedence. Consider, for example, the following statement:

```
print(5 + 2 * 3)
```

Using the Python **operator precedence** shown in Table 8.2, Python will first perform the multiplication followed by the addition, displaying the value 11. To control precedence, you can group expressions within parentheses. Python will always execute the expressions in parentheses first:

```
>>> print(5 + 2 * 3)
11
>>> print((5 + 2) * 3)
21
```

## Relational Operators

When you specify conditions within an if statement, you will often test whether one value is equal to another, greater than another, or less than another. To allow you to perform such operations, Python provides the relational operators described in **TABLE 8.3**.

TABLE 8.2  The Python Operators

| Operator | Meaning |
|---|---|
| ** | Exponentiation |
| ~, ± | Unary operator, such as minus or plus one |
| *, /, %, // | Multiply, divide, modulo, and floor division |
| +, − | Addition, subtraction |
| >>, << | Right and left bitwise shift |
| <= < > >= | Comparison operators |
| == <> != | Equality operators |
| = += −= *= /= %= //= **= | Assignment operators |
| is is not | Identity operators |
| in not in | Membership operators |
| and or not | Logical operators |

TABLE 8.3  The Python Relational Operators

| Operator | Purpose |
|---|---|
| == | Equality test |
| != | Not equal |
| < | Less than |
| > | Greater than |
| <= | Less than or equal to |
| >= | Greater than or equal to |

## Python Lists

An array is a data structure that contains multiple values of the same type within a single variable. Arrays can be one-dimensional or multidimensional. To access the values in an array, you use an index value, which you specify within left and right brackets []. Like most programming languages, the first element in a Python array is at the index location zero (array[0]), which developers call zero-based indexing.

Python does not have an array data structure, per se, but instead uses lists. The following statement, for example, creates a list of values:

```
numbers = [1, 5, 10]
```

In this case, to display the values, you would use the index values 0, 1, and 2:

```
>>> numbers = [1, 5, 10]
>>> print(numbers[0])
1
>>> print(numbers[1])
5
>>> print(numbers[2])
10
```

In a similar way, the following statement creates a list of days:

```
>>> days = ['Sunday', 'Monday', 'Tuesday', 'Wednesday',
'Thursday', 'Friday', 'Saturday']
>>> print(days[0])
Sunday
>>> print(days[3])
Wednesday
```

A Python list can have multiple dimensions. The following statement creates a two-dimensional list of values:

```
values = [[10, 20, 30], [40, 50, 60], [70, 80, 90]]
```

You can visualize this list as a table, as shown in **FIGURE 8.4**.

The following script, 2DList.py, creates a two-dimensional list and then uses a for loop (discussed later in this chapter) to display the values:

```
values = [[10, 20, 30], [40, 50, 60], [70, 80, 90]]

# print lists
for index in range(0, 3):
    print(values[index])
```

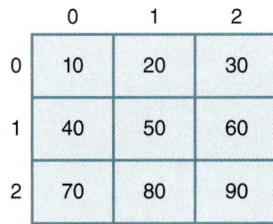

**FIGURE 8.4** A two-dimensional list of values.

```
# print individual values
for row in range(0, 3):
  for column in range(0, 3):
    print(values[row][column])
```

When you execute this script, it will display the following output:

```
[10, 20, 30]
[40, 50, 60]
[70, 80, 90]
10
20
30
40
50
60
70
80
90
```

As you can see, the first for loop displays the row values, and the second for loop displays the individual values.

When you use for and while loops to manipulate lists, you will often want to know the length of the list. To do so, you can use the Python len function:

```
count = len(someList)
```

To determine the number of rows and columns in a two-dimensional list, you would use:

```
rows = len(someList)
columns = len(someList[0])
```

## Python Groups Statements Based upon Statement Indentation

If you are familiar with programming languages such as Java, JavaScript, or C#, you know that such languages group related statements within left and right braces {}. Python does not use braces, but rather, uses indentation to group related statements. The following if-else statement illustrates Python's use of indentation to group related statements:

```
age = 21

if age >= 21:
    print("Going to Vegas!")
    print("Feeling lucky!")
else:
    print("One of these days ...")
```

If you examine the statement indentation, you will find the if statement has two related statements and the else statement has one. You will examine the if-else statements later in this section. For now, however, beyond the statement indentation, note that the Python **syntax** requires a colon after the if and else.

## Conditional Processing within Python

To provide your scripts the ability to make decisions, Python provides the if construct, the format of which is:

```
if condition:
    statement
[elif condition:
    statement]
[else:
    statement]
```

The brackets in the if-construct format indicate that the elif and else are optional. Note the colon that follows the conditions and the else—you must include the colon. Remember, Python, unlike many other programming languages, does not use braces to group related statements. Instead, Python relies on indentation to indicate the statements that go with the if, elif, and else.

### Python Ternary Operator

In addition to if-statement processing, Python supports the ternary operator, the format of which is:

```
result = (falseResult, trueResult) [condition]
```

The following statement uses the operator to assign the minimum of two values:

```
minimum = (b, a) [a < b]
```

The following Python script, Conditional.py, illustrates the use of the if, elif, and else statements:

```
pet = "dog"

if pet == 'dog':
  print("Remember to buy dog biscuits")
elif pet == 'cat':
  print("Buy some catnip")
else:
  print("Buy something")
```

When you execute this script, it will display the following output:

```
C:\python> python conditional.py
Remember to buy dog biscuits
```

## Logical Operators

When you specify a condition within a Python if or while statement, there will be times when you must test two or more conditions. To allow you to do so, Python provides the AND, OR, and NOT logical operators. The AND operator examines two conditions and results in true if both of the conditions are true, and false otherwise. In contrast, the OR operator returns true if either condition is true, and false only if both conditions are false.

The following Python script, Logical.py, illustrates the use of the Python logical operators:

```
day = 'Sunday'
season = 'fall'

if season == 'fall' and day == 'Sunday':
   print('Football season is here!')
else:
   print('Football season is coming!')

language = 'C#'

if language == 'Python' or language == 'R':
   print('Learn some machine language!')
else:
   print('Learn Python and R')
```

As you can see, the logical AND operator and the OR operator allow you to combine two conditions. Unlike other programming languages, Python does not require you to group your conditions within parentheses. When you execute this script, Python will display the following output:

```
C:\> python Logical.py
Football season is here!
Learn Python and R
```

## Iterative Processing

To let your programs repeat a set of statements, Python provides the for and while loops. The format of the Python for loop is different from that used by Java, C++, C#, and JavaScript. The following Python script, OneToTen.py, uses a for loop to display the numbers 1 through 10:

```
for i in range(1, 11):
   print(i)
```

The loop uses the variable i as its control variable. When the loop starts, Python initializes i with the value 1. Within the loop, the code prints the value of i and repeats the loop. Note that the range specified is 1–11. The script's goal is to display the numbers 1–10. If the loop were to use range(1, 10), the loop would end when i has the value 10 and the 10 would not be displayed. When you execute this script, it will display the following output:

```
1
2
3
4
5
6
7
8
9
10
```

The following Python script, ForList.py, uses a for loop to display the elements in a list:

```
week = ['Sunday', 'Monday', 'Tuesday', 'Wednesday', 'Thursday',
'Friday', 'Saturday']

for day in week:
    print(day)
```

In this case, the for loop uses the control variable day. Again, when the loop begins, Python will assign the variable day the first item in the list. With each iteration, the loop assigns the variable day the next list value. When you execute this script, it will display the following output:

```
C:\Python> python ForList.py
Sunday
Monday
Tuesday
Wednesday
Thursday
Friday
Saturday
```

Finally, the following Python script, ForDataSet.py, uses a for loop to display the rows and columns of a data set. You will make extensive use of data sets throughout this text. The script opens the Seattle.csv data set, which contains data about the Seattle housing market, which you can download from this text's catalog page at go.jblearning.com/DataMining. Within the script, the for loop uses two control variables. The first is assigned a row index and the second the actual row values. The loop then prints the value of two specific columns:

```
import pandas as pd

data = pd.read_csv('Seattle.csv')

for index, row in data.iterrows():
    print(row['price'], row['sqft_living'])
```

When you run the script, it will display the price and square footage of each home:

```
C:\python> python ForDataSet.py
467000.0 2660
385000.0 770
670000.0 1800
500000.0 2900
    :          :
669888.0 2550
405000.0 1310
518000.0 1430
```

Later in this chapter, you will examine the import statement and the read.csv function that reads the data from the file into the dataframe.

## Looping with While Loops

In addition to the for loop, Python provides a while loop, the format of which is:

```
while (condition):
    statement
```

The following Python script, WhileDemo.py, uses a while loop to plot data within two lists:

```python
import matplotlib.pyplot as plt

x = [35,34,32,37,33,33,31,27,35,34,62,54,57,47,50,57,59,52,61,
47,50,48,39,40, 45,47,39,44,50,48]

y = [79,54,52,77,59,74,73,57,69,75,51,32,40,47,53,36,35,58,59,
50,23,22,13,14, 22,7,29,25,9,8]

index = 0
while index < len(x):
   plt.scatter(x[index], y[index], marker='x', color='red')
   index += 1

plt.show()
```

As you can see, the script assigns values to each list and then uses a while loop to iterate through the list elements, plotting them. After the loop ends, the script displays the chart.

When you execute this script, it will display the chart shown in **FIGURE 8.5**.

## Python Supports Functions

Python is a procedural programming language in that it lets you define and later call functions to perform specific tasks. To create a function within Python, you use the def keyword, identifying

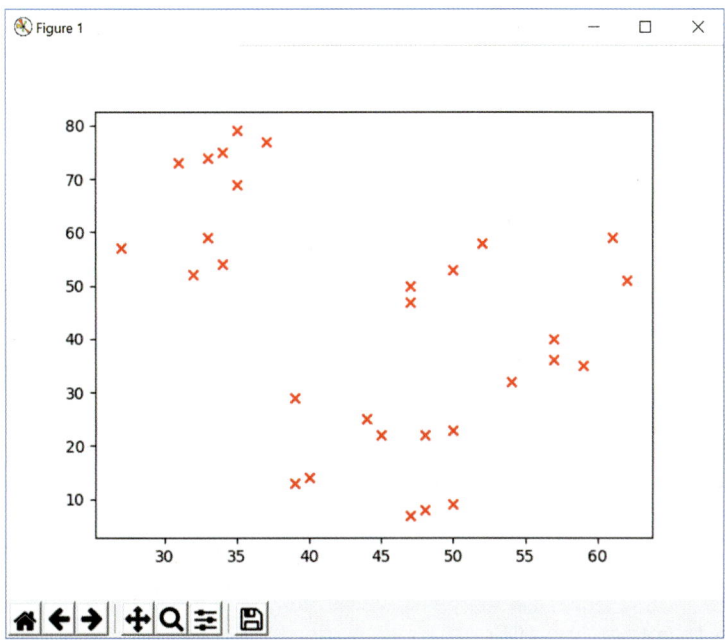

**FIGURE 8.5** Using a while loop to chart data in a dataframe.

Used with permission of Python Software Foundation

## Continue and Break Statements

Like most programming languages, Python supports the continue and break statements. When Python encounters a continue statement within a for or while loop, it will immediately branch to the next iteration of the loop. The following Python script, ShowOdd.py, uses the continue statement to display only odd values:

```
for i in range(0, 10):
    if i % 2 == 0:
        continue
    print(i)
```

The script uses the modulo (%) operator to get the remainder of the variable divided by 2. For even values, the remainder will be 0, which causes the code to continue with the next iteration of the loop. For odd values, the result of the modulo operation will be 1, causing the if statement to fail, so the script will print the value. When you execute this script, Python will display the following output:

```
C:\> python ShowOdd.py
1
3
```

```
5
7
9
```

When Python encounters a break statement within a for or while loop, it will immediately end the loop's processing, continuing the script's execution at the statement that follows the loop. The following Python script, StopAt5.py, illustrates the use of the break statement to end the loop's processing when the value 5 is encountered:

```
for i in range(0, 10):
   if i == 5:
      break;
   print(i)
```

Although continue and break are common to most programming languages, in most instances, you can refactor code that uses them to create a more structured solution. For example, the following code displays the odd values without the need of the continue statement:

```
for i in range(0, 10):
   if i % 2:
      print(i)
```

the function name, and use indentation to group the function statements. The following Python script, TwoFunctions.py, creates and calls two functions:

```
def Hello():
    print("Hello, world")

def AddValues(a, b):
    return(a + b)

# call the functions
Hello()
print("The sum of 1 + 2 is: ", AddValues(1, 2))
```

As you can see, the script first defines a function named Hello that contains one print statement, which displays the message "Hello, world!" Note the colon that follows the function declaration. The Hello function does not receive any parameters, which you indicate by following the function name with the empty parentheses.

The script also defines the AddValues function, which receives two parameter values that Python will assign to the local variables a and b. The function uses the return statement to return the sum of the two parameter values.

Within the main program, the script first calls the Hello function by referring to the function name. When you call a function, you must include the parentheses even if the function does not have any parameter values. To call the AddValues function, the script again refers to the function name, this time including values for each parameter within the parentheses.

## Using Default Function Parameters

Many of the Python functions you will examine throughout this text will make use of the default parameter values, meaning if you don't specify a value for the parameter when you call the function, Python will use the default.

When you create your own functions using def, you can specify a parameter's default values by using the assignment operator within the parameter list, as shown here:

```
def someFunction(a = 100, b = 200):
    return(a + b)
```

As you can see, to specify the default values, you use the assignment operator to assign a value to one or more of the parameter variables. The following Python script, UseDefault.py, illustrates the use of default parameter values:

```
def someFunction(a = 100, b = 200):
    return(a + b)

print(someFunction())
print(someFunction(500))
print(someFunction(0, 0))
print(someFunction(b=300))
```

The script calls the function with different parameter values, specifying no parameters, which uses both default values; one parameter based on order; and by name (b=300). When you execute this script, it will display the following output:

```
C:\Python> python usedefault.py
300
700
0
400
```

## Leveraging Python's Built-In Functions

Python provides a large set of built-in functions that you can call simply by referring to the function's name and providing any needed parameters, such as print("Hello").

The following Python script, BuiltIns.py, illustrates the use of several Python built-in functions:

```
print('Hello, world')
print(1 + 2 * 5)
print('Power of 5 raised to 2 is', pow(5, 2))
print('Absolute value of -3 is', abs(-3))
print('Sorted list', sorted([3,2,1,5,4]))
```

# CHAPTER 8 Programming Data Mining and Analytic Solutions

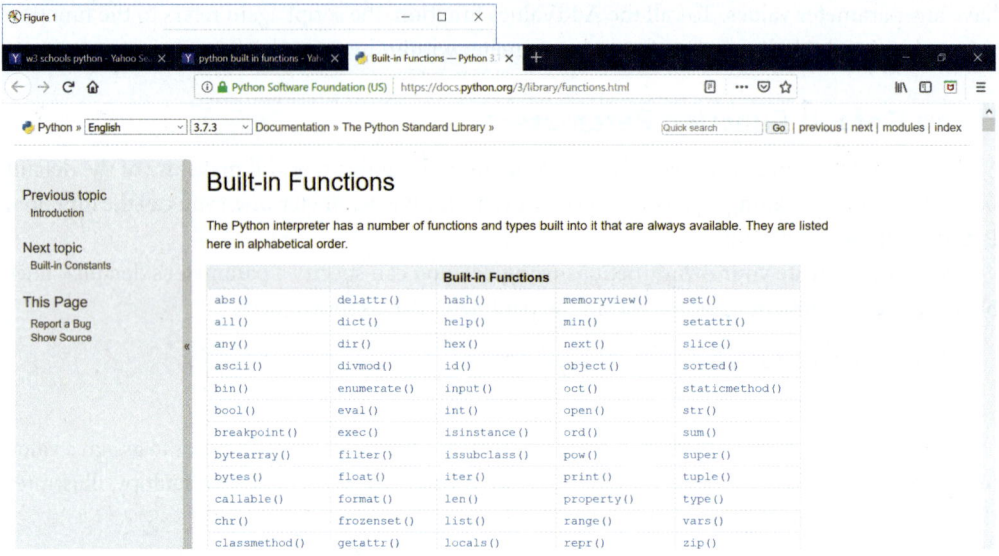

**FIGURE 8.6** Viewing specifics on Python's built-in functions.
Used with permission of Python Software Foundation

When you execute this script, it will display the following output:

```
C:\Python> python Built-Ins.py
Hello, world
11
Power of 5 raised to 2 is 25
Absolute value of -3 is 3
Sorted list [1, 2, 3, 4, 5]
```

To call each built-in function, you refer to the function name, specifying your parameter values, separated by commas, within parentheses.

You can find specifics on each Python function at the Python website, as shown in **FIGURE 8.6**.

## Python Is Object Oriented

Python is an object-oriented programming language that lets you create objects from classes that provide attribute values and methods. To access an object's attribute values or to call an object's methods, you use dot notation:

```
objectName.SomeAttribute = 7;
student.Name = "Bill Smith";
student.ShowGrades()
```

The following Python script, StudentObject.py, defines a student class and then uses it to create student objects:

```
class Student:
    def __init__(self, name, age, gpa):
        self.name = name
        self.age = age
        self.gpa = gpa

    def show(self):
        print('Name:', self.name)
        print('Age:', self.age)
        print('GPA:', self.gpa)

Jim = Student('Jim Smith', 25, 3.6)
Mary = Student('Mary Davis', 22, 4.0)

Jim.show()
Mary.show()
```

The script uses the def statement to define the Student class. Within the class, the script defines the __init__ function, which is a Python constructor method that Python automatically calls each time you create an object. In this case, the function assigns three values to the object attributes (name, age, and grade point average [GPA]). Within the function self refers to the current object. The script also defines a second function, show, which displays the student's attribute values.

To create an object, the script calls the Student method, passing to it the values to assign to the student attributes. As you can see, to refer to object attributes and methods, the script uses the dot operator.

## Understanding Python Modules

Python programmers store Python scripts within text files with the .py extension, such as Hello.py. Such a file can be a complete program, or it can be a **module** that contains function and class definitions. To use a Python module, within your script, you use the import statement:

```
import moduleName
```

The following Python script, Random100.py, imports the rand module and then uses the randint method the library contains to display 100 random values in the range 1–25:

```
import random

for i in range(0, 100):
  print(random.randint(1, 25))
```

As you can see, the program refers to functions defined within the module using dot notation: random.randint. When you run this script, it will display the following output:

```
C:\> python Random100.py
6
18
```

```
16
1
:
16
19
```

## Importing a Module and Creating an Alias

Depending on the name of the Python module you are importing, there may be times when you want to create an abbreviated alias name to refer to the module. To do so, you include the "as" alias name following your import statement, as shown here:

```
import random as rnd
```

The following Python script, Rnd100.py, illustrates the use of a module alias:

```
import random as rnd

for i in range(0, 99):
  print(rnd.randint(1, 25))
```

## Importing a Module Using from ... Import

As you have seen, when you import a Python module using an import statement, you later call the module's methods using dot notation:

```
moduleName.method()
or
aliasName.method()
```

To eliminate your need to use the dot notation, you can use a different form of the import statement:

```
from moduleName import functionName
```

The following Python script, FromImport.py, illustrates the use of this import form:

```
from random import randint

for i in range(0, 99):
  print(randint(1, 25))
```

## Understanding and Importing Packages

As you have learned, a module is a Python source file that provides function and class definitions. A Python package is similar to a module in that it provides specific functionality, but it differs in that it is not a single file, but rather, a folder of files. You can view packages within the lib subfolder within your Python folder, as shown in **FIGURE 8.7**.

Getting Started with Python 367

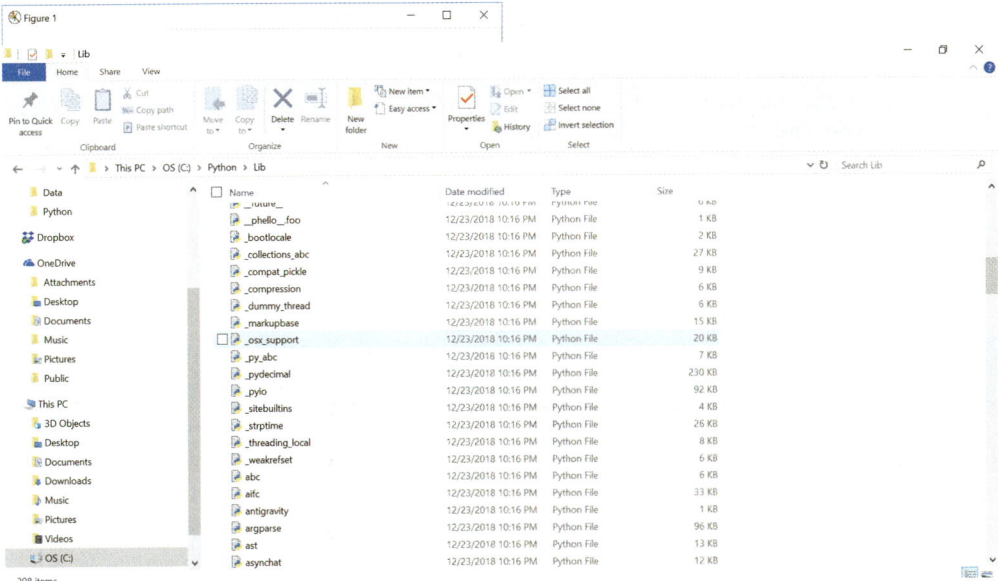

**FIGURE 8.7** Viewing packages installed in your Python folder.

Used with permission of Microsoft

**TABLE 8.4 Python Packages You Will Use throughout This Text**

| Package Name | Functionality |
| --- | --- |
| matplotlib | Contains functions you will use to plot and chart data |
| pandas | Data structure definitions, such as dataframe |
| numpy | numpy stands for numerical Python, and the numpy package supports such operations |
| plot.ly | Provides functions to plot and chart data |
| sklearn | Defines data structures and functions you will use to perform data mining and machine learning for clustering, classification, and prediction |

Before you can use a **package**, you must install it on to your system using a command-line tool called PIP.

Throughout this text, you will make use of the packages listed in **TABLE 8.4**.

Before you can use each package, you must install them on your system using PIP. The following PIP command installs the matplotlib package, which you will use to create charts:

```
C:\python> pip install matplotlib
```

If you try to import a package within a script and the package does not exist on your system, Python will display an error message similar to that shown here:

```
>>> import someLib
Traceback (most recent call last):
  File "<stdin>", line 1, in <module>
ModuleNotFoundError: No module named 'someLib'
>>>
```

Should this error occur, use PIP to install the package.

## Leveraging the Python Package Index (PyPI)

Since Python's release in 1991, developers have created over 170,000 packages that provide a wide range of functionality. The Python Package Index (**PyPI**) is a searchable website that provides you with access to many of these packages, as shown in **FIGURE A**.

For each package, you can find an overview, as well as the PIP command you must perform to download and install the package.

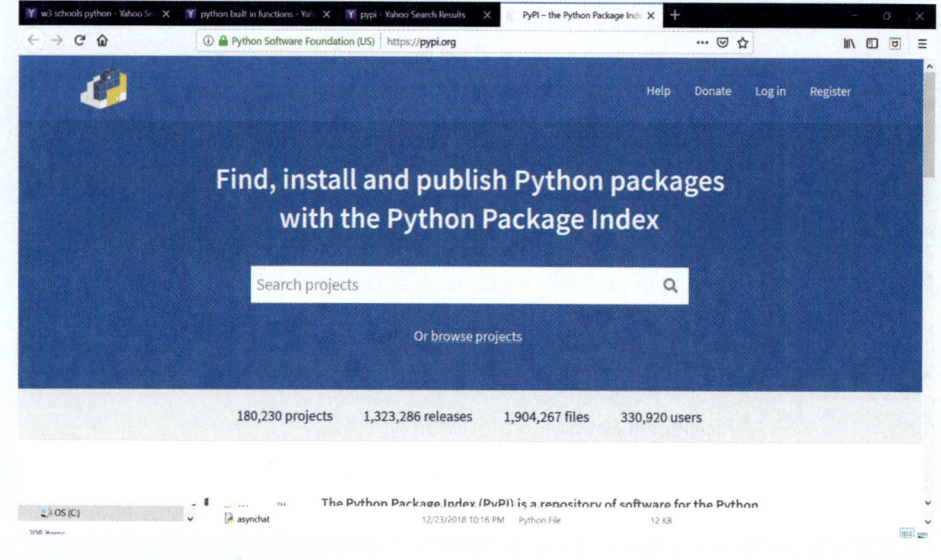

**FIGURE A** The PyPI website.

Used with permission of Python Software Foundation

## Understanding Python Dataframe Objects

Throughout this text, the Python scripts will make extensive use of dataframe objects to store various data sets. You can think of a dataframe as a two-dimensional container that stores a data-set's rows and columns. The following Python script, UseDataframe.py, builds several dataframes by hand:

```
from pandas import DataFrame

Data = {
        'x': [35,34,32,37,33,33,31,27,35,34,62,54,57,
              47,50,57,59,52,61,47,50,48,39,40,45],
        'y': [79,54,52,77,59,74,73,57,69,75,51,32,40,
              47,53,36,35,58,59,50,23,22,13,14,22]
       }

df = DataFrame(Data,columns=['x','y'])

Sales = {
        'Day': ['Mon', 'Tue', 'Wed', 'Thu', 'Fri'],
        'Count': [79,54,52,77,59,]
        }

salesdf = DataFrame(Sales,columns=['Day','Count'])

print(df.head())
print(df.size)
print(df.shape)

print(salesdf.head())
print(salesdf.size)
print(salesdf.shape)
```

As you can see, the script creates two dataframe objects. One dataframe contains only numeric data, and the second contains text and data. The script uses the size, shape, and head methods to display the number of elements in the dataframe, the dimensions, and the first rows of data. When you run this script, it will display the following output:

```
C:\Python> python UseDataframe.py
    x   y
0  35  79
1  34  54
2  32  52
3  37  77
4  33  59
50
(25, 2)
    Day  Count
0   Mon     79
1   Tue     54
2   Wed     52
3   Thu     77
```

```
4   Fri    59
10
(5, 2)
```

Most of the Python scripts this text presents will load dataframe objects from a .csv file. The following Python script, LoadDataframa.py, loads data from the Titanic data set, which contains data for passengers from the *Titanic*. You can download the .csv file for the data set from this text's catalog page at go.jblearning.com/DataMining.

As you can see, the script uses the read.csv function to read data from the Titanic.csv file. The script then uses the dataframe to describe the method to display specifics about each column:

```python
import pandas as pd
from pandas import DataFrame

df = pd.read_csv('Titanic.csv')
print(df.describe())
```

When you run this script, it will display the following output:

```
C:\Python> python LoadDataframe.py
       PassengerId      Survived        Pclass         Age          SibSp
Parch         Fare
count   1309.000000   1309.000000   1309.000000   1046.000000   1309.000000
1309.000000   1308.000000
mean     655.000000      0.377387      2.294882     29.881138      0.498854
   0.385027     33.295479
std      378.020061      0.484918      0.837836     14.413493      1.041658
   0.865560     51.758668
min        1.000000      0.000000      1.000000      0.170000      0.000000
   0.000000      0.000000
25%      328.000000      0.000000      2.000000     21.000000      0.000000
   0.000000      7.895800
50%      655.000000      0.000000      3.000000     28.000000      0.000000
   0.000000     14.454200
75%      982.000000      1.000000      3.000000     39.000000      1.000000
   0.000000     31.275000
max     1309.000000      1.000000      3.000000     80.000000      8.000000
   9.000000    512.329200
```

The dataframe class has a wide range of methods. You should take time to review specifics about the dataframe object at the website https://pandas.pydata.org/pandas-docs/stable/reference/api/pandas.DataFrame.html shown in **FIGURE 8.8**.

## Using the pandas Package for Numerical Data Structures

Throughout this text, you will make extensive use of the pandas library, which contains data structures, such as the dataframe, which your programs will use extensively. To get started, use PIP to install pandas:

```
C:\> pip install pandas   <Enter>
```

# Getting Started with Python

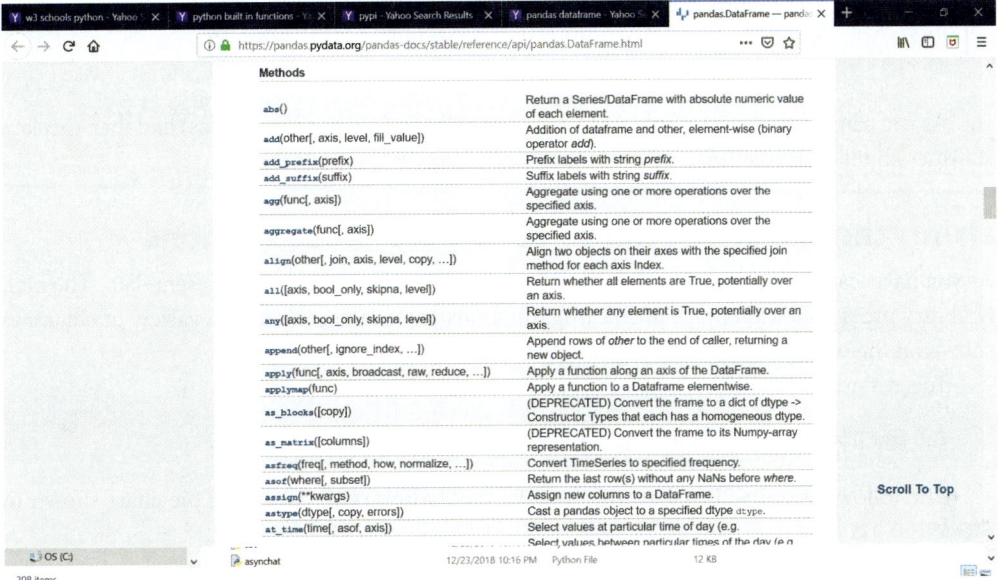

**FIGURE 8.8** Displaying the dataframe class methods.

Pandas data frame https://pandas.pydata.org/pandas-docs/stable/reference/api/pandas.DataFrame.html

If PIP displays a bad command error message, make sure you have installed it, as discussed earlier in this chapter, and that the Pip.exe file is in your current directory or command path.

The following Python script, UsePandas.py, uses pandas to create a dataframe object and then to load the iris data set, which you will use for many data-mining operations throughout this text. The script then displays several facts about the data set:

```
import pandas as pd
from pandas import DataFrame

df = pd.read_csv('iris.data.csv')
print(df.size)
print(df.shape)
print(df.describe())
```

When you run this script, it will display the following output:

```
C:\Python> python UsePandas.py
745
(149, 5)
                5.1          3.5          1.4          0.2
count    149.000000   149.000000   149.000000   149.000000
mean       5.848322     3.051007     3.774497     1.205369
std        0.828594     0.433499     1.759651     0.761292
min        4.300000     2.000000     1.000000     0.100000
25%        5.100000     2.800000     1.600000     0.300000
```

```
50%      5.800000    3.000000    4.400000    1.300000
75%      6.400000    3.300000    5.100000    1.800000
max      7.900000    4.400000    6.900000    2.500000
```

As you can see, the script displays the dataframe size and shape (dimensions) and then displays statistics about each column.

## Using the plot.ly Package to Create Visualizations

As you have learned, data analysts make extensive use of visualization to represent data. The plot.ly library provides a wide range of charting functions you can use to create a variety of charts, as shown on the plot.ly website shown in **FIGURE 8.9**.

To get started, use PIP to install the package:

```
C:\python> pip install plotly
```

The following script, PieChart.py, uses the plot.ly library to create the pie chart shown in **FIGURE 8.10**:

```
import plotly.plotly as py
import plotly.graph_objs as go

labels = ['Data Mining','Machine Learning','Statistics','Programming']
values = [150000,145000,135000,125000]

chart = go.Pie(labels=labels, values=values)

py.plot([chart])
```

## Using the matplotlib Package to Create Visualization

In addition to the plot.ly graphics library, Python developers make extensive use of the matplotlib library. To start, use PIP to install matplotlib:

```
C:\> pip install matplotlib    <Enter>
```

The following script, UseMatPlotLib.py, uses the matplotlib library to create a stacked plot chart, as shown in **FIGURE 8.11**:

```
import numpy as np
import matplotlib.pyplot as plt


N = 5
salesMay = (20, 35, 30, 35, 27)
salesJune = (25, 32, 34, 20, 25)
ind = np.arange(N)
width = 0.35
```

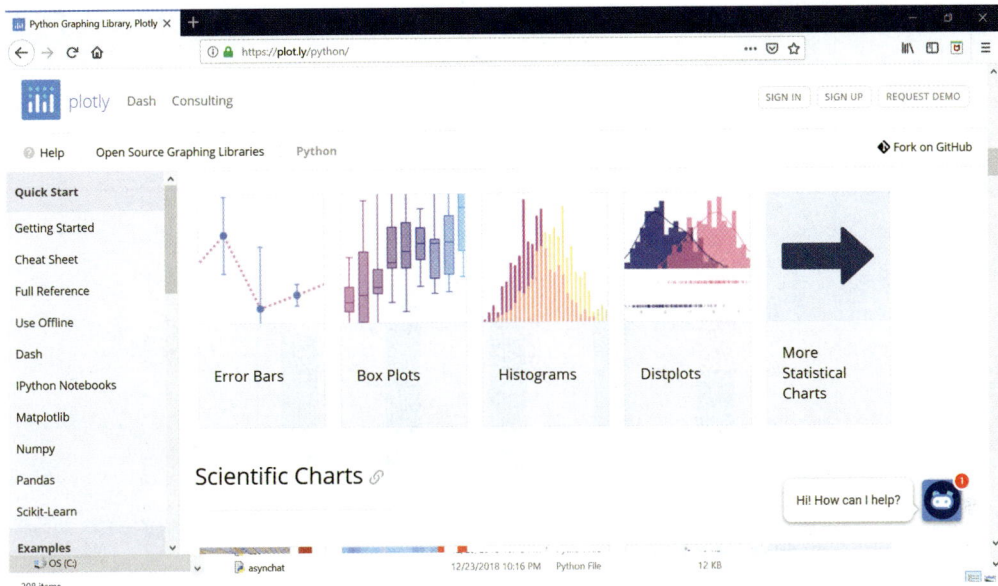

**FIGURE 8.9** Chart examples on the plot.ly website, located at http://plot.ly/python.

Used with permission of plotly

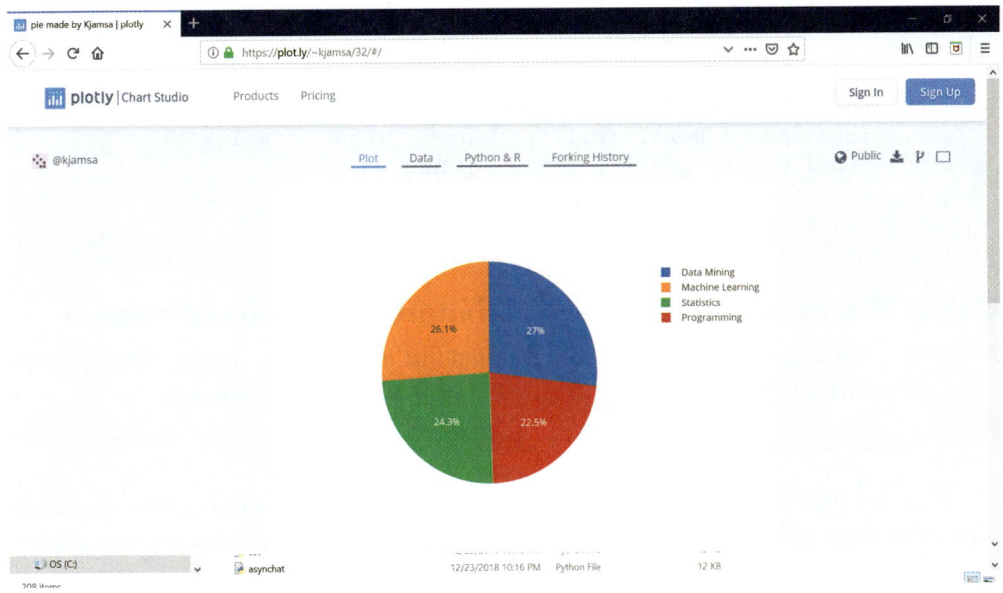

**FIGURE 8.10** Creating a pie chart using the plot.ly library.

Used with permission of plotly

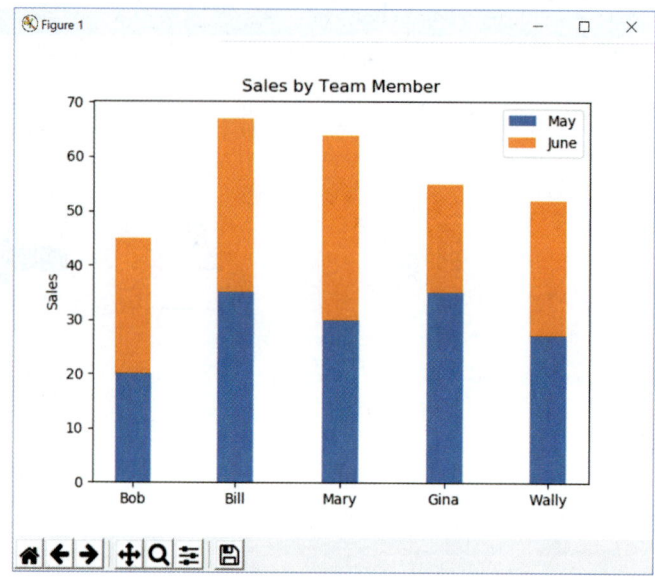

**FIGURE 8.11** Creating a stacked chart using matplotlib.

Used with permission of Python Software Foundation

```
p1 = plt.bar(ind, salesMay, width)
p2 = plt.bar(ind, salesJune, width, bottom=salesMay)

plt.ylabel('Sales')
plt.title('Sales by Team Member')
plt.xticks(ind, ('Bob', 'Bill', 'Mary', 'Gina', 'Wally'))
plt.legend((p1[0], p2[0]), ('May', 'June'))

plt.show()
```

## Using the numpy Package for Numerical Calculations

As you examine data-mining solutions, you will find that many use the numpy library. Numpy stands for numerical Python. To get started, use PIP to install the numpy package:

```
C:\python> pip install numpy   <Enter>
```

The following Python script, UseNumpy.py, uses numpy to create a 10 × 2 array of random values. The script then uses the matplotlib library previously discussed to create a scatter chart of the values, as shown in **FIGURE 8.12**:

```
import numpy as np
import matplotlib.pyplot as plt

x = np.random.rand(10,1)
y = np.random.rand(10,1)
```

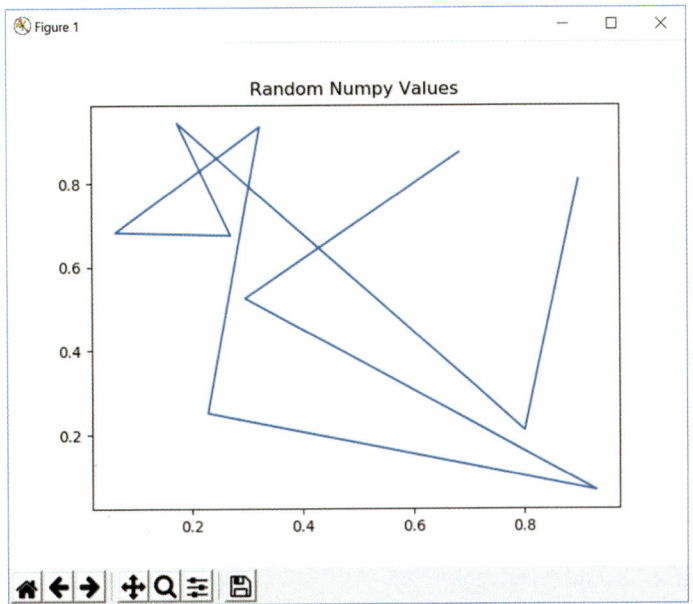

**FIGURE 8.12** Plotting random values created by the numpy random function.

Used with permission of Python Software Foundation

```
plt.title('Random Numpy Values')
plt.plot(x,y)

plt.show()
```

## Using the sklearn Package for Machine Learning and Data Mining

Throughout this text, your Python data-mining and machine-learning scripts will make extensive use of the scikit-learn library. As you will learn, the scikit-learn library contains functions your code will use to perform cluster analysis, data classification, linear regression for prediction, and more. To get started, use PIP to install the library on your system:

```
C:\python> pip install scikit-learn
```

As you can see, to download and install the library, you use the name scikit-learn. However, within the import statement in your scripts, you refer to sklearn:

```
import sklearn
```

The following Python script, UseSklearn.py, uses the library to cluster a dataframe's values:

```
import matplotlib.pyplot as plt
from sklearn.cluster import KMeans
```

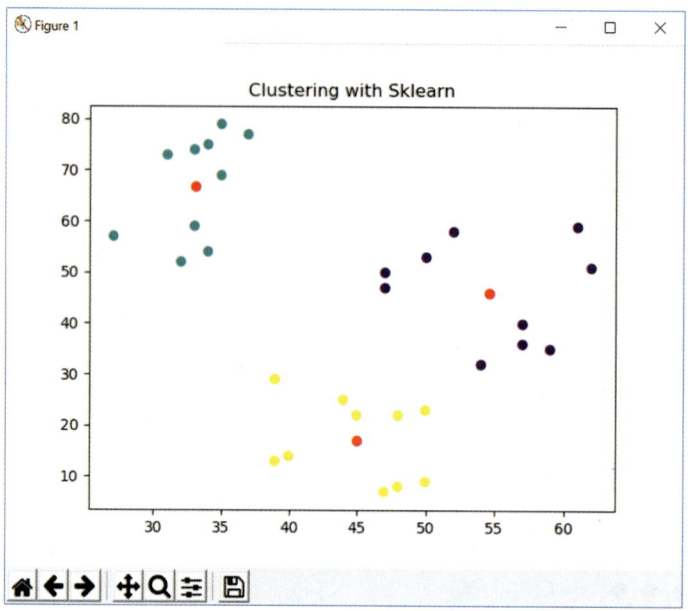

**FIGURE 8.13 Clustering data using sklearn.**
Used with permission of Python Software Foundation

```
from pandas import DataFrame

Data = {
        'x': [35,34,32,37,33,33,31,27,35,34,62,54,
              57,47,50,57,59,52,61,47,50,48,39,40,45,47,39,44,50,48],
        'y': [79,54,52,77,59,74,73,57,69,75,51,32,40,
              47,53,36,35,58,59,50,23,22,13,14,22,7,29,25,9,8]
       }

df = DataFrame(Data,columns=['x','y'])

kmeans = KMeans(n_clusters=3).fit(df)
centroids = kmeans.cluster_centers_
plt.title('Clustering with Sklearn')
plt.scatter(df['x'], df['y'], c=kmeans.labels_.astype(float))
plt.scatter(centroids[:, 0], centroids[:, 1], c='red')
plt.show()
```

When you run this script, it will display the chart shown in **FIGURE 8.13**.

# Getting Started with R

The R programming language was first released around the year 2000 to support data-mining, machine-learning, and statistical programming applications. In this section, you will get up and

## Using the iPython Development Environment

Throughout this text, you will make extensive use of the Python interpreter, which you run from the command line. In addition to using Python, many developers now use iPython (which stands for interactive Python). You can download and install iPython from the ipython.org website.

In Chapter 16, "Planning and Launching a Data Mining and Data Analytics Project," you will learn how to leverage Jupyter Notebooks to create interactive documents, similar to that shown in **FIGURE A**. Within a Jupyter Notebook users can run and view the output of embedded Python scripts, including visual charts. Behind the scenes, Jupyter Notebooks leverages iPython.

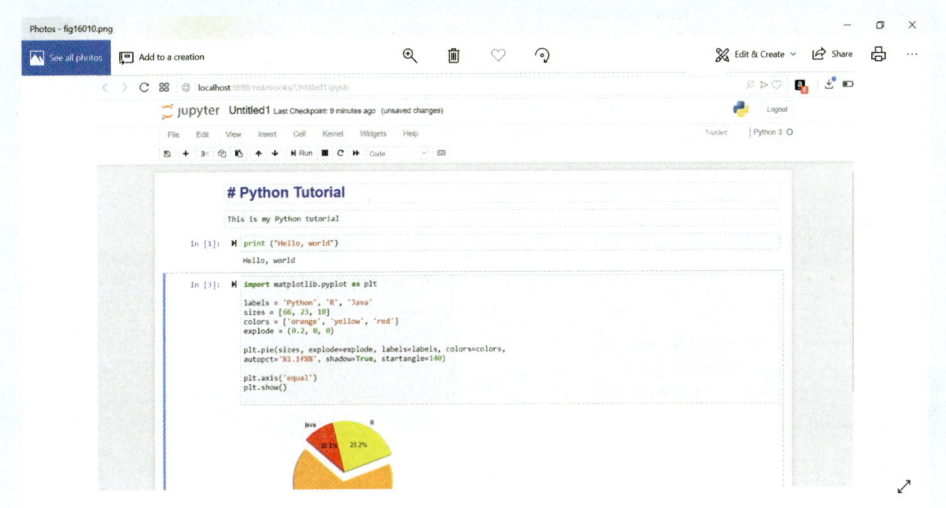

**FIGURE A** An interactive Jupyter Notebook.

Used with permission of Project Jupyter

running with R. Like Python, R is a very powerful and complex language on which many books have been written. This section's goal is to present the key aspects of R that you will need to know to understand the programs this text presents.

To get started, download and install R from the R website, located at https://www.r-project.org/, as shown in **FIGURE 8.14**.

After you install and run R, it will display its interactive development environment prompt, as shown in **FIGURE 8.15**.

At the R prompt, type the following print statement:

```
print("Hello, world!")
```

# CHAPTER 8 Programming Data Mining and Analytic Solutions

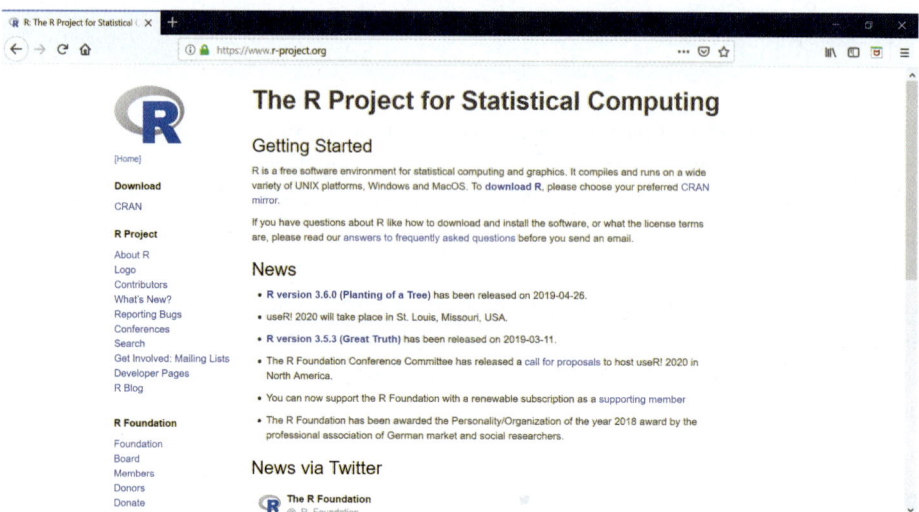

**FIGURE 8.14** Download and install R from the R website.
Used with permission of The R Foundation

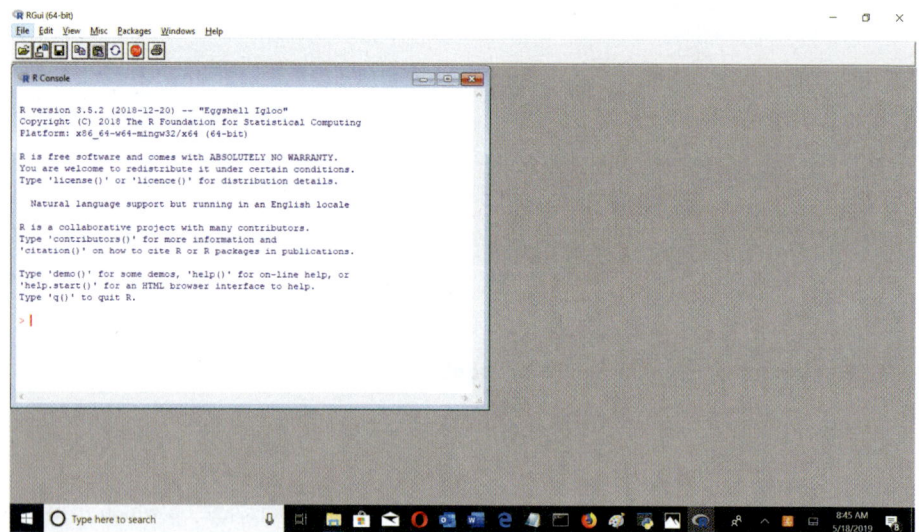

**FIGURE 8.15** The R interactive development environment.
Used with permission of The R Foundation

R will display the "Hello, world!" message, as shown in **FIGURE 8.16**.

R provides an interpreted environment, for which R executes one statement at a time, as opposed to a compiled programming language environment for which a compiler produces an executable file. As you work with R, you will find the ability to execute a few statements at a time is very convenient as you try new functions or troubleshoot your code.

```
R Console
> print('Hello, world!')
[1] "Hello, world!"
>
```

**FIGURE 8.16** Running the Hello, world! program within R.

Used with permission of The R Foundation

At the R prompt, issue the following statements:

```
> print(3)
[1] 3
> print(3 + 1)
[1] 4
> a <- 1000
> b <- 5
> print(a * b)
[1] 5000
> a <- c(1, 2, 3)
> print(a)
[1] 1 2 3
> print(a * b)
[1]  5 10 15
```

R uses the colon (:) to specify a range of values. 1:5, for example, means the values 1, 2, 3, 4, and 5. Consider the following examples:

```
> print(1:5)
[1] 1 2 3 4 5
> print(sum(1:5))
[1] 15
> print(mean(1:5))
[1] 3
```

To assign a value to a variable in R, you use the <- assignment operator. R also supports the equals sign (=) assignment operator, but the preference is to use the <- operator:

```
> a <- 100
> b = 50
> print(a + b)
[1] 150
```

When you create R programs, the <<– operator (two <<) assigns a value to a global variable. You can use the assignment from right to left:

```
> a <- 1
```

Or you can do the assignments from left to right:

```
> 1 -> a
```

## Creating Variables in R

Variables in R are dynamic, meaning that to use a variable in R, you simply refer to the variable name. Unlike many other programming languages, you do not need to specify a variable's type before you can use it. Instead, R will determine the type based on the value assigned. The following statements create several different variables in R:

```
> a <- 1
> b <- 2
> c <- d <- e <- 3
> d <- c(a, b, c, d, e)
> print(a)
[1] 1
> print(b)
[1] 2
> print(c)
[1] 3
> print(d)
[1] 1 2 3 3 3
> e <- 1:5
> print(e)
[1] 1 2 3 4 5
```

The c function in R creates a vector (one-dimensional list). R determines a variable's type based on the value assigned. To display a variable's type, you use the class function, as shown here:

```
> age <- 21
> class(age)
[1] "numeric"
> pi <- 3.14
> class(pi)
[1] "numeric"
> name = "Bo"
> class(name)
[1] "character"
> list = c(1, 2, 3)
> class(list)
[1] "numeric"
> list = c(age, pi, name)
> print(list)
```

## TABLE 8.5  R Keywords

| break | else   | for   | function | if   |
|-------|--------|-------|----------|------|
| in    | inf    | NA    | NA       | next |
| NULL  | repeat | while |          |      |

```
[1] "21"   "3.14" "Bo"
> class(list)
[1] "character"
```

To display the names of variables you have created during your current session, you use the ls function:

```
> ls()
[1] "a"    "age"  "b"    "c"    "d"    "e"    "list" "name" "pi"
```

Variable names in R must start with letters or a dot. Further, you cannot use the R keywords listed in **TABLE 8.5** for variable names. R is a case-dependent programming language in that it considers uppercase and lowercase letters as different. Therefore, R would consider the variables myList and mylist to be different.

Variable names in R can contain letters, dots, underscores, and numbers. The following variable names are valid in R:

```
> a <- 1
> .b <- 2
> a2 <- 3
> a_2 <- 4
```

## Comments in R

R, like Python, uses the pound sign (#) to indicate the start of a comment:

```
# This is a comment in R
```

When R encounters the pound sign, it will ignore the remainder of the current line. The following statements illustrate the use of comments in R:

```
> a <- 2   # assign the value 2
```

## Using R's Built-in Functions

Like most programming languages, R provides a set of built-in functions, such as print, sum, mean, median, and so on, which you have already used. As shown in **FIGURE 8.17**, the R development team provides a several-thousand-page document that describes the R functions in detail at https://cran.r-project.org/doc/manuals/r-release/fullrefman.pdf.

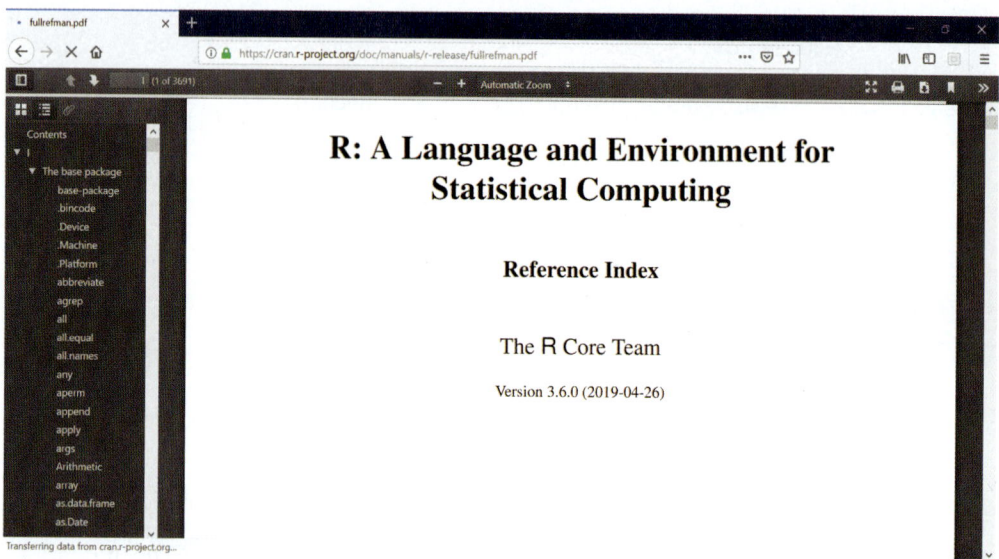

**FIGURE 8.17 Complete documentation on the R functions.**
Used with permission of The R Foundation

## Getting Additional Help in R

The R interpreter provides built-in help support, which you can invoke by typing a question mark (?) followed by a topic at the R prompt. The following statement displays help on the R for loop:

```
> ? "for"
```

When you execute this statement, R will display help text within a browser window on your screen, as shown in **FIGURE 8.18**.

## Operators within R

R supports the standard set of operators, such as + for addition, – for subtraction, * for multiplication, and / for division. **TABLE 8.6** lists the R operators.

The following illustrates the result of common operations in R:

```
> a <- 10
> b <- 3
> a + b
[1] 13
> a * b
[1] 30
> a / b
[1] 3.333333
> a %/% b
[1] 3
> a %% b
```

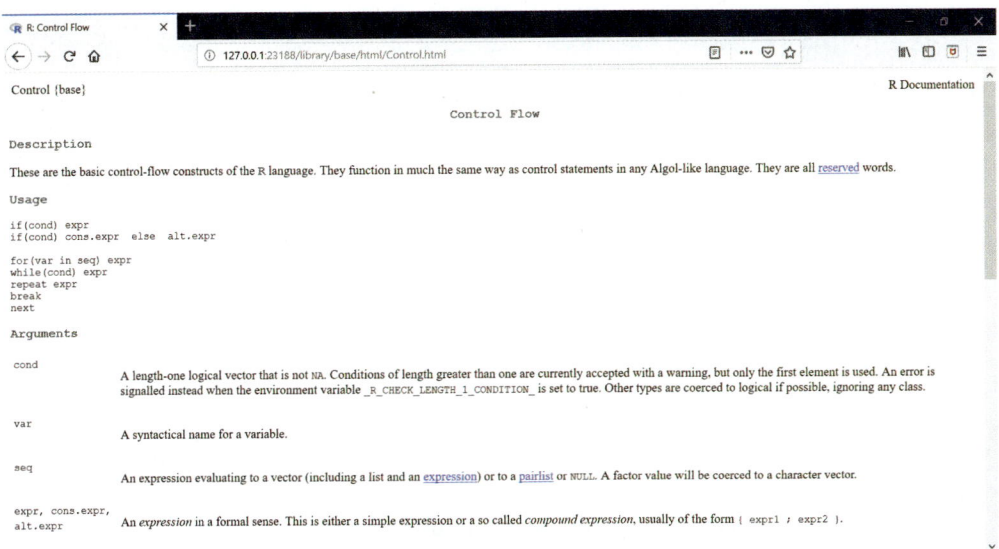

**FIGURE 8.18** Getting help on topics within R.
Used with permission of The R Foundation

**TABLE 8.6** The R Operators

| Operator | Purpose |
|---|---|
| * | Multiplication |
| / | Division |
| ^ or ** | Exponentiation |
| %/% | Integer result of a division |
| %% | Modulo (remainder) |
| + | Addition |
| − | Subtraction |

```
[1] 1
> a ^ b
[1] 1000
```

## Relational Operators

To allow your programs to compare values, R provides relational operators that let you test if one value is equal to, not equal to, less than, or greater than another value. **TABLE 8.7** lists R's relational operators.

### TABLE 8.7  The R Relational Operators

| Operator | Meaning |
|---|---|
| == | Equality |
| != | Not equal |
| > | Greater than |
| < | Less than |
| >= | Greater than or equal to |
| <= | Less than or equal to |

The following statements illustrate the operators' use:

```
> a <- 1
> b <- 2
> a == b
[1] FALSE
> a != b
[1] TRUE
> a < b
[1] TRUE
> a > b
[1] FALSE
```

In addition to common relational operators, R provides the %in% operator that returns true if a value is in a list or false otherwise:

```
> a = c(1, 2, 3)
> 1 %in% a
[1] TRUE
> 5 %in% a
[1] FALSE
```

## Logical Operators

To allow your programs to test multiple conditions at one time, R provides the AND (&&) and OR (||) operators. The AND operator returns true if both conditions are true and false otherwise. Likewise, the OR operator returns true if either condition is true. R also provides the NOT (!) operator. The following statements illustrate the use of R logical operators:

```
> a <- 1
> b <- 2
> a == 1 && b == 2
```

```
[1] TRUE
> (a == 1) && (b == 2)
[1] TRUE
> a < 1 && b < 2
[1] FALSE
> a < 1 && b == 2
[1] FALSE
> a < 1 || b == 2
[1] TRUE
> ! a < 1
[1] TRUE
```

## Conditional Operators in R

To allow your programs to make decisions, R supports the if-else statement. Within the statement, R uses left and right braces {} to group related statements. The following R program, Vegas.R, illustrates the use of the if-else statement:

```
age <- 21

if (age >= 21)
   {
     print("Vegas!")
   } else
   {
     print('Disneyland!')
   }
```

Note that the else is on the same line as the if statement's ending brace. If R encounters an end-of-line character at the end of a complete statement, it will consider the statement complete. As such, placing the else on its own line, following the ending brace, will create a syntax error:

```
if (age >= 21)
   {
     print("Vegas!")
   }
else    # this is a syntax error
   {
     print('Disneyland!')
   }
```

When you execute these statements, R will display the following error:

```
> if (age >= 21)
+   {
+      print("Vegas!")
+   }
[1] "Vegas!"
> else
Error: unexpected 'else' in "else"
```

Depending on your R environment, to execute a program's statements, you simply cut and paste the statements from your editor to the R prompt.

In addition to the if-else statement, R supports a switch statement, the format of which is:

```
result = switch(expression, case1, case2, case3 ...)
```

When R encounters a switch statement, it will evaluate the expression and match the result to one of the listed cases, where the cases correspond to the values 1 to *n*. If the expression is less than 1 or greater than *n*, the switch will return the value null:

```
> number = 1
> result = switch(number, "one", "two", "three")
> result
[1] "one"
> number = 0
> result = switch(number, "one", "two", "three")
> result
NULL
> number = 3
> result = switch(number, "one", "two", "three")
> result
[1] "three"
> number = 4
> result = switch(number, "one", "two", "three")
> result
NULL
```

In addition, R provides an ifelse function, the format of which is:

```
x <- ifelse (a < b, "true", "false")
```

In this case, R will evaluate the given expression (a < b) and return the true result if the expression is true and the false result otherwise.

## Repeating Statements with for, while, and repeat

To allow your programs to repeat statements, R provides the for, while, and repeat iterative (looping) statements, the format of which is:

```
for (value in sequence)
    statement

while (condition)
    statement

repeat
    statement
```

The following R program, Loop.R, illustrates the use of the R looping statements:

```
for (i in 1:3)
  print(i)

list = c('a', 'b', 'c')

for (i in list)
  print(i)

i = 0
while (i < 3)
  {
    print(i)
    i = i + 1
  }

i = 0
repeat {
  print(i)
  if (i == 3)
    break
  i = i + 1
}
```

As you can see, when the loop has multiple statements, you group the statements within left and right braces. When you execute this program, it will display the following output:

```
> for (i in 1:3)
+   print(i)
[1] 1
[1] 2
[1] 3
> list = c('a', 'b', 'c')
> for (i in list)
+   print(i)
[1] "a"
[1] "b"
[1] "c"
> i = 0
> while (i < 3)
+   {
+     print(i)
+     i = i + 1
+   }
[1] 0
[1] 1
[1] 2
> i = 0
> repeat {
+   print(i)
```

```
+   if (i == 3)
+      break
+   i = i + 1
+ }
[1] 0
[1] 1
[1] 2
[1] 3
```

Within the repeat loop, you use the break statement, discussed next, to end the loop's processing. Throughout this text, you will make extensive use of the for statement to iterate through data sets.

## Next and Break Statements

Like Python, R supports the next (similar to continue) and break statements. When R encounters a next statement within a for or while loop, R will immediately branch to the next iteration of the loop. The following R script, ShowOdd.R, uses the next statement to display only odd values:

```
for (i in 1:10)
  {
    if (i %% 2 == 0)
       next
    print(i)
  }
```

The script uses the modulo (%%) operator to get the remainder of the variable divided by 2. For even values, the remainder will be 0, which causes the code to continue with the next iteration of the loop. For odd values, the result of the modulo operation will be 1, causing the if statement to fail and the program to print the value. When you execute this script, R will display the following output:

```
1
3
5
7
9
```

When R encounters a break statement within a for, while, or repeat loop, it will immediately end the loop's processing, continuing the script's execution at the statement that follows the loop.

Although next (continue) and break are common to most programming languages, in most instances, you can refactor code that uses them to create a more structured solution. For example, the following code displays the odd values without the need of the next statement:

```
for (i in 1:10)
   if (i %% 2 == 1)
      print(i)
```

## Storing a List of Values as a One-Dimensional Vector

A vector is a one-dimensional collection of values such as [1, 2, 3, 4, 5]. The following statement creates an R vector with five values:

```
> myVector = c(10, 20, 30, 40, 50)
```

The statement uses the c function to create the vector. To access the individual values within the vector, you use an index. The first value in the vector is at the index location 1, the second at 2, and so on:

```
> myVector = c(10, 20, 30, 40, 50)
> myVector[1]
[1] 10
> myVector[3]
[1] 30
```

To specify a range of values within a vector, you can use the R colon (:) operator to specify a sequence, as shown here:

```
> myVector[2:4]
[1] 20 30 40
```

R lets you perform operations on a vector. For example, the following statement multiplies each item in the vector by 5:

```
> myVector * 3
[1]  30  60  90 120 150
```

In a similar way, the following statement performs an operation on a vector of values, assigning the result to a new vector:

```
> newVector <- myVector * 3 + 1
> newVector
[1]  31  61  91 121 151
```

To determine the number of items in an R vector, you use the length function:

```
> length(myVector)
[1] 5
```

The following R program, VectorFor.R, uses two for loops to display the values a vector contains:

```
myVector = c(10, 20, 30, 40, 50)
for (i in myVector)
  print(i)

for (i in 1: length(myVector))
  print(myVector[i])
```

The for loops illustrate two approaches to loop through a list. The first for loop uses the vector items, whereas the second uses an index to access the vector items.

When you execute this program, it will display the following output:

```
> myVector = c(10, 20, 30, 40, 50)
> for (i in myVector)
+    print(i)
[1] 10
[1] 20
[1] 30
[1] 40
[1] 50
>
> for (i in 1: length(myVector))
+    print(myVector[i])
[1] 10
[1] 20
[1] 30
[1] 40
[1] 50
```

## Performing a Vectored If Operation

When you work with vectors, there are often times when you will need to test each value within the list and perform a related operation. Using a for loop and nested if statement, you can perform such operations. However, to improve the readability of your code, R provides a vectored if statement. Consider the following example that creates a vector containing values 1–25. The statements then use the ifelse statement and the modulo operator (%%) to convert the odd values to the value 1 and the even values to the value 0:

```
> x <- 1:25
> x
 [1]  1  2  3  4  5  6  7  8  9 10 11 12 13 14 15 16 17 18 19 20
21 22 23 24 25
> x <- ifelse(x%%2, 1, 0)
> x
 [1] 1 0 1 0 1 0 1 0 1 0 1 0 1 0 1 0 1 0 1 0 1 0 1 0 1
```

The following statements illustrate the use of the ifelse statement with an array. The program uses the array function to create a two-dimensional array, as discussed in the next section. In this case, the statements use the ifelse to convert any values of 4 to the value 1 and all other values to 2:

```
> a <- c(1, 2, 3, 4)
> b <- c(3, 3, 3, 4)
> c <- array(c(a, b), dim=c(2,4))
> c
     [,1] [,2] [,3] [,4]
```

```
[1,]    1    3    3    3
[2,]    2    4    3    4
> c <- ifelse(c == 4, 1, 2)
> c
        [,1] [,2] [,3] [,4]
[1,]     2    2    2    2
[2,]     2    1    2    1
```

## Storing Multidimensional Values in an Array

As you have learned, a vector stores a one-dimensional list of values. An array, in contrast, can store multiple dimensions of values, such as *x* and *y* values; *x*, *y*, and *z* values; and more. The following statement creates a two-dimensional array of values:

```
> x = c(1, 3, 5)
> y = c(2, 4, 6)
> a = array(c(x,y), dim=c(3,2))
```

In this case, the statements first create a vector of *x* values followed by a vector of *y* values. The statements then create an array named a that combines the vectors and specifies a dimension of three rows by two columns. When you view the array, R will display the following:

```
> a
       [,1] [,2]
[1,]    1    2
[2,]    3    4
[3,]    5    6
```

To access the values for specify array elements, you use index values (starting with 1, not zero-based indexing), as shown here:

```
> a[1,1]
[1] 1
> a[1,2]
[1] 2
> a[2,1]
[1] 3
> a[2,2]
```

The following R program, plotArray.R, assigns an array of *x* and *y* values and then creates a scatter plot of the values using the plot function:

```
x = c(1, 3, 5)
y = c(2, 4, 6)
a = array(c(x,y), dim=c(3,2))
```

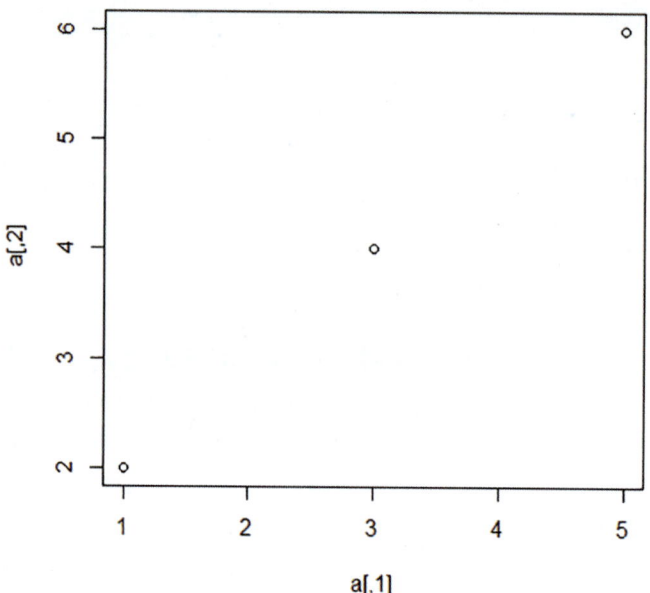

**FIGURE 8.19** Plotting a two-dimensional array of values.

```
plot(a)
```

When you execute this program, it will display the chart shown in **FIGURE 8.19**.

To determine the number of rows and columns in an array, you use the nrow and ncol functions, as shown here:

```
> nrow(a)
[1] 3
> ncol(a)
[1] 2
```

The following program, LoopArray.R, uses a for loop to display the elements in an array:

```
x = c(1, 3, 5)
y = c(2, 4, 6)
a = array(c(x,y), dim=c(3,2))

for (i in 1:nrow(a))
  for (j in 1:ncol(a))
    print(a[i,j])
```

When you execute this program, it will display the following results:

```
[1] 1
[1] 2
[1] 3
```

```
[1] 4
[1] 5
[1] 6
```

## Using a Dataframe to Store a Data Set

Throughout this text, you will make extensive use of R dataframe objects to perform data-mining and machine-learning operations on data sets. The following R program, DatasetDemo.R, creates a dataframe object and then displays the values it contains:

```
df = data.frame(
    x = c(35,34,32,37,33,33,31),
    y = c(79,54,52,77,59,74,44)
)
df
```

As the number of elements in your dataframe becomes large, you will often use the head function to display the first part of the data the dataframe contains:

```
> head(df)
```

Normally, you will load a .csv file that contains a data set into a dataframe, using the read.csv function:

```
df <- read.csv(file='filename.csv')
```

The following R program, LoadDataframe.R, loads the Auto-Mpg.csv data set that contains automotive gas mileage data. You can download the data set from this text's catalog page at go.jblearning.com/DataMining:

```
df <- read.csv(file='auto-mpg.csv')
head(df)
summary(df)
```

The program first loads the data set from the .csv file and then uses the head function to display the dataframe's starting data. Then the program uses the summary function to display a summary of the dataframe's fields. When you execute this program, it will display the following output:

```
> df <- read.csv(file='auto-mpg.csv')
> head(df)
  mpg cylinders displacement horsepower weight acceleration model.year origin
1  18         8          307        130   3504         12.0         70      1
2  15         8          350        165   3693         11.5         70      1
3  18         8          318        150   3436         11.0         70      1
4  16         8          304        150   3433         12.0         70      1
5  17         8          302        140   3449         10.5         70      1
6  15         8          429        198   4341         10.0         70      1
```

```
                    car.name
1 chevrolet chevelle Malibu
2          buick skylark 320
3          plymouth satellite
4              amc rebel sst
5                 ford torino
6           ford galaxie 500
> summary(df)
      mpg          cylinders       displacement      horsepower        weight
 Min.   : 2.40   Min.   :3.000   Min.   : 68.0   Min.   : 46.0   Min.   :1613
 1st Qu.:17.00   1st Qu.:4.000   1st Qu.:105.0   1st Qu.: 75.0   1st Qu.:2225
 Median :22.45   Median :4.000   Median :151.0   Median : 93.5   Median :2804
 Mean   :23.37   Mean   :5.472   Mean   :194.4   Mean   :104.5   Mean   :2978
 3rd Qu.:29.00   3rd Qu.:8.000   3rd Qu.:275.8   3rd Qu.:126.0   3rd Qu.:3615
 Max.   :46.60   Max.   :8.000   Max.   :455.0   Max.   :230.0   Max.   :5140

  acceleration      model.year         origin                   car.name
 Min.   : 8.00   Min.   :70.00    Min.   :1.000    amc matador      :  5
 1st Qu.:13.78   1st Qu.:73.00    1st Qu.:1.000    ford pinto       :  5
 Median :15.50   Median :76.00    Median :1.000    toyota corolla   :  5
 Mean   :15.54   Mean   :75.98    Mean   :1.577    amc gremlin      :  4
 3rd Qu.:17.02   3rd Qu.:79.00    3rd Qu.:2.000    amc hornet       :  4
 Max.   :24.80   Max.   :82.00    Max.   :3.000    chevrolet chevette:  4
                                                   (Other)          :365
```

After you load a data set, using the head and summary functions can provide you with insights into the dataframe's contents.

## Using Dataframe Column Names

When you work with dataframes, you may find it convenient to refer to columns using names. In such cases, you can use the names function to assign the column names:

```
names(df) <- c('a', 'b', 'c')
```

After you assign names to columns, you can refer to the columns using the $ and column name, as shown here:

```
df$a
```

The following statements illustrate the use of column names in R. The program loads sales data from a .csv file and then assigns names to each column:

```
sales = read.csv('somefile.csv')
colnames(df) <- c("March", "April", "May")
```

After you assign the names, you can refer to a column by name:

```
sales$May
[1] 30  40  35  55
```

Throughout this text, you will use column names to improve the readability of many data-set operations.

## Defining Your Own Functions

Throughout this text's section, you have made extensive use of R's built-in functions. R, like most programming languages, lets you define your own functions. To do so, you use the keyword function, specifying the name and parameters and grouping the statements within left and right braces, as shown here:

```
name <- function (arguments) {
          statement(s)
        }
```

As you can see, you assign a function to a variable with the function name you desire. The following statements, for example, create a function named Hello that uses print to display a message:

```
Hello <- function() {
  print("Hello, world!")
}
```

In this case, the function does not receive any parameter values. You must, however, include the empty parentheses. To call the function, you simply refer to its name:

```
> Hello()
[1] "Hello, world!"
```

The following statements create a function named addNumbers that returns the values of the three numbers it receives as parameters:

```
addNumbers <- function(a, b, c)
       return(a+b+c)
```

To use the function, you refer to the function name, providing the parameter values, as shown here:

```
> addNumbers(1, 2, 3)
[1] 6
```

When you pass parameters to an R function, you must specify variables (in the previous function, the variables a, b, and c) that will hold the parameter values. These variables and any other variables you create within the function are local to that function, meaning they are only known within the function and will not conflict with any variables outside of the function that have the same names.

R does support the concept of a global variable that is known throughout your program. To create a global variable, you use the global variable assignment operator (<<-) shown here:

```
someGlobalVariable <<- 1001
```

As you have learned, R assigns the functions you create to variable names. If you type the function variable name without the parentheses at the R prompt, R will display the function statements, as shown here:

```
> addValues
function(a, b, c) {
  return(a+b+c)
}
<bytecode: 0x0000000018abb738>
```

You can use this technique to display the statements for any R function. For example, the following displays the statements that comprise the Knn.reg function, which performs a K-nearest-neighbor's regression classification, which you will examine in Chapter 11, "Data Classification":

```
> library(FNN)
>
> knn.reg
function (train, test = NULL, y, k = 3, algorithm = c("kd_tree",
    "cover_tree", "brute"))
{
    algorithm <- match.arg(algorithm)
    train <- as.matrix(train)
    if (!is.null(test)) {
        if (is.null(dim(test)))
            dim(test) <- c(1, length(test))
        test <- as.matrix(test)
    }
    ntr <- nrow(train)
    p <- ncol(train)
    n <- ifelse(is.null(test), nrow(train), nrow(test))
    pred <- switch(algorithm, cover_tree = , kd_tree = , brute = {
        Z <- if (is.null(test)) get.knn(train, k, algorithm)
            else get.knnx(train,
              test, k, algorithm)
        rowMeans(matrix(y[Z$nn.index], ncol = k))
    })
    if (is.null(test)) {
        residuals <- y - pred
        PRESS <- sum(residuals^2)
        R2 <- 1 - PRESS/sum((y - mean(y))^2)
    }
    else {
        residuals <- PRESS <- R2 <- NULL
    }
    res <- list(call = match.call(), k = k, n = n, pred = pred,
        residuals = residuals, PRESS = PRESS, R2Pred = R2)
    class(res) <- if (!is.null(test))
        "knnReg"
    else "knnRegCV"
```

```
        return(res)
}
<bytecode: 0x0000000005778b18>
<environment: namespace:FNN>
```

By displaying function statements in this way, you can learn not only a function's underlying algorithm but you also will see many good R programming practices.

## Using Default Function Parameters

Many of the R functions you will examine throughout this text will make use of the default parameter values, meaning if you don't specify a value for the parameter when you call the function, R will use the default.

When you create your own functions, you can specify a parameter's default values by using the assignment operator within the parameter list, as shown here:

```
someFunction <- function(a = 100, b = 200)
    return(a + b)
```

As you can see, to specify the default values, you use the assignment operator to assign a value to one or more of the parameter variables. The following R script, UseDefault.R, illustrates the use of default parameter values:

```
someFunction <- function(a = 100, b = 200)
    return(a + b)

print(someFunction())
print(someFunction(500))
print(someFunction(0, 0))
print(someFunction(b=300))
```

The script calls the function with different parameter values, specifying no parameters, which uses both default values; one parameter based on order; and by name (b=300). When you execute this script, it will display the following output:

```
> print(someFunction())
[1] 300
> print(someFunction(500))
[1] 700
> print(someFunction(0, 0))
[1] 0
> print(someFunction(b=300))
[1] 400
```

## Using R Packages

An R package contains a set of functions you can use to perform specific tasks, such as clustering, classifying, or plotting data. To use a package within your R programs, you must first import the package using the import statement:

```
import packageName
```

The following R program, for example, KmeansPlusPlus.R, uses Kmeans++ clustering, discussed in Chapter 11, "Data Clustering," to cluster and chart data. The program imports several libraries, which it uses to perform its processing:

```
library(factoextra)
library(cluster)
library(fpc)
library(LICORS)

df = data.frame(
     x = c(35,34,32,37,33,33,31,27,35,34,62,54,57,
           47,50,57,59,52,61,47,50,48,39,40,45,47,39,44,50,48),
     y = c(79,54,52,77,59,74,73,57,69,75,51,32,40,
           47,53,36,35,58,59,50,23,22,13,14,22,7,29,25,9,8)
     )

clusters <- kmeanspp(df, 3)
plotcluster(df, clusters$cluster)

points <- fviz_cluster(clusters, geom = "point",   data = df) +
ggtitle("K = 3")
```

When you execute this program, it will display the output shown in **FIGURE 8.20**.

Before you can use a package, it must reside on your system. If, when you try to use a package, R displays a message that the package was not found, you will need to install it:

```
install.packages("packageName")
```

To display the packages installed on your system, you can use the installed.packages function:

```
> installed.packages()
                    Package
abind             "abind"
arules            "arules"
assertthat        "assertthat"
BH                "BH"
bitops            "bitops"
C50               "C50"
car               "car"
    :                 :
```

## Object-Oriented Programming with R

R is an object-oriented programming language, which lets you define classes and leverage inheritance. Throughout this text you will leverage many R-based objects as you perform different machine-learning and data-mining operations, such as the dataframe object, into which you will load and access data sets. As you work with such objects within your programs, you will make extensive use of the dot (.) operator, such as:

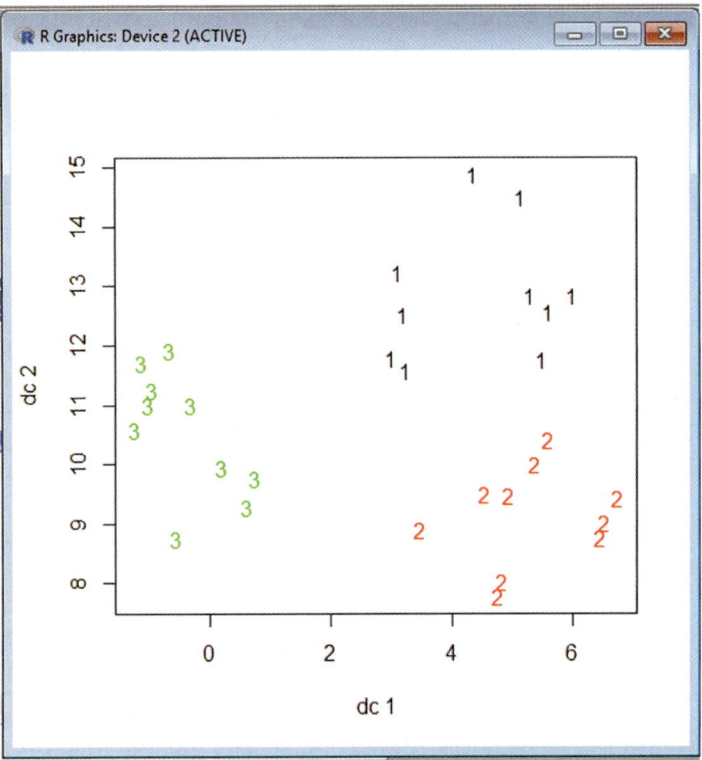

**FIGURE 8.20** Using KMeans++ clustering to group items.

```
df = read.csv("SomeDataSet.csv")
```

The R programs the text presents will not require you to create your own classes. As such, the class creation and inheritance process will not be covered.

## Hands-On Visual Studio

Programmers make extensive use of integrated development environments (IDEs) to create, run, and debug programs. For years, C# developers have used Microsoft Visual Studio to create .NET applications. Visual Studio is one of the most widely used IDEs. Because of the success and popularity of Python and R, Microsoft has extended Visual Studio to support them. Using Visual Studio, you can create, run, and debug the programs you create in Python and R. At the time of this writing, the current version of Visual Studio has turned off support for R; however, because the support was available in previous versions, I expect Visual Studio to start supporting it again.

In this section, you will use Visual Studio to create Python scripts. You will learn that Visual Studio not only lets you build and run Python scripts, it also provides several built-in templates you can use to quickly create applications that perform clustering, classification, and regression.

To start, download and install Visual Studio (Community Edition) from the Microsoft website, as shown in **FIGURE 8.21**.

Visual Studio uses a version of Python called IronPython, which you must install. To do so, download and install the software from the IronPython website shown in **FIGURE 8.22**.

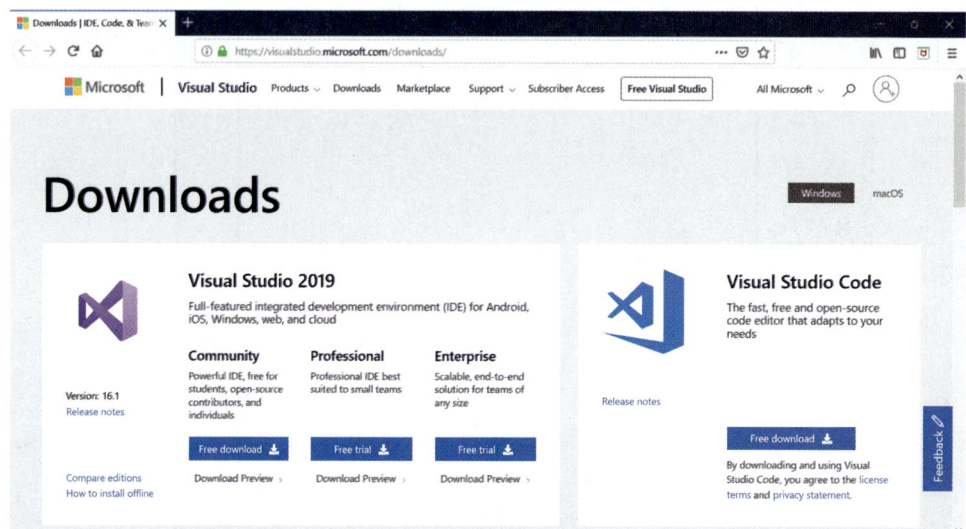

**FIGURE 8.21** Download and install Visual Studio (Community Edition) from the Microsoft website.

Used with permission of Microsoft

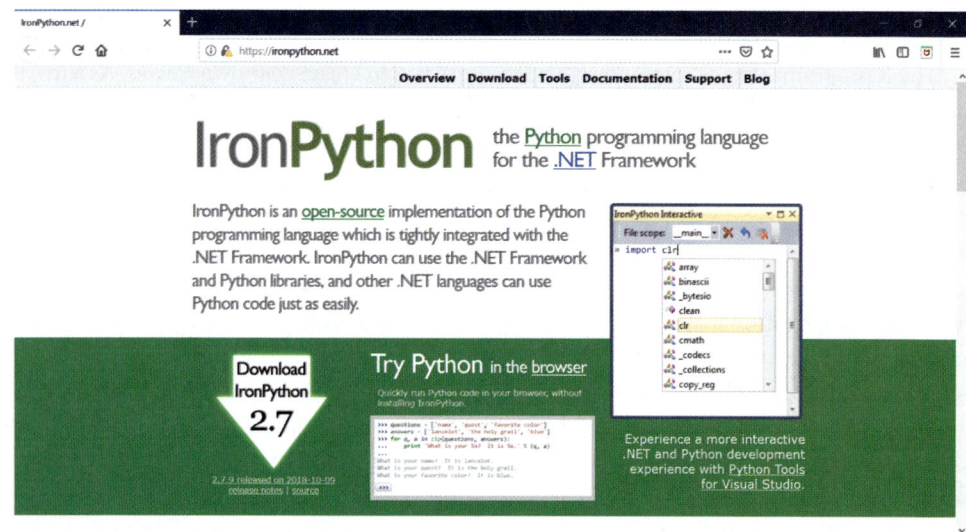

**FIGURE 8.22** Download and install IronPython.

Used with permission of .NET Foundation

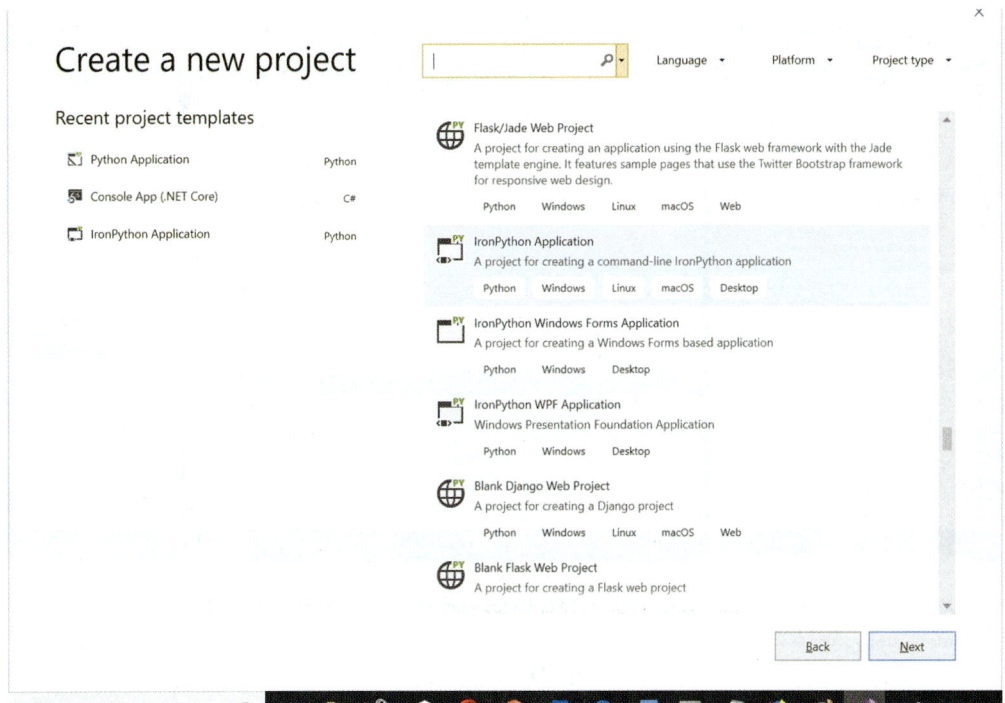

**FIGURE 8.23** Project templates within Visual Studio.

Used with permission of Python Software Foundation

After you start Visual Studio, click Create new project. Visual Studio will display its project templates, as shown in **FIGURE 8.23**.

Scroll through the Visual Studio project templates until you locate the IronPython application. If you do not find an IronPython project template, you will need to use the Visual Studio Installer (which you run from the Windows Start menu) to install the Python project templates, as well as the data science and analytical templates.

Locate and click on the IronPython application project template. Visual Studio will display a dialog box prompting you to specify a project name and folder location. Use the default values and click Create. Visual Studio will create a project that contains a "Hello, world" print statement, as shown in **FIGURE 8.24**.

Select the Debug menu Start without debugging option. Visual Studio will run the script, displaying the "Hello, world" message. If you encounter an error, make sure you have installed IronPython as previously discussed.

Select the File menu Close option. Then select the Create New Project option to create a new project. Visual Studio will again display its project templates. Scroll through the project list and click on the Classifier Project. Visual Studio will create and display the project, as shown in **FIGURE 8.25**.

Within the Cookie Cutter box that appears on the left side of your screen, click on python-sklearn-classify-cookiecutter and click Next. Visual Studio will display the Cookiecutter dialog box.

**402** CHAPTER 8 Programming Data Mining and Analytic Solutions

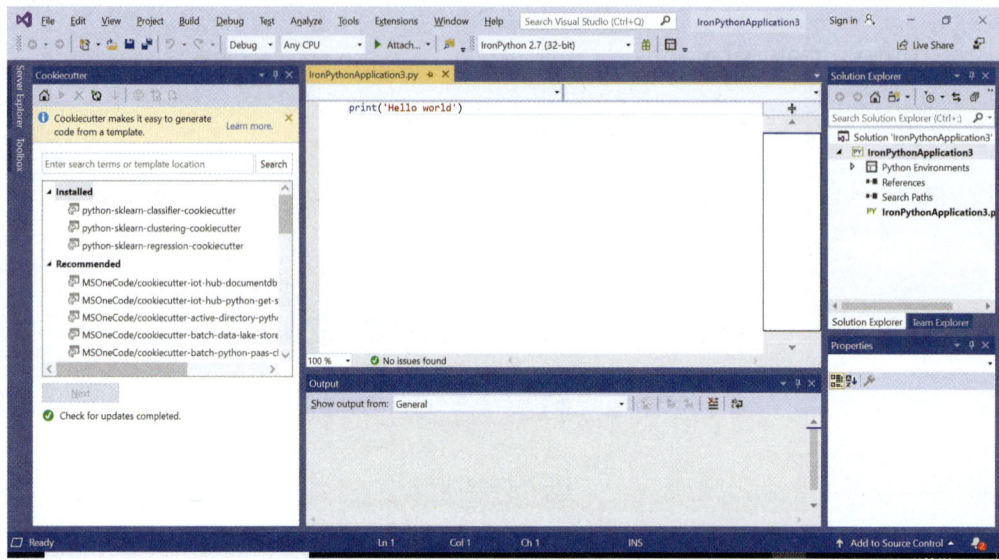

**FIGURE 8.24** Creating a "Hello, world" Python script within Visual Studio.
Used with permission of Python Software Foundation

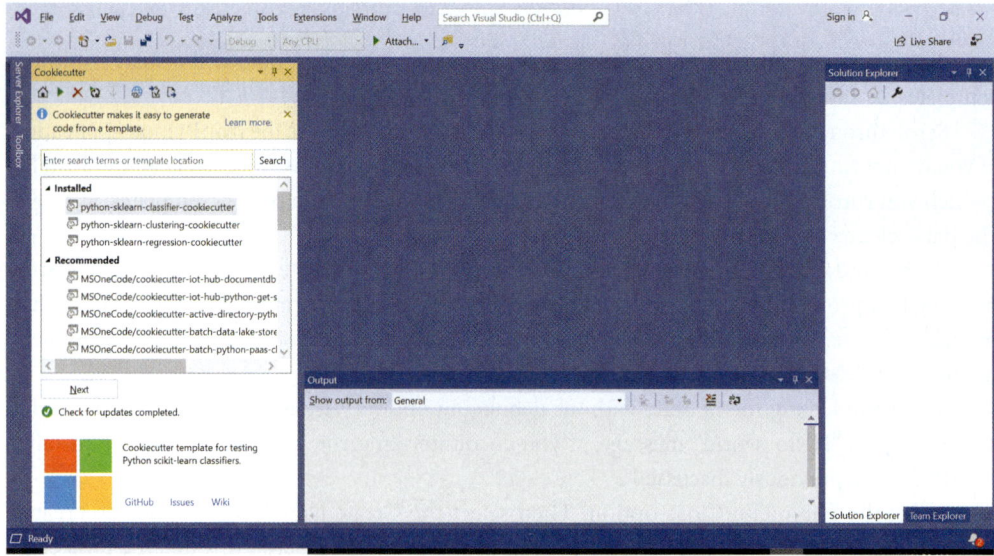

**FIGURE 8.25** Creating a machine-learning classification project in Visual Studio.
Used with permission of Python Software Foundation

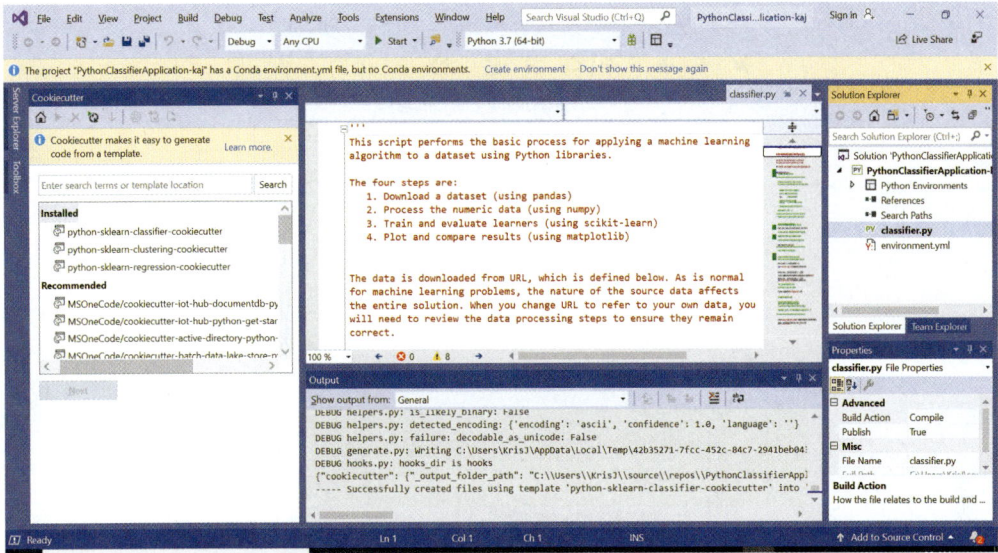

**FIGURE 8.26** The Visual Studio prompt to create an environment.

Used with permission of Python Software Foundation

Within the Cookiecutter box, click Create and Open project. Then select the Debug menu Start debugging option. Visual Studio will display a banner across the top of its window stating it must create an environment, as shown in **FIGURE 8.26**.

Within the banner, click the Create Environment link. Visual Studio will display the Add Environment dialog box prompting you to create an environment. Click the Create button. Visual Studio will create the environment, which may take a few moments. Select the Debug menu Continue option. You may have to press Enter to continue. Then select the Debug menu Debug option. Visual Studio will run the script, displaying the chart shown in **FIGURE 8.27**.

For now, it's not important that you examine and understand the code. You can revisit the code after you read Chapter 11, "Data Classification."

Within the Visual Studio code window, press Ctrl+A to select all the code and then press the Del key to delete the code. Then type the following code, which will create the clustering chart shown in **FIGURE 8.28**. The code, which you will examine in Chapter 10, "Data Clustering," uses the K-means algorithm to perform a clustering operation:

```
import matplotlib.pyplot as plt
from sklearn.cluster import KMeans
from pandas import DataFrame
```

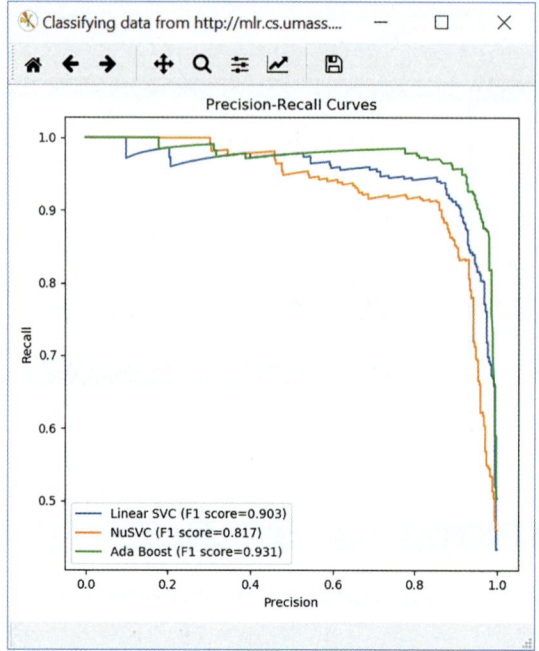

**FIGURE 8.27** Displaying a chart that summarizes classification results.

Used with permission of Python Software Foundation

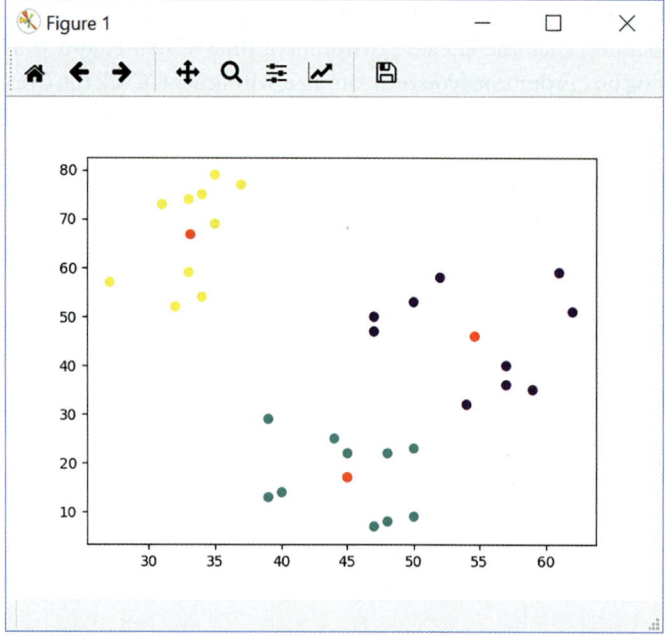

**FIGURE 8.28** Using Visual Studio to create and run your own clustering program.

Used with permission of Python Software Foundation

```
Data = {
        'x': [35,34,32,37,33,33,31,27,35,34,62,54,57,
              47,50,57,59,52,61,47,50,48,39,40,45,47,39,44,50,48],
        'y': [79,54,52,77,59,74,73,57,69,75,51,32,40,47,
              53,36,35,58,59,50,23,22,13,14,22,7,29,25,9,8]
       }

df = DataFrame(Data,columns=['x','y'])

kmeans = KMeans(n_clusters=3).fit(df)
centroids = kmeans.cluster_centers_

plt.scatter(df['x'], df['y'], c=kmeans.labels_.astype(float))
plt.scatter(centroids[:, 0], centroids[:, 1], c='red')
plt.show()
```

Click the Debug menu Start without debugging option. Visual Studio will run the script, displaying the cluster chart shown in Figure 8.28.

Use the File menu Close solution option to close the project.

## Using Visual Studio to Create a Regression Program

Select the Create new project option. Visual Studio will display its list of project templates. Within the list, scroll down and click on the Regression project. Visual Studio will open the project template. Within the Cookie Cutter box, click on the python-sklear-regression-cookiecutter and click Next. Visual Studio will display the Cookie Cutter dialog box. Click Create and open project to add it to your solution.

Select the Debug menu Start debugging option. Visual Studio will again display the yellow banner at the top of the window prompting you to create an environment. Click the Create environment link followed by Create to add the environment to your solution. Select the Debug menu Continue option. Again, you may have to press Enter through one or two screens. Then select the Debug menu Start debugging option. Visual Studio will run the script, displaying the output shown in **FIGURE 8.29**.

Again, you do not need to examine the code now. Rather, after you read Chapter 12, "Predictive Analytics," take time to circle back here to review the code.

Select the File menu Close solution option. Repeat the steps you just performed to create a clustering project. When you run the project, Visual Studio will display the output shown in **FIGURE 8.30**.

# CHAPTER 8 Programming Data Mining and Analytic Solutions

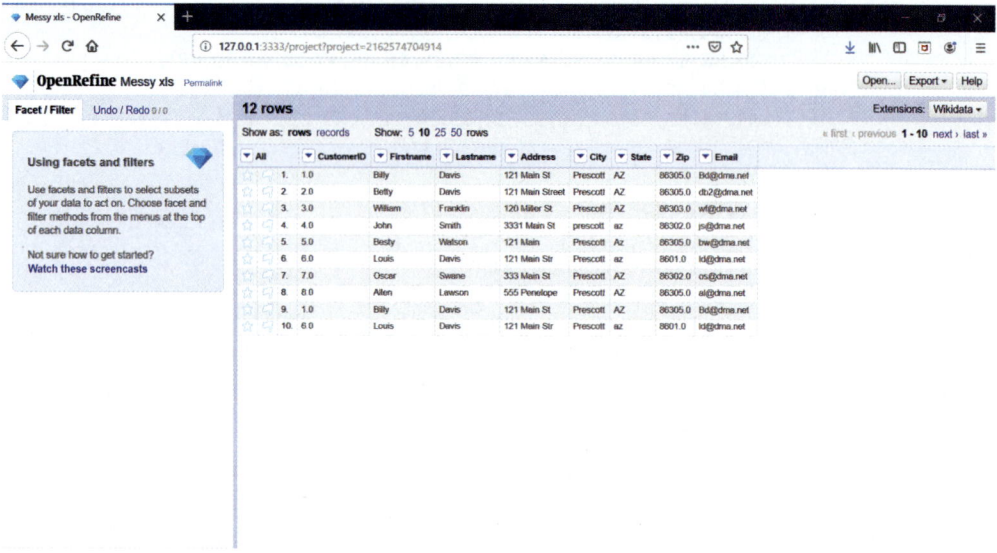

**FIGURE 8.29** Displaying the regression results within Visual Studio.

Used with permission from Microsoft

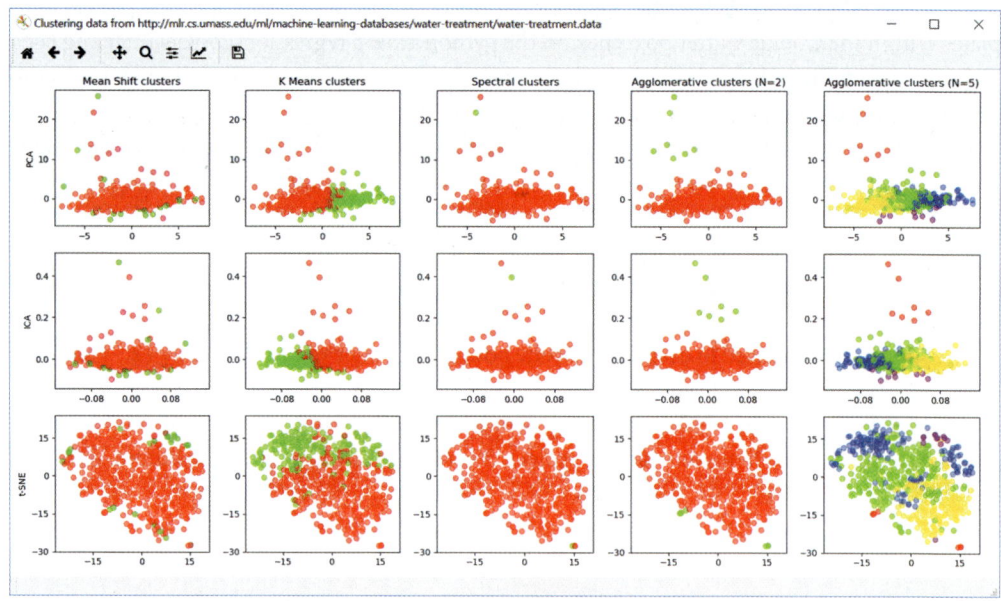

**FIGURE 8.30** Using the Visual Studio clustering template.

Clustering data from: http://mlr.cs.umass.edu/ml/machine-learning-databases/water-treatment/water-treatment.data

## Summary

Throughout this text, you will make extensive use of the Python and R programming languages to perform machine-learning and data-mining operations. As you learned, Python is one of the world's most popular programming languages and is used to create solutions that range from websites, data mining, machine learning, visualization, and more. Python is open-source software, which users can download, install, and use for free.

Python is an interpreted language, as opposed to a compiled language, for which the Python interpreter executes one statement at a time. Developers can interactively execute one statement at a time via the Python interpreter's prompt, or developers can group statements into a text file, called a Python script, which they then direct Python to execute.

Programmers use variables to store information as a program executes. In Python, a script creates a variable simply by assigning a value to the variable's name, using the equals sign (=), which is the Python assignment operator. Python variable names must start with a letter or underscore and cannot be the same as a Python reserved word. Data-mining programs often assign large amounts of data to a variable. In Python, when you are done using a variable, you can delete it to free up the memory the variable contained.

Python recognizes the pound sign (#) as the start of a comment. When Python encounters the #, it will ignore any remaining text on that line. Python provides arithmetic operators similar to those found in other programming languages, such as + for addition, - for subtraction, * for multiplication, and / for division. To allow scripts to make comparisons, Python provides a set of relational operators, such as < for less than, > for greater than, and so on. Often, scripts must test multiple conditions. As such, Python provides the AND and OR logical operators. In addition, Python provides a NOT operator.

An array is a data structure that can store multiple values of the same type. Python implements arrays using lists. A list can be one-dimensional (a vector) or multidimensional. To access the values within a list, developers specify an index that corresponds to the location they desire. Python uses zero-based indexing, which means the first item in the list resides at the index location 0 (someList[0]).

To allow scripts to evaluate a condition and perform statements accordingly, Python provides the if-elif-else statements. Unlike other programming languages that use braces {} to group related statements, Python instead relies on statement indentation to group statements.

Python provides a ternary operator, which is like a shorthand notation for an if-else statement, which takes the form (falseResult, trueResult)[condition]. To allow programs to repeat a set of statements until a condition is met, Python supports the for and while statements. Python is a procedural-programming language, in that it supports functions. A function is a named (related) group of statements that perform processing that solves a specific task. Python provides built-in functions, such as print, which you call by specifying the function name and parameter values within parentheses. Python developers use the def keyword to specify the function name and statements the function performs to accomplish its task. Within the function, developers indent the function statements to indicate their relationship to the function. Parameters are values passed to a function. Python supports default parameter values. If a function call does not include values for all parameters, Python will use the default values (if they exist, or it will display an error otherwise).

Python is an object-oriented language, in that it supports class definitions and object instances. To define an object class, developers use the Python def statement. To perform data-mining operations, Python scripts make extensive use of dataframe objects. You can think of a dataframe as a two-dimensional table that holds a data-set's values. Since Python's release in 1991, developers have created over 170,000 libraries, each of which holds code that performs specific tasks, which you may be able to use within the scripts you create. To use a Python library, the library code must exist on your system. To download and install a Python library, developers use the PIP command. Then you use the import statement to include the library code within your script.

To perform data-mining and machine-learning operations in this chapter, you will make extensive use of the following Python libraries:

- pandas, which defines the dataframe object
- numpy, which provides functions and data structures for numeric operations
- matplotlib for plotting charts
- sklearn, which defines data structures and functions that support machine-learning and data-mining operations such as clustering, classification, and regression

R has become one of the most popular programming languages for data mining and machine learning. It is open-source software, which users can download, install, and use for free. R is an interpreted language, as opposed to a compiled language, for which the R interpreter executes one statement at a time. Developers can interactively execute one statement at a time via the R interpreter's prompt, or developers can group statements into a text file, called an R program or script, which they then direct R to execute.

Programmers use variables to store information as a program executes. In R, a script creates a variable simply by assigning a value to the variable's name, using <-, which is the R assignment operator. R variable names must start with a letter or dot and cannot be the same as an R reserved word. To view a list of variables you have created in the current session, you use the R ls function.

R recognizes the pound sign (#) as the start of a comment. When R encounters the #, it will ignore any remaining text on that line.

R provides arithmetic operators similar to those found in other programming languages, such as + for addition, - for subtraction, * for multiplication, and / for division. To allow scripts to make comparisons, R provides a set of relational operators, such as < for less than, > for greater than, and so on. Often, scripts must test multiple conditions. As such, R provides the AND (&&) and OR (||) logical operators. In addition, R provides a NOT operator (!).

An array is a data structure that can store multiple values of the same type. An array can be one-dimensional (a vector) or multidimensional. To access the values within a list, developers specify an index that corresponds to the location they desire. R does not use zero-based indexing, which means the first item in the list resides at the index location 1 (someList[1]).

To allow scripts to evaluate a condition and perform statements accordingly, R provides the if-else statements. R uses left and right braces {} to group related statements. To allow programs to repeat a set of statements until a condition is met, R supports the for, repeat, and while statements.

R is a procedural programming language, in that it supports functions. A function is a named (related) group of statements that perform processing that solves a specific task. R provides built-in functions, such as print, which you call by specifying the function name and parameter values within parentheses. Using the function keyword, R developers specify the name of the function and the statements the function performs to accomplish its task. Within the function, developers group the function statements using left and right braces {} to indicate the statements' relationship to the function. Parameters are values passed to a function. R supports default parameter values. If a function call does not include values for all parameters, R will use the default values (if they exist, or it will display an error otherwise).

To perform data-mining operations, R scripts make extensive use of dataframe objects. You can think of a dataframe as a two-dimensional table that holds a data-set's values. R developers have created thousands of libraries, each of which holds code that performs specific tasks, which you may be able to use within the scripts you create. To use an R library, the library code must exist on your system. To download and install an R library, developers use the install.packages function. Then you use the import statement to include the library code within your script.

## Key Terms

| | | |
|---|---|---|
| Arithmetic operators | Module | Relational operators |
| Compiler | Operator precedence | Script |
| Conditional processing | Package | sklearn |
| Interpreter | pandas | Syntax |
| Iterative processing | PIP | Ternary operator |
| Logical operator | PyPi | Zero-based indexing |

## Review

1. Describe the Python features that make it well suited for data mining and machine learning.
2. Describe the R features that make it well suited for data mining and machine learning.
3. Compare and contrast a compiled versus an interpreted programming language.
4. Build and execute the Python code examples this chapter presents.
5. Build and execute the R code examples this chapter presents.

6. Using Python, load the Titanic data set as a data frame and then use the summary function to display specifics about the data set. You can download the Titanic data set from this text's catalog page at go.jblearning.com/DataMining.
7. Using R, load the Titanic data set as a data frame and then use the summary function to display specifics about the data set. You can download the Titanic data set from this text's catalog page at go.jblearning.com/DataMining.
8. Using a Python for loop, display the contents of the Titanic data set.
9. Using an R for loop, display the contents of the Titanic data set.
10. Using Visual Studio, create and run the projects presented in this chapter.

# CHAPTER 9

# Data Preprocessing and Cleansing

## Chapter Goals and Objectives

- Define and describe data cleansing.
- Describe data-quality attributes.
- Define and describe data governance.
- Describe the role of a data-quality assessment framework (**DQAF**).

Database developers today face greater amounts of data from more sources than ever before. Unfortunately, the many sources of data bring with them a greater chance of bad data. The decades-old adage of "garbage in, garbage out" remains an ever-present data threat. Data analysts and database developers must be constantly aware of the risks of bad data and must work to put in place safeguards against factors that reduce the quality of data and, ultimately, reduce the quality of the decisions made that are based upon such data.

**Data cleansing** is the process of detecting, correcting, and removing errors and inconsistencies from data. Such errors may be the result of bad user input, which may include incorrect spelling, numeric entry errors, inconsistent abbreviation of names and addresses, and so on. Likewise, some errors may occur due to a faulty sensor on an Internet of Things (IoT) device or a noisy data transmission line. Regardless of the cause of the error, the goal of data cleansing is higher quality data. Data cleansing is normally not a one-time event. Database developers and data analysts must constantly monitor and assess the quality of incoming data. The database developers may create and execute queries to clean up the data, which they then integrate into one or more data-cleansing scripts, which can run automatically in the future.

This chapter examines data-cleansing challenges and approaches. By the time you complete this chapter, you will understand the following key concepts:

- **Data quality** is a measure of the data's suitability for use.
- Attributes that contribute to data quality include accuracy, completeness, consistency, and conformity.
- Regardless of the content a data set contains, the techniques you will apply to validate the data will be similar.
- Data cleansing is the process of detecting, correcting, and removing errors and inconsistences from data.
- Governance describes the administrative steps an individual or group performs or oversees. Most companies establish a data-governance board to oversee data operations, master data management, and data quality. The goal of the data-governance board is to continually improve the quality of data.
- Database developers often refer to the steps they must perform to transform and cleanse data as "**data wrangling**." To wrangle data, developers can use Structured Query Language (SQL) queries, create a custom application, or use a third-party tool.
- To define quality in terms of a greater number of factors, many companies use the data quality assessment framework (DQAF), which specifies 48 quality factors.

## Understanding and Measuring Data Quality

Ask several different users within an organization about the quality of their data, and you will often get many different responses about the same data. Users who have experienced a past data glitch will be suspect of all data. In contrast, the developers who corrected the glitch will insist that the quality of the data is fine. Despite such differences of opinion, you will likely get everyone to agree that it should be a goal for the quality of data to continually improve, as shown in **FIGURE 9.1**.

With the goal of data quality in mind, you should begin the data-cleansing process by establishing a good definition of what quality data means. Data quality is a measure of the data's suitability for use. Data quality can range from high to low.

- Accuracy: the degree to which the data correctly represent the underlying real-world values, such as all temperatures from a sensor in the correct range.
- Completeness: the degree to which the data represent all required values, such as a data set that should contain an hour of data, for a sensor that reports every second, having 100% of the data values.
- Consistency: the degree to which similar or related data values align throughout the data set, such as each occurrence of an address having the same ZIP code.
- Conformity: the degree to which the data values align with the company's **business rules**, such as the company will measure and store sensor values in 1-second intervals.

Most business leaders will agree that for something to be manageable, it must be measurable. With respect to the data-quality attributes, you can assign a numeric score to each attribute that

## Installing This Text's Companion CHAPTER09 Database

This chapter presents many queries that leverage tables contained in the CHAPTER09 database, which you can download and install from this text's catalog page at go.jblearning.com/DataMining. To use this database, use the link to open the file within a text editor. Then cut and paste the SQL queries the file contains, as discussed in Chapter 6, "Keep SQL in Your Toolset," into the MySQL Workbench. When you execute the queries, SQL will create the CHAPTER09 databases, the tables they contain, and select CHAPTER09 as the database for use, as shown in **FIGURE A**.

```
CREATE Database CHAPTER09;

USE CHAPTER09;

CREATE TABLE Sensor (
    Record INT,
    SensorValue INT
);

INSERT INTO Sensor Values (1, 50);
INSERT INTO Sensor Values (2, 52);
INSERT INTO Sensor Values (3, 54);
INSERT INTO Sensor Values (4, 50);
INSERT INTO Sensor Values (5, 52);
INSERT INTO Sensor Values (6, 56);
INSERT INTO Sensor Values (8, 58);
INSERT INTO Sensor Values (9, 60);
INSERT INTO Sensor Values (10, 60);
INSERT INTO Sensor Values (11, 50);
INSERT INTO Sensor Values (12, 52);
INSERT INTO Sensor Values (13, 54);
INSERT INTO Sensor Values (14, 50);
```

**FIGURE A** Installing this chapter's data files from this text's catalog page within the MySQL Workbench.

Copyright Oracle and its affiliates. Used with permission

represents the attribute's current state. By combining the attribute measures, you can determine an overall data-quality assessment, as shown in **TABLE 9.1**.

To determine measures for each data-quality attribute, you will likely need to audit your data sources and perform statistical tests and analysis on the data. Such analysis will examine individual values, sets of related values, and the entire data set as a whole. Analysts often learn that the quality of data from one source can differ significantly from that of another, as shown in **FIGURE 9.2**. The sections that follow examine common data-quality considerations.

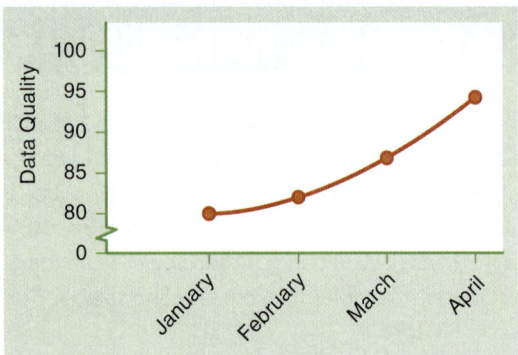

**FIGURE 9.1** Continually improving data quality should be a business goal and priority.

**TABLE 9.1** Calculating Data Quality Based upon Attribute Measurements

| Quality Attribute | Current State Score |
|---|---|
| Accuracy | 97 |
| Completeness | 99 |
| Consistency | 90 |
| Conformity | 88 |
|  |  |
| Data Quality (Average of 97, 99, 90, 88) | 93.5 |

# Common Data Validation Techniques

Depending on the volume and complexity of data your company processes, determining how to measure the underlying data quality may feel like a daunting task. Fortunately, regardless of the specific data content, you can apply the following techniques to assess your data. To begin, you can consider your data-set values one field at a time, evaluating the field's values with respect to the quality attributes just discussed.

## Testing for Nonexistent Records, Fields, and Null Values

Completeness is a measure of the degree to which the data represent all required values. To measure the completeness of your data, you can determine first what percentage of the expected data values are present within your data set. For example, if a process collects a sensor's values every second, for each hour of data, you should have 3,600 records:

```
(60 records/minute)*(60 minutes/hour) = 3,600 records/hour
```

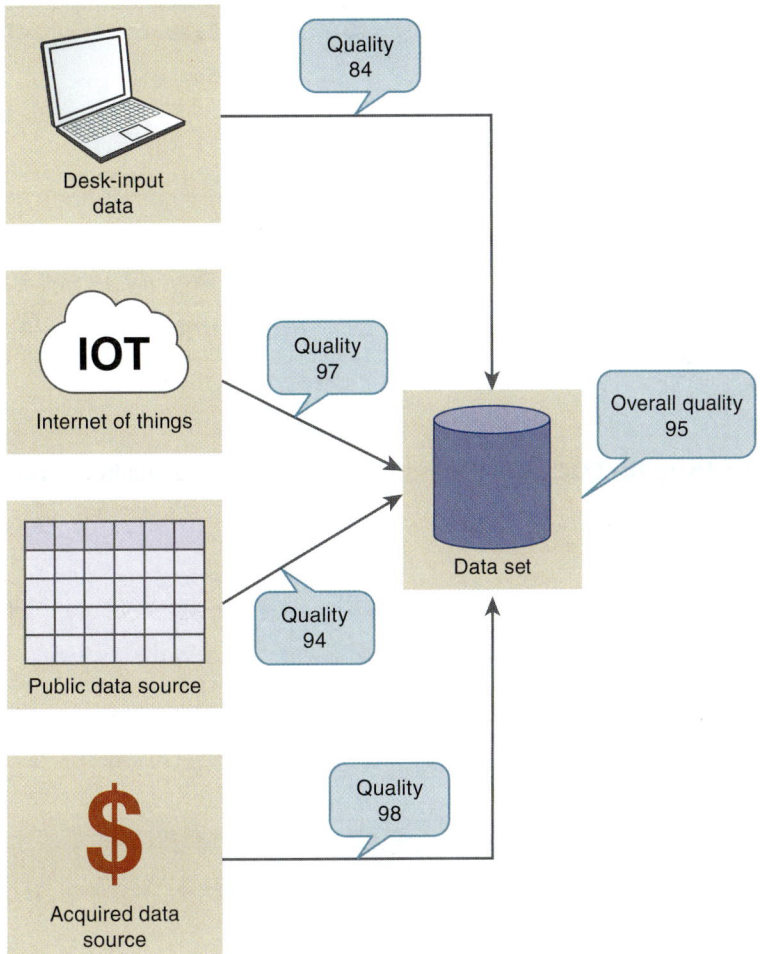

**FIGURE 9.2** The quality of data may vary by data source, which, in turn, affects the overall data-quality metric.

For simplicity, assume you record and store 1 minute of data (60 seconds). You can compare the number of records you have to the number of records you expect:

SELECT COUNT(*)/60 AS 'Completeness' FROM Sensor

When you execute this query, SQL will display the completeness value shown in **FIGURE 9.3**.

In this case, the completeness value is greater than 1—an indicator that your table has duplicate records. Later in this chapter, you will learn how to quickly identify the duplicate records.

Next, for each field within every record, you will want to determine the percentage of fields that do not have values:

SELECT COUNT(*) FROM SensorTable WHERE SensorValue IS NULL

# CHAPTER 9 Data Preprocessing and Cleansing

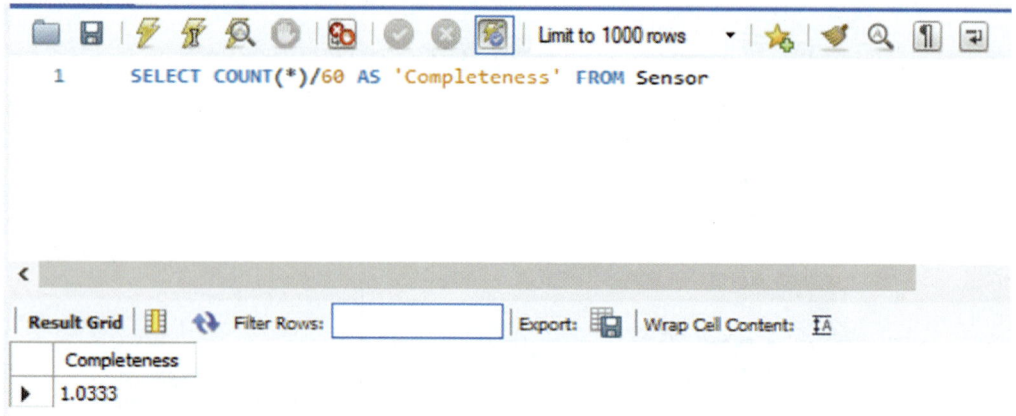

**FIGURE 9.3** Using the SQL COUNT function to determine the number of records a table contains.

Copyright Oracle and its affiliates. Used with permission

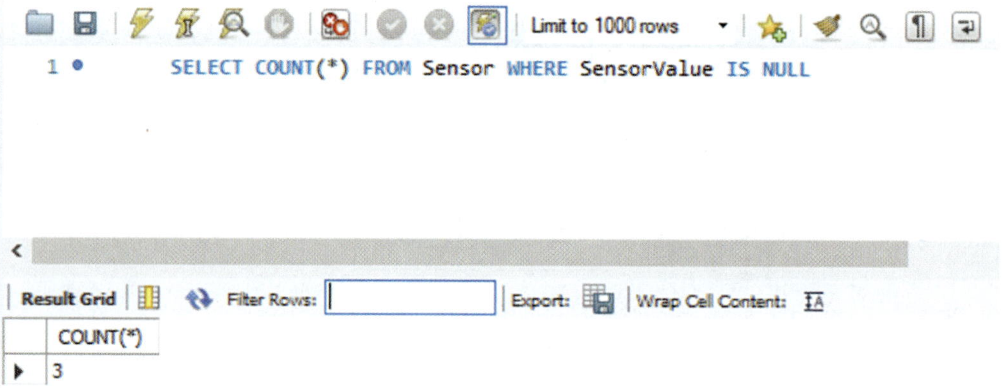

**FIGURE 9.4** Displaying a count of records for which a specified field is NULL.

Copyright Oracle and its affiliates. Used with permission

When you execute this query, SQL will display the count of records for which the SensorValue field contains the NULL value, as shown in **FIGURE 9.4**.

If you find that NULL values exist, you can display those records using the following query:

```
SELECT * FROM Sensor WHERE SensorValue IS NULL
```

When you execute this query, SQL will display the records shown in **FIGURE 9.5**.

## Understanding and Measuring Data Quality

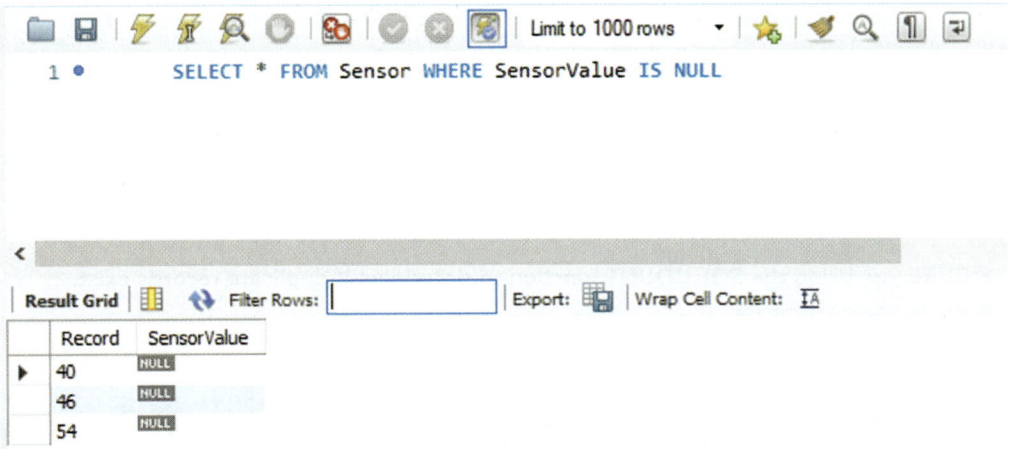

**FIGURE 9.5** Displaying field values in the Sensor table that have the NULL value.

*Note:* Many database systems use NaN (which stands for Not a Number) for values that cannot exist, such as some number divided by zero. As you audit your data, you may also want to search for fields with the NaN value. MySQL represents such values as NULL.

Copyright Oracle and its affiliates. Used with permission

## Testing for Duplicate Values

Depending on the size of your data set, quickly determining if duplicate records exists can seem a challenging process—you likely cannot determine the duplicate records at a glance. To determine if the data set contains duplicate records, first determine the number of records the data set contains:

```
SELECT COUNT(*) AS 'Actual Record Count' FROM Customers
```

Next, determine the number of DISTINCT records in the set:

```
SELECT DISTINCT COUNT(*) AS 'Distinct Record Count' FROM
Customers
```

If the two queries return the same count, the data set does not have duplicate records. If the first query contains more records than the second, duplicate records exist. **FIGURE 9.6** displays the results of these two queries.

Next, to determine which records have duplicates, issue the following query:

```
SELECT *, COUNT(*) FROM Customers
GROUP BY CustomerID, FirstName, LastName
HAVING Count(*) > 1
```

When you execute this query, SQL will display the duplicate records, as shown in **FIGURE 9.7**.

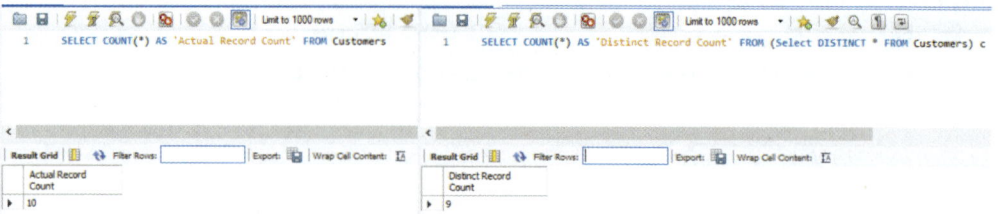

**FIGURE 9.6** Using the SQL COUNT function to determine if duplicate records exist.
Copyright Oracle and its affiliates. Used with permission

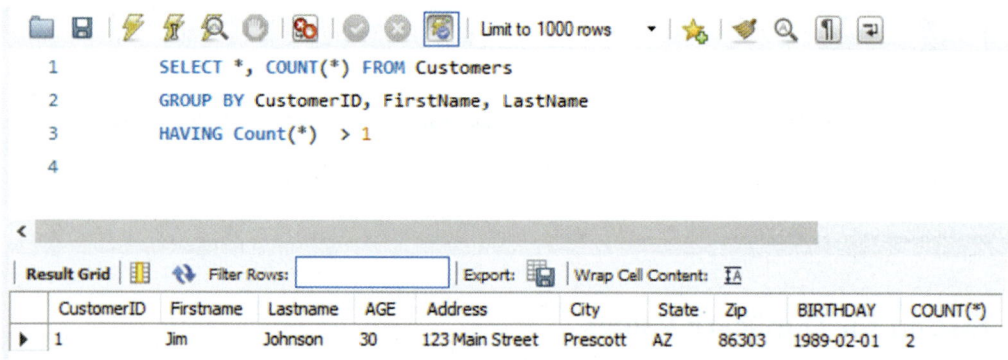

**FIGURE 9.7** Displaying duplicate records in the Customers table.
Copyright Oracle and its affiliates. Used with permission

In this case, by grouping on three key fields, we have a very high probability that the records are the same. To be exact, you can group on all the fields. In this case, if you examine the Customers table, you would find the duplicate records. This query, however, would not detect a customer who is in the system twice but with different customer IDs. To detect those customers, you would issue the following query that groups records on each field except the CustomerID:

```
SELECT *, COUNT(*) FROM Customers
GROUP BY FirstName, LastName, Age, Address, City, State, Zip, Birthday
HAVING COUNT(*) > 1
```

The following query performs a similar operation on the Sensors table to display duplicate records:

```
SELECT Record, SensorValue, COUNT(*) FROM Sensor
   GROUP BY Record, SensorValue HAVING Count(*) > 1
```

When you execute this query, SQL will display the duplicate records, as shown in **FIGURE 9.8**.

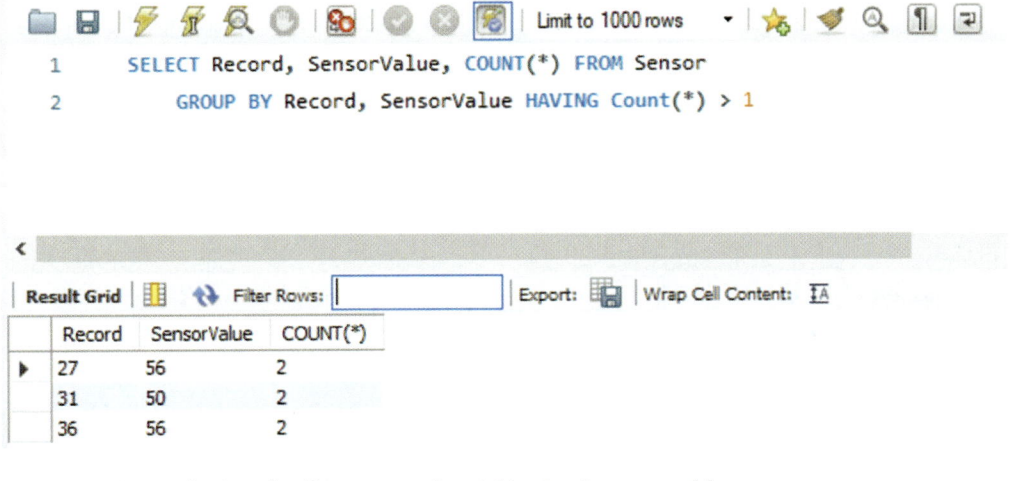

**FIGURE 9.8** Displaying duplicate records within the Sensors table.
Copyright Oracle and its affiliates. Used with permission

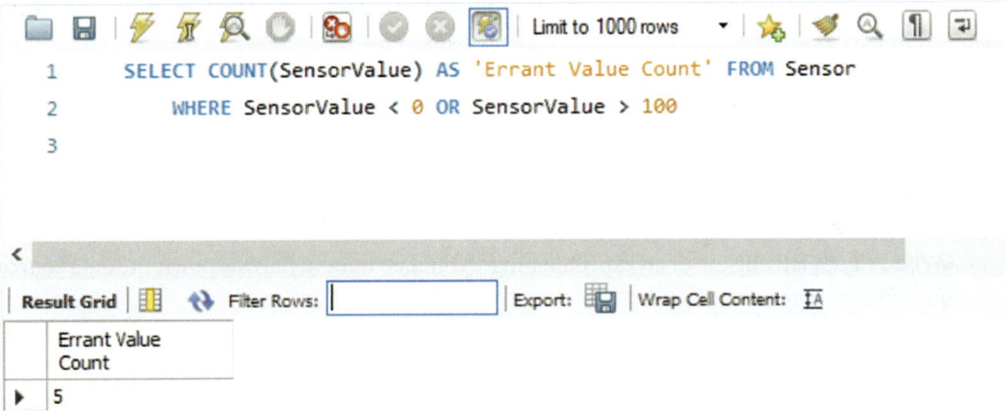

**FIGURE 9.9** Displaying a count of records, the values of which fall outside of an expected value.
Copyright Oracle and its affiliates. Used with permission

## Testing Value-Range Compliance

Accuracy is a measure of the degree to which the data correctly represent the corresponding real-world values. Assume, for example, that a sensor should only produce values in the range 0–100. To begin your accuracy measurement, you should test to ensure that all the data values are in the range:

```
SELECT COUNT(SensorValue) AS 'Errant Value Count' FROM Sensor
WHERE SensorValue < 0 OR SensorValue > 100
```

In this case, the query will display a count of records that have values outside of the range, as shown in **FIGURE 9.9**.

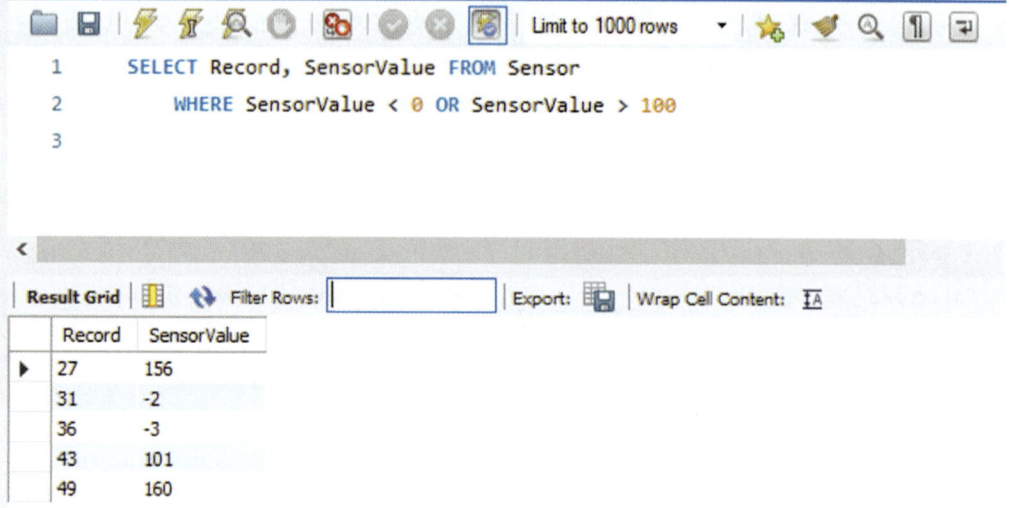

**FIGURE 9.10** Displaying records for which a field's value falls outside of an expected range.

Copyright Oracle and its affiliates. Used with permission

To display the actual value that falls outside of the expected value range, issue the following query:

```
SELECT Record, SensorValue FROM Sensor
    WHERE SensorValue < 0 OR SensorValue > 100
```

When you execute this query, SQL will display the output shown in **FIGURE 9.10**.

When values fall outside of an expected range, you may want to narrow down the data source in your effort to detect the cause.

## Testing Value-Pair Consistency

Depending on your data, there may be times when you can leverage two or more related fields to validate each. Assume, for example, you have the Customers table data shown in **FIGURE 9.11**.

As you can see, the table contains each customer's birth date data in the form yyyy-mm-dd, as well as a field containing the customer's age. Websites, for example, use a user's age to determine if they can collect information from them. A site, by law, cannot collect information from users under the age of 13. The following query leverages the value of these two fields to validate the age against the specified birth date.

```
SELECT * FROM Customers
Where Age != TIMESTAMPDIFF(YEAR, Birthday, CURDATE())
```

The SELECT statement leverages two MySQL functions. The CURDATE function returns the current system date. The TIMESTAMPDIFF function, in this case, subtracts the date within the Birthday field from the current date to return the corresponding number of years.

If you were to run this query on the date of its writing (the output may change each day as the current date changes) against the Customers table shown in Figure 9.11, the query would identify the errant records shown in **FIGURE 9.12**.

## Understanding and Measuring Data Quality

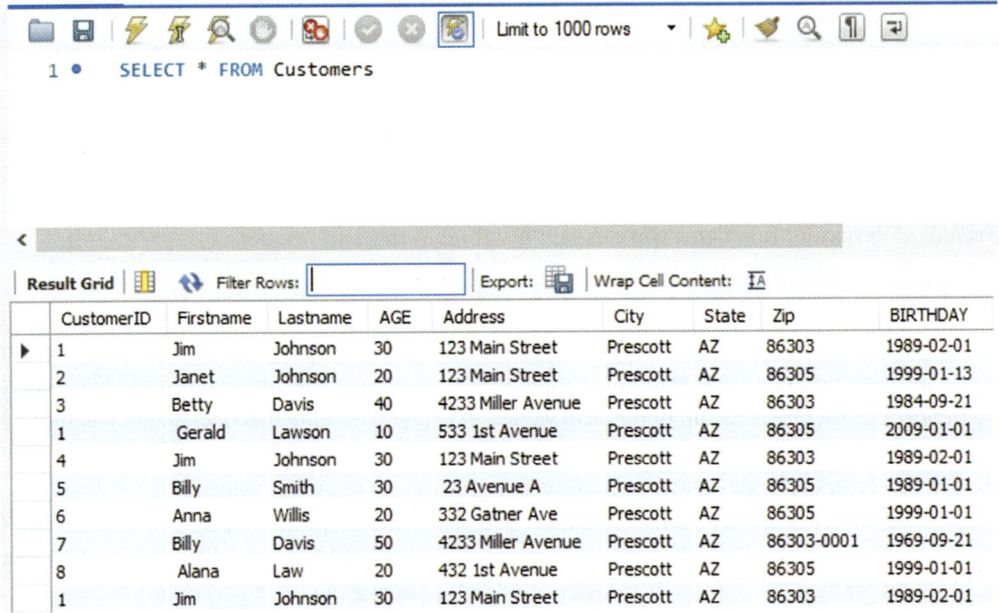

**FIGURE 9.11** A Customers data table.

Copyright Oracle and its affiliates. Used with permission

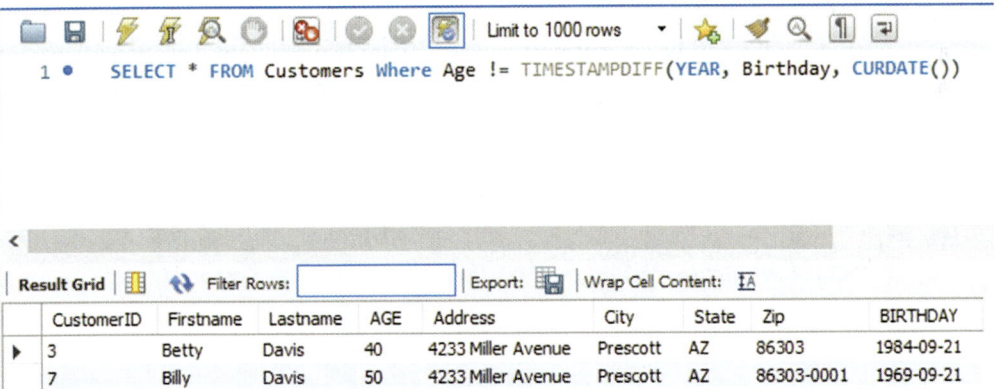

**FIGURE 9.12** Comparing two related Customers table data fields to determine errant records.

*Note:* Many database developers recommend that your tables should not contain fields that are calculatable, such as the total amount of a sale for which you know the quantity of products sold and their prices, or, in this case, the age of a customer for which you know the customer's birth date. The Age field is included in the example here to provide a simple way to demonstrate the process of validating data using value-pair consistency.

Copyright Oracle and its affiliates. Used with permission

## Examining a Field's Mean and Standard Deviation

As you evaluate the quality of your data, you may want to perform similar processing to identify potentially errant data. Further, you may want to perform simple statistics on a field's value to determine if you should continue to examine the field values for errors and inconsistencies. For example, assume your data contain records for a monitor device. Under normal operations, the device should return values in the range 50–60. Using the SQL AVG (average) and STDDEV (standard deviation) functions, you can gain insight into the field's values:

```
SELECT AVG(SensorValue), STDDEV(SensorValue) FROM Sensor
```

For a device returning values in the range 50–60, you would expect a small standard deviation and a mean value close to 55. Should the standard deviation become large, you would likely want to perform further exploration of the field values. When you execute this query, SQL will display the results shown in **FIGURE 9.13**.

In this case, the large standard deviation is an indication of outlier values.

Using the AVG and STDDEV functions, you can identify specific records that have values that do not necessarily align with others. For example, the following query will identify values that differ from the average by more than twice the standard deviation:

```
SELECT Record, SensorValue FROM Sensor WHERE
SensorValue > (SELECT AVG(SensorValue)+2*STDDEV(SensorValue)
   FROM Sensor) OR
SensorValue < (SELECT AVG(SensorValue)-2*STDDEV(SensorValue)
   FROM Sensor)
```

The query tests the SensorValue against values that are two standard deviations above the average and two standard deviations less than the average. By examining values that are greater

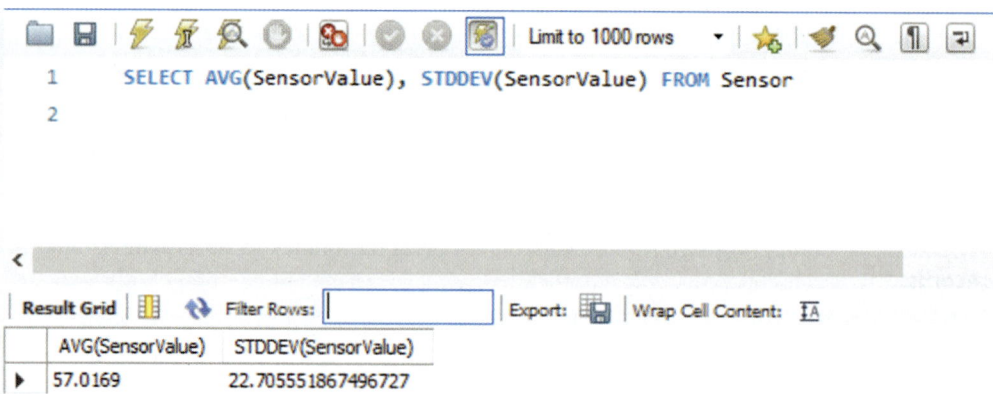

**FIGURE 9.13** Using the SQL AVG and STDDEV functions to analyze field values.
Copyright Oracle and its affiliates. Used with permission

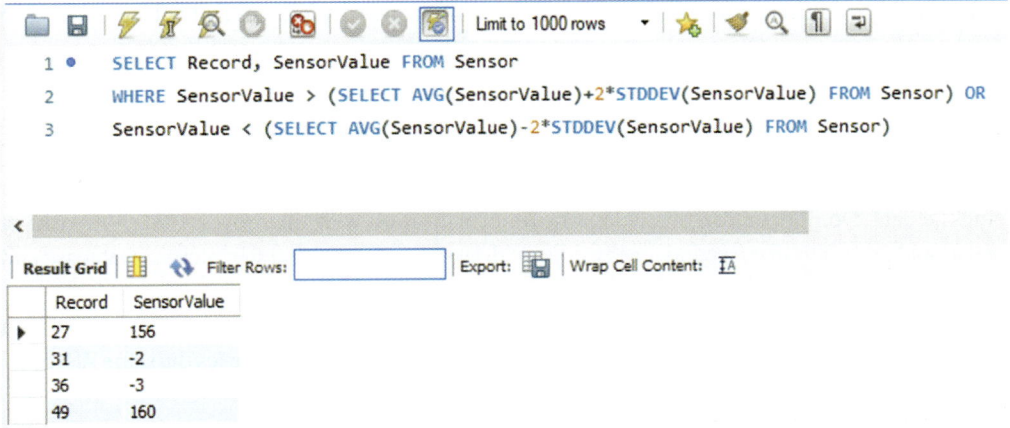

**FIGURE 9.14** Displaying records whose values fall outside of two standard deviations.

Copyright Oracle and its affiliates. Used with permission

than twice the standard deviation from the mean, you are likely to identify only data outliers. When you execute this query, SQL will display the records shown in **FIGURE 9.14**.

Assume that you decide to delete values that fall outside of the two standard deviation limit. You will find that after you do so, the standard deviation value will decrease significantly.

If you are examining a field for which the values do not fall into a consistent range, such as the sensor in the previous example, you should create a historical values table into which you store the mean and standard deviation values you gather over time. In this way, should your query produce results that differ significantly from your historical findings, you can drill deeper into the values.

## Identifying Data Inconsistences

Consistency is a measure of the degree to which similar or related data values align throughout the data set. For systems that store user-input values, **data consistency** is always a challenge. For example, assume that a call center user must enter a user's address:

```
123 North Main Street
```

The user might enter any of the following to represent the address:

```
123 N Main Street
123 N. Main Street
123 No. Main Street
123 North Main Street
123 North Main St.
123 North Main St
123 N. Main St.
123 N Main St.
123 N Main St.
123 N. Main St.
```

Although a mailperson will deliver mail to any of the listed addresses and will consider each address the same, an SQL query will not.

Sticking with addresses, one user might specify a five-digit ZIP code (86305), whereas another user may input a nine-digit ZIP code (86305-0001). Again, the data are conceptually the same, but not to an SQL query.

Database developers refer to the process of correcting such data inconsistences as normalizing the data. Do not confuse this type of field normalization with the process of decomposing a relational table into first, second, or third normal form, as discussed in Chapter 5, "Database and Data Warehouse Considerations."

As you might guess, because they are often entered by users, addresses are constantly a data consistency challenge. To start, you might test to confirm that each address uses the same ZIP code:

```
SELECT A.Address, A.Zip, B.Zip FROM Customers A
INNER JOIN (SELECT Address, Zip FROM Customers) B
ON A.Address = B.Address WHERE A.Zip != B.Zip
GROUP BY A.Address
```

The query performs a self-join (an inner join on itself, based on the address field). Then it compares the ZIP codes of the joined records, returning those that differ. As you can see, the query uses table aliases to specify fields, as discussed in Chapter 6. When you execute this query, SQL will display the records shown in **FIGURE 9.15**.

To determine if the same address is represented differently within the data set is more challenging. One approach is to leverage geolocation (latitude and longitude) data. To start, you can write an application program that uses an application programming interface (**API**), such as the Neutrino API, to convert the address into its corresponding latitude and longitude values. Then the application can use the API to convert those values back to a standard street address, which

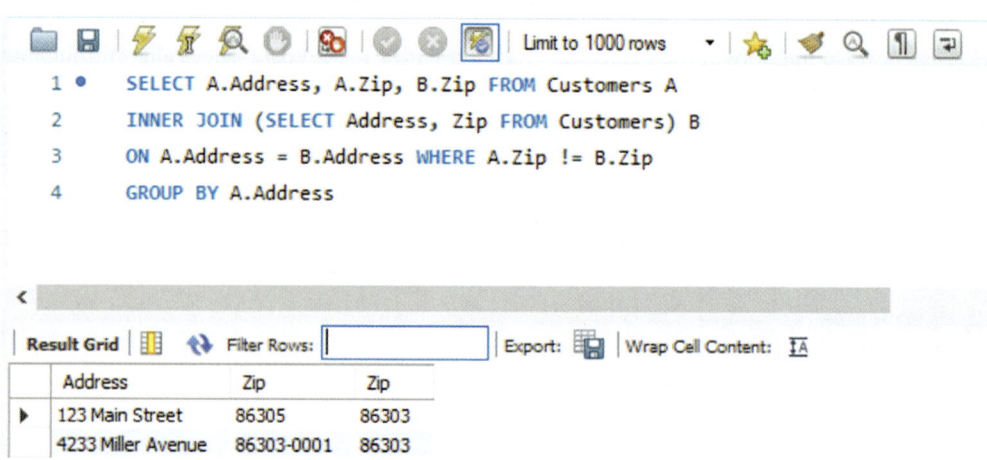

**FIGURE 9.15** Displaying addresses with an inconsistent ZIP code.

Copyright Oracle and its affiliates. Used with permission.

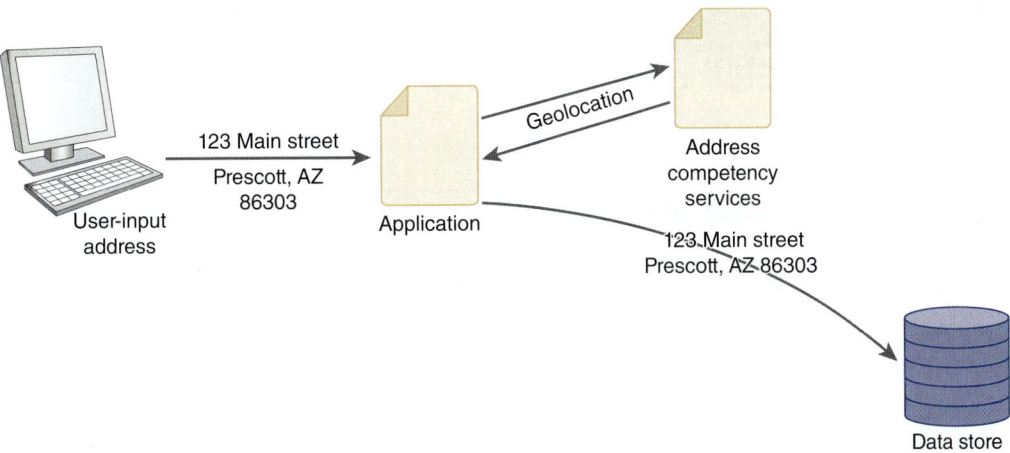

**FIGURE 9.16** Converting street addresses to geolocation coordinates and back again.

the application then stores. In this way, the records will contain only the address returned by the API, which produces one consistent address form, as shown in **FIGURE 9.16**.

## Eliminating Leading and Trailing Spaces

When a user enters data into a form, which a database later stores, there may be times when the user errantly types leading or trailing spaces before or after the values they type. Ideally, the application program storing the data will recognize and eliminate these extra characters. That said, as part of your data-cleansing process, you may need to eliminate them. In such cases, you can leverage the SQL RTRIM and LTRIM functions to remove the spaces:

```
UPDATE Customers SET Firstname=RTrim(LTrim(FirstName)),
Lastname=RTrim(LTrim(LastName)),
Address=RTrim(LTrim(Address)),
City=RTrim(LTrim(City)),
State=RTrim(LTrim(State)),
Zip=RTrim(LTrim(Zip))
```

In this case, the UPDATE query will assign the specified fields with the value each contains, minus leading spaces, which are removed by LTRIM, and without the trailing spaces, which are removed by RTRIM. When you execute the query, SQL will display the number of records it updated, as shown in **FIGURE 9.17**.

## Synchronizing Data Time Stamps

Often, a data integration process will collect data from a variety of sources, which may include servers that are dispersed around the country, as shown in **FIGURE 9.18**.

When you gather data from such sources, your integration process (which precedes your data-cleansing process) should ensure that your data are based upon a consistent time zone. To

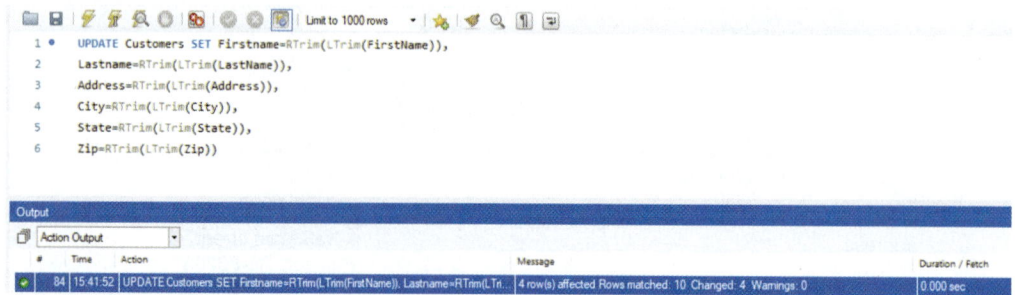

**FIGURE 9.17** Displaying a count of the number of updated records.

Copyright Oracle and its affiliates. Used with permission

**FIGURE 9.18** Aggregating data from sources dispersed across the country.

reduce the chance of misinterpreting time-based data, many applications will store the data in terms of Greenwich Mean Time (GMT). In this way, regardless of the time zone within which the server stores a record, the time fields will be consistent.

## Determining Whether to Correct or Delete Records

When you determine that your data contain errant or outlier data values, your challenge becomes determining whether to delete the records or to try to correct the field values the record contains. If, for example, you decide to discard records that contain errant fields, you will increase the accuracy of your data. However, in the process, you will decrease the completeness of your data. Further, you might delete a record for having an invalid ZIP code when your data-mining software ignores the ZIP code value and instead is interested only in the product and order quantity that the record contains.

If your analysis determines that the data are missing records, you would likely not try to reconstruct them. Instead, depending on the number of missing records, you may specify time intervals so that they are identifiable during future data analytic operations, or you may assign a lower confidence-level value to the data that the data analyst can consider. To make such confidence values readily available to data analysts, consider adding a column to your data into which you can store the record's corresponding confidence value.

Correcting errant data may sound like a good approach, but unfortunately, making such corrections is not always easy. For example, if a sensor's value falls outside of its 0–100 value range, the analyst may not know which replacement value best represents the missing data:

- The average field value
- The value in the record that precedes the record with the missing data
- The value in the record that follows the record with the missing data
- The average value of the 10 preceding values
- And so on

# Understanding the Role of Data Governance

Governance describes the administrative steps (processes, policies, and procedures) an individual or group performs or oversees. Data governance therefore describes the steps an organization performs to maximize the quality of data throughout its lifecycle.

Data have become operationally critical to most organizations. As such, having a data-governance process in place is equally key. In fact, most organizations will establish a data-governance board that consists of members from across the organization who have a knowledge or interest in the organization's data. The data-governance board will create and later enforce the company's data-governance plan.

Common goals of the data-governance board include:

- Continually improving the quality of data across the organization
- Establishing key performance indicators (**KPI**s) from which the board can determine and track the overall data quality
- Reducing cost and time associated with data acquisition and cleansing
- Standardizing data-related practices
- Creating an environment for effective data-driven decision-making

## Using a Data-Governance Framework

Regardless of the type of data companies use, the data-governance process is similar from one company to the next. **FIGURE 9.19**, for example, illustrates common data-governance operations.

To help your company establish a data-governance group and to define the tasks the board should perform, you may want to select one of the data-governance frameworks you can find on the web. A **framework** is a basic supporting structure—often a document that guides a group through a process. A good data-governance framework is the DGI Data Governance Framework, which you can find at the Data Governance Institute (DGI), as shown in **FIGURE 9.20**.

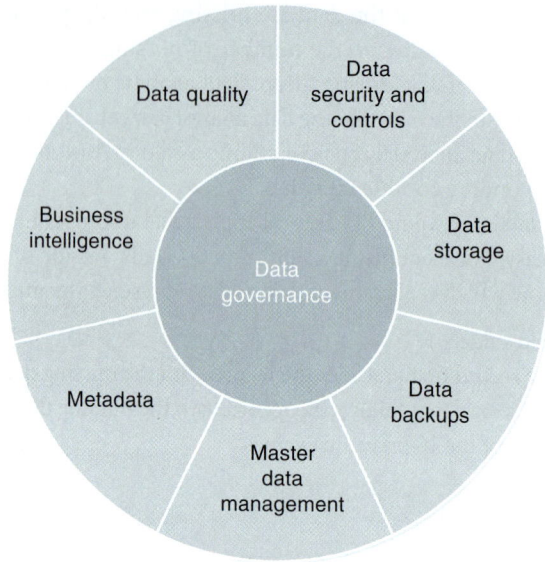

**FIGURE 9.19** Common data-governance operations.

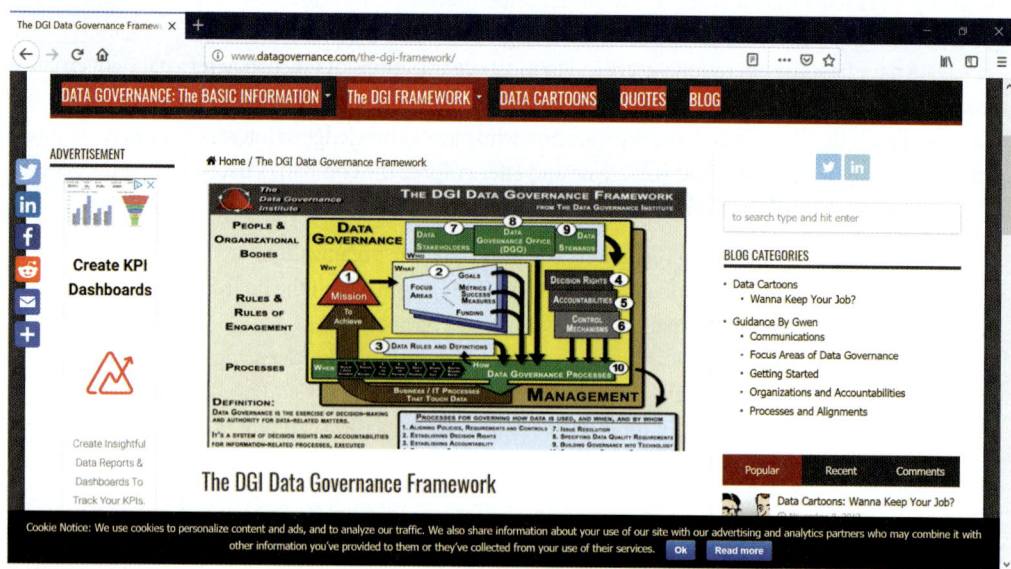

**FIGURE 9.20** The DGI Data Governance Framework.
Used with permission of the Data Governance Institute

## Understanding Data Stakeholders, Owners, Stewards, and Custodians

As your organization begins to formalize its data-governance plan, several closely related data roles will emerge:

- Data stakeholders
- Data owners
- Data stewards
- Data custodians

A **data stakeholder** is any individual with an interest in the data and their quality. A data stakeholder may be an end user who interacts with the data, application programmers who create programs that manipulate the data, and database developers who write data queries and reports or create dashboards. A data stakeholder may also fall into one of the other roles of data owner, steward, or custodian.

A **data owner** is often an executive who oversees the business unit associated with the data. The chief financial officer (CFO), for example, owns the financial data, the chief compliance officer owns the company's regulatory and compliance data, and the chief people officer would own the company's human resources (HR) data. As the data owner, the executive serves as the final arbitrator and decision maker for issues that affect the data. He or she, however, would not play a day-to-day, hands-on role with the data.

A **data steward** makes the day-to-day decisions for the data with respect to data quality, content, and metadata. The data steward, for example, would define the **master data** elements. The data steward has great knowledge of the data, their producers and consumers, and the business rules that guide data operations.

A **data custodian** is the technical expert who administers and manages the data. The data custodian would implement the tables (or, in the case of NoSQL, the collections) that store the data. In addition, the data custodian would implement the queries, stored procedures, and database solutions that implement the business rules. Finally, the data steward would implement the security and authorization controls that protect the data.

## Understanding the Data Lifecycle

Regardless of the type of data and the value they contain, most data follow a consistent lifecycle, as shown in **FIGURE 9.21**.

As you can see, data are created (or acquired from a source), stored, updated, archived, and eventually deleted. Using the data lifecycle as a guide, the data-governance board can specify best practices and policies the business should perform at each stage of the lifecycle, such as auditing changes, placing controls on who can access the data and how, or confirming proper backups of the data exist.

**FIGURE 9.21** The typical data lifecycle.

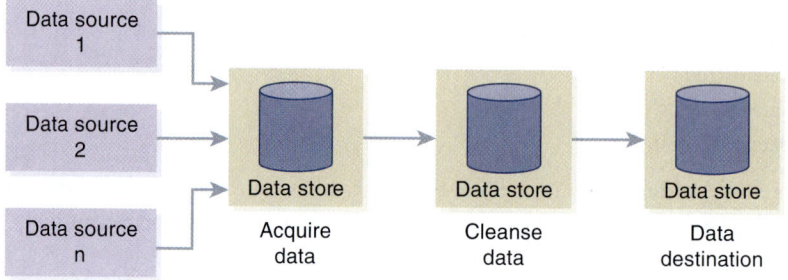

**FIGURE 9.22** Integrating data cleansing into the ETL process.

# Revisiting Extract, Transform, and Load Operations

As you have learned, one of the most common operations that database developers perform is to extract data from one source, change the data in some way (transform it), and then load the transformed data into a new source. When you automate your data-cleansing process, you should perform it prior to loading it into the destination, as shown in **FIGURE 9.22**.

As you can see, the extract, transform, and load (ETL) process extracts data from multiple sources, transforms the data into a standard format, and then cleanses that data before loading them.

# Data Wrangling Defined

As just discussed, database developers must often transform and cleanse data before loading into a destination system for analysis. Developers often refer to this process of transforming and cleansing data as "data wrangling," or, depending upon with whom you are speaking, "**data munging**."

## Leveraging a Data-Wrangling Tool

As mentioned earlier, database developers often refer to the data transformation and cleansing processes they perform as data wrangling. To wrangle data, the database developers may execute SQL queries or run applications that perform specific operations to manipulate the data. Often, such applications combine the ETL and data-cleansing processes.

Rather than write their own custom data-wrangling applications, many database developers turn to one of the many readily available third-party data-wrangling tools:

- OpenRefine
- R programing language
- Python and pandas
- DataWrangler

The "Hands-On" section of this chapter examines the use of the OpenRefine tool.

## Using Microsoft SQL Server Data Quality Services

If you are using Microsoft MS SQL, you should leverage the Microsoft SQL Server Data Quality Services (DQS) to cleanse your data. Using DQS, you can create a knowledge base of your commonly used cleansing values and techniques. DQS provides extensive capabilities, the functionality of which is beyond the scope of this text. For more information on DQS, visit the Microsoft website, as shown in **FIGURE A**.

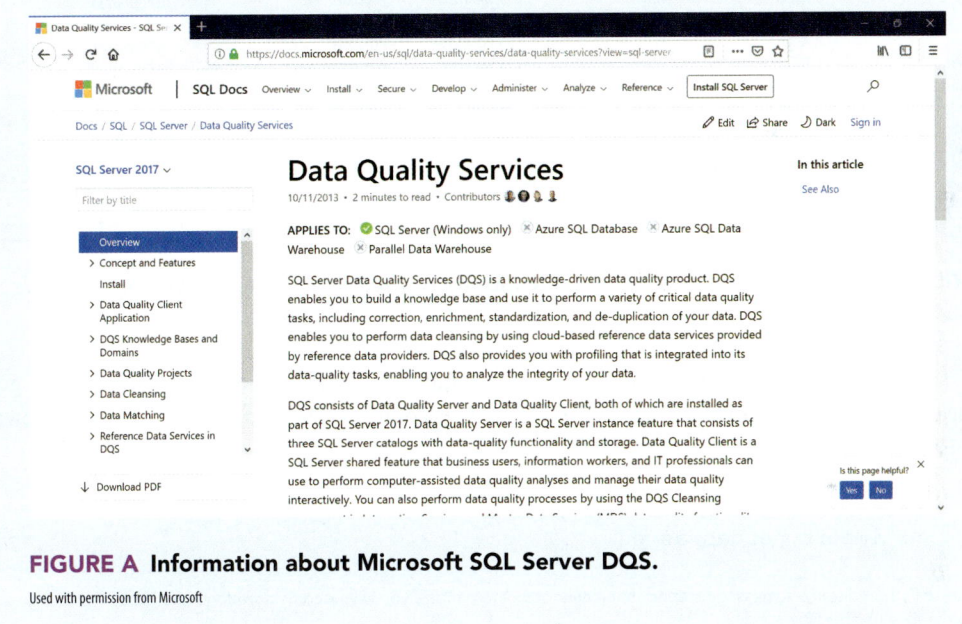

**FIGURE A** Information about Microsoft SQL Server DQS.
Used with permission from Microsoft

# Creating Your Own Custom Data Wrangler in Python

Depending on the complexity of the data they must transform or cleanse, database developers can use a programming language, such as Python, to create their own custom data-wrangling application. In this section, you will use Python to perform simple data-wrangling operations. You won't need to create a Python program in this case, but rather, you can execute the program statements using the Python interpreter. The purpose of this section is not to make you a Python programmer, but rather, to give you a feel for Python's data-cleansing capabilities. You will build more upon the concepts presented in Chapter 8, "Programming Data-Mining and Analytic Solutions."

If you have not yet installed Python, turn to Chapter 8, which examines the installation process in detail. Start Python, which will display its command prompt, which appears as three greater-than symbols:

```
>>>
```

From the command prompt, you can execute the statements we will present, one statement at a time.

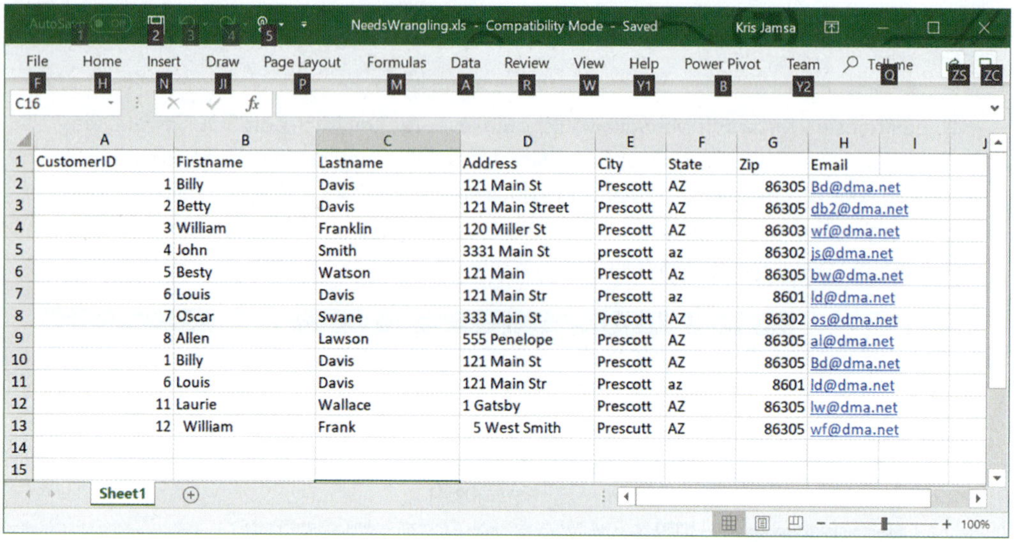

**CHAPTER 9** Data Preprocessing and Cleansing

**FIGURE 9.23** Download and display the contents of the Excel file NeedsWrangling.csv.
Used with permission from Microsoft

To start, download the Excel file NeedsWrangling.csv from this text's catalog page at go.jblearning.com/DataMining. When you view the file's contents, Excel will display the data shown in **FIGURE 9.23**.

To start, you must import the pandas library:

```
>>> import pandas as pd
```

*Note:* If Python displays a message stating that it cannot locate pandas, you will need to download and install the library as discussed in Chapter 8.

Next, direct Python to create a data frame to hold your data and to load into it the contents of the NeedsWrangling.csv file. You will need to modify the folder location to specify the folder into which you stored the NeedsWrangling.csv file:

```
>>> dataFile = pd.read_csv('C:/Databook/Chapter09/
    NeedsWrangling.csv')
```

Using Python's print method, you can display the number of rows and columns your data contains:

```
>>> print(dataFile.shape)
(12, 8)
```

If you examine the NeedsWrangling.csv file, you will find that, as shown, it contains 12 rows which are eight columns wide. To display the first five rows in your data, use the Python head method:

```
>>> dataFile.head()
```

```
   CustomerID  Firstname    Lastname  ...  State    Zip       Email
0       1      Billy        Davis     ...   AZ     86305   Bd@dma.net
1       2      Betty        Davis     ...   AZ     86305   db2@dma.net
2       3      William      Franklin  ...   AZ     86303   wf@dma.net
3       4      John         Smith     ...   az     86302   js@dma.net
4       5      Betsy        Watson    ...   Az     86305   bw@dma.net
[5 rows x 8 columns]
>>>
```

Note that the head method precedes each row of data with an index value. You will use these values later to refer to specific rows within the data.

The NeedsWrangling.csv file contains duplicate records. To view the duplicated records, use the duplicated method. The method returns a list of Boolean values that specify whether a row is a duplicate:

```
>>> dupList.head(12)
0      False
1      False
2      False
3      False
4      False
5      False
6      False
7      False
8      True
9      True
10     False
11     False
dtype: bool
>>>
```

If you examine the NeedsWrangling.csv file, you will find that pandas correctly identified the duplicate records. To remove the duplicate records, use the drop_duplicates method and assign the result to the data set:

```
>>> dataFile = dataFile.drop_duplicates('CustomerID')
>>> dataFile
    CustomerID  Firstname    Lastname  ...  State    Zip       Email
0       1       Billy        Davis     ...   AZ     86305   Bd@dma.net
1       2       Betty        Davis     ...   AZ     86305   db2@dma.net
2       3       William      Franklin  ...   AZ     86303   wf@dma.net
3       4       John         Smith     ...   az     86302   js@dma.net
4       5       Betsy        Watson    ...   Az     86305   bw@dma.net
5       6       Louis        Davis     ...   az     8601    ld@dma.net
6       7       Oscar        Swane     ...   AZ     86302   os@dma.net
7       8       Allen        Lawson    ...   AZ     86305   al@dma.net
10      11      Laurie       Wallace   ...   AZ     86305   lw@dma.net
11      12      William      Frank     ...   AZ     86305   wf@dma.net
[10 rows x 8 columns]
>>>
```

Several of the fields within the NeedsWrangling.csv file have leading and trailing spaces. To eliminate such whitespace from a column, perform the following:

```
>>> dataFile['Firstname'] = dataFile['Firstname'].map(str.strip)
```

If you examine the State column, you will find that some records use an uppercase value, some lowercase, and possibly some mixed case. To capitalize all the values in the State column, perform the following:

```
>>> dataFile['State'] = dataFile['State'].map(lambda s : s.upper())
>>> dataFile
   CustomerID Firstname   Lastname  ... State    Zip         Email
0           1     Billy      Davis  ...    AZ  86305   Bd@dma.net
1           2     Betty      Davis  ...    AZ  86305  db2@dma.net
2           3   William   Franklin  ...    AZ  86303   wf@dma.net
3           4      John      Smith  ...    AZ  86302   js@dma.net
4           5     Betsy     Watson  ...    AZ  86305   bw@dma.net
5           6     Louis      Davis  ...    AZ   8601   ld@dma.net
6           7     Oscar      Swane  ...    AZ  86302   os@dma.net
7           8     Allen     Lawson  ...    AZ  86305   al@dma.net
10         11    Laurie    Wallace  ...    AZ  86305   lw@dma.net
11         12   William      Frank  ...    AZ  86305   wf@dma.net
[10 rows x 8 columns]
>>>
```

The operation uses a lambda function to call the panda's built-in upper function.

As discussed, user-entered addresses and ZIP codes often yield inconsistent data. One way to identify potential problems is to display a count of values. The following operation displays a count of the different ZIP codes:

```
>>> dataFile['Zip'].value_counts()
86305 6
86302 2
86303 1
8601  1
Name: Zip, dtype: int64
```

As you can see, the operation identifies errant ZIP code 8601. Using a dataframe index, you can update a specific cell. In addition, if there are multiple occurrences of the invalid zip code, you can create a lambda function to update all cells with the ZIP code 8601.

Often, as you analyze data, you will want to sort the data based on a column's values. The following command directs Python to sort the data values by Lastname:

```
>>> dataFile.sort_values('Lastname')
```

```
    CustomerID  Firstname  Lastname  ...  State   Zip    Email
0       1         Billy     Davis    ...   AZ    86305  Bd@dma.net
1       2         Betty     Davis    ...   AZ    86305  db2@dma.net
5       6         Louis     Davis    ...   AZ    8601   ld@dma.net
11      12        William   Frank    ...   AZ    86305  wf@dma.net
2       3         William   Franklin ...   AZ    86303  wf@dma.net
7       8         Allen     Lawson   ...   AZ    86305  al@dma.net
3       4         John      Smith    ...   AZ    86302  js@dma.net
6       7         Oscar     Swane    ...   AZ    86302  os@dma.net
10      11        Laurie    Wallace  ...   AZ    86305  lw@dma.net
4       5         Betsy     Watson   ...   AZ    86305  bw@dma.net
[10 rows x 8 columns]
>>>
```

The following state directs Python to display only the Address column:

```
>>> dataFile["Address"]
Zip
86305    121 Main St
86305    121 Main Street
86303    120 Miller St
86302    3331 Main St
86305    121 Main
8601     121 Main Str
86302    333 Main St
86305    555 Penelope
86305    1 Gatsby
86305    5 West Smith
Name: Address, dtype: object
>>>
```

As you can see, there are several address values that are similar but differ by one or more characters.

Finally, analysts often want to know if NULL or NaN values exist. Using the isnull method, you can direct pandas to report whether or not a field is NULL or NaN. By default, Python will return a true or false value for every field. As an alternative, you can use the sum method to add up any such values:

```
>>> dataFile.isnull().sum()
CustomerID   0
Firstname    0
Lastname     0
Address      0
City         0
State        0
Zip          0
Email        0
dtype: int64
>>>
```

# Leveraging the Data Quality Assessment Framework

As you have learned, data quality is a measure of the suitability of data use. Throughout this chapter, we have defined data quality in terms of:

- Accuracy
- Completeness
- Consistency
- Conformity

Using these four measures as a starting point, you can create ways to analyze and, optionally, to cleanse your data.

As you might guess, all companies should continually evaluate their data to improve data quality. To help companies evaluate the quality of their data and to expand their data-quality evaluation beyond the metrics presented here, Ingenix (a subsidiary of United Health Group) created the DQAF. As previously defined, a framework provides a structure that users can follow to achieve a result. The DQAF provides 48 standard measurements based upon the following quality dimensions:

- Completeness: the degree to which data represent all required values.
- Timeliness: the degree to which data arrive in a favorable time frame.
- Validity: the degree to which data are logically correct.
- Consistency: the degree to which similar or related values align throughout the data set.
- Integrity: the degree to which data are accurate, complete, and truly representative of the real-world data.

For more information on DQAF, refer to Lauren Sebastian-Coleman's book, *Managing Data Quality for Ongoing Improvement* (Elsevier, 2012). Sebastian-Coleman was the architect of the DQAF. In addition, the International Monetary Fund (IMF) provides an excellent article on their application of DQAF on their website, as shown in **FIGURE 9.24**, as does the United Nations Educational, Scientific, and Cultural Organization (UNESCO), as shown in **FIGURE 9.25**.

## Master Data Management

Within most organizations you can identify the key data, such as customer, vendor, or employee data. To maintain consistency of such data, database designers and administrators will normally have one definition (schema) for the data and, ideally, store the data in one location. Database designers and administrators refer to such data as master data. Using master data, regardless of the number of applications that may use customer data, there is only one schema for the customer data. Master data management (MDM) is the process of defining and enforcing controls for such master data. Having strong master data management is a key to improving data quality.

# Leveraging the Data Quality Assessment Framework

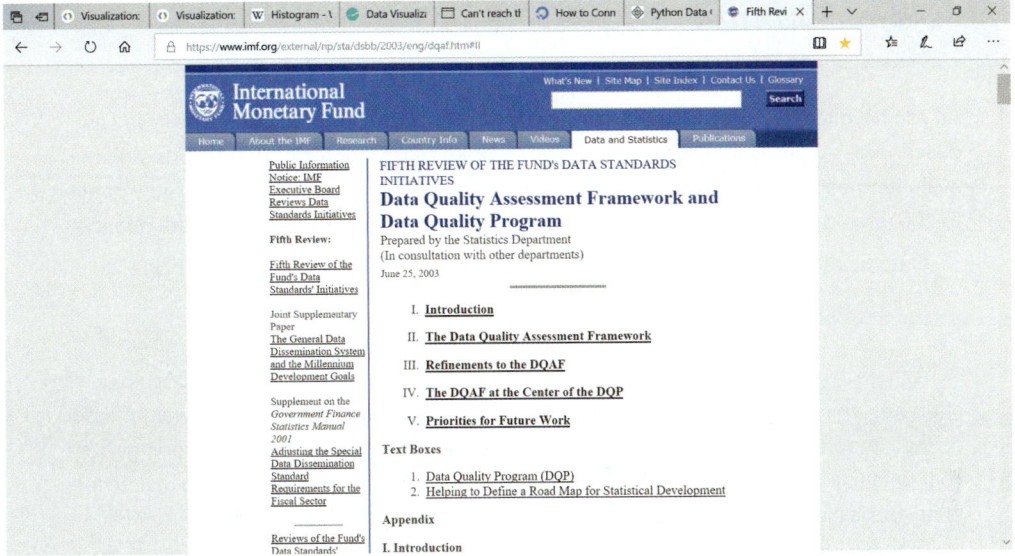

**FIGURE 9.24** An article summarizing the IMF application of DQAF.
Used with permission of International Monetary Fund

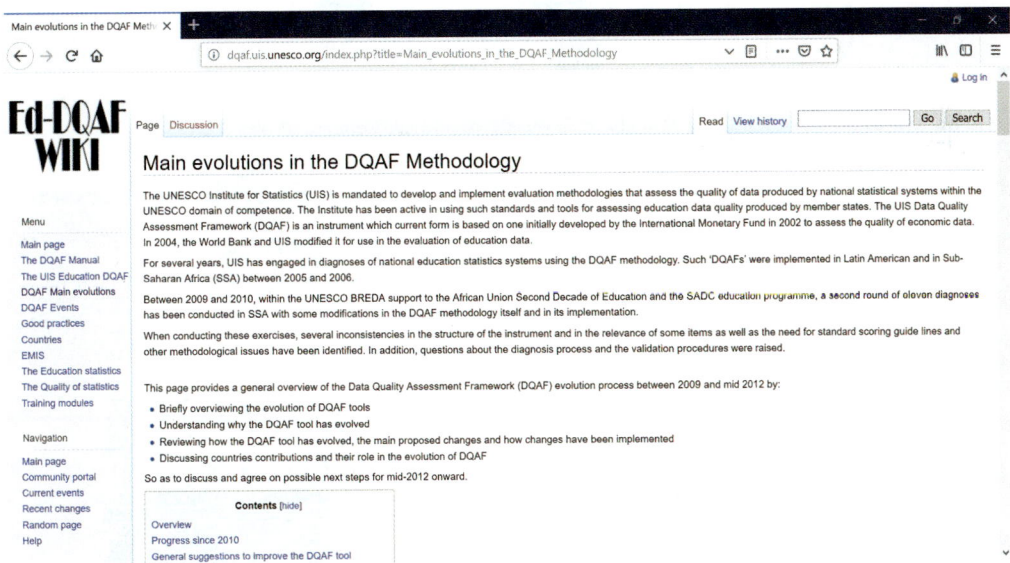

**FIGURE 9.25** An article on the use of DQAF at UNESCO.
Used with permission of UNESCO

## Data-Quality Key Performance Indicators

As you have learned, data quality is a measure of the data's suitability for use. You can describe data quality in terms of accuracy, completeness, conformity, and consistency. By evaluating each of these attributes in terms of a numeric percentage, from 0 (low quality) to 100 (high quality), you can use the percentage to calculate your overall data quality:

Data Quality = Average(Accuracy, Completeness, Conformity, Consistency)
= Average(97, 95, 99, 97)
= 97%

A more complex calculation of data quality, perhaps one based upon the DQAF 48 quality attributes, would increase the attributes, some of which your calculations might weight based on their importance. To determine values for the attributes, you can apply your findings from your data-analysis and data-cleansing processes. If, for example, you are running SQL scripts or an application to cleanse your data, you might modify your processes to produce KPIs, which you might then report on a dashboard to provide your data-governance board with current-state insights into the quality of your data, as shown in **FIGURE A**.

**FIGURE A** Displaying data-quality KPIs within a dashboard.

*Note:* Chapter 6, "Keep SQL in Your Toolset," presents how to create this dashboard using Microsoft Power BI.

Used with permission from Microsoft

## Hands-On: Data Cleansing Using OpenRefine

OpenRefine is an open-source data-cleansing tool originally developed by Google. Using OpenRefine, you can quickly perform many of the operations this chapter presents. In this section, you will use OpenRefine to trim leading and trailing blanks, remove duplicate records, correct capitalization, apply consistency to address values, and apply corrections across multiple records.

To start, download the data file Messy.xlsx from this text's catalog page at go.jblearning.com/DataMining. Your system will open the spreadsheet within Excel, displaying its contents, as shown in **FIGURE A**.

**FIGURE A** Downloading the Messy.xlsx file.

Used with permission from Microsoft

If you examine the file's contents, you will find that some cells have leading and trailing blanks. Several records reference the address 121 Main Street, but in different forms. Some state abbreviations are in uppercase, some in mixed case, and some in lowercase. Some ZIP codes are wrong. The spreadsheet contains duplicate rows, and the capitalization of the city is inconsistent. Save the Messy.xlsx file to a folder on your computer and close the Excel window.

You can download and install OpenRefine from the openrefine.org website, as shown in **FIGURE B**.

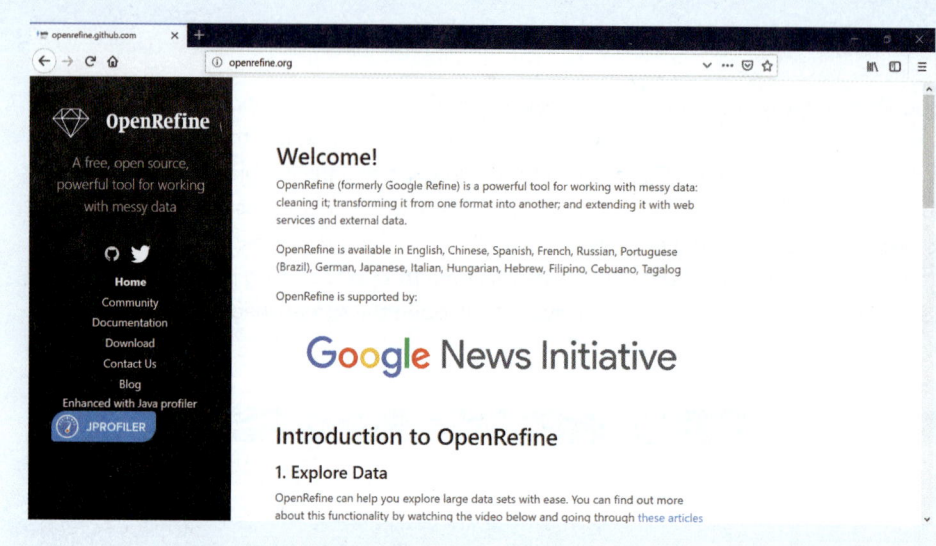

**FIGURE B** The openrefine.org website.

Used with permission of GitHub, Inc

After you download and install OpenRefine, it will run within a web browser, as shown in **FIGURE C**.

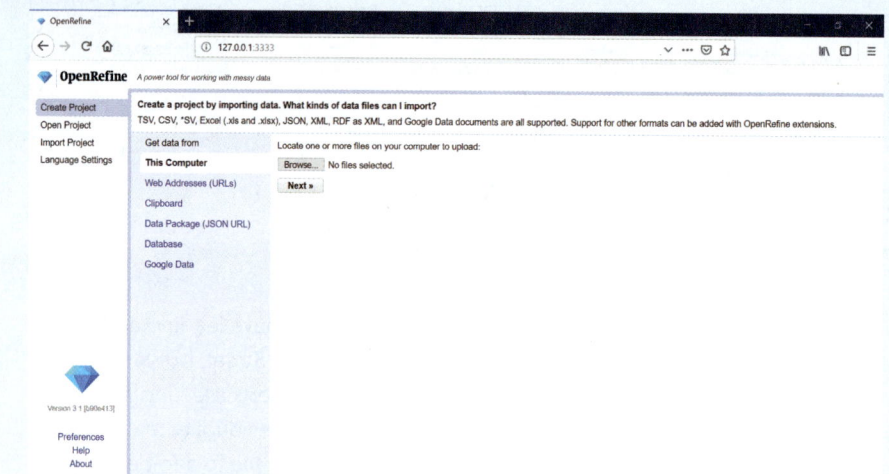

**FIGURE C** The OpenRefine data cleanser runs within a web browser.

Used with permission of GitHub, Inc

OpenRefine lets you open data from a wide range of sources. In this case, click the This computer option. OpenRefine will display a page from which you can browse your computer for the file. Click the Browse button. OpenRefine will display a dialog box within which you can locate and upload the file. After you select the Messy.xlsx file, click

## Leveraging the Data Quality Assessment Framework

Next. OpenRefine will load the spreadsheet contents and display its Configure Parsing Options screen, as shown in **FIGURE D**.

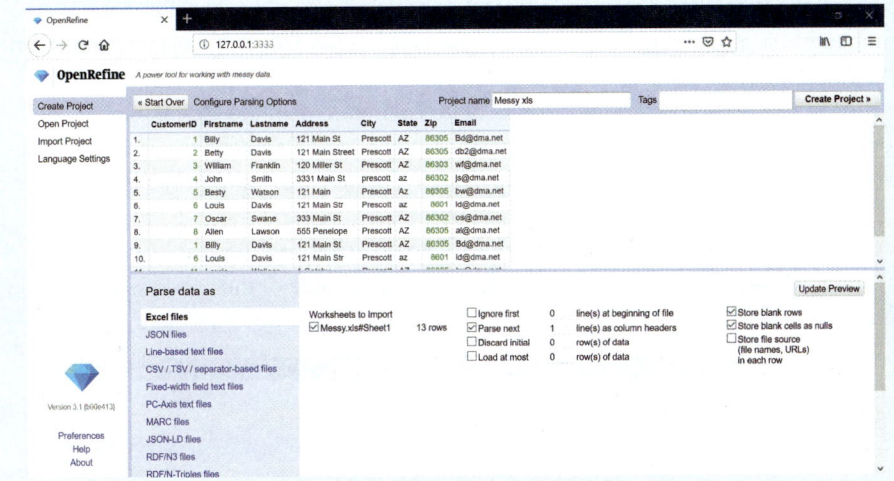

**FIGURE D** The OpenRefine Configure Parsing Options screen.
Used with permission of GitHub, Inc

Within this screen, you can direct OpenRefine to perform additional operations before you begin cleansing your data, such as skipping starting rows, including or excluding blank rows, and so on. For now, simply click the Create Project button. OpenRefine will display its editing page, as shown in **FIGURE E**. It may not be obvious, but OpenRefine has already eliminated duplicate rows.

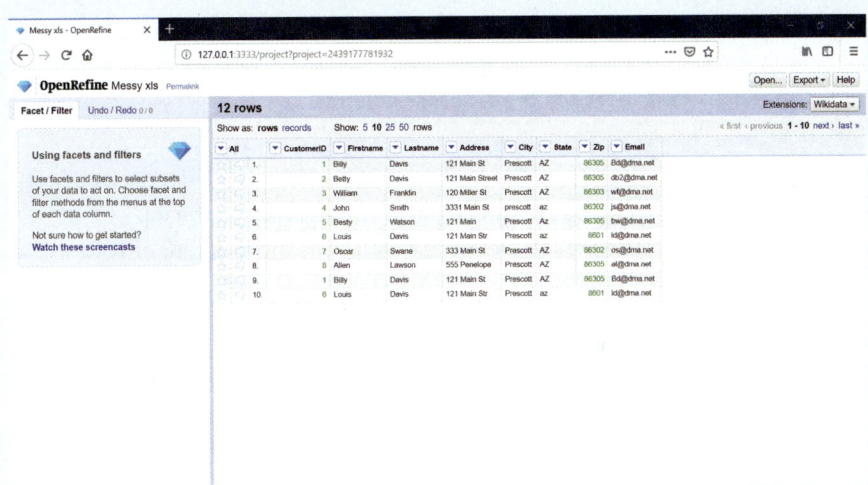

**FIGURE E** Loading the file Messy.xlsx into the OpenRefine Editing page.
Used with permission of GitHub, Inc

To start, click the down arrow next to the Firstname column. OpenRefine will display a drop-down menu. Within the menu, select the Edit Cells option Common Transformations entry and choose Trim leading and trailing whitespace. Repeat this step for the remaining columns. OpenRefine will remove the leading and trailing spaces from all fields.

Next, click the down arrow next to the State column. Within the OpenRefine menu, choose the Edit Cells entry Common Transformations option and choose To uppercase. OpenRefine will convert each state abbreviation to uppercase. Perform similar processing to the City column to select the To titlecase option.

Click the down arrow next to the Address field and choose the Facet option Text facet entry. OpenRefine will display a facet along the left side of the window, as shown in **FIGURE F**.

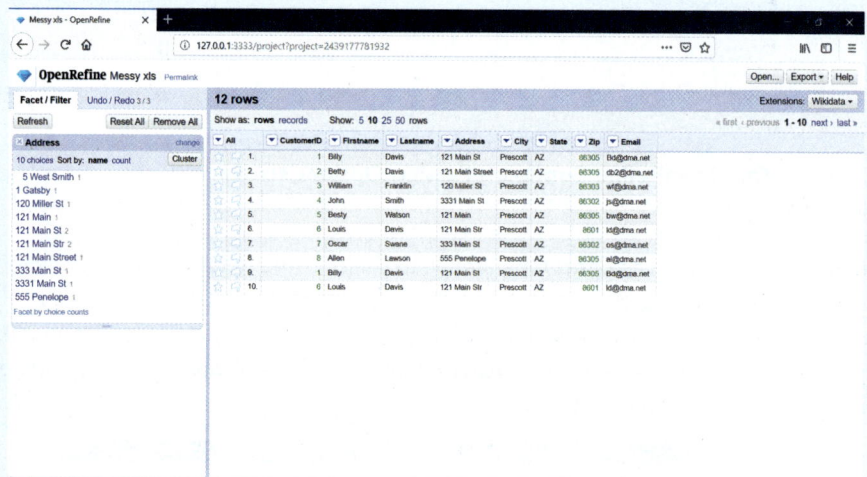

**FIGURE F** Creating a text facet for the Address column.

Used with permission of GitHub, Inc

Within the Address text facet, click the Cluster button. OpenRefine will display its Cluster & Edit window, which will initially be blank. Use the drop-down lists at the top of the window to try options until OpenRefine identifies a cluster, as shown in **FIGURE G**.

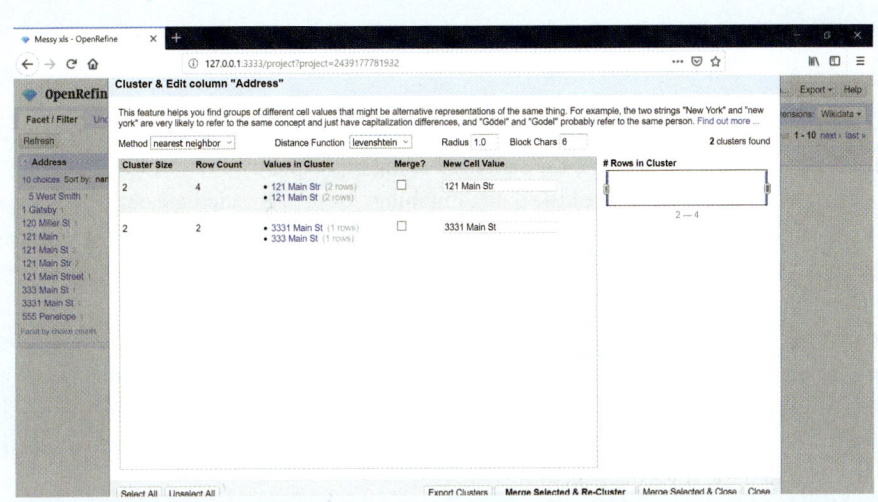

**FIGURE G** Identifying address clusters within OpenRefine.

Used with permission of GitHub, Inc

Click the Merge checkbox that appears next to the addresses that start with 121 Main. Then in the text box, type the complete address 121 Main Street. Click the Merge Selected & Close button. OpenRefine will close the window and update all matching addresses in the cluster. Close the Address facet. Within the record list, hover your mouse over the address 121 Main and click Edit. OpenRefine will display a dialog box within which you will type 121 Main Street and click Apply. OpenRefine will update the address.

Hover your mouse over the ZIP code 8601 and click Edit. OpenRefine will display a prompt for the desired value. Type 86301 and click Apply. Repeat this step for the other 8601 ZIP code.

Your data cleanse is now complete. Click the Export button and save the file's contents. Note that OpenRefine will save the file to a new name.

In this section you used OpenRefine to cleanse data in a variety of ways. The section only briefly touches upon OpenRefine's features. The OpenRefine website provides documentation that will guide you through its data-cleansing capabilities.

## Summary

Companies today are acquiring more data from a wider range of sources than ever before. Having large quantities of data, however, is not the same as having high-quality data. In this chapter, you learned that data quality is a measure of the data's suitability for use. To calculate data quality, data analysts often factor attributes such as consistency, completeness, accuracy, and conformity—each of which the analyst can quantify.

Improving data quality should be a constant goal of every business. To establish data-quality procedures, processes, and controls, companies often establish a data-governance board. Members of the board may include data stakeholders, who have an interest in the data; data owners, who are the executives over the business unit that creates the data; data stewards, who are the day-to-day data experts; and data custodians, who implement the data applications and data security. In this chapter, you examined the roles of each.

To provide the data-governance board with insights into the current state of data quality, many companies establish KPIs that measure the board's effort and intentions to improve data quality.

Data cleansing is the process of detecting, correcting, and removing errors and inconsistencies from data. Database developers describe the steps they perform to transform and cleanse data as data wrangling. To wrangle data, the database developers may use SQL scripts, custom applications, and third-party tools. The goal of such data wrangling is to improve overall data quality.

## Key Terms

| | | |
|---|---|---|
| Application Program Interface (API) | Data custodian | Data wrangling |
| Business rules | Data integrity | DQAF |
| Data accuracy | Data munging | Framework |
| Data cleansing | Data owner | Key Performance Indicator (KPI) |
| Data completeness | Data quality | Master data |
| Data conformity | Data steward | |
| Data consistency | Data timeliness | |
| | Data validity | |

## Review

1. Define and describe data quality to include the attributes that influence it.
2. Define and describe data cleansing.
3. Define and describe data wrangling.
4. Define and describe the DQAF.

5. Briefly describe several common data validation techniques a data analyst might perform.
6. Define and describe data governance. Include common goals of a data-governance process.
7. Describe the role of data-quality KPIs.
8. Describe the data lifecycle.
9. Compare and contrast data stakeholders, owners, custodians, and stewards.
10. Using Python, perform the data-cleansing operations this chapter presents, creating screen captures of your results.
11. Using OpenRefine, perform the data-cleansing operations this chapter presents, creating screen captures of your results.

# CHAPTER 10

# Data Clustering

## Chapter Goals and Objectives

- Define and describe data clustering.
- Compare and contrast hard and soft clustering.
- Compare and contrast different clustering algorithms.
- Describe the purpose of a dendrogram.
- Visually represent cluster assignments.

Often, one of the first steps a data analyst will perform when analyzing new data is to decompose a large data set into smaller groups of related data elements called clusters. The concept of **clustering** is that an item in one cluster more closely resembles other items in that cluster than it does items in another cluster.

Clustering uses unsupervised learning, in that it works with unlabeled data that have not been assigned to a category or group—the clustering process will form such groups (clusters). Business uses of clustering include:

- Assigning customers to a market segment
- Assigning website users into groups based upon their on-site behavior
- Identifying healthcare risks and causes
- Grouping sales by underlying product inventories
- Clustering results for a search engine to better match user requests
- Clustering housing and census data

There are two main types of clustering solutions. Hard clustering restricts each point to residing in only one cluster. **Soft clustering algorithms**, in contrast, allow points to reside in multiple clusters.

As you perform cluster analysis, you will find that some values fall outside of all clusters—making the points outliers. This chapter will discuss ways to best deal with such values.

There are hundreds of different clustering algorithms, which differ by the following:

- Performance
- Memory use
- Hardness or softness
- Data-set size
- Need for the analyst to specify the starting number of clusters

This chapter examines several commonly used clustering algorithms readily available in both Python and R. By the time you finish this chapter, you will understand the following key concepts:

- To explore data, analysts will often group data into related clusters.
- Analysts assume that data within the same cluster are more closely related (are more similar) than data within other clusters.
- Data-clustering algorithms use unsupervised learning, in that they identify structure and groups from uncategorized data.
- There are hundreds of data-clustering algorithms.
- The two primary clustering algorithm types are hard and soft algorithms. A hard data-clustering algorithm restricts each point to residing in only one cluster. A soft clustering algorithm, in contrast, allows a point to reside in multiple clusters.
- Commonly used clustering algorithms include:
    - Connectivity algorithms, such as **hierarchical clustering**
    - Centroid algorithms, such as **K-means clustering**
    - Density algorithms, such as Density-Based Spatial Clustering of Applications with Noise (**DBSCAN**) clustering
- Connectivity algorithms, such as hierarchical clustering algorithms, group points into clusters by merging (agglomerating) related clusters.
- Centroid algorithms, such as K-means, create clusters by grouping points based on minimizing the average distance between the cluster points and the center of the cluster, which is called the centroid.
- Density algorithms, such as DBSCAN, create clusters based on proximity to dense regions.
- To understand how a hierarchical clustering algorithm will group data, analysts often use a chart called a dendrogram.
- With respect to density-clustering algorithms, a data outlier is a data point that does not fall into any clusters.

# Common Clustering Approaches

There are hundreds of clustering algorithms from which a data analyst can choose. Clustering uses unsupervised learning, in that it does not start with categorized data. In general, you can group most clustering algorithms based on their underlying approach, as described in **TABLE 10.1**.

### TABLE 10.1 Common Clustering Approaches

| Cluster Model | Example Algorithms | Notes |
| --- | --- | --- |
| Centroid | K-means, K-means++ | Selects cluster members based upon a mean optimization vector. Requires the data analyst to specify the number of clusters. |
| Connectivity | Hierarchical | Agglomerates (combines) related clusters to build a larger cluster. Illustrated using a chart called a dendrogram. Not well suited for large data sets. |
| Density | DBSCAN | Clusters are collected based on each point's proximity to dense regions in the data's coordinate space. Does not require the analyst to specify the number of clusters. |

The sections that follow examine each of these clustering approaches, presenting real-world implementations of each using Python and R.

### Understanding Euclidian Distances

Many of the clustering algorithms include or exclude a point within or from a cluster based upon the point's distance from a cluster's center (which is called the **centroid**). Such distances are normally defined in terms of the Euclidian (or straight-line) distance between the points, which is calculated as shown in **FIGURE A**.

$$\text{distance}(a, b) = \sqrt{(a_1 - b_1)^2 + (a_2 - b_2)^2}$$

**FIGURE A** Calculating the Euclidian distance between points.

# Understanding K-Means Clustering

The K-means clustering algorithm groups data into K clusters, based on each point's distance from the center of the cluster, which is called the centroid. For example, **FIGURE 10.1** shows the same data using K = 3, K = 4, and K = 5 clusters.

When you use the K-means algorithm, you must specify the value of K, meaning the number of clusters you desire. If you specify too few clusters, you may lose valuable insights. Likewise, if you specify too many clusters, you will increase your processing time and you may not gain additional insights.

## Understanding K-Means Clustering

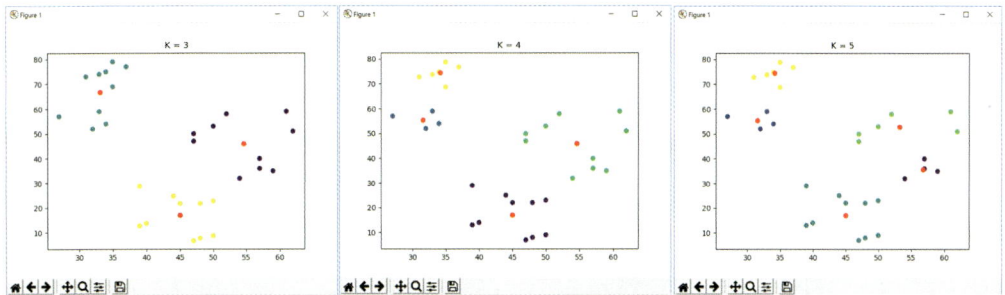

**FIGURE 10.1** K-means clustering groups points into K clusters.
Used with permission of Python Software Foundation

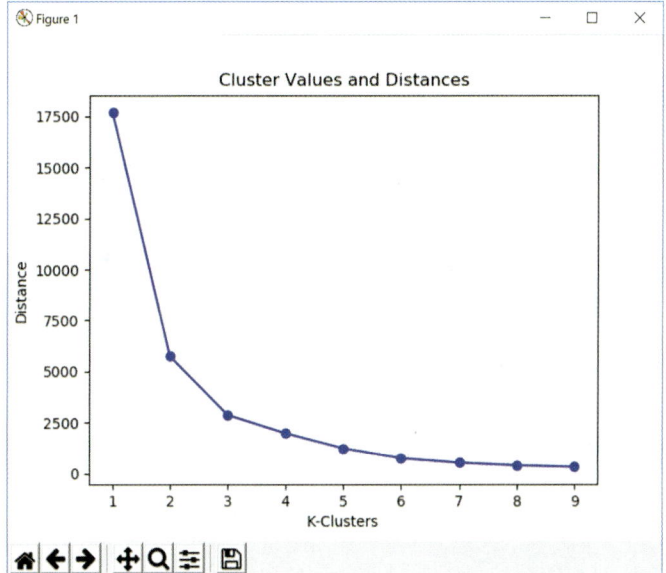

**FIGURE 10.2** Using the bent-elbow method to determine the proper number of clusters.
Used with permission of Python Software Foundation

You will need to determine and specify the number of clusters for each data set with which you work. Depending on the data-set values, you may find that for one set of values (possibly from the same data source), a cluster size of three is appropriate, whereas for other values, a cluster size of five provides better grouping. The only way to determine the appropriate cluster size is to create clusters and then to analyze the results (normally using the **sum of squared** distances).

Several algorithms exist to help you determine the proper number of clusters for your data. A common approach is called the "elbow method," so named because the chart that it produces resembles the bend in an elbow, as shown in **FIGURE 10.2**.

In this case, the bend at the elbow (the point where adding more clusters has minimal impact) occurs at three clusters. You create the elbow chart by charting the sum of the squares of each cluster result.

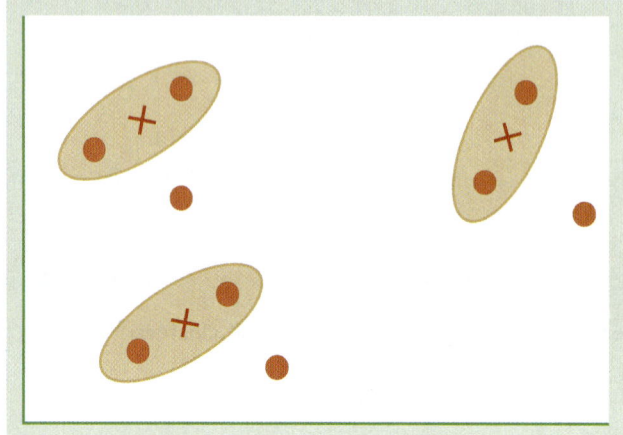

Assign Centroids X and Group

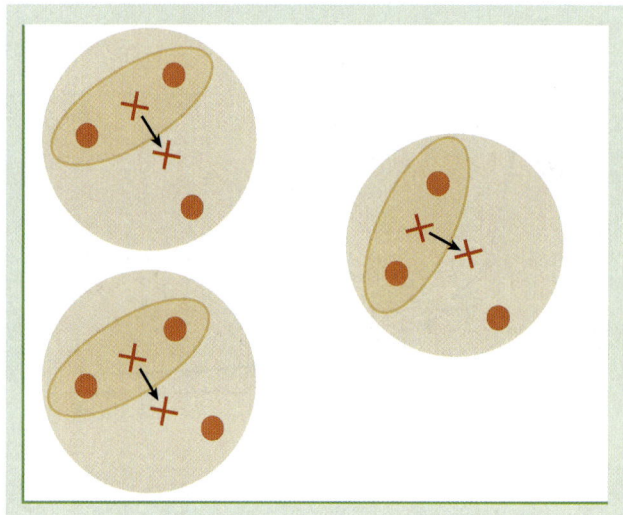

Move Centroids and Group

**FIGURE 10.3 Iterations within K-means to form three clusters.**

The following Python program, Elbow.py, creates the elbow chart previously shown in **FIGURE 10.3**:

```
import matplotlib.pyplot as plt
from sklearn.cluster import KMeans
from pandas import DataFrame

Data = {
        'x': [35,34,32,37,33,33,31,27,35,34,62,54,57,47,50,57,
              59,52,61,47,50,48,39,40,45,47,39,44,50,48],
```

```
            'y': [79,54,52,77,59,74,73,57,69,75,51,32,40,47,53,
                  36,35,58,59,50,23,22,13,14,22,7,29,25,9,8]
       }

df = DataFrame(Data,columns=['x','y'])

distances = []

K = range(1,10)
for k in K:
    ClusterInfo = kmeanModel = KMeans(n_clusters=k).fit(df)
    distances.append(ClusterInfo.inertia_)

plt.plot(K, distances, 'bo-')
plt.xlabel('K-Clusters')
plt.ylabel('Distance')
plt.title('Cluster Values and Distances')
plt.show()
```

In this case, the program loops, creating clusters for K = 1 to K = 10, plotting each cluster's distances (inertia).

The "means" in K-means clustering corresponds to the average distance for each point in the cluster to the cluster's center (centroid). K-means is an iterative algorithm that loops until either the maximum number of iterations is reached or the clusters do not change. To start the K-means clustering process, you will specify the number of clusters, the maximum number of iterations, and the starting location for K centroids (cluster centers for which you will normally specify K-random values). The locations that you choose for the starting centroids, as specified, can be random. The K-means algorithm will move the centroids to the ideal locations as it performs its processing. With each iteration, the K-means algorithm will perform these steps:

- Calculate K-centroid locations
- Move each point into the nearest cluster

In other words, with each iteration, the algorithm will move each cluster's centroid to the location that minimizes the average distance to the cluster's points. Figure 10.3 illustrates the process the algorithm performs to form three clusters.

The following Python script, KMeans.py, creates a three-cluster grouping:

```
import matplotlib.pyplot as plt
from sklearn.cluster import KMeans
from pandas import DataFrame

Data = {
        'x': [35,34,32,37,33,33,31,27,35,34,62,54,57,
              47,50,57,59,52,61,47,50,48,39,40,45,47,39,44,50,4
              8],
        'y': [79,54,52,77,59,74,73,57,69,75,51,32,40,47,
              53,36,35,58,59,50,23,22,13,14,22,7,29,25,9,8]
       }
```

## CHAPTER 10 Data Clustering

```
df = DataFrame(Data,columns=['x','y'])

kmeans = KMeans(n_clusters=3).fit(df)
centroids = kmeans.cluster_centers_

plt.scatter(df['x'], df['y'], c=kmeans.labels_.astype(float))
plt.scatter(centroids[:, 0], centroids[:, 1], c='red')
plt.show()
```

When you run the program, it will display the clusters shown in **FIGURE 10.4**.

As you can see, the script uses the KMeans function to create the clusters, specifying the parameter K = 3. The program also displays the ending centroids in red.

The following R program, KMeans.R, performs similar processing:

```
library(factoextra)
library(cluster)
library(fpc)

df = data.frame(
        x = c(35,34,32,37,33,33,31,27,35,34,62,54,57,
              47,50,57,59,52,61,47,50,48,39,40,45,47,39,44,50,48),
```

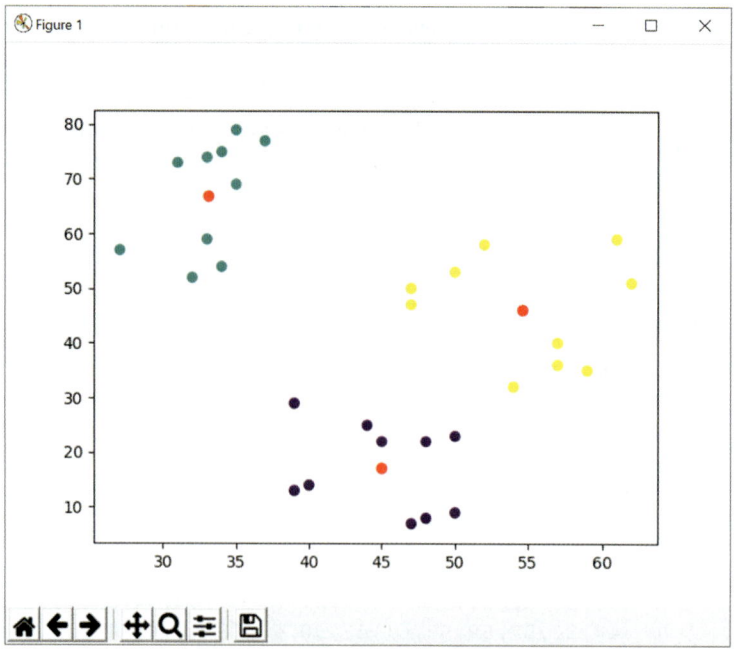

**FIGURE 10.4** Creating a three-cluster grouping using Python.
Used with permission of Python Software Foundation

## Understanding K-Means Clustering

```
        y = c(79,54,52,77,59,74,73,57,69,75,51,32,40,47,
              53,36,35,58,59,50,23,22,13,14,22,7,29,25,9,8)
        )

clusters <- kmeans(df, centers=3)
plotcluster(df, clusters$cluster)

points <- fviz_cluster(k3, geom = "point",  data = df) +
  ggtitle("K = 3")
```

When you run this program, it will display the clusters shown in **FIGURE 10.5**.

Depending on the plotting function you use to graph your clusters, you may find that the *x*- and *y*-axis chart values differ. The clusters in Figure 10.4, for example, use the actual data-point values for each axis, whereas Figure 10.5 plots the points based upon their related distances.

## Using K-Means++

When you use the K-means algorithm, you normally specify the starting centroid locations as random values. The K-means++ algorithm improves processing time by better calculating the starting centroid locations. The following Python program, KMeansPlusPlus.py, uses K-means to create the same three-cluster grouping:

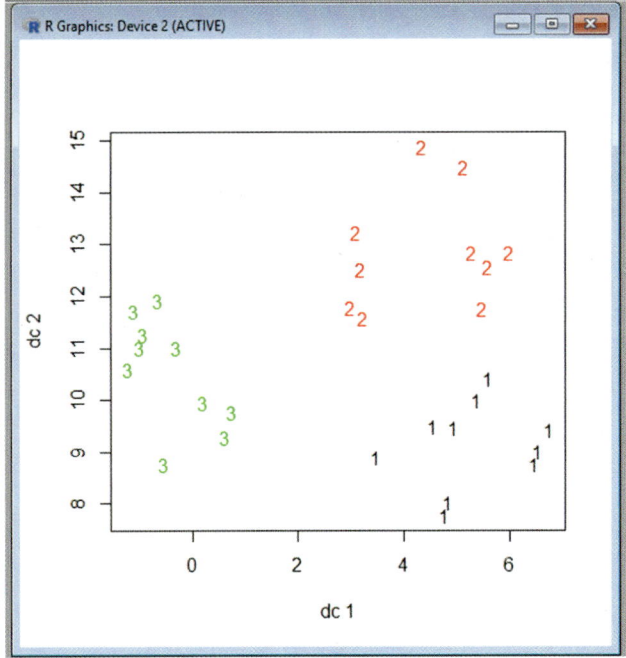

**FIGURE 10.5** Creating a three-cluster grouping using R.
Used with permission of The R Foundation

```
import matplotlib.pyplot as plt
from sklearn.cluster import KMeans
from pandas import DataFrame

Data = {
        'x': [35,34,32,37,33,33,31,27,35,34,62,54,57,
              47,50,57,59,52,61,47,50,48,39,40,45,47,39,44,50,48],
        'y': [79,54,52,77,59,74,73,57,69,75,51,32,40,47,
              53,36,35,58,59,50,23,22,13,14,22,7,29,25,9,8]
       }

df = DataFrame(Data,columns=['x','y'])

kmeans = KMeans(n_clusters=3, init='k-means++').fit(df)
centroids = kmeans.cluster_centers_

plt.scatter(df['x'], df['y'], c=kmeans.labels_.astype(float))
plt.scatter(centroids[:, 0], centroids[:, 1], c='red')
plt.show()
```

As you can see, the program passes the parameter init='k-means++' to the KMeans function. K-means++ should arrive at a solution faster than K-means. The following Python script, TimeClusters.py, uses the K-means and K-means++ algorithms to create clusters with K = 3, K = 4, and K = 5, timing the processing required.

```
import matplotlib.pyplot as plt
import time
from sklearn.cluster import KMeans
from pandas import DataFrame

Data = {
        'x': [35,34,32,37,33,33,31,27,35,34,62,54,57,
              47,50,57,59,52,61,47,50,48,39,40,45,47,39,44,50,48],
        'y': [79,54,52,77,59,74,73,57,69,75,51,32,40,
              47,53,36,35,58,59,50,23,22,13,14,22,7,29,25,9,8]
       }

df = DataFrame(Data,columns=['x','y'])

KMeansStartTime = time.time()

kmeans = KMeans(n_clusters=3).fit(df)
kmeansDistance = kmeans.inertia_

kmeans = KMeans(n_clusters=4).fit(df)
kmeansDistance += kmeans.inertia_

kmeans = KMeans(n_clusters=5).fit(df)
kmeansDistance += kmeans.inertia_
```

```
KMeansStopTime = time.time()

KMeansppStartTime = time.time()

kmeans = KMeans(n_clusters=3, init='k-means++').fit(df)
kmeansppDistance = kmeans.inertia_

kmeans = KMeans(n_clusters=4, init='k-means++').fit(df)
kmeansppDistance += kmeans.inertia_

kmeans = KMeans(n_clusters=5, init='k-means++').fit(df)
kmeansppDistance += kmeans.inertia_

KMeansppStopTime = time.time()

print('KMeans time ', KMeansStopTime - KMeansStartTime)
print('KMeans total distance ', kmeansDistance)
print('KMeans++ time ', KMeansppStopTime - KMeansppStartTime)
print('KMeans++ total distance ', kmeansppDistance)
```

As you can see, the script uses the time method to approximate the processing time required to perform a task—in this case, the clustering operation. As you perform different analytic operations, you may want to use the time function in this way to gain insights into the processing time. When you run this script, it will display the output shown here:

```
KMeans time    0.04100680351257324
KMeans total distance   6136.200000000001
KMeans++ time   0.03795266151428223
KMeans++ total distance   6136.200000000001
```

The following R program, KMeansPlusPlus.R, uses the kmeanspp function to implement K-means++ processing:

```
library(factoextra)
library(cluster)
library(LICORS)
library(pracma)

df = data.frame(
      x = c(35,34,32,37,33,33,31,27,35,34,62,54,57,
            47,50,57,59,52,61,47,50,48,39,40,45,47,39,44,50,48),
      y = c(79,54,52,77,59,74,73,57,69,75,51,32,40,
            47,53,36,35,58,59,50,23,22,13,14,22,7,29,25,9,8)
      )

clusters <- kmeanspp(df, 3)
plotcluster(df, clusters$cluster)
```

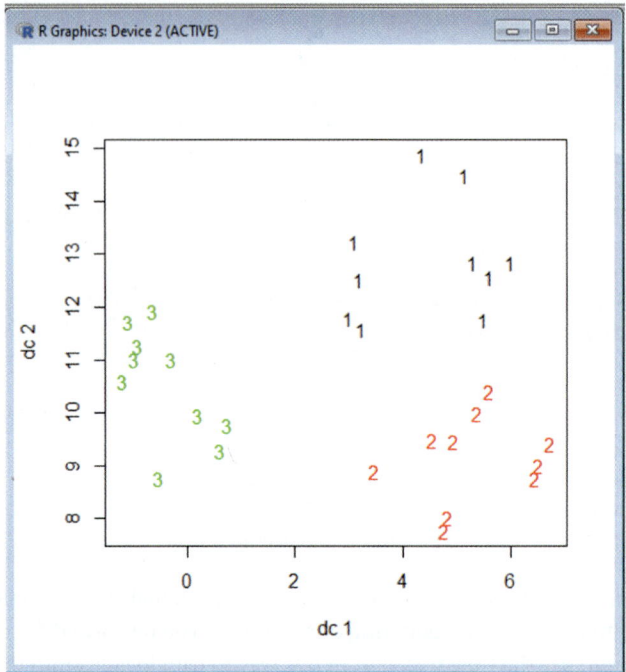

**FIGURE 10.6** Displaying the output of an R program that clusters data using K-means++.
Used with permission of The R Foundation

```
points <- fviz_cluster(k3, geom = "point", data = df) +
   ggtitle("K = 3")
```

When you run this program, it will display the output shown in **FIGURE 10.6**.

## Hierarchical Cluster

A hierarchical clustering algorithm takes a different approach to grouping data. There are two forms of hierarchical clustering algorithms: bottom-up and top-down. The bottom-up clustering algorithm is called an **agglomerative** algorithm because, with each iteration, it merges related clusters into a larger cluster. In other words, the bottom-up algorithm finds the two nearest clusters and merges them, repeating this process, as shown in **FIGURE 10.7**, until only one cluster exists.

In contrast, a top-down hierarchical clustering algorithm starts with one cluster and with each iteration, decomposes the cluster to form the lower-level clusters. Because it breaks apart a larger cluster into smaller clusters, the top-down approach is called a divisive algorithm.

To understand how the hierarchical algorithm groups clusters, analysts use a chart to show the cluster groupings called a dendrogram. **FIGURE 10.8** shows a dendrogram that illustrates the cluster groupings.

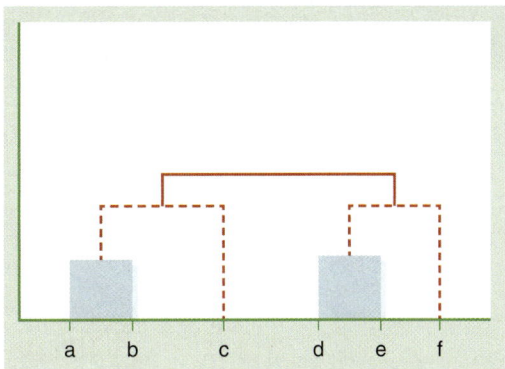

**FIGURE 10.7** Merging clusters using the hierarchical clustering algorithm.

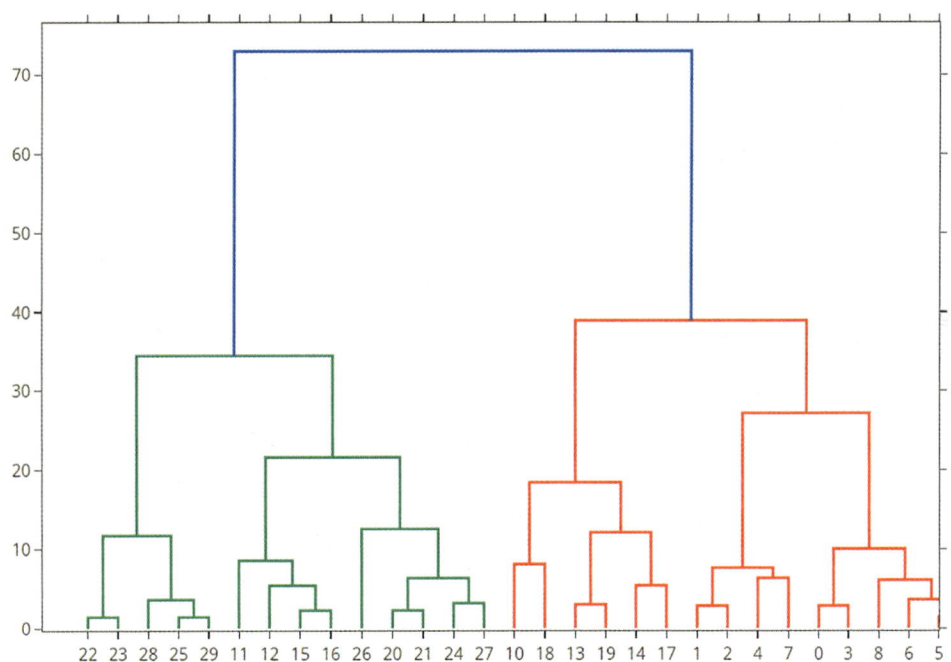

**FIGURE 10.8** Using a dendrogram to illustrate hierarchical cluster groupings.

To better understand the processing hierarchical clustering performs, take time to examine the data-point locations and groupings the dendrogram presents. The dendrogram provides you with insight as to how the hierarchical clustering algorithm will cluster data. Normally, you will use a scatter chart to display the clustered data, similar to that shown in **FIGURE 10.9**.

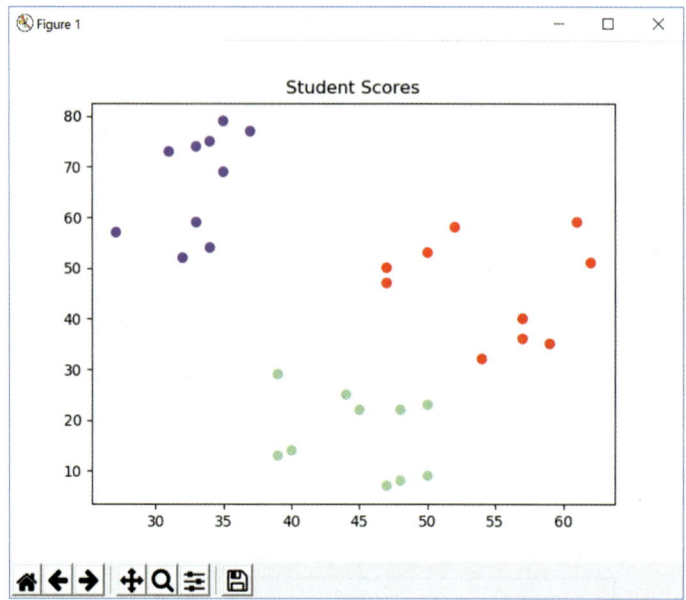

**FIGURE 10.9** A cluster chart produced by a hierarchical cluster algorithm.

Used with permission of Python Software Foundation

The previous discussion used the minimum distance between points to select the points assigned to a cluster. It turns out that hierarchical algorithms can use several different approaches to selecting points:

- Simple linkage: Select the closest neighbor.
- Complete linkage: Selects points furthest apart.
- Wards: Selects the point that results in the smallest increase to the group's sum of squares.
- Average linkage: Selects points to minimize the average distance between points.

Using the data previously used for the K-means clustering, **FIGURE 10.10** illustrates the dendrograms produced by each of the distance methods.

The following Python script, MultiDendrogram.py, creates the dendrograms previously shown in Figure 10.10:

```
import matplotlib.pyplot as plt
from pandas import DataFrame
from scipy.cluster.hierarchy import dendrogram, linkage

Data = {
        'x': [35,34,32,37,33,33,31,27,35,34,62,54,57,
              47,50,57,59,52,61,47,50,48,39,40,45,47,39,44,50,48],
        'y': [79,54,52,77,59,74,73,57,69,75,51,32,40,
              47,53,36,35,58,59,50,23,22,13,14,22,7,29,25,9,8]
       }
```

## Understanding K-Means Clustering

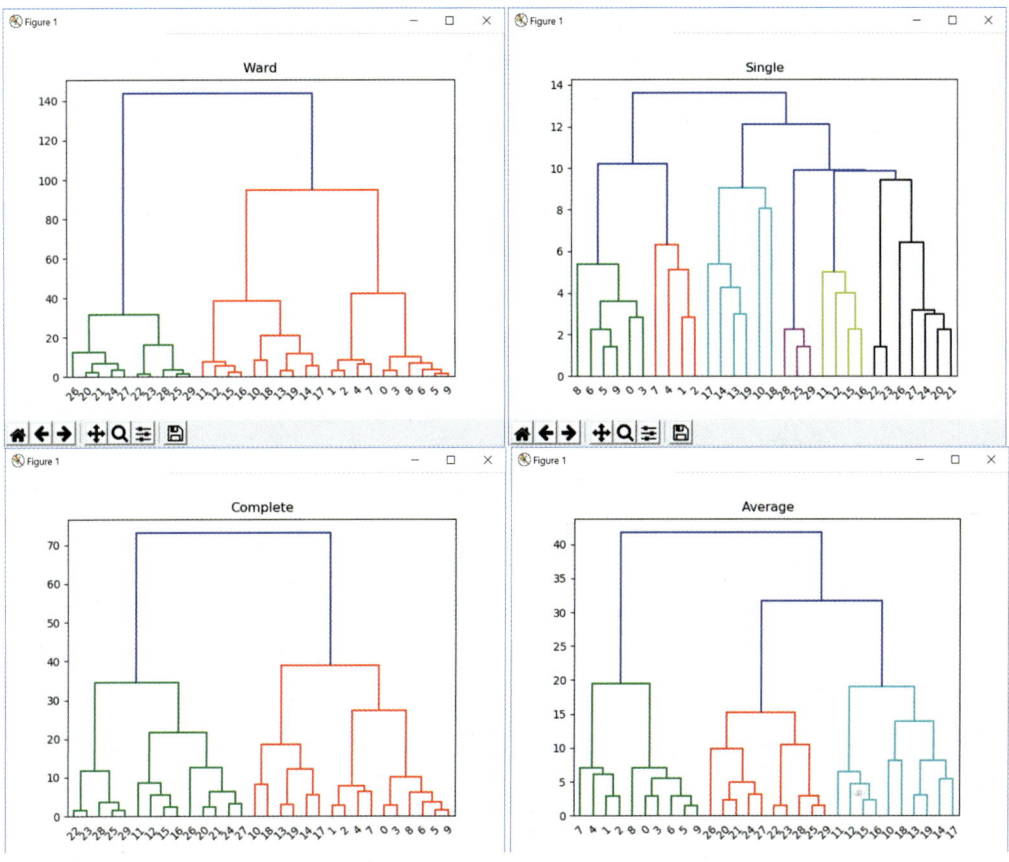

**FIGURE 10.10** Using different hierarchical clustering distance methods to produce dendrograms.

Used with permission of Python Software Foundation

```
df = DataFrame(Data,columns=['x','y'])

dendrogram(linkage(df, 'ward'))
plt.title('Ward')
plt.show()

dendrogram(linkage(df, 'single'))
plt.title('Single')
plt.show()

dendrogram(linkage(df, 'complete'))
plt.title('Complete')
plt.show()

dendrogram(linkage(df, 'average'))
plt.title('Average')
plt.show()
```

# CHAPTER 10 Data Clustering

The program uses the dendrogram function to create the dendrograms. Because a hierarchical algorithm combines clusters until only one cluster remains, you do not specify a cluster size.

In a similar way, the following R program, Hierarchical.R, creates a dendrogram based on the average linkage method that clusters points by minimizing the average distance between them:

```
library(cluster)
library(fpc)

df = data.frame(
        x = c(35,34,32,37,33,33,31,27,35,34,62,54,57,
              47,50,57,59,52,61,47,50,48,39,40,45,47,39,44,50,48),
        y = c(79,54,52,77,59,74,73,57,69,75,51,32,40,
              47,53,36,35,58,59,50,23,22,13,14,22,7,29,25,9,8)
        )

distances <- dist(df, method = "euclidean")

dendrogram <- hclust(distances, method = "average")
plot(dendrogram, labels = NULL, hang = 0.1, main = "Cluster Dendrogram",
sub = NULL, xlab = 'Distances', ylab = "Height")
```

When you run this program, R will produce the chart shown in **FIGURE 10.11**.

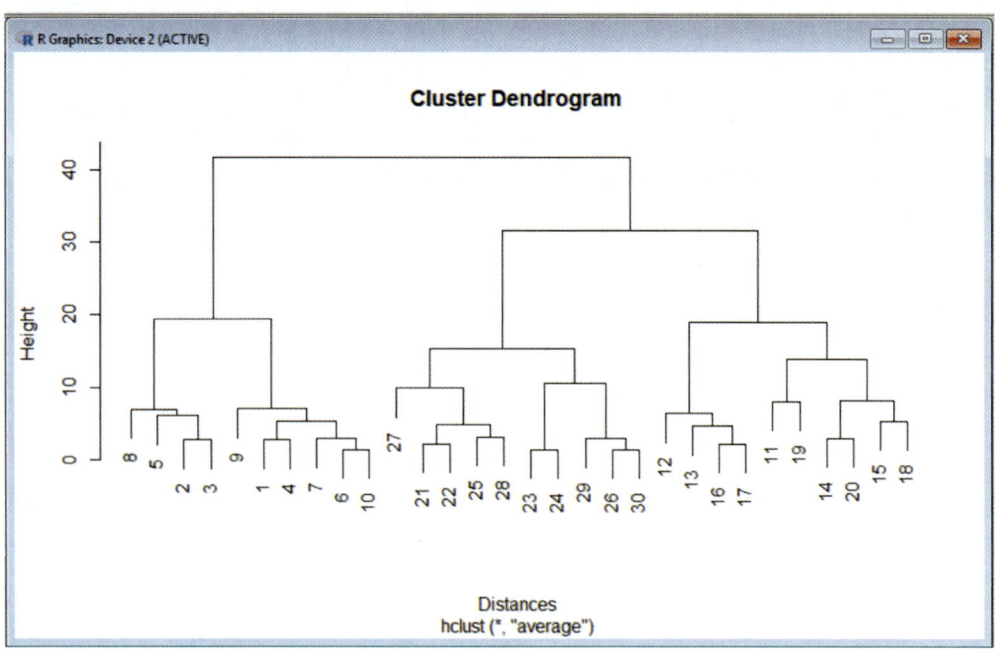

**FIGURE 10.11** Producing a dendrogram using R.
Used with permission of The R Foundation

To create clusters for other linkage methods, change the call to hclust to specify the method you desire, such as "compete."

The following Python program, HierchicalCharts.py, produces the cluster charts for each point-selection algorithm:

```python
import matplotlib.pyplot as plt
from pandas import DataFrame
from sklearn.cluster import AgglomerativeClustering

Data = {
        'x': [35,34,32,37,33,33,31,27,35,34,62,54,57,
              47,50,57,59,52,61,47,50,48,39,40,45,47,39,44,50,48],
        'y': [79,54,52,77,59,74,73,57,69,75,51,32,40,
              47,53,36,35,58,59,50,23,22,13,14,22,7,29,25,9,8]
       }

df = DataFrame(Data,columns=['x','y'])

cluster = AgglomerativeClustering(n_clusters=3,
  affinity='euclidean', linkage='ward')
cluster.fit_predict(df)
plt.scatter(df['x'], df['y'], c=cluster.labels_, cmap='rainbow')
  plt.title('Ward');
plt.show()

cluster = AgglomerativeClustering(n_clusters=3,
  affinity='euclidean', linkage='single')
cluster.fit_predict(df)
plt.scatter(df['x'], df['y'], c=cluster.labels_, cmap='rainbow')
plt.title('Single')
plt.scatter(df['x'], df['y'], c=cluster.labels_, cmap='rainbow')
plt.show()

cluster = AgglomerativeClustering(n_clusters=3,
  affinity='euclidean', linkage='complete')
cluster.fit_predict(df)
plt.scatter(df['x'], df['y'], c=cluster.labels_, cmap='rainbow')
plt.title('Complete')
plt.show()

cluster = AgglomerativeClustering(n_clusters=3,
  affinity='euclidean', linkage='average')
cluster.fit_predict(df)
plt.scatter(df['x'], df['y'], c=cluster.labels_, cmap='rainbow')
plt.title('Average')
plt.show()
```

When you run this script, it will display the charts as shown in **FIGURE 10.12**.

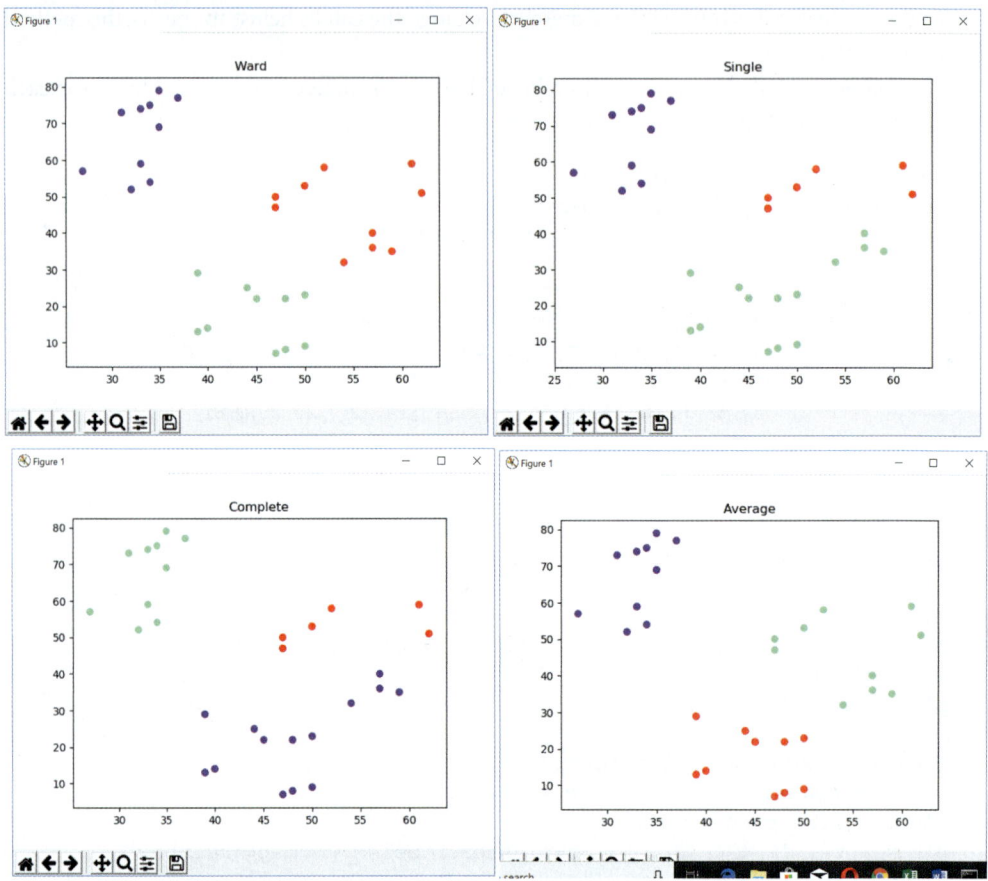

**FIGURE 10.12** Producing clusters using each of the hierarchical distance algorithms.

Used with permission of Python Software Foundation

To create each cluster, the program uses the AgglomerativeClustering method. Remember, agglomerative simply means merging. The function will merge related clusters. Within each function call, the affinity parameter directs the function to use a Euclidean distance. Likewise, the linkage parameter specifies which distance technique to use.

## Understanding DBSCAN Clustering

DBSCAN groups points within clusters based on the density of surrounding points. The DBSCAN algorithm begins by specifying a minimum number of points and a radius. Within a cluster, a "core point" has at least the minimum number of points surrounding it within the given radius. A "cluster border point," in contrast, falls within the radius distance but does not have the minimum

## Understanding the Sum of Squares

To analyze the effectiveness of a clustering algorithm, analysts calculate the sum of squares for distances from the mean value. To calculate the sum of squares, perform these steps:

- Calculate the cluster's mean distance.
- For each point in the cluster, determine the distance from the mean, square that value, and add the result to the sum:

$$\text{Sum of squares} = \sum_{i=1}^{n}(x_i - \bar{x})^2$$

number of points surrounding it. All other points fall outside of the cluster and are considered "noise," as shown in **FIGURE 10.13**.

The DBSCAN algorithm starts by determining the point types (core, border, and noise). It then creates a cluster for each core point, merging the clusters that fall within the radius. Finally, DBSCAN adds the border points to the cluster.

The following Python program, DBSCAN.py, uses the DBSCAN algorithm to group data into clusters:

```
import matplotlib.pyplot as plt
from sklearn.cluster import DBSCAN
from pandas import DataFrame

Data = {
        'x': [35,34,32,37,33,33,31,27,35,34,62,54,57,
              47,50,57,59,52,61,47,50,48,39,40,45,47,39,44,50,48],
        'y': [79,54,52,77,59,74,73,57,69,75,51,32,40,
              47,53,36,35,58,59,50,23,22,13,14,22,7,29,25,9,8]
       }

df = DataFrame(Data,columns=['x','y'])

clustering = DBSCAN(eps=5, min_samples=3).fit(df)
labels = clustering.labels_
numberofclusters = len(set(labels)) - (1 if -1 in labels else 0)
plt.title('DBSCAN Number of clusters: %d' % numberofclusters)
plt.scatter(df['x'], df['y'], c=clustering.labels_.astype(float))
plt.show()
```

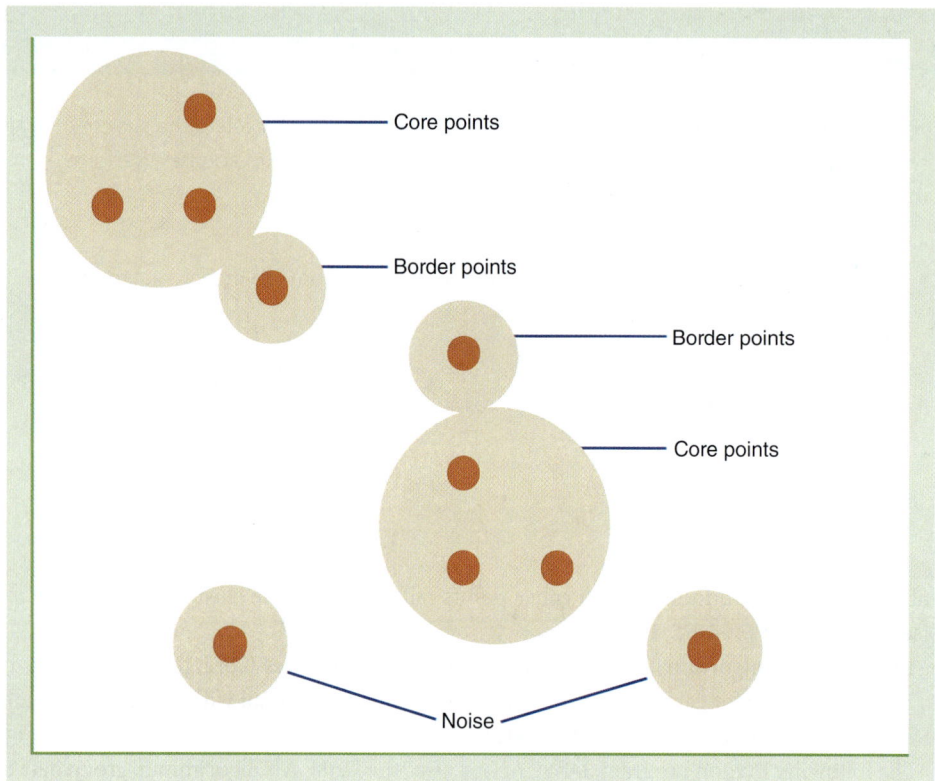

**FIGURE 10.13** Assigning points to clusters using DBSCAN.

Within the call to the DBSCAN function, the eps parameter specifies the maximum distance between two points for the points to be considered within the same cluster. When you execute this program, it will display the cluster chart shown in **FIGURE 10.14**.

The script creates the clusters by calling the DBSCAN function. The function will return a vector that specifies into which cluster each corresponding point falls. If a point is not in a cluster, meaning the point is noise (an outlier), the vector will contain the value −1. The code determines the number of clusters by counting cluster values that are not −1.

In a similar way, this R program uses DBSCAN to cluster data:

```
library(dbscan)

df = data.frame(
    x = c(35,34,32,37,33,33,31,27,35,34,62,54,57,
          47,50,57,59,52,61,47,50,48,39,40,45,47,39,44,50,48),
```

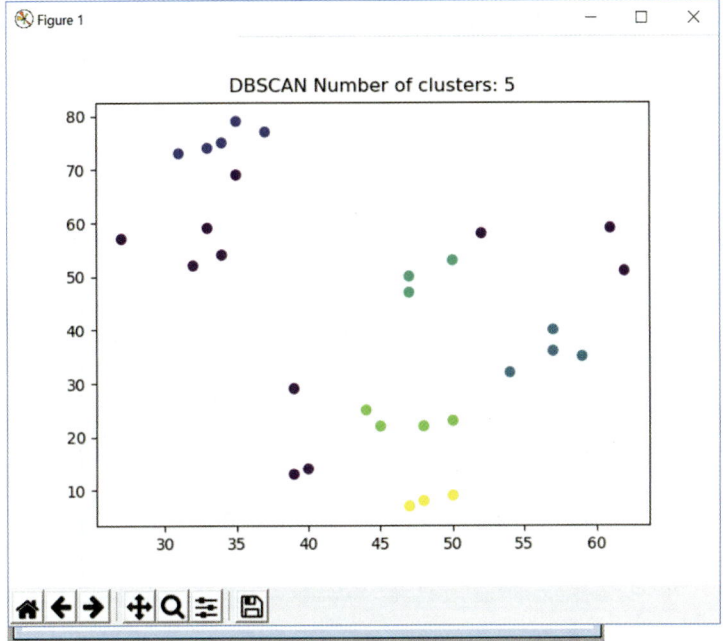

**FIGURE 10.14** Using DBSCAN to produce clusters.

Used with permission of Python Software Foundation

```
        y = c(79,54,52,77,59,74,73,57,69,75,51,32,40,
              47,53,36,35,58,59,50,23,22,13,14,22,7,29,25,9,8)
        )

clusters <- dbscan(df, eps=5.0, minPts = 3)

plot(df, col=clusters$cluster)
```

When you execute this program, it will display the clusters shown in **FIGURE 10.15**.

## Set Aside Cluster-Shape Biases

When data analysts first start clustering data, they often envision clusters as neat and orderly groups, as shown in **FIGURE 10.16**.

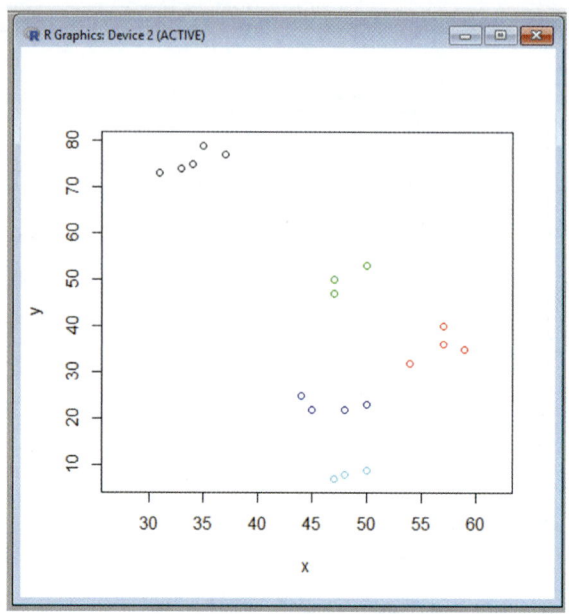

**FIGURE 10.15** Using R to chart clusters formed by DBSCAN.
Used with permission of The R Foundation

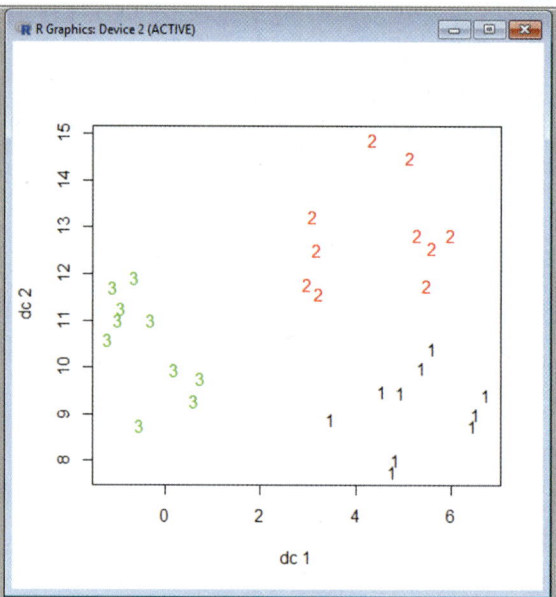

**FIGURE 10.16** Typical expectation of clustered data.
Used with permission of The R Foundation

## Set Aside Cluster-Shape Biases

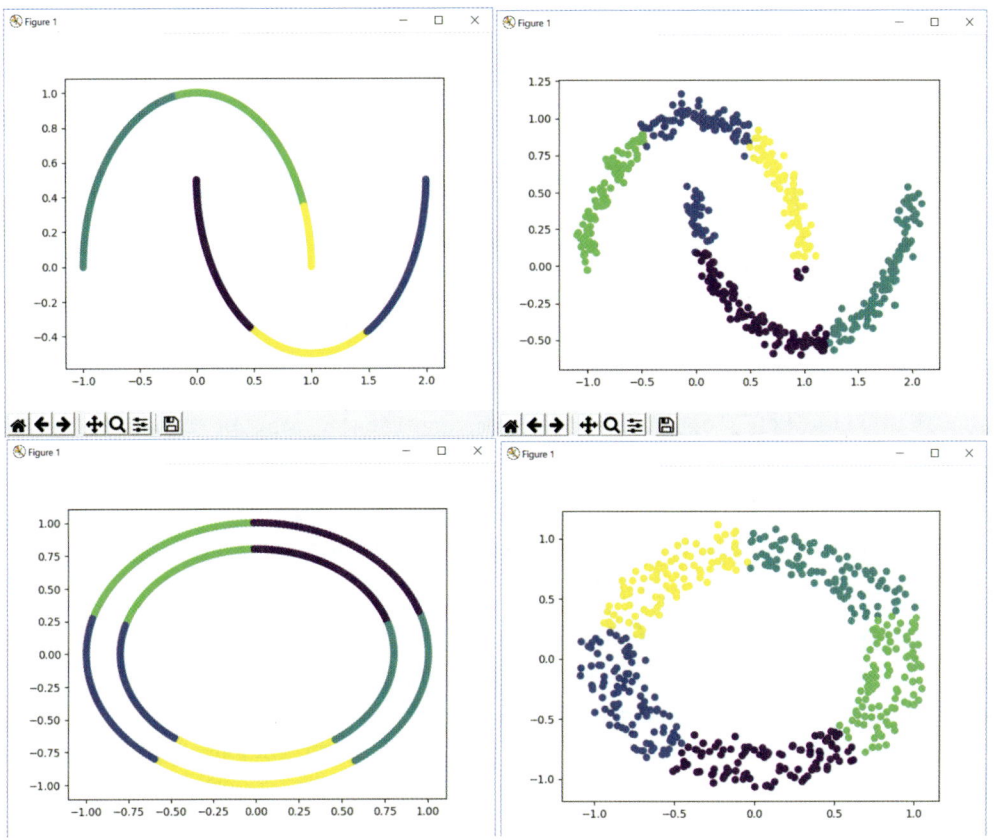

**FIGURE 10.17 Clusters can take on a variety of shapes and forms.**
Used with permission of Python Software Foundation

Clusters, however, can take on a variety of shapes and forms. **FIGURE 10.17**, for example, illustrates clusters produced by data in the Python sklearn make_moons and make_circles data sets.

The following Python program, Moons.py, creates the clusters previously shown in Figure 10.17:

```
import matplotlib.pyplot as plt
from sklearn.cluster import KMeans
from sklearn import datasets

X, y = datasets.make_moons(n_samples=500)

kmeans = KMeans(n_clusters=5).fit(X)
plt.scatter(X[:, 0], X[:, 1], c=kmeans.labels_.astype(float))
plt.show()
```

```
X, y = datasets.make_moons(n_samples=500, noise=0.05)

kmeans = KMeans(n_clusters=5).fit(X)
plt.scatter(X[:, 0], X[:, 1], c=kmeans.labels_.astype(float))
plt.show()

X, y = datasets.make_circles(n_samples=500)

kmeans = KMeans(n_clusters=5).fit(X)
plt.scatter(X[:, 0], X[:, 1], c=kmeans.labels_.astype(float))
plt.show()

X, y = datasets.make_circles(n_samples=500, noise=0.05)
kmeans = KMeans(n_clusters=5).fit(X)
plt.scatter(X[:, 0], X[:, 1], c=kmeans.labels_.astype(float))
plt.show()
```

The program uses the make_moons and make_circles data sets, using 500 points per chart. Within the data sets, the noise parameter adds jitter to the charts, slightly moving overlapping points.

## Viewing the Cluster Assignments

When you create your clusters, the functions will normally return a vector of values that specify to which cluster the corresponding point has been assigned. When you plot the clusters, your plotting functions will use this vector to assign different colors to each cluster. The following Python script, ShowClusters.py, prints the cluster vector returned by the Kmeans function:

```
from sklearn.cluster import KMeans
from pandas import DataFrame

Data = {
       'x': [35,34,32,37,33,33,31,27,35,34,62,54,57,
             47,50,57,59,52,61,47,50,48,39,40,45,47,39,44,50,48],
       'y': [79,54,52,77,59,74,73,57,69,75,51,32,40,
             47,53,36,35,58,59,50,23,22,13,14,22,7,29,25,9,8]
       }

df = DataFrame(Data,columns=['x','y'])

kmeans = KMeans(n_clusters=3).fit(df)

clusters = kmeans.labels_
i = 0
print("Cluster    X        Y")
for row in df.iterrows():
   print(clusters[i], '  ', row[1]['x'], '    ', row[1]['y'])
   i = i + 1
```

When you run this script, it will display the following output:

```
Cluster         X       Y
1               35      79
1               34      54
1               32      52
1               37      77
1               33      59
1               33      74
1               31      73
1               27      57
1               35      69
1               34      75
2               62      51
2               54      32
2               57      40
2               47      47
2               50      53
2               57      36
2               59      35
2               52      58
2               61      59
2               47      50
0               50      23
0               48      22
0               39      13
0               40      14
0               45      22
0               47      7
0               39      29
0               44      25
0               50      9
0               48      8
```

Similarly, this Python script, ShowHierarchicalClusters.py, displays the clusters returned for a hierarchical clustering:

```
from pandas import DataFrame
from sklearn.cluster import AgglomerativeClustering

Data = {
        'x': [35,34,32,37,33,33,31,27,35,34,62,54,57,
              47,50,57,59,52,61,47,50,48,39,40,45,47,39,44,50,48],
        'y': [79,54,52,77,59,74,73,57,69,75,51,32,40,
              47,53,36,35,58,59,50,23,22,13,14,22,7,29,25,9,8]
       }
```

```
df = DataFrame(Data,columns=['x','y'])

cluster = AgglomerativeClustering(n_clusters=3,
affinity='euclidean', linkage='ward')
cluster.fit_predict(df)

clusters = cluster.labels_
i = 0
print("Cluster     X       Y")
for row in df.iterrows():
    print(clusters[i], ' ', row[1]['x'], '   ', row[1]['y'])
    i = i + 1
```

When you run this program, it will display the following output:

```
Cluster         X       Y
0               35      79
0               34      54
0               32      52
0               37      77
0               33      59
0               33      74
0               31      73
0               27      57
0               35      69
0               34      75
2               62      51
2               54      32
2               57      40
2               47      47
2               50      53
2               57      36
2               59      35
2               52      58
2               61      59
2               47      50
1               50      23
1               48      22
1               39      13
1               40      14
1               45      22
1               47      7
1               39      29
1               44      25
1               50      9
1               48      8
```

## Identifying Data Outliers

An **outlier** is a value that falls outside of the expected range of values. Depending on the analysis you are performing, the presence of one or more outliers can have a significant impact on your results. The following Python program, BasicMetrics.py, calculates the mean and standard deviation for an array of values:

```
import statistics

values = [-100, -75, 1,2,3,4,5, 75, 100]
print('Mean', statistics.mean(values))
print('Standard Deviation', statistics.stdev(values))
```

When you run the program, it will display the following output:

```
Mean 1.6666666666666667
Standard Deviation 62.52999280345393
```

In this case, the large standard deviation, relative to the mean, is an indication that outlier values may exist. Next, the following program, IdentifyOutliers.py, examines the array values to identify values that fall outside of the standard deviation from the mean, and if so, identifies the corresponding value and index:

```
import statistics

values = [-100, -75, 1,2,3,4,5, 75, 100]
mean = statistics.mean(values)
stdev = statistics.stdev(values)

print('Mean ', mean)
print('Standard deviation ', stdev)

newvalues = []

for i in range(len(values)):
  if values[i] < (mean - stdev) or values[i] > (mean + stdev):
    print(i, values[i])
```

As you can see, the script uses an if statement to test if the value falls beyond the standard deviation and, if so, displays the value. When you run this script, it will display the following output:

```
Mean    1.6666666666666667
Standard deviation   62.52999280345393
0 -100
1 -75
7 75
8 100
```

Depending on your data analytic goal, you may actually pursue outliers. For example, within healthcare data, an outlier might provide you with a genetic trait key to a cause or cure. Often, however, you will simply delete the outlier values. The following Python program, NoOutliers.py, again performs the mean and standard deviation calculations, this time, however, with and without the outliers:

```
import statistics

values = [-100, -75, 1,2,3,4,5, 75, 100]
mean = statistics.mean(values)
stdev = statistics.stdev(values)
print('Starting values ', values)
print('Mean ', mean)
print('Standard deviation ', stdev)

newvalues = []

for i in range(len(values)):
  if values[i] > (mean - stdev) and values[i] < (mean + stdev):
    newvalues.append(values[i])

mean = statistics.mean(newvalues)
stdev = statistics.stdev(newvalues)

print('\nList without outliers ', newvalues)
print('Mean ', mean)
print('Standard deviation ', stdev)
```

As you can see, the script loops through the values, selecting only the values that fall within the standard deviation, which omits the outliers. When you execute this script, it will display the following output:

```
C:\Data> python NoOutliers.py
Starting values  [-100, -75, 1, 2, 3, 4, 5, 75, 100]
Mean   1.6666666666666667
Standard deviation   62.52999280345393

List without outliers   [1, 2, 3, 4, 5]
Mean   3
Standard deviation   1.5811388300841898
```

As you can see, when you eliminate the outlier values, you significantly change the data's mean and standard deviation.

## Identifying Outliers Using DBSCAN

When you cluster data sets, most cluster algorithms will assign all values to clusters, even outliers. As you have learned, the DBSCAN clustering algorithm will identify "core" values, "border" values, and noise. The following Python script, ShowNoise.py, displays the noise values identified by DBSCAN:

```python
from sklearn.cluster import DBSCAN
from pandas import DataFrame

Data = {
        'x': [35,34,32,37,33,33,31,27,35,34,62,54,57,
              47,50,57,59,52,61,47,50,48,39,40,45,47,39,44,50,48],
        'y': [79,54,52,77,59,74,73,57,69,75,51,32,40,
              47,53,36,35,58,59,50,23,22,13,14,22,7,29,25,9,8]
        }

df = DataFrame(Data,columns=['x','y'])

clustering = DBSCAN(eps=5, min_samples=3).fit(df)
labels = clustering.labels_

i = 0
print("Index     Cluster      X       Y")
for row in df.iterrows():
    if labels[i] == -1:
        print(i, '   ', labels[i], '     ', row[1]['x'], '   ',
            row[1]['y'])
    i = i + 1
```

When you run this program, it will display the following output:

```
C:\Data> python ShowOutliers.py
Index     Cluster      X       Y
1           -1         34      54
2           -1         32      52
4           -1         33      59
7           -1         27      57
8           -1         35      69
10          -1         62      51
18          -1         61      59
22          -1         39      13
23          -1         40      14
26          -1         39      29
```

# Hands-On: K-Means and Hierarchical Clustering in Excel Using Solver

If Python and R are not currently in your programming repertoire, you will likely leverage Excel to perform many data analytic operations. If so, you will want to download and install Solver (previously known as XLMiner) from the Frontline Solver's website at www.solver.com, as shown in **FIGURE 10.18**.

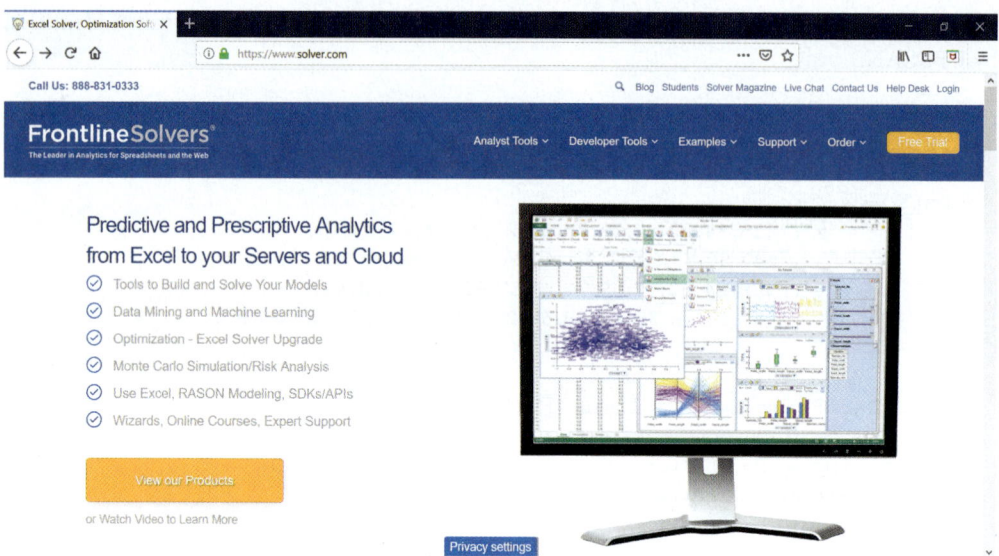

**FIGURE 10.18** The Frontline Solver website.

Used with permission of Frontline Systems

Using Solver, you can perform a wide range of data-mining and data-analytic operations, such as:

- Time-series analysis
- Text-data mining
- Predictive analysis
- Data classification
- K-means and hierarchical clustering

In this section, you will use Solver to perform K-means and hierarchical clustering.

## K-Means Clustering Using Solver

To start, download the Excel file HandsOn.xlsx from this text's catalog page at go.jblearning.com/DataMining. Excel will display the file's contents, as shown in **FIGURE 10.19**.

As you can see, the file contains data about wine contents and quality. You can find specifics on the data set at https://archive.ics.uci.edu/ml/datasets/wine.

Click the Add-Ins menu option and choose K-Means Clustering from the XLMiner menu, as shown in **FIGURE 10.20**.

Solver will display the dialog box shown in **FIGURE 10.21**, from which you can select the variables that you want to cluster.

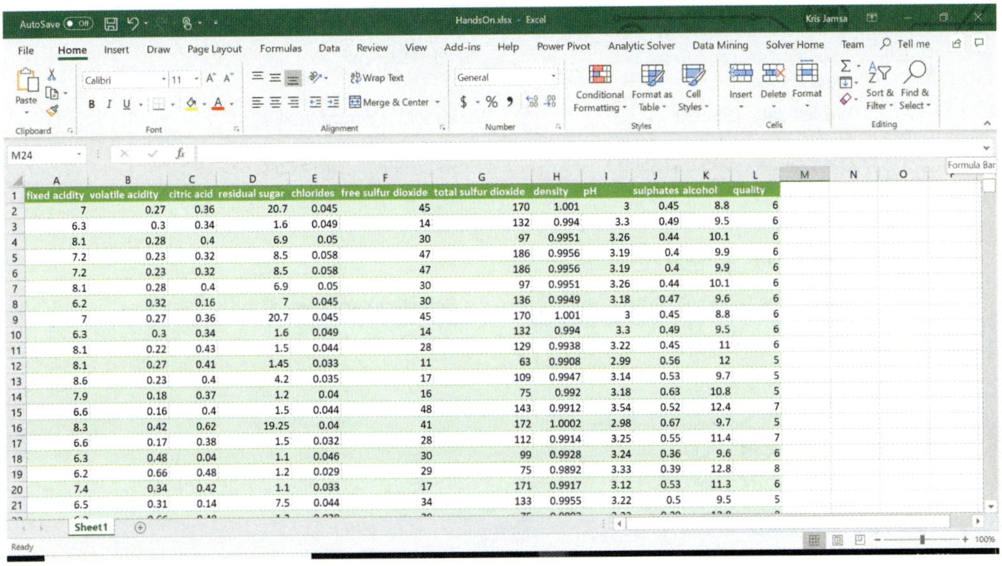

# Hands-On: K-Means and Hierarchical Clustering in Excel Using Solver

**FIGURE 10.19** The contents of the HandsOn.xlsx file.

Used with permission from Microsoft

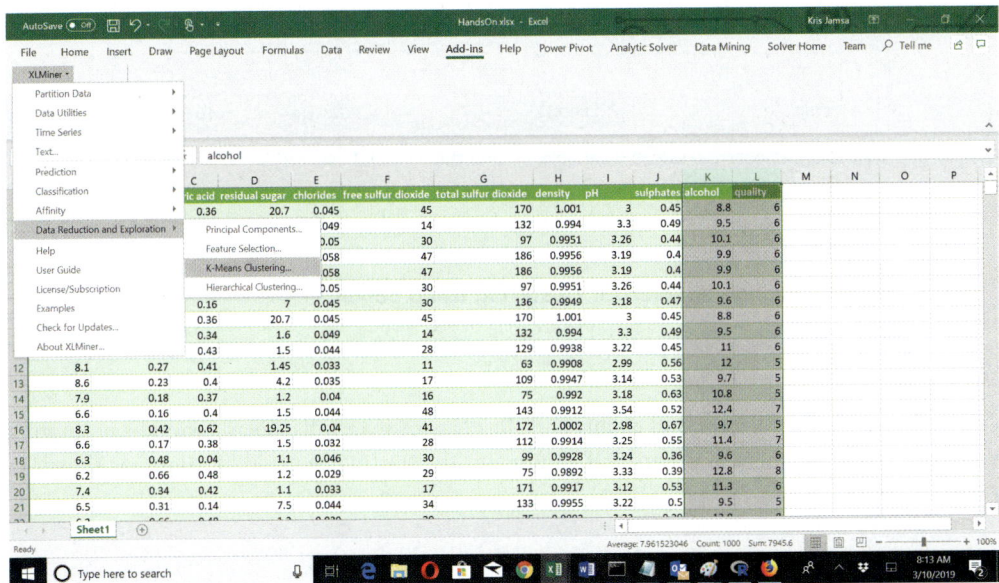

**FIGURE 10.20** Selecting K-Means Clustering.

Used with permission from Microsoft

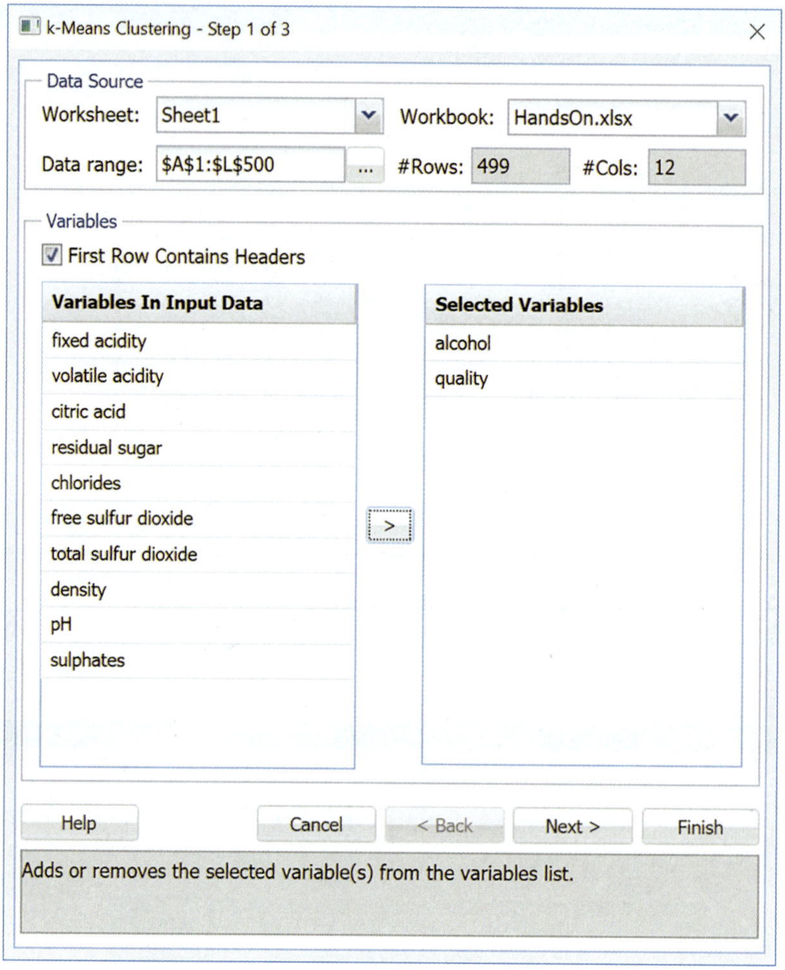

**FIGURE 10.21** **Selecting variables for clustering using Solver.**
Used with permission of Frontline Systems, Inc.

In this case, select alcohol and quality and click Next. Solver will display a window prompting you to enter the number of clusters and, optionally, the starting centroid locations, as shown in **FIGURE 10.22**.

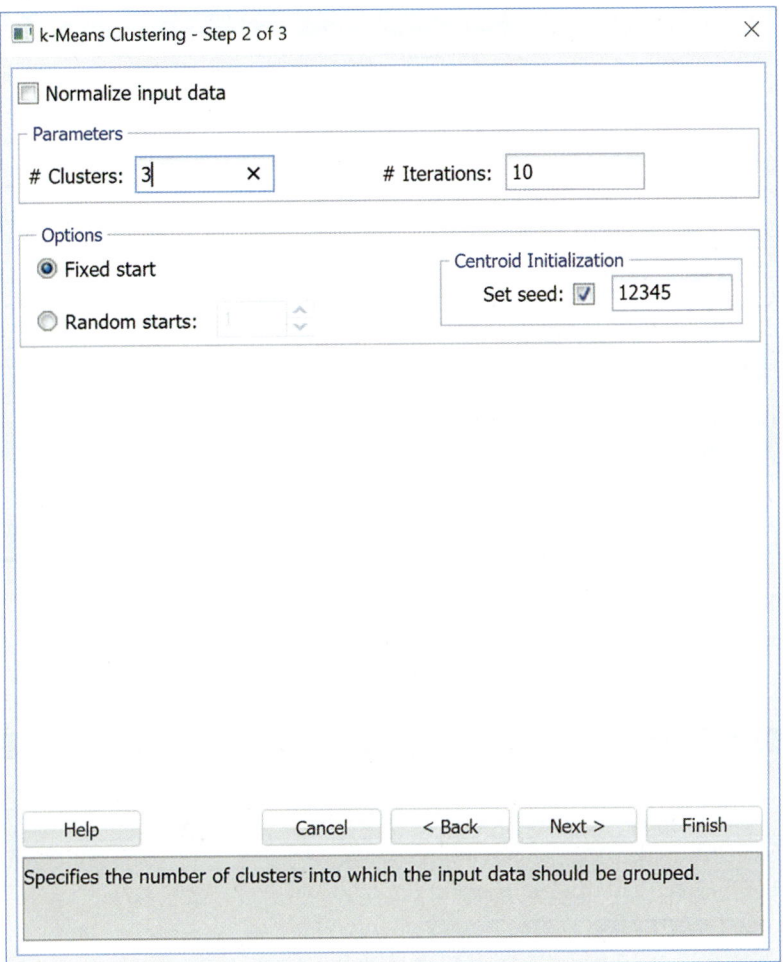

**FIGURE 10.22 Specifying the number of clusters and starting centroid locations.**
Used with permission of Frontline Systems, Inc.

Select four clusters and click Finish. Solver will display a summary of its results, as shown in **FIGURE 10.23**.

Within the summary, you will find:

- Cluster centers
- Cluster sizes
- Cluster average distances
- Cluster assignments

To view the cluster assignments, click on the KMC_Clusters sheet, as shown in **FIGURE 10.24**.

# CHAPTER 10 Data Clustering

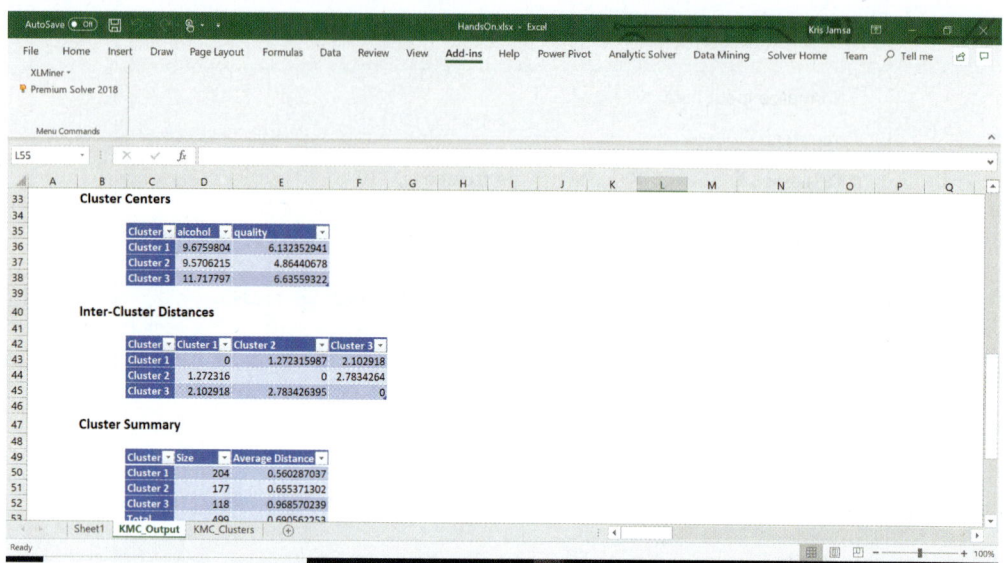

**FIGURE 10.23** Solver's clustering results.

Used with permission from Microsoft

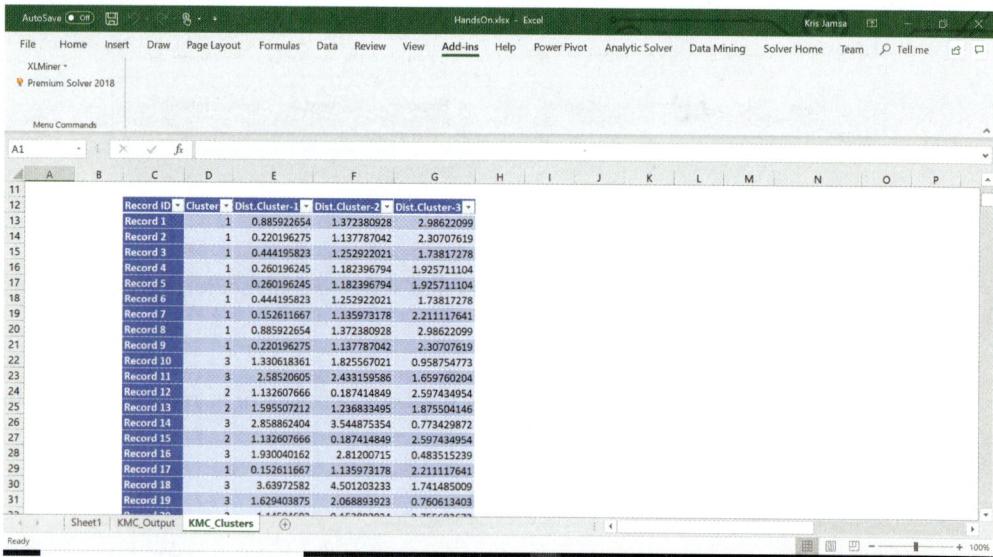

**FIGURE 10.24** Displaying the K-Means cluster assignments for alcohol and quality.

Used with permission from Microsoft

## Hierarchical Clustering Using Solver

Performing hierarchical clustering using Solver is similar. To start, within your data sheet, select the Add-ins XLMiner menu and choose Hierarchical Clustering, as shown in **FIGURE 10.25**.

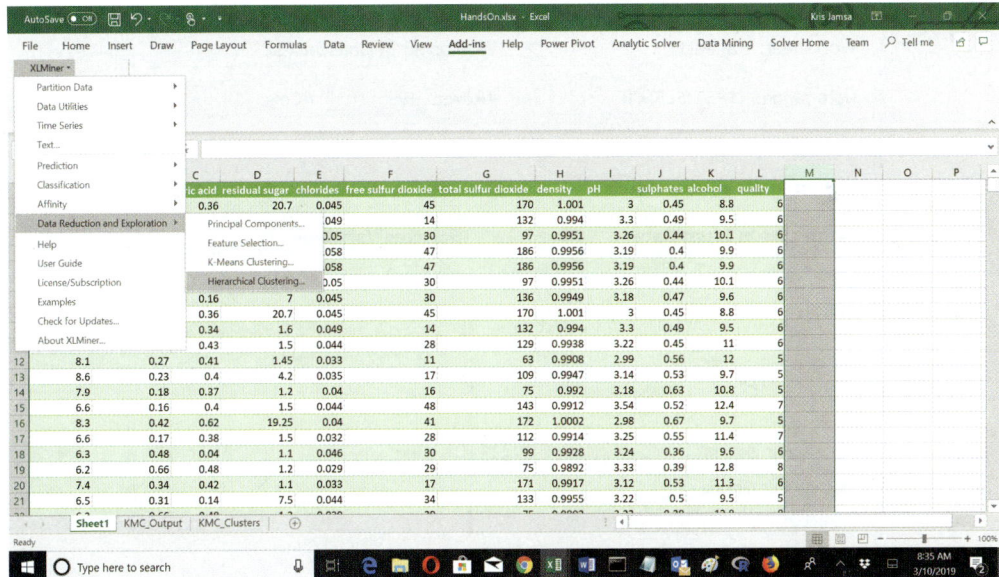

**FIGURE 10.25** Selecting XLMiner hierarchical clustering.

Used with permission from Microsoft

Solver will display a window within which you can select the fields to cluster. Again, choose alcohol and quality, as shown in **FIGURE 10.26**.

**FIGURE 10.26** Selecting fields for hierarchical clustering.
Used with permission of Frontline Systems, Inc.

When you click Next, Solver will display a window prompting you for the distance method you desire, as shown in **FIGURE 10.27**.

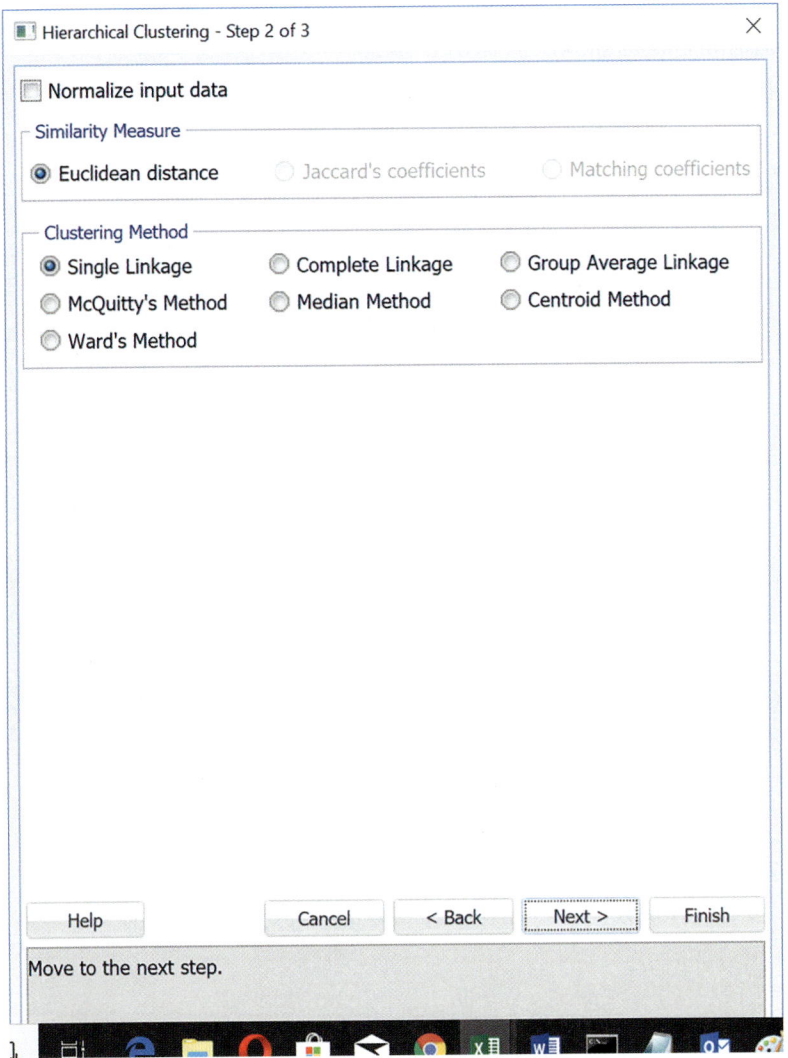

**FIGURE 10.27** Specifying the hierarchical clustering linkage method.
Used with permission of Frontline Systems, Inc.

Choose Wards and click Next. Solver will prompt you to specify the number of clusters you desire, as shown in **FIGURE 10.28**.

Enter 3 and click Finish. Solver will perform its calculations, displaying a summary result. To view the cluster assignments, click the HC_Clusters sheet, as shown in **FIGURE 10.29**.

Within the sheet, click on the HC_Dendrogram sheet. Solver will display the dendrogram for the cluster assignments, as shown in **FIGURE 10.30**.

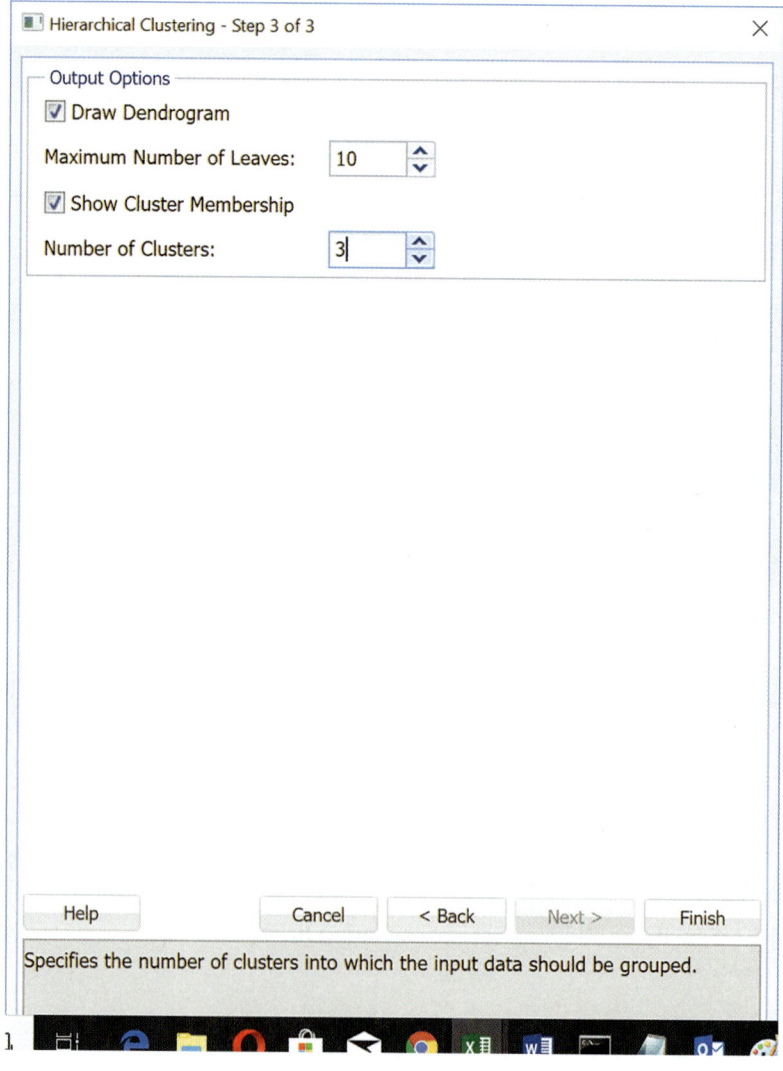

**FIGURE 10.28 Specifying the number of clusters.**

Used with permission of Frontline Systems, Inc.

# Hands-On: K-Means and Hierarchical Clustering in Excel Using Solver

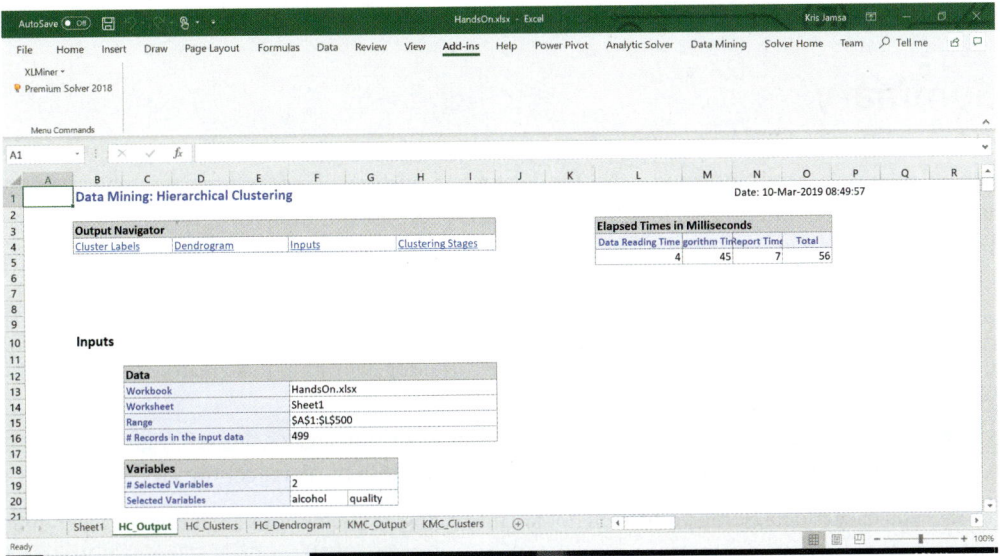

**FIGURE 10.29** Hierarchical cluster assignments.

Used with permission from Microsoft

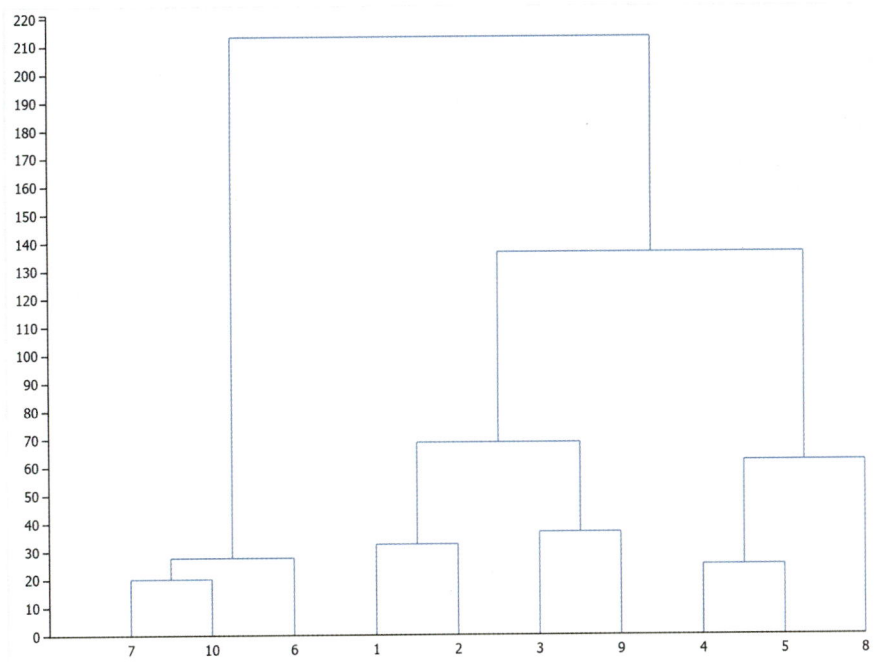

**FIGURE 10.30** The Solver dendrogram for alcohol and quality.

Used with permission of Frontline Systems, Inc.

## Summary

To better understand and analyze large data sets, analysts often group related data into clusters. The general premise behind clustering is that the data in one cluster will more closely resemble the data in that cluster than they do data in a different cluster. There are hundreds of clustering algorithms. In this chapter, you examined three commonly used clustering algorithms:

- K-Means Clustering: A clustering technique that groups points based on minimizing the average distance of each point from its cluster's center (centroid).
- Hierarchical Clustering: An agglomerative clustering algorithm that creates clusters by merging related (nearby) clusters.
- DBSCAN Clustering: The DBSCAN clustering algorithm creates clusters by grouping points based on their proximity to dense regions within the data's coordinate space.

As you cluster data, some points will not fall into a cluster. Such points are outliers. Depending on the analysis you are performing, you may want to further pursue the outliers to better understand their cause or implication, or you may simply want to remove the outliers from your data set. The cluster algorithms you examined in this chapter identify such outlier values.

## Key Terms

Agglomerative
Centroid
Clustering
Density-Based Spatial Clustering of Applications with Noise (DBSCAN)
Euclidian distance
Hierarchical clustering
K-means clustering
Outlier
Soft clustering algorithms
Sum of squares

## Review

1. Define and describe data clustering.
2. Describe the K-means clustering algorithm.
3. Describe the hierarchical clustering algorithm.
4. Describe the DBSCAN clustering algorithm.
5. Describe the expectations maximization clustering algorithm.
6. Perform each of the Python clustering applications this chapter presents using different cluster sizes. Describe your results.
7. Perform each of the R clustering applications this chapter presents using different cluster sizes. Describe your results.
8. Perform the Solver operations this chapter presents using different cluster sizes. Describe your findings.
9. Define and describe a data outlier.
10. Describe different approaches to handling data outliers.

# CHAPTER 11

# Classification

## Chapter Goals and Objectives

- Define and describe data classification.
- Compare and contrast binary and multiclass classification.
- Compare and contrast classification algorithms.
- Define and describe the role of training and testing data sets.
- Describe the steps to perform the classification process.

When data analysts mine data, they must often put data into specific groups (such as a pet is a dog, cat, or horse) or determine if an object is or isn't something (such as a loan being approved or disapproved). With respect to data mining, **classification** is the use of a supervised machine-learning algorithm to assign an observation into a specific category. Depending on the application, the classification may be binary:

- Is the customer male or female?
- Is the pet a dog or a cat?
- Should the loan be approved or disapproved?
- Is the wine a red or a white?
- Is the tumor benign or malignant?

Or the classification may use multiple classes (categories):

- Is a person's facial expression happy, sad, or angry?
- What breed of dog is my pet?
- Which user's biometric data were entered?

- Which voice recognition option did the caller select?
- How do we predict the book to sell (poorly, good, very good, great)?

Classification algorithms work by examining an input "training set" of data to learn how the data values combine to create a result. Such a training set, for example, might contain heights, weights, colors, and temperaments of different dogs and the resulting breeds, or it might contain the sizes, shapes, dimensions, and locations of tumors that are malignant, as well as similar data for tumors that are benign. In other words, the training data contain predictive values and the correct classification results.

After the learning algorithm learns from and models the test data, a "test" data set (for which the correct results are known) is tested against the model to determine its accuracy, such as 97%. With knowledge of the accuracy in hand, the data analyst can then use the model to classify other data values.

Normally, the training set and testing set come from the same data set of values that are known to be correct or observed. The data analyst will specify, for example, that 70% of the data will be training data and 30% will be used for testing. Across the web, you can find many different data sets of known or observed data that you can use to try different classification algorithms. This chapter will use several commonly used algorithms to:

- Determine to which type of iris a flower belongs.
- Determine if a breast cancer tumor is malignant or benign.
- Determine, based on chemical composition, a wine's type.
- Determine whether breast surgery patients should live 5 or more years post-surgery.

By the time you finish this chapter, you will understand the following key concepts:

- Classification is the process of assigning data to a specific group.
- Classification techniques are optimal for binary classifications, which use two target classes, such as a tumor being malignant or benign, or multiclass classifications, which have multiple target classes, such as a pet being a dog, cat, or horse.
- There are hundreds of classification algorithms that differ by:
  - Performance
  - Memory use
  - Support for **binary classification** and **multiclass classification**
  - Data-set size
  - Complexity
- Classification uses **supervised learning**, meaning it uses a **training data set** to teach the model how to assign data to correct classes and a training data set that evaluates the model's accuracy.
- To create the training and test data sets, the data must contain not only the predictor data values but also the correct class assignments for that data.
- Analysts normally use 70–80% of the known (complete) data to create the training data set and the rest for the **test data set**.
- After you train the model and test its accuracy, you can use the model to predict data classification.

- The classification process consists of three steps:
  - Train the model
  - Evaluate (test) the model's accuracy
  - Use the model to predict data classification
- After you test a model, you can examine the resulting confusion matrix to determine which classification assignments the model got wrong.
- The **K-nearest-neighbors** classifier assigns data to the class the data most resemble.
- The Naïve Bayes classifier uses the **Bayes Theorem** to classify data based on knowledge of known or related conditions, which are represented as probabilities.
- The **Naïve Bayes classifier** is called "naïve" because it treats each **predictor variable** as independent.
- The logarithmic-regression classifier, which is best suited for binary classification, assigns data to classes based upon the function (called a **logit**) that determines the probability that the data belong to the class.
- Neural networks are at the heart of machine learning and are used for many problems, including classification. Behind the scenes, neural networks use a collection of linear functions, called perceptrons, that simulate activities performed by the brain and nervous system.
- Many problems are not linear in nature. To use their underlying linear functions, **neural network** programs decompose such problems into a series of linear functions, creating multiple layers of perceptrons.
- The multilayer perceptron (**MLP**) classifier assigns data to classes using a neural-network model.
- A **decision tree** is a graph-based data structure that specifies a collection of decision points. By following a path through the decision points, a decision-tree classifier assigns data to specific classes.
- A **decision-tree classifier** creates a decision tree based on the training data set. The resulting tree may not be optimal. A random-forest classifier creates many decision trees and then selects and applies the decision tree that produces the best result (as voted upon by the decision trees).
- A support vector machine (**SVM**) classifier (often called a support vector classifier [**SVC**]) creates classes by dividing the data into groups using lines (called hyperplanes) to separate the data.
- To access data sets that you can use to learn and test data-mining algorithms, you can use the University of California, Irvine (UCI), data-set repository or the Kaggle website.
- Before you can use real-world data sets to classify data, you must often cleanse the data to remove missing or duplicate data.
- Many real-world data sets contain text-based categorical data. Unfortunately, many data-mining algorithms do not work well with text. Before you can use the data, you must convert the data from text to numeric data, such as converting gender data from "male" and "female" to values such as 0 and 1. To perform such conversions, data analysts often use a technique called hot encoding.

As discussed, there are many data-classification techniques. This chapter's goal is to introduce you to the several commonly used algorithms. As you examine each technique, you should drill down into the functions used to learn about different parameter options you may be able to leverage to provide a better result for your data set.

# Applying the K-Nearest Neighbors (KNN) Classification Algorithm

One of the most widely used data sets to understand machine learning is the Iris database, which you can find at the UCI Machine Learning Repository at https://archive.ics.uci.edu/ml/datasets/Iris/ and which is provided in the R programming language's built-in data sets. Within the data set, each record contains data for four values:

- The flower's sepal length
- The flower's sepal width
- The flower's petal length
- The flower's petal width

**FIGURE 11.1** shows an iris sepal and petal along with the corresponding length and width. Botanists categorize iris flowers into different types, three of which include:

- Iris setosa
- Iris versicolor
- Iris virginica

You can download the Iris data set from this text's catalog page at go.jblearning.com/DataMining. When you do so, Notepad will display the file's contents, as shown in **FIGURE 11.2**. Save the file to a folder on your disk.

Within the file, you will find that each record has measured sepal and petal lengths and widths, as well as the resulting flower classifications. The learning algorithm will use

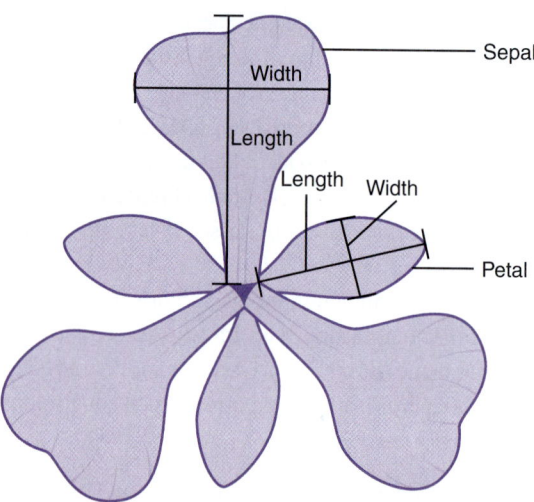

**FIGURE 11.1** Data-classification algorithms use the sepal and petal lengths and widths to classify iris flower types.

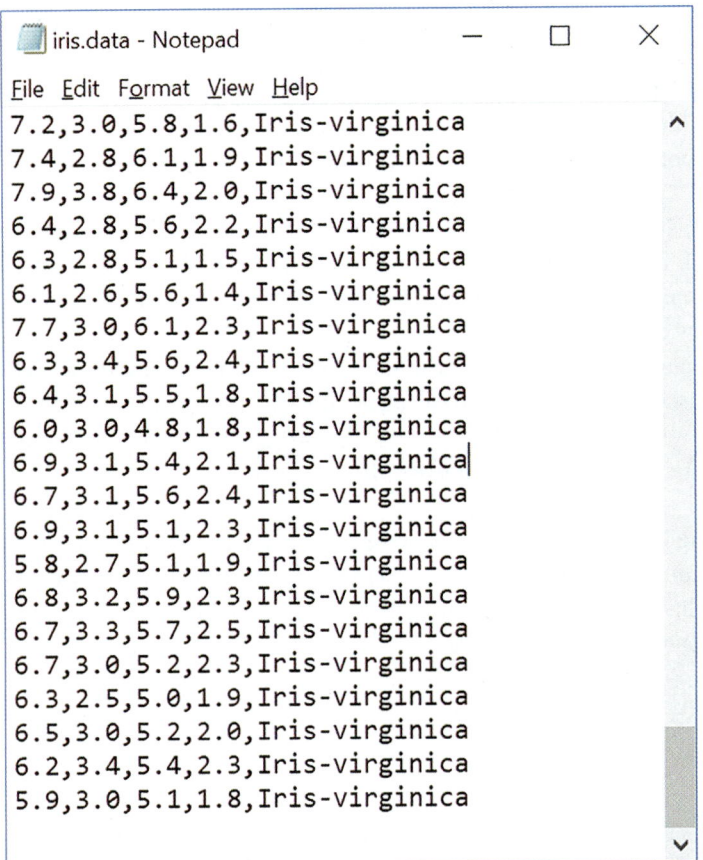

**FIGURE 11.2** The Iris data set.

Used with permission from Microsoft

## Specifying the Training Set and Testing the Set Size

As you have learned, to perform classification, you start with a data set of known (correct or observed) values. You then divide that data set into training and testing sets. Analysts often use 70% or 80% of the data for training and the remainder for testing. If you make the testing set too small, you may skew the model's accuracy, making you think the model is more accurate than it really is. Likewise, if you make the training set too small, you may omit key values that will influence the model's knowledge.

As you examine the classification algorithms this chapter presents, take time to experiment with the data-set sizes and note the result.

part of the data set for training and part for testing. You can then provide values you want to classify.

The KNN's classification algorithm is based on the premise "If it walks like duck and quacks like a duck, it's a duck." To use KNN, you provide a value for the number K that specifies the number of neighboring data-set values to which a value must be similar in order to be considered part of a group.

For example, assume, as shown in **FIGURE 11.3**, that you have three classes of data (Dogs, Cats, and Horses). The data point, in this case, has four neighbors in the Dogs class, one neighbor in the Cats class, and two neighbors in the Horse class. Using KNN with a value of 3, you would categorize the new data point as a Dog.

Behind the scenes, to determine the nearest neighbors, the algorithms use a Euclidean distance (a straight-line distance), which you can calculate using:

$$\text{Distance}(a,b) = \sqrt{(a_1 - b_1)^2 + (a_2 - b_2)^2}$$

The following Python script, IrisKNN.py, opens the Iris data set and loads the data into two arrays, one containing the petal and sepal data (X) and one containing the known classifications (y). The code then splits the arrays into a training data set that contains 70% of the values and a testing data set that contains the remaining 30%.

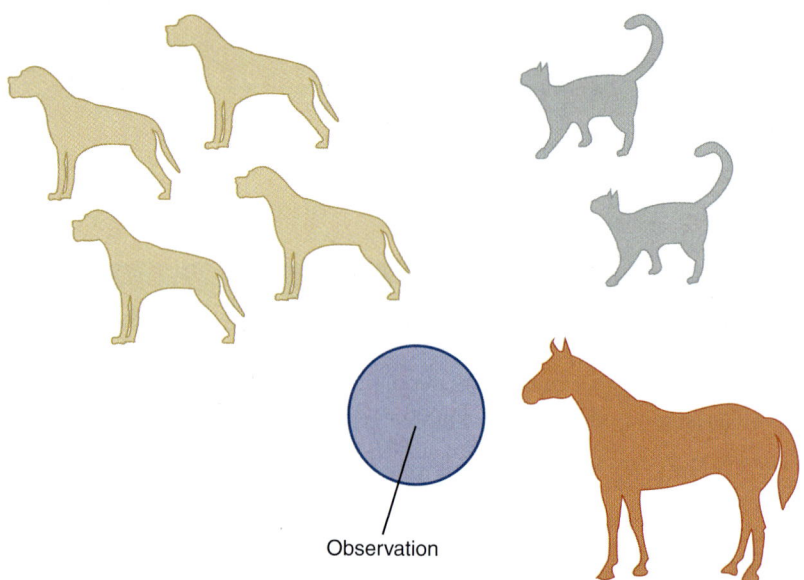

**FIGURE 11.3** Assigning a data point to a class using KNN.

The script then uses the KNN algorithm with K = 3 to calculate and display the model's accuracy. Using the model, the script then predicts the classification for three sets of sepal and petal lengths:

```
import pandas as pd
import numpy as np
from sklearn.model_selection import train_test_split
from sklearn.metrics import accuracy_score
from sklearn.neighbors import KNeighborsClassifier

names = ['sepal_length', 'sepal_width', 'petal_length', 'petal_
width', 'class']

df = pd.read_csv('iris.data.csv', header=None, names=names)
X = np.array(df.iloc[:, 0:4])
y = np.array(df['class'])

# split the data into the train and test sets
X_train, X_test, y_train, y_test = train_test_split(X, y,
test_size=0.30)

knn = KNeighborsClassifier(n_neighbors=3)
knn.fit(X_train, y_train)
pred = knn.predict(X_test)

print ('\nModel accuracy score: ', accuracy_score(y_test, pred))
print("\nFrom the test data")
print('Index\tPredicted\t\tActual')
for i in range(len(pred)):
  if pred[i] != y_test[i]:
    print(i, '\t', pred[i], '\t', y_test[i], '****')

DataToPredict =
np.array([[5.2,3.5,1.4,0.2],[5.7,2.9,3.6,1.3],[5.8,3.0,5.1,1.8]])
pred = knn.predict(DataToPredict)

print("\nPredicted Results")
for i in range(len(pred)):
    print('\t', DataToPredict[i], '\t', pred[i])
```

When you execute the script, it will display the following output:

```
C:\> python IrisKNN.py
Model accuracy score:   0.9555555555555556

From the test data
Index       Predicted               Actual
4           Iris-virginica          Iris-versicolor    ****
37          Iris-versicolor         Iris-virginica     ****
```

```
Predicted Results
        [5.2 3.5 1.4 0.2]    Iris-setosa
        [5.7 2.9 3.6 1.3]    Iris-versicolor
        [5.8 3.  5.1 1.8]    Iris-virginica
```

As you can see, the model has a 95% accuracy. The script also displays the test data values the model incorrectly classified. Finally, the script shows the predictions for three new data values.

The following R program, IrisKNN.R, loads the Iris.csv data set and performs similar processing for K = 3 and 70% training data and 30% test data:

```
library (class)

data(iris)

## Split in train + test set
indexes <- sample(1:nrow(iris),as.integer(0.7*nrow(iris)))

trainData <- iris[indexes,]
testData <- iris[-indexes,]

## A 3-nearest neighbors model with no normalization
## The number -5 in the follow says to drop column 5
pred <- knn(train = trainData[, -5], test = testData[, -5], cl =
trainData$Species, k=3)

confusionmatrix = as.matrix(table(Actual = testData$Species,
Predicted = pred))
accuracy = sum(diag(confusionmatrix))/length(testData$Species)

print('Accuracy')
print(accuracy)

DataToPredict <- matrix(c(5.2,3.5,1.4,0.2, 5.7,2.9,3.6,1.3,
5.8,3.0,5.1,1.8), nrow=3, ncol=4)
pred <- knn(train = trainData[, -5], test = DataToPredict[,], cl
= trainData$Species, k=3)
print(pred)
```

When you execute this program, it will display the following output:

```
[1] "Accuracy"
[1] 0.9777778
[1] versicolor setosa     versicolor
Levels: setosa versicolor virginica
```

## Determining the Value of K for the K-Nearest Neighbor's Algorithm

When you use the KNN algorithm to classify data, you must specify the value of K for the number of neighbors to which a point must be similar in order to be included in a group. If you specify a value of K that is too small, you may "overfit" the model, meaning the model may start to treat noise or errant data as valid training data. Likewise, if you specify too large a value for K, you may "underfit" the model, which means the model is not capable of correctly modeling the training data.

To determine the appropriate value of K, you can run your model with different values of K and note the model's resulting accuracy. The following Python script, EstimateK.py, plots the accuracy for K = 1–10 for the Iris data set:

```
import pandas as pd
import numpy as np
import matplotlib.pyplot as plt
from sklearn.model_selection import train_test_split
from sklearn.metrics import accuracy_score
from sklearn.neighbors import KNeighborsClassifier

names = ['sepal_length', 'sepal_width', 'petal_length',
'petal_width', 'class']

df = pd.read_csv('iris.data.csv', header=None, names=names)
X = np.array(df.iloc[:, 0:4])
y = np.array(df['class'])
# split the data into train and test sets
X_train, X_test, y_train, y_test = train_test_split(X, y,
test_size=0.25)

scores = []
K_Range = range(1, 10)

for K in K_Range:
    knn = KNeighborsClassifier(n_neighbors=K)
    knn.fit(X_train, y_train)
    y_pred = knn.predict(X_test)
    scores.append(accuracy_score(y_test, y_pred))

plt.plot(K_Range, scores)
plt.xlabel('Value of K for KNN')
plt.ylabel('Testing Accuracy')
plt.show()
```

When you execute this script, it will display the graph shown in **FIGURE A**.

As you can see, the KNN accuracy will differ by the value of K. In this case, you would likely choose K = 5.

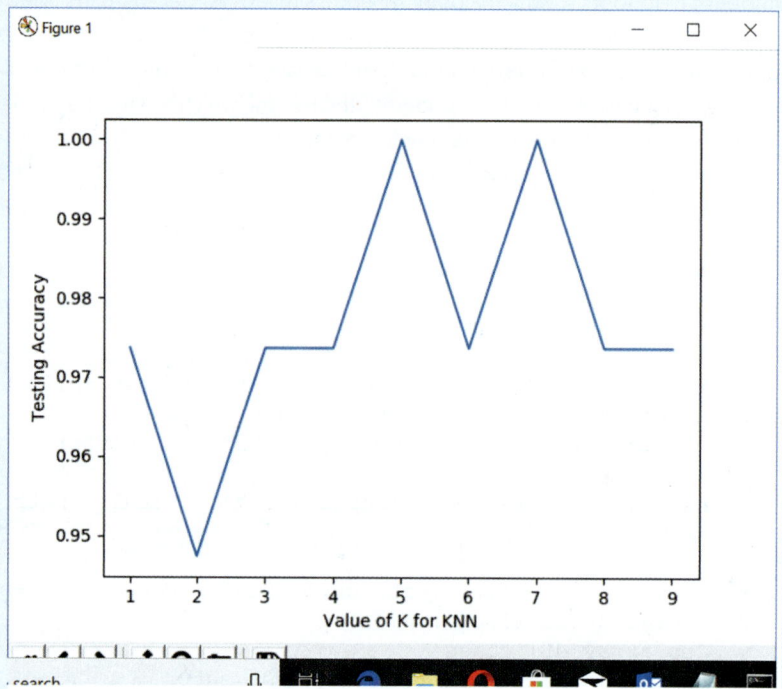

**FIGURE A** Plotting accuracy of KNN for values of K = 1–10.

Used with permission of Python Software Foundation

## Understanding the Confusion Matrix

When you use a classification algorithm, your code will load the training and test data sets, using them to fit the data model. After you fit the model, it will produce an accuracy score:

```
Model accuracy score:   0.9555555555555556
```

The accuracy score is a percentage of the number of correct predictions divided by the total number of predictions.

To help you understand which predictions the model got correct and which predictions were wrong, you can display the model's confusion matrix, which summarizes the prediction's results.

The following Python script, ConfusionIrisKNN.py, uses KNN to model the iris flower data. The script displays the accuracy score and the confusion matrix:

```python
import pandas as pd
import numpy as np
from sklearn.model_selection import train_test_split
from sklearn.metrics import accuracy_score
from sklearn.neighbors import KNeighborsClassifier
from sklearn.metrics import confusion_matrix

names = ['sepal_length', 'sepal_width', 'petal_length', 'petal_width', 'class']

df = pd.read_csv('iris.data.csv', header=None, names=names)
X = np.array(df.iloc[:, 0:4])
y = np.array(df['class'])

# split the data into the train and test sets
X_train, X_test, y_train, y_test = train_test_split(X, y, test_size=0.30)

knn = KNeighborsClassifier(n_neighbors=3)
knn.fit(X_train, y_train)
pred = knn.predict(X_test)

print ('\nModel accuracy score: ', accuracy_score(y_test, pred))
print("\nFrom the test data")
print('Index\tPredicted\tActual')
for i in range(len(pred)):
  if pred[i] != y_test[i]:
    print(i, '\t', pred[i], '\t', y_test[i], ' ****')

print('\nConfusion Matrix\n', confusion_matrix(y_test, pred))
```

When you run this script, it will display the following output:

```
Model accuracy score:    0.9777777777777777
```

```
From the test data
Index       Predicted               Actual
 20          Iris-virginica         Iris-versicolor     ****

Confusion Matrix
 [[16  0   0]
  [ 0 15   1]
  [ 0  0  13]]
```

As you can see, the model had a 97% accuracy, missing one prediction. The confusion matrix tells you that the model missed the classification of Versicolor assignment. Within the confusion matrix, the diagonal values correspond to the correct predictions. In this case, the model was correct for the first iris species, missed one for the second, and was correct for the third.

The following R program, ConfusionIrisKNN.R, performs similar processing:

```
library (class)

data(iris)

## Split in train + test set
indexes <- sample(1:nrow(iris),as.integer(0.7*nrow(iris)))

trainData <- iris[indexes,]
testData <- iris[-indexes,]

## A 3-nearest neighbors model with no normalization
pred <- knn(train = trainData[, -5], test = testData[, -5],
cl = trainData$Species, k=3)

confusionmatrix = as.matrix(table(Actual = testData$Species,
Predicted = pred))
accuracy = sum(diag(confusionmatrix))/length(pred)

print('Confusion Matrix')
print(confusionmatrix)
print('Accuracy')
print(accuracy)
```

When you run this program, it will display the following output:

```
[1] "Confusion Matrix"
              Predicted
Actual      setosa versicolor virginica
  setosa        10          0         0
  versicolor     0         17         1
  virginica      0          2        15
[1] "Accuracy"
[1] 0.9333333
```

Again, the confusion matrix diagonals tell you which predictions the model got correct and which it missed. To determine the model's accuracy, the code sums the confusion matrix diagonal (42) and divides it by the total number of predictions (45) to produce (42 / 45) 0.933333.

## Predicting Wine Types Using KNN

The Wine data set, available at the UCI data repository, contains 13 attributes that contribute to the quality of wine. The data set contains data for three types of wines, identified by the category values 1, 2, and 3. The data set consists of 178 records. To start, download the data set from this text's catalog page at go.jblearning.com/DataMining. Within Windows, Notepad will display the values, as shown in **FIGURE 11.4**.

The following Python script, WineKNN.py, uses the Wine data set with K=5 to predict the types for three sets of wine values:

```
import pandas as pd
import numpy as np
```

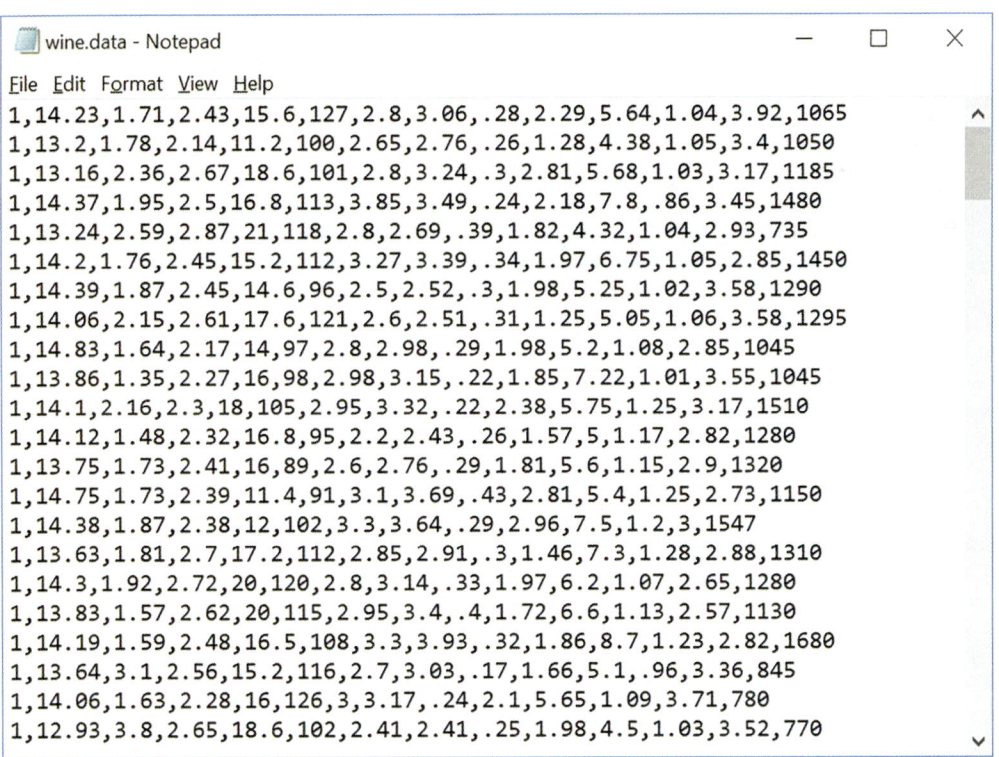

**FIGURE 11.4** The Wine data set.

Used with permission from Microsoft

```python
from sklearn.model_selection import train_test_split
from sklearn.metrics import accuracy_score
from sklearn.neighbors import KNeighborsClassifier
from sklearn.metrics import confusion_matrix

names = ['class', 'Alcohol','Malic Acid','Ash','Acadlinity','Magnisium','Total Phenols','Flavanoids', 'NonFlavanoid Phenols', 'Proanthocyanins', 'Color Intensity', 'Hue', 'OD280/OD315', 'Proline' ]

df = pd.read_csv('wine.data.csv', header=None, names=names)
X = np.array(df.iloc[:, 1:14])
y = np.array(df['class'])

# split into train and test
X_train, X_test, y_train, y_test = train_test_split(X, y, test_size=0.30)

knn = KNeighborsClassifier(n_neighbors=5)
knn.fit(X_train, y_train)
pred = knn.predict(X_test)

print ('\nModel accuracy score: ', accuracy_score(y_test, pred))
print(confusion_matrix(y_test, pred))

DataToPredict = np.array(
[[14.23,1.71,2.43,15.6,127,2.8,3.06,.28,2.29,5.64,1.04,3.92,1065],
[12.64,1.36,2.02,16.8,100,2.02,1.41,.53,.62,5.75,.98,1.59,450],
[12.53,5.51,2.64,25,96,1.79,.6,.63,1.1,5,.82,1.69,515],
[13.49,3.59,2.19,19.5,88,1.62,.48,.58,.88,5.7,.81,1.82,580]])

pred = knn.predict(DataToPredict)

print("\nPredicted Results")
for i in range(len(pred)):
    print('\t', DataToPredict[i], '\t', 'Class: ', pred[i])
```

When you execute this script, it will display the following output:

```
C:\> python WineKNN.py
Model accuracy score:  0.6851851851851852
[[18  0  2]
 [ 3 10  6]
 [ 3  3  9]]


Predicted Results
     [1.423e+01 1.710e+00 2.430e+00 1.560e+01 1.270e+02 2.800e+00 3.060e+00
 2.800e-01 2.290e+00 5.640e+00 1.040e+00 3.920e+00 1.065e+03]    Class:  1
```

```
    [ 12.64    1.36    2.02   16.8    100.     2.02    1.41    0.53    0.62    5.75
  0.98    1.59   450.   ]   Class:    2
    [ 12.53    5.51    2.64   25.      96.     1.79    0.6     0.63    1.1     5.
  0.82    1.69   515.   ]   Class:    3
     [1.349e+01 3.590e+00 2.190e+00 1.950e+01 8.800e+01 1.620e+00 4.800e-01
 5.800e-01 8.800e-01 5.700e+00 8.100e-01 1.820e+00 5.800e+02]   Class:    2
```

As you can see, the model has a low accuracy of 68%. The predicted data should have been classes 1, 2, 3, and 3. The model's results for the predicted data turned out to be 75% correct.

The following R program, WineKNN.R, performs similar processing:

```
library (class)
library (datasets)

Wine <- read.csv(file='wine.data.csv')

## Split in train + test set
indexes <- sample(1:nrow(Wine),as.integer(0.7*nrow(Wine)))

trainData <- Wine[indexes,]
testData <- Wine[-indexes,]

## A 3-nearest neighbors model with no normalization
pred <- knn(train = trainData[, -1], test = testData[, -1],
cl = trainData[,1], k=5)

confusionmatrix = as.matrix(table(Actual = testData[,1],
Predicted = pred))
accuracy = sum(diag(confusionmatrix))/length(pred)

print('Confusion Matrix')
print(confusionmatrix)
print('Accuracy')
print(accuracy)
```

When you execute this program, it will display the following output:

```
Confusion Matrix
       Predicted
Actual  1  2  3
     1 15  0  1
     2  1 18  4
     3  4  5  6
 [1]  "Accuracy"
 [1]  0.7222222
```

# Predicting Breast Cancer Malignancy Using KNN

The Breast Cancer data set, available at the UCI data repository, contains 9 attributes, which can be used to determine if a breast cancer tumor is malignant or benign. The data set contains 569 records. You can download the data set from this text's catalog page at go.jblearning.com/DataMining. Notebook will display the data set, as shown in **FIGURE 11.5**.

The following Python script, CancerPredictKNN.py, uses the data set with K=5 to train and test the model:

```
import pandas as pd
import numpy as np
from sklearn.model_selection import train_test_split
from sklearn.metrics import accuracy_score
from sklearn.neighbors import KNeighborsClassifier
```

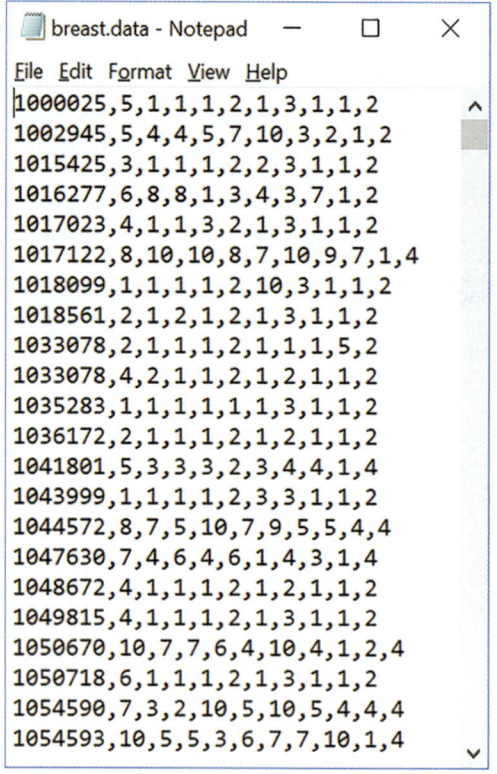

**FIGURE 11.5** The Breast Cancer data set.

Used with permission from Microsoft

```python
from sklearn.metrics import confusion_matrix

names = ['Sample', 'Clump Thickness','Uniformity of Cell
Size','Uniformity of Cell Shape','Marginal Adhesion','Single
Epithelial Cell Size','Bare Nuclei','Bland Chromatin', 'Normal
Nucleoli', 'Mitoses', 'class']

df = pd.read_csv('breast.data.csv', header=None, names=names)
X = np.array(df.iloc[:, 1:10])  # do not include sample field
y = np.array(df['class'])

# split into train and test
X_train, X_test, y_train, y_test = train_test_split(X, y,
test_size=0.30)

knn = KNeighborsClassifier(n_neighbors=5)
knn.fit(X_train, y_train)
pred = knn.predict(X_test)

print ('\nModel accuracy score: ', accuracy_score(y_test, pred))
print(confusion_matrix(y_test, pred))
```

When you execute this script, it will display the following output:

```
C:\> python CancerPredictionKNN.py
Model accuracy score:  0.9609756097560975
[[130   5]
 [  3  67]]
```

As you can see, KNN in this case produces an accuracy model of 96%.

The following R program, CancerPredictKNN.R, performs similar processing:

```
library (class)
library (datasets)

BreastCancer <- read.csv(file='breast.data.csv')
BreastCancer <- BreastCancer[-1] # drop sample column

## Split in train + test set
indexes <- sample(1:nrow(BreastCancer),
as.integer(0.7*nrow(BreastCancer)))

trainData <- BreastCancer[indexes,]
testData <- BreastCancer[-indexes,]

## A 5-nearest neighbors model with no normalization
pred <- knn(train = trainData[, -11], test = testData[, -11],
cl = trainData[,11], k=5)
```

```
confusionmatrix = as.matrix(table(Actual = testData[,11],
Predicted = pred))
accuracy = sum(diag(confusionmatrix))/length(testData[,11])

print('Confusion Matrix')
print(confusionmatrix)
print('Accuracy')
print(accuracy)
```

When you execute this script, it will display the following output:

```
[1] "Confusion Matrix"
       Predicted
Actual   2   4
     2 133   3
     4   3  66
[1] "Accuracy"
[1] 0.9707317
```

## Classification Using Naïve Bayes

In Chapter 10, "Clustering," you learned that there are many different clustering algorithms, each of which approaches the data-grouping process differently. There are many different classification algorithms. The Naïve Bayes classification algorithm is so named because it is based on the Bayes Theorem to calculate the probability that an item is a member of a category based upon knowledge of related conditions. The Naïve Bayes classification algorithm is called "naïve" because it treats the different data set attributes as independent and calculates a probability for each.

The formula for the Bayes Theorem is:

$$P(A|B) = \frac{P(B|A)P(A)}{P(B)}$$

Within the theorem, P(A|B) means the probability of A given B. Assume, for example, that you must determine if a bird is a duck, chicken, or ostrich and you are given the data shown in **TABLE 11.1**.

Your bird data set has 100 samples split evenly across each category (duck, chicken, and ostrich). Assume you have the following observations:

| Swim | Fly | Run |
| --- | --- | --- |
| False | True | True |

## Classification Using Naïve Bayes

**TABLE 11.1** Probabilities that a Duck, Chicken, and Ostrich Can Swim, Run, or Fly

|         | Swim | Fly | Run |
|---------|------|-----|-----|
| Duck    | 100  | 99  | 90  |
| Chicken | 5    | 90  | 95  |
| Ostrich | 1    | 0   | 100 |

You would determine the probability for each bird type as follows:

```
P(Duck | Fly, Run) = P(Fly | Duck) * P(Run | Duck) / P(Fly, Run)
                   = (0.99)*(0.9)/P(Fly, Run)
                   = 0.891 /P(Fly, Run)

P(Chicken | Fly, Run) = P(Fly | Chicken) * P(Run | Chicken) / P(Fly, Run)
                      = (0.9)*(0.95)/P(Fly, Run)
                      = 0.855 /P(Fly, Run)

P(Ostrich | Fly, Run) = P(Fly | Ostrich) * P(Run | Ostrich) / P(Fly, Run)
                      = (0)*(1.0)/P(Fly, Run)
                      = 0 /P(Fly, Run)
```

Given that P(Fly, Run) will be the same for each bird, we can ignore it, which yields:

```
P(Duck   | Fly, Run) = 0.891
P(Chicken| Fly, Run) = 0.855
P(Ostrich | Fly, Run) = 0
```

In this case, the probability for P(Duck | Fly, Run) is the highest, making the classification of the observation a duck.

The following Python script, NaiveBayes.py, uses the GaussianNB function to predict which class of iris a flower observation aligns with:

```
import pandas as pd
import numpy as np
from sklearn.model_selection import train_test_split
from sklearn.metrics import accuracy_score
from sklearn.naive_bayes import GaussianNB
```

```
names = ['sepal_length', 'sepal_width', 'petal_length', 'petal_
width', 'class']

df = pd.read_csv('iris.data.csv', header=None, names=names)
X = np.array(df.iloc[:, 0:4])
y = np.array(df['class'])

# split the data into the train and test sets
X_train, X_test, y_train, y_test = train_test_split(X, y,
test_size=0.30)

model = GaussianNB().fit(X_train, y_train)
pred = model.predict(X_test)

print ('\nModel accuracy score: ', accuracy_score(y_test, pred))
print("\nFrom the test data")
print('Index\tPredicted\tActual')
for i in range(len(pred)):
  if pred[i] != y_test[i]:
    print(i, '\t', pred[i], '\t', y_test[i], ' ****')

DataToPredict =
np.array([[5.2,3.5,1.4,0.2],[5.7,2.9,3.6,1.3],[5.8,3.0,5.1,1.8]])
pred = model.predict(DataToPredict)

print("\nPredicted Results")
for i in range(len(pred)):
    print('\t', DataToPredict[i], '\t', pred[i])
```

When you run this script, it will display the following output:

```
Model accuracy score:   0.9333333333333333

From the test data
Index       Predicted              Actual
13          Iris-virginica         Iris-versicolor    ****
17          Iris-virginica         Iris-versicolor    ****
26          Iris-versicolor        Iris-virginica     ****

Predicted Results
        [5.2 3.5 1.4 0.2]      Iris-setosa
        [5.7 2.9 3.6 1.3]      Iris-versicolor
        [5.8 3.  5.1 1.8]      Iris-virginica
```

As you can see, the Naïve Bayes model has an accuracy of 93% and assigns the correct predictions.

As discussed, Naïve Bayes will create probabilities for each attribute. To display the probabilities, you can use the predict_proba function, as shown here:

```
model = GaussianNB().fit(X_train, y_train)
pred = model.predict(X_test)
print('probabilities')
print (model.predict_proba(X_test))
```

Given the Iris data set, the statements would display the following probabilities:

```
probabilities
[[9.98343689e-260 5.58260527e-012 1.00000000e+000]
 [2.43619162e-240 7.83783100e-010 9.99999999e-001]
 [9.28563087e-135 1.92197421e-001 8.07802579e-001]
   :               :               :
 [1.00000000e+000 2.09063910e-019 6.57849667e-022]
 [5.20045931e-196 3.17490010e-004 9.99682510e-001]
 [2.56049132e-175 2.49560631e-003 9.97504394e-001]]
```

The following R program, NaiveBayes.R, performs similar processing:

```
library(e1071)

data(iris)

## Split in train + test set
indexes <- sample(1:nrow(iris),as.integer(0.7*nrow(iris)))

trainData <- iris[indexes,]
testData <- iris[-indexes,]

model <- naiveBayes(x=trainData[,-5], y=trainData[, 5])
pred <- predict(model, testData)

confusionmatrix = as.matrix(table(Actual = testData[, 5],
Predicted = pred))
accuracy = sum(diag(confusionmatrix))/length(pred)

print('Confusion Matrix')
print(confusionmatrix)
print('Accuracy')
print(accuracy)

plant1 <- data.frame(Sepal.Length=5.2, Sepal.Width=3.5, Petal.
Length=1.4, Petal.Width=0.2, Species='Unk')
plant2 <- data.frame(Sepal.Length=5.7, Sepal.Width=1.4, Petal.
Length=3.6, Petal.Width=1.3, Species='Unk')
```

```
plant3 <- data.frame(Sepal.Length=5.8, Sepal.Width=1.3, Petal.
Length=5.1, Petal.Width=1.8, Species='Unk')

pred <- predict(model, plant1)
print(pred)

pred <- predict(model, plant2)
print(pred)

pred <- predict(model, plant3)
print(pred)
```

When you execute this program, it will display the following output:

```
[1] "Confusion Matrix"
            Predicted
Actual      setosa versicolor virginica
  setosa       16        0          0
  versicolor    0       16          0
  virginica     0        0         13

[1] "Accuracy"
[1] 1

[1] setosa
Levels: setosa versicolor virginica

[1] versicolor
Levels: setosa versicolor virginica

[1] virginica
Levels: setosa versicolor virginica
```

In this case, the model was 100% correct. That will often not be the case. In fact, because the algorithm starts its processing using some random values, if you run the same program again, with the same data, you may get a different result. If you need your model to be repeatable, many of the functions allow you to specify the seed value used for the random-number generators.

## Classification Using Logistic Regression

The **logistic regression classifier** is best suited for binary-dependent variables—meaning classifications for which there are only two classes, such as gender, a tumor being malignant or benign, and so on. That said, you can use logistic regression for multiclass problems, but your results may not prove as accurate as other methods.

A logistic regression classifier does not use the **dependent variable** (the classes we are trying to group into) directly, but rather, it uses a function called a logit that uses each of the predictor variables. The logistic regression algorithm is often called the "logit" algorithm. Behind the scenes, the algorithm uses a series of odds that correspond to whether an event will occur. The logistic classifier determines the probability that data belong to each class based upon this series of odds, which it produces by analyzing each predictor variable.

The following Python script, LogitisticRegressionIris.py, uses the model to predict iris flower types:

```
import pandas as pd
import numpy as np
from sklearn.model_selection import train_test_split
from sklearn.metrics import accuracy_score
from sklearn.naive_bayes import GaussianNB
from sklearn.linear_model import LogisticRegression

names = ['sepal_length', 'sepal_width', 'petal_length', 'petal_width', 'class']

df = pd.read_csv('iris.data.csv', header=None, names=names)
X = np.array(df.iloc[:, 0:4])
y = np.array(df['class'])

# split the data into train and test sets
X_train, X_test, y_train, y_test = train_test_split(X, y, test_size=0.25)

model = LogisticRegression(solver='lbfgs', multi_class='multinomial', max_iter=200).fit(X_train, y_train)

pred = model.predict(X_test)

print('Accuracy score: ', accuracy_score(y_test, pred))

print('Index\tPredicted\tActual')
for i in range(len(pred)):
  if pred[i] != y_test[i]:
    print(i, '\t', pred[i], '\t', y_test[i], ' ****')

DataToPredict = np.array([[5.2,3.5,1.4,0.2],[5.7,2.9,3.6,1.3],[5.8,3.0,5.1,1.8]])
pred = model.predict(DataToPredict)

print("\nPredicted Results")
for i in range(len(pred)):
    print('\t', DataToPredict[i], '\t', pred[i])
```

When you execute this script, it will display the following output:

```
Accuracy score:   0.9736842105263158
Index      Predicted           Actual
31         Iris-versicolor     Iris-virginica   ****
```

```
Predicted Results
        [5.2 3.5 1.4 0.2]    Iris-setosa
        [5.7 2.9 3.6 1.3]    Iris-versicolor
        [5.8 3.  5.1 1.8]    Iris-virginica
```

As you can see, the logistic regression model returns a high accuracy. Also, the model is correct on the three predictions.

As stated, logistic regression is best suited for a binary-dependent variable. The following Python script, LogisticRegressionCancer.py, uses the approach to predict if a tumor is benign or malignant:

```
import pandas as pd
import numpy as np
from sklearn.model_selection import train_test_split
from sklearn.metrics import accuracy_score
from sklearn.linear_model import LogisticRegression
from sklearn.metrics import confusion_matrix

names = ['Sample','Clump Thickness','Uniformity of Cell
Size','Uniformity of Cell Shape','Marginal Adhesion','Single
Epithelial Cell Size','Bare Nuclei','Bland Chromatin', 'Normal
Nucleoli', 'Mitoses', 'class']

df = pd.read_csv('breast.data.csv', header=None, names=names)
X = np.array(df.iloc[:, 1:10])
y = np.array(df['class'])

# split the data into train and test sets
X_train, X_test, y_train, y_test = train_test_split(X, y,
test_size=0.30)

model = LogisticRegression(solver='lbfgs').fit(X_train, y_train)

pred = model.predict(X_test)

print('Accuracy score: ', accuracy_score(y_test, pred))
print(confusion_matrix(y_test, pred))
```

When you execute the script, it will display the following output:

```
C:\> python LogisticRegressionCancer.py
Accuracy score:  0.9658536585365853
[[126   4]
 [  3  72]]
```

The following R program, LogisticRegression.R, performs similar processing:

```
library(caTools)
```

```
BreastCancer <- read.csv(file='breast.data.csv',
stringsAsFactors=T)
BreastCancer <- BreastCancer[-1] # drop sample column
## Split in train + test set
indexes <- sample(1:nrow(BreastCancer),
as.integer(0.7*nrow(BreastCancer)))

trainData <- BreastCancer[indexes,]
testData <- BreastCancer[-indexes,]

model <- glm(formula = as.factor(trainData[,11])~.,
data=trainData[,-11], family=binomial('logit'), control =
list(maxit = 100, epsilon=3))

pred <- predict(model, testData, type = 'response')
pred_num <- ifelse(pred > 0.5, 4, 2)

confusionmatrix = as.matrix(table(Actual = testData[,11],
Predicted = pred_num))
accuracy = sum(diag(confusionmatrix))/length(testData[,11])

print('Confusion Matrix')
print(confusionmatrix)
print('Accuracy')
print(accuracy)
```

As you can see, the program calls the predict function to use the logistics regression model to predict the test data. Then the program uses ifelse to assign any percentage values greater than 0.5–class 4 (malignant) and the percentage values less than 0.5–class 2 (benign). With those assignments in place, the program can create a confusion matrix and use it to compute an accuracy.

## Classification Using a Neural Network

Neural networks are at the heart of machine learning and are used for a wide range of applications, including classification. In this section, you will examine the MLPClassifer function, so named because it uses MLPs to accomplish its processing, in this case, classifications.

In a neural network, a **perceptron** is a supervised learning algorithm that uses a linear function to convert inputs into outputs, as shown in **FIGURE 11.6**.

As shown in Figure 11.6, the inputs to a perceptron can be weighted and biased.

As discussed, a perceptron uses a linear function. Many real-world problems, however, are not linear in nature. As such, the problems must be decomposed into a series of linear components, and additional layers of perceptrons must be used. **FIGURE 11.7** illustrates an MLP solution.

The following Python script, MLPIris.py, uses an MLP model to predict iris flower types:

```
import pandas as pd
import numpy as np
```

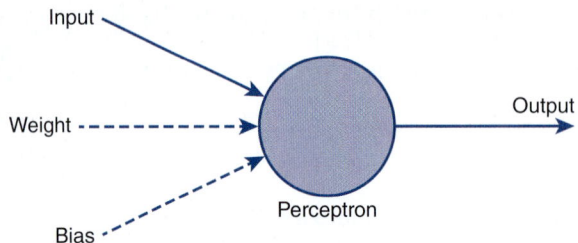

**FIGURE 11.6** A perceptron is an algorithm that converts inputs into outputs.

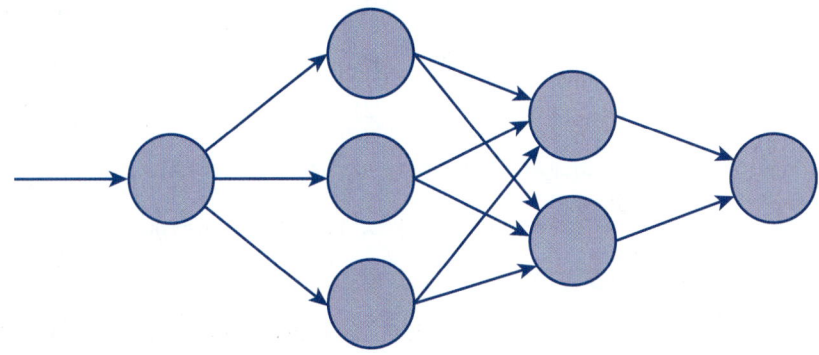

**FIGURE 11.7** An MLP solution.

```
from sklearn.model_selection import train_test_split
from sklearn.metrics import accuracy_score
from sklearn.neural_network import MLPClassifier

names = ['sepal_length', 'sepal_width', 'petal_length', 'petal_width', 'class']

df = pd.read_csv('iris.data.csv', header=None, names=names)
X = np.array(df.iloc[:, 0:4])
y = np.array(df['class'])

# split the data into train and test sets
X_train, X_test, y_train, y_test = train_test_split(X, y, test_size=0.30)

model = MLPClassifier(max_iter=1000)
model.fit(X_train, y_train)
pred = model.predict(X_test)

print ('Accuracy: ', accuracy_score(y_test, pred))

print('Index\tPredicted\tActual')
for i in range(len(pred)):
```

```
    if pred[i] != y_test[i]:
      print(i, '\t', pred[i], '\t', y_test[i], ' ****')

DataToPredict =
np.array([[5.2,3.5,1.4,0.2],[5.7,2.9,3.6,1.3],[5.8,3.0,5.1,1.8]])
pred = model.predict(DataToPredict)

print("\nPredicted Results")
for i in range(len(pred)):
    print('\t', DataToPredict[i], '\t', pred[i])
```

When you execute this script, it will display the following output:

```
Accuracy:   0.9555555555555556
Index       Predicted           Actual
25          Iris-virginica      Iris-versicolor     ****
42          Iris-virginica      Iris-versicolor     ****

Predicted Results
            [5.2 3.5 1.4 0.2]   Iris-setosa
            [5.7 2.9 3.6 1.3]   Iris-versicolor
            [5.8 3.  5.1 1.8]   Iris-virginica
```

## Classification Using Decision Trees

A decision tree is a graph-based data structure that a program can use to follow a series of decision paths to arrive at a decision. **FIGURE 11.8**, for example, illustrates a decision tree that determines a student's test grade.

Within machine learning, a decision-tree classifier creates a similar structure with decision points that are based upon the different data-set attributes. As you might guess, as the number and complexity of the attributes increase, so, too, does the complexity of the underlying decision tree.

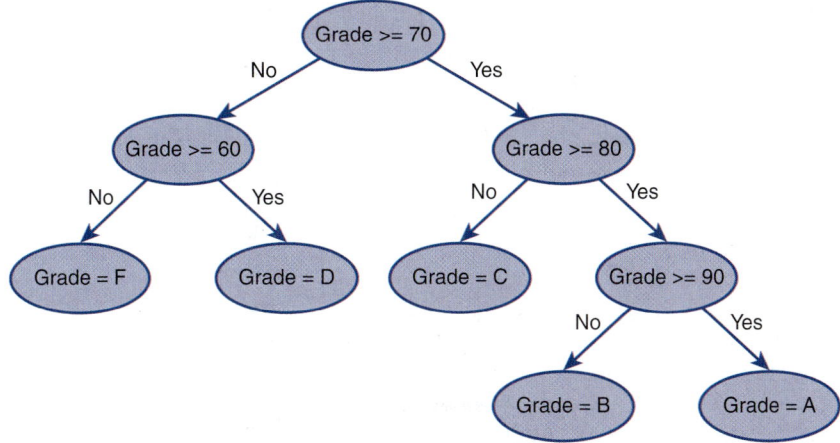

**FIGURE 11.8** A decision tree to calculate a student's grade.

The following Python script, DecisionTreeCancer.py, uses a decision tree to predict if a breast cancer tumor is benign:

```python
import pandas as pd
import numpy as np
from sklearn.model_selection import train_test_split
from sklearn.metrics import accuracy_score
from sklearn.neural_network import MLPClassifier
import sklearn.tree as tree
from sklearn.metrics import confusion_matrix

names = ['Sample', 'Clump Thickness','Uniformity of Cell
Size','Uniformity of Cell Shape','Marginal Adhesion','Single
Epithelial Cell Size','Bare Nuclei','Bland Chromatin', 'Normal
Nucleoli', 'Mitoses', 'class']

df = pd.read_csv('breast.data.csv', header=None, names=names)
X = np.array(df.iloc[:, 1:10])
y = np.array(df['class'])

# split the data into train and test sets
X_train, X_test, y_train, y_test = train_test_split(X, y,
test_size=0.30)

DT = tree.DecisionTreeClassifier()
DT.fit(X_train, y_train)
pred = DT.predict(X_test)
print ('Accuracy Score: ', accuracy_score(y_test, pred))
print('\nConfusion Matrix\n', confusion_matrix(y_test, pred))
```

When you execute this script, it will display the following output:

```
Accuracy Score:   0.9707317073170731

Confusion Matrix
 [[128    6]
  [  0   71]]
```

As you can see, the decision-tree model creates a very accurate solution. The following R program, DecisionTreeCancer.R, performs similar processing:

```r
library(C50)
library (datasets)

BreastCancer <- read.csv(file='breast.data.csv')
BreastCancer <- BreastCancer[-1] # drop sample column
## Split in train + test set
indexes <- sample(1:nrow(BreastCancer),
as.integer(0.7*nrow(BreastCancer)))
```

```
trainData <- BreastCancer[indexes,]
testData <- BreastCancer[-indexes,]

treeFit <- C5.0(x=trainData[,-10], y=as.factor(trainData[,10]))
pred <- predict(treeFit, testData)

confusionmatrix = as.matrix(table(Actual = testData[,10],
Predicted = pred))
accuracy = sum(diag(confusionmatrix))/length(testData[,10])

print('Confusion Matrix')
print(confusionmatrix)
print('Accuracy')
print(accuracy)
```

When you run this program, it will display the following output:

```
Confusion Matrix
      Predicted
Actual  2    4
     2 134   4
     4   6  61
[1] "Accuracy"
[1] 0.9512195
```

## Viewing the Decision Tree

When you use the DecisionTreeClassifier function to create a decision-tree model, you can actually view the tree the model creates. The following Python script, ViewDecisionTree.py, displays the decision tree created to model the breast cancer data:

```
import pandas as pd
import numpy as np
from sklearn.model_selection import train_test_split
from sklearn.metrics import accuracy_score
from sklearn.neural_network import MLPClassifier
from sklearn.tree import export_graphviz
import graphviz
import sklearn.tree as tree
from sklearn.metrics import confusion_matrix

names = ['Sample', 'Clump Thickness','Uniformity of Cell
Size','Uniformity of Cell Shape','Marginal Adhesion','Single
Epithelial Cell Size','Bare Nuclei','Bland Chromatin', 'Normal
Nucleoli', 'Mitoses', 'class']

df = pd.read_csv('breast.data.csv', header=None, names=names)
X = np.array(df.iloc[:, 1:10])
y = np.array(df['class'])
```

```python
# split the data into train and test sets
X_train, X_test, y_train, y_test = train_test_split(X, y,
test_size=0.30)

DT = tree.DecisionTreeClassifier()
DT.fit(X_train, y_train)
pred = DT.predict(X_test)
print ('Accuracy Score: ', accuracy_score(y_test, pred))
print('\nConfusion Matrix\n', confusion_matrix(y_test, pred))

export_graphviz(DT, out_file='DecisionTree.dot')

with open('DecisionTree.dot') as f:
  dot_graph = f.read()
g = graphviz.Source(dot_graph)
g.render()
print('PDF created')
```

When you run this script, it will produce a Portable Document File (PDF) you can use to view the decision tree, as shown in **FIGURE 11.9**.

As you can see, the decision tree the script creates is more complex than our previous decision tree for student grades. That said, the processing performed is similar—the algorithm will follow the tree's decision paths to classify data.

## Classifying Data Using Random Forests

In the previous section you learned how to use decision-tree modeling to classify data. Depending on the data set and model, there may be times when the decision tree becomes very deep (many levels of nodes). Often, such decision trees will overfill the data and will have a large variance.

A random-forest classification model creates many different decision trees for a data set and then, based on each tree's prediction, the trees essentially vote to select the tree that produces the best result.

The following Python script, RandomForests.py, uses a random forest to predict whether a tumor is benign or malignant:

```python
import pandas as pd
import numpy as np
from sklearn.model_selection import train_test_split
from sklearn.metrics import accuracy_score
from sklearn.neural_network import MLPClassifier
import sklearn.tree as tree
from sklearn.metrics import confusion_matrix
from sklearn.ensemble import RandomForestClassifier

names = ['Sample','Clump Thickness','Uniformity of Cell
Size','Uniformity of Cell Shape','Marginal Adhesion','Single
```

**FIGURE 11.9** The decision tree used to predict iris flower data.

```
Epithelial Cell Size','Bare Nuclei','Bland Chromatin', 'Normal
Nucleoli', 'Mitoses', 'class']

df = pd.read_csv('breast.data.csv', header=None, names=names)
X = np.array(df.iloc[:, 1:10])
y = np.array(df['class'])

# split the data into train and test sets
X_train, X_test, y_train, y_test = train_test_split(X, y,
test_size=0.30)

model = RandomForestClassifier()
model.fit(X_train, y_train)
pred = model.predict(X_test)
print ('Accuracy Score: ', accuracy_score(y_test, pred))
print('\nConfusion Matrix\n', confusion_matrix(y_test, pred))
```

When you execute this script, it will display the following output:

```
Accuracy Score:   0.975609756097561

Confusion Matrix
 [[131    4]
 [  1   69]]
```

The following R program, RandomForests.R, performs similar processing:

```
library(randomForest)
library (datasets)

BreastCancer <- read.csv(file='breast.data.csv')
BreastCancer <- BreastCancer[-1] # drop sample column
## Split in train + test set
indexes <- sample(1:nrow(BreastCancer),
as.integer(0.7*nrow(BreastCancer)))

trainData <- BreastCancer[indexes,]
testData <- BreastCancer[-indexes,]

treeFit <- randomForest(x=trainData[,-10],
y=as.factor(trainData[,10]))
pred <- predict(treeFit, testData)

confusionmatrix = as.matrix(table(Actual = testData[,10],
Predicted = pred))
accuracy = sum(diag(confusionmatrix))/length(testData[,10])

print('Confusion Matrix')
print(confusionmatrix)
```

```
print('Accuracy')
print(accuracy)
```

When you execute this program, it will display the following output:

```
Confusion Matrix
      Predicted
Actual   2    4
     2 129    4
     4   2   70
  [1] "Accuracy"
  [1] 0.9707317
```

## Classifying Data Using a Support Vector Machine

The SVM, also called an SVC, classifies data by separating values with a line called a hyperplane, as shown in **FIGURE 11.10**.

Classes that you can separate using a line in this way are said to be linearly separable. As you can see in **FIGURE 11.11**, there are many lines you can use to divide the classes.

The goal of SVC is to find the line that creates the widest separation between the classes. To calculate the best separation line, the algorithm uses two additional lines called support vectors, as shown in **FIGURE 11.12**.

As you might guess, many classes are not linearly separable, as shown in **FIGURE 11.13**.

The SVC algorithm extends the separation capabilities to support such nonlinear solutions.

SVC is ideal for binary classification problems, such as whether a loan will be approved or disapproved. That said, you can use SVC to multiclass problems; however, your solution may not be as accurate as other methods.

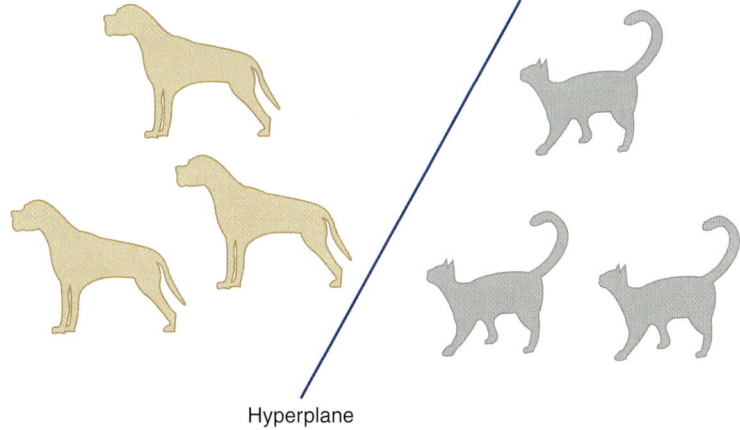

**FIGURE 11.10** Separating data into classes using a hyperplane.

**FIGURE 11.11 Using different lines to separate data classes.**

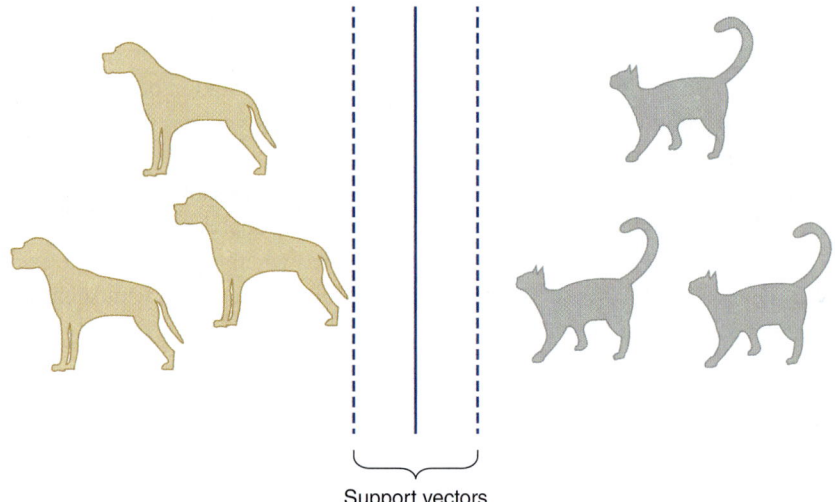

**FIGURE 11.12 Using support vectors to determine the best separation line.**

The following Python script, SVCIris.py, uses SVC to predict iris flower types:

```
import pandas as pd
import numpy as np
from sklearn.model_selection import train_test_split
from sklearn.metrics import accuracy_score
from sklearn.svm import SVC

names = ['sepal_length', 'sepal_width', 'petal_length', 'petal_width', 'class']
```

**FIGURE 11.13** Many data sets are not linearly separable.

```
df = pd.read_csv('iris.data.csv', header=None, names=names)
X = np.array(df.iloc[:, 0:4])
y = np.array(df['class'])

# split the data into the train and test sets
X_train, X_test, y_train, y_test = train_test_split(X, y,
test_size=0.30)

model = SVC(gamma='auto').fit(X_train, y_train)
pred = model.predict(X_test)

print ('\nModel accuracy score: ', accuracy_score(y_test, pred))
print("\nFrom the test data")
print('Index\tPredicted\tActual')
for i in range(len(pred)):
  if pred[i] != y_test[i]:
    print(i, '\t', pred[i], '\t', y_test[i], ' ****')
```

```
DataToPredict =
np.array([[5.2,3.5,1.4,0.2],[5.7,2.9,3.6,1.3],[5.8,3.0,5.1,1.8]])
pred = model.predict(DataToPredict)

print("\nPredicted Results")
for i in range(len(pred)):
    print('\t', DataToPredict[i], '\t', pred[i])
```

When you execute this script, it will display the following output:

```
Model accuracy score:  0.9555555555555556

From the test data
Index        Predicted              Actual
7            Iris-virginica         Iris-versicolor    ****
40           Iris-virginica         Iris-versicolor    ****

Predicted Results
        [5.2 3.5 1.4 0.2]     Iris-setosa
        [5.7 2.9 3.6 1.3]     Iris-versicolor
        [5.8 3.  5.1 1.8]     Iris-virginica
```

As discussed, SVC is ideal for binary classifications. The following Python script, SVCcancer.py, uses SVC to predict whether a breast tumor is malignant or benign:

```
import pandas as pd
import numpy as np
from sklearn.model_selection import train_test_split
from sklearn.metrics import accuracy_score
from sklearn.svm import SVC

names = ['Sample', 'Clump Thickness','Uniformity of Cell
Size','Uniformity of Cell Shape','Marginal Adhesion','Single
Epithelial Cell Size','Bare Nuclei','Bland Chromatin', 'Normal
Nucleoli', 'Mitoses', 'class']

df = pd.read_csv('breast.data.csv', header=None, names=names)
X = np.array(df.iloc[:, 1:10])
y = np.array(df['class'])

# split the data into the train and test sets
X_train, X_test, y_train, y_test = train_test_split(X, y,
test_size=0.30)

model = SVC(gamma='auto').fit(X_train, y_train)
pred = model.predict(X_test)

print ('\nModel accuracy score: ', accuracy_score(y_test, pred))
```

When you execute this program, it will display the following output:

```
C:\python> python SVCcancer.py
Model accuracy score:  0.975609756097561
```

# Hands-on: Real-World Data Sets

Throughout this book, you will work with many data sets that originate from the UCI data repository, as shown in **FIGURE 11.14**.

Take time to become familiar with the available data sets. To get started, locate the Zoo data set, which you can use to categorize animals into one of seven classes:

```
1 -- (41) aardvark, antelope, bear, boar, buffalo, calf, cavy,
cheetah, deer, dolphin, elephant, fruitbat, giraffe, girl,
goat, gorilla, hamster, hare, leopard, lion, lynx, mink, mole,
mongoose, opossum, oryx, platypus, polecat, pony, porpoise,
puma, pussycat, raccoon, reindeer, seal, sealion, squirrel,
vampire, vole, wallaby, wolf
2 -- (20) chicken, crow, dove, duck, flamingo, gull, hawk, kiwi,
lark, ostrich, parakeet, penguin, pheasant, rhea, skimmer, skua,
sparrow, swan, vulture, wren
3 -- (5) pitviper, seasnake, slowworm, tortoise, tuatara
```

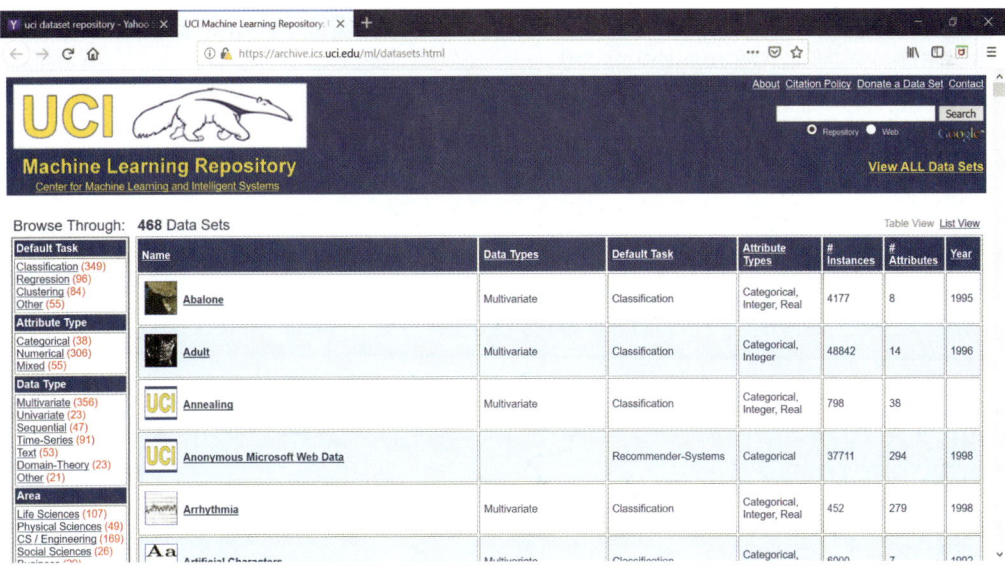

**FIGURE 11.14** The UCI data-set repository.

Used with permission of UC Regents

```
4 -- (13) bass, carp, catfish, chub, dogfish, haddock, herring,
pike, piranha, seahorse, sole, stingray, tuna
5 -- (4) frog, frog, newt, toad
6 -- (8) flea, gnat, honeybee, housefly, ladybird, moth,
termite, wasp
7 -- (10) clam, crab, crayfish, lobster, octopus, scorpion,
seawasp, slug, starfish, worm
```

The data set contains 101 records, each containing 17 attributes. There are no missing values within the data set. From the UCI website, click on the zoo.data link. Your browser will display the data shown in **FIGURE 11.15**.

Press the Ctrl+A keyboard combination to select all the data and Ctrl+C to copy the data to the Clipboard. Then open a text editor, such as Notepad, and press Ctrl+V to paste the data. Save the data file to your disk using the name Zoo.csv.

The following Python script, ZooKNN.py, uses the KNN classifier to classify the data:

```python
import pandas as pd
import numpy as np
from sklearn.model_selection import train_test_split
from sklearn.metrics import accuracy_score
from sklearn.neighbors import KNeighborsClassifier

df = pd.read_csv('zoo.csv', header=0)
```

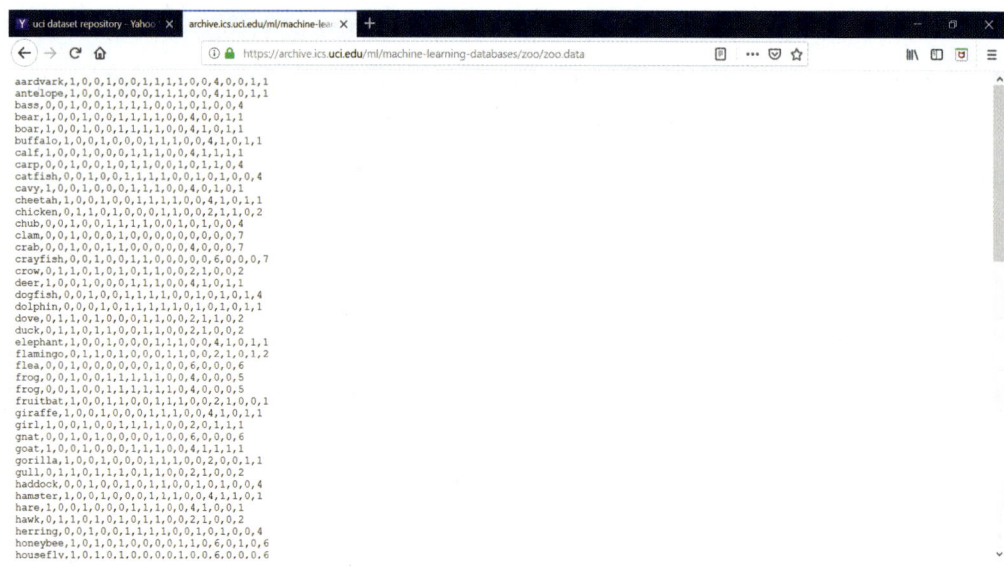

**FIGURE 11.15** The contents of the Zoo data set.

Dua, D., and Graff, C. 2019. *UCI Machine Learning Repository*. Irvine, CA: University of California, School of Information and Computer Science. http://archive.ics.uci.edu/ml

```
# Drop column 0 which has the class names
X = np.array(df.iloc[:, 1:17])
y = np.array(df['class_type'])

# split the data into train and test sets
X_train, X_test, y_train, y_test = train_test_split(X, y,
test_size=0.30)

knn = KNeighborsClassifier(n_neighbors=3)
knn.fit(X_train, y_train)
pred = knn.predict(X_test)

print('Index\tPredicted\tActual')
for i in range(len(pred)):
  if pred[i] != y_test[i]:
    print(i, '\t', pred[i], '\t\t', y_test[i], ' ****')

print (accuracy_score(y_test, pred))
```

When you run this script, it will display the following output:

```
C:\Python> python zooknn.py
Index    Predicted       Actual
8           6              7   ****
0.967741935483871
```

As you can see, the script reads the Zoo.csv file, using the file's header row to define the column names. The script uses all the data-set values except the first column, which contains the animal names, which is text based as opposed to numeric. Later in this chapter, you will learn how to work with such text data within a data set.

## Data Sets from Kaggle

The Kaggle.com website, shown in **FIGURE 11.16**, is a premier gathering space for data scientists and want-to-be data scientists. The site houses blogs, thousands of code samples, and tutorials, as well as a large repository of data sets. Kaggle also regularly holds machine-learning and data-mining competitions (with high-dollar winnings).

To use Kaggle, you must first register on the site. Do so and then download the Heart Disease data set shown in **FIGURE 11.17**, which contains over 300 records with 13 attributes you can use to predict the presence of heart disease.

Save the data-set file to your disk. Then create the following Python script, Heart.py, that uses the KNN classifier to predict the presence of heart disease:

```
import pandas as pd
import numpy as np
from sklearn.model_selection import train_test_split
from sklearn.metrics import accuracy_score
```

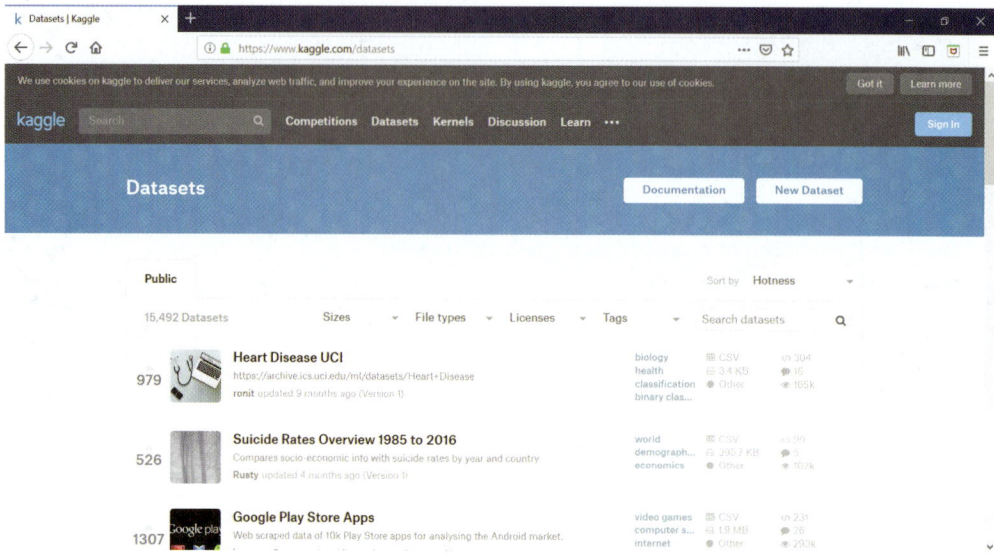

**FIGURE 11.16** The Kaggle website is a must-visit site for data scientists.

Used with permission from Kaggle Inc.

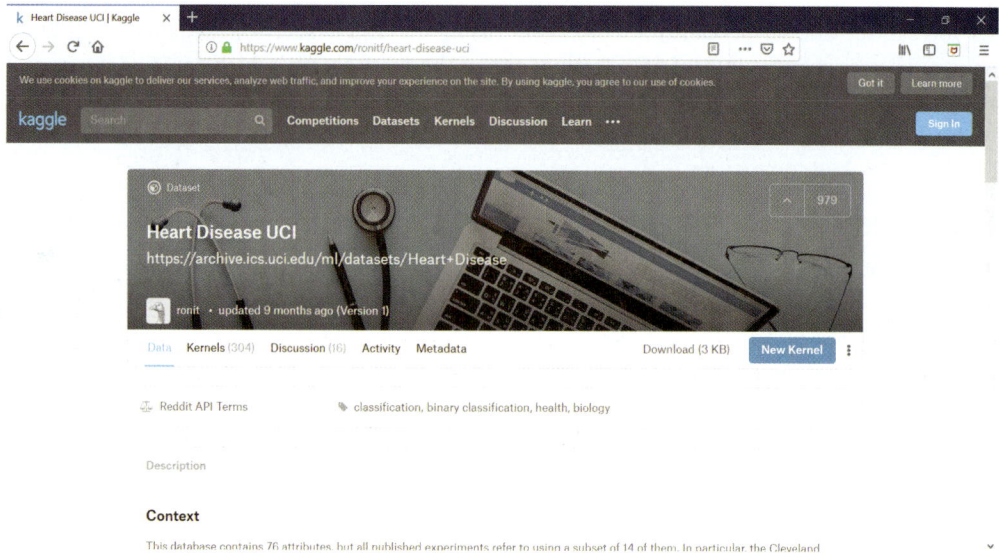

**FIGURE 11.17** The Heart Disease data set.

Used with permission from Kaggle Inc.

```
from sklearn.neighbors import KNeighborsClassifier

df = pd.read_csv('heart.csv', header=0)

X = np.array(df.iloc[:, 0:13])
y = np.array(df['target'])

# split the data into train and test sets
X_train, X_test, y_train, y_test = train_test_split(X, y,
test_size=0.30)

knn = KNeighborsClassifier(n_neighbors=3)
knn.fit(X_train, y_train)
pred = knn.predict(X_test)

print('Index\tPredicted\tActual')
for i in range(len(pred)):
  if pred[i] != y_test[i]:
    print(i, '\t', pred[i], '\t', y_test[i], ' ****')

print (accuracy_score(y_test, pred))
```

As you can see, the script reads the data set, the header row of which defines the column names. The script then uses K=3 nearest neighbors to predict the presence of heart disease.

## Filtering Non-Numeric Data

For simplicity, all the examples this chapter presents have used data sets for which all the data are numeric. Often, however, that won't be the case and your data set will contain text-based categorical data. Unfortunately, many machine-learning algorithms don't work with text data, and you will need to convert the data to a numeric value, possibly using hot encoding. In Chapter 2, "Data Mining," you learned that data analysts use a technique called "hot encoding" to perform such conversion. For example, using hot encoding, you might convert gender data from "male" and "female" to the values 0,1 and 1,0.

To keep the code simple and focused, the following programs will hand-edit such fields using values such as 0 for male and 1 for female. Although such edits will let you run the machine-learning algorithms, they introduce biases that will affect your result—for a correct result, you would need to use hot encoding, as discussed in Chapter 2. Depending on your Python and R programming skills, you may have your programs convert the data. Or you may use Excel or a text editor to perform your edits.

The UCI data-set repository, for example, contains the Congressional Voting Records data set, the goal of which was to determine whether members of the 1984 Congress could be classified as Republican or Democrat based on the member's voting record on the following key issues:

- Handicapped infants
- Water project cost sharing

- Adoption of the budget resolution
- Physician fee freeze
- El Salvador aid
- Religious groups in schools
- Anti-satellite test ban
- Aid to Nicaraguan Contras
- MX missile
- Immigration
- Synfuels corporation cutback
- Education spending
- Superfund right to sue
- Crime
- Duty-free exports
- Export administration act for South Africa

The data set contains voting records for 435 members of Congress (267 Democrats and 168 Republicans). When you download the data set, you will find that it contains categorical data, as shown in **FIGURE 11.18**.

Using a text editor, make the following changes to the data set:

- Replace republican with 0
- Replace democrat with 1
- Replace y with 2

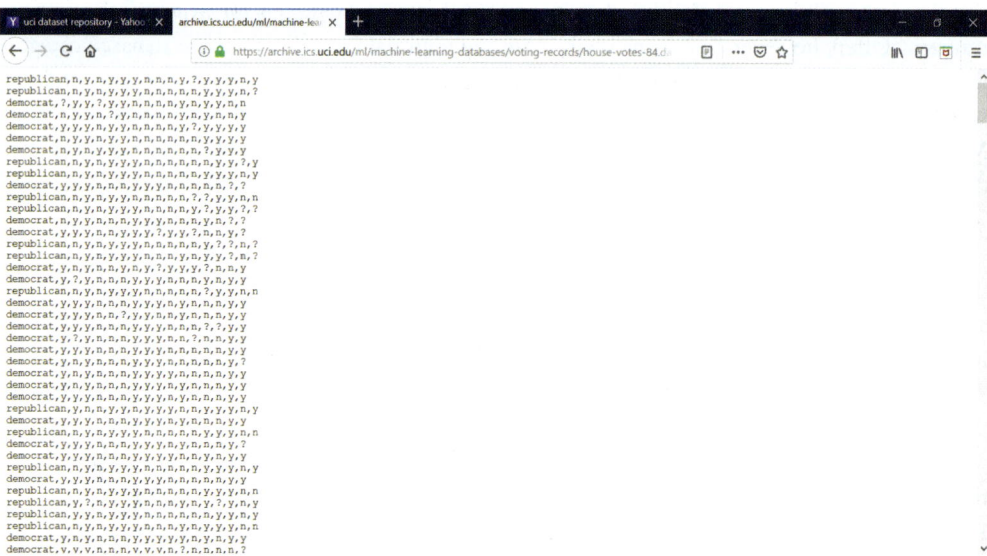

**FIGURE 11.18** Categorical data within the Congressional Voting Records data set.

Dua, D., and Graff, C. 2019. UCI Machine Learning Repository. Irvine, CA: University of California, School of Information and Computer Science. http://archive.ics.uci.edu/ml

- Replace n with 1
- Replace ? with 0

Following your edits, the data set should appear as shown in **FIGURE 11.19**.

The following Python script, Congress.py, uses the KNN classifier with K=3 to categorize the members of Congress as Democrat or Republican based upon voting records:

```
import pandas as pd
import numpy as np
from sklearn.model_selection import train_test_split
from sklearn.metrics import accuracy_score
from sklearn.neighbors import KNeighborsClassifier
from sklearn.metrics import confusion_matrix

names = ['Party', 'A', 'B','C','D','E','F','G','H','I','J','K',
'L','M','N','O','P']

df = pd.read_csv('congress.csv', header=None, names=names)
X = np.array(df.iloc[:, 1:17])
y = np.array(df['Party'])

# split into train and test
X_train, X_test, y_train, y_test = train_test_split(X, y,
test_size=0.30)

knn = KNeighborsClassifier(n_neighbors=3)
knn.fit(X_train, y_train)
pred = knn.predict(X_test)
```

```
congress - Notepad
File Edit Format View Help
0,1,2,1,2,2,2,1,1,1,2,0,2,2,2,1,2
0,1,2,1,2,2,2,1,1,1,1,2,2,2,1,0
1,0,2,2,0,2,2,1,1,1,1,2,1,2,2,1,1
1,1,2,2,1,0,2,1,1,1,1,2,1,2,1,1,2
1,2,2,2,1,2,2,1,1,1,1,2,0,2,2,2,2
1,1,2,2,1,2,2,1,1,1,1,1,2,2,2,2
1,1,2,1,2,2,2,1,1,1,1,1,0,2,2,2
0,1,2,1,2,2,2,1,1,1,1,1,2,2,0,2
0,1,2,1,2,2,2,1,1,1,1,1,2,2,2,1,2
1,2,2,2,1,1,1,2,2,2,1,1,1,1,1,0,0
0,1,2,1,2,2,1,1,1,1,1,0,0,2,2,1,1
0,1,2,1,2,2,2,1,1,1,1,1,2,0,2,2,0,0
1,1,2,2,1,1,1,2,2,2,1,1,1,2,1,0,0
1,2,2,2,1,1,2,2,2,0,2,2,0,1,1,2,0
0,1,2,1,2,2,2,1,1,1,1,1,2,0,0,1,0
0,1,2,1,2,2,2,1,1,1,2,1,2,2,0,1,0
1,2,1,2,1,1,2,1,2,0,2,2,2,0,1,1,2
1,2,0,2,1,1,1,2,2,2,1,1,1,2,1,2,2
```

**FIGURE 11.19** Representing categorical data with numeric values.

Used with permission from Microsoft

```
print ('\nModel accuracy score: ', accuracy_score(y_test, pred))
print(confusion_matrix(y_test, pred))
```

When you run this script, it will display the following output:

```
C:\> python Congress.py

Model accuracy score:   0.916030534351145
[[49  3]
 [ 8 71]]
```

As you work with real-world data, you will find that you must cleanse your data for missing and duplicate values, and you will often need to replace text-based categorical data with numeric representations.

## Summary

Classification is the process of assigning data to specific groups. Classification uses supervised machine learning, meaning the algorithm learns from a training data set. To determine the accuracy of a classification model, you use a test data set.

Classification algorithms work by examining an input "training set" of data to learn how the data values combine to create a result. Such a training set, for example, might contain heights, weights, colors, and temperaments of different dogs and the resulting breeds, or it might contain the sizes, shapes, dimensions, and locations of tumors that are malignant, as well as similar data for tumors that are benign. In other words, the training data contain values and the correct classification results.

After the algorithm learns and models the test data, a "test" data set (for which the correct results are known) is tested against the model to determine its accuracy, such as 97%. With knowledge of the accuracy in hand, the data analyst can then use the model to classify other data values.

Normally, the training set and testing set come from the same data set of values that are known to be correct or observed. The data analyst will specify, for example, that 70% of the data will be training data and 30% will be used for testing. Across the web, you can find many different data sets of known or observed data that you can use to try different learning algorithms.

Classification uses supervised learning, meaning it uses a training data set to teach the model how to assign data to correct classes and a test data set that evaluates the model's accuracy. To create the training and test data sets, the data must contain not only the predictor data values but also the correct class assignments for that data. Analysts normally use 70–80% of the known (complete) data to create the training data set and the rest for the test data set. After you train the model and test its accuracy, you can use the model to predict data classification. The classification process consists of three steps:

- Train the model.
- Evaluate (test) the model's accuracy.
- Use the model to predict data classification.

After you test a model, you can examine the resulting confusion matrix to determine which classification assignments the model got wrong.

Before you can use real-world data sets to classify data, you must often cleanse the data to remove missing or duplicate data. Many real-world data sets contain text-based categorical data. Unfortunately, many data-mining algorithms do not work well with text. Before you can use the data, you must convert the data from text to a numeric value, such as converting gender data from "male" and "female" to values such as 0 and 1.

This chapter examined several commonly used classification algorithms, each of which performs different processing to categorize data and each of which may better support binary or multiclass problems. As you examine classification algorithms, you will find that they differ by:

- Performance
- Memory use
- Support for binary classification and multiclass classification
- Data-set size
- Complexity

## Key Terms

Bayes Theorem
Classification
Decision tree
Decision-tree classifier
Dependent variable
K-nearest-neighbor classifiers
Logistic regression classifier
Logit

Multilayer Perceptron (MLP)
Multiclass classification
Naïve Bayes classifier
Neural network
Overfitting data
Perceptron
Predictor variable
Random tree classifier

Supervised learning
Support Vector Classifier (SVC)
Support Vector Machine (SVM)
Test data set
Training data set
Underfitting data
Unsupervised learning

## Review

1. Define and describe data classification.
2. Compare and contrast the data-classification algorithms presented in this chapter.
3. Using Python, implement the classification programs this chapter presents.
4. Using R, implement the classification programs this chapter presents.
5. Select a data set from the UCI data-set repository. Perform a KNN classification of the data and describe your results.
6. Select a data set from the Kaggle data-set repository. Perform a decision tree classification of the data, and describe your results.

# CHAPTER 12

# Predictive Analytics

## Chapter Goals and Objectives

- Define and describe predictive analysis.
- Compare and contrast predictive and prescriptive analysis.
- Define and describe the regression process.
- Define and describe regression techniques.
- Compare and contrast regression algorithms.

Data mining is the process of analyzing data to discover patterns and relationships. If you are working with sales data, for example, it makes sense that you would analyze data to determine facts such as:

- Which customer purchased the most products?
- Which customer purchased the least?
- What was the average sales per customer order?
- What was the average number of days between orders?
- What customers have not yet ordered the new product?
- And so on.

Using data in this way to describe past events is **descriptive analytics**. As you might imagine, being able to analyze data to determine such historical facts is very important and very valuable to businesses. To perform descriptive analytics, you can use statistical tools to generate metrics, you can use visualization tools to chart data, you can use clustering to group data, and more.

This chapter, however, is about using data to predict future events—predictive analytics. Companies today use predictive analytics for a wide range of applications:

- Estimate the revenue opportunity associated with an upcoming product sale.
- Predict the length of time machines will run without failing.
- Determine the loan amount to offer a customer.
- Which customers are likely to become long-term customers?
- For what price will a seaside home in Seattle sell?
- And more.

In Chapter 11, "Data Classification," you examined one form of predictive analytics: classification. Using supervised learning, you can predict in which class (category) an object should reside given predictor variables. Classification works with discrete categories, meaning data that have finite values, such as the type of a car, breed of a dog, color of hair, number of students (you can't have a fractional student), and so on. In contrast, continuous values have an infinite set of values, such as a company's projected revenue, the average basketball player's height, and the range of temperatures in Phoenix.

This chapter focuses on predicting continuous values using a technique called regression, the goal of which is to produce an equation that you can then use to predict results. By the time you finish this chapter, you will understand the following key concepts:

- **Descriptive analytics** is the use of statistics and data mining to describe what has happened in the past.
- **Predictive analytics** is the use of statistics, data mining, and machine learning to analyze data for the purpose of making predictions about the future.
- **Prescriptive analytics** relates to descriptive and predictive analytics. It attempts to recommend (prescribe) the best approach among various choices.
- Two primary forms of predictive analytics are classification and regression.
- **Regression** is a technique that produces an equation that models the relationships between variables.
- **Linear regression** is a technique that produces a linear equation that represents the relationships among variables. The linear equation normally minimizes the sum of each point's squared distance from the line.
- **Simple linear regression** is the use of linear regression to represent the relationship between the dependent variable and one predictor variable, such as $y = mx + b$.
- **Multiple linear regression** is the use of linear regression to represent the relationship between a dependent variable and two or more predictor variables, such as $y = ax_0 + bx_1 + cx_2$.
- There are many regression algorithms that differ by:
  - Ease of use
  - Data-set appropriateness
  - Performance
  - Memory use
- Many of the classification algorithms, such as K-nearest-neighbor, decision tree, and random forest, have regression counterparts.

# Understanding Linear Regression

Linear regression is a statistical technique that produces a linear equation that best models a set of data, as shown in **FIGURE 12.1**.

Beginning with the basics, the equation for a line is:

$$y = mx + b$$

where *m* is the slope coefficient and *b* is a constant that corresponds to the *y*-intercept—the value of *y* when *x* is zero.

When analysts use linear regression to create an equation that predicts one variable, such as relating a customer's age to sales, the process is called simple regression. In contrast, when more than one predictor variable is used, such as age and gender to predict salary, the process is called multiple regression.

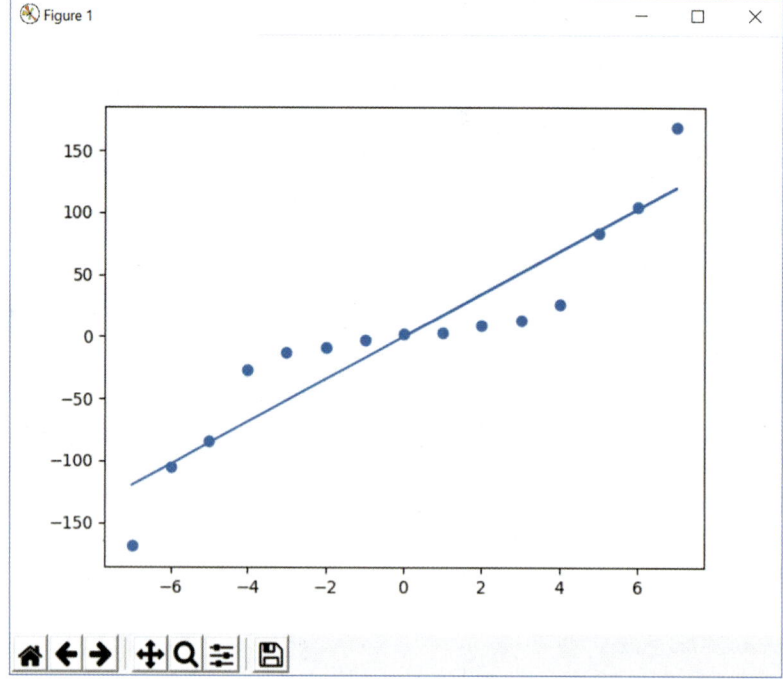

**FIGURE 12.1** Using linear regression to produce a linear equation that best models the data set.

Used with permission of Python Software Foundation

## Looking at a Simple Example

Assume that you have the following data points:

| X | Y |
|---|---|
| 0 | 2 |
| 1 | 3 |
| 2 | 4 |
| 3 | 5 |

If you chart the data, as shown in **FIGURE 12.2**, you will find that the data are linear, that the *y*-intercept is 2 and the slope is 1.

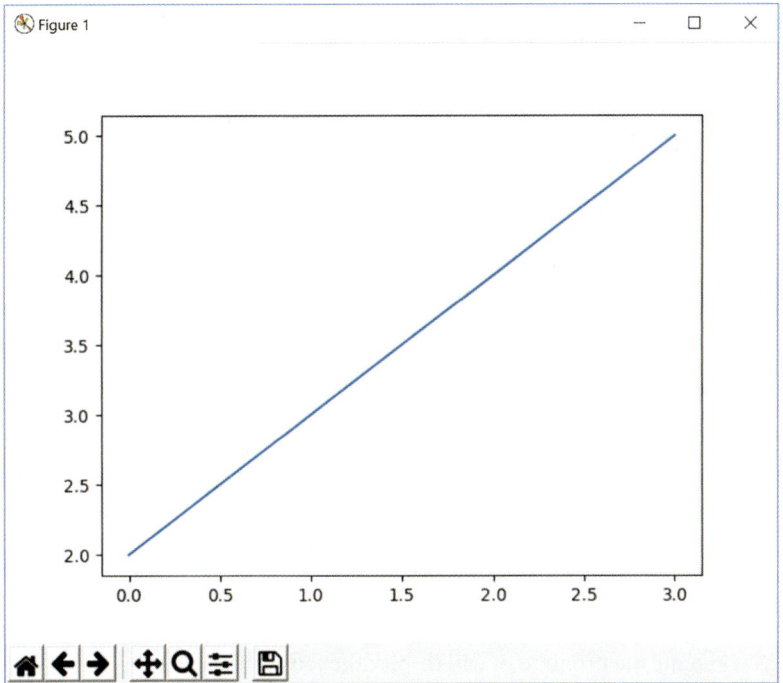

**FIGURE 12.2** Charting a simple data set.

Used with permission of Python Software Foundation

The following Python script, Plot.py, uses the data set to create the chart previously shown in Figure 12.2:

```python
import numpy as np
import matplotlib.pyplot as plt

X = np.array([[0],[1],[2],[3]])
y = np.array([2,3,4,5])

plt.plot(X, y)
plt.show()
```

The following Python script, SimpleLR.py, uses the linear_model library LinearRegression function to perform a simple (one predictor value) linear regression using the data set previously shown:

```python
import pandas as pd
import numpy as np
from sklearn.linear_model import LinearRegression

X = np.array([[0],[1],[2],[3]])
y = np.array([2,3,4,5])

model = LinearRegression()
clf = model.fit(X, y)
print ('Coefficient: ', clf.coef_)
print('Y intercept: ', clf.intercept_)
```

When you execute this script, it will display the following output:

```
C:\Python>python SimpleLR.py
Coefficient:   [1.]
Y intercept:   2.0
```

The following R program, Simply.r, performs similar processing:

```r
df <- data.frame(
     x = c(0,1,2,3),
     y = c(2,3,4,5))

lm(formula = y ~ x, data=df)
```

When you execute the program, it will display the following output:

```
Coefficients:
(Intercept)                    x
     2                         1
```

As you can see, the slope coefficient is 1 and the *y*-intercept is 2. In this case, our data happened to be linear, which will most often not be the case. Assume, for example, that you are given the following data:

| X | Y |
|---|---|
| 0 | 2 |
| 1 | 3 |
| 2 | 9 |
| 3 | 13 |
| 4 | 27 |
| 5 | 84 |
| 6 | 105 |
| 7 | 169 |

If you plot the data, you will find that the data are not linear, as shown in **FIGURE 12.3**.

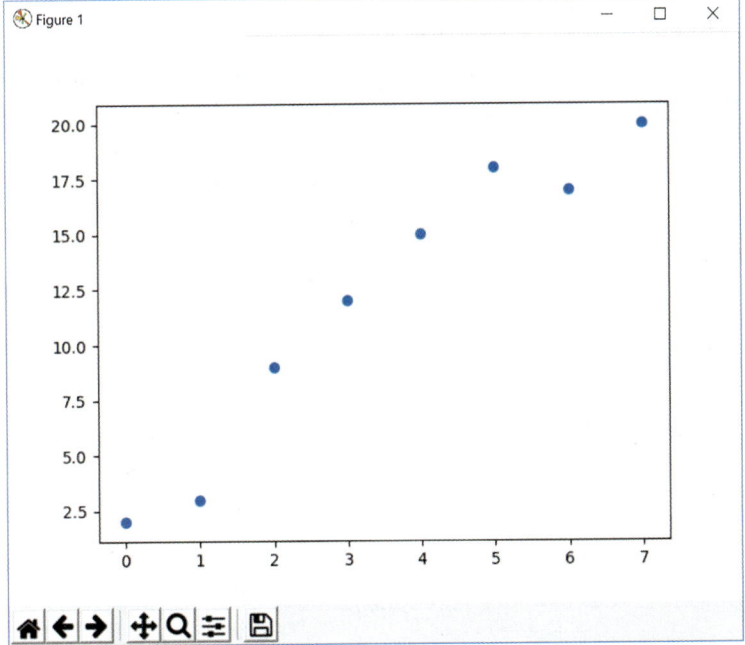

**FIGURE 12.3** Plotting a simple nonlinear data set.

Used with permission of Python Software Foundation

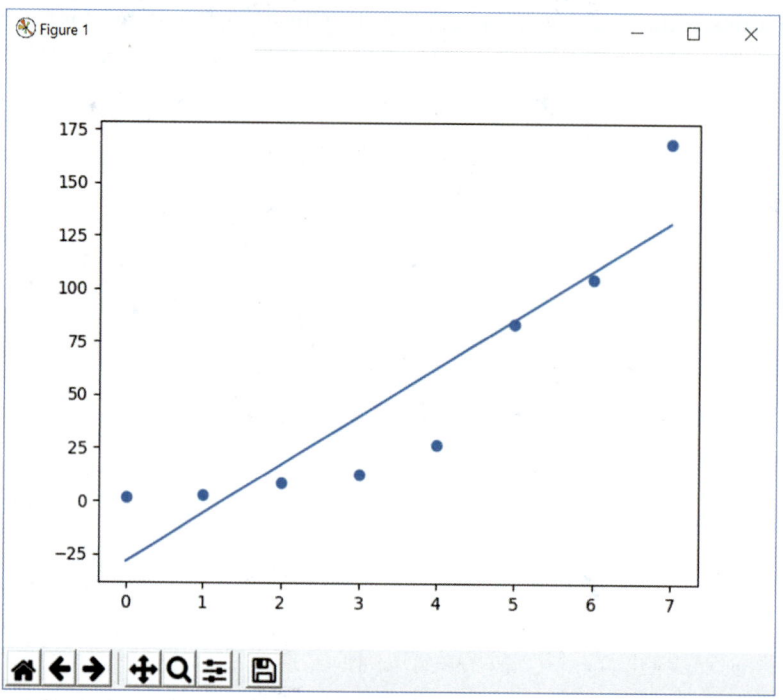

**FIGURE 12.4** Plotting data and the corresponding line produced by linear regression.

Used with permission of Python Software Foundation

The following Python script, PlotLR.py, uses the LinearRegression function to determine the line that best represents the data and then plots the data and line, as shown in **FIGURE 12.4**:

```
import numpy as np
import matplotlib.pyplot as plt
import pandas as pd
import numpy as np
from sklearn.linear_model import LinearRegression

X = np.array([[0],[1],[2],[3],[4],[5],[6],[7]])
y = np.array([2,3,9,13,27,84,105,169])
plt.scatter(X,y)

model = LinearRegression()
clf = model.fit(X, y)
predictions = np.dot(X, clf.coef_)

for index in range(len(predictions)):
 predictions[index] = predictions[index] + clf.intercept_

plt.plot(X, predictions)

plt.show()
```

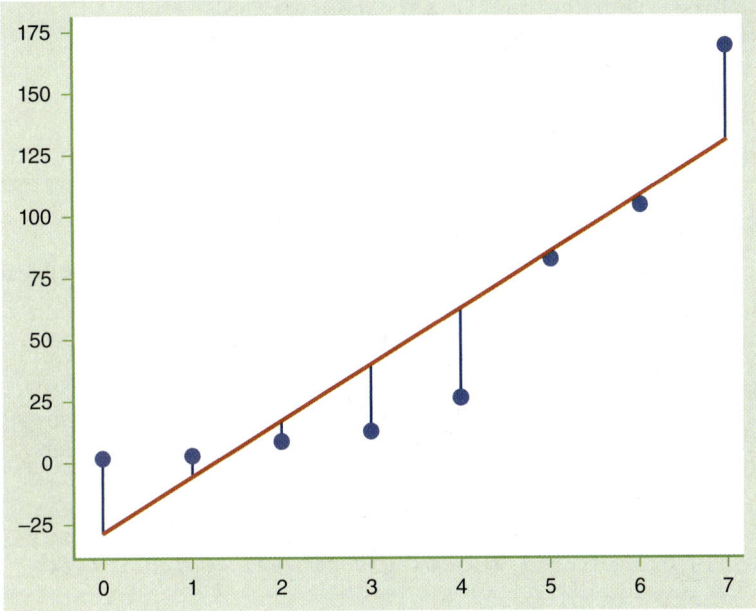

**FIGURE 12.5** Linear regression produces a line that minimizes each point's distance from the line.

To model an equation, a linear regression algorithm produces a line that will minimize the sum of the squared distances of each point to the line, as shown in **FIGURE 12.5**.

## Looking at a Real-World Example of Simple Linear Regression

The University of California, Irvine (UCI) data-set repository provides the Auto-MPG data set, which contains average miles per gallon (MPG), horsepower, weight, number of cylinders, and so on for many different car types. The following Python script, WeightMPG.py, uses the data set to create an equation that models the relationship between automobile weight and MPG:

```
import pandas as pd
import numpy as np
from sklearn.linear_model import LinearRegression

data = pd.read_csv('auto-mpg.csv')

X = data[['weight']].values
y = data['mpg']
```

```python
model = LinearRegression(fit_intercept=False)
clf = model.fit(X, y)
print ('Coefficient: ', clf.coef_)

predictions = model.predict(X)
for index in range(len(predictions)):
  print('Actual: ', y[index], 'Predicted: ', predictions[index],
'Weight: ', X[index,0])
```

To start, download and save the file from this text's catalog page at go.jblearning.com/DataMining. When you execute this script, it will display the following output:

```
C:\> python WeightMPG.py
Coefficient:  [0.00669058]
Actual:  18.0 Predicted:   23.443794170864074 Weight:  3504
Actual:  15.0 Predicted:   24.708313890696637 Weight:  3693
Actual:  18.0 Predicted:   22.988834694945478 Weight:  3436
Actual:  16.0 Predicted:   22.968762953360834 Weight:  3433
Actual:  17.0 Predicted:   23.07581224181227  Weight:  3449
Actual:  15.0 Predicted:   29.04381007297972  Weight:  4341
   :       :        :              :             :       :
Actual:  14.0 Predicted:   29.130787619846508 Weight:  4354
Actual:  14.0 Predicted:   28.849783237661494 Weight:  4312
Actual:  14.0 Predicted:   29.605818837349748 Weight:  4425
Actual:  15.0 Predicted:   25.758735033626333 Weight:  3850
Actual:  15.0 Predicted:   23.838538422028734 Weight:  3563
Actual:  14.0 Predicted:   24.14630512632661  Weight:  3609
```

In this case, based only on the weight, the linear regression's prediction of the MPG is not as accurate as we would like. Later in this chapter, we will use the same data with a multiple linear regression that uses several predictor values. As you will see, the multiple predictors improve the model's accuracy. This chapter also examines the Auto-MPG data set with several prediction algorithms.

The following R program, WeightMPG.r, performs similar processing:

```
df <- read.csv(file='auto-mpg.csv')

model <- lm(formula = mpg ~ weight, data=df)

prediction <- predict(model,df)

print(cbind(df$mpg, prediction))
```

When you execute this program, it will display the following output:

```
        prediction
1   18.0  19.382198
2   15.0  17.950670
3   18.0  19.897245
```

```
4   16.0   19.919968
5   17.0   19.798780
6   15.0   13.042575
7   14.0   12.944110
8   14.0   13.262227
:    :        :
```

## Multiple Linear Regression

When you must predict values based on two or more predictor variables, you can perform multiple linear regression. Assume, for example, you are given the following data set:

| $x_0$ | $x_1$ | $x_2$ | Y |
|---|---|---|---|
| 0 | 6 | 11 | 46 |
| 2 | 7 | 12 | 52 |
| 3 | 8 | 13 | 58 |
| 4 | 9 | 14 | 64 |
| 5 | 10 | 15 | 70 |

The equation to compute $y$, in this case, becomes:

$$y = ax_0 + bx_1 + cx_2 + y\_intercept$$

The following Python script, MultipleLR.py, uses multiple linear regression to determine the coefficients:

```
import pandas as pd
import numpy as np
from sklearn.linear_model import LinearRegression

X = np.array([[0, 6, 11],[2, 7, 12],[3, 8, 13],[4, 9, 14],[5, 10, 15]])
y = np.array([46,52,58,64,70])

model = LinearRegression()
clf = model.fit(X, y)
print ('Coefficient: ', clf.coef_)
print('Y intercept: ', clf.intercept_)
```

When you run the script, it will display the following output:

```
C:\> python MultipleLR.py
Coefficient:  [3.62415977e-15 3.00000000e+00 3.00000000e+00]
Y intercept:  -5.0
```

Take time to perform the math that applies the coefficients to the $x$ values and that adds the $y$-intercept.

The following R program, MultipleLR.r, performs similar processing:

```
df <- data.frame(
     y = c(46, 52, 58, 64, 70),
     x0 = c(0, 2, 3, 4, 5),
     x1 = c(6, 7, 8, 9, 10),
     x2 = c(11, 12, 13, 14, 15))

print(lm(y~x0+x1+x2, data=df))
```

When you run the program, it will display the following output:

```
Coefficients:
(Intercept)           x0           x1           x2
   1.00e+01     2.77e-15     6.00e+00           NA
```

If you multiply the coefficients specified and add the $y$-intercept, you will find that the results closely approximate the values of $y$. That said, the equation is much different from that produced by the Python script.

## Looking at a Real-World Multiple Linear Regression

Earlier in this chapter you examined the use of the Auto-MPG data set to predict the MPG based on the weight of a car. The following Python script, AutoMPGMR.py, extends the previous script used for multiple predictor variables:

```
import pandas as pd
import numpy as np
from sklearn.linear_model import LinearRegression

data = pd.read_csv('auto-mpg.csv')

X = data[['weight', 'horsepower', 'cylinders', 'acceleration',
'displacement', 'model year', 'origin']].values
y = data['mpg']

model = LinearRegression(fit_intercept=False)
clf = model.fit(X, y)
print ('Coefficient: ', clf.coef_)
```

```
y2 = model.predict(X)
for index in range(len(y2)):
  print('Actual: ', y[index], 'Predicted: ', y2[index], 'Weight: ',
X[index,0])
```

When you execute this script, it will display the following output:

```
Coefficient:  [-0.00607987 -0.03489977 -0.62739129 -0.06569545
 0.01930388  0.5804971
  1.10007702]
Actual:  18.0 Predicted:  16.012841738633064 Weight:  3504.0
Actual:  15.0 Predicted:  14.505168381684879 Weight:  3693.0
Actual:  18.0 Predicted:  16.006316011283417 Weight:  3436.0
Actual:  16.0 Predicted:  15.688605843780202 Weight:  3433.0
Actual:  17.0 Predicted:  16.000260921193057 Weight:  3449.0
Actual:  15.0 Predicted:  11.037267543836581 Weight:  4341.0
   :            :              :                 :
Actual:  44.0 Predicted:  32.78280001168392 Weight:  2130.0
Actual:  32.0 Predicted:  31.15033959891936 Weight:  2295.0
Actual:  28.0 Predicted:  28.569053628005296 Weight:  2625.0
Actual:  31.0 Predicted:  27.814906055815655 Weight:  2720.0
```

The following R program, AutoMPGMR.r, performs similar processing:

```
df <- read.csv(file='auto-mpg.csv')
df = df[-8] # drop car name

model <- lm(formula = mpg ~ ., data=df)

prediction <- predict(model, df[,2:8])
actual <- df[,1:1]
print(cbind(actual, prediction))
```

When you execute this program, it will display the following output:

```
    actual prediction
1    18.0  16.188217
2    15.0  15.000000
3    18.0  18.000000
4    16.0  16.000000
5    17.0  17.000000
6    15.0  13.170741
7    14.0  12.231707
8    14.0  13.291063
9    14.0  12.473394
  :    :      :
391  28.0  28.000000
392  31.0  31.000000
```

Seattle (King County, Washington) is home to many successful high-tech companies (along with waterfront property), and this is reflected in the prices of its housing. The Kaggle website (discussed in Chapter 11) has the House Sales in King County, USA, data set that contains 19 house attributes and the prices for which each house sold.

The following Python script, SeattleHousing.py, uses several of the attributes to generate an equation with which you can predict a house price:

```
import pandas as pd
import numpy as np
from sklearn.linear_model import LinearRegression

data = pd.read_csv('Seattle.csv')

X = data[['bedrooms', 'bathrooms', 'sqft_living', 'sqft_
lot','floors', 'waterfront', 'view', 'condition', 'grade',
'sqft_above', 'sqft_basement', 'yr_built', 'yr_renovated',
'zipcode', 'lat', 'long', 'sqft_living15', 'sqft_lot15']].values
y = data['price']

model = LinearRegression(fit_intercept=False)
clf = model.fit(X, y)
print ('Coefficient: ', clf.coef_)

predictions = model.predict(X)
for index in range(len(predictions)):
   print('Actual: ', y[index], 'Predicted: ', predictions[index])
```

When you run this script, it will display the following output:

```
C:\> python SeattleHousing.pyd
Coefficient:   [-3.55429634e+04   4.10775605e+04   1.10335560e+02
1.33179788e-01
  5.27005384e+03   5.83351196e+05   5.24194027e+04   2.72350677e+04
  9.55767038e+04   7.14334345e+01   3.89021245e+01  -2.56410126e+03
  2.04290662e+01  -5.19355977e+02   6.02267189e+05  -2.18124673e+05
  2.30910133e+01  -3.75943742e-01]
Actual:     221900.0 Predicted:   214074.58212646507
Actual:     538000.0 Predicted:   736220.0183605829
Actual:     180000.0 Predicted:   376666.3118561058
Actual:     604000.0 Predicted:   459571.47462631756
    :          :         :              :
Actual:     510000.0 Predicted:   441180.97865572694
Actual:    1230000.0 Predicted:  1460407.4176293113
Actual:     257500.0 Predicted:   270625.0717223288
```

As you can see, before displaying the actual and predicted values, the program displays the coefficient for each predictor variable.

The following R program, SeattleHousing.r, performs similar processing:

```r
df <- read.csv(file='seattle.csv')

df <- df[1:15]
df <- df[-2] # drop date
df <- df[-1] # drop id

model <- lm(formula = price ~ ., data=df)

prediction <- predict(model, df[,2:13])
actual <- df[,1:1]
print(cbind(actual, prediction))
```

When you execute this program, it will display the following output:

```
  actual  prediction
1 221900   293017.8
2 538000   627366.4
3 180000   216295.5
4 604000   481500.6
5 510000   432790.1
6 1230000 1448260.9
:    :         :
```

## Decision Tree Regression

In Chapter 11, "Classification," you used decision trees to classify data. As it turns out, you can use decision trees to perform **decision tree regression** to predict continuous data. The following Python script, SimpleDecisionTreeRegression.py, uses the data set previously shown:

```python
import numpy as np
from sklearn import tree
from sklearn.tree import export_graphviz
import graphviz

X = np.array([[0],[1],[2],[3]])
y = np.array([2,3,4,5])

model = tree.DecisionTreeRegressor()
model.fit(X, y)
predictions = model.predict(X)

print(model.feature_importances_)

for index in range(len(predictions)):
  print('Actual: ', y[index], 'Predicted: ', predictions[index])
```

```
export_graphviz(model, out_file='DecisionTree.dot')

with open('DecisionTree.dot') as f:
  dot_graph = f.read()
g = graphviz.Source(dot_graph)
g.render()
print('PDF created')
```

When you execute this script, it will display the following output:

```
C:\> python SimpleDecisionTreeRegression.py
[1.]
Actual:   2  Predicted:   2.0
Actual:   3  Predicted:   3.0
Actual:   4  Predicted:   4.0
Actual:   5  Predicted:   5.0
PDF created
```

After the script applies the decision tree, the code creates a Portable Document File (PDF) that shows the decision tree used, as shown in **FIGURE 12.6**.

The following Python script, SeattleDT.py, uses decision tree regression to create an equation you can use to predict housing values in Seattle:

```
import pandas as pd
import numpy as np
from sklearn import tree
```

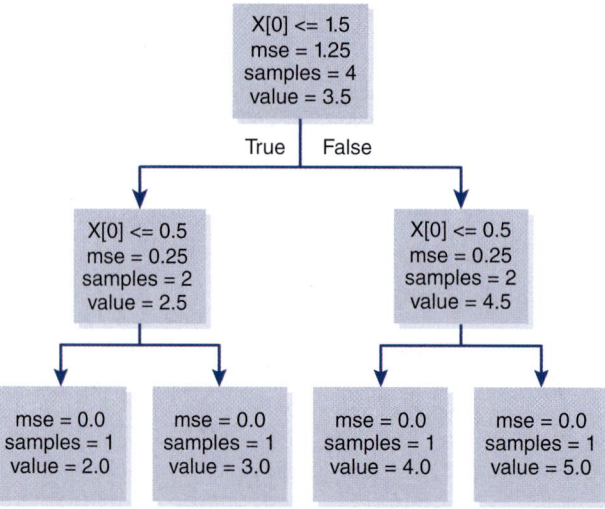

**FIGURE 12.6** The decision tree produced to perform a simple regression.

```
data = pd.read_csv('Seattle.csv')

X = data[['bedrooms', 'bathrooms', 'sqft_living', 'sqft_
lot','floors', 'waterfront', 'view', 'condition', 'grade',
'sqft_above', 'sqft_basement', 'yr_built', 'yr_renovated',
'zipcode', 'lat', 'long', 'sqft_living15', 'sqft_lot15']].values
y = data['price']

model = tree.DecisionTreeRegressor()
model.fit(X, y)
predictions = model.predict(X)

print(model.feature_importances_)

for index in range(len(predictions)):
  print('Actual: ', y[index], 'Predicted: ', predictions[index])
```

When you execute this script, it will display the following output:

```
C:\>python SeattleDT.py
[0.00297262 0.00499896 0.25291043 0.01392607 0.00099653
0.03304663
 0.00810034 0.00216407 0.33917602 0.02858094 0.00470583 0.01701006
 0.00161078 0.01197595 0.1651831  0.06439105 0.02724414 0.0210065 ]
Actual:   221900.0 Predicted:    221900.0
Actual:   538000.0 Predicted:    538000.0
Actual:   180000.0 Predicted:    180000.0
   :         :         :            :
Actual:   323000.0 Predicted:    323000.0
Actual:   662500.0 Predicted:    662500.0
Actual:   468000.0 Predicted:    468000.0
```

The following R program, SeattleDT.r, performs similar processing:

```
library(rpart)
df <- read.csv(file='seattle.csv')

df <- df[1:15]
df <- df[-2] # drop date
df <- df[-1] # drop id

model <- rpart(price~., data=df)

prediction <- predict(model, df[,2:13])
actual <- df[,1:1]
print(cbind(actual, prediction))
```

When you execute this program, it will display the following output:

```
   actual   prediction
1  221900   383389.7
2  538000   691658.9
3  180000   383389.7
4  604000   383389.7
5  510000   383389.7
6 1230000  1435002.9
:    :         :
```

## Random Forest Regression

A decision tree may not be optimal for the data set, as you learned in Chapter 11. A random-forest algorithm will create many decision trees and then apply the one that best represents the best prediction (based upon a vote of the other trees). The following Python script, AutoMPGRF.py, uses **random-forest regression** to produce coefficients for multiple predictor variables:

```
import pandas as pd
import numpy as np
from sklearn.ensemble import RandomForestRegressor

data = pd.read_csv('auto-mpg.csv')

X = data[['weight', 'horsepower', 'cylinders', 'acceleration',
'displacement','model year', 'origin']].values
y = data['mpg']

model = RandomForestRegressor(n_estimators=100)
model.fit(X, y)
predictions = model.predict(X)

print(model.feature_importances_)

for index in range(len(predictions)):
  print('Actual: ', y[index], 'Predicted: ', predictions[index],
'Weight: ', X[index,0])
```

When you execute this script, it will display the following output:

```
[0.17717852 0.13261749 0.19222058 0.03029727 0.34146629
 0.11504438 0.01117547]
Actual:   18.0  Predicted:   17.265  Weight:   3504.0
Actual:   15.0  Predicted:   14.74   Weight:   3693.0
Actual:   18.0  Predicted:   17.121  Weight:   3436.0
Actual:   16.0  Predicted:   16.23   Weight:   3433.0
Actual:   17.0  Predicted:   17.108  Weight:   3449.0
Actual:   15.0  Predicted:   14.63   Weight:   4341.0
```

```
Actual:   14.0  Predicted:   13.85  Weight:  4354.0
   :        :        :          :       :      :
Actual:   27.0  Predicted:   26.959  Weight:  2790.0
Actual:   44.0  Predicted:   42.382000000000005 Weight: 2130.0
Actual:   32.0  Predicted:   31.47  Weight:  2295.0
Actual:   28.0  Predicted:   28.552 Weight:  2625.0
Actual:   31.0  Predicted:   29.666 Weight:  2720.0
```

The following Python script, RandomForestSeattle.py, uses random-forest regression to produce an equation you can use to predict house values:

```
import pandas as pd
import numpy as np
from sklearn.ensemble import RandomForestRegressor

data = pd.read_csv('Seattle.csv')

X = data[['bedrooms', 'bathrooms', 'sqft_living', 'sqft_
lot','floors', 'waterfront', 'view', 'condition', 'grade',
'sqft_above', 'sqft_basement', 'yr_built', 'yr_renovated',
'zipcode', 'lat', 'long', 'sqft_living15', 'sqft_lot15']].values
y = data['price']

model = RandomForestRegressor(n_estimators=100)
model.fit(X, y)
predictions = model.predict(X)

print(model.feature_importances_)

for index in range(len(predictions)):
  print('Actual: ', y[index], 'Predicted: ', predictions[index])
```

When you execute this script, it will display the following output:

```
C:\Python>python SeattleRF.py | more
[0.00319293 0.00700491 0.26444561 0.01461835 0.00201871 0.02925467
 0.01147557 0.00282201 0.32199856 0.02180377 0.00566249 0.02696517
 0.0020755  0.01387127 0.1603682  0.06795986 0.03098179 0.01348064]
Actual:     221900.0 Predicted:    232241.58
Actual:     538000.0 Predicted:    518312.94
Actual:     180000.0 Predicted:    225074.07
Actual:     604000.0 Predicted:    561910.8333333334
   :           :          :            :
Actual:     510000.0 Predicted:    519553.0
Actual:    1230000.0 Predicted:   1302415.0
Actual:     257500.0 Predicted:    265736.01
Actual:     291850.0 Predicted:    256230.9
Actual:     229500.0 Predicted:    258336.0
```

The following R program, SeattleDT.r, performs similar processing:

```
library(rpart)
df <- read.csv(file='seattle.csv')

df <- df[1:15]
df <- df[-2] # drop date
df <- df[-1] # drop id

model <- rpart(price~., data=df)

prediction <- predict(model, df[,2:13])
actual <- df[,1:1]
print(cbind(actual, prediction))
```

When you execute this program, it will display the following output:

```
    actual prediction
1   221900   383389.7
2   538000   691658.9
3   180000   383389.7
4   604000   383389.7
5   510000   383389.7
6  1230000  1435002.9
:      :         :
```

## K-Nearest-Neighbors Regression

In Chapter 11, you used the K-nearest-neighbors algorithm to classify data. The K-nearest-neighbor algorithm groups data that are similar to that around it. It turns out that K-nearest-neighbors can also be used for regression. To predict values, the algorithm matches values to its nearest neighbors and then calculates an average.

The following Python script, KNNRegression.py, uses the Auto-MPG data set to predict MPG based on a car's weight:

```
import pandas as pd
import numpy as np
from sklearn import neighbors

data = pd.read_csv('auto-mpg.csv')

X = data[['weight', 'horsepower', 'cylinders', 'acceleration',
'displacement','model year', 'origin']].values
y = data['mpg']

model = neighbors.KNeighborsRegressor(n_neighbors = 5)
```

```
model.fit(X, y)
predictions = model.predict(X)

for index in range(len(predictions)):
  print('Actual: ', y[index], 'Predicted: ', predictions[index],
'Weight: ', X[index,0])
```

When you run this script, it will display the following output:

```
C:\> python AugoMPGKNN.py
Actual:  18.0 Predicted:  18.240000000000002 Weight:   3504.0
Actual:  15.0 Predicted:  15.280000000000001 Weight:   3693.0
Actual:  18.0 Predicted:  17.04 Weight:   3436.0
Actual:  16.0 Predicted:  17.04 Weight:   3433.0
Actual:  17.0 Predicted:  17.04 Weight:   3449.0
    :             :              :
Actual:  27.0 Predicted:  23.2 Weight:   2950.0
Actual:  27.0 Predicted:  24.8 Weight:   2790.0
Actual:  44.0 Predicted:  36.96 Weight:   2130.0
Actual:  32.0 Predicted:  21.220000000000002 Weight:   2295.0
Actual:  28.0 Predicted:  29.5 Weight:   2625.0
Actual:  31.0 Predicted:  26.580000000000002 Weight:   2720.0
```

The following R program, KNNRegression.r, performs similar processing:

```
library(FNN)

df <- read.csv(file='auto-mpg.csv')

## Split in train + test set
indexes <- sample(1:nrow(df),as.integer(0.7*nrow(df)))

trainData <- df[indexes,1:7]
testData <- df[-indexes,1:7]

## A 3-nearest neighbors model
model <- knn.reg(train = trainData, test = testData, y =
trainData$mpg, k=3)
prediction <- model$pred

actual <- testData[,1:1]
print(cbind(actual, prediction))
```

When you execute this program, it will display the following output:

```
     actual prediction
[1,]    18    17.40000
[2,]    14    14.83333
[3,]    14    14.00000
```

```
[4,]    15   18.73333
[5,]    14   15.33333
[6,]    18   23.03333
 :       :       :
```

In a similar way, the following R program, SeattleKNN.r, uses K-nearest-neighbors regression to predict Seattle housing:

```
library(FNN)

df <- read.csv(file='Seattle.csv')

## Split in train + test set
indexes <- sample(1:nrow(df),as.integer(0.7*nrow(df)))

trainData <- df[indexes,3:17]
testData <- df[-indexes,3:17]

## A 3-nearest neighbors model with no normalization
model <- knn.reg(train = trainData, test = testData, y =
trainData$price, k=3)
prediction <- model$pred

actual <- testData$price
print(cbind(actual, prediction))
```

When you execute this program, it will display the following output:

```
     actual prediction
[1,] 221900   221333.3
[2,] 604000   603983.3
[3,] 323000   322666.7
[4,] 662500   663166.7
[5,] 650000   650000.0
[6,] 189000   190000.0
  :      :        :
```

## Polynomial Regression

As you have learned, a line is not often a perfect fit for the underlying data. In such cases, you may find that a curved line better matches the data, as shown in **FIGURE 12.7**.

To create such a curved line, you can use **polynomial regression**. A **polynomial** is a mathematical expression that consists of variables, coefficients, and exponents:

$$y = 2x^2 + 4x^1 + 3$$

The degree of a polynomial corresponds to the expression's highest exponent. In the previous expression, the degree is 2. In the following expression, the degree is 3:

$$y = 4x^3 + 2x^2 + x - 3$$

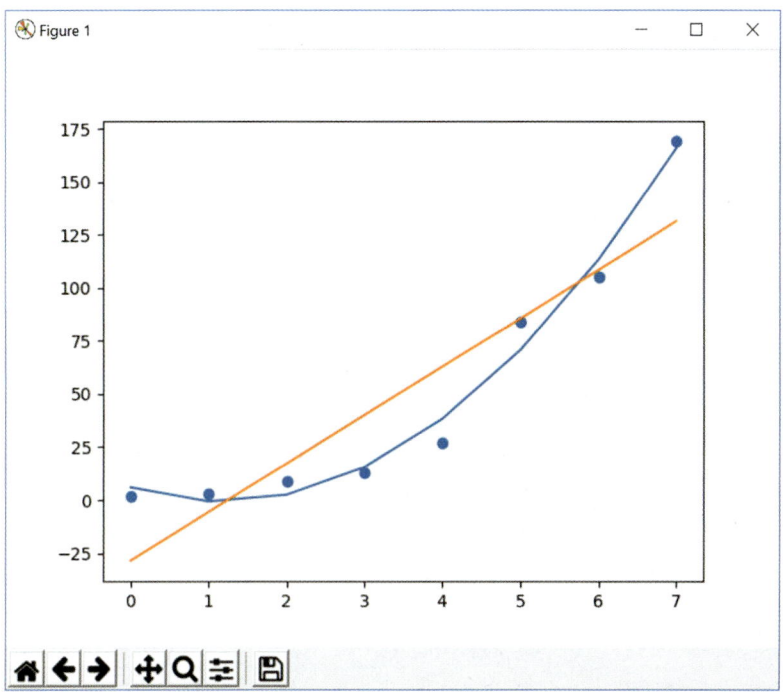

**FIGURE 12.7** A curved line may better represent the data set.

Used with permission of Python Software Foundation

Assume, for example, that you have the following data set:

| X | Y |
|---|---|
| 0 | 2 |
| 1 | 3 |
| 2 | 9 |
| 3 | 12 |
| 4 | 15 |
| 5 | 18 |
| 6 | 19 |
| 7 | 20 |

The following Python script, SimplePoly.py, uses the data to perform polynomial regression:

```
import matplotlib.pyplot as plt
import pandas as pd
import numpy as np
from sklearn.linear_model import LinearRegression
from sklearn.preprocessing import PolynomialFeatures

X = np.array([[0],[1],[2],[3],[4],[5],[6],[7]])
y = np.array([2,3,9,12,15,18,19,20])

plt.scatter(X,y)
poly = PolynomialFeatures(degree=2)
X_poly = poly.fit_transform(X)

model = LinearRegression()
model.fit(X_poly, y)
predictions = model.predict(X_poly)

plt.plot(X, predictions)

plt.show()
```

When you execute this script, it will display the chart shown in **FIGURE 12.8**. As you can see, the script's call to PolynomialFeatures uses a degree of 2. If you make the degree too small, you may underfit the data. Likewise, if you make the degree too large, you may overfit the data, introducing noise.

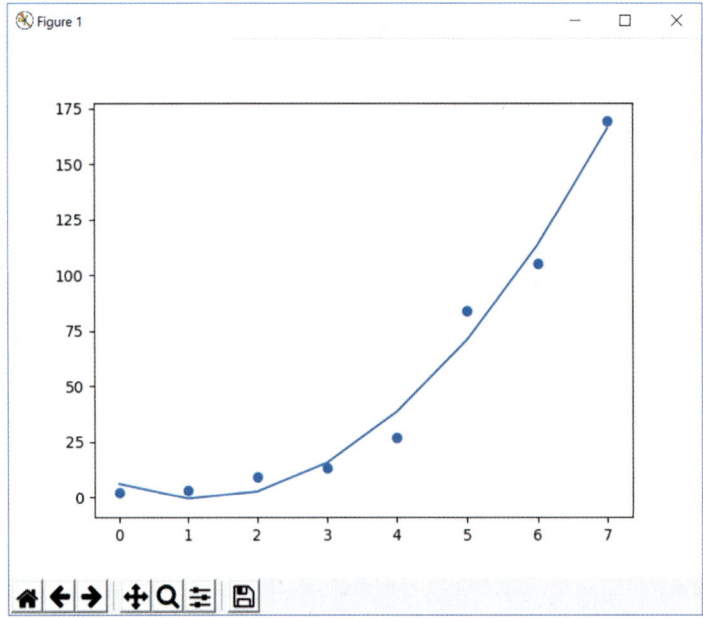

**FIGURE 12.8** Using a polynomial regression to better match the data set.

Used with permission of Python Software Foundation

The following Python script, SeattlePoly.py, uses polynomial regression to predict Seattle housing prices:

```
import pandas as pd
import numpy as np
from sklearn.linear_model import LinearRegression
from sklearn.preprocessing import PolynomialFeatures

data = pd.read_csv('Seattle.csv')

X = data[['bedrooms', 'bathrooms', 'sqft_living', 'sqft_
lot','floors', 'waterfront', 'view', 'condition', 'grade',
'sqft_above', 'sqft_basement', 'yr_built', 'yr_renovated',
'zipcode', 'lat', 'long', 'sqft_living15', 'sqft_lot15']].values
y = data['price']

poly = PolynomialFeatures(degree=2)
X_poly = poly.fit_transform(X)

model = LinearRegression()
model.fit(X_poly, y)
predictions = model.predict(X_poly)

for index in range(len(predictions)):
  print('Actual: ', y[index], 'Predicted: ', predictions[index])
```

When you execute this script, it will display the following:

```
C:\>python SeattlePoly.py
Actual:    221900.0 Predicted:   281513.63063812256
Actual:    538000.0 Predicted:   597503.946231842
Actual:    180000.0 Predicted:   465796.1729660034
Actual:    604000.0 Predicted:   374529.4194984436
Actual:    510000.0 Predicted:   440017.6208114624
    :          :           :            :
Actual:   1230000.0 Predicted:  1593494.9352798462
Actual:    257500.0 Predicted:   148664.48342895508
Actual:    291850.0 Predicted:   198388.18183135986
Actual:    229500.0 Predicted:   361355.69786453247
Actual:    323000.0 Predicted:   322805.03552627563
Actual:    662500.0 Predicted:   748746.6836776733
```

## Hands-on: RapidMiner

Throughout this text, you have performed machine-learning and data-mining operations using R and Python. RapidMiner is an integrated environment that lets you perform many of the operations without having to write code. Instead, you can drag and drop data and the operations you want to

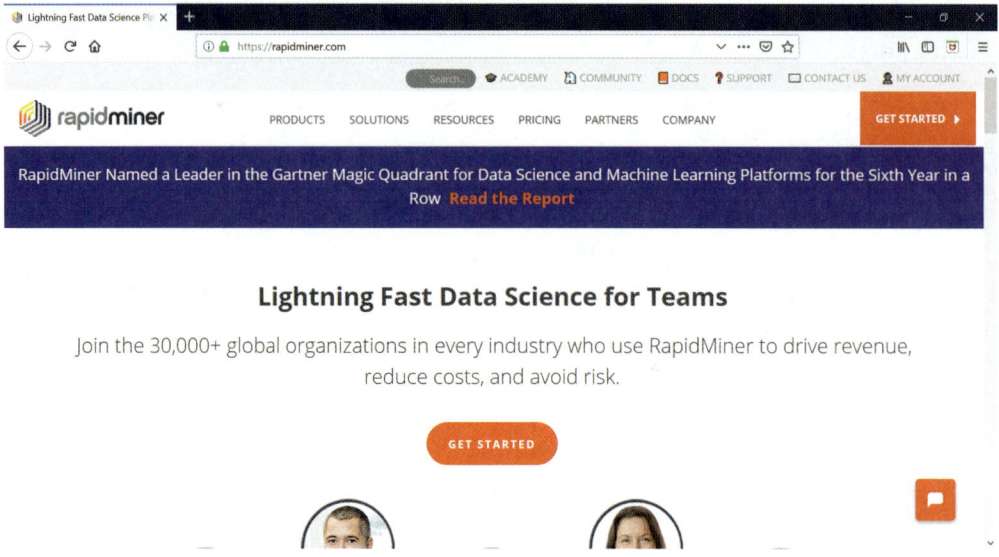

**FIGURE 12.9** The RapidMiner website.

Used with permission of RapidMiner

perform on to your workspace. RapidMiner will then use them to perform the operations to produce a result. You can use RapidMiner to cluster data, cleanse data, classify data, predict data, and more.

To get started, download and install the RapidMiner trial from the RapidMiner website at www.RapidMiner.com, as shown in **FIGURE 12.9**.

After you download and run RapidMiner, select the File menu New Process option. RapidMiner will display its Start Layout screen, as shown in **FIGURE 12.10**.

Choose the Auto Model option. RapidMiner will display the Auto Model screen, as shown in **FIGURE 12.11**, which will guide you through your operations.

Within the Samples folder Data subfolder, select the Deals data set, which you can use to predict whether someone will become a future customer. RapidMiner will display a prompt asking you to specify the operation that you want to perform, as shown in **FIGURE 12.12**.

Choose the Predict option. Then click on the Future Customer column and click Next. RapidMiner will display two bar charts that show the original counts of individuals who are and are not future customers. Click Next. RapidMiner will display a screen letting you choose the predictive columns, as shown in **FIGURE 12.13**.

Use the default setting (all the columns) and click Next. RapidMiner will display a screen, as shown in **FIGURE 12.14**, within which you can select the algorithms you want to apply.

Use the default (all models) and click Next. RapidMiner will apply each model, showing a screen that summarizes each model's accuracy, as shown in **FIGURE 12.15**.

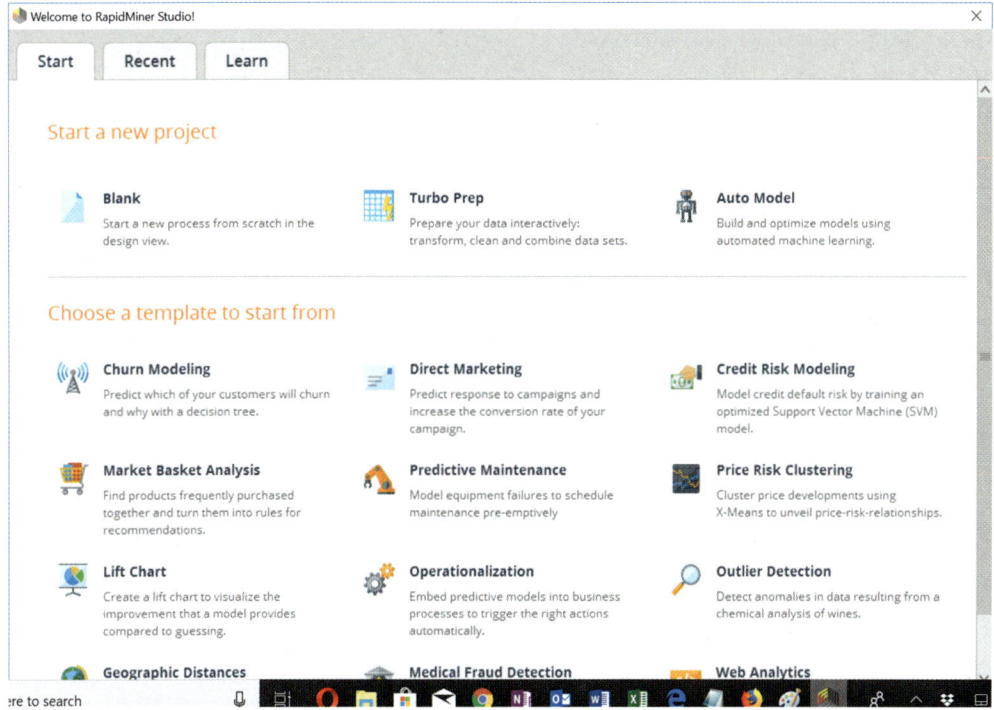

**FIGURE 12.10** The RapidMiner Start Layout screen.

Used with permission of RapidMiner

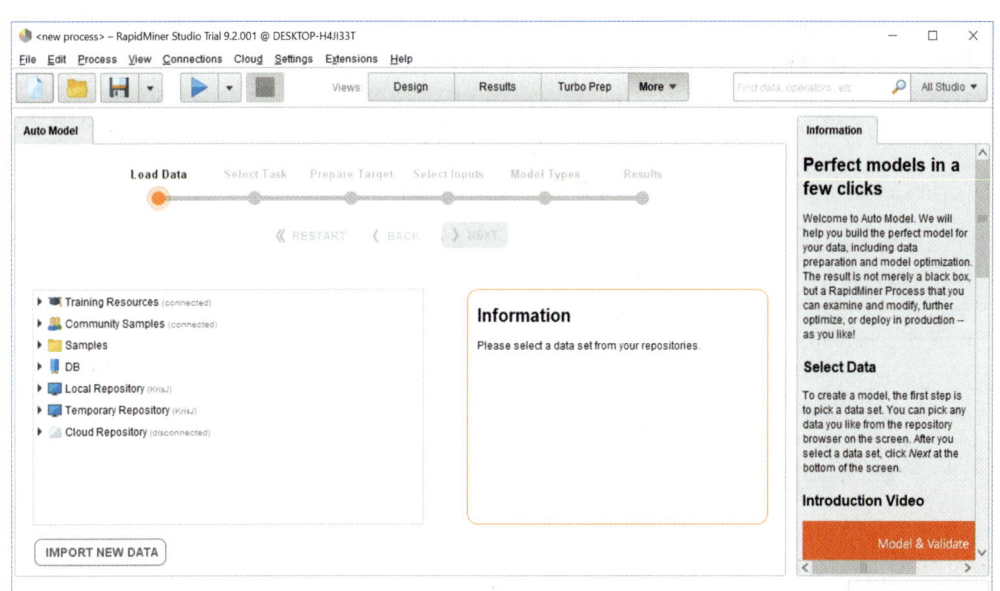

**FIGURE 12.11** The RapidMiner Auto Model screen.

Used with permission of RapidMiner

**556**    **CHAPTER 12** Predictive Analytics

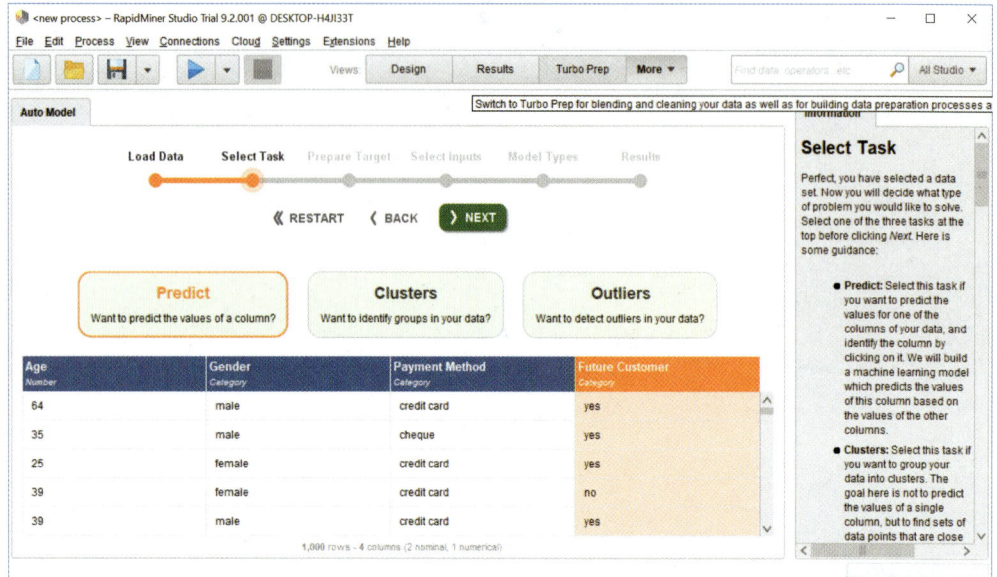

**FIGURE 12.12** Selecting an operation within RapidMiner.
Used with permission of RapidMiner

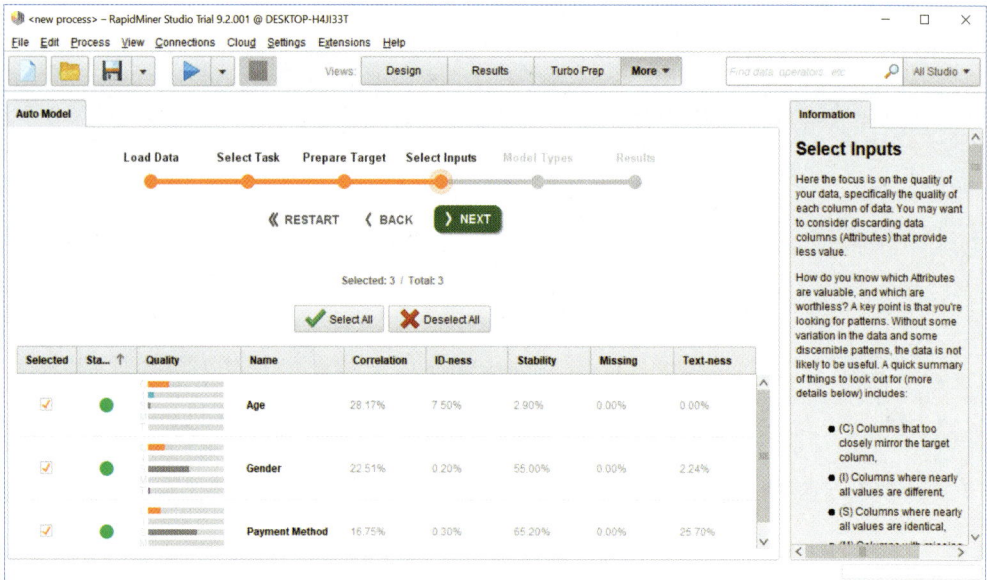

**FIGURE 12.13** Selecting prediction variables.
Used with permission of RapidMiner

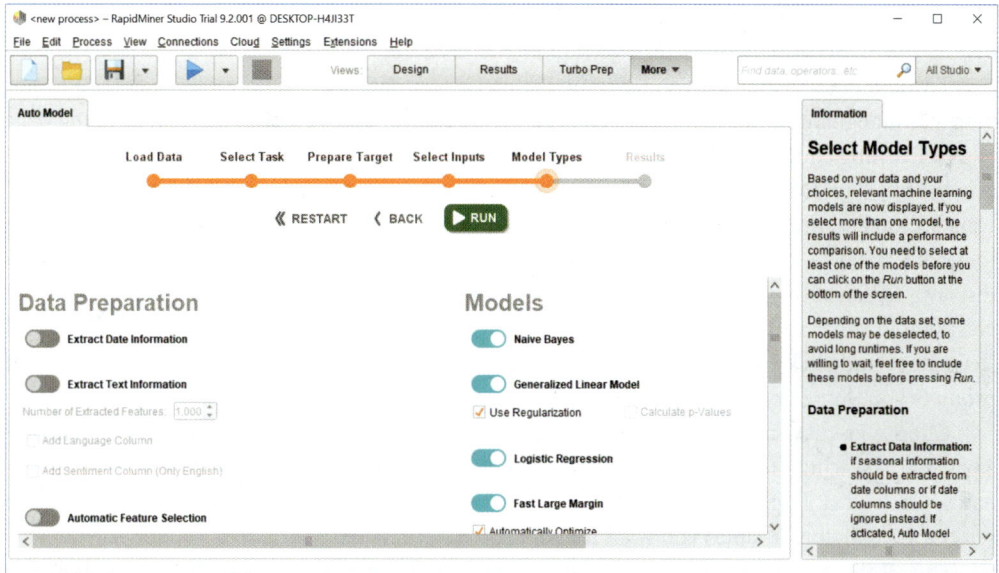

**FIGURE 12.14** Selecting prediction algorithms.

Used with permission of RapidMiner

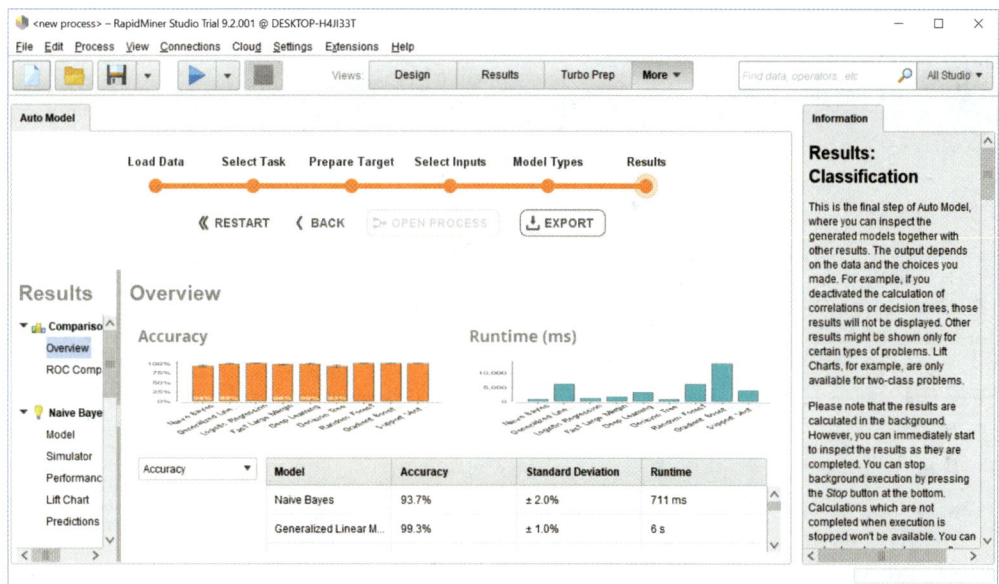

**FIGURE 12.15** Displaying the accuracy of prediction models.

Used with permission of RapidMiner

From the left side of your screen, select the Predictions list for Naïve Bayes. RapidMiner will display the model's predictions, as shown in **FIGURE 12.16**.

Throughout Chapter 11, you used the Breast Cancer data set to determine whether a tumor biopsy is malignant or benign. Download the Breast Cancer data set from this text's catalog page at go.jblearning.com/DataMining.

Within RapidMiner, select the Restart button to start a new analysis. Click the Import New Data button and import the file BreastHeader.csv. RapidMiner will display a screen allowing you to modify the data format. You do not need to make any changes, so click Next. RapidMiner will display a screen letting you format columns. Again, you do not need to make any changes, so click Next. RapidMiner will display a screen asking you where you want to store the data. Select Local Repository and click Finish. RapidMiner will display a screen, as shown in **FIGURE 12.17**, that prompts you to specify the operation you want to perform.

Choose Predict and then click on the "class" column and click Next. RapidMiner will display a bar chart showing the number of records that correspond to class 2 (benign) and class 4 (malignant). Click Next. RapidMiner will display the screen shown in **FIGURE 12.18** prompting you to select the predictor variables you want to include.

Use all the predictor variables and click Next. RapidMiner will display the screen shown in **FIGURE 12.19**, prompting you to select the models you want to apply.

Use all the models and click Run. RapidMiner will calculate its predictions, displaying the screen shown in **FIGURE 12.20** that shows each model's accuracy.

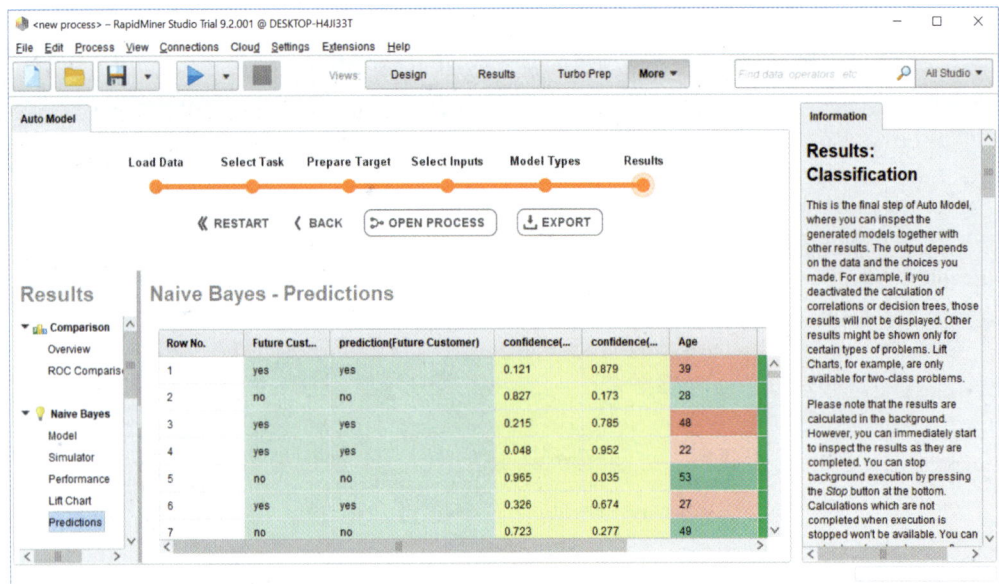

**FIGURE 12.16** Displaying the Naïve Bayes predictions.

Used with permission of RapidMiner

Hands-on: RapidMiner 559

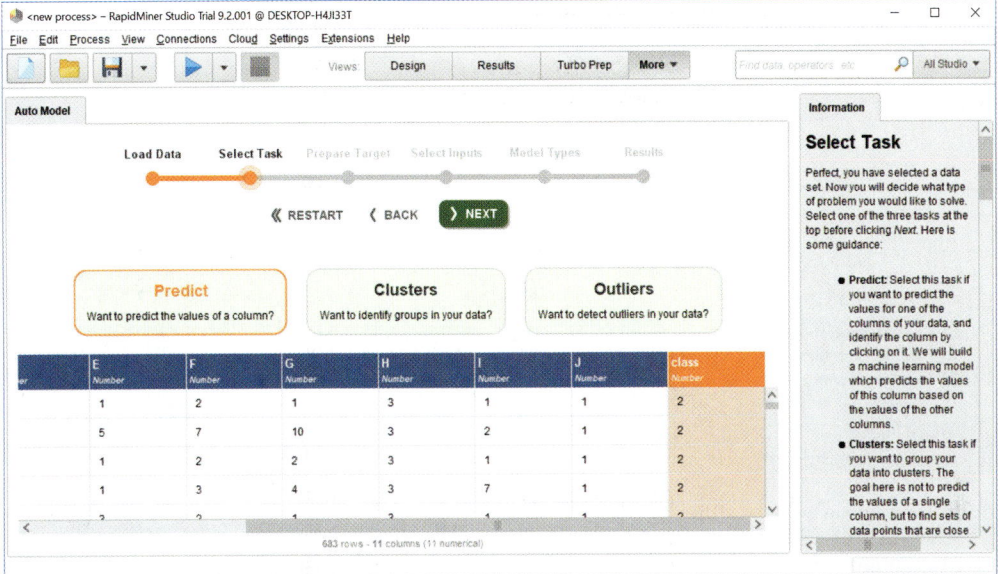

**FIGURE 12.17** Selecting an operation within RapidMiner.
Used with permission of RapidMiner

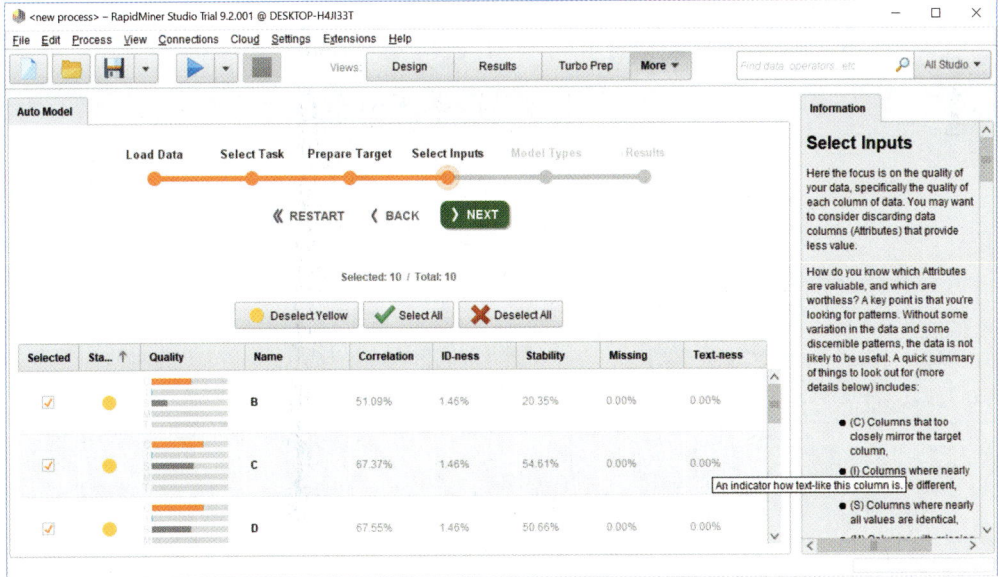

**FIGURE 12.18** Selecting predictor variables within RapidMiner.
Used with permission of RapidMiner

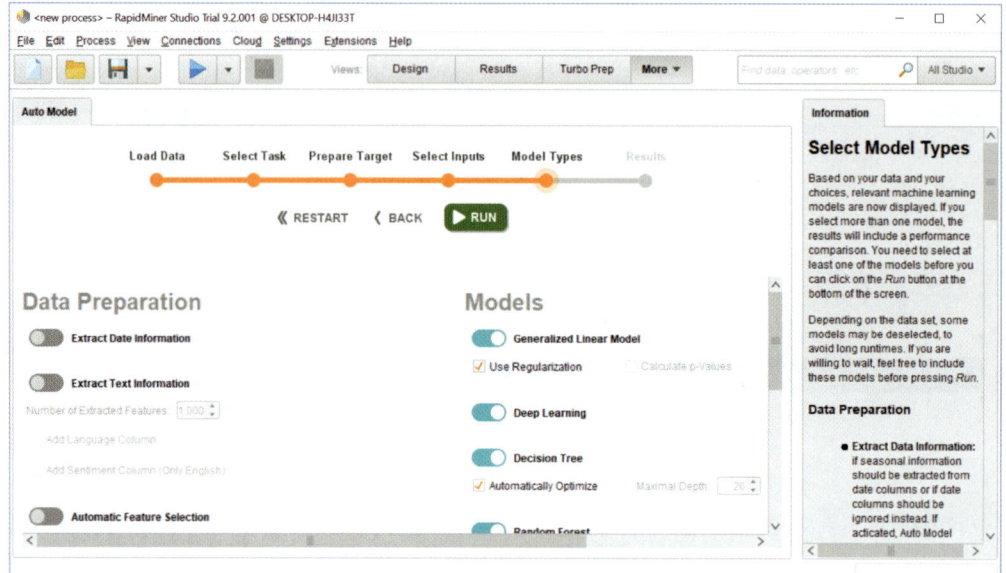

**FIGURE 12.19** Selecting prediction models within RapidMiner.

Used with permission of RapidMiner

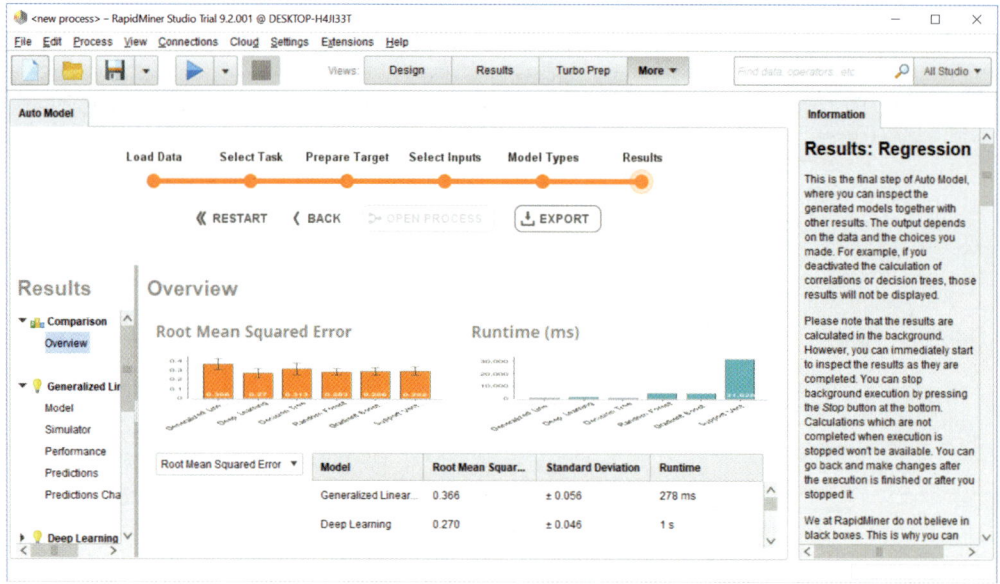

**FIGURE 12.20** Displaying prediction model accuracy within RapidMiner.

Used with permission of RapidMiner

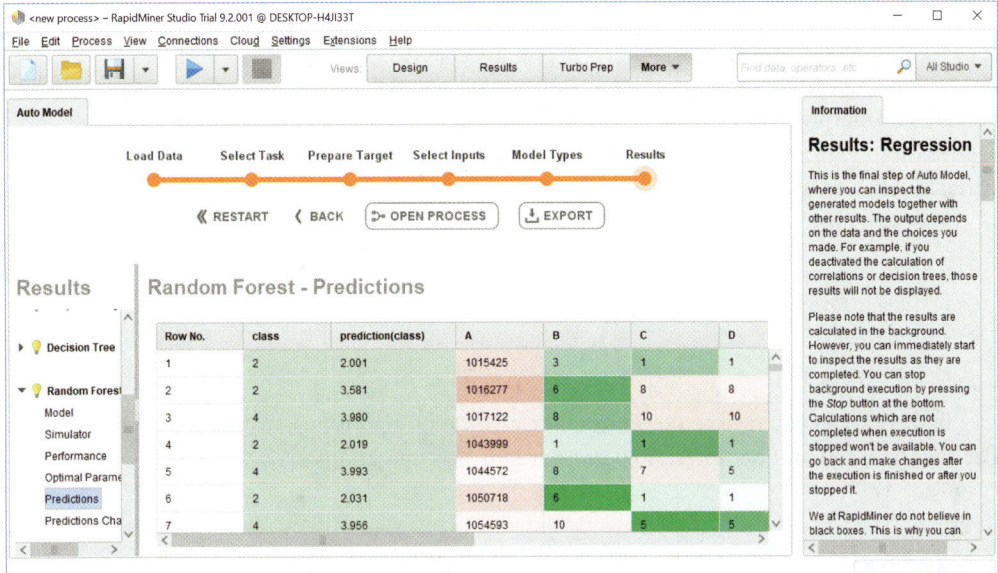

**FIGURE 12.21** Using a random forest prediction for breast cancer data within RapidMiner.
Used with permission of RapidMiner

Within the left-hand side of your screen, select Random Forest and select Predictions. RapidMiner will display its class predictions, as shown in **FIGURE 12.21**.

The purpose of this section was to get you started with RapidMiner. Using RapidMiner's Auto Model option, you can quickly perform many common operations. That said, the Auto Model capability only begins to scratch the surface of RapidMiner's capabilities. Fortunately, RapidMiner comes with a great set of tutorial videos you can use to drill deeper into its functionality.

# Summary

Descriptive analytics is the use of statistics and data mining to describe what has happened in the past. Predictive analytics is the use of statistics, data mining, and machine learning to analyze data for the purpose of making predictions about the future. Prescriptive analytics relates to descriptive and predictive analytics. It attempts to recommend (prescribe) the best approach among various choices.

Two primary forms of predictive analytics are classification and regression. In Chapter 11, you examined many different supervised learning classification algorithms. Regression is a technique that produces an equation that models the relationships between variables. Linear regression is a technique that produces a linear equation that represents the relationships among variables. The linear equation normally minimizes the sum of each point's squared distance from the line. Simple linear regression is the use of linear regression to represent the relationship between the dependent variable and one predictor variable, such as $y = mx + b$. Multiple linear regression is the use of linear regression to represent the relationship between a dependent variable and two or more predictor variables, such as $y = ax_0 + bx_1 + cx_2$.

There are many regression algorithms that differ by:

- Ease of use
- Data-set appropriateness
- Performance
- Memory use

In this chapter you revisited several of the classification algorithms, such as K-nearest-neighbor, decision tree, and random forest, to perform regression operations.

## Key Terms

Decision tree regression
Descriptive analytics
Linear regression
Multiple linear regression
Polynomial
Polynomial degree
Polynomial regression
Predictive analytics
Prescriptive analytics
Random-forest regression
Simple linear regression

## Review

1. Compare and contrast descriptive, predictive, and prescriptive data analytics.
2. Compare and contrast classification and regression.
3. Compare and contrast simple and multiple linear regression.
4. Implement and run the Python regression programs this chapter presents.
5. Implement and run the R regression programs this chapter presents.
6. Perform the RapidMiner operations this chapter presents, presenting screen captures of your operations.

# CHAPTER 13

# Data Association

## Chapter Goals and Objectives

- Define and describe data association.
- Define and describe market-basket analysis.
- Define and describe support, confidence, conviction, and lift.
- Use visual programming to implement machine-learning and data-mining solutions.

Throughout this text, you have performed a wide range of data operations that relate different data within a data set: visual charts, clustering, and classification. In this chapter, you will learn how to use **association** to identify patterns within data sets, such as the items a customer often purchases together at a grocery store, the links on a website upon which a customer clicks before making a purchase, and the snacks a fan purchases together at a ball game.

As you will learn, one of the most well-known association applications is the shopping-cart problem, which identifies the association between buying diapers and beer. You can think of this association process as looking in each shopping cart as customers leave the market and taking note of the items they bought. By noting that many of the carts that contained diapers also contained beer, you form an association. Data analysts often refer to this process as **market-basket analysis**.

In this chapter, you will perform association operations. By the time you finish this chapter, you will understand the following key concepts:

- Data association is the process of identifying patterns (relationships) between variables in a data set.
- Market-basket analysis is the use of data association to analyze consumer data for patterns, such as the products a shopper adds to their shopping cart (called consequent products) based upon an item that already resides in the cart (called the antecedent product).

As mentioned previously, a well-known pattern is the purchase of beer based on the presence of diapers in the shopping cart.

- Data association uses four measures to identify patterns:
  - Support
  - Confidence
  - Lift
  - Conviction
- **Support:** In market-basket analysis, support is a ratio measure that provides the relative frequency of an item in the basket.
- **Lift:** In market-basket analysis, lift is the ratio of the confidence to the expected confidence. Lift values close to 1 do not show an association, but rather, more likely indicate coincidence.
- **Confidence:** In market-basket analysis, confidence is a ratio measure that indicates the likelihood of the consequent based on a rule to all occurrences of the antecedent.
- **Conviction:** In market-basket analysis, conviction is a measure that examines the frequency with which the consequent occurs in spite of the absence of the antecedent.
- **Visual programming:** The process of creating a program by dragging and dropping objects on to a workspace, as opposed to writing programming language statements. The RapidMiner and Orange environments allow data analysts to use visual programming to create data-mining and machine-learning solutions.

## Understanding Support, Confidence, and Lift

To determine the level of association between two variables (the **antecedent**, which was the first variable that existed, and the **consequent**, which is the variable that occurred following or as a result of the antecedent), we will examine four measures: support, confidence, lift, and conviction. Assume, for example, that you have the data set shown in **FIGURE 13.1**.

Because the data set is small, you may see associations at a glance, such as the purchase of beer often accompanying the purchase of diapers. In addition, you may see an association between beer and chips. As your data sets become large, you must automate the identification of such associations.

**FIGURE 13.1** The shopping cart data set.

Used with permission from Microsoft

Data analysts express associations in the form of rules, such as:

```
{ diapers } -> { beer }
{ beer } -> { chips }
```

In the first rule, diapers is the antecedent and beer is the consequent. Likewise, in the second rule, beer is the antecedent and chips, the consequent.

Support is a measure that specifies the frequency with which an item occurs within a data set. To calculate support, use:

$$\text{Support}(x) = \frac{\text{Frequency}(x)}{\text{Total Transactions}}$$

If you examine the data set shown in Figure 13.1, there are five records. If you count the number of records that contain diapers, you should find three. Using these two counts, you would calculate support as:

$$\text{Support (Diapers)} = \frac{\text{Frequency (Diapers)}}{\text{Total Transactions}}$$
$$= \frac{3}{5}$$
$$= 0.6$$

Likewise, to determine the support for { diapers } -> { beer } you would use:

$$\text{Support (Diapers} \rightarrow \text{Beer)} = \frac{\text{Frequency (Diapers} \rightarrow \text{Beer)}}{\text{Total Transactions}}$$
$$= \frac{2}{5}$$
$$= 0.4$$

Confidence is a measure that indicates the likelihood of the consequent based on a rule to all occurrences of the antecedent. To calculate confidence, use:

$$\text{Confidence}(x \rightarrow y) = \frac{\text{Support}(x \cup y)}{\text{Support}(x)}$$

To calculate confidence for { diapers } -> {beer } you would perform:

$$\text{Confidence (Diapers} \rightarrow \text{Beer)} = \frac{\text{Support (Diapers} \cup \text{Beer)}}{\text{Support (Diapers)}}$$
$$= \frac{0.4}{0.6}$$
$$= 0.667$$

Next, lift is a measure that shows the ratio of confidence to the expected confidence. To calculate lift, use:

$$\text{Lift}(x \rightarrow y) = \frac{\text{Support}(x \cup y)}{\text{support}(x) \times \text{support}(y)}$$

Lift values close to 1 do not show an association, but rather, more likely indicate coincidence. To calculate the lift for { diapers } -> { beer } you would use:

$$\text{Lift}(\text{Diapers} \rightarrow \text{Beer}) = \frac{\text{Support}(\text{Diapers} \cup \text{Beer})}{\text{Support}(\text{Diapers}) \times \text{Support}(\text{Beer})}$$

$$= \frac{0.4}{0.6 \times 0.8}$$

$$= 0.833$$

Finally, conviction is a measure that examines the frequency with which a consequent occurs in spite of the absence of the antecedent. To measure conviction, use:

$$\text{Conviction}(x \rightarrow y) = \frac{1 - \text{Support}(y)}{1 - \text{Confidence}(x \rightarrow y)}$$

To calculate the conviction for { diapers } -> { beer }, you would perform:

$$\text{Conviction}(\text{Diapers} \rightarrow \text{Beer}) = \frac{1 - \text{Support}(\text{Diapers})}{1 - \text{Confidence}(\text{Diapers} \rightarrow \text{Beer})}$$

$$= \frac{1 - 0.6}{1 - 0.667}$$

$$= 1.2$$

## Calculating the Association Measures

The following Python script, DiapersAndBeer.py, uses a data set similar to that shown in Figure 13.1, which you can download from this text's catalog page at go.jblearning.com/DataMining, to calculate support, confidence, and lift:

```
import pandas as pd
from apyori import apriori

data = pd.read_csv('DiapersAndBeer.csv', header=None)

records = []
for i in range(0, len(data)):
    records.append([str(data.values[i,j]) for j in range(0,
len(data.columns))])

rules = apriori(records, min_length=2)
results = list(rules)
```

```
for item in results:
    print()
    print(item)
    print()
    print("----------------------")
```

The script uses the apyori package, which you can download from this text's catalog page at go.jblearning.com/DataMining (download the text file and save it as apyori.py). Place the apyori.py file within your Project folder. As you can see, the script first loads the DiapersAndBeer.csv data set. The apriori function requires a list of lists parameter, so the script loops through the rows and columns of the data set, appending records to the list of lists. After the script creates the association rules, it uses a for loop to display them. When you run this script, it will display the following output:

```
C:\> python DiapersAndBeer.py
RelationRecord(items=frozenset({'Beer'}), support=0.8, ordered_
statistics=[OrderedStatistic(items_base=frozenset(), items_
add=frozenset({'Beer'}), confidence=0.8, lift=1.0)])
----------------------
RelationRecord(items=frozenset({'Bread'}), support=0.2, ordered_
statistics=[OrderedStatistic(items_base=frozenset(), items_
add=frozenset({'Bread'}), confidence=0.2, lift=1.0)])
----------------------
       :      :       :
----------------------
RelationRecord(items=frozenset({'Beer', 'Bread'}),
support=0.2, ordered_statistics=[OrderedStatistic(items_
base=frozenset({'Beer'}), items_add=frozenset({'Bread'}),
confidence=0.25, lift=1.25), OrderedStatistic(items_
base=frozenset({'Bread'}), items_add=frozenset({'Beer'}),
confidence=1.0, lift=1.25)])
----------------------
RelationRecord(items=frozenset({'Beer', 'Candy'}),
support=0.2, ordered_statistics=[OrderedStatistic(items_
base=frozenset({'Beer'}), items_add=frozenset({'Candy'}),
confidence=0.25, lift=1.25), OrderedStatistic(items_
base=frozenset({'Candy'}), items_add=frozenset({'Beer'}),
confidence=1.0, lift=1.25)])
----------------------
RelationRecord(items=frozenset({'Beer', 'Diapers'}),
support=0.4, ordered_statistics=[OrderedStatistic(items_
base=frozenset({'Beer'}), items_add=frozenset({'Diapers'}),
confidence=0.5, lift=0.8333333333333334), OrderedStatistic(items_
base=frozenset({'Diapers'}), items_add=frozenset({'Beer'}),
confidence=0.6666666666666667, lift=0.8333333333333334)])
----------------------
```

As you can see, the program displays the results for each item and the combinations of items that occur in the shopping cart (called item sets). Within the combinations, you will see items_base, which specifies the antecedent.

The following R program, DiapersAndBeer.r, performs similar processing:

```r
install.packages("arules")
library(arules)

df <- read.csv(file='DiapersAndBeer.csv')

rules <- apriori(df)
inspect(rules)
```

When you execute this script, it will display the following output:

```
     lhs                    rhs              support  confidence
[1]  {Formula=Candy}    => {Diapers=Diapers}  0.25     1
[2]  {Formula=Candy}    => {Beer=Beer}        0.25     1
[3]  {Formula=Candy}    => {Fritos=Chips}     0.25     1
[4]  {Diapers=Flour}    => {Formula=Milk}     0.25     1
[5]  {Formula=Milk}     => {Diapers=Flour}    0.25     1
[6]  {Diapers=Flour}    => {Fritos=Cheetos}   0.25     1
[7]  {Fritos=Cheetos}   => {Diapers=Flour}    0.25     1
[8]  {Diapers=Flour}    => {Beer=Beer}        0.25     1
[9]  {Formula=Milk}     => {Fritos=Cheetos}   0.25     1
[10] {Fritos=Cheetos}   => {Formula=Milk}     0.25     1
[11] {Formula=Milk}     => {Beer=Beer}        0.25     1
[12] {Fritos=Cheetos}   => {Beer=Beer}        0.25     1
[13] {Diapers=Bread}    => {Formula=Straws}   0.25     1
  :          :                   :             :       :
[75] {Diapers=Bread,Formula=Straws,Fritos=Chips} => {Beer=Beer}        0.25 1
[76] {Diapers=Bread,Beer=Beer,Fritos=Chips}      => {Formula=Straws}   0.25 1
[77] {Formula=Straws,Beer=Beer,Fritos=Chips}     => {Diapers=Bread}    0.25 1
[78] {Diapers=Diapers,Formula=Corn,Beer=Sugar}   => {Fritos=Chips}     0.25 1
[79] {Formula=Corn,Beer=Sugar,Fritos=Chips}      => {Diapers=Diapers}  0.25 1
[80] {Diapers=Diapers,Formula=Corn,Fritos=Chips} => {Beer=Sugar}       0.25 1
[81] {Diapers=Diapers,Beer=Sugar,Fritos=Chips}   => {Formula=Corn}     0.25 1
```

As you can see, the program identifies each **item set**, showing the corresponding support and lift.

## Associating Real-World Data

You could perform the calculations by hand, if desired, to confirm the association processing—the DiapersAndBeer.csv file limited the number of data items. Professor Eric Seuss, at California State University, East Bay, provides the Groceries.csv data set, the contents of which are shown in **FIGURE 13.2**.

Download the Groceries data set from this text's catalog page at go.jblearning.com/DataMining and save the file to a folder on your disk.

The following Python script, RealWorldApriori.py, uses the data set to calculate support, confidence, and lift:

```python
import pandas as pd
from apyori import apriori
data = pd.read_csv('Groceries.csv', header=None)
```

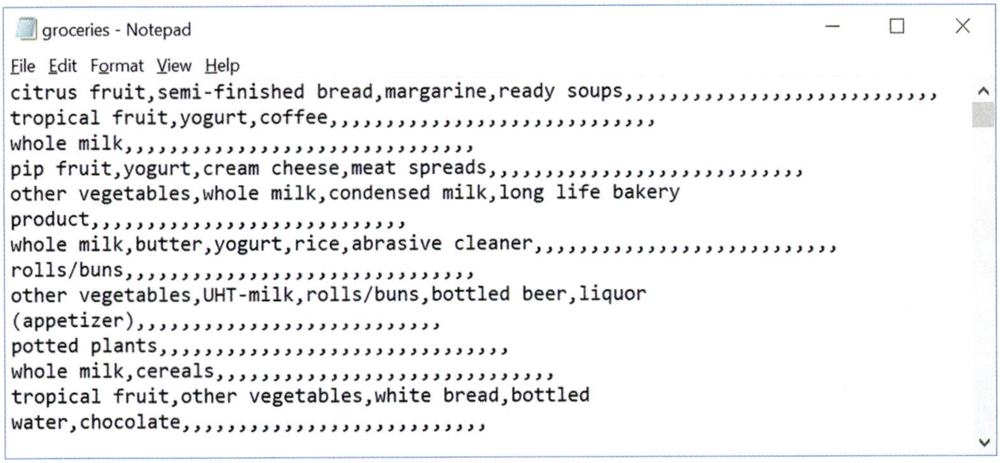

```
groceries - Notepad
File Edit Format View Help
citrus fruit,semi-finished bread,margarine,ready soups,,,,,,,,,,,,,,,,,,,,,,,,,,,,,
tropical fruit,yogurt,coffee,,,,,,,,,,,,,,,,,,,,,,,,,,,,,
whole milk,,,,,,,,,,,,,,,,,,,,,,,,,,,,,,
pip fruit,yogurt,cream cheese,meat spreads,,,,,,,,,,,,,,,,,,,,,,,,,,,,,
other vegetables,whole milk,condensed milk,long life bakery
product,,,,,,,,,,,,,,,,,,,,,,,,,,,,
whole milk,butter,yogurt,rice,abrasive cleaner,,,,,,,,,,,,,,,,,,,,,,,,,,,
rolls/buns,,,,,,,,,,,,,,,,,,,,,,,,,,,,,,
other vegetables,UHT-milk,rolls/buns,bottled beer,liquor
(appetizer),,,,,,,,,,,,,,,,,,,,,,,,,,,,
potted plants,,,,,,,,,,,,,,,,,,,,,,,,,,,,,
whole milk,cereals,,,,,,,,,,,,,,,,,,,,,,,,,,,,,
tropical fruit,other vegetables,white bread,bottled
water,chocolate,,,,,,,,,,,,,,,,,,,,,,,,,,,
```

**FIGURE 13.2 The Groceries data set.**

Used with permission from Microsoft

```
records = []
for i in range(0, len(data)):
    records.append([str(data.values[i,j]) for j in range(0,
len(data.columns))])

rules = apriori(records, min_support=0.025, min_length=2,
min_lift=1.1)
results = list(rules)

for item in results:
 if not 'nan' in str(item):
   print()
   print(item)
   print()
   print("----------------------")
```

As you can see, the program opens the data set and then uses the apriori function to determine the association rules. The function call specifies the minimum number of items to consider as two and, to reduce uninteresting output, specifies minimum support and lift parameters. When you run this script, it will display the following output:

```
C:\> python RealWorldApriori.py
RelationRecord(items=frozenset({'soda', 'bottled
water'}), support=0.028978139298423997, ordered_
statistics=[OrderedStatistic(items_base=frozenset({'bottled
water'}), items_add=frozenset({'soda'}),
confidence=0.2621895124195032, lift=1.5035765916302124),
OrderedStatistic(items_base=frozenset({'soda'}), items_
add=frozenset({'bottled water'}), confidence=0.1661807580174927,
lift=1.5035765916302124)])
----------------------
```

```
RelationRecord(items=frozenset({'bottled water',
'whole milk'}), support=0.03436705643111337, ordered_
statistics=[OrderedStatistic(items_base=frozenset({'bottled
water'}), items_add=frozenset({'whole milk'}),
confidence=0.31094756209751606, lift=1.2169396232507244),
OrderedStatistic(items_base=frozenset({'whole
milk'}), items_add=frozenset({'bottled water'}),
confidence=0.13450059689614005, lift=1.2169396232507244)])
----------------------
RelationRecord(items=frozenset({'brown bread',
'whole milk'}), support=0.0251606507371632, ordered_
statistics=[OrderedStatistic(items_base=frozenset({'brown
bread'}), items_add=frozenset({'whole milk'}),
confidence=0.3887147335423197, lift=1.5212930379581036),
OrderedStatistic(items_base=frozenset({'whole milk'}), items_
add=frozenset({'brown bread'}), confidence=0.09868682849184242,
lift=1.5212930379581036)])
----------------------
RelationRecord(items=frozenset({'butter', 'whole
milk'}), support=0.0275465175394001, ordered_
statistics=[OrderedStatistic(items_base=frozenset({'butter'}),
items_add=frozenset({'whole milk'}),
confidence=0.4972477064220184, lift=1.9460530014566455),
OrderedStatistic(items_base=frozenset({'whole milk'}), items_
add=frozenset({'butter'}), confidence=0.1078392359729407,
lift=1.9460530014566455)])
----------------------
       :         :         :
----------------------
RelationRecord(items=frozenset({'whipped/sour cream',
'whole milk'}), support=0.032231825114387394, ordered_
statistics=[OrderedStatistic(items_base=frozenset({'whipped/
sour cream'}), items_add=frozenset({'whole milk'}),
confidence=0.449645390070922, lift=1.759754242478121),
OrderedStatistic(items_base=frozenset({'whole
milk'}), items_add=frozenset({'whipped/sour cream'}),
confidence=0.12614405093513728, lift=1.7597542424781207)])
----------------------
RelationRecord(items=frozenset({'yogurt', 'whole
milk'}), support=0.05602440264361973, ordered_
statistics=[OrderedStatistic(items_base=frozenset({'whole
milk'}), items_add=frozenset({'yogurt'}),
confidence=0.21925984878631116, lift=1.5717351405345263),
OrderedStatistic(items_base=frozenset({'yogurt'}), items_
add=frozenset({'whole milk'}), confidence=0.40160349854227406,
lift=1.5717351405345266)])
----------------------
```

To help you get started with market-basket analysis, R provides the built-in Groceries data set. The following program, BuiltInGroceries.r, uses the data set:

```
library(arules)
library(datasets)

data(Groceries)

rules <- apriori(Groceries, parameter = list(supp = 0.001, conf = 0.5))

inspect(rules)
```

When you run this program, it will display the following output:

|     | Lhs              |    | rhs           | support | confidence | lift | count |
|-----|------------------|----|---------------|---------|------------|------|-------|
| [1] | {honey}          | => | {whole milk}  | 0.0011  | 0.73       | 2.9  | 11    |
| [2] | {tidbits}        | => | {rolls/buns}  | 0.0012  | 0.52       | 2.8  | 12    |
| [3] | {cocoa drinks}   | => | {whole milk}  | 0.0013  | 0.59       | 2.3  | 13    |
| [4] | {pudding powder} | => | {whole milk}  | 0.0013  | 0.57       | 2.2  | 13    |
| :   | :                |    | :             | :       |            |      |       |

## FP-Growth Association Using RapidMiner

Apriori is one way to perform association analysis. A second is FP-Growth, so named because it performs its processing using a frequent pattern tree (FP-Tree). The FP-Growth algorithm has been shown to have better performance than other approaches. Across the web, you can find libraries you can use to perform FP-Growth association in Python and R. In this section, you will use the RapidMiner environment (introduced in Chapter 12, "Predictive Analytics") to perform FP-Growth data association.

To start, download and install RapidMiner, as discussed in Chapter 12. RapidMiner will display its interface, as shown in **FIGURE 13.3**.

Within RapidMiner, select Blank Project. Next, download the data set FPGrowthGroceries.csv from this text's catalog page at go.jblearning.com/DataMining. Save the file to a folder on your disk.

Within RapidMiner, click the Input Data button. RapidMiner will start a wizard you can use to load the FPGrowthGroceries.csv data set. Use the wizard to load the file. RapidMiner will display the file's contents, as shown in **FIGURE 13.4**.

The RapidMiner FP-Growth algorithm requires the data in a binary format. Each row of the data set represents a transaction. The value 1 within a transaction indicates the corresponding item was purchased—the value 0 means it was not.

Click the Design tab. RapidMiner will display a blank workspace, as shown in **FIGURE 13.5**.

Drag and drop the FPGrowthGroceries.csv data set onto the workspace, as shown in **FIGURE 13.6**.

**572** **CHAPTER 13** Data Association

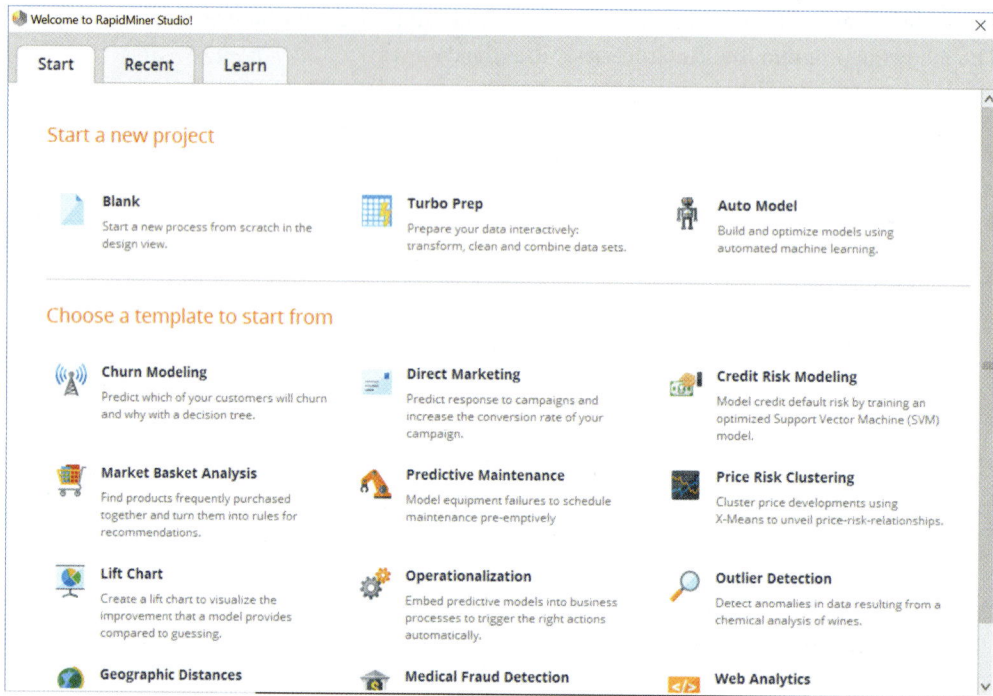

**FIGURE 13.3** The RapidMiner interface.

Used with permission of RapidMiner

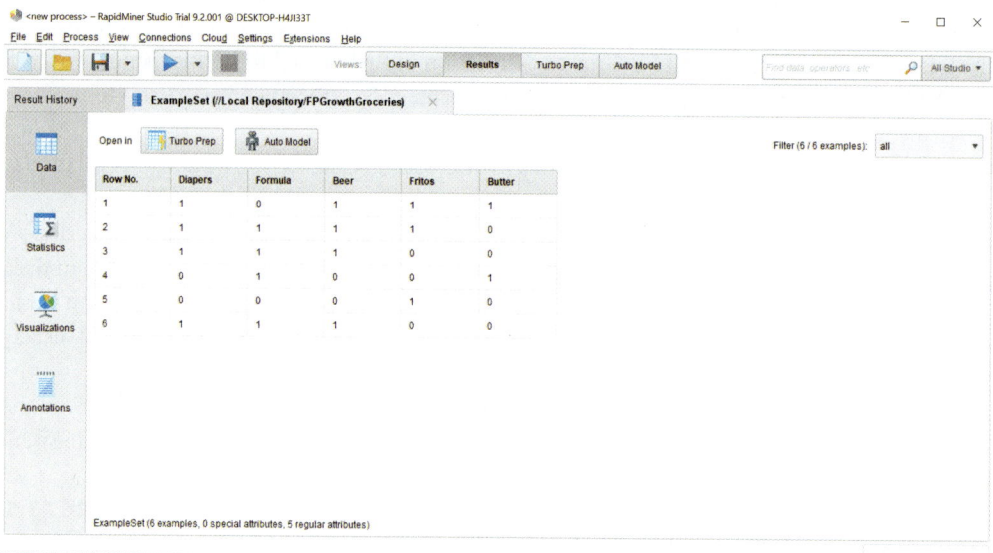

**FIGURE 13.4** Displaying the FPGrowthGroceries data set.

Used with permission of RapidMiner

## FP-Growth Association Using RapidMiner

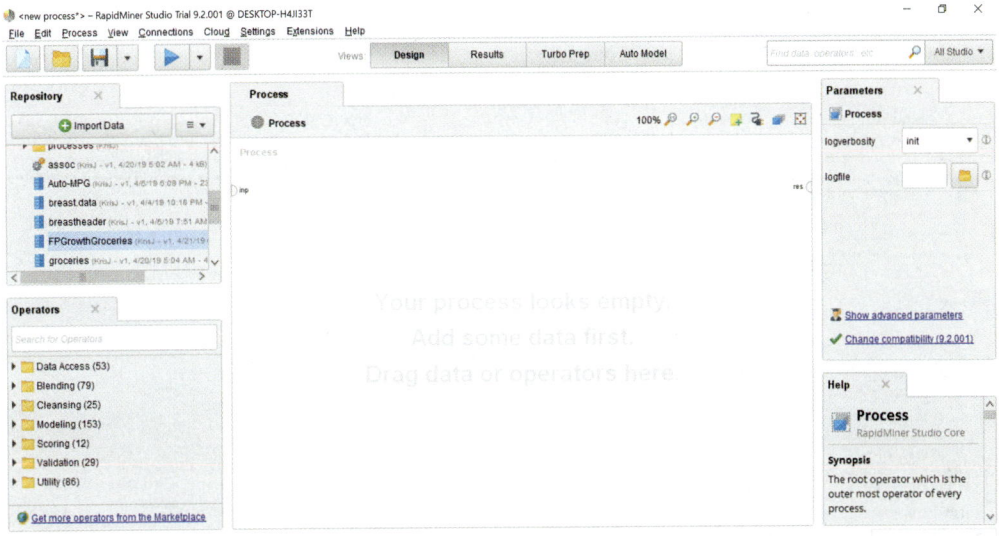

**FIGURE 13.5** A RapidMiner workspace.
Used with permission of RapidMiner

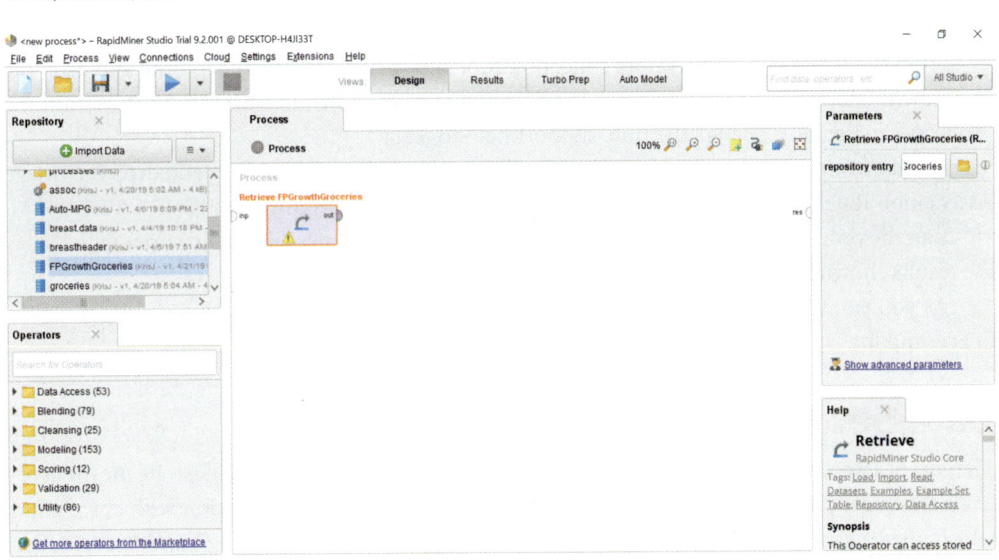

**FIGURE 13.6** Dragging the FPGrowthGroceries data set on to the RapidMiner workspace.
Used with permission of RapidMiner

RapidMiner will display a window prompting you to specify the data format. Make sure the column separator is a comma. Then, within the RapidMiner Operators collection Blending\Attributes\Types folder, drag the Numerical to Binary operator onto the workspace and connect it to the data set, as shown in **FIGURE 13.7**.

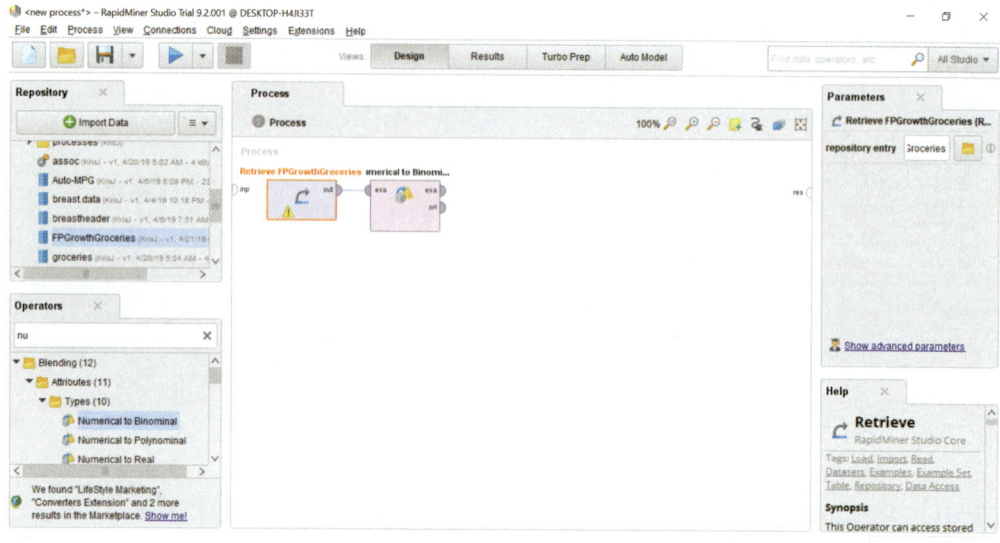

**FIGURE 13.7** Connecting the FPGrowthGroceries data set to the Numerical to Binary operator.

Used with permission of RapidMiner

From the RapidMiner Operators collection Modeling\Associations folder, drag and drop the FP-Growth operator on to the workspace and connect it, as shown in **FIGURE 13.8**. Within the Properties dialog box, change the min-support field to 0.25.

Finally, from the Operators collection Modeling\Associations folder, drag and drop the Create Association Rules operator on to the workspace, connecting it, as shown in **FIGURE 13.9**.

Run the process and then click the Results tab Association Rules tab. RapidMiner will display the results shown in **FIGURE 13.10**.

As you can see, RapidMiner displays the item sets and their corresponding support, confidence, and lift.

# Data-Set Summaries and Correlation

The goal of association is to identify relationship patterns within a data set that illustrate the influence of an antecedent variable on a consequent variable. Do not confuse association with correlation, which identifies a statistical relationship between two variables. As shown in **FIGURE 13.11**, correlation can be negative, positive, or nonexistent.

The following Python script, Summary.py, loads the Auto-MPG data set that contains data about different car models, such as the horsepower, weight, and miles per gallon (MPG). The script then uses the describe function to provide a summary of the data-set values, which includes each column's min, max, mean, standard deviation, and so on:

```
import pandas as pd
data = pd.read_csv('auto-mpg.csv')
print(data.describe())
```

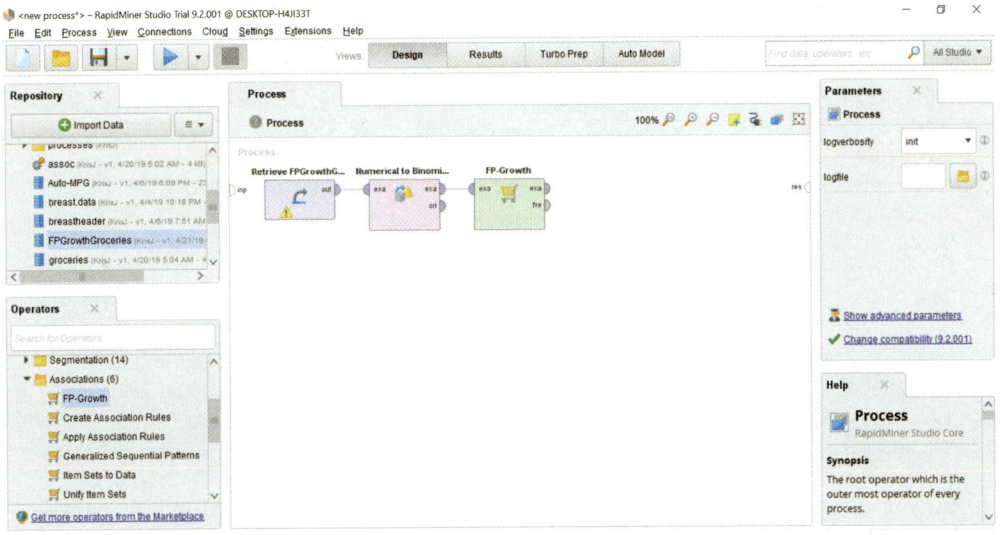

**FIGURE 13.8** Connecting the FP-Growth operator.
Used with permission of RapidMiner

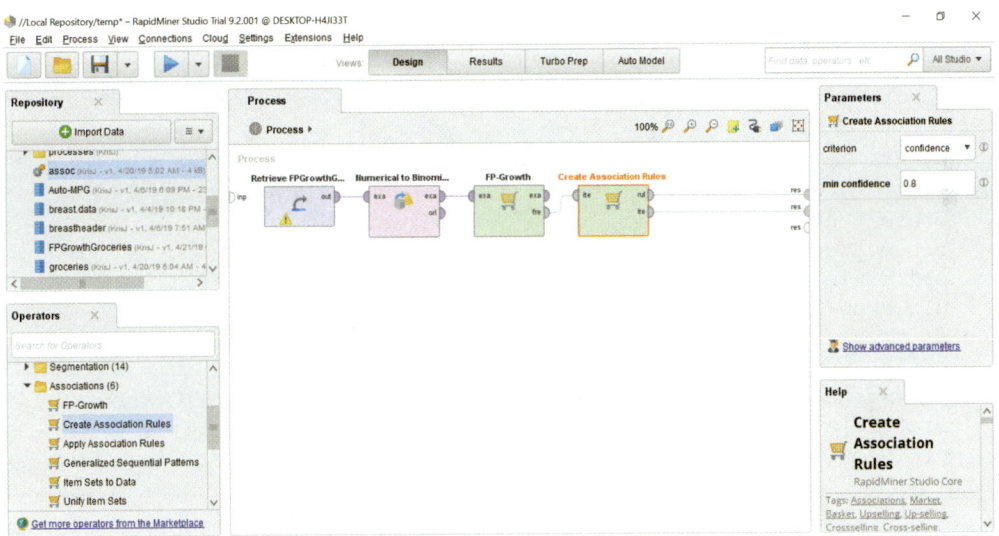

**FIGURE 13.9** Connecting the Create Association Rules operator.
Used with permission of RapidMiner

When you run this script, it will display the following output:

```
C:\Python>python Summary.py
            mpg    cylinders   displacement   horsepower      weight
acceleration   model year      origin
```

```
count   392.000000   392.000000    392.000000   392.000000    392.000000
392.000000   392.000000    392.000000
mean     23.369388     5.471939    194.411990   104.469388   2977.584184
 15.541327   75.979592      1.576531
std       7.863843     1.705783    104.644004    38.491160    849.402560
  2.758864    3.683737      0.805518
min       2.400000     3.000000     68.000000    46.000000   1613.000000
  8.000000   70.000000      1.000000
25%      17.000000     4.000000    105.000000    75.000000   2225.250000
 13.775000   73.000000      1.000000
50%      22.450000     4.000000    151.000000    93.500000   2803.500000
 15.500000   76.000000      1.000000
75%      29.000000     8.000000    275.750000   126.000000   3614.750000
 17.025000   79.000000      2.000000
max      46.600000     8.000000    455.000000   230.000000   5140.000000
 24.800000   82.000000      3.000000
```

As you can see, the describe function returns the count, mean, min, max, and standard deviation, as well as quartile values. Using the describe function, you can quickly gain insights into the data a data set contains.

The following Python script, MPGCorrelation.py, displays the correlation between MPG and other vehicle attributes:

```
import pandas as pd
import numpy as np
import matplotlib.pyplot as plt

data = pd.read_csv('auto-mpg.csv')

coefs = np.corrcoef(data['mpg'], data['weight'])
plt.scatter(data['mpg'], data['weight'])
plt.title('MPG and Weight Correlation: ' + str(coefs[0,1]))
plt.show()

coefs = np.corrcoef(data['mpg'], data['horsepower'])
plt.scatter(data['mpg'], data['horsepower'])
plt.title('MPG and Weight Horsepower: ' + str(coefs[0,1]))
plt.show()

coefs = np.corrcoef(data['mpg'], data['acceleration'])
plt.scatter(data['mpg'], data['acceleration'])
plt.title('MPG and Weight Acceleration: ' + str(coefs[0,1]))
plt.show()
```

When you execute this script, it will display the output shown in **FIGURE 13.12**.

As you can see, the weight and horsepower correlations are negative, meaning in the case of weight, as the weight goes up, the MPG goes down. The correlation for the weight and horsepower is approaching −1, which makes them more significant than the acceleration.

## Data-Set Summaries and Correlation

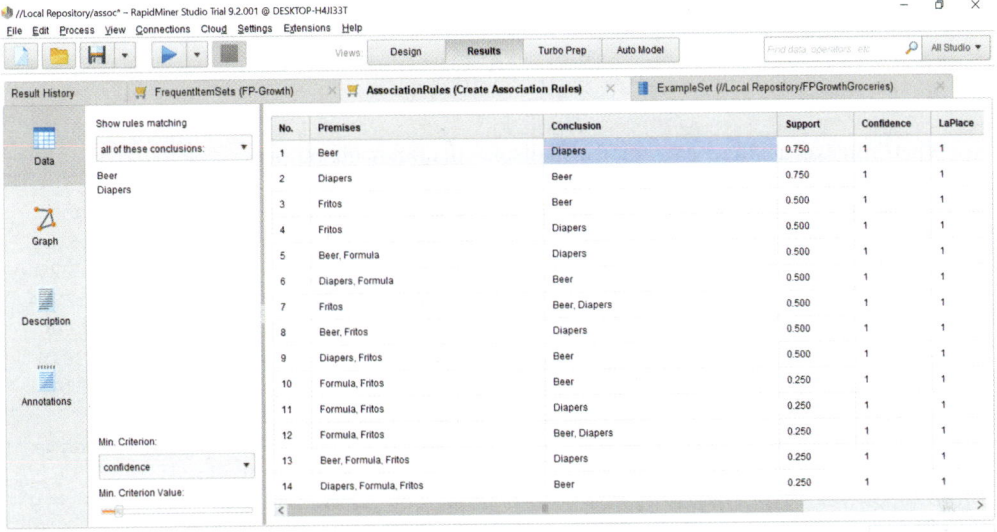

**FIGURE 13.10** Displaying the results of the market-basket analysis.

Used with permission of RapidMiner

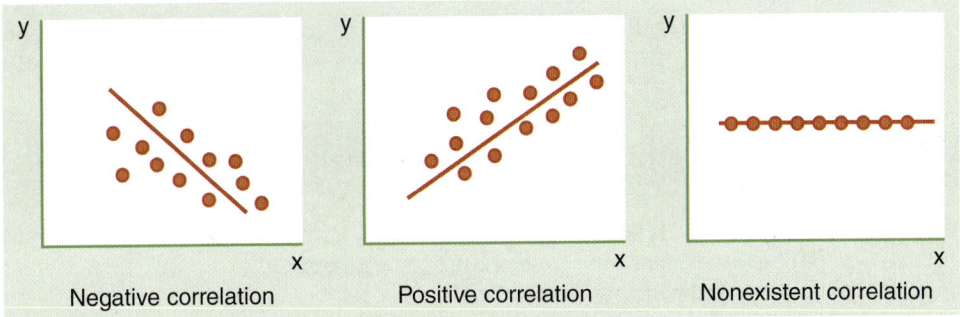

**FIGURE 13.11** Correlation between variables can be positive, negative, or nonexistent.

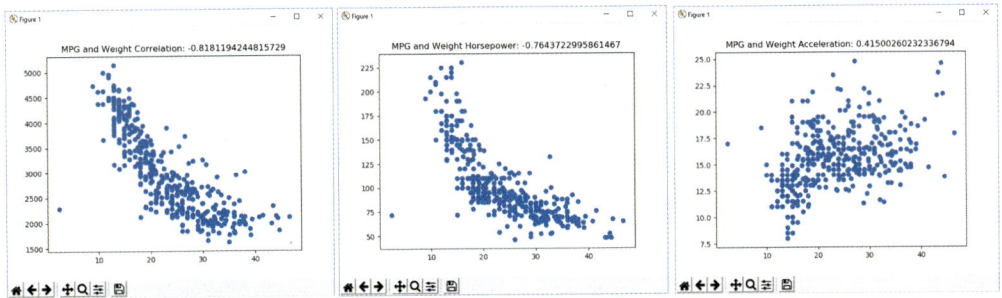

**FIGURE 13.12** Representing the correlation between MGP and other automobile attributes.

Used with permission of Python Software Foundation

The following R program, Summary.R, displays a summary of the Auto-MPG data set:

```
df <- read.csv(file='/python/auto-mpg.csv')
print(summary(df))
```

When you execute this program, it will display the following output:

```
     mpg           cylinders       displacement      horsepower         weight
 Min.   : 2.40   Min.   :3.000   Min.   : 68.0    Min.   : 46.0    Min.   :1613
 1st Qu.:17.00   1st Qu.:4.000   1st Qu.:105.0    1st Qu.: 75.0    1st Qu.:2225
 Median :22.45   Median :4.000   Median :151.0    Median : 93.5    Median :2804
 Mean   :23.37   Mean   :5.472   Mean   :194.4    Mean   :104.5    Mean   :2978
 3rd Qu.:29.00   3rd Qu.:8.000   3rd Qu.:275.8    3rd Qu.:126.0    3rd Qu.:3615
 Max.   :46.60   Max.   :8.000   Max.   :455.0    Max.   :230.0    Max.   :5140

  acceleration      model.year        origin                  car.name
 Min.   : 8.00    Min.   :70.00    Min.   :1.000    amc matador       :   5
 1st Qu.:13.78    1st Qu.:73.00    1st Qu.:1.000    ford pinto        :   5
 Median :15.50    Median :76.00    Median :1.000    toyota corolla    :   5
 Mean   :15.54    Mean   :75.98    Mean   :1.577    amc gremlin       :   4
 3rd Qu.:17.02    3rd Qu.:79.00    3rd Qu.:2.000    amc hornet        :   4
 Max.   :24.80    Max.   :82.00    Max.   :3.000    chevrolet chevette:   4
                                                    (Other)           :365
```

The following R program, MPGCorrelation.r, displays the correlation between MPG and other automobile attributes:

```
df <- read.csv(file='/python/auto-mpg.csv')

plots <- par(mfrow=c(1, 3))

corr <- cor(df$mpg, df$weight)
title <- paste("MPG Weight ", sprintf("%s", corr))
plot(df$weight, df$mpg, main=title,
   xlab="Car Weight ", ylab="Miles Per Gallon ")

corr <- cor(df$mpg, df$horsepower)
title <- paste("MPG Horsepower ", sprintf("%s", corr))
plot(df$weight, df$mpg, main=title,
   xlab="Car Horsepower ", ylab="Miles Per Gallon ")

corr <- cor(df$mpg, df$acceleration)
title <- paste("MPG Acceleration ", sprintf("%s", corr))
plot(df$weight, df$mpg, main=title,
   xlab="Car Acceleation ", ylab="Miles Per Gallon ")

par(plots)
```

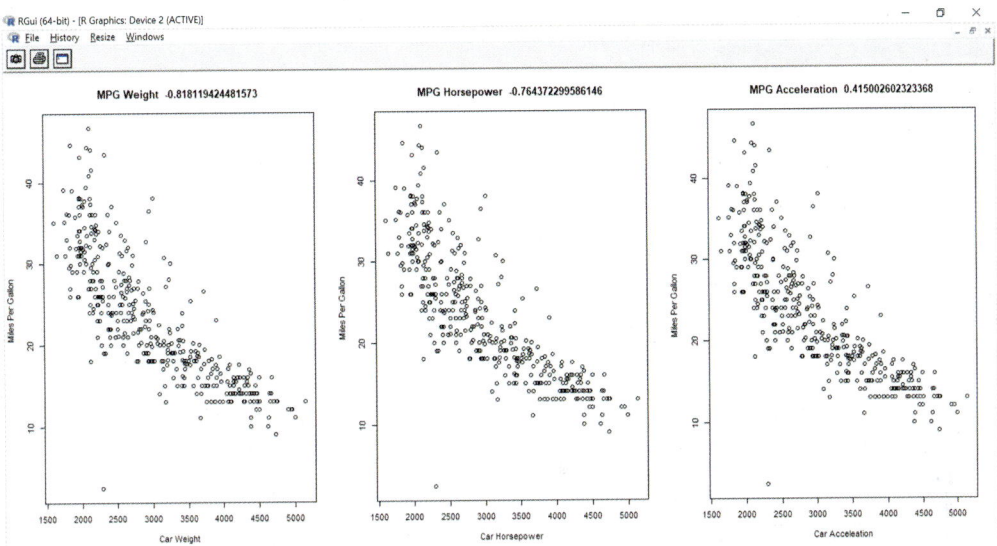

**FIGURE 13.13** Using R to display the correlation between beer and other shopping cart items.

Used with permission from The R Foundation

As you can see, the program loads the data set and uses the cor function to calculate the correlations. The code uses the par function to group the plots. When you execute this program, it will display the output shown in **FIGURE 13.13**.

## Hands-on: Data Mining with Orange

Throughout this text, you have made extensive use of Python and R to perform data-mining and machine-learning operations. Orange is a data-mining tool that supports visual programming, meaning rather than writing programming language statements to accomplish a task, with Orange, you drag and drop components that perform the tasks on to your workspace and then link them together to accomplish specific tasks, as shown in **FIGURE 13.14**.

To start, download and install Orange from the Orange website at http://Orange.Biolab.si, as shown in **FIGURE 13.15**.

When you run Orange, it will display the screen shown in **FIGURE 13.16**.

To start, click on the Data collection and drag a File widget onto the workspace, as shown in **FIGURE 13.17**.

Right-click on the File widget and select Open. Orange will display the File dialog box. Within the dialog box, click the Browse documentation data sets. Orange will display a dialog box with its built-in data sets, as shown in **FIGURE 13.18**.

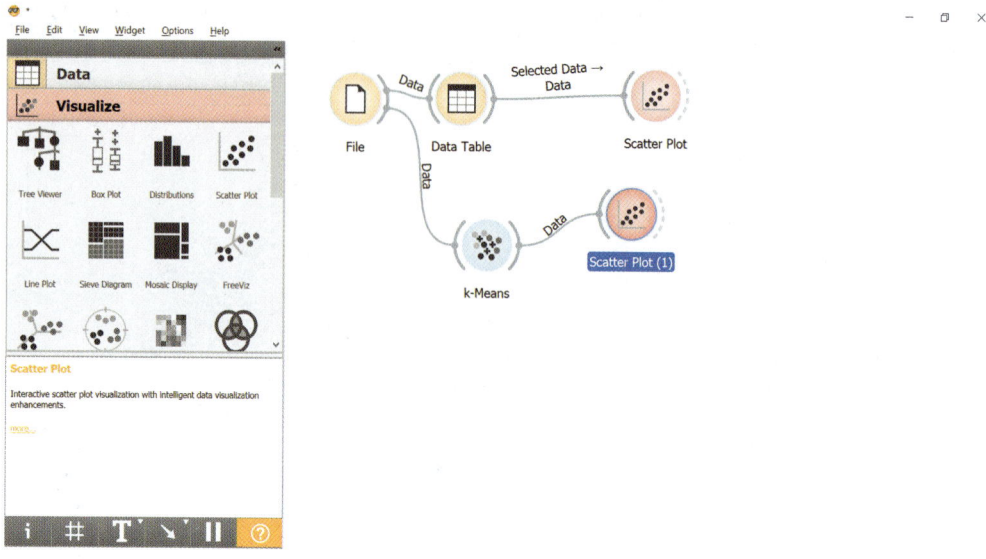

**FIGURE 13.14** Using visual programming in Orange to perform data-mining tasks.

Orange Software. Used with permission from University of Ljubljana

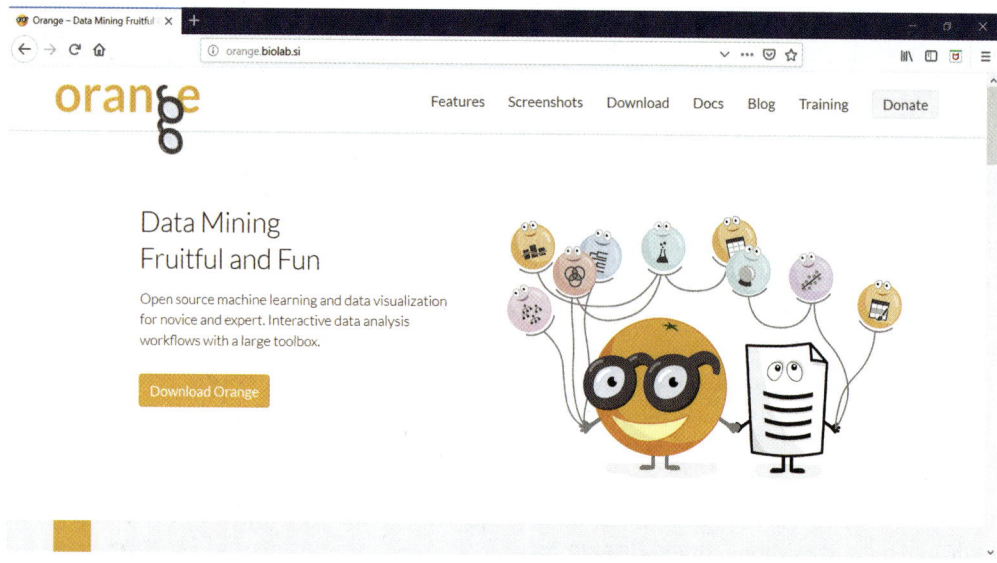

**FIGURE 13.15** Download Orange from the product website.

Orange Software. Used with permission from University of Ljubljana

Hands-on: Data Mining with Orange

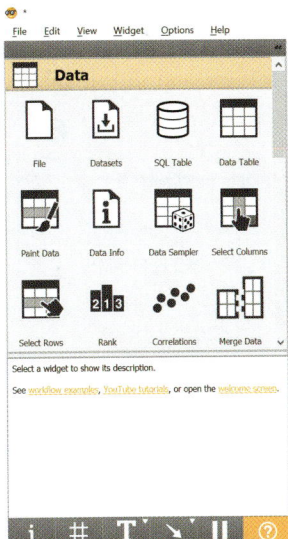

**FIGURE 13.16** The Orange development environment.

Orange Software. Used with permission from University of Ljubljana

**FIGURE 13.17** Placing a File widget on the Orange workspace.

Orange Software. Used with permission from University of Ljubljana

# CHAPTER 13 Data Association

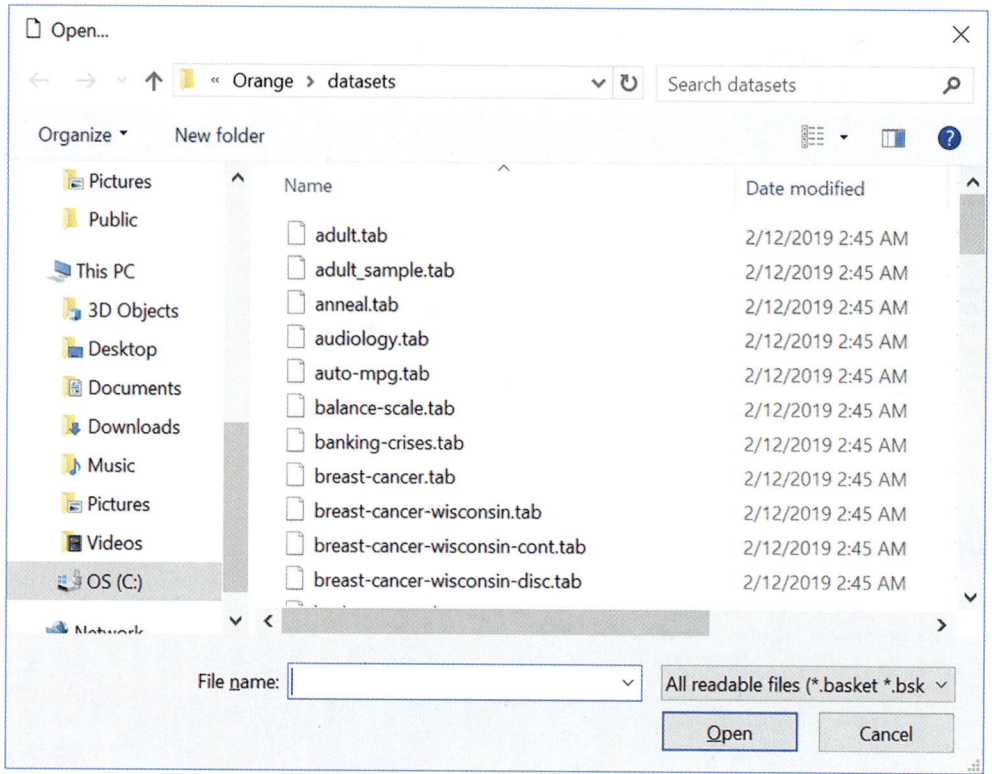

**FIGURE 13.18** Data sets built into Orange.

Used with permission from Microsoft

Within the dialog box, click on the iris.tab and choose Open. Orange will display the file's columns, as shown in **FIGURE 13.19**.

Close the File dialog box. From the Data collection, drag the Data Table on to the workspace. Then drag your mouse between the File and Data Table widgets, connecting the widgets with a line, as shown in **FIGURE 13.20**.

Double-click on the Data Table widget. Orange will display the table's contents, as shown in **FIGURE 13.21**.

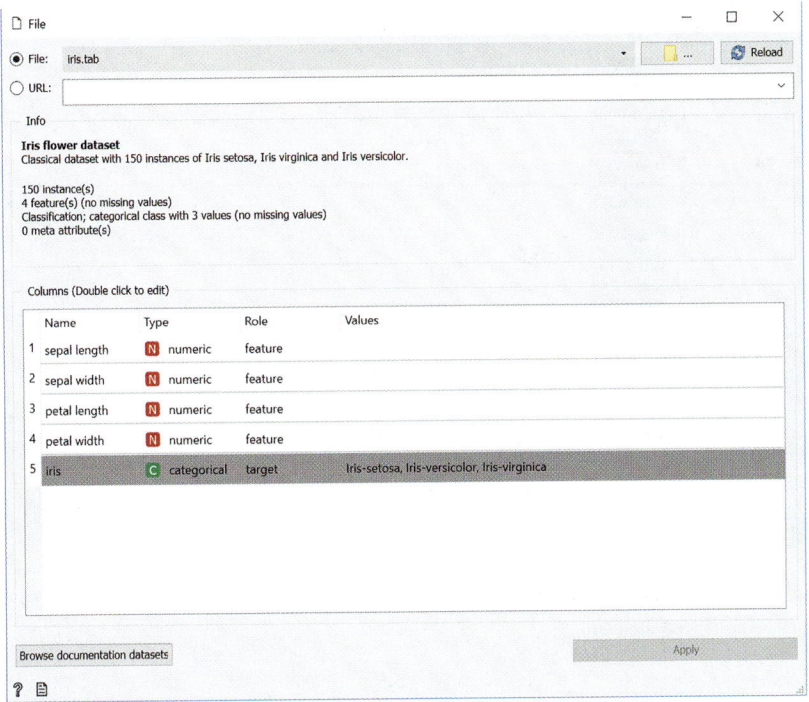

**FIGURE 13.19** Viewing the iris.tab file's columns.

Orange Software. Used with permission from University of Ljubljana

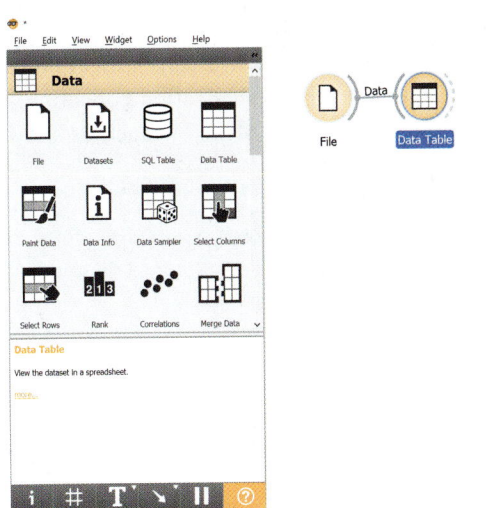

**FIGURE 13.20** Connecting widgets on the Orange workspace.

Orange Software. Used with permission from University of Ljubljana

**584** CHAPTER 13 Data Association

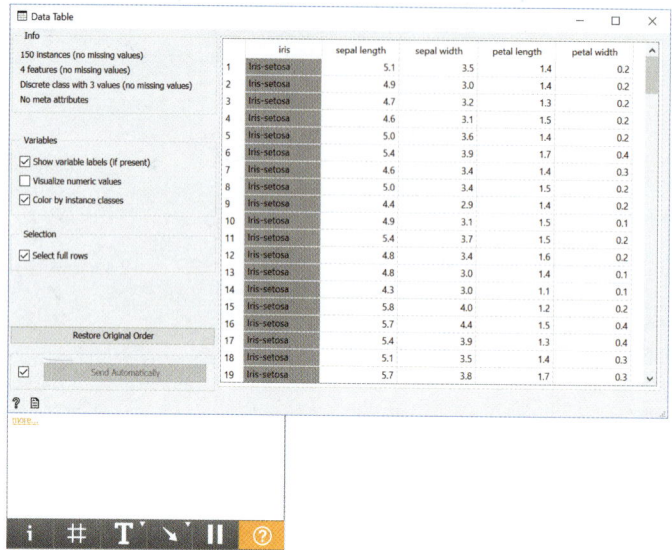

**FIGURE 13.21 Displaying a data table's contents.**

Orange Software. Used with permission from University of Ljubljana

Press Ctrl+A to select the table's rows and columns. Close the table and click on the Visualize collection. Drag a Scatter Chart widget on to the workspace, and drag your mouse to connect the Scatter Chart to the Data Table widget. Double-click your mouse on the Scatter Plot widget. Orange will display the chart shown in **FIGURE 13.22**.

Click your mouse on the Unsupervised collection. Drag the k-Means widget on to the workspace and connect it to the File widget. Then, from the Visualization collection, drag a Scatter Plot widget on to the workspace. Connect it to the k-Means widget, as shown in **FIGURE 13.23**.

# Hands-on: Data Mining with Orange 585

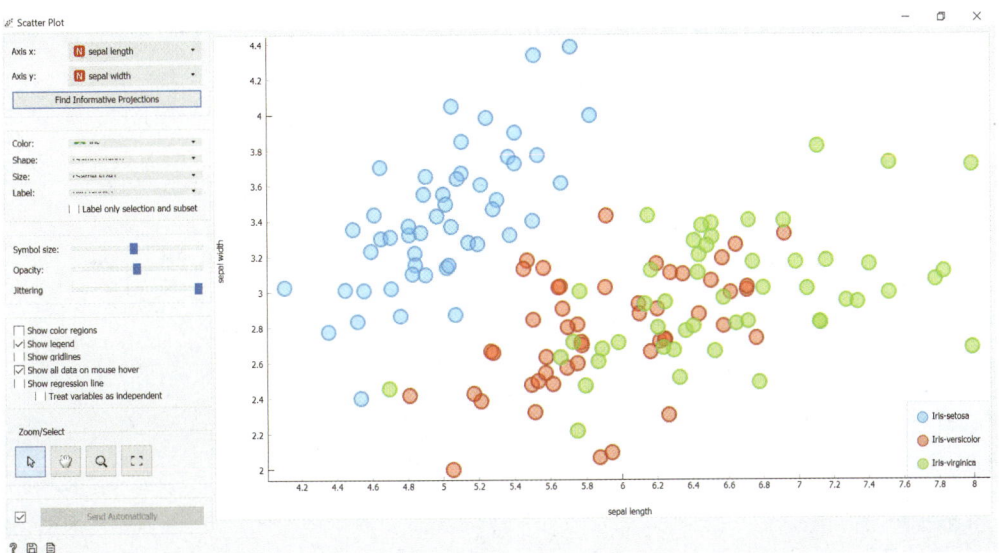

**FIGURE 13.22** Displaying a scatter chart within Orange.

Orange Software. Used with permission from University of Ljubljana

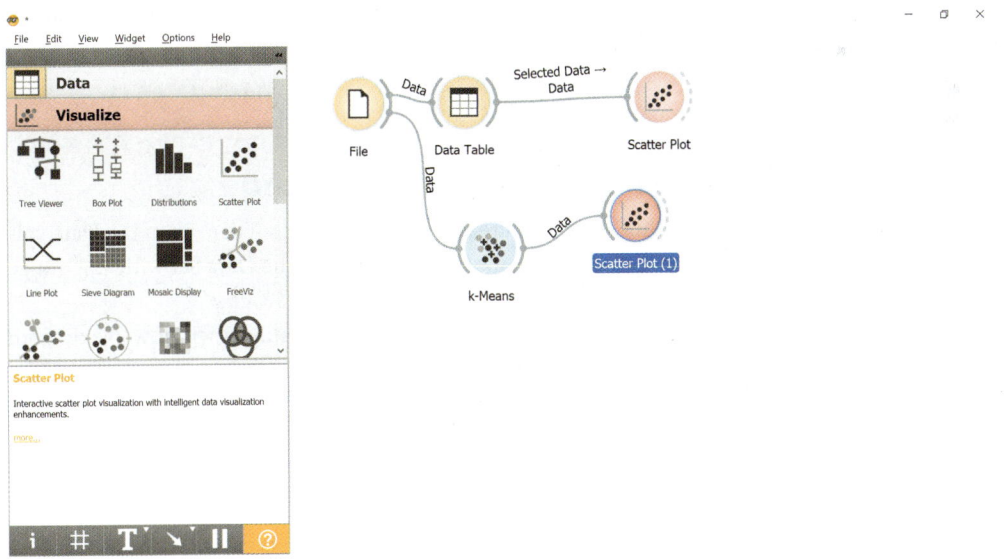

**FIGURE 13.23** Connecting a Scatter Chart widget to the k-Means widget.

Orange Software. Used with permission from University of Ljubljana

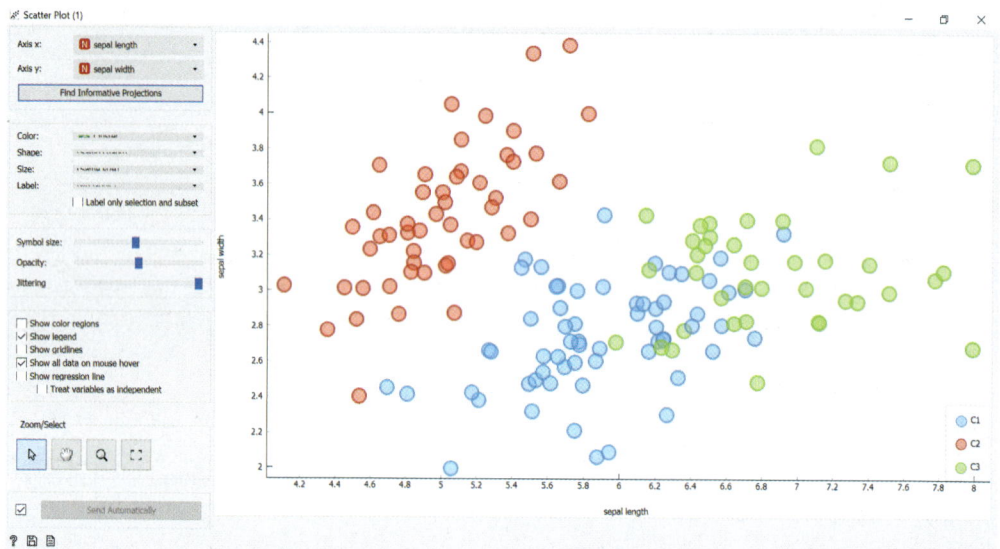

**FIGURE 13.24 Displaying cluster assignments within a Scatter Chart widget.**

Orange Software. Used with permission from University of Ljubljana

Double-click your mouse on the Scatter Plot widget. Orange will display a chart. Within the chart, click on the color property and choose Cluster. Orange will display the clusters, as shown in **FIGURE 13.24**.

## Performing Predictive Analysis within Orange

Select the Orange File menu and choose New to create a new workspace. Then, from the Data collection, drag a Data Set widget on to the workspace. Double-click on the Data Set widget. Orange will open a window within its built-in data sets, as shown in **FIGURE 13.25**.

Click on the AutoMpg data set and click Send Data. Close the data-set window. Next, from the Models collection, drag a Linear Regression widget on to the workspace, and from the Data collection, drag a Data Table widget on to the workspace, connecting them, as shown in **FIGURE 13.26**.

# Hands-on: Data Mining with Orange

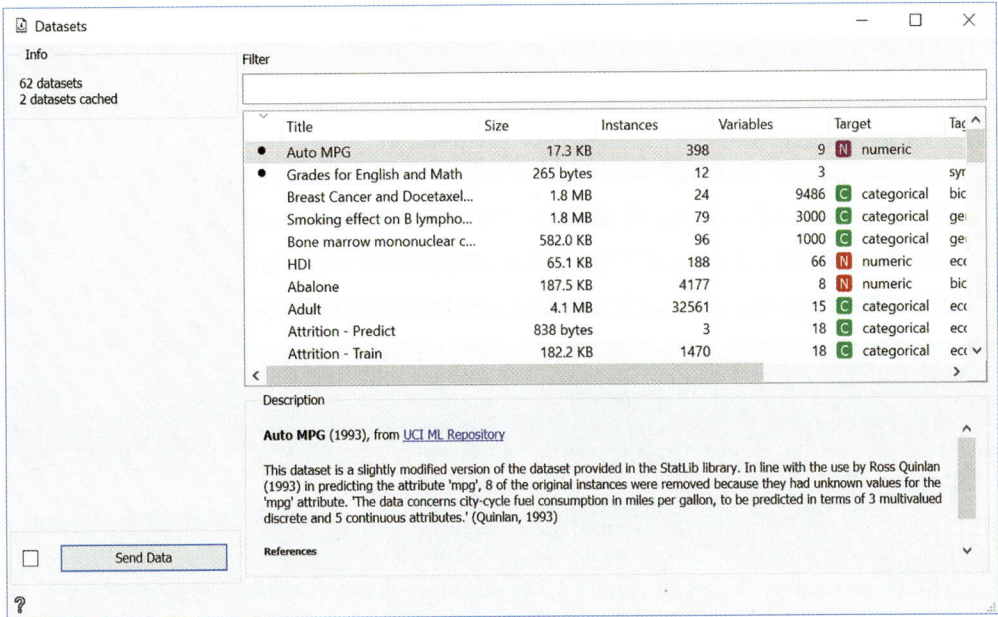

**FIGURE 13.25** Displaying the data sets built into Orange.
Orange Software. Used with permission from University of Ljubljana

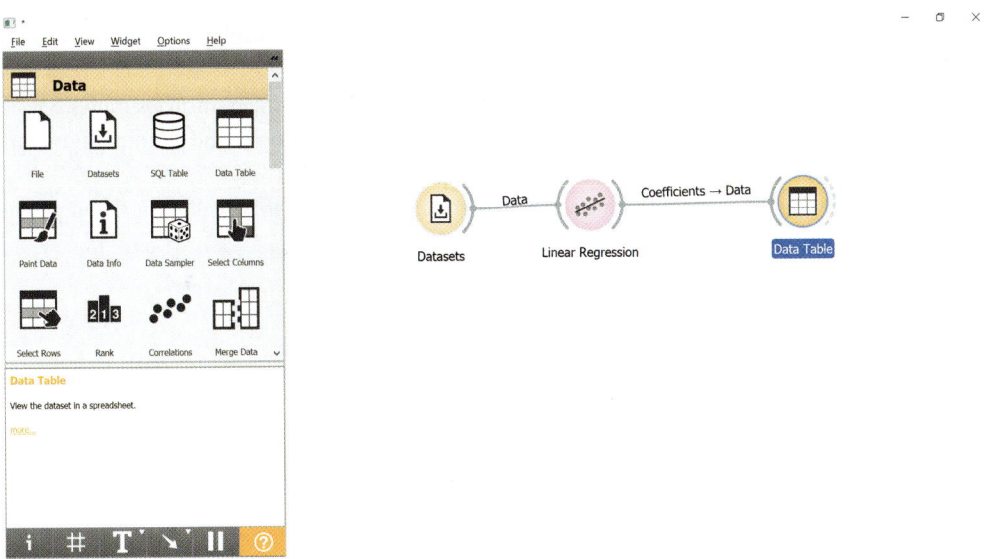

**FIGURE 13.26** Connecting the AutoMpg data set to the Data Table widget.
Orange Software. Used with permission from University of Ljubljana

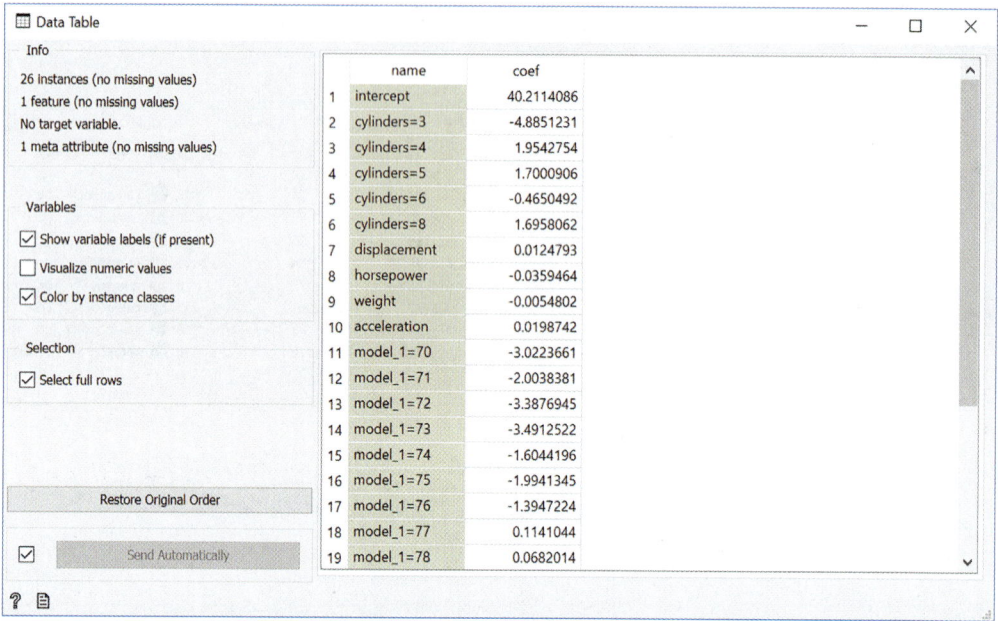

**FIGURE 13.27** Displaying linear regression coefficients within Orange.

Orange Software. Used with permission from University of Ljubljana

Double-click your mouse on the Data Table widget. Orange will display the coefficients, as shown in **FIGURE 13.27**.

To help you develop more complex workflows, Orange provides several built-in examples. Select the Orange Help menu and choose Workflow Examples. Orange will open the window shown in **FIGURE 13.28**, presenting the sample workflows.

From the Orange Help menu, you can also find several videos that walk you through the process of building advanced workflows.

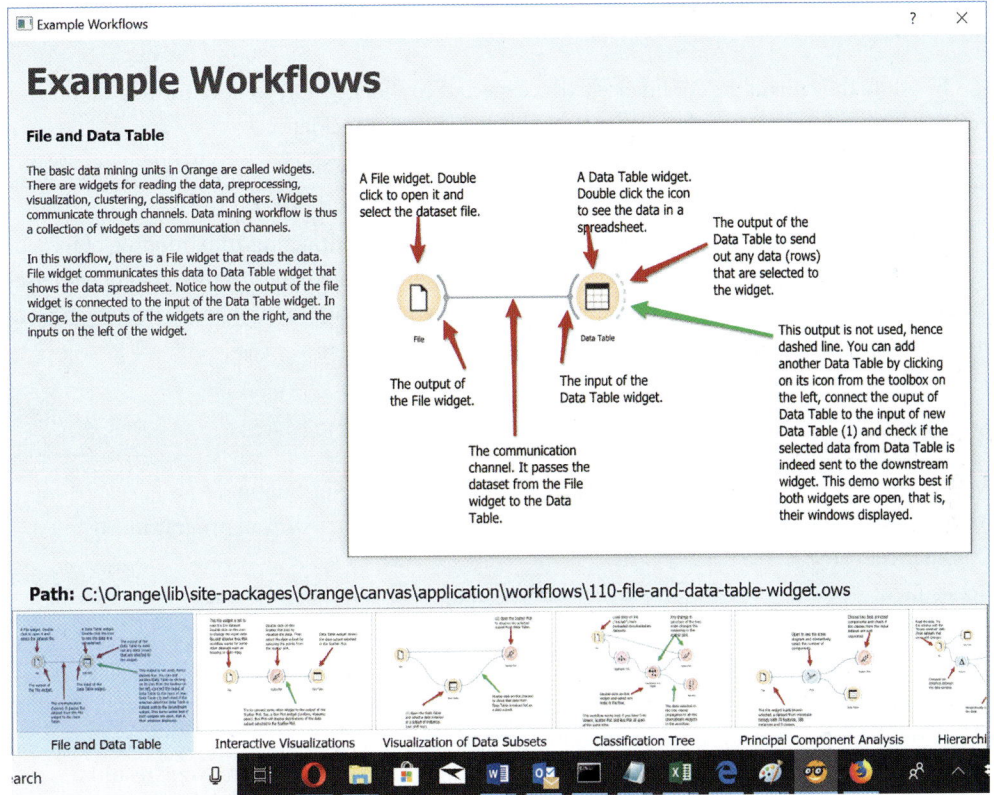

**FIGURE 13.28** Displaying sample workflows within Orange.

Orange Software. Used with permission from University of Ljubljana

# Summary

In this chapter, you examined data association, the process of identifying patterns (relationships) between variables in a data set. As you learned, market-basket analysis is the use of data association to analyze consumer data for patterns, such as the products a shopper adds to their shopping cart (called consequent products) based upon an item that already resides in the cart (called the antecedent product). Throughout this chapter, you performed several analyses of shopping carts using Python, R, and RapidMiner.

As you learned, data association uses four measures to identify patterns:

- Support: a ratio measure that provides the relative frequency of an item in the basket.
- Confidence: a measure that examines the frequency with which a consequent occurs in spite of the absence of the antecedent.

- Lift: the ratio of the confidence to the expected confidence. Lift values close to 1 do not show an association, but rather, more likely indicate coincidence.
- Conviction: a measure that examines the frequency with which the consequent occurs in spite of the absence of the antecedent.

Visual programming is the process of creating a program by dragging and dropping objects on to a workspace, as opposed to writing programming language statements. In this chapter, you used the RapidMiner and Orange environments to perform visual programming to create data-mining and machine-learning solutions.

## Key Terms

Antecedent
Association
Confidence
Consequent
Conviction
Item set
Lift
Market-basket analysis
Support
Visual programming

## Review

1. Compare and contrast association and correlation.
2. Using Python, re-create the examples shown in this chapter, presenting your results.
3. Using R, re-create the examples shown in this chapter, presenting your results.
4. Use RapidMiner to perform the market-basket analysis presented in this chapter.
5. Using Orange, create a histogram showing the number of samples in the iris.tab file provided by Orange.
6. Using Python, load the Breast Cancer data set from go.jblearning.com/DataMining and display a data-set summary.
7. Using R, load the Breast Cancer data set from go.jblearning.com/DataMining and display a data-set summary.
8. Using Python, load the Breast Cancer data set from go.jblearning.com/DataMining and display the correlation between variables.
9. Using R, load the Breast Cancer data set from go.jblearning.com/DataMining and display the correlation between variables.

# CHAPTER 14

# Mining Text and Images

## Chapter Goals and Objectives

- Perform text sentiment analysis and categorization.
- Perform facial recognition.
- Perform image classification.
- Understand that text and image mining use the same data-mining techniques you have used throughout this text.

As you have learned, data mining is the process of examining data sets for meaningful patterns. Throughout this text, you have examined many different ways to mine numeric data. Across the web, much data, however, is either text or image based. Such text and image data are ripe for data mining. For example, companies collect and mine Twitter posts, email messages, and other forms of customer feedback. Further, government organizations make extensive use of image and facial recognition.

In general, text and image mining include many of the data-mining operations you have performed throughout this text:

- Clustering: Grouping related text fragments, documents, or images
- Classification: Categorizing text or images
- Prediction: Determining the next text in a sequence

This chapter examines text and image processing. By the time you finish this chapter, you will understand the following key concepts:

- To perform text and image processing, you will use many of the data-mining techniques you have used throughout this text. To do so, you will first convert the text or image into a numeric representation the algorithms require.

- **Text mining** is the application of data-mining techniques with text files. Text mining includes sentiment analysis, text clustering, text classification, and text prediction.
- **Text clustering** is the grouping of related words and sentences. Document clustering is the grouping of documents based on the text or image contents the document contains.
- **Text classification** is the process of categorizing text based upon the words the text contains.
- **Image mining** is the application of data-mining techniques to image files. Image mining includes image recognition (computer vision), image clustering, and image classification.
- Across the web, you can find many text- and image-processing libraries.
- **Computer vision**: the ability for a software application to analyze and understand images.
- **Facial recognition**: the analysis of patterns within photos to identify and recognize faces.
- **Sentiment analysis** is the analysis of text to determine the underlying attitude, such as positive, neutral, or negative.

# Getting Started with Text Mining

Text mining is the application of data-mining techniques to text files. Text mining includes sentiment analysis, text clustering, and text classification. Companies use text data for a wide range of applications that include:

- National security applications
- Document or email classification
- Customer sentiment analysis
- Natural-language processing

We hear many stories, for example, of how government agencies were able to stop terrorist acts by mining Facebook posts, emails, Twitter tweets, and texts. As you can imagine, the amount of data such organizations must classify as a threat or nonthreat is vast, making automated text mining a must.

Similarly, many companies have many (in some cases, millions) of emails and documents they must organize (possibly for archival) or to search for specific content. Again, the sheer volume of such data makes some form of automated text mining essential.

Finally, voice-driven applications, such as Siri or Amazon Alexa, perform **natural-language processing**, which leverages text mining. For example, when a voice-driven application cannot recognize one or two words, it often uses text processing to make a best guess for the missing words.

## Performing Sentiment Analysis

Sentiment analysis is the process of examining text to determine if it corresponds to negative, neutral, or positive feedback. To perform sentiment analysis, you can take advantage of several existing packages, which are readily available on the web.

For example, the following R program, Sentiment.R, uses the RSentiments package:

```
install.packages("RSentiment")
library(RSentiment)

calculate_total_presence_sentiment(c("The meal was excellent",
"The service was bad!", "The wine was too expensive.", "The
parking was horrible", "The service was awesome."))
calculate_sentiment(c("The meal was excellent", "The service
was bad!", "The wine was too expensive.", "The parking was
horrible", "The service was awesome."))
calculate_score(c("The meal was excellent", "The service
was bad!", "The wine was too expensive.", "The parking was
horrible", "The service was awesome."))
```

The program uses three functions to perform its sentiment analysis:

- calculate_total_presence_sentiment: Calculates the number of sentences in each category of sentiment.
- calculate_score: Calculates the score of sentences from –1 (negative) to 1 (positive).
- calculate_sentiment: Predicts the sentiment of sentences.

When you run this program, it will display the following output:

```
> calculate_total_presence_sentiment(c("The meal was excellent",
"The service was bad!", "The wine was too expensive.", "The
parking was horrible", "The service was awesome."))
[1] "Processing sentence: the meal was excellent"
[1] "Processing sentence: the service was bad"
[1] "Processing sentence: the wine was too expensive"
[1] "Processing sentence: the parking was horrible"
[1] "Processing sentence: the service was awesome"
     [,1]       [,2]       [,3]            [,4]       [,5]        [,6]
[1,] "Sarcasm" "Negative" "Very Negative" "Neutral" "Positive"
"Very Positive"
[2,] "0"       "3"        "0"             "0"       "2"         "0"
>
> calculate_sentiment(c("The meal was excellent", "The service
was bad!", "The wine was too expensive.", "The parking was
horrible", "The service was awesome."))
[1] "Processing sentence: the meal was excellent"
[1] "Processing sentence: the service was bad"
[1] "Processing sentence: the wine was too expensive"
[1] "Processing sentence: the parking was horrible"
[1] "Processing sentence: the service was awesome"
                         text sentiment
1    The meal was excellent   Positive
2    The service was bad!     Negative
3    The wine was too expensive.   Negative
```

```
4    The parking was horrible   Negative
5    The service was awesome.   Positive
>
> calculate_score(c("The meal was excellent", "The service
was bad!", "The wine was too expensive.", "The parking was
horrible", "The service was awesome."))
[1] "Processing sentence: the meal was excellent"
[1] "Processing sentence: the service was bad"
[1] "Processing sentence: the wine was too expensive"
[1] "Processing sentence: the parking was horrible"
[1] "Processing sentence: the service was awesome"
[1]  1 -1 -1 -1  1
```

As you can see, the program correctly determines the sentiments of the text data. The calculate_score function returns a value from −1 (negative) to 1 (positive) that corresponds to the sentiment.

## Text Processing in Python

TextBlob is a widely used text-processing library for Python. The TextBlob library supports a wide range of text-processing operations, which include natural-language processing, language translation, and sentiment analysis.

To get started, use PIP to install TextBlob:

`C:\> pip install TextBlob`

Next, to install supporting libraries, execute the following script (you may need to run the script as an administrator):

`C:\python> python -m textblob.download_corpora`

The following Python script, SimpleSentiment.py, uses a Naïve Bayes classifier to determine the sentiment (negative or positive) of several text strings:

```
from textblob.classifiers import NaiveBayesClassifier

trainingData = [
    ("The service was great!.", "pos"),
    ("Our waiter was awesome!", "pos"),
    ("They have great appetizers.", "pos"),
    ("Happy hour was busy and fun.", "pos"),
    ("Great place for a quick meal.", "pos"),
    ("Our foot took forever to arrive.", "neg"),
    ("The waiter was slow.", "neg"),
    ("The drinks were weak", "neg"),
    ("It was very crowded and noisy!", "neg"),
    ("My pasta was horrible.", "neg"),
    ("The cost was reasonable.", "pos"),
```

```
        ("The drinks were cold.", "pos"),
        ("The hostess was ditsy.", "neg")
]
testingData = [
        ("The wine list was complete.", "pos"),
        ("There was no place to park.", "neg"),
        ("I really liked the bread.", "pos"),
        ("I want to come back!", "pos"),
        ("The food was not that good.", "neg"),
        ("The beer was great!", "pos")
]
classifier = NaiveBayesClassifier(trainingData)
print("Accuracy: {0}".format(classifier.accuracy(testingData)))

# Classify some text
print("The food was awesome.", classifier.classify("The food was
awesome."))        # "pos"
print("I didn't like my pasta.", classifier.classify("I didn't
like my pasta."))    # "neg"

classifier.show_informative_features(10)
```

The script creates the training and testing data sets by specifying a sentence and the corresponding sentiment: "pos" or "neg." The program calls the show_informative_features to show you how the classifier uses specific words in its decision process.

When you execute this script, it will display the following output:

```
C:\python> python SimpleSentiment.py
Accuracy: 0.5
The food was awesome. pos
I didn't like my pasta. neg
Most Informative Features
    contains(great) = False          neg : pos    =       1.4 : 1.0
    contains(was) = False            pos : neg    =       1.2 : 1.0
    contains(weak) = False           pos : neg    =       1.2 : 1.0
    contains(slow) = False           pos : neg    =       1.2 : 1.0
    contains(noisy) = False          pos : neg    =       1.2 : 1.0
    contains(It) = False             pos : neg    =       1.2 : 1.0
    contains(forever) = False        pos : neg    =       1.2 : 1.0
    contains(took) = False           pos : neg    =       1.2 : 1.0
    contains(arrive) = False         pos : neg    =       1.2 : 1.0
    contains(ditsy) = False          pos : neg    =       1.2 : 1.0
```

As you might expect, the greater the amount of data in the training set, the more accurate your sentiment results. In fact, because of the small training data set, you can experiment with the script by adding more positive or negative sentiments. As you do, you can see how your new examples directly influence the result.

The following Python script, DecisionTreeText.py, uses a DecisionTree classifier. To improve the results, several training data-set records have been added:

```python
from textblob.classifiers import DecisionTreeClassifier
trainingData = [
    ("The service was great!.", "pos"),
    ("Our waiter was awesome!", "pos"),
    ("They have great appetizers.", "pos"),
    ("Happy hour was busy and fun.", "pos"),
    ("Great place for a quick meal.", "pos"),
    ("Our food took forever to arrive.", "neg"),
    ("The waiter was slow.", "neg"),
    ("The drinks were weak", "neg"),
    ("It was very crowded and noisy!", "neg"),
    ("My pasta was horrible.", "neg"),
    ("My pasta was yummy.", "pos"),
    ("The cost was reasonable.", "pos"),
    ("The drinks were cold.", "pos"),
    ("The hostess was ditsy.", "neg"),
    ("Very good pasta.", "pos"),
    ("They didn't have dessert.", "neg"),
    ("They didn't want to help us.", "neg")
]
testingData = [
    ("The wine list was complete.", "pos"),
    ("There was no place to park.", "neg"),
    ("I really liked the bread.", "pos"),
    ("I want to come back!", "pos"),
    ("The food was not that good.", "neg"),
    ("The beer was great!", "pos")
]
classifer = DecisionTreeClassifier(trainingData)

# Classify new text
print("The food was awesome.", classifer.classify("The food was awesome."))      # "pos"
print("I didn't like my pasta.", classifer.classify("I didn't like my pasta."))    # "neg"

print("Accuracy: {0}".format(classifer.accuracy(testingData)))
print(classifer.pprint())
```

When you execute this script, it will display the following output:

```
C:\python> python DecisionTreeText.py
The food was awesome. pos
I didn't like my pasta. neg
Accuracy: 0.6666666666666666
contains(to)=False? ......................... neg
contains(crowded)=False? .............. .. neg
contains(weak)=False? .................... neg
```

```
contains(did)=False? ....................... pos
contains(did)=True? ........................ neg
contains(weak)=True? ...................... neg
contains(crowded)=True? .............. neg
contains(to)=True? ......................... neg
```

In this case, the script uses the pprint function to display part of its decision tree, which will give you insights into the classification decisions the script performs.

## Using the Natural Language Toolkit

One way to increase your training data is to use the Natural Language Toolkit (NLTK) data set, which you can install using the following commands:

```
C:\python> pip install NLTK
```

Within Python, issue the following statement:

```
>>> import NLTK
>>> NLTK.download()
```

Python will display a dialog box, which you will use to install the desired files.

The following Python script, AskSentiment.py, uses the NLTK data set. The script prompts the user to enter a response to a question regarding their meal. The script then determines the corresponding customer sentiment:

```
import nltk
from nltk.sentiment.vader import SentimentIntensityAnalyzer

feedback = input("How was your meal?")

sia = SentimentIntensityAnalyzer()

score = sia.polarity_scores(feedback)
for i in score:
   print('{0}: {1}, '.format(i, score[i]), end='')
```

The script uses the SentimentIntensityAnalyzer function to determine the sentiment of the text you enter. When you execute this script, it will display the following output:

```
C:\python> python AskSentiment.py
How was your meal? The food was lousy.
neg: 0.538, neu: 0.462, pos: 0.0, compound: -0.5423,
```

In this case, the sentiment analyzer considers the text mostly negative. If you change your input, you will see a different result:

```
C:\python> python AskSentiment.py
How was your meal? It was delicious!
neg: 0.0, neu: 0.334, pos: 0.666, compound: 0.6114,
```

## Clustering Related Text

As you have learned, clustering groups together relates data items. Text clustering is similar, in that the text processor will cluster similar terms or sentences. The following Python script, ClusterText.py, clusters similar text using a K-Means clustering algorithm:

```
from gensim.models import Word2Vec
from nltk.cluster import KMeansClusterer
import nltk
import numpy as np

sentences = [['We', 'should', 'watch', 'a', 'movie'],
             ['Babe', 'Ruth', 'was', 'a', 'great', 'baseball', 'player'],
             ['Lou', 'Gehrig', 'played', 'baseball'],
             ['Do', 'not', 'discuss', 'politics', 'at', 'work'],
             ['Baseball', 'hotdogs', 'Apple', 'Pie', 'and', 'Chevrolet'],
             ['Data', 'mining', 'can', 'use', 'machine', 'learning'],
             ['Clustering', 'uses', 'unsupervised', 'machine', 'learning'],
             ['My', 'company', 'does', 'machine', 'learning'],
             ['Bill', 'Gates', 'was', 'a', 'programmer'],
             ['The', 'movie', 'was', 'bad']]

model = Word2Vec(sentences, min_count=1)
Data = []
for sentence in sentences:
    vector = []
    wordCount = 0
    for word in sentence:
        if wordCount == 0:
            vector = model[word]
        else:
            vector = np.add(vector, model[word])
        wordCount += 1
    Data.append(np.asarray(vector)/wordCount)
km = KMeansClusterer(5, nltk.cluster.util.euclidean_distance, repeats=10)
assigned_clusters = km.cluster(Data, assign_clusters=True)

for index, sentence in enumerate(sentences):
    print (str(assigned_clusters[index]) + ":" + str(sentence))
```

The script specifies several sentences. Because Word2Vec will cluster based upon words, the script specifies the sentences as individual words. You could instead specify strings and later parse the strings into the individual words, but for simplicity, the script does that step for you.

The K-Means clustering algorithm works with numbers, not words. As such, the script uses Word2Vec to model the words:

```
model = Word2Vec(sentences, min_count=1)
```

After this step, you can view each word's numeric representation as follows:

```
>>> model['machine']
array([-4.3701948e-04, -4.1765548e-04, -3.3977258e-03,  4.6074861e-03,
       -1.3499127e-03, -2.1755672e-04,  2.6213960e-03, -1.3710246e-03,
       -2.1278115e-03,  2.2482695e-03, -5.8523717e-04, -4.6008956e-03,
        4.2010406e-03,  1.4054523e-03, -5.6426268e-04,  2.0363431e-03,
       -3.2825542e-03, -4.3889945e-03,  3.9440817e-03, -1.6822156e-03,
        9.7015130e-05,  4.6269833e-03,  8.9539506e-05,  3.1995103e-03,
       -2.1887616e-05,  4.0066866e-03, -1.7019135e-03, -1.5717789e-03,
        1.3924072e-03, -1.6640263e-03,  1.6413350e-03,  1.2646630e-04,
       -3.3646333e-03,  4.3520234e-03, -3.6120508e-04,  3.9923214e-03,
       -2.9524292e-03,  2.6546794e-03,  1.4842564e-03, -2.1809882e-03,
       -3.5368311e-03,  4.3866793e-03,  1.2987041e-03, -3.5056521e-03,
        4.1798898e-03,  3.6463665e-05,  3.5490831e-03, -3.6608097e-03,
        2.3095852e-03, -3.8255258e-03,  4.6909922e-03, -4.6192901e-04,
        3.1994435e-03,  1.9685237e-03, -4.4092243e-03, -4.5141769e-03,
        4.2088828e-03,  1.7347093e-03,  9.0792199e-04,  3.3861864e-03,
       -4.0160106e-03, -3.9825616e-03, -9.1505743e-04,  3.6950472e-03,
        1.1776804e-04,  1.3436123e-03, -2.8758326e-03, -1.9213930e-03,
        3.1923591e-03, -1.4453450e-03, -2.9942589e-03,  3.6989921e-03,
        3.9833374e-03,  1.8041521e-06, -3.5127513e-03,  1.7112205e-03,
        3.5855153e-03,  2.0155928e-03, -3.3114783e-03, -4.8972722e-03,
       -3.9096046e-03, -4.9450919e-03, -2.1619292e-03,  4.6911356e-03,
        3.9994833e-04, -3.7127771e-04,  1.8114785e-03,  1.5441969e-03,
        3.5771835e-03,  7.1355415e-04,  1.7560926e-03,  3.0955451e-03,
       -2.0211767e-03, -1.5374318e-03, -2.1277661e-03, -4.9432628e-03,
        1.4247042e-03,  3.7711598e-03, -1.6805201e-03, -2.9403025e-03],
      dtype=float32)
```

The script then uses for loops to build a collection of vectors, each of which contains a sentence's numeric model of its original words. The script then passes the vectors to the K-Means clusterer. When you execute this script, it will display the following output:

```
C:\python> python ClusterText.py
3:['We', 'should', 'watch', 'a', 'movie']
3:['Babe', 'Ruth', 'was', 'a', 'great', 'baseball', 'player']
0:['Lou', 'Gehrig', 'played', 'baseball']
1:['Do', 'not', 'discuss', 'politics', 'at', 'work']
1:['Baseball', 'hotdogs', 'Apple', 'Pie', 'and', 'Chevrolet']
2:['Data', 'mining', 'can', 'use', 'machine', 'learning']
2:['Clustering', 'uses', 'unsupervised', 'machine', 'learning']
2:['My', 'company', 'does', 'machine', 'learning']
4:['Bill', 'Gates', 'was', 'a', 'programmer']
4:['The', 'movie', 'was', 'bad']
```

As you can see, some of the cluster groups are more accurate than others. To improve the results, the following script, RevisedCluster.py, edits the sentences to use only key words (eliminating words such as "was," "a," and "do"):

```
from gensim.models import Word2Vec
from nltk.cluster import KMeansClusterer
import nltk
import numpy as np

sentences = [['watch', 'movie'],
            ['Ruth', 'baseball', 'player'],
            ['Gehrig', 'played', 'baseball'],
            ['politics', 'work'],
            ['Baseball', 'hotdogs', 'Apple', 'Pie', 'Chevrolet'],
            ['Data', 'mining', 'machine', 'learning'],
            ['Clustering', 'unsupervised', 'machine', 'learning'],
            ['machine', 'learning'],
            ['Gates', 'programmer'],
            ['movie', 'bad']]
model = Word2Vec(sentences, min_count=1)
Data = []

for sentence in sentences:
    vector = []
    wordCount = 0
    for word in sentence:
        if wordCount == 0:
            vector = model[word]
        else:
            vector = np.add(vector, model[word])
        wordCount += 1

    Data.append(np.asarray(vector)/wordCount)

km = KMeansClusterer(5, nltk.cluster.util.euclidean_distance, repeats=10)
assigned_clusters = km.cluster(Data, assign_clusters=True)

for index, sentence in enumerate(sentences):
    print (str(assigned_clusters[index]) + ":" + str(sentence))
```

When you run this script, it will display the following output:

```
C:\python> python RevisedCluster.py
0:['watch', 'movie']
1:['Ruth', 'baseball', 'player']
1:['Gehrig', 'played', 'baseball']
```

```
4:['politics', 'work']
3:['Baseball', 'hotdogs', 'Apple', 'Pie', 'Chevrolet']
3:['Data', 'mining', 'machine', 'learning']
3:['Clustering', 'unsupervised', 'machine', 'learning']
3:['machine', 'learning']
2:['Gates', 'programmer']
0:['movie', 'bad']
```

As you can see, the groupings are better. To further improve the results, but at the cost of processing time, you can increase the number of iterations the K-Means clusterer performs:

```
km = KMeansClusterer(5, nltk.cluster.util.euclidean_distance,
repeats=100)
```

# Getting Started with Image Mining

Image mining is the application of data-mining techniques to image data. Image mining includes facial recognition, object identification, image clustering, and image classification. Across the web, applications make extensive use of image processing for a wide range of operations:

- Weather image analysis
- Medical image analysis
- National security
- Facial recognition
- And more

## Creating a Simple Facial Recognition Application

Facial recognition is a software process that identifies a person (or people) within a photo. The government, for example, makes use of facial recognition for national security applications, tracking who is entering and exiting the country. Similarly, mobile phone apps and many computer applications make use of facial recognition to authenticate users.

The following Python script, Recognize.py, leverages the Facial_Recognition and DLib modules to create a simple facial recognition solution. The DLib module requires that your system have CMake and Boost installed, which you can download and install from the following websites:

- http://cmake.org/download
- https://www.boost.org/users/download/

After you install these two applications, use PIP to install the Facial_Recognition and DLib modules:

```
C:\> pip install Dlib
C:\> pip install Facial_Recognition
```

The script will compare the image that you specify within the command line to a collection of photos. If the application finds a match, it will display the corresponding filename:

```
import os
import sys
import face_recognition

# Get the images to compare
images = os.listdir('photos')

# load the image to match
image_to_be_matched = face_recognition.load_image_file(sys.argv[1])

# Convert the image into a feature vector
image_to_be_matched_encoded = face_recognition.face_encodings(image_to_be_matched)[0]
# Loop through the images comparing each
for image in images:
    current_image = face_recognition.load_image_file("photos/" + image)
    current_image_encoded = face_recognition.face_encodings(current_image)[0]
    result = face_recognition.compare_faces(
        [image_to_be_matched_encoded], current_image_encoded)
    if result[0] == True:
        print("Matched the image: " + image)
    else:
```

Before you run the script, create a folder called *photos* into which you will place the images you want to compare. To make the script's output more meaningful, consider using the names of people who appear in each photo as the filenames.

Assume, for example, you have the images shown in **FIGURE 14.1**, which you can download from this text's catalog page at go.jblearning.com/DataMining.

To run the script, specify the name of the file you want the application to analyze within the Python command line:

```
C:\Python>python recognize.py photos rump.jpg
Did not match the image: bush.jpg
Did not match the image: bush02.jpg
Did not match the image: bushsr.jpg
Did not match the image: carter.jpg
Did not match the image: clinton.jpg
Did not match the image: clinton02.jpg
Did not match the image: obama.jpg
Did not match the image: obama02.jpg
Did not match the image: reagan.jpg
Did not match the image: reagan02.jpg
Matched the image: trump.jpg
Matched the image: trump01.jpg
Matched the image: trump02.jpg
```

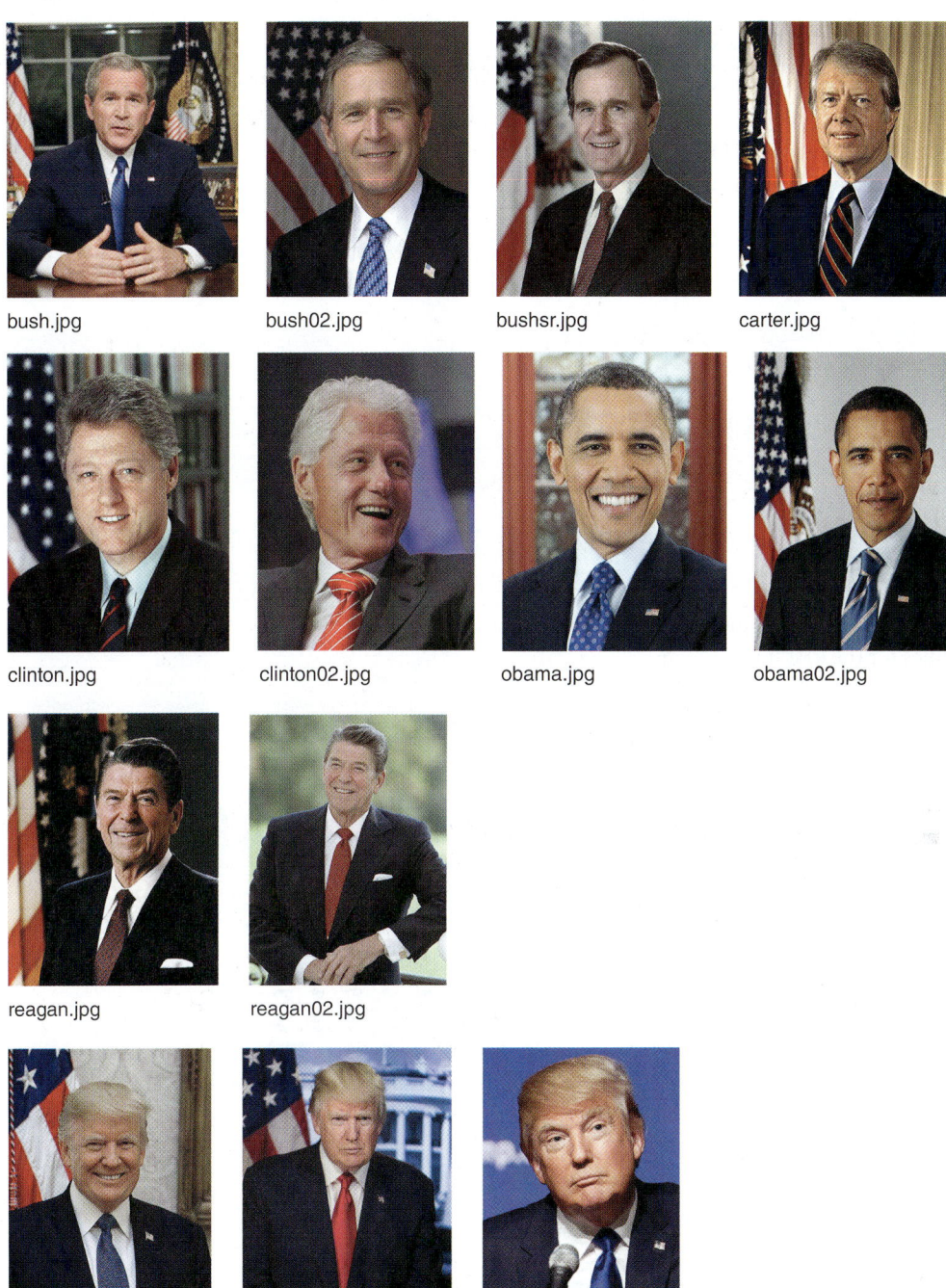

**FIGURE 14.1** **Images used for facial recognition.**

Courtesy of USA.gov

trump02.jpg: © stocklight/Shutterstock

## Handwriting Classification

One of the most commonly used image classification examples on the web is the classification of handwritten digits (0–9), using images contained in the Modified National Institute of Science and Technology (MNIST) digits data set, as shown in **FIGURE 14.2**. The MNIST data set contains 60,000 images, stored in an 8 × 8 matrix (64 attributes). Each attribute value is represented using a value from 0 to 255.

The following script, ShowDigit.py, loads a 1,797-image subset into the data set, which is built into sklearn, and displays the first digit:

```
from sklearn import datasets
import matplotlib.pyplot as plt

digits = datasets.load_digits()

plt.imshow(digits.images[0], cmap=plt.cm.gray_r,
interpolation='nearest')
plt.show()
```

When you run this script, it will display the first image, as shown in **FIGURE 14.3**.

The following Python script, DigitAttributes.py, loads the data set and displays the attribute values for the first image:

```
from sklearn import datasets

digits = datasets.load_digits()

print(digits.data[0])
```

**FIGURE 14.2** Handwritten digit images within the MNIST data set.

Source: Josef Steppan (2017). Sample image from MNIST test dataset. Licensed under the Creative Commons Attribution-Share Alike 4.0 International license

# Getting Started with Image Mining

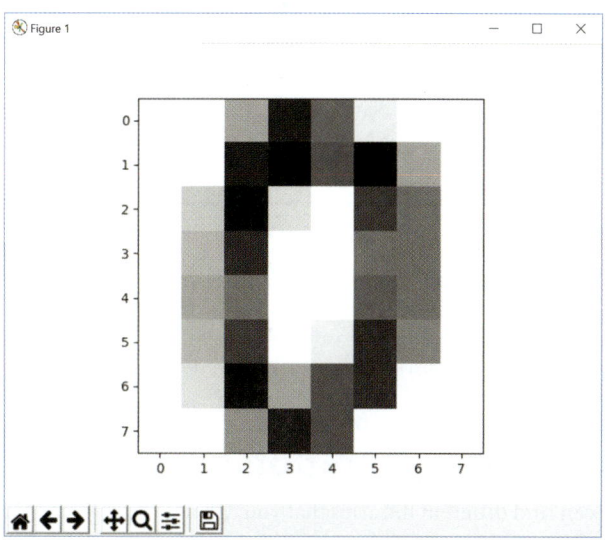

**FIGURE 14.3** Displaying a handwritten digit from the digits data set.
Used with permission of Python Software Foundation

When you execute this code, it will display the following output:

```
C:\python> python DigitAttributes.py
[ 0.   0.   5.  13.   9.   1.   0.   0.   0.  13.  15.  10.  15.   5.   0.   0.   3.
 15.   2.   0.  11.   8.   0.   0.   4.  12.   0.   0.   8.   8.   0.   0.   5.   8.   0.
  0.   9.   8.   0.   0.   4.  11.   0.   1.  12.   7.   0.   0.   2.  14.   5.  10.  12.
  0.   0.   0.   0.   6.  13.  10.   0.   0.   0.]
```

The following Python script, DigitsClassify.py, uses K-nearest-neighbor (KNN) classification, discussed in Chapter 10, "Data Clustering," to classify the handwritten digits as a number from 0 to 9:

```
from sklearn.neighbors import KNeighborsClassifier
from sklearn.model_selection import train_test_split
from sklearn.metrics import accuracy_score
from sklearn import datasets

digits = datasets.load_digits()
X = digits.data
y = digits.target
X_train, X_test, y_train, y_test = train_test_split(X, y, test_
size = 0.2)

knn = KNeighborsClassifier(n_neighbors=5)

# Fit the classifier to the training data
knn.fit(X_train, y_train)
pred = knn.predict(X_test)
```

```
print ('\nModel accuracy score: ', accuracy_score(y_test, pred))

# Predict a handwritten digit, reshape the 1D array as a 2D array
pred = knn.predict(digits.data[500].reshape(1, -1))
print('Predicted:', pred, 'Actual:', digits.target[500])
```

When you run this script, it will display the following output:

```
C:\python> python DigitClassify.py
Model accuracy score:  0.9833333333333333
Predicted: [8] Actual: 8
```

As you can see, the script has a 98% accuracy and correctly classifies the text-written digit as an 8.

## Hands-on: Facial Recognition Using OpenCV

Across the web, you can find different libraries that you can use to perform image recognition. One of the most complete is OpenCV, which you can download and install from the OpenCV website, shown in **FIGURE 14.4**, at http://opencv.org. OpenCV is an open-source library designed to support computer vision—the ability of an application to analyze and understand images.

After you install OpenCV, use PIP to install the CV2 package:

```
C:\python> pip install cv2
```

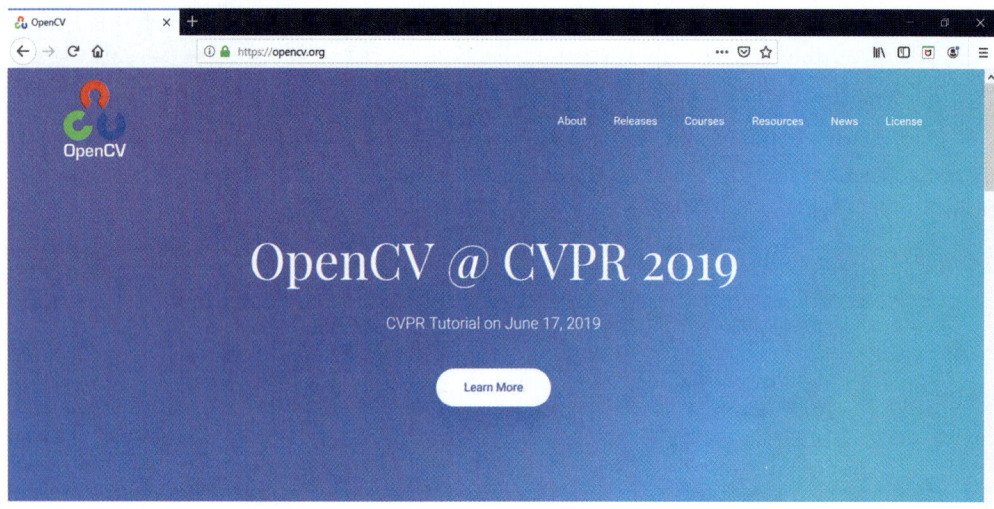

**FIGURE 14.4** Download and install OpenCV from the OpenCV website.

Used with permission from OpenCV team

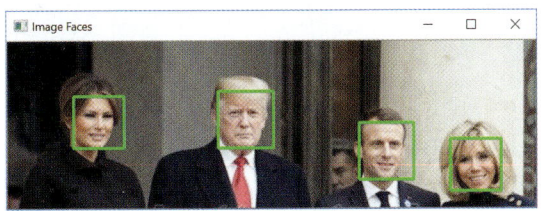

**FIGURE 14.5** Using OpenCV to identify faces in a photo.

Used with permission from OpenCV team

The following Python script, BoxFace.py, uses OpenCV to recognize faces within a photo. The script draws squares around the faces, as shown in **FIGURE 14.5**.

```
import cv2
import sys

cascPath = "haarcascade_frontalface_default.xml"
faceCascade = cv2.CascadeClassifier(cascPath)

imagePath = sys.argv[1]
image = cv2.imread(imagePath)
gray = cv2.cvtColor(image, cv2.COLOR_BGR2GRAY)

faces = faceCascade.detectMultiScale(gray, scaleFactor=1.1,
minNeighbors=5, minSize=(25, 25))

# Draw a square around each face
for (x, y, width, height) in faces:
    cv2.rectangle(image, (x, y), (x+width, y+height), (0, 255, 0), 2)

cv2.imshow("Image Faces ", image)
cv2.waitKey(0)
```

The script will analyze the photo you specify as a command-line argument when you run the script:

```
C:\python> python BoxFace.py yourFilename.jpg
```

To recognize faces, the script uses the haarcascade_frontalface_default.xml file that contains the attributes of a frontal face. You can download the file from this text's catalog page at go.jblearning.com/DataMining. As it turns out, you can find other "haar_cascade" files on the web that you can use to recognize different objects. In addition, you can use OpenCV to create your own. In this way, if you wanted to recognize dogs, cars, or license plates, you could use the same code, changing only the XML file. In fact, across the web, you can find several tutorials and code repositories that can help you get started.

## Summary

This chapter introduced text and image mining. To perform text and image processing, you used many of the data-mining techniques you have used throughout this text. To do so, you first converted the text or image into a numeric representation the algorithms require. Across the web, you can find many text- and image-processing libraries.

## Key Terms

Computer vision
Facial recognition

Image mining
Natural-language processing

Sentiment analysis
Text mining

## Review

1. Define and describe text mining.
2. Define and describe image mining.
3. Modify the text sentiment script DecisionTreeText.py this chapter presents to use your own text. Describe how modifying your words or format influences your results.
4. Modify the text-clustering script ClusterText.py this chapter presents to use a different clustering algorithm.
5. Modify the Python script digitsClassify.py this chapter presents to use a different clustering algorithm.
6. Implement the Python face recognition program this chapter presents.
7. Modify the Python script BoxFace.py this chapter presents to draw a circle around each face.

# CHAPTER 15

# Big Data Mining

## Chapter Goals and Objectives

- Define and describe big data.
- Define and describe common data capacities such as megabytes, terabytes, and petabytes.
- Describe the role of Hadoop in big data processing.
- Define and describe the MapReduce process.

My first IBM PC had two 360-KB floppy drives—when I purchased the system, I upgraded it to add the second drive. Two years later, when I upgraded to a PC AT with a 10-MB hard drive, I knew I was set for disk space! Ten years later, the typical PC had a 1-gigabyte (1-GB) hard drive. By the time of this writing, most PCs ship with a 1-terabyte (1-TB) or larger hard drive (**FIGURE 15.1**).

Throughout this text, you have examined many tools that let you manage and manipulate data. Each of these tools has a limit on the amount of data they can store or process. The term "**big data**" applies to data sets that exceed the size our data programs can hold. For Excel, that might be a data set that is larger than the available memory, and for MySQL, that might be the size of the largest file supported by the underlying operating system. The point is, most software applications have size limits, which the size of big data solutions exceed.

Normal questions you may have probably include: Where is all the big data coming from, how quickly, and how much?

In general, so much data are being created so quickly that best-guess estimates are that more than 2 quintillion bytes (2,000,000,000,000,000,000 bytes) are created annually. Much of that data

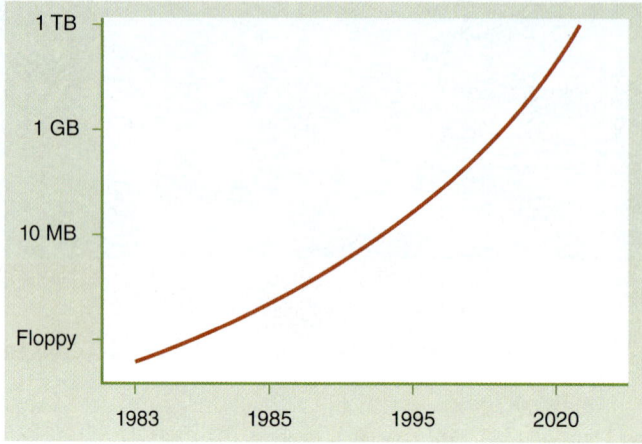

**FIGURE 15.1** The evolution of PC hard drive sizes.

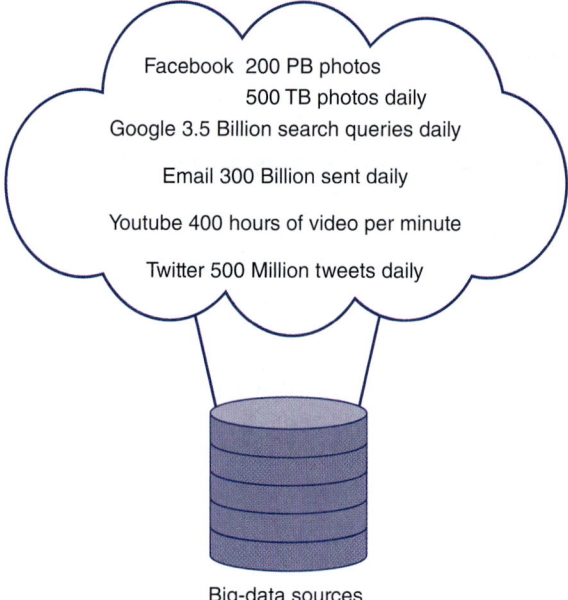

**FIGURE 15.2** Social media sources of data.

comes from social media, for which **FIGURE 15.2** provides estimates. Keep in mind that these numbers grow daily.

In the future, the greatest source of data will be devices on the Internet of Things (**IoT**). Looking forward, big data is only going to become bigger and the demand for big data solutions greater.

This chapter examines big data. By the time you finish this chapter, you will understand the following key concepts:

- The amount of total data worldwide doubles nearly every 2 years.
- Most applications, from the operating system to Excel or a database, have a maximum amount of data they can handle.
- Big data is data that are larger in size than traditional software applications can handle.
- The size of data is expressed in terms of bytes, **kilobytes**, **megabytes**, and so on. In general, you can determine the exact number of bytes a category of data can store by raising the value 1,024 to the category's corresponding value:
  - Byte = $1,024^0$ byte
  - Kilobyte (KB) = $1,024^1$ bytes
  - Megabyte (MB) = $1,024^2$ bytes
  - Gigabyte (GB) = $1,024^3$ bytes
  - Terabyte (TB) = $1,024^4$ bytes
  - Exabyte (EB) = $1,024^5$ bytes
  - Petabyte (PB) = $1,024^6$ bytes
  - Zettabyte (ZB) = $1,024^7$ bytes
  - Yottabyte (YB) = $1,024^8$ bytes
- Within an operating system, special software called the file system creates, writes, reads, and manages files.
- Like applications, file systems have a maximum file size they can store.
- To store very large files, specialized file systems have been created that store files across multiple systems, the most commonly used distributed file system being the Hadoop Distributed File System (**HDFS**).
- HDFS stores large files across nodes, which comprise a **cluster**.
- HDFS uses a master/slave model within which the slave stores data and the master tracks on which systems the data are stored. When a data request arrives, the master node redirects the request to the correct node.
- To reduce the overhead of transferring large amounts of data across a network, **Hadoop** uses a model that does not bring data to the process, but rather, brings the processing to be performed to the data nodes—a process developers call bringing the process to the data.
- To analyze big data, Hadoop uses a two-step MapReduce process. During the Map phase, a function maps (specifies) the desired data, and during the Reduce phase, a function reduces matching data down to the desired result.
- Hadoop is more than a file system. It also provides the framework that distributes and coordinates the parallel processing across the nodes.

## Revisiting the Numbers

It used to be easy to make sense of file and disk sizes. A character of data was a **byte**, 1,024 bytes were 1 KB, and 1024 × 1,024, or 1,048,576 bytes, were 1 MB, as shown in **TABLE A**.

Today, the size of most hard drives is expressed in terms of **gigabytes** or **terabytes**, as described in **TABLE B**.

Driven by big data, we now speak in terms of **exabytes**, **petabytes**, **zettabytes**, and **yottabytes**, as shown in **TABLE C**.

### TABLE A Understanding Bytes, Kilobytes, and Megabytes

| Capacity | Symbol | Size | Example |
| --- | --- | --- | --- |
| Byte | B | 1 byte | A character of the alphabet |
| Kilobyte | KB | $2^{10}$ or 1,024 bytes | A page of text |
| Megabyte | MB | $2^{20}$ or 1,024 × 1,024 or 1,048,576 bytes | A book |

### TABLE B Understanding Gigabytes and Terabytes

| Capacity | Symbol | Size | Example |
| --- | --- | --- | --- |
| Gigabyte | GB | $2^{30}$ or $1,024^3$ or 1,073,741,824 bytes | A library of 1,000 books |
| Terabyte | TB | $2^{40}$ or $1,024^4$ or 1,099,511,627,776 bytes | 1 million books |

### TABLE C Understanding Exabytes, Petabytes, Zettabytes, and Yottabytes

| Capacity | Symbol | Size | Example |
| --- | --- | --- | --- |
| Exabyte | EB | $2^{50}$ or $1,024^5$ or 1,125,899,906,842,624 bytes | 2 days of Facebook photo posts |
| Petabyte | PB | $2^{60}$ or $1,024^6$ or 1,152,921,504,606,846,976 bytes | Google |
| Zettabyte | ZB | $2^{70}$ or $1,024^7$ | The web |
| Yottabyte | YB | $2^{80}$ or $1,024^8$ | "Big" |

## The V's of Big Data

As users and developers discuss big data, they often speak in terms of the following V's:

- Volume
- Velocity
- Variety
- Veracity
- Value

Volume corresponds to the amount of data. Facebook, for example, stores over 200 PB of photos. Velocity describes how fast the data accumulate and are accessed. Facebook users post over 500 TB of photos daily. Twitter users post 500 million tweets per day. Google processes over 3.5 billion queries per day. Over 300 billion emails are exchanged daily, and YouTube users upload over 400 hours of video every minute. Variety specifies the different types of data. Facebook, for example, has posts, likes, and photos. Finally, veracity relates to data accuracy. Recently, many people speak about a fifth V: value. Simply having a ton of data is not enough. You must be able to convert the data into something of value.

To view current data statistics for social media sites, visit the Internet Live Stats website at http://www.InternetLiveStats.com.

## Big Data Requires a Big Number of Servers

As you can imagine, it takes a lot of disks and servers to store and process big data. As of this text's writing, estimates place the number of servers at big data sites as shown in **TABLE 15.1**.

Facebook, for example, has very large data centers distributed across the country, each capable of storing tens of thousands of servers. **FIGURE 15.3**, for example, shows the size of such a data center.

**TABLE 15.1** The Number of Servers at Well-Known Big Data Site

| Site | Server Estimate |
| --- | --- |
| Amazon | 1+ million |
| Microsoft | 1+ million |
| Google | 1+ million |

# CHAPTER 15 Big Data Mining

**FIGURE 15.3** Google Datacenter in the Netherlands.
© Rudmer Zwerver/Shutterstock

## Understanding the Role of File Systems

Operating systems, such as Windows or Linux, exist to let users run programs and store and retrieve data using files. Within an operating system, the file system is responsible for storing and retrieving files. Regardless of the size of the underlying disk, an operating system has a maximum file size. To support larger files, new file systems have emerged that let systems store data across collections of systems (nodes) called clusters. The most commonly used big data file system is HDFS, shown in **FIGURE 15.4**.

As you know, the more devices used in a system, the greater the risk of failure. To reduce such risks, HDFS provides redundant nodes within a cluster, which may reside in different data centers, as shown in **FIGURE 15.5**. Should one node fail, the redundant node can take over.

HDFS uses a master/slave relationship for which one node manages the others to coordinate the data storage and retrieval, as shown in **FIGURE 15.6**.

The master node tracks where specific data are stored within a cluster. When a request for data comes in, the master node routes the request to the correct slave node.

## Bring the Process to the Data

When programs retrieve data from a disk, the time required to get the data from the disk directly affects the application's performance. When you distribute files across a network, the network's transmission speed will become the longest delay in the process, as shown in **FIGURE 15.7**.

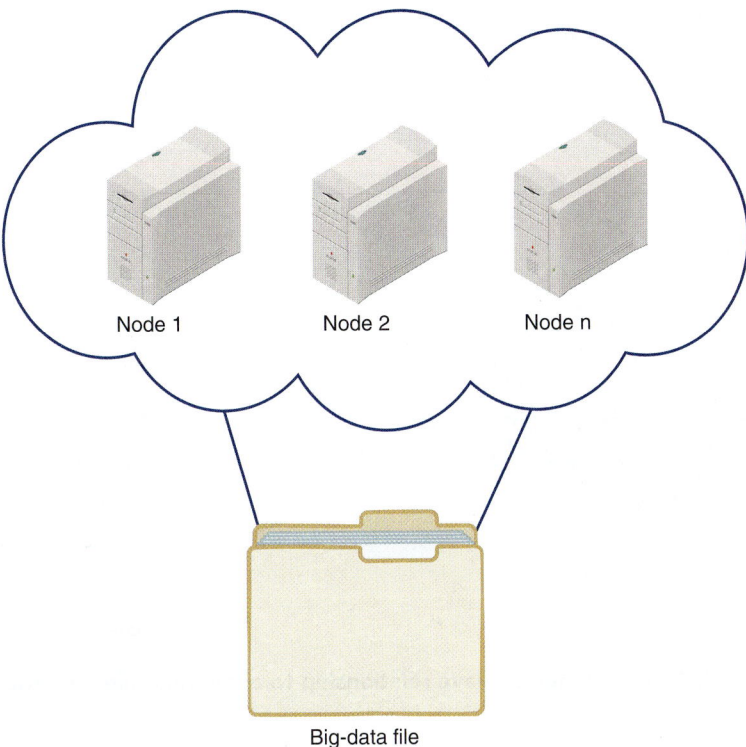

**FIGURE 15.4 Storing a file in a distributed file system.**

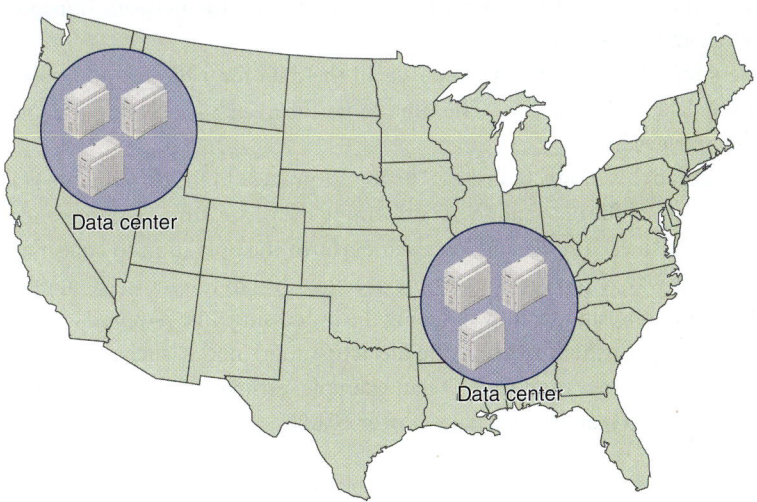

**FIGURE 15.5 Storing nodes in an HDFS cluster in different data centers.**

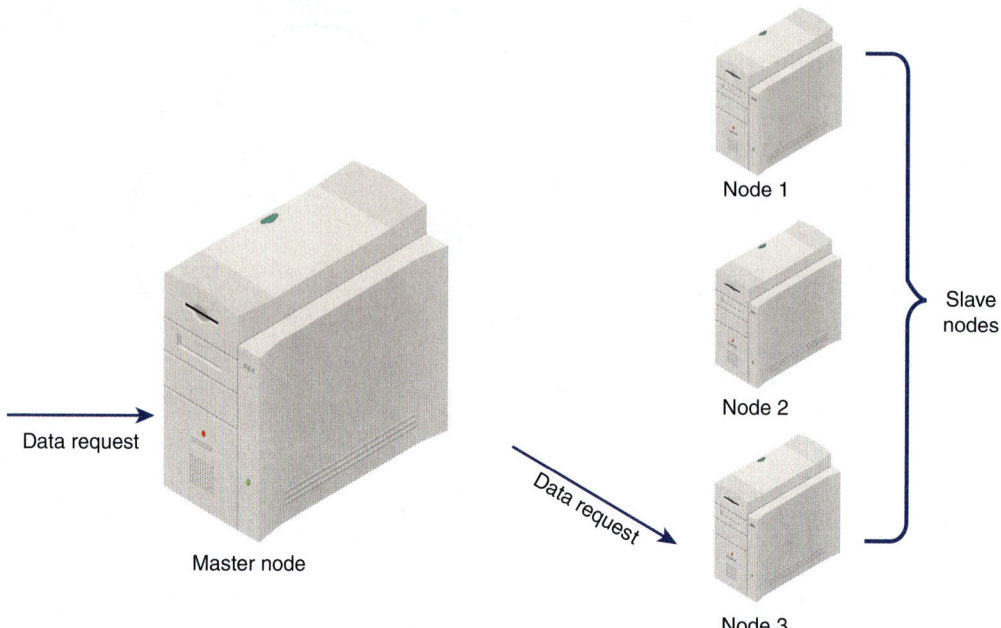

**FIGURE 15.6** HDFS uses a master/slave relationship to coordinate file operations.

Assume, for example, that you must read a 10-GB file to find each occurrence of the phrase "data mining." On a local drive, a system may read the file (based on a 100-MB/S disk) in about 100 seconds. If you move the file to a distributed file system, the network transportation speed will increase that amount of time.

Developers refer to solutions that retrieve all the data for a file for processing in this way as "bringing the data to the process." The time to perform such processing is dependent on the amount of data retrieved.

Hadoop changed this model to instead "bring the process to the data." In the Hadoop model, rather than returning all the data and then performing the processing, Hadoop sends the processing to be performed to each node and lets each perform the operation to collect and return the desired data. In this way, if you break apart the previous 10-GB file across 20 nodes, Hadoop can parallelize the operations, significantly reducing the processing time required—in this case, down to 5–10 seconds. If you further distribute the file across more nodes, such as 100, you can quickly distribute much of the processing time. As an example, estimates place the number of Hadoop nodes driving the Yahoo search index page at over 10,000.

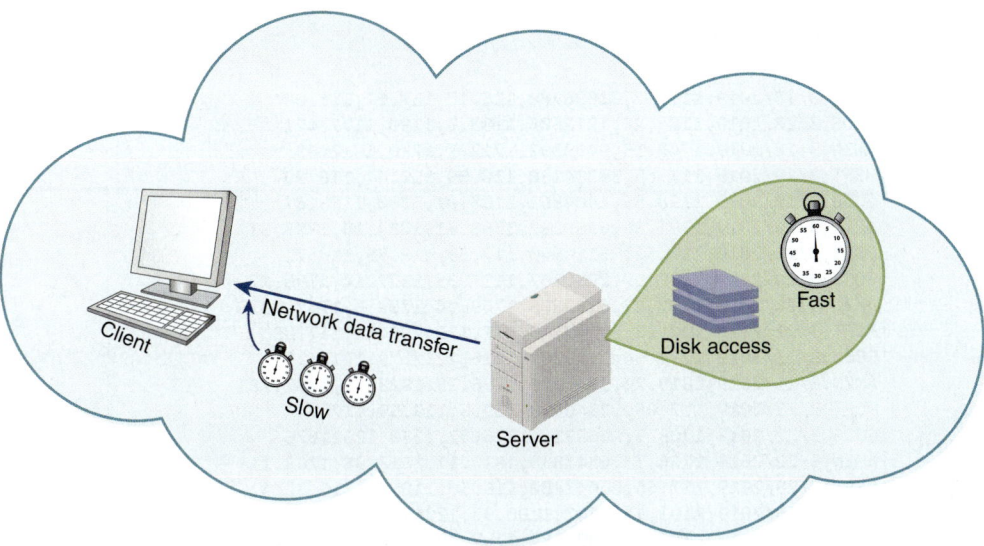

**FIGURE 15.7** Network transfer times directly affect an application's distributed file performance.

# Enter MapReduce

As you have learned, HDFS distributes large files across many nodes within a cluster. To perform big data analytics, applications normally use a two-step process called MapReduce.

During the first step, the application maps the data that it reads into key–value pairs. Assume, for example, you have stock market data for technology stocks (date, symbol, open, low, high, and close) since the year 2000. Your goal is to know the date of each company's highest closing stock price. The file stores the fields separated by commas, as shown in **FIGURE 15.8**.

Our data of interest, in this case, are the date of each record and the closing price. The Map phase will identify the key–value pair of interest (date, high price). The query, as such, would provide data for each record. The Reduce phase, then, will examine that data to determine the desired result (the date and price of the highest price found), as shown in **FIGURE 15.9**.

To implement MapReduce processing, developers define two functions: one to perform the mapping and one to perform the reduction. Using Hadoop, developers can implement these functions using Java, C++, Python, and other languages.

## Looking at a Simple MapReduce Example

To better understand the MapReduce process, consider the following simple Python scripts that use the data file Stocks.csv, which you can download from this text's catalog page at go.jblearning.com/DataMining.

**618**    **CHAPTER 15** Big Data Mining

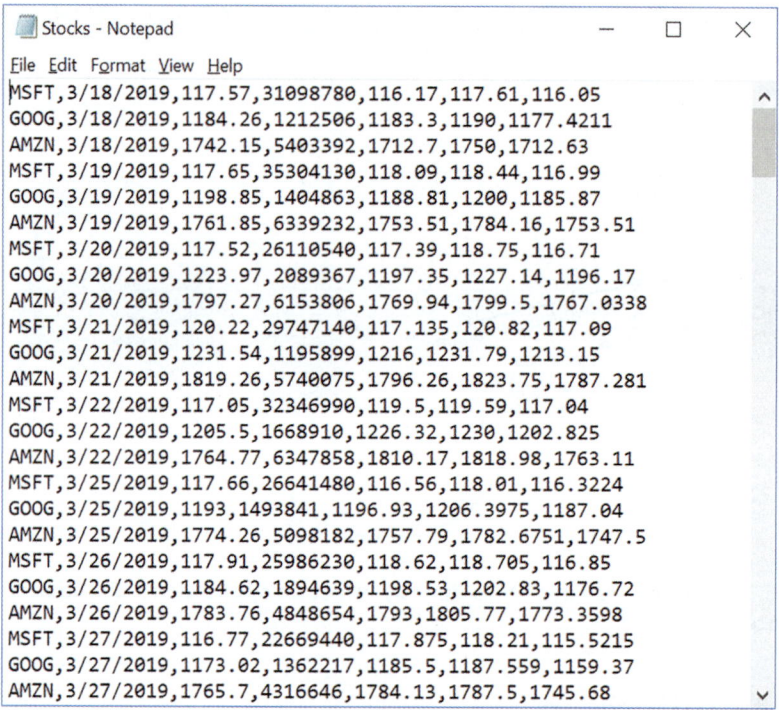

**FIGURE 15.8** The format of the stock data file.

Used with permission from Microsoft

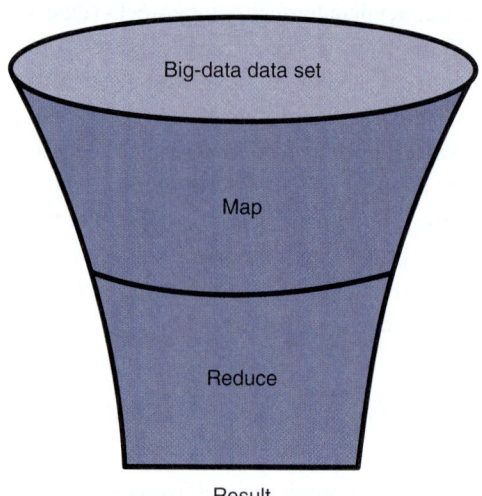

**FIGURE 15.9** Using MapReduce to funnel big data down to a desired result.

The first script, Mapper.py, reads the file, searching for the MSFT symbol, and outputs matching dates and closing prices:

```python
import sys

for line in sys.stdin:
    data = line.split(',')
    if (data[0] == 'MSFT'):
      print(data[1] + ',' + data[2])
```

To run the script, you can redirect the contents of the Stocks.txt file to the script, as shown here:

```
C:\python> stocks.txt < python Mapper.py
```

As you can see, the Mapper returns the data for each MSFT record, along with the closing price, but does not calculate the date of the highest price—that's the role of the Reduce function, which the script Reduce.py implements:

```python
import sys

high = 0

for line in sys.stdin:
    data = line.split(',')
    close = float(data[1].rstrip())    # get rid of newline

    if (close > high):
      high = close
      date = data[0]

print(date + ',' + str(high))
```

To combine the scripts, we will sort the output of the Mapper script and pipe those results to the Reduce script, as shown here:

```
C:\> python Mapper.py < stocks.csv | python Reduce.py
6/18/2019,135.16
```

As you can see, the command displays the date and closing price for Microsoft's highest closing price.

Admittedly, this example was very simple. In a real-world example, Hadoop would pass the functions to each node, which, in turn, would use it to process its data.

## Data Lakes

When applications, such as a data warehouse, deal with files, as opposed to databases, developers refer to the file as a data lake. Such a file can be a structured file, possibly in Extended Markup Language (XML) or JavaScript Object Notation (JSON), or it can be an unstructured comma-separated value (CSV), text, or binary file. A data lake may get its data from many different sources.

To store a large data lake, systems use a specialized file system, such as HDFS, to store data across different nodes. In addition to Hadoop, to store such large files, Amazon provides S3, Microsoft Azure provides Data Lake, and Google Cloud Platform provides Cloud Dataproc.

## A Word on Spark

Beyond Hadoop, one of the most widely used analytic engines is Apache Spark, an open-source project. Spark was designed and engineered for performance, and developers find that it can be 100 times faster than Hadoop. What makes Spark fast is that it performs most operations in memory. Also, Spark is written in Scala, which, unlike Java (Hadoop is written in Java), produces a compiled machine code, as opposed to bytecode that the Java Virtual Machine must translate during execution.

Spark can sit on top of Hadoop, Kubernetes, and other platforms, as well as run as a stand-alone process. Developers can use R, Java, Python, and other programming languages to call Spark application programming interfaces (APIs). Spark provides built-in libraries, as shown in **FIGURE A**.

As you can see, Spark provides libraries for data connections, for performing machine learning, for creating charts and graphs, and more.

In addition to writing programs that interact with Spark, users can access Spark from the R, Python, Scala, or Structured Query Language (SQL) shells. For more information on Spark, or to download it, visit the Spark website at http://spark.apache.org, as shown in **FIGURE B**.

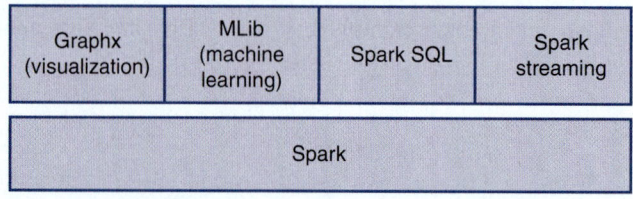

**FIGURE A** The Spark libraries.

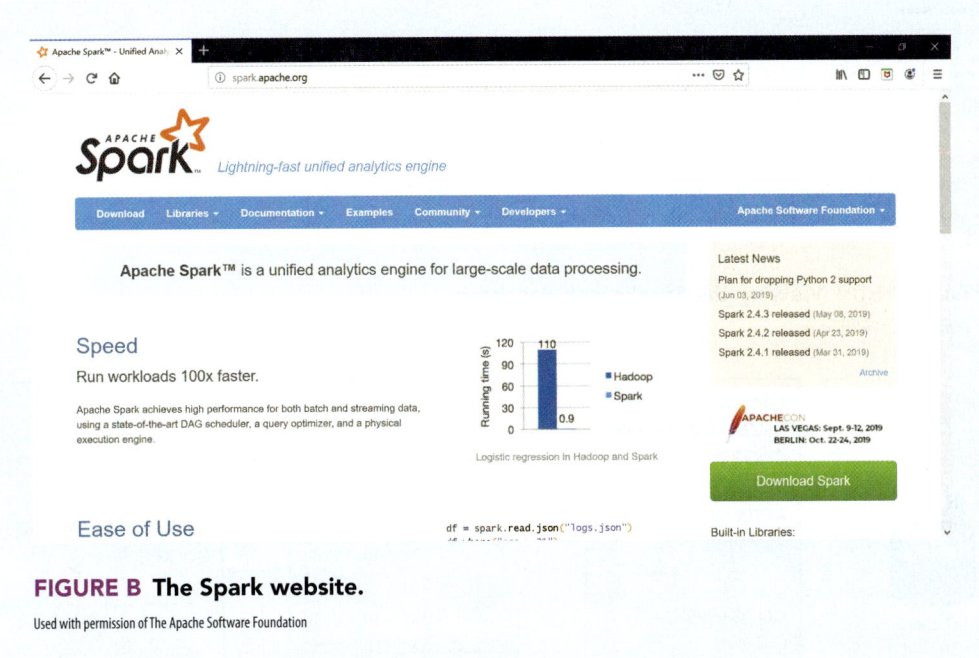

**FIGURE B** The Spark website.

Used with permission of The Apache Software Foundation

# Hands-On: Performing MapReduce Options Using MongoDB

As you have learned, using shards, MongoDB can distribute data across nodes. To provide support for big data analytics, MongoDB provides support for MapReduce operations. Chapter 7, "NoSQL Data Analytics," examines MongoDB in detail.

In this section, you will perform MapReduce operations within MongoDB. To start, download the Stocks.json database schema from this text's catalog page at go.jblearning.com/DataMining. If you view the file's contents using Notepad, you will find that it contains the MongoDB queries to create the stock market data (date, symbol, open, low, high, close) for several tech stocks, as shown in **FIGURE 15.10**.

Save and open the file. Then, within Notepad, press the Ctrl+A keyboard combination, select the file's contents, and press Ctrl+C to copy the contents to the Clipboard. Then, using the MongoDB windows Control menu, paste the queries at the MongoDB prompt.

To better understand MapReduce processing, consider the flow shown in **FIGURE 15.11**. The Map phase consumes the collection and emits the key–value pairs needed, moving them to the Reduce phase as a key (in this case, the stock symbol) and an array of data values (which in this case, includes the dates and closing prices). The Reduce phase performs an aggregation (in this case, finding the max value in the values received).

**622**   CHAPTER 15 Big Data Mining

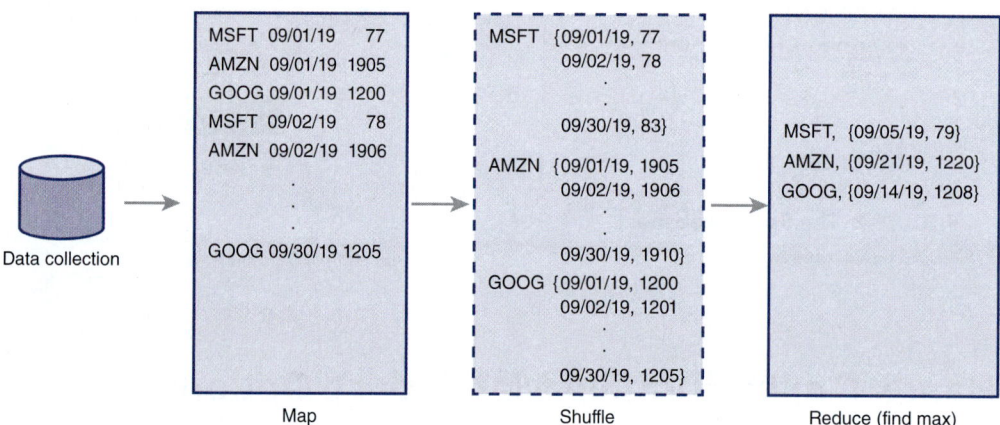

**FIGURE 15.10** Viewing the Stocks.json database.

Used with permission from Microsoft

**FIGURE 15.11** The MapReduce process flow.

Next, to perform a MapReduce operation, you must define two functions, map and reduce, as shown next:

```
var map = function() {
  emit(this.Symbol, { date: this.Date, close: this.Close});
};

reduce = function (key, values) {
  output = { date: "", close: 0 }

  for (i = 0; i < values.length; i++)
     if (values[i].close > output.close)
        {
           output.close = values[i].close;
           output.date = values[i].date;
        }

  return(output);
}
```

The map function provides the stock symbol, date, and closing price for each record. The reduce function receives a group of related records (same key) and determines and returns the highest stock closing price within the group. Note that the reduce function returns a result in the form emitted by the map function. That is because the reduce function may be called with partial group data (such as some of the MSFT data) and will be called repeatedly until the aggregation is complete. To use the two functions to perform a MapReduce operation, use the mapReduce class, as shown here:

```
> db.Data.mapReduce(map, reduce, { out: { inline: 1}})
```

In this case, the operation will return the following results:

```
> db.Data.mapReduce(map, reduce, { out: { inline:1}});
{
        "results" : [
                {
                        "_id" : "AMZN",
                        "value" : {
                                "date" : "5/3/2019",
                                "close" : 2162.46
                        }
                },
                {
                        "_id" : "GOOG",
                        "value" : {
                                "date" : "4/29/2019",
                                "close" : 1287.58
                        }
                },
                {
                        "_id" : "MSFT",
                        "value" : {
                                "date" : "6/18/2019",
                                "close" : 135.16
                        }
                }
        ],
        "timeMillis" : 26,
        "counts" : {
                "input" : 196,
                "emit" : 196,
                "reduce" : 6,
                "output" : 3
        },
        "ok" : 1
}
```

As you can see, the operation returns the highest closing price for each stock symbol.

Assume that rather than wanting to know the date and highest price, you want to know the day the stock price had the highest change (from opening price to closing price). To do so, you would need to change the map function to return the date and opening and closing prices:

```
var map = function() {
  emit(this.Symbol, { date: this.Date, open: this.Open, close: this.Close});
};
```

Then you would have to change the reduce function to calculate the largest change:

```
reduce = function (key, values) {
  output = { date: "", close: 0 }

  for (i = 0; i < values.length; i++)
     if (values[i].close > output.close)
        {
          output.close = values[i].close;
          output.date = values[i].date;
        }

  return(output);
}
```

When you run the MapReduce process, MongoDB will display the following:

```
> db.Data.mapReduce(map, reduce, { out: { inline:1}});
{
        "results" : [
                {
                        "_id" : "AMZN",
                        "value" : {
                                "date" : "5/3/2019",
                                "open" : 1949,
                                "close" : 2162.46
                        }
                },
                {
                        "_id" : "GOOG",
                        "value" : {
                                "date" : "5/15/2019",
                                "open" : 1117.87,
                                "close" : 1164.21
                        }
                },
                {
                        "_id" : "MSFT",
                        "value" : {
                                "date" : "6/3/2019",
                                "open" : 123.85,
                                "close" : 119.84
```

```
                                }
                        }
                ],
                "timeMillis" : 15,
                "counts" : {
                        "input" : 196,
                        "emit" : 196,
                        "reduce" : 6,
                        "output" : 3
                },
                "ok" : 1
}
```

Again, although these examples were quite simple, they illustrate the MapReduce process using MongoDB.

## Apache HBase

Throughout this text you have examined several different SQL and NoSQL databases. If you are working with big data and need to work with very large tables (billions of rows by millions of columns), you should consider Apache HBase, an open-source NoSQL database. To achieve support for such large tables, HBase runs on top of Hadoop. HBase provides an interactive shell, as well as APIs for program integration. For more information on HBase, or to download and install it, visit the HBase website at http://hbase.apache.org, shown in **FIGURE A**.

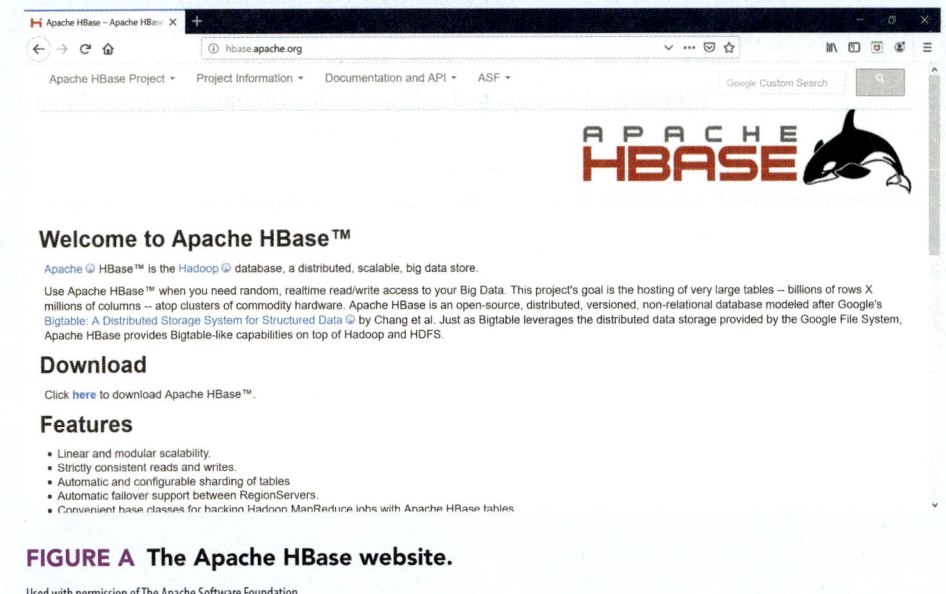

**FIGURE A** The Apache HBase website.

Used with permission of The Apache Software Foundation

## Summary

The amount of total data worldwide doubles nearly every 2 years. Much of this data comes from social media. In the future, much more will come from devices on the IoT.

Most applications, from operating systems to Excel or a database, have a maximum amount of data they can handle. Big data is data that is larger in size than traditional software applications can handle. Users and developers express the size of data in terms of bytes, kilobytes, megabytes, and so on. In general, you can determine the exact number of bytes a category of data can store by raising the value 1,024 to the category's corresponding value:

- Byte = $1,024^0$ byte or $2^0$ bytes
- Kilobyte = $1,024^1$ bytes or $2^{10}$ bytes
- Megabyte = $1,024^2$ bytes or $2^{20}$ bytes
- Gigabyte = $1,024^3$ bytes or $2^{30}$ bytes
- Terabyte = $1,024^4$ bytes or $2^{40}$ bytes
- Exabyte = $1,024^5$ bytes or $2^{50}$ bytes
- Petabyte = $1,024^6$ bytes or $2^{60}$ bytes
- Zettabyte = $1,024^7$ bytes or $2^{70}$ bytes
- Yottabyte = $1,024^8$ bytes or $2^{80}$ bytes

Within an operating system, special software called the file system creates, writes, reads, and manages files. Like applications, file systems have a maximum file size they can store. To store very large files, specialized file systems have been created that store files across multiple systems, with the most commonly used distributed file system being HDFS. HDFS stores large files across nodes, which comprise a cluster. HDFS uses a master/slave model within which the slave stores data and the master tracks upon which systems the data are stored. When a data request arrives, the master node redirects the request to the correct node. To reduce the overhead of transferring large amounts of data across a network, Hadoop uses a model that does not bring data to the process, but rather, brings the processing to be performed to the data nodes. To analyze big data, Hadoop uses a two-step MapReduce process. During the Map phase, a function maps (specifies) the desired data, and during the Reduce phase, a function reduces matching data down to the desired result. Hadoop is more than the HDFS, however. It also provides the framework that distributes and coordinates the processing across the nodes, which they perform in parallel.

## Key Terms

Big data
Byte
Cluster
Exabyte (EB)
Gigabyte (GB)
Hadoop

Hadoop Distributed File
  System (HDFS)
Internet of Things (IoT)
Kilobyte (KB)
MapReduce
Megabyte (MB)

Petabyte (PB)
Terabyte (TB)
Yottabyte (YB)
Zettabyte (ZB)

## Review

1. Define and describe big data. Identify sources of big data.
2. Define the following and try to include an example that represents the amount of data in a form meaningful to a user:
   a. Byte
   b. Kilobyte
   c. Megabyte
   d. Gigabyte
   e. Terabyte
   f. Exabyte
   g. Petabyte
   h. Zettabyte
   i. Yottabyte
3. Define and describe HDFS.
4. Describe the MapReduce process.
5. Using Python, create simple Map and Reduce scripts that calculate the average stock price for the stock symbol MSFT. You can download the data file from this text's catalog page at go.jblearning.com/DataMining.
6. Using MongoDB create a simple MapReduce application that calculates the average stock price for the stock symbol MSFT. You can download the data file from this text's catalog page at go.jblearning.com/DataMining.
7. Describe the four (or five) V's of big data.

# CHAPTER 16

# Planning and Launching a Data-Mining and Data-Analytics Project

## Chapter Goals and Objectives

- Define and describe data governance.
- Describe and calculate a return on investment (ROI).
- Describe and perform a SWOT analysis.
- Define and describe the PDCA process.

Throughout this text, you have examined many data-mining and data-analytics operations. If someone asks you to cleanse data, create a predictive model, and cluster related data, you know your approach and how to technically achieve it. That said, many organizations are new to data mining and data analytics, and beyond their initial efforts, most organizations are, at best, still performing such operations on a one-off or ad hoc process.

Companies that become successful with data analytics will put together and deploy a formal data plan. This chapter presumes that because you may now have the most data-analytic and data-mining knowledge and skills in your company, you will be asked to lead the company's data projects. To help you get started, this chapter addresses key issues you should consider and recommends practices you should implement. By the time you finish this chapter, you will understand the following key concepts:

- Regardless of the type of data-analytic project you are considering, the steps you will perform to get started will be similar.
- Each data-analytic project should begin with the question: "What do we want to show?"
- If you do not have one in place, you should form a data governance board very early in your project. The data governance board should approve and prioritize data projects, should ensure solid data processes (such as backups, disaster recovery, and security) are in place, and should continually strive to improve the quality of data.
- As you start a data-analytics project, make sure you identify the data owner who has ultimate responsibility and decision-making for the data, as well as the data custodian, who will implement and secure the data operations.
- Regardless of the type and source of your data, you can normally leverage the same set of questions to drill down into the facts you must know about the data.
- Data security is always a key aspect of any project. **Role-based security** is an effective security approach for most projects. With role-based security, you map users to specific roles (such as administrator, power user, user, and report/visualization creator). Then you will specify the access and capabilities each role needs.
- During the initial stages of most data projects, decisions must be made with respect to the location of the data (on-premise, cloud, or in a managed service), the underlying storage mechanism (SQL or NoSQL), the tools you will use to manipulate and visualize the data, and so on. To determine the best choices for such decisions, analysts often perform a Strengths, Weaknesses, Opportunities, and Threats (**SWOT**) analysis.
- All data projects require time, people, resources, and money. As such, you should create a business case for each project that justifies the project's implementation. Within the business case, you will normally include a return-on-investment (**ROI**) analysis.
- After implementing a data-analytics project, you should evaluate your solution to see if valuable improvements can be made. Analysts often use the Plan, Do, Check, and Act (**PDCA**) methodology to perform such evaluations.

## Creating an Enterprise Data Ecosystem

Integrating data solutions into an organization is a big undertaking, which, as shown in **FIGURE 16.1**, includes many key concepts.

The sections that follow will drill into each of these considerations in detail.

## Defining Your Data Goal

As you can imagine, trying to tackle all the data-related tasks previously shown in Figure 16.1 is a daunting exercise, with many risks and opportunities for failure. Further, such tasks will require people and budgets. As an early step in the data-planning process, therefore, you

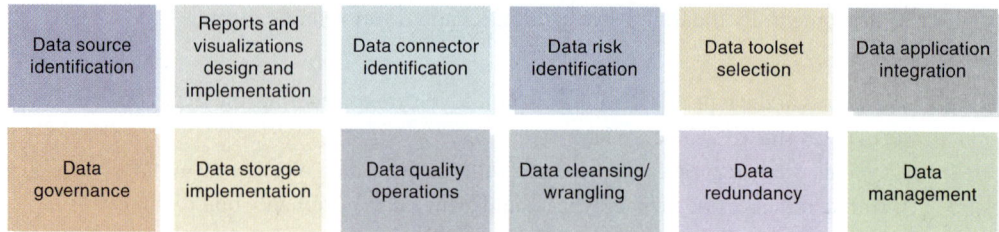

**FIGURE 16.1** Issues to consider when integrating a data solution.

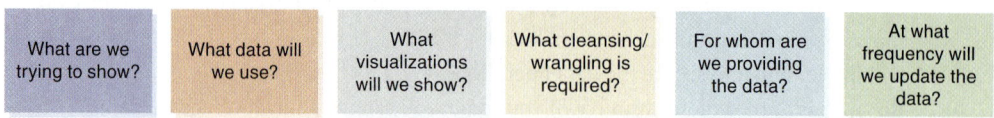

**FIGURE 16.2** Defining the question the data project is trying to answer.

should identify specific goals from which you can build a business case and justification for the implementation.

Data analysts often refer to this process as identifying the question: "What do we want to show?" phase, as shown in **FIGURE 16.2**.

## Establishing a Data Governance Board

As you learned in Chapter 8, "Data Preprocessing and Cleaning," a data governance board oversees all aspects of data with the goal of continually improving the quality of data across the organization. Your data governance board should be represented by members from across the organization. To start, you should identify your organization's key data buckets, similar to those shown in **FIGURE 16.3**.

Using the data buckets as your guide, you can identify data users, stakeholders, and custodians, which Chapter 8 defines as follows:

- Data custodian: A technical expert who administers and manages the data. The data custodian would implement the tables (or, in the case of NoSQL, the collections) that store the data. The data custodian might implement the queries, stored procedures, and database solutions that implement the business rules and security controls.
- Data owner: Often an executive who oversees the business unit associated with the data. The data owner serves as the final arbitrator and decision maker for issues that affect the data. However, he or she would not play a day-to-day, hands-on role with the data.
- Data stakeholder: An individual or group with interest in data quality and the data process.

Creating an effective data governance board takes time and should be a constantly maturing process. Common operations the board will perform include:

- Ensuring the continual improvement of data quality.
- Approving and prioritizing data projects.

# Identifying and Accessing Key Data Sources

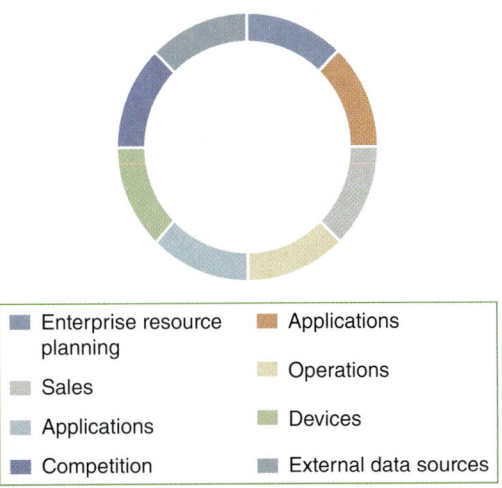

**FIGURE 16.3 Common organizational data buckets.**

- Auditing and verifying data, data quality, and data controls.
- Ensuring data safeguards (backups, replication, and disaster recovery) are in place.
- Championing data operations.

## Identifying and Accessing Key Data Sources

Depending on your project, you may receive data from a variety of sources, as shown in **FIGURE 16.4**. For each data source, you should identify the following:

- How do we access the data (database connection, Excel file upload, flat file read, and so on)?
- Do the data have existing access controls that require authentication (username, password, and connection string information)?
- Do we pay to acquire and store the data?
- Do we perform any cleansing of the data or transformations on the data?
- Do we have any assessment of the data quality?
- Who are the data owner and the data custodian?
- What is the size of the data?
- Is there a data schema?
- Do any models exist for the data?
- Where will the data reside?
- How will we report, visualize, and interact with the data?
- Do any of our applications consume the data?
- How will we store the data (SQL or NoSQL)?

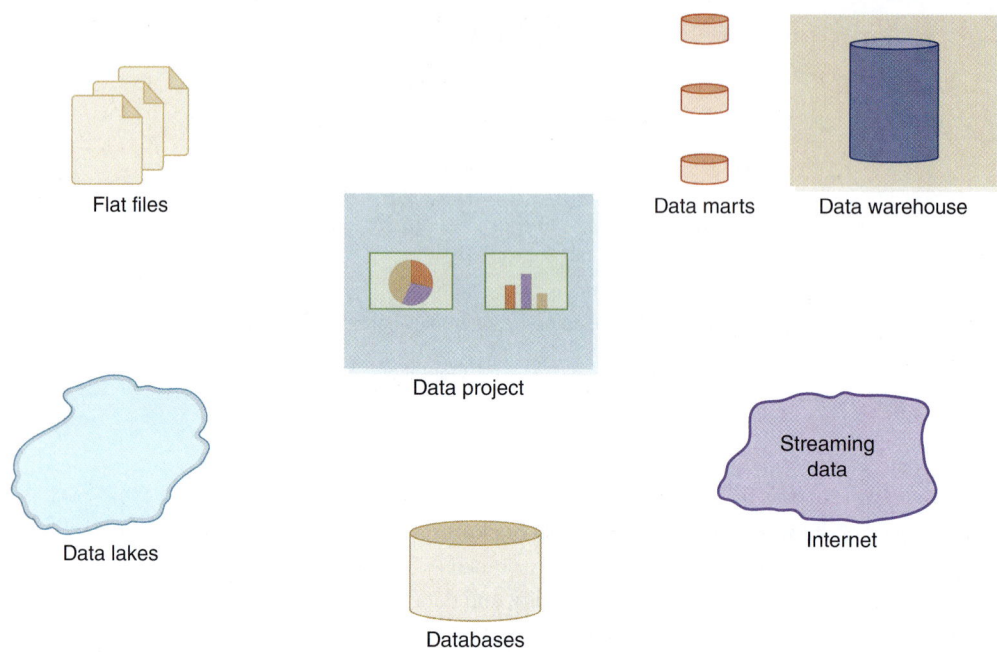

**FIGURE 16.4 Common data sources.**

## Establishing Data Quality Expectations

As discussed in Chapter 8, quality is a measure of the data's suitability for use. Data analysts often measure quality in terms of the following factors:

- Accuracy: The degree to which the data correctly represent the underlying real-world values, such as all temperatures from a sensor in the correct range.
- Completeness: The degree to which the data represent all required values, such as a data set that should contain an hour of data, for a sensor that reports every second, having 100% of the data values.
- Consistency: The degree to which similar or related data values align throughout the data set, such as each occurrence of an address having the same zip code.
- Conformity: The degree to which the data values align with the company's business rules, such as the company will measure and store sensor values in one-second intervals.

As you start a data project, you may not yet have measures you can use to determine data quality. You should, however, identify your plan to do so in the future:

- How will you measure the data-quality metrics?
- What key performance indicators (KPIs) relate to your quality metrics?
- How will you track and communicate the quality metrics?

# Identifying Your Data Toolsets

In order to establish a budget, as well as to ensure you have the tools you or others will need to perform data-analytic operations, you should first identify the data operations you expect to perform:

- Data storage (what database will store your data)
- Extract, transform, and load operations
- Visualization
- Reporting
- Exploration and mining
- Dashboards
- Applications
- Machine learning
- Ad hoc queries

Next, estimate the number of users who will perform the different tasks. With your lists in hand, you can then evaluate your purchasing options, such as buying desktop solutions, downloading open-source solutions, or using cloud-based Software-as-a-Service (SaaS) tools.

## On-Premise, Cloud, or Managed Services

Years ago, to perform data analytics, you would spin up one or more on-premise databases. Today, a cost-effective and fast way to get up and running with a scalable data store is to leverage cloud-based managed services in a pay-as-you-go environment. Throughout this text, you have seen managed services for SQL, MongoDB, and even Hadoop for big data.

Depending on your staffing and skillsets, you may find that using a managed service is not only cost-effective but also lets you focus your time on performing analytics and providing solutions as opposed to administering systems.

# Identifying Security Considerations

Depending on the data you must store, the security steps you must perform will vary. For example, if you have HIPAA-based healthcare information or PCI-based credit card data, your security focus will significantly increase. That said, regardless of the security levels you require, you will normally establish user roles, such as administrator, power user, user, and so on, and determine the level of access each requires. Then, you can implement role-based access controls (RBAC) to define the roles and access capabilities of each.

## Identifying Data Controls and Logging

By establishing role-based security controls, you provide a solid foundation from which you can continue to expand your data security. A database administrator, for example, can access (read, update, and delete) all system data. To prevent potential data misuse, you will want to define additional controls and logging (which records who has accessed the data and how). Such controls are your data safeguards, and your logs provide auditing transparency to confirm the controls are effective and working.

## Creating a "SMART" Approach

As you begin to define your data approaches, you should leverage the **SMART** acronym to assess your plan:

- Specific: Many data-analytic projects fail because they are too large from the start. A better approach is to start with a well-defined target better suited for success and from which you can learn and later build upon.
- Measurable: The adage "If you can't measure it, you can't manage it" applies to data projects. Clearly define measurable goals, which might include:
  - A specific budget amount
  - The specific deliverables, such as three dashboards that include specific visualizations
  - Your expected level of quality, such as 95%
- Achievable: Do you have the resources and time to complete the project as scheduled? If you cannot deliver the solution, the rest does not matter.
- Realistic: Do you have the time, people, skills, and knowledge to complete the project?
- Time-based: Specify the dates by which will you provide certain deliverables. A project without time-based deliverables is destined to fail.

## Making Your Business Case

Regardless of whether you choose open-source tools, pay-as-you-go managed services, or a high-end enterprise solution, a data-analytics project takes time, people, and money. **FIGURE 16.5** illustrates many common budget factors associated with a data project.

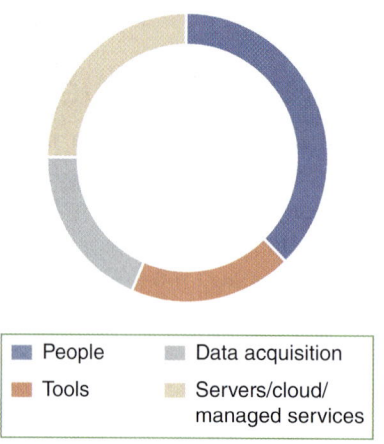

**FIGURE 16.5** Common budget factors for a data project.

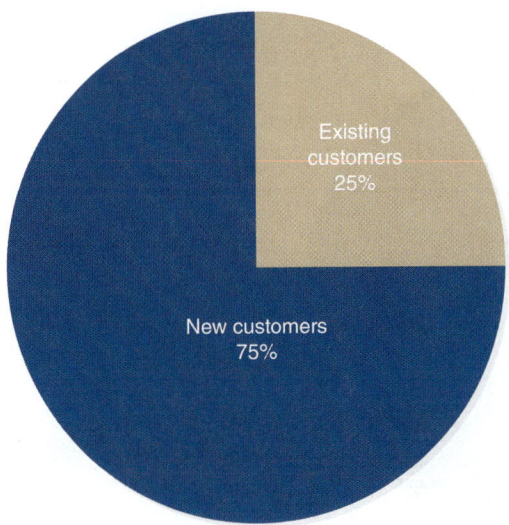

**FIGURE 16.6  Current company sales.**

As you have learned, a data-analytics project should begin with, and be driven, by the question:

What do we want to show?

With your question in hand, you can then ask the question:

What is the value of showing it?

Assume, for example, that your company sales is $1 million, with 75% of the sales coming from new customers and 25% coming from existing customer reorders, as shown in **FIGURE 16.6**.

Your company's vice president of sales has expressed the fact that acquiring new customers is expensive and that it makes sense to better leverage the existing customer base. She estimates that the company can easily increase reorder sales by 20% this year, growing reorder sales from $250,000 to $300,000. She has come to you requesting a data-analytics project to better understand the existing customer base. Knowing you will ask the "What do we want to show?" question, she tells you:

We want to show how we can get our existing customers to reorder more.

Although not perfect, you at least have a starting question. By applying the SMART acronym, you can create a series of specific questions:

- Who is reordering products?
  - Gender
  - Age
  - Location
- How soon after ordering do they reorder?
- Do they reorder more than once?

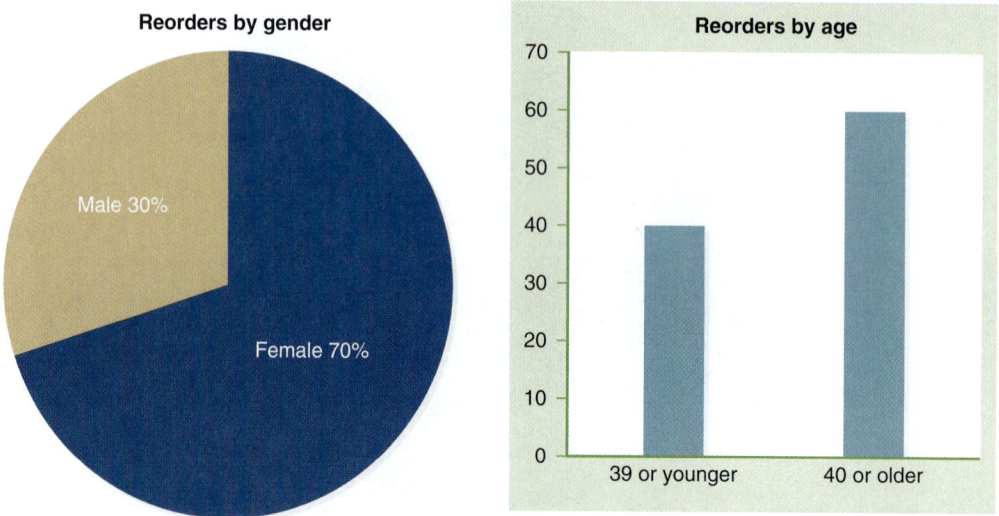

**FIGURE 16.7 Possible visuals to represent customer reorders.**

After your sales VP approves and possibly prioritizes your questions, you can determine the visuals you might use to represent each, as shown in **FIGURE 16.7**.

Next, you can estimate your costs to produce such a dashboard:

| | | |
|---|---|---|
| Dashboard Design and Implementation | 80 hours at $50 an hour | $4,000 |
| Power BI | Free | $0 |
| ETL Operations | 20 hours at $50 an hour | $1,000 |
| Data-Analytics Server | | $5,000 |
| Total | | $10,000 |

Business people often use the ROI metric to determine whether they should pursue an opportunity. To calculate the ROI, you divide the potential gain by the cost:

$$\text{Return on Investment} = \text{Gain}/\text{Cost} \times 100$$

For your sales dashboard, the ROI would become:

$$\text{ROI} = 50{,}000/10{,}000 \times 100$$

$$\text{ROI} = 500$$

In this case, your management team would eagerly approve your project.

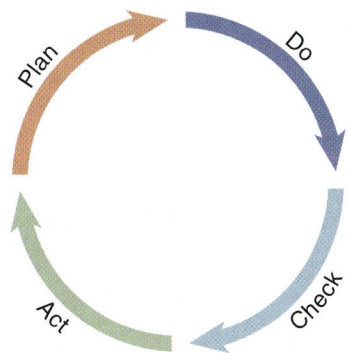

**FIGURE 16.8** Using PDCA to review and improve a solution or process.

# Applying Plan, Do, Check, and Act

You have learned that the data governance board exists to ensure the quality of your data is continually improving. In a similar way, as you create and deploy data-analytics projects, you should have a plan to evaluate and improve upon your solutions. A good process to follow is the PDCA methodology, which, as shown in **FIGURE 16.8**, is an iterative process that leads to regular review and improvement.

With each PDCA iteration, you should identify potential opportunities and then leverage a metric such as ROI to determine whether you should proceed with the improvement.

# Leveraging SWOT Analysis

As you plan for your data-analytics project, you will need to make a variety of decisions:

- Should data be stored on-premise, in the cloud, or within a managed-service solution?
- Which visualization tool should you use?
- Should data reside within an SQL or NoSQL database?
- And more.

To approach such questions, you should leverage a SWOT analysis, which measures each alternative's strengths, weaknesses, opportunities, and threats. **FIGURE 16.9**, for example, shows SWOT diagrams for on-premise, cloud, and managed service implementations.

# Strive to Deliver Self-Service Solutions That Empower Others

When you roll out your data-analytics solution, your first step will often answer the questions asked:

- Who is reordering products?
  - Gender: 70% of reorders are female, and 30% are male.

|  | On-premise | | Cloud | | Managed service | |
|---|---|---|---|---|---|---|
| **Strengths** | **Weaknesses** | **Strengths** | **Weaknesses** | **Strengths** | **Weaknesses** |
| • Hands-on management<br>• Speed of applying changes | • Admin skill set<br>• Cost | • Hands-on management<br>• Speed of applying changes and spin up | • On-going monthly costs | • Speed of applying changes and spin up<br>• No administration | • On-going monthly costs |
| **Opportunities** | **Threats** | **Opportunities** | **Threats** | **Opportunities** | **Threats** |
| • Leverage team to administer other projects | • Scalability | • Admin staff reduction or reassignment | • Security concerns | • Admin staff reduction or reassignment | • Security concerns |

**FIGURE 16.9** Using SWOT analysis to evaluate alternatives.

- Age: 60% of reorders come from users age 40 or older.
- Location: 35% of reorders come from the west, 25% from the south, 15% from the east, and 25% from the north.

▸ How soon after ordering do they reorder? 75% of reorders occur after 6 months and 25% in the first 6 months.
▸ Do they reorder more than once? 50% reorder more than once.

A better approach, however, is to provide a self-service solution that others can use to find answers themselves. You might, for example, create a visual dashboard that provides clickable metrics that allow users to drill deeper into data without having to know how to perform query operations. As you design your solutions, ask yourself how you can provide users with self-service capabilities.

# Hands-On: Documenting Projects Using Jupyter Notebook

As you work with data stakeholders, owners, custodians, developers, and the data governance board, you will need to document your work. Jupyter Notebook is a Python-based documentation tool you can use to create documents that contain text, source code, and visualizations, as shown in **FIGURE 16.10**.

What makes a Jupyter Notebook document unique is that your documents are live, meaning that if you change the source code it contains, you can run that source code within the document, and related visualizations will automatically update. Jupyter Notebook is not only good for documenting your completed project, but you can use it to present proofs of concepts to stakeholders and even to create tutorials.

You can use many different programming languages within Jupyter Notebook. After you create your document, you can save and easily share using email, a shared file folder, or even GitHub.

Depending on the Python version you are running, you may already have Jupyter Notebook installed on your system. If not, you can find installation specifics at the Jupyter Notebook website (http://jupyter.org), as shown in **FIGURE 16.11**.

# Hands-On Documenting Projects Using Jupyter Notebook

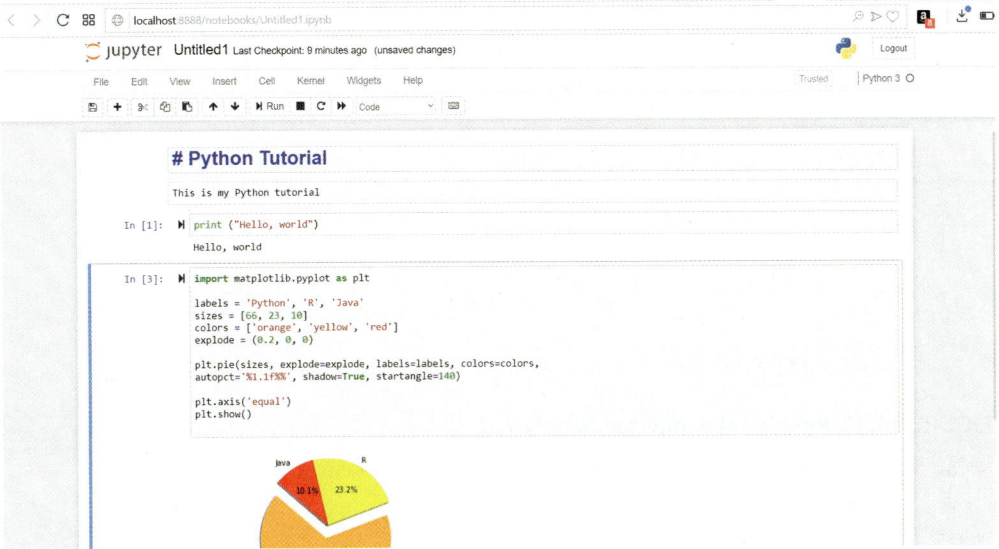

**FIGURE 16.10** Using Jupyter Notebook to document a data-analytics project.

Used with permission of Project Jupyter

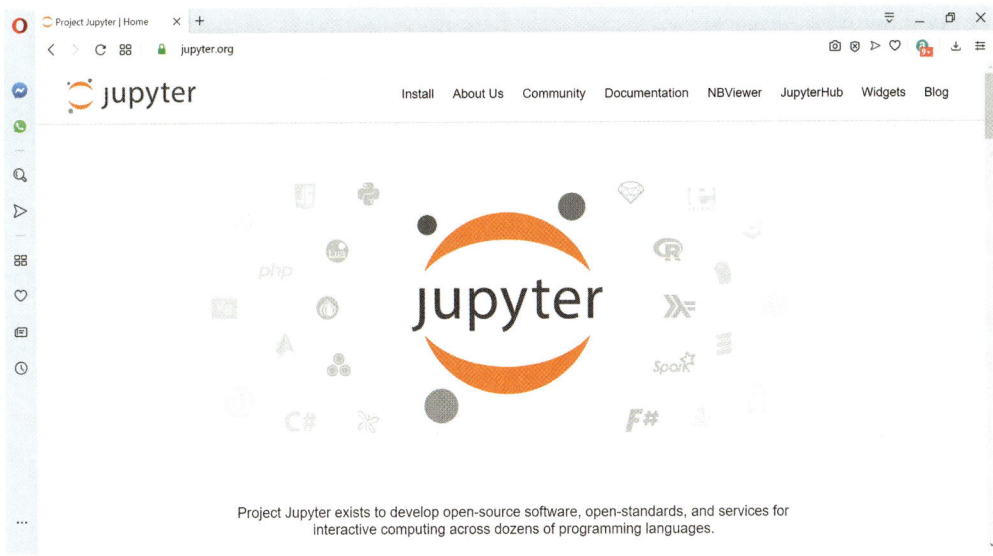

**FIGURE 16.11** The Jupyter Notebook website.

Used with permission of Project Jupyter

# CHAPTER 16 Planning and Launching a Data-Mining and Data-Analytics Project

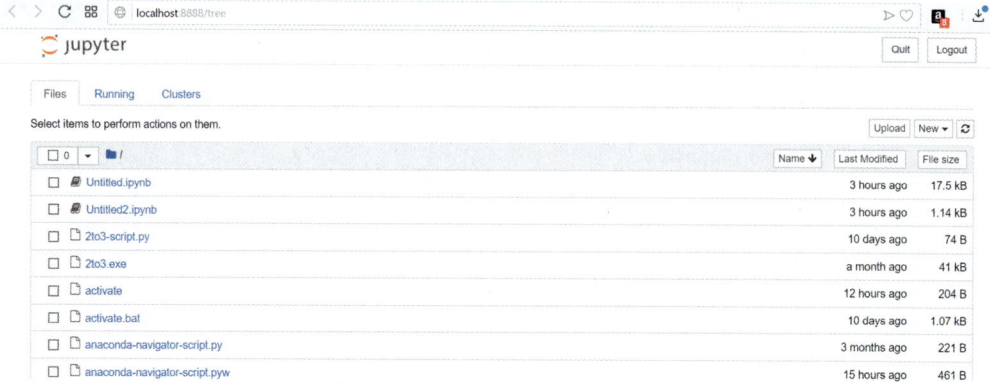

**FIGURE 16.12** Running the Jupyter Notebook.

Used with permission of Project Jupyter

To start Jupyter Notebook, run the following command:

C:\> Jupyter Notebook

Jupyter Notebook, in turn, will start its server (which runs at localhost:8888) and will open a browser window within which you will create and edit your notebooks, as shown in **FIGURE 16.12**.

Within Jupyter Notebook, create a new notebook. Jupyter Notebook will display a blank notebook as shown in **FIGURE 16.13**.

Within the cell, type:

Python Tutorial

Use the toolbar pull-down menu to change the cell from code to a heading. Jupyter Notebook will display the heading as shown in **FIGURE 16.14**.

Next, insert a new cell and type:

This is my Python tutorial

Use the toolbar pull-down menu to change the cell to Markdown. Jupyter Notebook will display your text as shown in **FIGURE 16.15**.

Insert a new cell and type:

```
print ("Hello, world")
```
Insert your final cell and insert the following code:

```
import matplotlib.pyplot as plt

labels = 'Python', 'R', 'Java'
sizes = [66, 23, 10]
colors = ['orange', 'yellow', 'red']
explode = (0.2, 0, 0)
```

# Hands-On Documenting Projects Using Jupyter Notebook 641

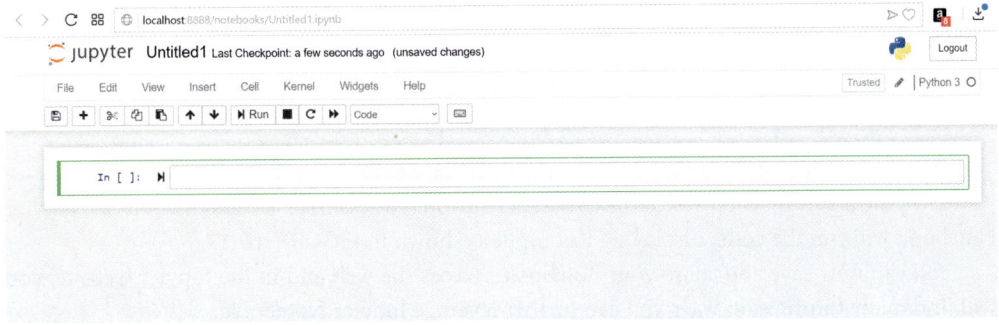

**FIGURE 16.13** A blank Jupyter Notebook.
Used with permission of Project Jupyter

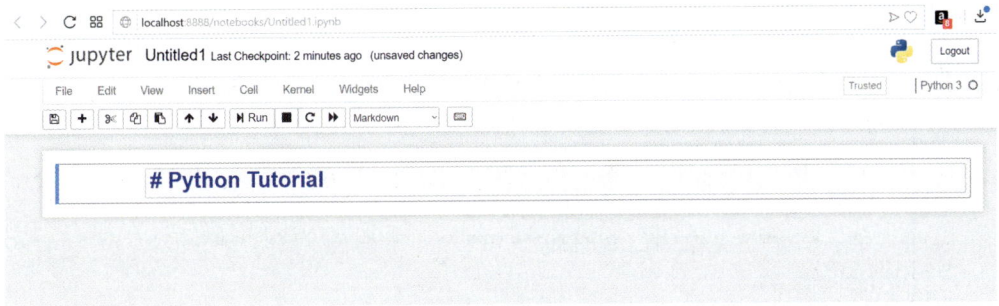

**FIGURE 16.14** Adding a heading to a notebook.
Used with permission of Project Jupyter

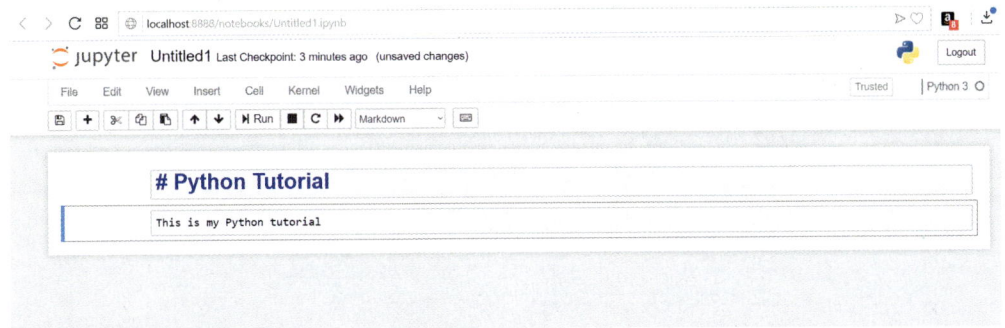

**FIGURE 16.15** Adding text to a notebook.
Used with permission of Project Jupyter

```
plt.pie(sizes, explode=explode, labels=labels, colors=colors,
autopct='%1.1f%%', shadow=True, startangle=140)

plt.axis('equal')
plt.show()
```

Your notebook should appear as shown in **FIGURE 16.16**.

Click the arrow that appears to the left of each of your code cells (the cell's run button). Jupyter Notebook will run the code, displaying its output as shown in **FIGURE 16.17**.

You can now save and share your notebook. Across the web and in the Jupyter website, you will find many tutorials on ways you can further leverage Jupyter Notebook.

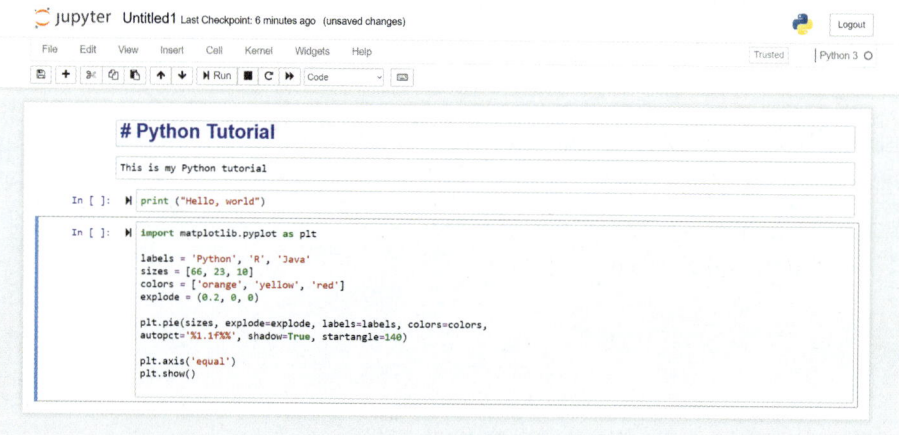

**FIGURE 16.16** Adding code to notebook.

Used with permission of Project Jupyter

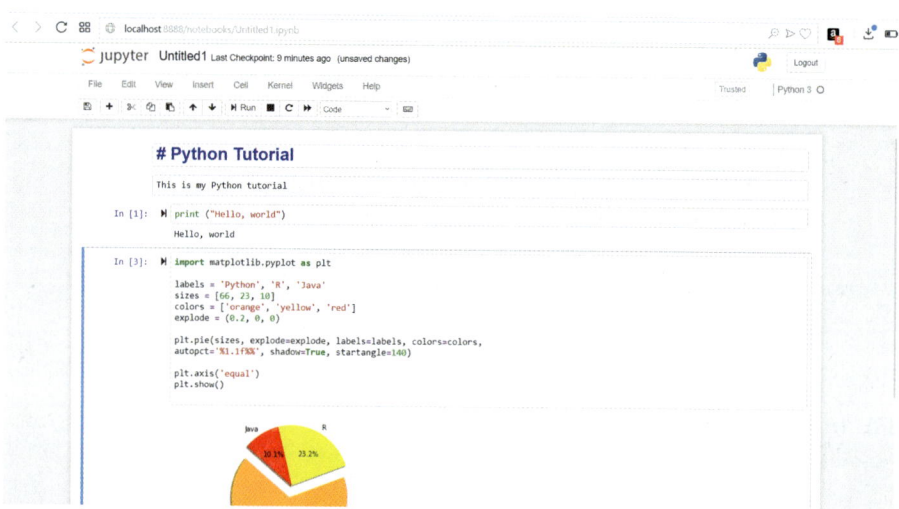

**FIGURE 16.17** Running code within Jupyter Notebook.

Used with permission of Project Jupyter

## Summary

For over 50 years, computer scientists, programmers, administrators, and project managers have been tasked to complete projects. Despite improvements in project management, better project management tools, and even methodologies such as Agile, over half of all information technology projects fail, are late, or are over budget. This chapter discusses many factors you should consider when you initiate data-analytics projects.

To start, make sure you have a well-defined answer to the question:

> What do we want to show?

Using the SMART (Specific, Measurable, Achievable, Realistic, and Time-based) metric, you can improve the question's quality.

When you are designing a new data-analytics project, there will be many unknowns, new things that pop up, and unexpected delays. You should plan for such events and decompose your project into a phased collection of more feasible projects. Meaning, don't try to implement everything at once—but rather plan for incremental success. With each phase, you should leverage the PDCA methodology to determine if there are opportunities for future additional value.

## Key Terms

Plan, Do, Act, and Change (PDCA)
Return on Investment (ROI)
Role-based security
SMART (Specific, Measurable, Achievable, Realistic, and Time-based)
Strengths, Weakness, Opportunities, and Threats (SWOT)

## Review

1. Describe common tasks and responsibilities of the data governance board.
2. Perform a SWOT analysis that provides insight into whether you should choose the R or Python programming language as your data-analytics programming tool.
3. Assume you are asked to use census data to create a dashboard for potential healthcare customers. List the questions you would ask about the data source.
4. Describe role-based security and how you would use it for a data-analytics project.
5. Describe the SMART acronym and how and when you might use it.
6. Assume a computer company can increase the price at which it sells computers by $5 a system by adding a $3 memory chip. What is the potential ROI?
7. Describe how you would use the Plan, Do, Check, and Act methodology for a new business intelligence dashboard.
8. Using Jupyter Notebook, create the notebook presented in the Hands-On section of this chapter.

# GLOSSARY

**Agglomerative:** A synonym for merging. A hierarchical clustering algorithm is agglomerative in that it merges related clusters to form a larger cluster.

**Aggregate:** A group. Structured Query Language (SQL) provides several aggregation queries that group values. SQL also provides aggregation functions, such as COUNT, SUM, and AVG, which perform operations on a group of records.

**Antecedent:** Something that existed before another. In the case of market-basket analysis, the antecedent corresponds to an item that existed in the cart prior to the selection of another.

**API:** An acronym for application programming interface, which describes code (often a library) a program can call (use) to accomplish a specific task. To create charts, Python programmers use the plot.ly API.

**Area chart:** A chart, similar to a line chart, that represents how values change over time. The area chart fills the area under the line that connects the data points with a solid color.

**Arithmetic mean:** The sum of the data values divided by the number of values

$$\text{Average} = \frac{\sum_{i=1}^{n} x_i}{n}$$

**Arithmetic operator:** Within a programming language, an arithmetic operator is a symbol that represents addition (+), subtraction (−), multiplication (*), division (/), and so on.

**Artificial intelligence:** The science of making intelligent machines that can perceive visual items, recognize voices, make decisions, and more. Machine learning is an application of artificial intelligence.

**Association:** In market-basket analysis, association is the process of relationships between variables, such as identifying items that a customer frequently purchases together, such as diapers and beer.

**Bar chart:** A chart that represents data using horizontal bars, the lengths of which are proportional to the underlying data value.

**Bayes Theorem:** A theorem that produces a probability based upon known or related events.

**Big data:** The term to describe a data set the size of which exceeds the amount of data with which our common applications can work.

**Binary classification:** A classification that assigns data to one of two classes, such as a loan being approved or disapproved.

**Box and whiskers chart:** A chart that represents data quartiles (Q1, Q2, and Q3)—which are based on the data set's media value. Within the chart, the box groups the values from Q1 to Q3, and the whiskers that protrude from the box group the majority (often 96%) of the remaining values. The 2% of values not included on each end are often considered outliers.

**Bubble chart:** A chart that represents three dimensions of data using x and y coordinates and the size of the bubble, which is proportional to the underlying data value.

**Business intelligence:** The use of tools (data mining, machine learning, and visualization) to convert data into actionable business insights and recommendations.

**Business rule:** Defines or constrains a specific business operational process. A business rule, for example, might specify that employee overtime cannot exceed 10 hours per week.

**Byte:** The amount of data required to store an ASCII character: $1,024^0$ bytes.

**Candlestick chart:** A chart used for financial data that represents a stock's open, close, high, and low values, with the color of the box representing whether the stock closed positive or negative.

**Cardinality:** With respect to database entities, describes a relationship type. Common cardinalities include one-to-one, one-to-many, and many-to-many.

**Category-based comparison chart:** A chart that represents how two or more categories of values compare. Common category-based comparison charts include bar charts and column charts.

**Centroid:** The center of a cluster. The centroid does not have to correspond to a data point within the data set.

**Classification:** A supervised machine-learning solution that assigns data items to specific categories.

**Cluster:** In database management, a cluster is a collection of notes within a distributed database. In data mining, a cluster is a group of related data.

**Clustering:** The process of grouping related data. Clustering is an unsupervised learning process in that it works with unlabeled data.

**Collection:** A group of documents within a NoSQL database, similar to a table within a relational database.

**Column chart:** A chart that represents data using vertical bars, the lengths of which are proportional to the underlying data value.

**Combo chart:** A chart that combines a bar chart with a line chart, often for comparative purposes.

**Comma-delimited file:** A field that contains field values separated by commas. Database developers often use comma-delimited files, also called comma-separated (CSV) files, to move data between a database and an application, such as a spreadsheet.

**Compiler:** A program that examines a source code file for syntax errors and, if none exist, creates an executable file.

**Composition chart:** A chart that represents how one or more values relate to a larger whole. Common composition charts include pie charts and sunburst charts.

**Computer vision:** The ability for a software application to analyze and understand images.

**Conceptual model:** A high-level database model that shows the entities that make up a system and their relationships, but not the attributes that make up the entities.

**Conditional formatting:** The process of highlighting (using fonts and colors) cells in a spreadsheet that satisfy a specific condition.

**Conditional processing:** In programming, conditional processing identifies a set of instructions (statements) a program executes when a specified condition is true or false. The Python and R programming languages implement conditional processing using an if-else statement.

**Confidence:** In market-basket analysis, confidence compares the number of times the pair was purchased to the number of times one of the items in the pair was purchased.

**Confidence interval:** A range of values between which the probability of a value falling into the range is defined as the confidence interval.

**Consequent:** Something that occurred based on the presence of another. In the case of market-basket analysis, the consequent is the item that a customer places in the cart based on the presence of another item—the antecedent.

**Conviction:** In market-basket analysis, conviction is a measure that examines the frequency with which a consequent occurs in spite of the absence of the antecedent.

**Correlation:** A measure that shows the relationship between two variables. Variables with a correlation approaching 1 have a strong correlation—as you increase the value of one of the variables, the value of the second will also increase. Likewise, if you decrease the value of one of the variables, the value of the second will decrease. Variables with a correlation approaching −1 are inversely correlated. As you increase the value of one variable, the other variable's value will decrease. Variables with a correlation approaching 0 are not correlated.

**Correlation chart:** A chart that represents how two or more variables relate. A common correlation chart is the scatter chart.

**Covariance:** A measure of similarity between two variables. If the large values of one variable align with the large values of a second variable, the covariance is positive. If instead, the large values of one variable align with the small values of the other variable, the covariance is negative.

**Cross join:** A join operation that returns a row for each combination of a field in the right table combined with a field in the left table.

**Crow's foot:** Within an entity relationship diagram, a crow's foot is a symbol used to represent a "many" relationship (such as one-to-many). The symbol is so named because it resembles the shape a crow's foot might leave in dirt as the crow walks across it.

**CRUD:** An acronym for create, read, update, and delete, which correspond to common database operations. Structured Query Language (SQL) and MongoDB provide specific queries for each of these operations.

**Dashboard:** A visual (and often interactive) collection of charts and graphs that correspond to the metrics for a business's key performance indicators.

**Dashboard chart:** A chart that represents key performance indicators (KPIs) that companies use to track initiatives. Common dashboard charts include the gauge chart and calendar chart.

**Data accuracy:** The degree to which data correctly represent underlying real-world values.

**Data anomalies:** Inconsistencies that occur within data due to duplicate or unnormalized data. Data anomalies normally occur during insert, update, or delete operations.

**Data association:** The process of identifying relationships between variables. A well-known data association problem is market-basket analysis for which the items in a customer's shopping cart are examined in order to determine relationships between the items that influence the shopper's behavior.

**Data cleansing:** The process of detecting, correcting, and removing errors and inconsistencies from data.

**Data completeness:** The degree to which data represent all required values.

**Data conformity:** The degree to which data values align with business rules.

**Data consistency:** The degree to which similar or related values align throughout the data set.

**Data custodian:** A technical expert who administers and manages the data. The data custodian would implement the tables (or, in the case of NoSQL, the collections) that store the data. The data custodian might implement the queries, stored procedures, and database solutions that implement the business rules and security controls.

**Data integrity:** The degree to which data are accurate, complete, and truly representative of the real-world data.

**Data lake:** A collection of data outside of a database stored in a more natural form, such as a binary or text file.

**Data mart:** A specialized data warehouse that contains information for a specific group, such as sales or manufacturing.

**Data munging:** A synonym for data wrangling—the steps a database developer performs to transform and cleanse data.

**Data owner:** Often an executive who oversees the business unit associated with the data. The data owner serves as the final arbitrator and decision maker for issues that affect the data. He or she, however, would not play a day-to-day, hands-on role with the data.

**Data quality:** The measure of data's suitability for use.

**Data steward:** An individual who makes the day-to-day decisions for the data with respect to quality, content, and metadata. The data steward has great knowledge of the data, its producers and consumers, and the business rules that guide data operations.

**Data timeliness:** The degree to which data arrive in a favorable time frame.

**Data validity:** The degree to which data are logically correct.

**Data visualization:** The process of using charts and graphs (visuals) to represent data.

**Data warehouse:** A database optimized for reporting, decision support, and other analytical operations.

**Data wrangling:** The steps a database developer performs to transform and cleanse data.

**Database:** A collection of data organized within a database management system (DBMS) for fast storage and retrieval.

**DBMS:** An acronym for database management system—the software that surrounds and operates the database. Common DBMS software includes Oracle, Microsoft SQL, and MySQL, as well as NoSQL DBMS software such as MongoDB.

**DBSCAN:** An acronym for density-based spatial clustering of applications with noise. The DBSCAN clustering algorithm creates clusters by grouping points based on their proximity to dense regions within the data's coordinate space.

**Decision tree:** A graph-based data structure that contains decision points. By following paths through the decision points, a decision tree classifier can determine to which class it should assign data.

**Decision tree classifier:** A classification technique that creates a decision tree, which it applies to assign data to a class.

**Decision tree regression:** A regression technique that produces an expression that relates predictor variables to the dependent variable.

**Deep learning:** A hierarchically structured process that leverages layers of machine learning for which the output of one layer becomes the input to the next.

**Delimiter:** A value used to separate values within a file. Comma delimiters include the comma and tab.

**Dependent variable:** In data classification, the dependent variable is the class to which the algorithm will assign the data.

**Descriptive analytics:** The use of statics and data mining to explain (describe) what happened based on historical data.

**Diff chart:** A chart that compares two data sets by representing the differences between them.

**Distributed database:** A database that runs on multiple servers located (distributed) within a network or the cloud.

**Distribution chart:** A chart that represents the frequency of values within a data set. The common distribution chart is the histogram.

**Document:** A data item within a NoSQL database, similar to a record within a relational database.

**DQAF:** An acronym for data quality assessment framework, a guide that presents 48 factors to consider when measuring data quality.

**Dynamic chart:** A web-based chart, the contents of which update automatically when the underlying data set values change.

**Entity:** A term for a thing or object.

**Entity relationship diagram (ERD):** A drawing that represents the entities (things) that make up a system, along with the relationships between entities.

**ETL:** An acronym for extract, transform, and load. Database developers commonly perform ETL operations. The extract operation retrieves data from one or more database tables. The transform operation changes the data in some way. The load operation stores the transformed data into a different destination.

**Euclidian distance:** The straight-line distance between two points, calculated as follows:

$$\text{distance } (a, b) = \sqrt{(a_1 - b_1)^2 + (a_2 - b_2)^2}$$

**Exabyte (EB):** $1,024^5$ bytes.

**Export:** The process of extracting data from an application or database to another destination.

**Facial recognition:** Analyzing patterns within photos to identify and recognize faces.

**Filter:** A query operation performed on a subset of records based upon a condition specified within a WHERE or HAVING clause.

**Filtering:** The process of displaying only selected values.

**Foreign key:** A field in one table that corresponds to a primary-key field in a different table. Foreign keys exist to support databases' referential integrity. A database enforces many of the same rules for a foreign key that it would for the primary key, such as a foreign key cannot have a NULL value.

**Framework:** A structure (often a document) users can follow to achieve a desired result.

**Funnel chart:** A chart, the shape of which resembles a funnel, for which the top of the funnel represents 100% of the whole and the area of each section below represents the section's underlying value.

**Gauge chart:** A chart that appears similar to a dial on an automobile dashboard that represents a value. Analysts often display gauge charts on a key performance indicator (KPI) dashboard.

**Geochart:** A chart that represents how the values from one location compare to values in a different location.

**Geomap chart:** A chart that includes a map.

**Geometric mean:** An arithmetic mean calculated by taking the product of a group of numbers as opposed to the sum

$$\text{Geometric mean} = \sqrt[n]{x_1 x_2 x_3 \cdots x_n}$$

**Gigabyte (GB):** $1,024^3$ bytes.

**Graph database:** A database designed to store the many relationships an entity may have. Graph databases store entities as nodes and the relationships between entities as edges. Graph databases are NoSQL databases.

**Graphical user interface:** A visual environment within which a user interacts with an application. The MySQL Workbench provides a graphical user interface within which a user can execute SQL queries.

**GUI:** An acronym for graphical user interface. MongoDB provides the Compass GUI.

**Hadoop:** An open-source distributed framework for processing big data.

**Hard clustering algorithm:** A clustering algorithm that restricts each point to residing in only one cluster.

**Harmonic mean:** The product of the data values divided by the number of values. The harmonic mean may reduce the impact of outliers

$$\text{Harmonic mean} = \frac{n}{\left(1/x_1 + 1/x_2 + 1/x_3 \cdots 1/x_n\right)}$$

**HDFS:** An acronym for Hadoop Distributed File System, a file system that distributes big data files across multiple nodes, which combine to create an HDFS cluster.

**Hierarchical clustering:** An agglomerative clustering algorithm that creates clusters by merging related (nearby) clusters.

**Histogram chart:** A chart that represents a data set's frequency distribution, which shows a count (the frequency) of occurrence of values within defined ranges, called bins.

**Horizontal scaling:** Scaling a database or application across additional servers.

**Image mining:** The application of data-mining techniques to image files. Image mining includes image recognition (computer vision), image clustering, and image classification.

**Import:** The process of loading data into an application or database from another source.

**Index:** A value that points to a specific record used to improve database performance. An index normally contains a field value and a pointer to the corresponding record within a table. To assign an index to a field, database developers use the CREATE INDEX query.

**Inner join:** A join operation that returns rows that include fields from the left and right tables for which the tables have matching values on the specified field.

**Interpreter:** A program that examines a programming language statement for syntax errors and, if none exist, executes the statements. Unlike a compiler that converts an entire source code file into an executable file at one time, an interpreter executes one statement at a time. R and Python use an interpreter.

**IoT:** An acronym for Internet of Things, which describes the collection of billions of devices on the internet.

**Item set:** A collection of items within a market-basket.

**Iterative processing:** In programming, iterative processing identifies a set of instructions (statements) a program executes as long as a specific condition is true. Programmers refer to such statements as a loop. When the condition becomes false, the program continues its execution at the first statement that follows the loop. To implement iterative processing, Python provides the for and while loops, and R provides the for, while, and repeat loops.

**JOIN:** A Structured Query Language (SQL) query operation that temporarily combines two tables based upon a related field.

**JSON:** An acronym for JavaScript Object Notation, a format used to describe an object. NoSQL databases make extensive use of JSON to store data.

**Kilobyte (KB):** $1,024^1$ bytes.

**K-means clustering:** A clustering technique that groups points based on minimizing the average distance of each point from its cluster's center (centroid).

**K-nearest-neighbor classifier:** A data classification technique that assigns data to the class it most closely resembles.

**KPIs:** Key performance indicators—a measurable value that indicates how well a company is achieving a specific business objective. Data KPIs are measures the company can use to determine the effectiveness of their data-quality objectives. Data analysts often display KPIs within a dashboard to make the metrics easily accessible by others.

**Left join:** A join operation that returns the matching rows from the left and right tables, as well as rows from the left table. Structured Query Language (SQL) will assign the null value to fields that do not have matching values in the right table.

**Lift:** In market-basket analysis, lift is the ratio of the actual confidence to the expected confidence. Lift values close to 1 do not show an association, but rather, more likely indicate coincidence.

**Lightweight:** Less overhead.

**Line chart:** A chart that uses line segments to connect data point markers, ideally to better visualize trends.

**Linear regression:** A regression technique that produces a linear equation that represents predictor variables to the dependent variable.

**Logical model:** A database model that represents the things (entities) that make up a system and their relationships. A logical model will include attribute (field) names, but not the underlying field data types.

**Logical operator:** Within a programming language, a logical operator allows programmers to combine two or more conditions. R and Python provide the AND, OR, and NOT logical operators.

**Logistic regression classifier:** A classification algorithm that assigns data to classes by determining the probability that the data belong to a class. Logistic regression classifiers are best suited for binary classification.

**Logit:** A function used in logistic regression that determines the probability that data belong to a class.

**Machine learning:** The use of data pattern recognition algorithms to solve problems. There are two primary forms of machine learning: supervised and unsupervised. In supervised machine learning, the algorithm examines a training data set to learn how to identify patterns. Unsupervised learning, in contrast, does not use a training set.

**Managed database server:** A cloud-based database for which the cloud provider manages the database software, performing the administrative tasks, such as applying updates and patches. A managed database server can also be configured to scale on demand. MongoDB provides the Atlas managed database server.

**MapReduce:** A two-phase process that applications use to perform big data analytics. During phase one, the mapping phase, the code maps (identifies) the data of interest and groups the data based on the key portion of a key–value pair. During the reduction phase, the code aggregates (combines) the results for the reduced groups.

**Marker:** The symbol used to represent a data point on a chart. The market might be a circle, an X, or some other meaningful shape.

**Market-basket analysis:** The process of analyzing items in a shopping cart to determine items that a consumer purchases together, such as diapers and beer.

**Master data:** The key data within a business, such as its customers, vendors, employees, and so on. Using master data management (MDM), database designers and administrators try to have only one definition/schema for these key data.

**Median:** The middle value in a list of sorted numbers.

**Megabyte (MB):** $1{,}024^2$ bytes.

**MLP:** An acronym for multilayer perceptron. The MLP classifier is a neural network solution that uses multiple layers of perceptrons to assign data to groups.

**Module:** In Python, a module is a source file that contains the data structure definitions and functions to perform a specific task.

**Multiclass classification:** A classification that assigns data to one of many classes, such as a wine being a white, red, or rose.

**Multiple linear regression:** A linear regression that produces an equation that relates two or more predictor variables to the dependent variable.

**Naïve Bayes classifier:** A classification technique that assigns data to groups by applying Bayes Theorem to determine the probability that data belong to a class. The classifier is called "naïve" in that it treats each predictor variable as independent.

**Natural-language processing:** The ability of software applications to understand written and spoken words. Amazon Alexa uses natural-language processing.

**Nested query:** A query within another query, such as a SELECT query within an UPDATE query that returns values that tell UPDATE which records to modify. You place the nested query within parentheses. Database developers also refer to a nested query as a subquery.

**Network port:** A numeric value that corresponds to the port that a network application listens to for connections and commands. Web browsers listen to port 80. MySQL, by default, listens to port 3306. The network port follows an Internet Protocol (IP) address or domain name, separated from each with a colon (:), such as 127.0.0.1:3306 or DataMiningAndAnalysis.com:3306.

**Neural network:** A machine learning algorithm that simulates the activities of the brain and nervous system. Behind the scenes, neural networks use mathematical functions (called perceptrons).

**Normalization:** A process of refining a relational database table, often by decomposing data into one or more tables, to achieve specific data conditions that correspond to a normal form. By normalizing database tables, database designers reduce the possibility of data anomalies that occur during insert, update, and delete operations.

**NoSQL:** An acronym for not only SQL. A NoSQL database does not store data within tables, but rather files (often in JavaScript Object Notation [JSON] or Extended Markup Language [XML]) and does not use Structured Query Language (SQL) as its primary query language.

**Object-oriented database:** A database that allows database developers to store and retrieve data using objects.

**OLAP:** An acronym for online analytical processing. A data warehouse that exists for reporting, decision support operations, and other analytics uses OLAP.

**OLTP:** An acronym for online transaction processing. A database that stores and retrieves data that describe a transaction, such as a customer order or an employee timecard update, uses OLTP.

**On-premise server:** A server that resides within a company's local data center.

**OODBMS:** An acronym for object-oriented database management system. A database management system that provides support for storing and retrieving objects and their attributes.

**Operator precedence:** In a programming language, operator precedence specifies the order in which the language will perform arithmetic operations when an expression contains more than one operator. In Python and R, for example, the multiplication operator has a higher precedence than addition, so the language will evaluate the following expression to 17: $2 + 3 \times 5$.

**Outer join:** A join operation that returns the matching rows from the left and right tables, as well as rows from the left or right table, as specified by LEFT OUTER JOIN or RIGHT OUTER JOIN. Structured Query Language (SQL) will assign the null value to fields that do not have matching values in the right table.

**Outlier:** A value that falls outside of the clusters.

**Overfitting data:** With respect to the K-nearest-neighbor's algorithm to classify data, if you specify a value of K that is too small, you may "overfit" the model, meaning the model may start to treat noise or errant data as valid training data.

**Package:** In Python, a package is a directory (folder) of Python module files.

**Pandas:** The library Python developers import into their program that provides data structure definitions and functions for data analytic operations. The pandas library also defines the dataframe object, into which Python programs often load data sets.

**PDCA:** An acronym for Plan, Do, Check, Act—an iterative process of reevaluating a solution or process to determine if solutions can be made.

**Perceptron:** A linear function used in neural networks. Because many problems are not linear, they must be further decomposed into linear models by creating additional layers of perceptrons, creating a multilayer perceptron (MLP) solution.

**Petabyte (PB):** $1,024^6$ bytes.

**Physical model:** A database model that represents the entities that make up a system and their relationships that include each entity's attribute name and data type. Using the physical model, a database developer can quickly create entities using the CREATE TABLE query.

**Pie chart:** A chart that represents 100% of the whole as a circle and the values of the components as proportional slices.

**PIP:** A command-line utility program that Python developers use to download and install packages on their computer.

**Pivot table:** A capability provided by Excel that lets users group data, identify relationships, and format data for reporting.

**Polynomial:** A mathematical expression that consists of variables, coefficients, and exponents.

**Polynomial degree:** The highest exponent within the polynomial.

**Polynomial regression:** A regression technique that produces a polynomial expression that represents the relationships between variables.

**Predictive analytics:** The use of statistics, data mining, and machine learning to analyze historical data to predict what will happen in the future.

**Predictor variable:** A data set value used by a classification algorithm to predict the class to which the data should be assigned.

**Prescriptive analytics:** Within descriptive and predictive analytics, recommends the best choice among available options.

**Primary key:** A field within a database table that uniquely identifies each record. Examples of primary keys include CUSTOMER_ID or ORDER_ID.

**PyPi:** An acronym for Python Package Index, a website that features over 180,000 installable packages.

**Pyramid chart:** A chart, the shape of which resembles a triangle, for which the bottom of the pyramid represents 100% of the whole and the area of each section represents the section's underlying value.

**Quartile:** A number in a sorted list that identifies 25% of the data. The second quartile value is also the median—the number below which 50% of the numbers fall and above which the other 50% reside.

**Query:** A command that directs a database to perform a specific task, such as creating a table or retrieving specific records from a table.

**Radar chart:** A chart that represents multiple variables across two or more axes, the origin of which is the center of the chart.

**Random forest regression:** A regression technique that uses a random forest algorithm to produce an expression that represents the relationship between variables.

**Random tree classifier:** A data classification technique that creates many decision trees and then, based on the predictions each tree produces, selects and applies the decision tree that best represents the solution with the best result (as voted upon by the other trees).

**RDBMS:** An acronym for relational database management system. A database management system that stores entities within tables, tracking the relationships that exist between them.

**Referential integrity:** A database concept that specifies related attributes in different tables are treated consistently.

**Reinforced machine learning:** The use of feedback loops to reward correct predictions and to punish mistakes.

**Relational database:** A database that stores entities (the things that make up the system) in individual tables for which the rows correspond to records and the columns to the attributes (fields) that make up the record. A relational database also stores information about the relationships between tables. Relational databases are often called SQL databases because developers make extensive use of Structured Query Language (SQL) to manipulate them.

**Relational operator:** In a programming language, a relational operator lets programs test the relationship between two values, such as whether the values are equal, one value is greater than the other, and so on.

**Remote database:** A database that does not reside on the current computer, but rather, on a network or cloud-based server.

**Replica set:** A collection of MongoDB databases that back up (replicate) other databases.

**Right join:** A join operation that returns the matching rows from the left and right tables, as well as rows from the right table. SQL will assign the null value to fields that do not have matching values in the left table.

**ROI:** An acronym for return on investment—a metric businesspeople use to determine whether they should proceed with an opportunity.

**Role-based security:** A security approach that identifies common roles within a system (such as administrator, power user, user, report/visualization creator), maps users to specific roles, and grants access levels to each role.

**Scaling:** The process of increasing (scaling up) or decreasing (scaling down) computing resources based on demand.

**Scatter chart:** A chart that represents the x–y relationships between two data sets as markers.

**Schema:** A representation of something in an outline or model form. Database designers often use entity relationship diagrams to visually represent a database schema.

**Script:** A file containing programming language statements that an interpreter will execute.

**Self-describing:** An item, the contents of which not only provide values but also specify the item's structure. JavaScript Object Notation (JSON) objects consist of field–value pairs that specify structure and values.

**Sentiment analysis:** The analysis of text to determine the underlying attitude, such as positive, neutral, or negative.

**Shard:** A database within a collection (cluster) of related databases distributed to improve performance and reliability.

**Simple linear regression:** A linear regression that produces an equation that relates one predictor variable to the dependent variable.

**Sklearn:** The package name Python developers use to import the scikit-learn library that provides functions to perform classification, clustering, regression, and more.

**SMART:** An acronym for specific, measurable, achievable, realistic, and time based—an approach to improving goals and processes.

**Snowflake schema:** A schema commonly used to represent the fact and dimension tables that make up a data warehouse. A snowflake schema differs from a star schema in that it includes levels of dimension tables to create a structure that resembles a snowflake in appearance.

**Soft-clustering algorithms:** A clustering algorithm that allows a point to reside within multiple clusters.

**Stacked-area chart:** A chart that displays two or more area charts on the same graph, often for comparative purposes or to represent each area's percentage of the whole.

**Stacked-bar chart:** A bar chart for which the primary (aggregate) rectangular bar is composed of two or more component rectangles, the lengths of which are proportional to the component value.

**Stacked-column chart:** A column chart for which the primary (aggregate) rectangular column bar is composed of two or more component rectangles, the lengths of which are proportional to the component value.

**Standard deviation:** A measure of the difference between a value and the mean. A large standard deviation indicates values are dispersed, whereas a small standard deviation indicates that the values are closely grouped.

**Star schema:** A data warehouse schema so named because it resembles the shape of a star. At the center of the star is a fact table that contains specific data metrics, surrounded by dimension tables that contain supporting data.

**Static chart:** A chart that does not automatically update based upon changes to the underlying data set. A static chart might be a graphics image within a Hypertext Markup Language (HTML) file. To change the values the chart displays, a developer must replace the graphic.

**Subquery:** A synonym for nested query.

**Sum of squares:** An algorithm to summarize the variance within a data set. Each value's distance from the mean is squared and added to the sum of values. The smaller the sum of the squares, the more closely the values align with the mean.

**Sunburst chart:** A chart that displays hierarchically related data using a multilayer circular shape, similar to multiple layers of pie charts.

**Supervised learning:** The use of an algorithm that uses labeled data to produce a training data set from which the algorithm can learn. Machine learning solutions that use supervised learning include classification.

**Support:** In market-basket analysis, support is a ratio measure that provides the relative frequency of an item in the basket.

**SVC:** An acronym for support vector classifier, a classification technique that creates classes using a series of lines (vectors) that divide the classes.

**SVM:** An acronym for support vector machine, a machine learning algorithm. When applied to classification, the term support vector classifier (SVC) is often used.

**SWOT:** An acronym for strengths, weaknesses, opportunities, and threats—an analysis technique for evaluating opportunities.

**Syntax:** The grammar rules for a language. In Python, for example, the syntax specifies that variable names start with a letter or an underscore. If you violate the language syntax, the interpreter will display a syntax error message and will not execute the statement.

**Terabyte (TB):** $1,024^4$ bytes.

**Ternary operator:** In a programming language, a ternary operator is a conditional operator that returns one of two values based upon a tested condition being true or false.

**Test data set:** A data set with predictor variables and correct results for the dependent variable that is used by a machine learning algorithm to test the accuracy of a model.

**Testing data set:** A data set that contains values for independent variables, as well as a value for the dependent variable, which a supervised learning algorithm uses to test the accuracy of its model.

**Text mining:** The application of data-mining techniques with text files. Text mining includes sentiment analysis, text clustering, text classification, and text prediction. Test clustering is the grouping of related words and sentences. Text classification is the process of categorizing text based upon the words the text contains.

**Time-based comparison chart:** A chart that represents how one or more sets of values change over time. Common time-based comparison charts include line charts and area charts.

**Training data set:** A data set with predictor variables and correct results for the dependent variable that is used by a machine learning algorithm to create a model.

**Treemap chart:** A chart that represents hierarchically related data using rectangular boxes nested within other boxes to represent a parent/child relationship. The area of a box is proportional to its underlying data value.

**Underfitting data:** With respect to the K-nearest-neighbor's algorithm, if you specify a value of K that is too large, you may "underfit" the model, which means the model is not capable of correctly modeling the training data.

**Unsupervised learning:** Machine learning that does not use labeled data, and hence, does not use a training data set. Unsupervised learning algorithms discover their solutions. Common unsupervised learning solutions include clustering and data association.

**Variance:** A measure of the difference between a value at the mean, which is equal to the square of the standard deviation.

**Vertical scaling:** Scaling a database or application server by adding processing power, random-access memory (RAM), and/or disk storage capacity.

**Visual programming:** The process of creating a program by dragging and dropping objects on to a workspace as opposed to writing programming language statements. The RapidMiner and Orange environments allow data analysts to use visual programming to create data-mining and machine learning solutions.

**Visualization:** The visual representation of data with the goal of improving communication.

**Waterfall chart:** A chart that represents the sequential impact of applying positive (increments) and negative (decrements) values to a starting value.

**Wildcard:** A symbol used within a query operation to match values. Structured Query Language (SQL) supports the percent sign (%) wildcard that matches one or more characters to the wildcard and the underscore (_) wildcard that matches any character to the wildcard. Database developers use wildcard characters with the LIKE clause.

**Yottabyte (YB):** $1,024^8$ bytes.

**Zero-based indexing:** In a programming language, zero-based indexing specifies that the first element of an array will reside at the index location zero. Python uses zero-based indexing; R does not. In R, the first element of an array resides at index location 1.

**Zettabyte (ZB):** $1,024^7$ bytes.

# INDEX

**Note:** Page numbers followed by *f* and *t* indicate material in figures and tables, respectively.

## A

Actian, 222*t*
agglomerative hierarchical clustering algorithm, 456
Amazon Alexa, 592
Amazon Aurora, 215, 222*t*
Amazon DynamoDB, 332
Amazon Web Services (AWS), 332
antecedent product, 563, 564, 589
application programming interface (API), 106, 327, 424
apriori function, 28, 567, 571
area chart, 118–119, 118*f*, 119*f*
arithmetic functions, 247–250, 248*t*–249*t*, 249*f*–250*f*
arithmetic mean, 175, 176*f*
arithmetic operations, 245–247, 245*f*–246*f*, 246*t*–247*t*
    bitwise operators, 246, 247*t*
    compound operators, 247, 247*t*
artificial intelligence (AI), 46, 47*f*
association, 3, 563, 589–590
    antecedent, 563, 564, 589
    apriori function, 567, 571
    calculating, 566–568
    confidence, 564, 565, 589
    consequent, 563, 564, 589
    conviction, 564, 566, 590
    definition, 27, 563
    FP-Growth, 571–574, 572*f*–575*f*, 577*f*
    item sets, 567, 568
    lift, 564, 566, 590
    Python script, 27–29
    real-world data, 568–571, 569*f*
    shopping cart data set, 564*f*
    shopping-cart problem, 563
    support, 564, 565, 589
    Weka, 40–41, 41*f*
asynchronous JavaScript (AJAX), 111
Auto-MGP.csv data set, 160
AVEDEV function, 188, 189*f*
AVERAGE function, 175, 176*f*
AVERAGEIF function, 177, 177*f*
AVERAGEIFS function, 178
AVG function, 422, 422*f*

## B

bad data, risks of, 411
bar charts, 120–121, 120*f*, 121*f*
Bayes theorem, 487, 502
bent-elbow method, 449, 449*f*
big data, 609, 611, 626. *See also* Hadoop; Hadoop Distributed File System (HDFS)
    data mining, 29–30, 30*f*
    servers, 613, 613*t*
    size of data, 611, 612, 612*t*, 626
    sources, 609–610, 610*f*
    V's of, 613
binary classification, 486, 487
bottom-up hierarchical clustering algorithm, 456, 457*f*
box and whisker charts, 145–146
Breast Cancer data set
    dimensionality reduction, 59, 59*f*, 60
    KNN classification, 500–502, 500*f*
bubble chart, 137–138, 138*f*
built-in aggregate functions
    AVG and STDDEV functions, 244, 244*f*
    COUNT function, 244, 244*f*
    SUM, MIN, and MAX functions, 244, 245*f*
business intelligence, 2, 15–17
business rules, 412
bytes, 612, 612*t*. *See also specific bytes*

## C

calendar chart, 139–141, 140*f*
candlestick chart, 141–142, 141*f*
cardinality, 76, 78, 78*f*, 79, 98
Cascading Style Sheets (CSS), 221
Cassandra, 333, 333*f*, 334*f*
category-based comparison charts, 4
    bar and column charts, 120–121, 120*f*, 121*f*
    clustered bar and column charts, 121–122, 122*f*
    combo chart, 122, 123*f*
    diff chart, 122–125, 124*f*
    radar chart, 122, 123*f*
    waterfall chart, 125, 125*f*
Census data set, 64–65, 64*f*
centroid, 448*f*, 448*t*
CFO. *See* chief financial officer (CFO)
ChartData.R program, 10–11, 10*f*, 11*f*
charting data with Excel, 164–167, 165*f*–167*f*
Chen diagram, 79, 79*f*, 80*f*, 82
chief financial officer (CFO), 429
classification, 23–25, 485–529, 531
    algorithms, 45, 47, 48
    decision-tree classifier, 511–514, 511*f*, 515*f*
    definition of, 485, 528
    handwriting, 604–606, 604*f*, 605*f*
    KNN classifier (*see* K-nearest-neighbors (KNN) classifier)
    logistic regression classifier, 506–509
    Naïve Bayes classifier, 502–506, 503*t*
    neural networks, 509–511
    random-forest classifier, 514, 516–517
    real-world data sets, 521–528
    steps in, 487
    supervised learning, 486, 528
    SVM classifier, 517–521, 517*f*–519*f*
    test data set, 486, 528
    text, 592
    training data set, 486, 528
    Weka, 36, 39, 39*f*
cloud services, 633
cloud-based databases, 267, 267*f*
clustered bar and column charts, 121–122, 122*f*

657

# INDEX

clustering, 20–23, 20f, 446–484
  algorithms, 447, 448, 448t
  centroid, 448f
  cluster assignments, 468–470
  concept of, 446
  definition of, 2, 35
  Euclidean distances, 448f
  hard, 446, 447
  hierarchical, 447, 448t
    bottom-up algorithm, 456, 457f
    cluster chart, 457, 458f
    dendrograms, 456, 457f, 459f
    Python script, 458–459, 461–462, 462f
    R program, 460, 460f
    top-down algorithm, 456
  K-means, 447
    bent-elbow method, 449, 449f
    cluster formation, 448, 449f, 450f
    description of, 448t
    Python script, 450–452, 452f
    R program, 452, 453, 453f
    steps in, 451
  K-means++, 448t, 453
    Python script, 453–455
    R program, 455–456, 456f
  shapes and forms, 467, 467f
  soft, 446, 447
  stock data, 56–57, 57f
  text, 592, 598–601
  Weka, 35, 36, 37f, 38f
clusters, 332, 611, 614
column charts, 120–121, 120f, 121f
combo chart, 122, 123f
comma-separated values (CSV) files, 30, 30f
compiler, 347, 378
composition charts, 4
  donut chart, 129–130, 130f
  funnel chart, 135–136, 135f
  pie chart, 126–129, 126f–129f
  pyramid chart, 136, 136f
  stacked area chart, 132–133, 133f
  stacked bar and column charts, 130–132, 132f
  sunburst chart, 130, 131f
  treemap chart, 134, 134f
computer vision, 592, 606
conceptual database model, 76, 80–81, 81f
conditional formatting, 160, 167
  in Excel, 168f
  to highlight specific values, 167–169, 168f

  steps in, 167
conditional operators, 385–386
conditional processing, 357–358
confidence, in market-basket analysis, 564, 565, 589
confidence interval, 198
confusion matrix, 487, 494–497
Congressional Voting Records data set, 525–528, 526f
consequent product, 563, 564, 589
conviction, in market-basket analysis, 564, 566, 590
"correct" chart, 105
CORREL function, 188–190, 190f
correlation charts, 4, 188, 190f
  bubble chart, 137–138, 138f
  scatter chart, 136–137, 137f
correlation, data-set, 576, 577f, 578, 579f
CouchDB, 327–330, 328f–331f
COUNT function, 184, 185f
covariance, 190, 192f
COVARIANCE.S and COVARIANCE.P function, 190–191, 192f
cross join, 261, 261f
crow's foot diagram, 79, 80f, 81f
CRUD operation, 214, 215t, 318, 318t
CURDATE function, 420
Cypher, 89

# D

dashboard charts, 4, 5f, 6, 31
  calendar chart, 139–141, 140f
  candlestick chart, 141–142, 141f
  gauge chart, 138–139, 139f
data accuracy, 2, 19, 42, 412, 419, 632
data analysis, Excel
  forecast sheet, 198–200, 199f–201f
  Goal Seek dialog box, 197f
  pivot tables, 200–208, 202f–208f
  what-if processing, 196–198, 197f, 198f
data anomalies, 77, 99
data buckets, 630, 631f
data centers
  Facebook, 613, 614f
  in HDFS clusters, 614, 615f
data cleansing, 19, 411–444
  correcting errant data, 426–427
  data governance, 427–430
  data quality assessment framework, 436, 437f
  data validation (see data validation techniques)

data-quality KPIs, 438f
  definition of, 411
  deleting errant data, 426
  ETL process, 430, 430f
  OpenRefine, 439–443, 439f–443f
data completeness, 412, 414, 436, 632
data conformity, 2, 19, 42, 412, 632
data consistency, 2, 19, 42, 423, 436, 632. See also data inconsistences
data controls and logging, 634
data custodian, 429, 630
data governance
  data lifecycle and, 429, 430f
  definition of, 427
  DGI Data Governance Framework, 427, 428f
  operations, 427, 428f
  stakeholders, owners, stewards, and custodians in, 429
data inconsistencies, 423–425, 424f, 425f
data integrity, 436
data lakes, 76, 95, 620
data lifecycle, 429, 430f
data marts, 78, 93
data mining
  definition of, 530
  future of, 31
  text and photo, 19–20
data munging, 430
data owner, 429, 629, 630
data quality, 436, 444
  accuracy, 2, 19, 42, 412, 419, 632
  attribute measurements, 413, 414t
  conformity, 2, 19, 42, 412, 632
  consistency, 2, 19, 42, 423, 436, 632
  definition of, 2
  improving, 412, 414f, 444
  key performance indicators, 438f
  multiple data sources vs., 414, 415f
  understanding, 412
data quality assessment framework (DQAF), 436, 437f
Data Quality Services (DQS), 431f
data science, 4
data sets, 18, 18f, 19f. See also specific data sets
data sources, 631, 632f
data stakeholder, 429, 630
data steward, 429
data timeliness, 436
data toolsets, 633
data validation techniques, 414–426

# INDEX

data inconsistences, 423–425, 424f, 425f
duplicate values, 417–418, 418f, 419f
field's mean and standard deviation, 422–423, 422f, 423f
leading and trailing spaces, 425, 426f
nonexistent records, fields, and null values, 415–416, 416f, 417f
synchronizing data time stamps, 425, 426, 426f
value-pair consistency, 420, 421f
value-range compliance, 419–420, 419f, 420f
data validity, 436
data visualization, 2, 4–11, 5f
  best practices, 104
  category-based comparison charts
    bar and column charts, 120–121, 120f, 121f
    clustered bar and column charts, 121–122, 122f
    combo chart, 122, 123f
    diff chart, 122–125, 124f
    radar chart, 122, 123f
    waterfall chart, 125, 125f
  composition charts
    donut chart, 129–130, 130f
    funnel chart, 135–136, 135f
    pie chart, 126–129, 126f–129f
    pyramid chart, 136, 136f
    stacked area chart, 132–133, 133f
    stacked bar and column charts, 130–132, 132f
    sunburst chart, 130, 131f
    treemap chart, 134, 134f
  "correct" chart, 105
  correlation charts
    bubble chart, 137–138, 138f
    scatter chart, 136–137, 137f
  dashboard charts
    calendar chart, 139–141, 140f
    candlestick chart, 141–142, 141f
    gauge chart, 138–139, 139f
  distribution charts
    box and whisker charts, 145–146
    histogram chart, 142–145, 142f–145f
  geocharts, 146–149, 148f
  Google Charts, 6, 7f, 41
  plotting data, 149
  Python script, 8–9, 9f

Tableau dashboard, 106, 152–156, 156f
Tableau website, 150–152, 151f
time-based comparison charts
  area chart, 118–119, 118f, 119f
  dual y-axis chart, 116–118, 117f
  line chart, 111–112, 112f
  multiline charts, 113, 113f
  smoothing line chart data, 115–116, 115f
  top x-axis line chart, 113–115, 113f
web solutions
  real-time dynamic chart, 111, 111f
  static chart, 107–111, 107f
data volume, 613
data warehouses, 76
  analytics data into, 91f
  data lakes, 95
  data marts, 93
  Lucidchart drawing environment, 96–98, 96f
  normalization process, 93
  relational schema, 93–95
  snowflake schema, 95, 95f
  Snowflake website, 92, 92f
  star schema, 94
data wrangling, 19, 412, 430
  in Python, 431–435, 432f
  tools, 430
data-analytics project, 628–629, 643
  budget factors, 634, 634f
  data governance board, 629–631
  data sources, 631, 632f
  data toolsets, 633
  defining the question, 629, 630, 630f
  integrating data solutions, 629, 630f
  Jupyter Notebook documentation, 638–642, 639f–642f
  organizational data buckets, 630, 631f
  PDCA methodology, 629, 637, 637f
  quality expectations, 632
  ROI analysis, 629, 636
  security considerations, 633
  self-service solutions, 637, 638
  SMART approach, 634
  SWOT analysis, 629, 637, 638f
  visual representation, 636, 636f
database administrator, 633
database as a service (DBaaS), 2

database developers, 411
database management systems (DBMS), 76, 99
databases
  entity relationship diagrams, 79
  graph, 89–90, 90f
  models
    conceptual database model, 80–81, 81f
    logical database model, 81–82, 81f
    physical database model, 82–84, 83f
  normalization, 85–87
  NoSQL, 88
  object-oriented, 88–89
  relational, 87–88, 88f, 89f
  role of, 17–18
  schemas, 85
data-governance board, 427, 444, 629–631
data-set correlation, 576, 577f, 578, 579f
data-set summaries, 574–576, 578
DBSCAN. See Density-Based Spatial Clustering of Applications with Noise (DBSCAN)
decision tree, 487, 511
decision tree regression, 543–546, 544f
decision-tree classifier, 487, 511–514, 511f, 515f
deep machine learning, 45, 47
degree of a polynomial, 550
DELETE operation, 274–275, 275f
dendrograms, 456, 457f, 459f
Density-Based Spatial Clustering of Applications with Noise (DBSCAN), 447, 448t, 484
  border point, core point and noise, 462, 464f
  identifying outliers using, 472–473
  using Python, 463, 464, 465f
  using R, 464, 465, 466f
dependent variable, 506
descriptive analytics, 25, 530, 531, 561
DEVSQ function, 188, 189f
DGI Data Governance Framework, 427, 428f
DiapersAndBeer data set, 40n 40f
diff chart, 122–125, 124f
dimensionality reduction
  linear discriminant analysis, 63–64
  primary component analysis, 60–63

# INDEX

distributed database system
  horizontal scaling, 323, 324f
  vertical scaling, 323, 324f
distribution charts, 6
  box and whisker charts, 145–146
  histogram chart, 142–145, 142f–145f
DLib modules, 601
donut chart, 129–130, 130f
Dow Jones Stocks data, 56–57, 56f–57f
DQAF. *See* data quality assessment framework (DQAF)
DQS. *See* Data Quality Services (DQS)
DROP operation, 275–276, 276f
dual *y*-axis chart, 116–118, 117f
duplicate values, testing for, 417–418, 418f, 419f

## E

e-commerce system, 78, 78f, 80, 81f
  Chen diagram, 82f
  conceptual view of, 80, 81f
  fact table, 94f
  logical view of, 81–82, 81f, 82f
  physical model of, 82–84, 83f
"elbow method," for clustering, 449, 449f
enterprise data ecosystem, 629, 630f
entity relationship diagram (ERD), 76, 78, 79
  Chen diagram, 79, 79f, 80f, 82
  crow's foot, 79, 80f, 81f
  labeling relationships within, 79f
  primary- and foreign-key fields, 84, 84f
  school ERD, entities, 98f
  for school's registration system, 97f
errors and inconsistences, 411. *See also* data cleansing
ETL process. *See* extract, transform, and load (ETL) process
Euclidean distances, 448f, 490
exabyte (EB), 612, 612t
Excel
  charting data, 164–167
  concepts of, 159–160
  conditional formatting, 167–169
  data analysis
    forecast sheet, 198–200, 199f–201f
    Goal Seek dialog box, 197f
    pivot tables, 200–208, 202f–208f
    what-if processing, 196–198, 197f, 198f

file formats
  comma-separated value files, 170, 170f
  JavaScript object notation files, 172–174, 173f
  markup language files, 172, 172f
  open document specification files, 170–171, 171f
  portable document format files, 171–172, 171f
  .xlsx file extension, 174, 174f
filtering data, 161–164
sorting data values, 160–161
statistical functions
  AVEDEV function, 188, 189f
  AVERAGE function, 175, 176f
  AVERAGEIF and AVERAGEIFS function, 177–178, 177f
  CORREL function, 188–190, 190f
  COUNT function, 184, 185f
  COVARIANCE.S and COVARIANCE.P function, 190, 192f
  DEVSQ function, 188, 189f
  FREQUENCY function, 194–196, 196f
  GEOMEAN function, 179–180, 180t
  HARMEAN function, 179–180, 180t
  LARGE and SMALL functions, 184, 184f
  LINEST function, 191, 194f
  LOGEST function, 193–194, 195f
  MAX and MIN functions, 181–182, 182f
  MEDIAN function, 180–181, 181f
  QUARTILE function, 183, 183f
  SLOPE and INTERCEPT functions, 191, 193f
  TRIMMEAN function, 178–179, 179f
  VAR and STDEV function, 185–187, 186f–187f, 186t–187t
executing queries
  command-line shell interface
    SHOW DATABASES query, 218, 219f
    using Windows, 218, 218f
  workbench
    built-in databases, 220, 221f

chapter's creation, 223, 224f
companion databases, 224, 224f
lightning-bolt icon, 219, 220f
SHOW DATABASES query, 219
using Windows, 219, 219f
export operations
  comma-separated file, 264, 264f
  MongoDB
    index, 322, 322f
    noSQL databases, 322, 322f
  spreadsheet program, 264
Extensible Markup Language (XML), 294, 620
extract, transform, and load (ETL) process, 266, 430, 430f

## F

Facebook, 613, 614f
facial recognition, 592, 601–602, 603f
  definition, 601
  OpenCV, 606–607, 606f, 607f
  Python script, 602, 607
fashion-mnist data set, 71f
file formats, in Excel
  comma-separated value files, 170, 170f
  JavaScript object notation files, 172–174, 173f
  markup language files, 172, 172f
  open document specification files, 170–171, 171f
  portable document format files, 171–172, 171f
  .xlsx file extension, 174, 174f
file systems, 611, 614, 626. *See also* Hadoop Distributed File System (HDFS)
filters, 303
filtering data, in Excel, 161–164, 162f–164f
Firebird, 222t
first-normal form (1NF), 77, 85–86, 85f
forecast worksheet, 198, 200f
foreign key, 77, 83–84
FP-Growth data association, 571–574, 572f–575f, 577f
framework
  definition of, 427
  DGI Data Governance Framework, 427, 428f
  Resource Description Framework, 89

FREQUENCY function, 194–196, 196f
funnel chart, 135–136, 135f

## G

gauge chart, 138–139, 139f
geocharts, 146–149, 148f
GEOMEAN function, 179–180, 180t
geometric mean, 179–180, 180t
gigabyte (GB), 612, 612t
Goal Seek tool, 196–198, 197f
Google, 613
Google Charts, 6, 7f, 41, 106, 106f–108f, 107
Google Colab, 69
Google "crash course" in machine learning, 68, 68f
governance, 427. *See also* data governance
grade point average (GPA), 229
graph database, 77, 89–90, 90f
graphical user interface (GUI), 216
    MongoDB
        arithmetic functions, 309, 310t
        arithmetic operator, 309, 310t
        compass GUI, 301, 302f
        grouping operations, 311–314, 312f–314f
        insert method, 314–315, 315f
        limit method, 309, 311f
        logical operator, 306–307, 307f–308f, 307t
        relational operators, 304–306, 305t, 306f
        sort method, 308, 309f
        specific collections, 302–304, 303f–304f
        third-party vendors, 302, 303f
Groceries data set, 568–571, 569f
GROUP BY clause
    data groups, 250, 251f
    displaying records, 250, 251f
    ROLLUPs
        COALESCE statement, 253, 254f
        grand total, 252, 253f
        product summary, 254, 254f
        subtotals, 252, 253f
        two fields, 255, 255f
    syntax error message, 251, 251f

## H

Hadoop, 611, 626
    "bring the process to the data," 614, 616, 617f
    example of, 617, 619

MapReduce process (*see* MapReduce process)
Hadoop Distributed File System (HDFS)
    clusters in, 611, 614
    definition, 611, 626
    master/slave model, 611, 614, 616f, 626
    use of different data centers, 614, 615f
handwriting classification, 604–606, 604f, 605f
hard clustering, 446, 447
HARMEAN function, 179–180, 180t
harmonic mean, 179–180, 180t
HBase, 333–334, 334f, 625, 625f
HDFS. *See* Hadoop Distributed File System (HDFS)
Heart Disease data set, 523, 524f, 525
hierarchical clustering, 22, 22f, 447, 448t, 484
    bottom-up algorithm, 456, 457f
    cluster chart, 457, 458f
    dendrograms, 456, 457f, 459f
    top-down algorithm, 456
    using Python, 458–459, 461–462, 462f
    using R, 460, 460f
    using Solver, 474–478, 475f–478f
histogram chart, 142–145, 142f–145f
horizonal scaling, 323, 324f
hot encoding, 24, 487, 525
HTML file
    calendar chart, 140–141
    candlestick chart, 141–142
    diff chart, 124
    dual *y*-axis chart, 116–118
    gauge chart, 138–139
    geochart, 148–149
    line chart, 114
    smoothing line chart data, 115
    static bar chart, 108
    static pie chart, 107
hyperplane, 487, 517, 517f
hypertext markup language (HTML), 221

## I

IBM DB2, 215, 222t
image mining
    applications, 601
    definition, 592, 601
    facial recognition, 601–602, 603f
    handwriting classification, 604–606, 604f, 605f

import operations
    MongoDB
        index, 321, 321f
        NoSQL databases, 321, 321f
    one table into another, 264–265
    spreadsheet program, 264
    tab-delimited files, 263, 264f
index
    MongoDB
        business-intelligence tools, 326–327
        distributed database system, 323–325, 324f
        export operations, 322, 322f
        import operations, 321, 321f
        real-time replications, 325–326, 325f–326f
        third-party tools, 322–323, 323f
    SQL
        performance improvement, 277, 278t
        time-consuming process, 277, 278t
inner join, 258, 258f
INSERT operation, 271–272, 272f
insert/update documents, MongoDB
    creating collection within database, 317, 318f
    CRUD operations, 318, 318t
    deleteOne/deleteMany method, 316–317, 317f
    dropping collection and database, 317, 318f
Insurance.csv data set, 26
INTERCEPT function, 191, 193f
Internet of Things (IoT), 18, 29, 31, 610
interpreter, 344
INTERSECT operation, 262, 263f
IoT. *See* Internet of Things (IoT)
iPython
    download and installation, 377, 377f
    Jupyter Notebook, 377, 377f
Iris data set, 21, 35, 36, 488–490, 488f, 489f
IronPython, 401, 402f
item sets, 567, 568

## J

Java Database Connectivity (JDBC), 333
JavaScript Object Notation (JSON), 620
JOIN operation

advantages, 297
component of, 297, 298f
cross join, 261, 261f
inner join, 258, 258f
left join, 258–259, 258f–259f
MySQL documentation, 319, 319f
nested objects, 295
orders and customers tables, 255, 256f
relational database table, 296, 297f
right join, 260, 260f
self-describing objects, 295–296
send and receive data, 292, 293f
storing, 295
temporary tables, 256, 256f
validating JSON content, 296, 297f
Windows Notepad accessory, 296, 296f
JSON files, 172–174, 173f
Jupyter Notebook, 377, 377f
documentation, 638–642, 639f–642f

## K

Kaggle website, 18, 19f, 41, 523, 524f
key performance indicators (KPIs), 427
data-quality, 438f
values, 281
kilobyte (KB), 611, 612t
K-means clustering, 21–22, 22f, 447, 484
bent-elbow method, 449, 449f
description of, 448t
formation of clusters, 448, 449f, 450f
steps in, 451
text clustering, 598–601
using Python, 450–452, 452f
using R, 452, 453, 453f
using Solver, 474–478, 475f–478f
K-means++ clustering, 453
description of, 448t
using Python, 453–455
using R, 455–456, 456f
K-nearest-neighbors (KNN)
classifier, 24–25, 487
accuracy score, 494–497
assigning data point to class, 490, 490f
Breast Cancer data set, 500–502, 500f
confusion matrix, 494–497
Euclidean distance, 490
for handwritten digits, 605–606

Iris data set, 488–490, 488f, 489f
training and testing data sets, 489
value of K, 493–494, 494f
Wine data set, 497–499, 497f
Zoo data set, 522, 523
K-nearest-neighbors (KNN) regression, 548–550
KNN classifier. *See* K-nearest-neighbors (KNN) classifier
KPIs. *See* key performance indicators (KPIs)

## L

LARGE function, 184, 184f
LDA. *See* linear discriminant analysis (LDA)
leading and trailing spaces, elimination of, 425, 426f
left join, 258–259, 258f–259f
lift, in market-basket analysis, 564, 566, 590
lightweight, JSON, 292, 294
line chart, 111–112, 112f
linear discriminant analysis (LDA), 63–64
linear regression, 531, 561
definition, 532
example of, 533–537, 533f, 535f–537f
linear equation, 532, 532f, 561
multiple regression, 531, 532, 539–543, 562
simple regression, 531, 532, 537–539
LINEST function, 193, 194f
LOGEST function, 193–194, 195f
logical database model, 76, 81–82, 81f
logical operators
AND, 238, 238t
NOT, 238t, 239, 239f
OR, 238, 239, 238t, 239f
Python script, 357–359
R program, 384–385
logistic regression classifier, 487, 506–509
logit, 487, 506
LTRIM function, 425
Lucidchart drawing environment, 96–98, 96f

## M

machine learning
algorithms, 47–48
*vs.* artificial intelligence, 46, 47f
clustering stock data, 56–57, 57f

concept of, 44
data clustering, 20–23, 20f
*vs.* data mining, 3
deep learning, 45, 47
definition of, 2, 3
dimensionality reduction
linear discriminant analysis, 63–64
primary component analysis, 60–63
fashion-mnist data set, 71f
Google "crash course" in, 68f
mapping categorical variables, 64–68
operation tools, 3
programming data mining, 17
reinforced learning, 45, 47, 48f
scaling data-set values, 57–59
spam data set, 51f, 53–55, 54f
supervised learning, 45, 46, 50f
accuracy model, 52, 53
machine-learning model, 52–53
perform steps, 48
Python program, 51, 52
training and testing data sets, 49–52, 51f
TensorFlow website, 69–71, 70f
for desktop, web, and mobile solutions, 69f
downloadable software and details, 70f
Google Colab tutorial on, 70f
unsupervised learning, 45, 47
managed database server, 268, 335
managed service provider (MSP), 92, 92f
managed services, 633
mapping categorical variables, 64–68
MapReduce process, 611, 626
example of, 617–619, 618f
using MongoDB, 621–625, 622f
MariaDB, 215
marker, 104, 111
market-basket analysis, 563, 589
markup language files, 172, 172f
master data, 429
master data management (MDM), 436
matplotlib package, 372, 374, 374f
MAX function, 181, 182f
mean
arithmetic, 175, 176f
examining the field's values, 422–423, 422f, 423f
geometric, 179–180, 180t

# INDEX

MEDIAN function, 180–181, 181f
median value, 180–181, 181f
megabyte (MB), 611, 612t
Microsoft Access, 222t
Microsoft MS SQL Server, 222t
Microsoft Power BI
   accuracy value, 285, 285f
   canvas, 284, 284f
   data source, 282, 282f
   data window, 283, 283f
   data-quality charts, 285, 285f
   data-quality KPIs, 281, 281f
   Fields section, 284, 284f
   gauge chart, 286, 286f
   Modeling tab, 283, 283f
   Power Query Editor, 282, 282f
   state-of-the-art visualization, 279, 280f
   trial version, 280, 280f
MIN function, 181, 182f
MLP classifier. *See* multilayer perceptron (MLP) classifier
MLP solution, 509, 510f
Modified National Institute of Science and Technology (MNIST) data set, 604, 604f
MongoDB
   collections, 298, 299f, 300f
   command-line shell, 298, 300f
   download and installation, 298, 299f
   graphical user interface
      arithmetic functions, 309, 310t
      arithmetic operator, 309, 310t
      compass GUI, 301, 302f
      grouping operations, 311–314, 312f–314f
      insert method, 314–315, 315f
      limit method, 309, 311f
      logical operator, 306–307, 307f–308f, 307t
      relational operator, 304–306, 305t, 306f
      sort method, 308, 309f
      specific collection, 302–304, 303f–304f
      third-party vendors, 302, 303f
   index
      business-intelligence tools, 326–327
      distributed database system, 323–325, 324f
      export operations, 322, 322f
      import operations, 321, 321f
      real-time replications, 325–326, 325f–326f
      third-party tools, 322–323, 323f
   insert/update documents
      creating collection within database, 317, 318f
      CRUD operations, 318, 318t
      deleteOne/deleteMany method, 316–317, 317f
      dropping collection and database, 317, 318f
   managed database server, 335–338, 336f–338f
   MapReduce operations, 621–625, 622f
   text's catalog page, 300–301
   visualization tool, 338–339, 339f–340f
multiclass classification, 486
multilayer perceptron (MLP) classifier, 487
multiline charts, 113, 113f
multiple linear regression, 531, 532, 539–543, 562
MySQL
   cloud-based managed database service, 268, 269f
   command-line shell interface
      chapter's creation, 225, 225f
      SHOW DATABASES query, 218, 219f
      using Windows, 218, 218f
   database creation, 268–271, 270t–271t
   Downloads page, 215, 216f
   implementation of, 215
   installation process, 215, 216f
   licenses, 215
   phpMyAdmin, 267–268, 267f–268f
   stores data and client programs, 216, 217f
   workbench
      built-in databases, 220, 221f
      chapter's creation, 221, 224f
      companion databases, 225, 225f
      lightning-bolt icon, 219, 220f
      SHOW DATABASES query, 219
      using Windows, 219, 219f

## N

Naïve Bayes classifier, 487, 502–506, 503t
natural language processing, 31, 592
Natural Language Toolkit (NLTK) data set, 597
Neo4j website, 89, 90f
nested query, 276–277
network port, 212
neural network(s), 487
   classification using, 509–511
   MLP solution, 509, 510f
   perceptrons, 487, 509, 510f
Neutrino API, 424
NLTK data set. *See* Natural Language Toolkit (NLTK) data set
non-numeric data, filtering, 525–528
normalization, 85–87, 93
NoSQL databases, 75, 77, 87–89, 99
   Amazon DynamoDB, 332
   Cassandra, 333, 333f, 334f
   CouchDB, 327–330, 328f–331f
   JSON
      advantages, 297
      component of, 297, 298f
      MySQL documentation, 319, 319f
      nested objects, 295
      relational database table, 296, 297f
      self-describing objects, 295–296
      send and receive data, 292, 293f
      storing, 295
      validating content, 296, 297f
      Windows Notepad accessory, 296, 296f
   MongoDB
      arithmetic functions, 309, 310t
      arithmetic operator, 309, 310t
      business-intelligence tools, 326–327
      collections, 298, 299f, 300f
      command-line shell, 298, 300f
      compass GUI, 301, 302f
      create a collection, 317, 318f
      CRUD operations, 318, 318t
      deleteOne/deleteMany method, 316–317, 317f
      distributed database system, 323–325, 324f
      download and installation, 298, 299f
      dropping a collection, 317, 318f
      export operations, 322, 322f
      grouping operations, 311–314, 312f–314f
      import operations, 321, 321f
      insert method, 314–315, 315f
      limit method, 309, 311f

logical operator, 306–307, 307f–308f, 307t
managed database server, 335–338, 336f–338f
real-time replications, 325–326, 325f–326f
relational operator, 304–306, 305t, 306f
sort method, 308, 309f
specific collections, 302–304, 303f–304f
text's catalog page, 300–301
third-party tools, 322–323, 323f
third-party vendors, 302, 303f
visualization tool, 338–339, 339f–340f
Redis, 330–332, 332f, 333f
RocksDB, 335, 335f
null/not-a-number (NaN) values, 2
numerical calculations
matplotlib package, 372, 374, 374f
numpy package, 374–375, 375f
plot.ly package, 372, 373f
numpy package, 374–375, 375f

## O

object-oriented database, 77, 88–89
object-oriented database management systems (OODBMSs), 88
Online Analytical Processing (OLAP), 77, 90, 90f, 100
Online Transaction Processing (OLTP), 77, 90, 90f, 100
Open Document Specification (.ods) file format, 170, 171f
OpenCV, facial recognition, 606–607, 606f, 607f
OpenRefine, data cleansing, 439–443, 439f–443f
Oracle, 211, 215, 222, 222t, 229, 268, 287
Oracle Warehouse Builder (OWB), 266
Orange, 45
data mining, 579–586, 580f–586f
predictive analysis, 586–589, 587f–589f
outer join, 260
outliers, 471–473

## P

pandas, 346
PC hard drive sizes, 609, 610f
PDCA methodology. *See* Plan, Do, Check, and Act (PDCA) methodology
perceptrons, 487, 509, 510f
petabyte (PB), 612, 612t
physical database model, 76, 82–84, 83f
pie chart, 126–129, 126f–129f
PIP command, 346
pivot tables
data preparation, 201–202, 202f
filter data using slicers, 207–208, 208f
pivot table creation, 202–205, 204f
pivoting data, 205–207, 207f
Plan, Do, Check, and Act (PDCA) methodology, 629, 637, 637f
plot.ly package, 372, 373f
plotting data, 149
polynomial, definition of, 550
polynomial regression, 550–553, 551f, 552f
portable document format (.pdf) files, 171–172, 171f
PostgreSQL, 222t
predictive analysis with Orange, 586–589, 587f–589f
predictive analytics, 33–35, 530–562
definition of, 3
linear regression, 25, 25f
multivariate regression, 25, 26f
Python script, 26–27
predictor variable, 487
prescriptive analytics, 531, 561
primary component analysis (PCA), 60–63
primary key, 77, 83–84
pyramid chart, 136, 136f
Python
association measures, 27–29, 566–570
break statements, 361–362
built-in functions, 363–364, 364f
classification algorithms, 24–25
decision-tree classifier, 512–514
KNN classifier, 490–492, 495–496, 497–501
logistic regression classifier, 507–508
Naïve Bayes classifier, 503–505
neural network-based classifier, 509–511
random-forest classifier, 514, 516
SVM classifier, 518–521
clustering algorithms, 21, 22f
handwriting, 604–606
hierarchical clustering, 457–458, 461–462, 462f
K-means clustering, 450–452, 452f
K-means++ clustering, 453–455
text clustering, 598–601
comment symbol, 355
conditional process, 357–358
continue statement, 361–362
creating, 351–352, 352f
data visualization, 8–9, 9f
data wrangling, 431–435, 432f
dataframe object, 369–370, 371f
data-set summaries and correlation, 574–576
deleting variables, 350–351
download and install, 348, 348f
equals-sign assignment operator, 350
ETL operations, 266
execute, 351–352
facial recognition, 602, 607
group related statements, 356–357
importing packages, 366–368, 367f, 367t
iterative process, 358–360, 361f
launching, 348, 349f
logical operator, 358
machine learning
Breast Cancer data set, 60
clustering stock data, 56–57
linear discriminant analysis, 63–64
mapping categorical variables, 65–68
primary component analysis, 61–63
scaling data-set values, 58–59
spam data set, 53–55
supervised machine learning, 51, 52
module, 365–366
numerical calculations
matplotlib package, 372, 374, 374f
numpy package, 374–375, 375f
plot.ly package, 372, 373f
numerical data structures, 370, 371, 372
object-oriented programming, 364–365
operator precedence, 353, 354t
PyPI, 368, 368f

regression algorithms
  decision tree regression, 543–545
  KNN regression, 548–549
  linear regression, 536
  multiple linear regression, 539–542
  polynomial regression, 552, 553
  random forest regression, 546–547
  simple linear regression, 534, 537–538
relational operator, 353, 354*t*
sklearn package, 375–376, 376*f*
supports functions, 360, 362, 363
syntax requires, 357
ternary operator, 357–358
text processing, 594–597
value list, 354–356, 355*f*
variables, 355
visual programming, 12
W3Schools, 350
Python Package Index (PyPI), 368, 368*f*

## Q
QUARTILE function, 146, 147*f*, 183, 183*f*

## R
R program
  additional support in, 382, 383*f*
  association measures, 568, 571
  break statements, 388
  built-in functions, 381, 382*f*
  classification algorithms
    decision-tree classifier, 512–513
    KNN classifier, 492, 496, 499, 501–502
    logistic regression classifier, 508–509
    Naïve Bayes classifier, 505–506
    random-forest classifier, 516–517
  clustering algorithms, 23
    hierarchical clustering, 460, 460*f*
    K-means clustering, 452, 453, 453*f*
    K-means++ clustering, 455–456, 456*f*
  comments in, 381
  common operations, 382, 383
  conditional operators, 385–386
  creating variables, 380–381, 381*t*

data visualization, 10–11, 10*f*, 11*f*
dataframe objects, 393–395
data-set summaries and correlation, 578
download and installation, 377, 378*f*
interactive development, 377, 378*f*
logical operators, 384–385
machine learning, spam data set, 53–55
multidimensional collection, 391–393, 392*f*
next statements, 388
object-oriented programming, 398, 399
one-dimensional collection, 389–390
own functions, 395–397
packages, 397–398, 399*f*
regression algorithms
  decision tree regression, 545–546
  KNN regression, 549–550
  multiple linear regression, 540, 541, 543
  random forest regression, 548
  simple linear regression, 538–539
repeating statement, 386–388
sentiment analysis, 593–594
radar chart, 122, 123*f*
random forest regression, 546–548
random-forest algorithm, 36, 39, 39*f*
random-forest classifier, 487, 514, 516–517
RapidMiner, 12, 13, 553–554
  accuracy of prediction models, 554, 557*f*, 558, 560*f*
  Auto Model option, 554, 555*f*, 561
  auto model wizard, 13, 14*f*
  data prediction, 13, 15*f*
  FP-Growth data association, 571–574, 572*f*–575*f*, 577*f*
  Naïve Bayes predictions, 558, 558*f*
  new project window, 13, 14*f*
  operations within, 554, 556*f*, 558, 559*f*
  prediction algorithms, 557*f*, 560*f*
  prediction variables within, 554, 556*f*, 558, 559*f*
  predictive models in, 13, 16*f*
  random forest prediction, 561*f*
  Start Layout screen, 554, 555*f*
  Titanic data set, 13, 15*f*, 17*f*
  website, 554, 554*f*

RBAC. *See* role-based access controls (RBAC)
real-time dynamic chart, 111, 111*f*
real-world data association, 568–571
real-world data sets, 487, 521–529
Redis, 330–332, 332*f*, 333*f*
referential integrity, 77
regression, 531, 561
  decision tree, 543–546, 544*f*
  K-nearest-neighbors, 548–550
  linear, 531, 561
    definition, 532
    example of, 533–537, 533*f*, 535*f*–537*f*
    linear equation, 532, 532*f*, 561
    multiple regression, 531, 532, 539–543, 562
    simple regression, 531, 532, 537–539
  polynomial, 550–553, 551*f*, 552*f*
  random forest, 546–548
reinforced machine learning, 45, 47, 48*f*
relational database, 77, 87–88, 88*f*, 89*f*
relational operator
  BETWEEN, 233*t*, 234, 235*f*
  IN, 233*t*, 234, 235*f*
  greater than or equal, 232, 233*t*, 234*f*
  less than, 233*t*, 234, 234*f*
  Python, 353, 354*t*
  R program, 382, 383–384, 383*t*, 384*t*
relational schema, 93–95
remote database, 212
remote dictionary server, 330
replication sets, 325, 326*f*
Resource Description Framework (RDF), 89
return-on-investment (ROI) analysis, 629, 636
right join, 260, 260*f*
RocksDB, 335, 335*f*
ROI analysis. *See* return-on-investment (ROI) analysis
role-based access controls (RBAC), 633
role-based security, 629, 633
ROUND function, 250, 250*f*
RTRIM function, 425

## S
scaling data-set values, 57–59
scatter chart, 136–137, 137*f*

Seattle.csv data set file, 33–34
second-normal form (2NF), 77, 86–87, 86f
security considerations, 629, 633
SELECT statement, 420
self-describing objects, 292, 295–296
self-service solutions, 637, 638
sentiment analysis, 592–594
servers, big data, 613
simple linear regression, 531, 532, 537–539, 561–562
SimpleKMeans algorithm, 37f
Siri, 592
sklearn package, 375–376, 376f
Slicer button, filter data, 207–208, 208f
SLOPE and INTERCEPT functions, 191, 193f
SMALL function, 184, 184f
SMART approach, 634, 643
smoothing line chart data, 115–116, 115f
snowflake schema, 95, 95f
Social Security number, 277
soft clustering, 446, 447
Solver, 473–474, 474f
  hierarchical clustering, 479–483, 479f–483f
  K-means clustering, 474–478, 475f–478f
Sort Options field, 160–161, 160f, 161f
spam data set, 51f, 53–55, 54f
Spark, 620, 620f, 621f
SQL DCL queries, 214, 214t
SQL DDL queries, 213, 213t
SQL DML queries, 214, 214t
SQLite, 222t
stacked area chart, 132–133, 133f
stacked bar and column charts, 130–132, 132f
standard deviation
  data-set values, 186, 187f, 187t
  examining the field's values, 422–423, 422f, 423f
star schema, 77, 94
static chart, 106–111, 107f
statistical functions, Excel
  AVEDEV function, 188, 189f
  AVERAGE function, 175, 176f
  AVERAGEIF and AVERAGEIFS functions, 177–178, 177f
  CORREL function, 188–190, 190f
  COUNT function, 184, 185f
  COVARIANCE.S and COVARIANCE.P functions, 190, 192f
  DEVSQ function, 188, 189f
  FREQUENCY function, 194–196, 196f
  GEOMEAN function, 179–180, 180t
  HARMEAN function, 179–180, 180t
  LARGE and SMALL functions, 184, 184f
  LINEST function, 191, 194f
  LOGEST function, 193–194, 195f
  MAX and MIN functions, 181–182, 182f
  MEDIAN function, 180–181, 181f
  QUARTILE function, 183, 183f
  SLOPE and INTERCEPT functions, 191, 193f
  TRIMMEAN function, 178–179, 179f
  VAR and STDEV functions, 185–187, 186f–187f, 186t–187t
statistics vs. data mining, 4
STDDEV function, 422, 422f
Stocks.json database, 621, 622f
strengths, weaknesses, opportunities, and threats (SWOT) analysis, 629, 637, 638f
Structured Query Language (SQL), 75, 87
  arithmetic operations, 247t, 248–249, 248t–249t, 249f–250f
  bitwise operators, 246, 247t
  compound operators, 247, 247t
  multiplication operator, 245, 245f
  built-in aggregate functions
    AVG and STDDEV functions, 244, 244f
    COUNT function, 244, 244f
    SUM, MIN, and MAX functions, 244, 245f
  cloud-based databases, 267, 267f
  CRUD operation, 214, 215t
  database vendors, 222–225, 222t, 223f–225f
  DCL queries, 214, 214t
  DDL queries, 213, 213t
  DELETE operation, 274–275, 275f
  DML queries, 214, 214t
  DROP operation, 275–276, 276f
  ETL operation, 266
  exporting data
    comma-separated file, 264, 264f
    spreadsheet program, 266
  GROUP BY clause
    data groups, 250, 251f
    displaying records, 250, 251f
    ROLLUPs, 252–255, 252f–255f
    syntax error message, 251, 251f
  importing data
    one table into another, 264–265
    spreadsheet program, 264
    tab-delimited files, 263, 264f
  index, 277, 278t
  INSERT operation, 271–272, 272f
  INTERSECT operation, 262, 263f
  JOIN operation
    cross join, 261, 261f
    inner join, 258, 258f
    left join, 258–259, 258f–259f
    orders and customers tables, 255, 256f
    right join, 260, 260f
    temporary table, 256, 256f
  LIMIT keyword, 229, 229f
  nested query, 276–277
  notepad accessory, 223, 223f
  retrieving rows (records)
    multiple field values, 228, 228f
    relational database, 227, 227f
    SHOW DATABASES query, 225, 226f
    SHOW TABLES query, 226, 226f
    single field, 227, 227f
    wildcard character, 228, 228f
  single query exists, semicolon, 221
  sorting records
    ASC keyword, 229, 229f
    DESC keyword, 229, 230f
    multiple fields, 230, 231f
  UNION operation, 262, 262f
  UPDATE operation, 272–274, 273f–274f
  WHERE clause condition
    asterisk wildcard, 231, 232f, 233f
    AS keyword, 241–243, 242f–243f
    LIKE operator, 235, 236t, 236f–237f

logical operators, 237–238, 238*t*, 238*f*–239*f*
relational operators, 232–237, 233*t*, 234*f*–235*f*
remote server, connection information, 240, 241*f*
uppercase and lowercase letters, 240, 240*f*
W3Schools tutorial, 221–222
subquery, 263, 277
sum of squares, 449, 463
summaries, data-set, 574–576, 578
sunburst chart, 130, 131*f*
supervised learning, 486, 528, 531
supervised machine learning, 23, 36, 41, 45, 50*f*
accuracy model, 52, 53
machine-learning model, 52–53
Python program, 51, 52
training and testing data sets, 49–52, 51*f*
support, in market-basket analysis, 564, 565, 589
support vector classifier (SVC). *See* support vector machine (SVM) classifier
support vector machine (SVM) classifier, 487, 517–521, 517*f*–519*f*
SWOT analysis. *See* strengths, weaknesses, opportunities, and threats (SWOT) analysis

## T

tab-delimited files, 263, 264*f*
Tableau dashboard, 152–156, 156*f*
Tableau website, 150–152, 151*f*
table-based relational databases, 18
TensorFlow website
for desktop, web, and mobile solutions, 69, 69*f*
downloadable software and details, 70*f*
Fashion-mnist data set, 71*f*
Google Colab tutorial on, 69, 70*f*
terabyte (TB), 612, 612*t*
test data set, 486, 528
testing data set, 36, 48–52, 51*f*, 56
text classification, 592
text clustering, 592, 598–601
text mining, 592
sentiment analysis, 592–594
text clustering, 598–601
text processing, 594–597
using NLTK data set, 597

text processing, 594–597
text-based categorical data, 525–528
TextBlob library, 594
third-normal form (3NF), 77, 87, 87*f*
time-based comparison charts, 4
area chart, 118–119, 118*f*, 119*f*
dual *y*-axis chart, 116–118, 117*f*
line chart, 111–112, 112*f*
multiline charts, 113, 113*f*
smoothing line chart data, 115–116, 115*f*
top *x*-axis line chart, 113–115, 113*f*
time-consuming process, 277
timeliness, 436
TIMESTAMPDIFF function, 420
TitanicFields data set, 12
top *x*-axis line chart, 113–115, 113*f*
top-down hierarchical clustering algorithm, 456
trailing spaces, elimination of, 425, 426*f*
training data set, 2, 23, 36, 42, 45, 49–52, 51*f*, 486, 528
transaction control language (TCL) queries, 214
treemap chart, 134, 134*f*
TRIMMEAN function, 178–179, 179*f*
Twitter, 613

## U

UCI data-set repository, 18, 18*f*, 41, 521, 521*f*, 525, 537
underfitting data, 493
UNION operation, 262, 262*f*
unsupervised machine learning, 2, 20, 41, 45
UPDATE operation, 272–274, 273*f*–274*f*

## V

value-pair consistency, 420, 421*f*
value-range compliance, 419–420, 419*f*, 420*f*
VAR and STDEV function, 185–187, 186*f*–187*f*, 186*t*–187*t*
variance, data-set values, 185–186, 186*f*, 186*t*
vertical scaling, 323
virtual data warehouses, 92
visual programming, 11–15, 564, 590
definition of, 2
environment, 12, 13*f*

Visual Studio
classification results, 403, 404*f*
cluster program, 403, 404*f*
Cookiecutter box, 403, 403*f*
Create new project option, 401, 402*f*
IronPython, 400, 400*f*
Microsoft, 399, 400*f*
project templates, 401, 401*f*
regression program, 405, 406*f*
visualization tools, 103, 103*t*
V's of big data, 613

## W

waterfall chart, 125, 125*f*
Weka (Waikato Environment for Knowledge Analysis)
data association, 40–41, 41*f*
data classification, 36, 39, 39*f*
data cleansing, 31–33
data clustering, 35, 36, 37*f*, 38*f*
data visualization, 33, 34*f*, 35*f*
download and installation, 31, 32*f*
predictive analytics, 33–35
running, 31, 32*f*
website, 32*f*
WHERE clause condition
asterisk wildcard, 231, 232*f*, 233*f*
AS keyword, 241–243, 242*f*–243*f*
LIKE operator
percent sign wildcard, 235, 236*t*, 236*f*, 237*f*
underscore wildcard, 235, 236*t*, 237, 237*f*
logical operators
AND, 238, 238*t*
NOT, 238*t*, 239, 239*f*
OR, 238, 239, 238*t*, 239*f*
relational operators
BETWEEN, 233*t*, 234, 235*f*
IN, 233*t*, 234, 235*f*
greater than or equal, 232, 233*t*, 234*f*
less than, 233*t*, 234, 234*f*
remote server, connection information, 240, 241*f*
uppercase and lowercase letters, 240, 240*f*
wildcards, 228
Wine data set, 497–499, 497*f*
workbench
built-in databases, 220, 221*f*
chapter's creation, 223, 224*f*

companion database, 225, 225*f*
lightning-bolt icon, 219, 220*f*
SHOW DATABASES query, 219
using Windows, 219, 219*f*
W3Schools
  CSS, 221
  HTML, 221
  JavaScript, 221
  SQL tutorial, 221, 222

# X

XML. *See* Extensible Markup
    Language (XML)
XML file grouping, 172, 172*f*–174*f*

# Y

yottabyte (YB), 612, 612*t*
YouTube, 613

# Z

zero-based indexing, 345
zettabyte (ZB), 612, 612*t*
Zoo data set, 521–523, 522*f*